Publications of the
CENTRE FOR RENAISSANCE AND REFORMATION AND STUDIES

Essays and Studies, 48

SERIES EDITOR KONRAD EISENBICHLER

Victoria University
in the
University of Toronto

NERIDA NEWBIGIN

Making a Play for God:

The *Sacre Rappresentazioni* of Renaissance Florence

Volume 1

Toronto
Centre for Renaissance and Reformation Studies
2021

CRRS Publications
Centre for Renaissance and Reformation Studies
Victoria University in the University of Toronto
Toronto, Ontario M5S 1K7, Canada
Tel: 416/585–4465 Fax: 416/585–4430
Email: crrs.publications@utoronto.ca Web: www.crrs.ca

The CRRS gratefully acknowledges the generous financial support it receives for its publishing activities from Victoria University in the University of Toronto.

Library and Archives Canada Cataloguing in Publication
Title: Making a play for God : the sacre rappresentazioni of Renaissance Florence / Nerida Newbigin.
Names: Newbigin, Nerida, author. | Victoria University (Toronto, Ont.). Centre for Renaissance and Reformation Studies, publisher.
Series: Essays and studies (Victoria University (Toronto, Ont.). Centre for Renaissance and Reformation Studies) ; 48
Description: Series statement: Essays and studies ; 48 | Includes bibliographical references and indexes. | Contents: Volume 1. The Manuscript Evidence of Florentine Sacre Rappresentazioni -- Plays in Churches -- Youth Confraternities and Their Plays -- Edifici for the Feast of St. John the Baptist -- Playing Outdoors -- Antonia Pulci, Antonio Miscomini, and the Transition to Print. | Text in English; some text in Italian.
Identifiers: Canadiana (print) 20210147911 | Canadiana (ebook) 20210148071 | ISBN 9780772725011 (v. 1 ; softcover) | ISBN 9780772724939 (set) | ISBN 9780772725059 (v. 1 ; PDF)
Subjects: LCSH: Italian drama—Italy—Florence—History and criticism. | LCSH: Italian drama—To 1700—History and criticism. | LCSH: Religious drama, Italian—History and criticism. | LCSH: Mysteries and miracle-plays, Italian—History and criticism.
Classification: LCC PQ5904.F572 N49 2021 | DDC 852/.209382—dc23

Cover image:
La festa di sancta Eufroxina ([Florence: Bartolomeo de' Libri, not after 1495]), fol. a1[r]. Milan, Archivio Storico Civico e Biblioteca Trivulziana, Inc. C 278. © Comune di Milano — All rights reserved.

Typesetting and cover design:
Iter Press

Contents

Volume 1

Acknowledgements   7
Transcriptions and Other Essentials   11
Illustrations   17

Introduction   37

1. The Manuscript Evidence of Florentine *Sacre Rappresentazioni*   59

2. Plays in Churches   89

3. Youth Confraternities and Their Plays   157

4. *Edifici* for the Feast of St. John the Baptist   307

5. Playing Outdoors   373

6. Antonia Pulci, Antonio Miscomini, and the Transition to Print   439

Volume 2

7. Defying Anonymity: Belcari, Poliziano, Bellincioni, and Lorenzo de' Medici   515

8. Bartolomeo de' Libri, Antonio Miscomini, and the Illustrated Editions   567

9. Savonarola and Beyond: Castellano Castellani   665

10. The Afterlife of the Plays   783

Tables

1 *Rappresentazioni* and *Frottole* in Manuscript 811
2 Printed *Rappresentazioni* 828
3 Major Collectors and Sales 851

Appendix 855
Cited Works 889
Index 983

ACKNOWLEDGMENTS

> If you want to see the show, be the show.
> St. Augustine[1]

This book has been many years in the making. My first taste of fourteenth- and fifteenth-century theatre came with a course taught by Jennifer Lorch at the University of Sydney in 1969. It was followed by her production that summer of Nativity plays from the Perugian *laudario*, accompanied by the anonymous humanist comedy, the *Lamentatio Uxor Cavichioli*, translated and directed by Frederick May. Those experiences remain fundamental to my understanding of how theatre works in social groups and in education. Research for my doctoral thesis on sixteenth-century Sienese comedy led me to the manuscript collections of Florentine libraries, and the often-incomplete descriptions available only in manuscript catalogue volumes. I took notes on 6×4-inch filing cards of all the plays that I called up and resolved to return to them later. The opportunity to do so came in 1980: I was awarded a period of study leave in Florence to work on *sacre rappresentazioni*. I sat myself down in the Sala Manoscritti of the Biblioteca Nazionale Centrale and the wonderful anthology of Conventi Soppressi F.3.488 was placed on my reading-stand. I stared at the chicken-scratchings on the page, and wondered, with tears welling, what I was doing there.

The next five decades have been a period of continuous learning and unending pleasure that I now hope to share. I worked initially on a group of texts that circulated widely in manuscript before the first printed editions, and with the assistance and support of the late Raffaele Spongano, I published a group of thirteen texts in 1983. At that stage, there was little available material on how these plays were performed, and with the support of a fellowship in 1984 at the Harvard Center for Italian Renaissance Studies Villa I Tatti, I turned my attention from the libraries to the archives. John Henderson introduced me to the resources of the various *fondi* of confraternities and to the rich documentation of plays that they contained. Since 1984 I have worked to put flesh on the bones of documents that I found there. This book is the one projected in 1984, more than thirty-five years late, but delayed by the need

---

[1] Augustine, *Enarratio in Psalmum* 39.9, *PL* 36 (1865): 440: "Spectare vis, esto spectaculum."

7

to re-explore much of the territory already mapped by others. I look back on my publications in the intervening years with satisfaction but also with occasional embarrassment: some of what I proposed in the past has proved wrong in the light of new research; some of my readings of manuscripts are infelicitous. This volume offers me a chance to set the record straight to some extent, and also to acknowledge the research being carried out by a new generation of scholars in Italy and abroad.

My debts are too many to list in full. I thank Villa I Tatti and its successive directors, staff, and fellows, for welcoming me back each year. I thank the staff of all the libraries and archives where I have worked, for their cheerfulness and humanity as well as their expertise: at the University of Sydney's Fisher Library; in Florence at the Riccardiana, Medicea Laurenziana, Marucelliana, and National libraries (and particularly Piero Scapecchi at the BNCF), as well as the Academia della Crusca, the Archivio di Stato (both at the Uffizi and at Piazza Beccaria) and the Archivio dell'Ospedale degli Innocenti; at the Archivio dell'Opera del Duomo (and particularly Lorenzo Fabbri); at the Biblioteca Comunale degli Intronati in Siena; at the Trivulziana, Poldi Pezzoli and Ambrosiana libraries and the Archivio provinciale dei Cappuccini Lombardi in Milan; the Estense Library in Modena; at the Marciana and the Fondazione Cini in Venice; at the Vallicelliana, Corsiniana, Casanatense, Angelica, and National libraries in Rome; at the Library (and the late Father Leonard Boyle) and Archives (and The Most Reverend Sergio Pagano) of the Vatican. Outside Italy, I have been assisted by the Österreichische Nationalbibliothek in Vienna; the Musée Condé Library at Chantilly; the Mazarin and National libraries in Paris; the Staats- und Stadtbibliothek of Augsburg; the British Library in London (especially Dennis E. Rhodes, John Goldfinch, and Stephen Parkin), the Bodleian in Oxford, and the private library of the Marquess of Northampton at Compton Wynyates; the Biblioteca Capitular Colombina in Seville; the Morgan Library and Museum in New York, and the New York Public Library; and the Lilly Library of the Indiana University at Bloomington. I am in the debt of librarians and library assistants and interns who have greeted me warmly, answered questions patiently, and arranged photography and permissions. The final stages of preparation of this book were undertaken as COVID-19 threw every aspect of our lives into disarray. I thank Konrad Eisenbichler and the Centre for Renaissance and Reformation Studies first for expressing their confidence in this project, and then for continuing to work with me. I am in awe of the people who helped me in this period, and offer them my heartfelt thanks.

I have been fortunate also to enjoy the benefits of major cultural investment in digital projects that have totally overtaken my filing cards and boxes of microfilm. ISTC (the Incunabula Short Title Catalogue), Edit16 (Censimento nazionale delle edizioni italiane del XVI secolo), BEIC (Bibioteca Europea di Informazione e Cultura), Internet Culturale (Cataloghi e collezioni digitali delle biblioteche italiane), and PatrimonIt (database of sixteenth-century Italian popular editions in the British Library), as well as the amazing achievements of Google Books and Archive.org, Gallica, and the major German libraries have brought to my desktop resources that I might never have discovered on my own. Manus and Biblioteca Agiografica Italiana and continue to grow. Francesco Bini (Sailko) has made precious images available through Wikimedia Commons. I am profoundly grateful to the individuals who have laboured to establish and maintain these activities.

The support and interest of colleagues has enriched this research beyond measure, and as I look through my files of letters — handwritten and typed through to electronic — I am almost overwhelmed by the recollection of generosity and friendship. For many years during this book's gestation, I worked with Barbara Wisch on another project, and with her I shared the pleasure of close reading and analysis. With Kathleen Olive I gained an appreciation of the importance of *volgarizzamenti* of devotional texts through our edition of the *Codice Rustici*. From Pietro Delcorno and Federico Bottana I gained precious insights into *misericordia* and alms-giving. Albinia de la Mare, Christopher de Hamel, and Mirjam Foot assisted in locating and identifying confraternal statutes. Joseph and Françoise Connors, Father John O'Malley, Lino Pertile and Anna Bensted, Riccardo Bruscagli, Nicole Lebrun Carew-Reid, Louis A. Waldman, Amy Namowitz Worthen, Neil Harris, Laura Riccò, Laura Carnelos, Marzia Pieri, Elissa Weaver, Anna Esposito, Cristelle Baskins, Konrad Eisenbichler, Cyrilla Barr, Diane Cole Ahl, Ludovica Sebregondi, Davide Baldi, Arthur L-F. Askins, Nicholas Terpstra, Antonio Lanza, Patrizia Ceccarelli, Paola Ventrone, Monica Azzolini, Christa Gardner von Teuffel and Julian Gardner, Sydney and Anna Higgins, Richard Goldthwaite, Robert and Jane Black, Emily Michelson, Daniel Stein Kokin, Michelle O'Malley, Jane Tylus, Lucia Ricciardi, Antonella Schena, Bruno Santi, and scholars sadly no longer with us, including Gene Brucker, Richard C. Trexler, Graham A. Runnalls, Lynette Muir, and Thomas Worthen, among others, offered friendship and hospitality as well as asking or answering questions that led to a new understanding of my subject. Colleagues at conferences in Kalamazoo and Leeds, Viterbo and Anagni, Florence, Camerino, Toronto,

Bristol, and Washington all reminded me that Florence *is* different and deserving of its own chapter in theatre history. In a fairly late stage of research, spirited discussions with Charles Dempsey, and a draft of his chapter on the St. John the Baptist procession of 1454, led me to a new reading of the Sibyls for which I thank him.

I also thank my fellow researchers in Australia: Ros Pesman, Dale Kent, Peter Howard, Robert Gaston, John Stinson, Lorenzo Polizzotto, Louise Marshall, Carolyn James, Nicholas Eckstein, John Gagné, and all those who have followed the late Louis Green and Bill (F.W.) Kent to constitute a dynamic 'Australian School' of Italian Renaissance studies. Penny Crino and Sandra Pitronaci were patient and painstaking research assistants in early stages of the project. My colleagues and my students in Italian Studies at the University of Sydney have also contributed their insights, not least through play-readings — most memorably with Cristina Mauceri as Santa Cristina who continues to speak even after her tongue is cut out. To Patricia Simons, Kathleen Olive, Nicole Lebrun Carew-Reid, to my anonymous readers, to Konrad Eisenbichler as General Editor of this series, and to Dylan Reid, who read my work from beginning to end and provided precious commentary, and to Anabela Piersol who transformed my typescript into a book, my deepest thanks. They have done their best to save me from errors, and those that remain are my own.

This project received ongoing support and regular periods of study leave from the University of Sydney, as well as funding from the Australian Research Council. Retirement at the end of 2008, however, brought the leisure to think and to write, to revisit the mass of documentation accumulated over forty years, and to use new research tools unimagined when my research began. This book is the result. I dedicate it to my family, who have lived with it for so long.

NERIDA NEWBIGIN

Transcriptions and Other Essentials

I have not been entirely consistent in my transcriptions. In principle, in transcribing manuscript documents and play texts, I have standardized the text, normalizing ç/z, i/j/y, and u/v according to modern usage, and introducing in italics the orthographic *i* where necessary, as in *cioè*. I have separated words and introduced accents, capitalization and punctuation. Where necessary, I have amended hypo- and hypermetric lines verse to conform with the expectations of the hendecasyllable; for the most part, editions of previously unpublished texts are forthcoming in the journal *Letteratura italiana antica*. In transcribing titles of works in manuscript, I have followed this practice, but in transcribing titles of early works in print, and particularly when I am referring to a specific early edition, I have maintained the spelling of the original — without word-division, apostrophes or accents or capitalization — rather than using the uniform title proposed by modern catalogues such as ISTC and Edit16, but to facilitate their location I have included their ISTC or CNCE number.

I have translated all the Italian and Latin texts that I cite into English. Play texts in verse are accompanied by parallel metrical translations, with the aim of transmitting some of the rhetorical *brio* of the original and avoiding the flat banality of prose. Prose texts are cited in English and the original is provided in footnotes or in the Appendix.

Saints, Their Feast Days, and Their Churches

Saints are called by their common English name, where one is available, and by their Italian name where it is not. Feast days are generally given in English, with the exception of San Giovanni, which designates the Feast of the Nativity of St. John the Baptist on 24 June. With the exception of St. Peter's Basilica in Rome and St. Mark's in Venice, Italian churches are called by their Italian names: San Marco, Santa Croce, Santa Maria del Fiore.

Feste and rappresentazioni

Sacra rappresentazione is a term of modern literary historiography that refers specifically to the fifteenth-century Florentine religious plays in octaves, introduced and closed by an angel; *rappresentazioni sacre* is a more generic term for religious plays. The printed editions bear the title of *La rappresentazione di…*, *La festa di…*, *La divota rappresentazione di…* (with various spellings), or occasionally *L'esempio di…* or *La storia di…*, although this last term would normally refer to a verse narrative or *cantare*. Except where the full title is germane to my argument, I cite all these play texts by short title: *La rappresentazione di Santa Dorotea Vergine e Martire* becomes simply *Santa Dorotea*. Sometimes the title is conventional rather than simply a shortening: in particular, Belcari's *Rappresentazione d'Abram quando volse fare sacrificio d'Isac suo figliuolo* becomes *Abramo*; the *Rappresentazione quando la Nostra Donna Vergine Maria quando fu annunziata dall'Angelo Gabriello* becomes, by convention, the *Annunciazione*; while the *Rappresentazione di San Giovanni Battista quando fu decollato* becomes *San Giovanni decollato*, as in the printed editions.

Rappresentazione almost always refers to a play, with actors, costumes, dialogue, and gestures. *Festa*, however, is ambiguous, and may refer to a play, or to a feast day and all the mimetic and celebratory elements that are incorporated into it. The financial accounts of the confraternities are only rarely unambiguous in their distinction between *festa* and *rappresentazione* and it is only when there is expenditure on wigs or costumes or scenery that it is it possible to assert that the *festa* encompasses some kind of performance. The annual Ascension Day *festa* in Santa Maria del Carmine clearly contained a play, but the men who staged it called it "La festa nostra della Scensione" (our Ascension *festa*).[2]

A further distinction is necessary, between plays for which we assuredly have a text and those for which we only have a name. Where there is certainty, I will use the Italian title, in italics; where there is not, I will use a more generic English title: a play of the Nativity, as distinct from the *Natività* published in Florence, c. 1484.

Calendar

Until the reform of the calendar in 1750, the Florentine year began not on 1 January but on the following 25 March. In order to minimize ambiguity, whenever I discuss an event that falls between those two dates, both years are given, as for example with the birth of Feo Belcari on 4 February 1410/11

---

[2] On nomenclature, see D'Ancona, *Origini*, 1:369–379.

(that is, 1410 Florentine style *ab incarnatione,* or 1411 modern style), as clear indication that I have checked sources. Where only one year is given, it is an indication of uncertainty. Furthermore, until the Gregorian reform of 1582, when ten days, 5–14 October, were suppressed, the solar year was increasingly ahead of the calendar year. Thus, in the fifteenth century, the shortest day was celebrated on St. Lucy's Day, 13 December, and the feasts of San Giovanni and Christmas were somewhat dislocated, falling almost two weeks after the summer and winter solstice.

Telling the Time

In Florence, the hours were counted from sundown. Thus, "alle ore 24" is at sunset, a time that can be 5 pm in winter and 8 pm in summer. From the mid-fourteenth century, Florence also had public clocks: one on the Torre di Arnolfo of the Palazzo Vecchio, first installed in 1353; the other on the interior of the facade wall of the cathedral, installed in 1443. Both of these were adjusted daily in accordance with sunset or vespers and offered a more regular mechanical division of time.

Weights and Measures

The Florentine pound weighed 339 grams, and was divided into 12 ounces, with each ounce, at 28.3 grams, being the near equivalent of an imperial ounce. The most commonly used measure of length is the *braccio,* the equivalent of 0.583 metres.

Money

Florentines used a range of coins in daily life: *grossi, soldi, quattrini* and *danari* — groats, shillings, fourpenny coins, and pence — while their written accounts were calculated in *lire, soldi* and *denari* — pounds, shillings and pence, with one lira consisting of 20 *soldi* or 240 *danari.* The value of the gold *fiorino largo d'oro* inflated over time: in 1455, its value in silver coin was *lire* 4 *di piccioli* or £4, and in 1497, £7.[3] In 1461, a skilled craftsman like the artist Neri di Bicci could charge 2 *lire* or 40 *soldi* a day; an unskilled labourer, 10 *soldi.*[4]

---

[3] De Roover, *The Rise,* 373 and 484 n. 79.
[4] Neri di Bicci, *Le ricordanze,* 164.

Biblical Citations

Biblical citations in English of canonical and deuterocanonical works are taken from the Douay-Rheims translation, American edition 1899, which closely reflects the Latin (and the inaccuracies) of the Vulgate. For Psalms, the numbering of the Vulgate is followed in parentheses by the numbering in the King James Version. Where relevant, vernacular Italian translations of single books are also cited.

Convents and Monasteries

Among the many 'false friends', *conventi* and *monasteri* are the most difficult to accommodate. In Italian, both terms can be used for male and female religious, although there is a tendency to speak of a *convento di frati* and a *monastero di suore*. In general, I have used 'convent' for a house of female religious, 'friary' for a *convento di frati* (even though convention allows San Marco to be called a 'convent'), 'female convent' for a *monastero di suore*, and 'monastery' for a house of monks. I leave *Badia* untranslated. Company and confraternity are used interchangeably. The sources also use a third term, *scuola*.

Abbreviations

AASS	*Acta Sanctorum: quotquot toto orbe coluntur.* 72 vols. Antwerp: various publishers, 1643–1971.
AAV	Archivio Apostolico Vaticano
AOIF	Archivio dell'Ospedale degli Innocenti, Florence
AOSMF	Archivio dell'Opera di Santa Maria del Fiore, Florence
APCLM	Archivio Provinciale Cappuccini Lombardi, Milan
ASF	Archivio di Stato, Florence
BACF	Biblioteca dell'Accademia della Crusca, Florence
BAI	*Biblioteca Agiografica Italiana,* online database at http://www.mirabileweb.it/p_agiografico.aspx
BAnR	Biblioteca Angelica, Rome
BAV	Biblioteca Apostolica Vaticana, Vatican City
BCIS	Biblioteca Comunale degli Intronati, Siena
BCoR	Biblioteca Corsiniana, Rome
BEIC	Biblioteca Europea di Informazione e Cultura, online digital library at https://www.beic.it/it/articoli/biblioteca-digitale

BEUMo	Biblioteca Estense Universitaria, Modena
BHL	*Bibliotheca Hagiographica Latina*
BMC	*Catalogue of Books Printed in the XVth Century now in the British Museum.* 12 vols. London: Trustees of the British Museum 1908–1985.
BMLF	Biblioteca Medicea Laurenziana, Florence
BMoF	Biblioteca Moreniana, Florence
BMVe	Biblioteca Marciana, Venice
BNCF	Biblioteca Nazionale Centrale, Florence
BNCR	Biblioteca Nazionale Centrale Vittorio Emanuele II, Rome
BnF	Bibliothèque nationale de France, Paris
BRF	Biblioteca Riccardiana, Florence
Briquet	Charles-Moïse Briquet, *Les filigranes: dictionnaire historique des marques du papier dès leur apparition vers 1282 jusqu'en 1600.* Rpt. Amsterdam: Paper Publications Society, 1968. Briquet online: http://www.ksbm.oeaw.ac.at/_scripts/php/BR.php.
CCRSPL	Capitoli delle Compagnie Religiose soppresse da Pietro Leopoldo
CNCE	Censimento Nazionale Cinquecentine — Edizioni, providing a unique number by which a specific edition can be located, at Edit16, http://edit16.iccu.sbn.it/
CRSPL	Compagnie Religiose Soppresse da Pietro Leopoldo
CUIthaca	Cornell University Library, Ithaca NY
GKW	Gesamtkatalog der Wiegendrucke, online at https://www.gesamt-katalogderwiegendrucke.de/
IGI	Teresa Maria Guarnaschelli and Enrichetta Valenziani, eds. *Indice generale degli incunaboli delle biblioteche d'Italia.* 6 vols. Rome: Libreria dello Stato, 1943–1981.
ISTC	Incunabula Short Title Catalogue, providing a unique number by which editions can be located, at https://data.cerl.org/istc/_search
LIA	*Letteratura italiana antica*
MAP	Mediceo Avanti il Principato
MiBACT	Ministero per i beni e le attività culturali e per il turismo, Italy
MLMNY	Morgan Library and Museum, New York
oct.	octave
PG	*Patrologiae Cursus Completus: Serie Graeca*, ed. J.-P. Migne. 162 vols. Paris: various printers, 1857–1887.
PL	*Patrologiae Cursus Completus: Serie Latina*, ed. J.-P. Migne. 217 vols. Paris: various printers, 1844–1893.
VBAMi	Veneranda Biblioteca Ambrosiana, Milan

ILLUSTRATIONS

All images are reproduced by kind permission from their respective copyright holders. Any reproduction, in whatever form, of the images in this volume is strictly forbidden.

0.1   André Barsacq, Set design for *Sant'Uliva*, cloister of Santa Croce, May 1933. From Corrado D'Errico, ed., *La rappresentazione di Santa Uliva, libero rifacimento* (Rome: Edizioni Sud, 1936), plate following p. 12. Author's collection.

1.1   Piero di Mariano Muzi, *Qui si chomincierà l'annutiatione del Vangielo del figliuolo prodigho (La festa del vitel sagginato)*. 1448–1464. Ink on paper. Copied by Filippo Benci. BAV, Chigi L.VII.266, fol. 62^v, col. 2.

1.2   Feo Belcari, *Festa di Abramo*, dedicatory sonnet addressed to Giovanni de' Medici. Before 1463. Ink, tempera, and gold leaf on vellum. BNCF, Magl. VII.744, fol. 1^r. © By permission of MiBACT/BNCF. All rights reserved.

1.3   Feo Belcari, *Questa è la rappresentatione d'Abram quando volse fare sacrificio di Isac*, stage direction after octave 60. Before 1484. Black and red ink on vellum. Formerly owned by the author's son, Jacopo di Feo Belcari (fol. 173^v); his grandson, Feo di Jacopo di Feo Belcari (guard leaf 2^r); and Giovanni di Pagolo Davanzati "che l'hebbe da Feo" (who got it from Feo; fol. 173^v). Prov. Gaddi. BNCF, Magl. VII.690, fol. 118^v. © By permission of MiBACT/BNCF. All rights reserved.

1.4   Feo Belcari, *Rappresentazione d'Abramo* with space left for rubricated stage directions. c. 1455. Black ink on paper. Copied by Jacopo di Niccolò di Cocco Donati. BRF, Ricc. 1721, fol. 56^r. © By permission of MiBACT/BRF. All rights reserved.

1.5   Feo Belcari, *Le stanze d'Abramo* without stage directions. 1461. Black and red ink on paper. BRF, Ricc. 1429, fols. 134^v–135^r. © By permission of MiBACT/BRF. All rights reserved.

1.6   Feo Belcari, *La rappresentatione d'abram quando volle fare sacrificio d'Isac*. 1464–1465. Black, red, and blue ink on paper. Copied by Lorenzo di ser Nicolaio di Diedi. Prov. Camaldoli. BNCF, Conv. Soppr. F.3.488, fol. 35^r. © By permission of MiBACT/BNCF. All rights reserved.

1.7   *Rappresentazioni*, with first folio of *Una notabile rappresentatione chiamata la Creazione del mondo*. 1464–1465. Black, red, and blue ink on

17

vellum and paper. Copied by Lorenzo di ser Nicolaio di Diedi. Prov. Camaldoli. BNCF, Conv. Soppr. F.3.488, inside cover and fol. 1ʳ. © By permission of MiBACT/BNCF. All rights reserved.

1.8   Feo Belcari, *La representatione delle dispute delle Virtù* (*La festa dell'Annunciazione*). 1450–1475. Ink and tempera on paper. Owned by Suor Arcangela, daughter of Domenico Alamanni. BRF, Ricc. 2893, fols. 48ᵛ–49ʳ. © By permission of MiBACT/BRF. All rights reserved.

1.9   *La diuota Rapresentatione di Sancto G‹i›ovanBatista cioè quando fue dicollato,* last page with word teloσ. 1450–1475. Red and black ink on paper. BRF, Ricc. 2816, fol. 44ʳ. © By permission of MiBACT/BRF. All rights reserved.

1.10 End of *La festa del pellegrino,* beginning of *La festa de·rre superbo.* Third quarter, fifteenth century. Red and black ink on paper, copied by Giovanni d'Antonio di Scarlatto Scarlatti. BAMi, C 35 sup., fol. 131ʳ. © Veneranda Biblioteca Ambrosiana.

1.11 End of Piero di Mariano Muzi, *Le stanze del figliuol prodigho* (*La festa del vitel sagginato*), and beginning of *La festa del pellegrino.* 1450–1475. Ink on paper. BRF, Ricc. 2971/1, fols. 49ᵛ–50ʳ. © By permission of MiBACT/BRF. All rights reserved.

1.12 End of *La rapresentatione d'uno santo padre e d'uno monacho dove si dimostra quando il monacho andò al servigio d'Iddio e chome ebbe molte tentazioni et era buono servo d'Iddio,* and beginning of *La festa di sancta Eufemia che è una bellissima festa ed ebbe più martiri.* First quarter of sixteenth century. Ink on paper. Prov. Riccardi, Guadagni, Poggiali. BNCF, Pal. 445, fol. 39ᵛ. © By permission of MiBACT/BNCF. All rights reserved.

1.13 *La festa de la representatione di Susanna.* 1482. Ink on paper, with red and blue decorations. Copied by Tommaso Leone. BNCR, VE 483, fol. 67ᵛ. © By permission of MiBACT/BNCR. All rights reserved.

2.1   Bonaccorso Ghiberti (1451–1516), *Nugola,* incorporating disappearing-light device. Fifteenth century. BNCF, Banco Rari 228, fol. 115ʳ. © By permission of MiBACT/BNCF. All rights reserved.

2.2   Bonaccorso Ghiberti (1451–1516), *Nugola,* with roof anchors and under-stage winch. Fifteenth century. BNCF, Banco Rari 228, fol. 115ᵛ. © By permission of MiBACT/BNCF. All rights reserved.

2.3   Pacino di Bonaguida, *Ascension.* Leaf from the dismembered *Laudario* of the Compagnia di Santa Maria delle Laude e di Sant'Agnese, originally fol. ʟxxvıɪᵛ. About 1340. Tempera and gold on parchment, 44.4

× 31.8 cm. Los Angeles, The J. Paul Getty Museum, Ms. 80a (2005.26). Open content.

2.4   *Santa Maria del Carmine*, hypothetical reconstruction. Legend: A. the oratorio of Santa Maria delle Laude e di Sant'Agnese; B. spiral staircase onto the *tramezzo* and up into the roof; C. the *tramezzo*; D: the *castello*; E: the *monte* with *Paradiso* above it; and F: the *Stella* above the choir; G: *Cielo* in the wall above the high altar. Based on Fabbri, Garbero Zorzi, and Petrioli Tofani, eds., *Il luogo teatrale*, 58, no. 1.18.

2.5   Filippo Lippi (1406–1469), *Martelli Annunciation*. About 1440. Tempera on panel, 175 cm × 183 cm. Florence, Basilica di San Lorenzo, Martelli Chapel. Wikimedia Commons / CC BY-SA-3.0. Photo Sailko.

2.6   Jacopo di Cione and Workshop, *Ascension*. 1370–1371. Tempera on wood, 95.5 × 49 cm. Upper tier panel of the altarpiece from San Pier Maggiore. London, National Gallery, NG577. Wikimedia Commons / CC BY-SA-3.0. Photo: National Gallery.

2.7   Compagnia di Santa Maria delle Laude e dello Spirito Santo, detta del Piccione, *Laudario*. Fourteenth century (or later replacement folio?). Miniated scene with the Descent of the Holy Spirit on Mary and the Apostles, with St. Augustine and St. Nicholas of Tolentino. BNCF, Banco Rari 18 (formerly II.i.122), fol. 2ᵛ. © By permission of MiBACT/ BNCF. All rights reserved.

2.8   Fra Angelico (Giovanni da Fiesole, 1395–1455), *Pentecost*. 1451–1453. Tempera on wood; 38.5 × 37.5 mm. Panel from the *Armadio degli Argenti*, formerly church of the Santissima Annunziata, Florence. Florence, Museo Nazionale di San Marco, inv. 1890, no. 8502. Wikimedia Commons / CC BY-SA-3.0. Photo: Sailko.

2.9   *Meditatione de la vita del nostro Signore Ihesu Christo*. The Virtues Justice, Truth, Mercy and Peace kneel before God. Fourteenth century. Ink and tempera on paper. Paris, BnF, Ms. italien 115, fol. 4ʳ. By courtesy of Bibliothèque nationale de France.

2.10   Bicci di Lorenzo (with Neri di Bicci), *Annunciation*. 1440. Tempera on wood. From church of San Michele Arcangelo, Legnaia (FI). Florence, Museo Diocesano di Santo Stefano al Ponte. By courtesy of the Fondazione Zeri, inv. no. 33804. Photographer unknown.

2.11   Ludovico Zorzi and Cesare Lisi, *Hypothetical reconstruction of the "ingegno brunelleschiano" in San Felice in Piazza, c. 1430*. 1975. Wooden model. Florence, property of Regione Toscana; present location: Parco di Pratolino, Scuderia. Photo: Ugo Scaletti, Studio 72.

2.12   Vincenzo Foppa, *Dome with dancing angels, and scene of the Annunciation*. 1462–1468. Painted vault with terracotta angels; fresco. Milan, Basilica di Sant'Eustorgio, Portinari Chapel. Photo: by courtesy of Museo di Sant'Eustorgio.

2.13   Francesco Botticini, *The Assumption of the Virgin*. 1475–1476. Tempera on wood. 228.6 × 377.2 cm. London, National Gallery, Accession no. NG1126. Wikimedia Commons / CC BY-SA-3.0. Photo: Sailko.

2.14   Alessandro di Mariano Filipepi, called Sandro Botticelli (1445–1510), *The Descent of the Holy Ghost*. 1495–1505. Oil on panel, 207.0 × 229.8 cm (originally 8 × 5 *braccia*, or 466.9 × 291.8 cm). Birmingham, UK. Birmingham Museum and Art Gallery, accession no. 1959P31. Wikimedia Commons / CC BY-SA-3.0. Photo: Terminators.

2.15   Alessandro di Mariano Filipepi, called Sandro Botticelli (1445–1510), *Gentiles at the gate after Pentecost*. 1495–1505. Black chalk, pen, and brown ink, brown wash with white gouache, on paper, 231 × 365 mm. Darmstadt, Hessisches Landesmuseum, Accession no. AE.1285. Photo: by courtesy of Hessisches Landesmuseum, Graphische Sammlung.

2.16   Filippino Lippi (1457–1504), *Assumption of the Virgin*, with *Annunciation* altarpiece. 1489. Fresco. Rome, Santa Maria Sopra Minerva, Carafa Chapel. Wikimedia Commons / CC BY-SA-3.0. Photo: Urnes.

2.17   Alessandro di Mariano Filipepi, called Botticelli (1445–1510), *Mystic Nativity*. 1500/1. Oil on canvas, 108.6 × 74.9 cm. London, National Gallery, Accession no. NG1034. Wikimedia Commons / CC BY-SA-3.0. Photo: Crisco 1492.

2.18   *La festa della annuntiatione di nostra donna* ([Florence: Bartolomeo de' Libri, not after 1495]), fol. a1ʳ. Rome, Biblioteca Casanatense, Inc. 1670; ISTC ia00757400. BEIC / CC BY-SA-4.0.

2.19   *La rapresentazione dell'annunziazione della gloriosa Vergine. Recitata in Firenze il di .x. di Marzo 1565. Nella Chiesa di Santo Spirito. Con Privilegio* (Florence: [Heirs of Lorenzo Torrentino] for Alessandro Ceccherelli, 1565[/6]), fol. a1ʳ. BNCF, Banco Rari 179.21; CNCE 42745. © By permission of MiBACT/BNCF. All rights reserved.

3.1   Compagnia della Purificazione della Gloriosa Vergine Maria e di San Zanobi. *Libro di Statuti*, fol. 1ʳ. February 1447/8–April 1448. Manuscript on parchment, copied by Fra Bartolomeo, and decorated by Battista di Biagio Sanguigni. Bloomington, Indiana University, Lilly Library, Ms. Medieval and Renaissance 26. By courtesy of the Lilly Library.

3.2   Benozzo Gozzoli, *Presentation of Christ at the Temple and Purification of the Virgin*. 1461–1462. Predella panel, tempera and gold on wood, 24.8 × 36.5 cm. Philadelphia Museum of Art, Cat. 38. Wikimedia Commons / CC BY-SA-3.0. Photo: Sailko.

3.3   Piero di Mariano Muzi, *La festa del uitel sagginato* ([Florence: Bartolomeo de' Libri, not after 1495]), fol. a1ʳ. BMVe, Rari 501.35; ISTC iv00305500. BEIC / CC BY-SA-4.0.

3.4   *Church and cloister of Santa Maria Maddalena in Cestello in Borgo Pinti.* Marco di Bartolomeo Rustici, *Codice Rustici: Dimostrazione*, fol. 19ʳ. Before 1459. Ink on paper. Florence, Seminario Maggiore Arcivescovile. By kind permission of the librarian, Dott. Elena Gurrieri.

3.5   Feo Belcari, *Qui comincia la rapresentatione dabramo quando uolle fare sacrificio disac suo caro figliuolo* (Florence: Maestro Franco [Cenni, c. 1485]), fol. a1ʳ. Paris, BnF, RES–YD–520; ISTC ib00297250. By courtesy of Bibliothèque nationale de France.

3.6   Filippo Brunelleschi, *Abraham and Isaac*. 1401. Competition panel, gilded bronze, 45 × 38 cm Florence, Museo Nazionale del Bargello. Wikimedia Commons / CC BY-SA-3.0. Photo: Sailko.

3.7   Lorenzo Ghiberti, *Abraham and Isaac*. 1401. Competition panel, gilded bronze, 45 × 38 cm. Florence, Museo Nazionale del Bargello. Wikimedia Commons / CC BY-SA-3.0. Photo: Sailko.

3.8   Lorenzo Ghiberti, *Abraham and Isaac*. 1425–1452. Gilded bronze quatrefoil panel, 79 × 79 cm. Florence, Museo dell'Opera del Duomo, Porta del Paradiso of the Battistero di San Giovanni Battista. Wikimedia Commons / CC BY-SA-3.0. Photo: Sailko.

3.9   Fra Angelico, *Last Judgment*, detail of the Blessed in Paradise. 1432–35. Tempera on wood. Full panel 105 × 210 cm. Florence, Museo di San Marco. Formerly Santa Maria degli Angeli. Wikimedia Commons / CC BY-SA-3.0. Photo: WGA.

3.10 *Storia di Iacob ed Esaù*. Manuscript on paper. BNCF, Landau Finaly 249, fol. 32ʳ. © By permission of MiBACT/BNCF. All rights reserved.

3.11 Lorenzo Ghiberti, *Jacob and Esau*. 1425–1452. Gilded bronze quatrefoil panel, 79 × 79 cm. Florence, Museo dell'Opera del Duomo, Porta del Paradiso of the Battistero di San Giovanni Battista. Wikimedia Commons / CC BY-SA-3.0. Photo: Sailko.

3.12 *La representatione di Moisè e di Faraone re d'Egitto* (title from *explicit*, fol. 48v). Black, red, and blue ink on paper. BRF, Ricc. 2893, fol. 38ʳ. © By permission of MiBACT/BRF. All rights reserved.

3.13 Benozzo Gozzoli, *Childhood of Moses* (detail). Fresco. Pisa, Camposanto, 1468–1484. Archivi Alinari, Florence. Photo: Brogi.

3.14 Beato Angelico (1395–1455), *Thebaid*. About 1420. Tempera on wood, 73.5 × 208 cm. Florence, Galleria degli Uffizi, inv. 1890, no. 447. Wikimedia Commons / CC BY-SA-3.0.

3.15 *Representatione dell'Abbataccio* (Florence: Jacopo Chiti, 1572), fol. a1^r. BNCF, Pal. E.6.5.1$^{1.1}$; CNCE 53491. © By permission of MiBACT/BNCF. All rights reserved.

3.16 Domenico Ghirlandaio, *Death and Assumption of the Virgin Santa*, detail showing the Convento di San Girolamo. 1490. Fresco. Florence, Santa Maria Novella, Tornabuoni Chapel. Wikimedia Commons / CC BY-SA-3.0. Photo: Sailko.

3.17 Giuseppe Zocchi, designer, and Petro Monaco, engraver. *Villa Medici and the Convento di San Girolamo. Villa della luna delli SS. Mar. Guadagni*, detail. 1744. Copperplate engraving on paper.

3.18 *Rappresentatione del Re superbo* ([Florence: Antonio Tubini and Andrea Ghirlandi] for Francesco di Giovanni Benvenuto, [c. 1515]), fol. a1^r. BNCF, Palat. E.6.5.1$^{V.1}$; CNCE 62333. © By permission of MiBACT/ BNCF. All rights reserved.

3.19 *La rappresentatione di Susanna* ([Florence: Antonio Tubini and Andrea Ghirlandi, before 8 Augut, 1515]), fol. a1^r. Venice, Biblioteca della Fondazione Cini, FOAN TES 842; CNCE 62391. By kind permission of the Fondazione Cini.

3.20 *Rappresentatione di S. Alexo* (Florence: [Antonio Tubini and Andrea Ghirlandi] for Francesco di Giovanni Benvenuto, 7 August 1517), fol. a1^r. BNCF, Banco Rari 179.15; CNCE 61519. © By permission of MiBACT/BNCF. All rights reserved.

3.21 Bernardo Pulci, *La rappresentatione divota di Barlaam et Iosafat* ([Florence: Antonio Miscomini, 1492–1494]), fol. a1^r. BNCF, Banco Rari 189.e; ISTC ip01105500. © By permission of MiBACT/BNCF. All rights reserved.

3.22 *La Diuota Rapresentatione Di Sancto Eustachio* ([Florence: Antonio Miscomini, 1492–1494]), fol. a4^v. BNCF, Banco Rari 189.k; ISTC ie00130700. © By permission of MiBACT/BNCF. All rights reserved.

3.23 The Tobit Master, *The Story of Tobit and Tobias*. Detail of Tobias's mother with the dog. 1350s. Detached fresco panel. Florence, Museo del Bigallo. Photo: Author.

3.24 Biagio d'Antonio (1446–1516), *The Story of Joseph*. About 1485. *Spalliera* panel, tempera and gold leaf on panel, 66.7 × 149.2 cm. Los Angeles, J. Paul Getty Museum, Object Number 70.PB.41. Open Content.

3.25 Biagio d'Antonio (1446–1516), *The Story of Joseph*. About 1482. *Spalliera* panel, tempera and gold leaf on panel, 68.6 × 149.9 cm. New York, Metropolitan Museum of Art, Accession no. 32.100.69. Public Domain.

3.26 *Giuseppe figliuolo di Giacobbe* (Florence: Salani, 1888). Back and front cover, each 145 × 100 mm. BNCF, C.10.54.210.bis. © By permission of MiBACT/BNCF. All rights reserved.

3.27 *Miracoli della gloriosa vergine Maria* ([Florence: Bartolomeo de' Libri] for Piero Pacini, 15 June 1500), fol. a3ᵛ, cap. ii *Come fu uno signore lo quale tenendo in casa lo demonio fu liberato dalla gloriosa Vergine Maria*. BNCF, Magl. L.7.46. ISTC im00619600. © By permission of MiBACT/BNCF. All rights reserved.

3.28 *La rapresentatione di Salamone* ([Florence: Antonio Miscomini, 1492–1494]), fol. a1ʳ. Milan, Archivio Storico Civico e Biblioteca Trivulziana, Rar. H 423. ISTC is00093800. © Comune di Milano. All rights reserved.

3.29 *Capitoli* of the youth confraternity of San Giovanni Evangelista, fol. a1ʳ. c. 1440. Tempera and gold leaf on vellum. 25 × 18.5 cm. Attributed to Battista di Biagio Sanguigni (1392/3–1451). Private collection. Photo by courtesy of Sotheby's.

3.30 *Capitoli* of the youth confraternity of San Giovanni Evangelista, back cover. c. 1440. Brown goatskin over wooden boards. 25 × 18.5 cm. Private collection. Photo by courtesy of Sotheby's.

3.31 End of *La festa del beato Zohanni Colombino*, and beginning of *La representatione di sancta Cicilia*. 1482. Ink on paper, with red and blue decorations. Copied by Tommaso Leone. BNCR, VE 483, fol. 110ʳ. © By permission of MiBACT/BNCR. All rights reserved.

3.32 *La rappresentatione di Sancta Cecilia uergine & martyre* ([Florence: Antonio Tubini and Andrea Ghirlandi, c. 1510]), fol. a1ʳ. BNCF, Banco Rari 189.g; CNCE 54152. © By permission of MiBACT/BNCF. All rights reserved.

3.33 *La rappresentatione di Sancta Cecilia uergine & martyre* ([Florence: Antonio Tubini and Andrea Ghirlandi, c. 1510]), fol. a8ᵛ. BNCF, Banco Rari 189.g; CNCE 54152. © By permission of MiBACT/BNCF. All rights reserved.

3.34   *La festa di sancta Agata uirgine & martyre* ([Florence: Bartolomeo de' Libri, not after 1495]), fol. a1^r. BNCF, Banco Rari 189.a; ISTC ia00157450. © By permission of MiBACT/BNCF. All rights reserved.

3.35   Mariano Bellandini, *La rappresentatione di Sancto Romolo martyre Vescouo di Fiesole* ([Florence: Antonio Tubini and Andrea Ghirlandi, before 8 August 1515]), fol. a1^r. London, British Library, 11426.dd.6; CNCE 4861. © The British Library Board.

3.36   *Traditional site of the Martyrdom of St. Romulus.* Fiesole, Via Vecchia Fiesolana, opposite Villa Medici. Photo: Author.

3.37   Pietro d'Antonio Dei, called Bartolomeo della Gatta, *Four Scenes from the Life of St. Julian the Hospitaller*, as displayed in 1909, in the order 2, 1, 3, 4. About 1485. Tempera on panel, each 22 × 58 cm. Panels 1 and 4: Castiglion Fiorentino, Pinacoteca Comunale. Panels 2 and 3: whereabouts unknown since 1909. By courtesy of the Fondazione Zeri, inventory number 47147. Photographer unknown.

4.1   Anonymous, *The Triumphal Entry of Alfonso of Aragon into Naples, 1443.* Third quarter, fifteenth century. *Cassone* panel, tempera and gold on wood, 43.2 × 167.7 cm. Naples, private collection. Photo: Author.

4.2   Porters carrying the Macchina di Santa Rosa called *La Gloria.* Viterbo 2015. Photo: Acistampa.

4.3   Castellano Castellani, *Meditatione della Morte* ([Florence: Antonio Tubini and Andrea Ghirlandi, before 8 August 1515]), fol. a1^r. BNCF, Banco Rari 182.37; CNCE 9923. © By permission of MiBACT/BNCF. All rights reserved.

4.4   Castellano Castellani, *La Canzona de Morti* ([Florence: Bartolomeo de' Libri or Giovanni Stefano di Carlo, before 30 October 1518]), fol. a1^r. BNCF, Pal. E.6.6.154$^{I.15}$; CNCE 9918. © By permission of MiBACT/BNCF. All rights reserved.

5.1   Boundary marker: Città Rossa Florence, Church of Sant'Ambrogio, south-west corner on Borgo La Croce. Lower stone, before 1486; upper stone, 1577. Wikimedia Commons / CC BY-SA-3.0. Photo: Sailko.

5.2   Andrea della Robbia (attr.), St. Bartholomew, *St. Francis receiving the Stigmata with Brother Leo, and Tobias and the Angel*; below: "Holy Father Bartholomew, pray for us" with two hooded *confratelli*. About 1475. Altar dossal with central ciborium, in glazed polychrome terracotta, from the altar of the Compagnia di San Bartolomeo, Santa Croce. Florence, Museo dell'Opera di Santa Croce, Room 3. Wikimedia Commons / CC BY-SA-3.0. Photo: Sailko.

5.3   Francesco di Lorenzo Rosselli (designer), Lucantonio degli Uberti (engraver), *Pianta della catena* (c. 1472), detail of Porta al Prato della Giustizia. 1500–1510. Woodcut on paper, eight sheets, 57.8 × 131.6 cm. Wikimedia Commons / CC BY-SA-3.0. Photo: Sailko.

5.4   *La rapresentatione di sancto Giouanni dicollato* ([Florence: Bartolomeo de' Libri, not after 1495]), fol. a1ʳ. BNCF, Banco Rari 189.0; ISTC ij00254700. © By permission of MiBACT/BNCF. All rights reserved.

5.5   *La rapresentatione di sancto Giorgio martyre* ([Florence: Bartolomeo de' Libri, not after 1495]), fol. a1ʳ. Rome, Biblioteca Casanatense, Vol. Inc. 1671; ISTC ig00146500. BEIC / CC BY-SA-4.0.

5.6   *La rapresentatione di sancto Giorgio martyre* ([Florence: Bartolomeo de' Libri, not after 1495]), fol. b4ᵛ. Rome, Biblioteca Casanatense, Vol. Inc. 1671; ISTC ig00146500. BEIC / CC BY-SA-4.0.

5.7   *Il secondo dì di San Giorgio:* "+ quivi chomincia la storia dell sechondo dì di san Giorgio." BNCF, Magl. vii.293, fol. 71ʳ. © By permission of MiBACT/BNCF. All rights reserved.

5.8   *Rappresentatione duno mracolo di tre Peregrini che andauono a sancto Iacopo di Galitia* ([Florence: Antonio Tubini and Andrea Ghirlandi, not after 1515]), fol. a1ʳ. BNCF, Banco Rari 183.22; CNCE 62082. © By permission of MiBACT/BNCF. All rights reserved.

5.9   *La rapresentatione d'uno miracolo di Tre Pellegrini che andauano a .S. Iacopo di Galitia* (Florence: n.p., 1555), fol. a4ʳ. BNCF, Pal. E.6.5.1ᴵⱽ·³⁸; CNCE 61839. © By permission of MiBACT/BNCF. All rights reserved.

5.10   *Larapresentatione duno miracolo del corpo di Christo* ([Florence: Bartolomeo de' Libri, not after 1495]), fol. a1ʳ. London, British Library, IA.27488. ISTC ir00029550. © The British Library Board.

5.11   Bartolomeo della Gatta (attr.), *Miracle of the Profanation of the Host.* About 1485. Predella panel, tempera on wood, 15 × 35 cm. St. Petersburg, The Hermitage State Museum, inv. ГЭ 7657. Photograph © The State Hermitage Museum. Photography by Pavel Demidov.

5.12   Benozzo Gozzoli, *St. Peter and the Fall of Simon Magus.* 1461. Predella panel, tempera on wood, 24.3 × 34.5 cm. Formerly, oratory of the Company of the Purification. London, Hampton Court, Royal Collection, RCIN 403372. Wikimedia Commons / CC BY-SA-3.0. Photo: WGA.

6.1   Antonia Pulci, *Incomincia La rapresentatione di sancta Domitilla uergine* ([Florence: Antonio Miscomini, c. 1484]), fol. a1ʳ. BNCF, P.6.37/1; ISTC ir00029680. © By permission of MiBACT/BNCF. All rights reserved.

6.2   Antonia Pulci, *Incomincia La rapresentatione di sancta Domitilla uergine* ([Florence: Antonio Miscomini, c. 1484]), fol. c2^r. BNCF, P.6.37/1; ISTC ir00029680 © By permission of MiBACT/BNCF. All rights reserved.

6.3   *Qui comincia lahistoria & leggenda di sancta Apollonia uergine & martyre di christo* ([Florence: Antonio Miscomini, c. 1484]), fol. f8^v. BNCF, P.6.36/3; ISTC ir00029700. © By permission of MiBACT/BNCF. All rights reserved.

6.4   *La rapresentatione divota di Sancta Apollonia* ([Florence: Antonio Miscomini, 1492–1494]), fol. b4^v. BNCF, Banco Rari 189.d; ISTC ia00922600. © By permission of MiBACT/BNCF. All rights reserved.

6.5   *La rapresentatione divota di Sancta Apollonia* ([Florence: Antonio Miscomini, 1492–1494]), fol. a1^r. BNCF, Banco Rari 189.d; ISTC ia00922600. © By permission of MiBACT/BNCF. All rights reserved.

6.6   Jean Fouquet, *The Martyrdom of St. Apollonia*, from *Le Livre d'Heures d'Étienne Chevalier.* 1452–1460. Vellum. Chantilly, Musée Condé, Ms. 71, fragment. Wikimedia Commons / CC BY-SA-3.0.

6.7   *La Passion et Résurrection de nostre saulveur et rédempteur Jhesucrist, ainsi qu'elle fut juée en Valenchiennes, en le an 1547, par grâce de maistre Nicaise Chamart, seigneur de Alsembergue, alors prevost de la ville,* fol. 89^v. Manuscript on paper, 292 × 205 mm. Paris, BnF, Ms. français 12536, fol. 89^v. By courtesy of Bibliothèque nationale de France.

6.8   *La rapresentatione di sancto Antonio abbate* ([Florence: Bartolomeo de' Libri, not after 1495]), fol. 10^v. BNCF, E.6.7.56^{t.9}; ISTC ia00888500. © By permission of MiBACT/BNCF. All rights reserved.

6.9   *La rapresentatione della Natiuita di Christo* ([Florence: Bartolomeo de' Libri, not after 1495]), fol. a1^r. London, British Library, IA27473; ISTC ir00028500. © The British Library Board.

6.10–6.14 *La rapresentatione divota di Stella: cioe un miracolo di Nostra Donna* ([Florence: Bartolomeo de' Libri or Giovanni Stefano di Carlo, not after 1515]), fols. a1^r, a3^v, a4^r, a4^v, and c4^v. BNCF, Pal. E.6.5.1^{V.16bis}; CNCE 19120. © By permission of MiBACT/BNCF. All rights reserved.

6.15   Antonia Pulci, *La rapresentatione della distructione di Saul & del pianto di Dauit* ([Florence, Bartolomeo de' Libri, not after 1495]), fol. a1^r. BRF, Edizioni Rare 686[17]; ISTC ir00029500. © By permission of MiBACT/BRF. All rights reserved.

6.16   *Larapresentatione disancto Lorenzo quando fu martyrizato* ([Florence: Bartolomeo de' Libri, not after 1495]), fol. a1^r. Milan, Archivio Storico

Civico e Biblioteca Trivulziana, Inc. C 322⁶; ISTC il00091500. BEIC / CC BY-SA-4.0.

6.17 Bernardo Daddi, *Martyrdom of St. Lawrence*. About 1320. Florence, Basilica di Santa Croce, Pulci-Berardi Chapel. Wikimedia Commons / CC BY-SA-3.0. Photo: Sailko.

7.1 Portrait of Feo Belcari, with sonnet to Giovanni di Cosimo de' Medici, and *La rappresentazione d'Abramo*. BNCF, Magl. VII.744, fol. 1ʳ. © By permission of MiBACT/BNCF. All rights reserved.

7.2 Antonio di Matteo di Meglio, Herald of the Signoria, with Feo Belcari, *Larapresentatione del di del giudicio* ([Florence: Bartolomeo de' Libri, not after 1495]), fol. a1ʳ. BRF, Edizioni Rare 686²; ISTC ir00028950. © By permission of MiBACT/BRF. All rights reserved.

7.3 Feo Belcari and Tommaso Benci, *Rappresentatione devota di san Giovanni Baptista quando ando nel deserto* ([Florence:] Andrea Tubini and Antonio Ghirlandi, [before 1515–1516]), fol. a1ᵛ. New York, New York Public Library, Spencer Coll., Ital. c. 1515; CNCE 62092.

7.4 Feo Belcari, *La rappresentatione di sancto Panuntio* ([Florence: Bartolomeo de' Libri, 1492–1494]), fol. a1ʳ. BRF, Edizioni Rare 686¹⁴; ISTC ib00297950. © By permission of MiBACT/BRF. All rights reserved.

7.5 Leonardo da Vinci, *Study for the mountain that rotates and then opens to reveal the Underworld*. London, British Library, Arundel Codex 263, detail of fol. 224ʳ, flipped horizontally. © The British Library Board.

7.6 Leonardo da Vinci, *Study for the palace of Pluto*. London, British Library, Arundel Codex 263, detail of fol. 231ᵛ, flipped horizontally. © The British Library Board.

7.7 Angelo Poliziano, *Cose volgare del Politiano* [with *La festa di Orfeo*] ([Florence: Bartolomeo de' Libri, after 9 August 1494]), fol. e2ʳ. BNCF, Pal. E.6.4.36; ISTC ip00900600. © By permission of MiBACT/BNCF. All rights reserved.

7.8 Angelo Poliziano, *La giostra di Giuliano de Medici* [with] *La festa di Orpheo* ([Florence: Antonio Tubini, Lorenzo de Alopa and Andrea Ghirlandi, c. 1500]), fols. c6ᵛ and c7ʳ. ISTC ip00900700. New York, Metropolitan Museum of Art, inv. 25.30.22. Harris Brisbane Dick Fund, 1925. Public domain.

7.9 Lorenzo de' Medici, *La rappresentatione di San Giovanni et Paulo composta pel magnifico Laurentio de Medici* ([Florence:] Francesco Bonaccorsi, [1491–1492]), fol. [a1ʳ]. BNCF, Pal. E.6.7.57¹; ISTC im00427180. © By permission of MiBACT/BNCF. All rights reserved.

7.10 *The former loggia of the Buca di San Paolo*. Florence, ex-Istituto di
Sant'Agnese (formerly Santa Trinita Vecchia), Via Guelfa 79. From Se-
bregondi, "I luoghi teatrali," 343, fig. 2. Photo: courtesy of the Facoltà di
Architettura, Università degli Studi di Firenze.

7.11 *Ground plan of the Buca di San Paolo*, showing loggia and open space.
Florence, ex-Istituto di Sant'Agnese (formerly Santa Trinita Vecchia),
Via Guelfa 79. From Sebregondi, "Istituto di Sant'Agnese," 44. Photo:
courtesy of the Facoltà di Architettura, Università degli Studi di Firenze.

7.12 [Castellano Castellani], *Rappresentatione di Constantino imperadore: di
sancto Silvestro papa et di sancta Helena imperatrice* ([Florence, Bartolomeo de' Libri or Giovanni Stefano di Carlo,] for Francesco di Giovanni Benvenuto, [not before 1511]), fol. a1ʳ. BNCF, Banco Rari 180.21;
CNCE 61540. © By permission of MiBACT/BNCF. All rights reserved.

8.1 Feo Belcari, *La rappresentazione d'Abramo*. Tempera, manuscript with
gold leaf and tempera on vellum. BNCF, Magl. VII.744, fol. 1ᵛ. © By permission of MiBACT/BNCF. All rights reserved.

8.2 Giacomo Ceruti, called *Il Pitocchetto* (1698–1767), *Portrait of a Print
Seller* (detail). Sold at auction in 2006, Heritage Fine Art, Dallas, TX,
Sale 638, lot. 24057. Present whereabouts unknown.

8.3 Feo Belcari, *Incomincia larapresentatione di Habraam ed di Ysaac* ([Flor-
ence: Lorenzo Morgiani and Johannes Petri, c. 1492]), fol. a1ʳ. Vienna,
Österreichische Nationalbibliothek, Ink 12.H.11; ISTC ib00297350.

8.4 Feo Belcari, *La representatione di Habraam et de Isaac* ([Rome: Stephan
Plannck, c. 1493–1500]), fol. a1ʳ. Venice, Fondazione Cini, FOAN TES
950; ISTC ib00297800. BEIC / CC BY-SA-4.0.

8.5 *Alcuni miracoli della gloriosa uergine Maria* ([Florence: Bartolomeo de'
Libri, not after 1495]), fol. c1ʳ. London, British Library, IA.27465; ISTC
im00619325. © The British Library Board.

8.6 *La rappresentatione di sancta Guglielma* ([Florence: Bartolomeo de'
Libri, after 1497 and no later than 1511]), fol. a1ʳ. BNCF, Banco Rari
189.q; ISTC ip01103600. © By permission of MiBACT/BNCF. All rights
reserved.

8.7 *Alcuni miracoli della gloriosa uergine Maria* ([Florence: Bartolomeo de'
Libri, not after 1495]); BL IA.27465) fol. d4ʳ. London, British Library,
IA.27465; ISTC im00619325. © The British Library Board.

8.8 *La rapresentatione di sancta Caterina uirgine & martyre* ([Florence: Bartolomeo de' Libri, not after 1495]), fol. a1ʳ. BRF, Edizioni Rare 686⁵; ISTC
ic00278800. © By permission of MiBACT/BRF. All rights reserved.

8.9 *La rapresentatione di sancta Caterina uirgine & martyre* ([Florence: Bartolomeo de' Libri, not after 1495]), fol. b2ʳ. BRF, Edizioni Rare 686⁵; ISTC ic00278800. © By permission of MiBACT/BRF. All rights reserved.

8.10 *La rapresentatione di sancto Antonio abbate* ([Florence: Bartolomeo de' Libri, not after 1495]), fol. a1ʳ. BNCF, E.6.7.56^{1.9}; ISTC 00888500. © By permission of MiBACT/BNCF. All rights reserved.

8.11 Feo Belcari, *La festa di san giouanni quando fu uisitato da christo nel diserto* ([Florence: Bartolomeo de' Libri, not after 1495]), fol. a1ʳ. BRF, Edizioni Rare 686⁹; ISTC ib00297900. © By permission of MiBACT/BRF. All rights reserved.

8.12 Feo Belcari and Tommaso Benci, *Rappresentatione devota di san Giovanni Baptista quando ando nel deserto* ([Florence:] Andrea Tubini and Antonio Ghirlandi, [before 1515–1516]), fol. a1ʳ. New York, New York Public Library, Spencer Coll., Ital. c. 1515; CNCE 62092.

8.13 Feo Belcari, *Rappresentatione devota di san Giovanni Baptista quando ando nel diserto* ([Florence:] Andrea Tubini and Antonio Ghirlandi for Maestro Francesco di Giovanni Benvenuto, 28 November 1518), fol. a1ʳ. BNCF, E.6.7.53²³; CNCE 42736. © By permission of MiBACT/BNCF. All rights reserved.

8.14 *La festa della annuntiatione di nostra donna* ([Florence: Bartolomeo de' Libri, not after 1495]), fol. A4ᵛ. Rome, Biblioteca Casanatense, Inc. 1670; ISTC ia00757400. BEIC / CC BY-SA-4.0.

8.15–8.16 *La Festa della Annuntiatione di nostra Donna Con una aggiunta di dua Capitoli* ([Florence:] for Francesco di Giovanni Benvenuto, [c. 1516]), fols. a1ʳ and a4ᵛ. BNCF, Pal. E.6.7.53¹⁶; CNCE 41313. © By permission of MiBACT/BNCF. All rights reserved.

8.17 *La Diuota Rapresentatione Di Sancto Eustachio* ([Florence: Antonio Miscomini, 1492–1494]), fol. a1ʳ. BNCF, Banco Rari 189.k; ISTC ie00130700. © By permission of MiBACT/BNCF. All rights reserved.

8.18 *La Diuota Rapresentatione Di Sancto Eustachio* ([Florence: Antonio Miscomini, 1492–1494]), fol. a4ʳ. BNCF, Banco Rari 189.k; ISTC ie00130700. © By permission of MiBACT/BNCF. All rights reserved.

8.19 *La rapresentatione di sancta Domitilla* ([Florence: Antonio Miscomini, 1492–1494]), fol. a1ʳ. BNCF, Banco Rari 189.i; ISTC ip01102500. © By permission of MiBACT/BNCF. All rights reserved.

8.20–8.23 *La rapresentatione divota di Ioseph figluolo di Iacob* ([Florence: Antonio Miscomini, 1492–1494]), fols. a1ʳ, a4ʳ, b1ᵛ, and b3ᵛ. Washington

DC, Library of Congress, Lessing J. Rosenwald Collection (ex Dyson Perrins), PQ4230.R3; ISTC ir00029000. By courtesy of the Library of Congress.

8.24 Bernardo Pulci, *La rapresentatione divota di Barlaam et Iosafat* ([Florence: Antonio Miscomini, 1492–1494]), fol. a8^r. BNCF, Banco Rari 189.e; ISTC ip01105500.

8.25 *La rapresentatione della reina Hester* ([Florence: Antonio Miscomini, 1492–1494]), fol. a1^r. Milan, Archivio Storico Civico e Biblioteca Trivulziana, Inc. H 431; ISTC ie00111500.

8.26 *Larapresentatione di Rosana* ([Florence: Antonio Miscomini, 1492–1494]), fol. a1^r. BNCF, Pal. E.6.5.1$^{V.5}$; ISTC ir00338300.

8.27 Luigi Pulci, *Morgante maggiore* (Florence: [Antonio Tubini] for Ser Piero Pacini da Pescia, 22 January 1500/1), fol. n7^r (103^r). Vienna, Österreichische Nationalbibliothek, Ink 5.G.9; ISTC ip01125050.

8.28 *Lafesta del miracolo dello spirito sancto* ([Florence: Bartolomeo de' Libri, not after 1495]), fol. a1^r. Milan, Archivio Storico Civico e Biblioteca Trivulziana, Inc. C 32212; ISTC ir00029650.

8.29 *La rapresentatione di sancto Giorgio martyre* ([Florence: Bartolomeo de' Libri, not after 1495]), fol. a1^r. BCoR, Deposito 34–I, formerly 92.f.22[29]; ISTC ig00146500. From Cioni, *Bibliografia*, 187, 27.

8.30 *La rapresentatione di san Giouanni & Paulo* ([Florence: Bartolomeo de' Libri, c. 1498]), fol. a1^r. BNCF, Pal. E.6.7.57[2]; ISTC im00427300.

8.31 Domenico Ghirlandaio (1449–1494) and workshop, *Octavian and the Sibyl*. 1482–1485. Fresco. Florence, Basilica di Santa Trinita, Sassetti Chapel, outer arch. Photo: Sailko.

8.32 *Stanze della festa di Otaviano imperadore* ([Florence: Antonio Miscomini, 1492–1494]), fol. a1^r. Milan, Archivio Storico Civico e Biblioteca Trivulziana, Inc. C 281; ISTC is00688800.

8.33 Antonia Pulci, *La rappresentatione di san Francesco* ([Florence: Bartolomeo de' Libri, not after 1495]), fol. a1^r. BNCF, Banco Rari 189.m; ISTC ip01103300.

8.34 Domenico Ghirlandaio (1449–1494) and Workshop, *St. Francis Receives the Stigmata*. 1482–1484. Fresco. Florence, Basilica di Santa

Trinita, Sassetti Chapel. Wikimedia Commons / CC BY-SA-3.0. Photo: Sailko.

8.35 Domenico (abbot), *La Rapresentatione di Dieci Mila Martiri Crocifis-si nel Monte Arat, Appresso alla Citta d'Alexandria, come riferisce San Hieronimo al tempo di Adriano: & Antonino Imperadori. Anno Domini CXVIIII. Et adi .xxii. di Giugno* (Florence: n.p., 1558), fol. a1ʳ. BNCF, E.6.5.1ᴵᴵ·³¹; CNCE 17585. © By permission of MiBACT/BNCF. All rights reserved.

8.36 Luigi Pulci, *Morgante maggiore* (Florence: [Antonio Tubini] for Ser Pie-ro Pacini da Pescia, 22 January 1500/1), fol. D2ʳ (218ʳ). Vienna, Öster-reichische Nationalbibliothek, Ink 5.G.9; ISTC ip01125050.

8.37 *La festa di sancta Felicita hebrea quando fu martyrizata con septe figluoli* ([Florence: Bartolomeo de' Libri, not after 1495]), fol. a1ʳ. BNCF, Banco Rari 189.l; ISTC if00059200. © By permission of MiBACT/BNCF. All rights reserved.

8.38 Neri di Bicci (1419–1491), *Santa Felicita and her Seven Sons.* 1464. Tempera on wood. 158.5 × 190 cm. Florence, Church of Santa Felici-ta, Sacristy. Until 1824, in the chapel dedicated to Santa Felicita. Photo: Bruno Santi.

8.39a–g Neri di Bicci (1419–1491), *Santa Felicita and her Seven Sons.* 1464. Predella, tempera on wood. Florence, Church of Santa Felicita, Sacris-ty. Until 1824, in the chapel dedicated to Santa Felicita. Photo: Bruno Santi.

8.40 *La rapresentatione di san Giouanni gualberto* ([Florence: Bartolo-meo de' Libri, not after 1495]), fol. a1ʳ. BNCF, Banco Rari 189.p; ISTC ij00334900. © By permission of MiBACT/BNCF. All rights reserved.

8.41 Niccolò di Pietro Gerini (active 1368–1414/15), *Scene from the Life of San Giovanni Gualberto.* Tempera on wood, gold ground, 146.7 × 72.4 cm. Washington, National Gallery, Accession No. 58.135. Public Do-main.

8.42 Bernardo Giambullari, *Questa è lastoria & miracoli di san Giouan-ni Gualberto nostro cittadino Fiorentino fondatore del ordine diuallem-brosa* ([Florence: Bartolomeo de' Libri, not after 1497]), fol. a1ʳ. BNCF, Magl. K.5.44; ISTC ig00303500. © By permission of MiBACT/BNCF. All rights reserved.

8.43 *Lafesta di sancta Eufroxina* ([Florence: Bartolomeo de' Libri, not after 1495]), fol. a1ʳ. Milan, Archivio Storico Civico e Biblioteca Trivulziana, Inc. C 278. © Comune di Milano — All rights reserved.

8.44   *La rapresentatione duno miracolo di nostra donna che per mezo duno peregrino risuscito elfigliuolo duno Re che chascava di quel malmale* ([Florence: Bartolomeo de' Libri, not after 1494]), fol. a1^r. Milan, Archivio Storico Civico e Biblioteca Trivulziana, Inc. C 270; ISTC ir00029600. BEIC / CC BY-SA-4.0.

8.45   *La representatione di Teofilo che sidette aldiauolo* ([Florence: Bartolomeo de' Libri, not after 1494]), fol. a1^r. BCoR, Deposito 34–I, formerly 92.F.22^{12}; ISTC it00153800. BEIC / CC BY-SA-4.0.

8.46   *Larappresentatione di dua hebrei che siconuertirono* ([Florence: Bartolomeo de' Libri, not after 1494]), fol. a1^r. Milan, Archivio Storico Civico e Biblioteca Trivulziana, Inc. C 273; ISTC ir00029400. BEIC / CC BY-SA-4.0.

8.47   *Miracoli della gloriosa vergine Maria* (Florence: [Bartolomeo de' Libri] for Ser Piero Pacini da Pescia, 15 June 1500), fol. g4^v. BNCF, Magl. L.7.46; ISTC im00619600. © By permission of MiBACT/BNCF. All rights reserved.

8.48   [Castellano Castellani,] *Rappresentatione di Santo Ignatio: vescovo et martire* ([Florence: Antonio Tubini and Andrea Ghirlandi for Zanobi della Barba, before 8 August 1515]), fol. a1^r. London, British Library, C.34.h.43; CNCE 54166. © The British Library Board.

8.49   Giuliano Dati, Bernardo di Antonio Romano, and Mariano Particappa, *Incomenza la passione di Christo historiata in rima vulgari secondo che recita e representa de parala a parola la dignissima compagnia dela Confalone di Roma lo Uenerdi santo in luocho dicto Coliseo* ([Rome:] Andreas Freitag and Johann Besicken [c. 1496]), fol. a1^r. Paris, Bibliothèque Mazarine, Inc 755 Pièce 11; ISTC id00046500. In the public domain.

8.50   [Castellano Castellani,] *Rappresentatione di Santo Ignatio: vescovo et martire* ([Florence: n.p., 1558]), fol. a1^r. BNCF, Banco Rari 182.49; CNCE 53233. © By permission of MiBACT/BNCF. All rights reserved.

8.51   *La Rappresentatione & festa di Ottaviano imperadore* (Florence: presso al Vescovado, 1558), fol. a1^r. BNCF, Pal. E.6.5.1$^{IV.29}$; CNCE 61829. © By permission of MiBACT/BNCF. All rights reserved.

9.1   *Incomincia la rapresentation del popolo d'Isdrael*. New York, The Morgan Library and Museum, Ms. B.37, fol. 1^r. Bequest of Curt F. Bühler, 1985.

9.2   Anastasius, *La passione de diecimila Martyri crucifixi di Iesu Christo* ([Florence: Giovanni Stefano di Carlo da Pavia, c. 1510]), fol. a1^r.

Washington DC, Library of Congress, Rosenwald Collection, Incun. X.A86; ISTC ih00283000. Image courtesy of the Library of Congress.

9.3   *Incomincia Lafesta di Nabucdonasor Re di Babillonia* ([Florence: Antonio Tubini and Andrea Ghirlandi, before December 1515]), fol. a1ʳ. Seville, Biblioteca Capitular Colombina, 6-3-28(12); CNCE 62281 (= CNCE 79370).

9.4   *Festa di Agnolo hebreo che sibaptezo per miracolo di nostra donna* ([Florence: Bartolomeo de' Libri or Giovanni Stefano di Carlo da Pavia] for Bartolomeo di Matteo Castelli, [c. 1520]), fol. a1ʳ. BNCF, Pal. D.10.2.15^{I.11}; CNCE 18888. © By permission of MiBACT/BNCF. All rights reserved.

9.5   *Miracoli della gloriosa Vergine Maria* (Florence: [Bartolomeo de' Libri] for Ser Piero Pacini da Pescia, 15 June 1500), fol. f8ʳ. BNCF, Magl. L.7.46; ISTC im00619600. © By permission of MiBACT/BNCF. All rights reserved.

9.6–9.7 Castellano Castellani, *La rappresentatione di Sancto Venantio Martyre* ([Florence:] Antonio Tubini and Andrea Ghirlandi, [before 8 August 1515]), fols. a1ʳ and b4ᵛ. BNCF, Pal. E.6.5.1^{V.27}; CNCE 9929. © By permission of MiBACT/BNCF. All rights reserved.

9.8   Master of St. Ursula, *St. Ursula rescues Pisa from the flood*. About 1380–1400. Tempera and gold on panel, 1.85 × 3.58 m. Pisa, Museo Nazionale di San Matteo, formerly in the church of San Paolo a Ripa d'Arno. Pisa, Museo di San Matteo, cod. 09 00405700. Wikimedia Commons / CC BY-SA-3.0. Photo: Miguel Hermoso Cuesta.

9.9   [Castellano Castellani], *La Rapresentatione di S. Orsola Vergine & Martire* (Florence: [Giunti?], March 1554), fol. b4ʳ. BNCF, Pal. E.6.5.1^{IV.26}; CNCE 52871. © By permission of MiBACT/BNCF. All rights reserved.

9.10   Castellano Castellani, *Rappresentatione della Cena et passione di Christo, correpta di nuouo con aggiunta di alquante stanze, Composta per messer Castellano Castellani* (Florence: [Antonio Tubini and Andrea Ghirlandi] for Francesco di Giovanni Benvenuto, 15 March 1519/20), fol. a1ʳ. BNCF, Pal. E.6.6.1^{II.20}; CNCE 9933. © By permission of MiBACT/BNCF. All rights reserved.

9.11   [Castellano Castellani], *La Rapresentatione della Resurrectione di Christo Nuouamente composta* ([Florence: Bernardo Zucchetta, after 1517]), fol. a1ʳ. BRF, Edizioni Rare 685^{15}; CNCE 71221. © By permission of MiBACT/BRF. All rights reserved.

9.12   Castellano Castellani, *Rapresentatione di sancto Honofrio, composta per messer Castellano Castellani* ([Florence: Antonio Tubini and Andrea Ghirlandi, between 22 October 1509, and 15 April 1511]), fol. a1^r. BNCF, Banco Rari 182.46; CNCE 9928. © By permission of MiBACT/BNCF. All rights reserved.

9.13   *Rappresentatione quando Abram caccio Aghar sua ancilla con Ismael suo figluolo. Et prima e/ per annuntiatione un padre con dua figluoli: Vno cattiuo chiamato Antonio. Laltro buono chamato Benedecto* ([Florence]: Antonio Tubini and Andrea Ghirlandi, [not after 8 August 1515]), fol. a1^r. BNCF, Banco Rari 179.6; CNCE 61516. © By permission of Mi-BACT/BNCF. All rights reserved.

9.14   *Froctola duno padre che haueua dua figliuoli vno buono chiamato Benedecto Laltro captiuo chiamato Antonio* ([Florence: Bernardo Zucchetta, 15..]), fol. a1^r. Milan, Archivio Storico Civico e Biblioteca Trivulziana, Inc. C 258/6; ISTC if00325600; CNCE 19915. © Comune di Milano — All rights reserved.

9.15   Giuntino d'Antonio Berti, *Larapresentatione & diuota historia: & festa di sancto Paulino Vescouo: & una oratione di Sancta Croce* ([Florence: Antonio Miscomini, 1492–1494]), fol. a6^v. Rome, Biblioteca Casanatense, Inc. 1582; ISTC ib00515500. BEIC / CC BY-SA-4.0.

9.16   [Castellano Castellani?], *Rappresentatione di sancta Barbara nuouamente composta* ([Florence: Antonio Tubini and Andrea Ghirlandi] for Francesco di Giovanni Benvenuto, [after 17 February 1516/17]), fol. a1^r. BNCF, Banco Rari 179.27; CNCE 61521. © By permission of MiBACT/BNCF. All rights reserved.

9.17   [Castellano Castellani?], *Festa di S. Margherita* (Florence: [Antonio Tubini and Andrea Ghirlandi] for Francesco di Giovanni Benvenuto, [after 22 November 1514]), fol. a1^r. BNCF, Pal. E.6.7.56$^{VI.6}$; CNCE 18893. © By permission of MiBACT/BNCF. All rights reserved.

9.18   *Reconstruction of the Purification company's oratory on the north-western corner of San Marco, in relation to the other confraternities of San Marco, Florence, 1444–1506.* Drawing: Teresa Flanigan; photo: Ann Matchette and Theresa Flanigan; from Matchette, "The Compagnia," 77, Plate 17.

9.19   *Comincia la devota rappresentatione di Iudith hebrea* ([Florence: Antonio Tubini and Andrea Ghirlandi] for Francesco di Giovanni Benvenuto, 30 [--] 1519), fol. a1^r. BNCF, Pal. E.6.5.1$^{IV.9}$; CNCE 32695. © By permission of MiBACT/BNCF. All rights reserved.

9.20 *La rapresentatione di santa Uliva Nuouamente mandata in Luce* (Florence: n.p., 1568), fol. a1ʳ. BRF, Edizioni Rare 674³⁷; CNCE 62404. © By permission of MiBACT/BRF. All rights reserved.

9.21 Giuliano Bugiardini, *Martyrdom of St. Catherine of Alexandria.* About 1530–1540, oil on canvas, 425 × 295 cm. Florence, Basilica of Santa Maria Novella, Rucellai Chapel. Wikimedia Commons / CC BY-SA-3.0. Photo: Sailko.

10.1 *Il primo libro di rappresentationi et feste. Di diuersi Santi & Sante del Testamento Vecchio, & Nuouo, composte da diuersi auttori, nuouamente ricorrette & ristampate: Fra le quali ue ne sono di molte non piu uenute in luce. Con una tavola di tutto quello. Che nel presente libro si contiene* (Florence: Giunti, 1555), fol. ♣ii^{r–v}. Milano, Biblioteca del Museo Poldi Pezzoli, Sezione antica; CNCE 53303. Internet Culturale / CC BY-NC-SA 3.0.

10.2 *Il terzo libro di feste, rappresentationi, Et Comedie Spirituali, Di Diuersi Santi, e Sante, del Testamento vecchio, & nuouo, Composte da Diuersi Autori. Nuouamente poste insieme, e parte non piu stampate. Aggiuntoui nel fine vna Scelta di Laude Spirituali. Con la Tauola di quel che nell'opera si contiene* (Florence: [Giunti], 1578), fol. AAAiiiʳ. Venice, Biblioteca Marciana, Rari 591; CNCE 53305. Internet Culturale / CC BY-NC-SA 3.0.

10.3 Antonio di Matteo di Meglio, Herald of the Signoria, with Feo Belcari, *Larapresentatione del di del giudicio* ([Florence: Bartolomeo de' Libri, c. 1495]), fol. a4ʳ. Annotations by Anton Maria Salvini. BRF, Edizioni Rare 686²; ISTC ir00028950. © By permission of MiBACT/BRF. All rights reserved.

10.4 *Rappresentationi et feste di diversi santi, e sante Del Testamento Vecchio, & Nuouo, Composte da Diuersi Autori. Nuouamente messe insieme. Con la Tauola di quel che nell'Opera si contiene* (Florence: [Giunti], 1581). Undated facsimile, in the Author's collection.

10.5–10.6 Bindings by Vincenzo Moggi, using French marbled paper. Florence, 1829. BNCF, Pal. E.6.7.56^{I.9}; Pal. E.6.7.56^{IV–10}. © By permission of MiBACT/BNCF. All rights reserved.

10.7 Feo Belcari, *Qui comincia la representatione di Habraam quando idio gli comando che gli facessi sacrificio in sul monte di Isaac suo figluolo* (Florence: [Printer of Vergilius (C 6061)], April 1490), inside front cover. Binding signed by the Parisian binder Bauzonnet-Trautz, gold tooling on red morocco, with marbled endpapers in nonpareil pattern, before 1851. BNCF, Pal. E.6.7.47; ISTC ib00297300. © By permission of Mi-BACT/BNCF. All rights reserved.

INTRODUCTION

> The extraordinary rarity of all these singular
> productions, termed Mysteries or Miracle-
> Plays, is too well known to require comment.
>
> Guglielmo Libri, 1859[1]

The *sacre rappresentazioni* of Renaissance Florence were not a single and unchanging phenomenon. Both ephemeral, since they existed only in the moment of their performance, and increasingly permanent, as they were copied for posterity, and printed first for an elite market and then to feed an insatiable appetite for devotional entertainment, they existed in a variety of ways and in various environments. To the people who took part in them, the plays were sociable and pleasurable performances of devotion to God and all the saints of the heavenly court, they were serious play. While it is possible to see the plays as a form of preaching through which actors and their audiences were instructed in doctrinal matters, this study sees the primary beneficiaries of the plays to be the performers themselves, who found an unprecedented outlet for collective creativity. To printers and booksellers from the 1490s to the 1630s, they were profitable merchandise: printed booklets of one or two quires, recognizable by the form of their title (usually *rappresentazione*, but also *festa* and *miracolo*) and by the woodcuts below, typically of the Angel of the Annunciation, holding a lily, above a larger scene depicting the climactic moment of the action. The market for the plays was the devout laity to whom the plays offered an alternative to the secular excess of Carnival. From the seventeenth century onwards, the plays appealed to lexicographers, who combed them for words and phrases of purest *toscana favella*; to collectors, who began to collect and list them; and to literary historians who accounted for them in short paragraphs relating to dramatic literature.

Few major authors could be found among their creators. Lorenzo de' Medici stood out as a poet of singular ability; Feo Belcari was relatively prolific and an industrious self-promoter; Bernardo Pulci, on the margins of Lorenzo's *brigata*, was the brother of a major poet, while his wife Antonia may well have been the first European woman to see her works through the printing press. Castellano Castellani was a prolific writer of *rappresentazioni*

---

[1] Libri, *Catalogue* (1859), 299.

after his academic career had faltered. The fact of having an author's name attached to them has brought many of these plays unwarranted attention, but the majority of the one hundred and thirty or so *rappresentazioni* that survived into modern consciousness are anonymous and demand to be read on their own terms, speaking to us directly, unmediated by biographies and reputations.

The *rappresentazioni* come to us as books, as dramatic texts, but the relationship of a text to a performance is seldom documented. We do not know if the book represents the starting point of a performance, or a literary reworking after the event. As modern readers, we must piece together disparate fragments: texts, descriptions, letters, account books, fictional narratives, and government records, in order to begin to understand the plays on their own terms.[2] This volume aims to read those texts at a variety of levels and to reconstruct their performance context. It combines the histories of the text, the book, social groups and their rituals, and theatre, viewed against the social history of Renaissance Florence.

Words, pictures, and people set Florence apart from other cities in the period and make its *rappresentazioni* worthy of their own investigation. In a brief introduction to religious theatre, Marzia Pieri outlined three factors that allowed religious spectacle to attain a remarkable level of "cultural worth" in Florence, creating sets and machinery that set standards throughout Italy, and formalizing texts into a new literary genre. The figurative traditions of Florentine painting and of ceremonial provided a backdrop against which the plays emerged; the Florentine vernacular had the status and the expressive capacity to communicate across all levels of society; and individuals and groups provided collective engagement and financial support for the plays.[3] Florentines were proud of their reputation for mounting *feste*, both for private devotions and for public and diplomatic display, and they willingly made their *festaiuoli* (people responsible for organising *feste*) and their expertise available to courts throughout Italy. The focus of this study is necessarily on Florence but students of other European dramas will find much to compare. They will also note the absence of performance-based research such as has flourished for other European dramas. I hope, however, that the wealth of documentation may lead to new insights into contacts between Florence and the Low Countries and Britain, influences that have long been suspected but never established.

---

[2] See Ferrone, "Scrivere per lo spettacolo"; Ventrone, "'Philosophia,'" 137.

[3] M. Pieri, *La nascita*, 43–44. For a different view of the process, see Ventrone, "Simbologia," 299–301.

Broad studies of the *rappresentazioni* date only from the Unification of Italy. In an important departure from the antiquarianism of the late seventeenth and eighteenth century,[4] romance philologists brought a new and nationalistic historicism to the study of the origins of Italian drama. In 1872, Alessandro D'Ancona (1835–1914), who spent all his academic life at the University of Pisa, published a three-volume anthology of *sacre rappresentazioni* covering the full range of compositions, from the earliest surviving text of the *Dì del Giudizio*, in which Feo Belcari built on an earlier text by the Florentine herald, through to sixteenth-century *commedie spirituali*. The plays were arranged approximately by subject matter, Old and New Testament followed by saints, without reference to chronology, so that texts composed almost a century apart sat in promiscuous proximity. Each text was preceded by a short introduction, listing the known editions, outlining the usually anonymous author's sources, and contained no discussion of performance. This absence was to some extent remedied in the first edition of his *Origini del teatro italiano* (1877), published in two small volumes as a companion to the anthology, for which he scoured print and manuscript sources for play texts and descriptions of performances, in Florence and beyond. And when he came to revise that work for a second edition in 1891, his study was enriched by a vast amount of additional material that had been shared with him by scholars from Europe.[5] The great contribution of this work, which has remained in print for the last fifty years, lies in the chapters on the *sacre rappresentazioni* of Florence.

Ernesto Monaci (1844–1918) was responsible for the dissemination of information about newly discovered texts of Umbrian drama.[6] When D'Ancona was preparing the second edition of his *Origini*, he lamented that the texts of the vast tradition of *laude drammatiche* — texts in ballad metres ranging from short dialogues to extended plays — from Perugia and Assisi, which Monaci and others had discovered, were still unpublished.[7] Monaci's student Vincenzo De Bartholomaeis (1867–1953) went on to publish a study of them — with a bold definite article — in *Le origini della poesia drammatica* (1924; substantial revision completed 1940 and published 1952). He also

---

[4] See, for example, Cionacci, "Sopra *Le rime sacre*" (1680); Walker, *An Historical and Critical Essay* (1808).

[5] See for example the addition of Abraham of Suzdal's description of the Annunciation and Ascension plays, D'Ancona, *Origini*, 1:246–253.

[6] Monaci, "Appunti."

[7] D'Ancona, *Origini*, 1:114, n. 5.

edited two anthologies: *Il teatro abruzzese nel medioevo* (1924) and much later *Laude drammatiche e rappresentazioni sacre* (1943). De Bartholomaeis, a native of L'Aquila, was somewhat partisan in his assertion of the priority of the Abruzzese *rappresentazioni* over the Florentine ones. Some of his claims do not withstand close scrutiny,[8] but the wealth of information his study contains on both Latin and vernacular drama from the tenth to the sixteenth century, and its geographical spread from Piedmont to Sicily, ensures that it is still useful. The edition of Umbrian *laude* promised in 1960 by Ignazio Baldelli did not materialize, but monumental scholarly editions of the *laudari* from Perugia, Assisi, and Orvieto, edited by Maurizio Perugi and Gina Scentoni, and of Orvieto, edited by Gina Scentoni, have recently appeared.[9]

Despite the place given to the *sacre rappresentazioni* in the great Enlightenment histories of Italian literature by Crescimbeni, Quadrio, and Tiraboschi,[10] for Apostolo Zeno, arbiter of taste in mid-eighteenth-century Venice, they were better forgotten:

> Apart from a few that have some trace of flavour, mixed however with an unpleasant sourness, they are old and stale and worthless, drawn from apocryphal legends and from contaminated sources, with a base pedestrian style, devoid of art and poetic grace, and where, from time to time, the verse and rhyme are barely, even with adjustment, sustained.[11]

Francesco De Sanctis dismissed them out of hand. For De Sanctis, whose *Storia della letteratura italiana* (1871–1872) was the received wisdom for generations of schoolchildren,

---

[8] For example, his assertion that the play of *Abramo* in a manuscript copied in Chieti in 1576, is earlier than Feo Belcari's *Abramo e Isac*; see De Bartholomaeis, *Le origini*, 415; Newbigin, "Il testo e il contesto," 19–21.

[9] *Il Laudario assisano 36*; *Il laudario perugino*; *Laudario orvietano*.

[10] Crescimbeni, *L'istoria della volgar poesia*, 1:300–305, vol. 1, lib. iv, cap. 13; Quadrio, *Della storia e della ragione*, 3.1:53–103, vol. 3. lib. i, dist. 1, cap. iv, part. 1–3; Tiraboschi, *Storia della letteratura italiana*, 6.2:182–183, lib. III, cap. 3, par. xxix.

[11] Zeno, "Annotazioni," 1:489, note (a): "Trattone alquante, che hanno qualche suco di buon sapore, mescolato però di agro, e di spiacevole, son rancidumi ed inezie, cavate anche da leggende apocrife, e da impure fonti, con basso, e pedestre stile, e d'arte prive e di grazia poetica, e dove di quando in quando appena il verso, e la rima aggiustatamente sostengonsi."

the action is pedestrian and bourgeois, prosaically clear, not enlivened by sentiment, nor transformed by imagination. It is the world of Dante in everyday dress. [...] If there is any serious purpose left in these spectacular performances, staged with such pomp of scenery and decoration, it is just a memory and an echo of a world weakened in its conscience. [...] The mystery play is an abortion, a sacred genre that no longer speaks to the heart and to the soul, it is without serious intent, transformed by men of learning into a game purely of the imagination.[12]

The process by which De Sanctis arrived at this point of view helps us to understand the kinds of distortion that have plagued the study of the *rappresentazioni*. In his description of BNCF, Ms. Palatino 445, the starting point of a rambling essay on the history of the *rappresentazioni*, the Palatine librarian Francesco Palermo began by eulogizing the play of the *Monaco che andò al servizio di Dio*, declaring that it was copied in (rather than after) 1485 and opining: "I certainly think it is older than the early years of that century."[13] Palermo included lengthy extracts that were taken up, separately, by two German scholars, Adolf Ebert and J. L. Klein, whose validation of the play allowed Francesco De Sanctis to momentarily set aside a small part of his hostility to the genre.[14] In 1870, he published in *Nuova antologia* a 'full' edition of the play, at the same time damning its author, whom he assumed to be a friar: "The friar has neither felt nor comprehended the magnificence of the concept before him, and he loses the most interesting dramatic conflicts

---

[12] De Sanctis, *Storia*, 1:365–366: "l'azione è pedestre e borghese, di una prosaica chiarezza, non animata dal sentimento, non trasformata dall'immaginazione. È il mondo dantesco vestito alla borghese. [...] Se alcuna serietà rimane ancora in queste spettacolose rappresentazioni, apparecchiate con tanta pompa di scene e di decorazioni, è reminiscenza ed eco di un mondo indebolito nella coscienza. [...] Il mistero è un aborto, è una materia sacra che non dice più nulla alla mente ed al cuore, senza alcuna serietà di motivi, e trasformata da uomini colti in un puro giuoco d'immaginazione." The view did not change in subsequent editions.

[13] BNCF, Pal. 445, fols. 26v–39v; Palermo, *I manoscritti palatini*, 1853–1868, 2 (1860): 337: "a noi par per certo più antica de' primi anni di esso secolo." See De Sanctis, "Un dramma claustrale," for praise of *Un monaco che andò al servizio di Dio*, and also D'Ancona, *Origini*, 1:210–215.

[14] Ebert, "Studien," 73–79; Klein, *Geschichte*, 1:157.

in the void."[15] That edition was subsequently reprinted in the many editions of his *Nuovi saggi critici,* and De Bartholomaeis then used it in his edition of *Laude drammatiche e rappresentazioni sacre.*[16] It tells of a son who disappoints his parents and godfather by leaving home to become a monk. The hermit who takes him in asks whether the boy will be saved and is told by an Angel that he will be damned. But after the hermit sees him resist the temptation of the Devil-disguised-as-the-godfather, the Angel returns to tell him that the young man will after all be saved. Joyful singing ends the play. But De Sanctis's edition is radically different from the manuscript version because he systematically purged the stage directions to deliver a very slight play. Many of the stage directions are indeed redundant but others, with their indication of emotion and intention and concurrent action, seem indispensable. The one after the Angel's prologue, for example: "Now, to begin the play, the young man is represented before he became a monk, and how he took leave of his father and mother, and is deep in thought about taking the cloth, and fearful of displeasing his father and mother; and his mother, seeing him lost in thought, speaks to him as follows"[17] is replaced by two words: "The Mother." The dialogue is decontextualized by these interventions, and ultimately misrepresented; the misrepresentations found their way to encyclopedias, and thence to webpages, and are difficult to correct.[18]

Between the great wars of the twentieth century, Fascist administrations sponsored various attempts to revive and indeed re-invent the popular festivals of late medieval and Renaissance Italy: the Palio in Siena, the Joust of the Saracen in Arezzo, and the Calcio Storico in Florence.[19] The revival of interest in the *sacre rappresentazioni* was probably more fortuitous. In 1933, in its very first season, the Florentine Maggio Musicale invited the French director Jacques Copeau — who had already achieved a radical renewal of

---

[15] De Sanctis, "Un dramma claustrale," 457: "Il frate non ha sentito, nè compreso quale magnificenza di concetto aveva innanzi, e lascia cadere nel vuoto i più interessanti contrasti drammatici."

[16] De Sanctis, "Un dramma claustrale," 439–452; reprinted in De Bartholomaeis, ed., *Laude drammatiche,* 2:403–422; see also De Bartholomaeis, *Le origini,* 416–417.

[17] BNCF, Pal. 445, fol. 27r: "Ora per dare forma alla rapresentatione, s'infignie che il giovane, innanzi che ssi amonachò, e in che modo si parte dal padre et dalla madre, sta pensoso d'andare alla religione e tteme di non dispiacere al padre e alla madre; e·lla madre, veggiendolo stare pensoso, gli parla chome seghuita."

[18] Oelsner, "Italian Literature," in *Encyclopaedia Britannica* (1911), 14:899; https://en. wikipedia.org/wiki/Italian_literature.

[19] Civai and Toti, "Fabio Bargagli Petrucci"; Lasansky, *The Renaissance Perfected.*

Figure 0.1 André Barsacq, Set design for *Sant'Uliva*, cloister of Santa Croce, May 1933. From Corrado D'Errico, ed., *La rappresentazione di Santa Uliva*, libero rifacimento (Rome: Edizioni Sud, 1936), plate following p. 12. Author's collection.

French theatre and of actor preparation — to devise and direct a production of *La rappresentazione di Santa Uliva* (The Play of Santa Uliva), billed as a "medieval mystery play," but not known before 1568.[20] The text had been substantially reworked, and the production, in the cloister of the Franciscan friary of Santa Croce, was a major event (fig. 0.1). *Santa Uliva* was followed in 1937 by another "mystery play," commissioned by the mayor of Padua for the Giotto celebrations of that year. The students of Silvio D'Amico's Accademia d'Arte Drammatica performed the *Mistero della Natività, Passione e Resurrezione di Nostro Signore,* which D'Amico (with the help of Paolo Toschi) had assembled from a selection of Umbrian *laude* and designed for performance on a 'medieval' stage, divided into *luoghi deputati* (appointed places).[21] The following year, the newly formed Compagnia dell'Accademia took the *Mistero*

---

[20] Aliverti, "Copeau" (1979), "Copeau" (1986), and "La *Rappresentazione di Santa Uliva*"; D'Amico, "*Santa Uliva*." Further discussion below, chapter 9.

[21] D'Amico, ed., *Mistero*. See also Toschi, "Il Mistero"; and Costa, "Regia," 343, describing Tatiana Pavlova's production of 1937 and his own production of 1938.

della Natività and Jacopone da Todi's *Donna del Paradiso* on tour throughout Italy.[22] These re-inventions of medieval drama were immensely important for the interest they generated in the drama of the past, but they had little to do with the historical and social realities of the genre, and — more importantly — the authority of their promoters guaranteed that there could be no interrogation of the assumptions underpinning the productions.[23]

Anthologies continued to appear. Like Paolo Toschi's *L'antico dramma sacro italiano* (1926–1927),[24] Mario Bonfantini's anthology, *Le sacre rappresentazioni italiane* (1942) brought together texts from the Umbrian and Florentine traditions as a seamless entity, without close examination of the performance contexts. The years after the Second World War brought incremental gains to our knowledge of the *sacre rappresentazioni*. The great arbiter of the Italian literary canon, Benedetto Croce, although wistful at the (imagined) demise of the *rappresentazioni* in the sixteenth century at the hands of post-Tridentine reformers, did not include these anonymous works in the Laterza collection of "Scrittori d'Italia."[25] Luigi Banfi added the play of the *Ortolano elemosiniere* (Beneficent gardener) to the published *corpus* in his *Sacre rappresentazioni del Quattrocento* (1963; latest reprint 1997); Erhard Lommatzsch's *Beiträge* (1959–1963) published transcriptions of twenty-seven plays contained in a bound anthology in the Herzog August Bibliothek of Wolfenbüttel, all printed between 1558 and 1569, and many without modern editions; and Giovanni Ponte complemented his study of Castellano Castellani and his attribution of new plays to this author, whom he regarded as essentially a follower of Savonarola,[26] with his own anthology of *Sacre rappresentazioni fiorentine del Quattrocento* (1974). Nevertheless, the study of these texts remained largely in the realm of philology and history of

---

[22] Pedullà in D'Amico, *Cronache*, 4.1 (2004): 41–42; Tinterri, *Arlecchino*, 125–134, 159–224.

[23] Silvio D'Amico, who shaped Italy's Accademia Nazionale d'Arte Drammatica that now bears his name, worked as a theatre critic, founded and edited a succession of important journals, and was the first editor (succeeded by his son) of the *Enciclopedia dello spettacolo* (11 vols., 1954–1975).

[24] Paolo Toschi, author of *Le origini del teatro italiano* (1955; rpt. 1997), held the chair of Storia delle Tradizioni Popolari (History of Folk Traditions) at Rome's La Sapienza University from 1938 to 1968. For his hostility to D'Ancona's philological approach, see Toschi, ed., *L'antico dramma*, 1:vii–xvi.

[25] Croce, "La fine delle sacre rappresentazioni," 346.

[26] Ponte, *Attorno al Savonarola*.

language.[27] Where the study of early English drama was invigorated by the towering literary respectability of Shakespeare, and by large-scale community performances revived in 1951,[28] no such stimuli were available in the study of the Florentine plays.

The appointment in 1972 of the Venetian scholar Ludovico Zorzi (1928–1983) to the first Italian chair of History of Theatre and Spectacle at the University of Florence marked a significant change in the intellectual climate surrounding the study of early modern theatre. In Florence, Zorzi dedicated himself to exploring the realities of Italian theatrical culture from the fifteenth to the eighteenth century. His monumental contributions were two exhibitions, *Il luogo teatrale a Firenze* (1975), and *La scena del principe* (1980), for which he worked with his wife Elvira Garbero Zorzi and the architect Cesare Lisi to produce architectural models that illustrated his reconstructions of stage machinery and stage design from Brunelleschi to the sixteenth-century Medici court.[29] His catalogue essay for the 1975 exhibition was reworked in *Il teatro e la città: saggi sulla scena italiana* (1977), along with essays on Ferrara and Venice. But even more significant than these are the scholars he trained in the course of his career, cut tragically short in 1983. Among them is Paola Ventrone, to whose many publications on Florentine theatre and spectacle I shall refer repeatedly in the course of this study. The exhibition she curated, *"Le tems revient" — "'l tempo si rinuova": feste e spettacoli nella Firenze di Lorenzo il Magnifico* (1992), together with her three monographic studies, *Gli araldi della commedia: teatro a Firenze nel Rinascimento* (1993), *Lo spettacolo religioso a Firenze nel Quattrocento* (2008) and *Teatro civile e sacra rappresentazione a Firenze nel Rinascimento* (2016), combine a wealth of scholarship and a spectacular command of a wide range of historical disciplines and of festive genres.[30]

---

[27] For important contributions, see Del Popolo, "Restauri testuali," "Altri appunti," "Leggendo le sacre rappresentazioni," and *Tra sacro e profano: saggi di filologia varia.*

[28] Rogerson, *Playing a Part in History*; on a challenge to the Lord Chamberlain's injunctions against representing the deity on stage, see pp. 44–45.

[29] The models appeared again in Florence in the 2001 exhibition *Teatro e spettacolo nella Firenze dei Medici: modelli dei luoghi teatrali,* curated by Elvira Garbero Zorzi and Mario Speranzi; and in Washington, D.C., in the 2018 exhibition *Sacred Drama: Performing the Bible in Renaissance Florence,* curated by Giorgio Bonsanti, Silvia Castelli, and Anna Maria Testaverde. They are currently housed in the Scuderia of the Parco di Pratolino, north of Florence.

[30] See also her review of her own approach in Ventrone, "Dall'osservatore," and her review of confraternal drama scholarship in Ventrone, "I teatri delle confraternite."

North American scholarship in the 1970s and 1980s brought about a significant shift in direction. In the vanguard of this change was a conference, *The Pursuit of Holiness in Late Medieval and Renaissance Religion*, held at the University of Michigan in 1972. The proceedings, edited by Charles E. Trinkaus and Heiko A. Oberman, brought together leading social and cultural historians, including a young and relatively unknown scholar, Richard C. Trexler. Trexler's subsequent essays on Florentine social and cultural history and his *Public Life in Renaissance Florence* (1980) opened the eyes of scholars in Italy and abroad to the wealth of material still to be uncovered in the Florentine archives. Trexler explored issues of gender, power, and ritual, and the function of saints, their cults and images, in fifteenth-century Florence, providing a new context for Rab Hatfield's earlier exemplary essay on the company of the Magi (1970) that had allowed us to glimpse the intersections of patronage, lay piety, and humanism in the procession of the Magi that the Medici would make their own. Similarly ground-breaking was Ronald F.E. Weissman's *Ritual Brotherhood in Renaissance Florence* (1982), that opened up the field of confraternity studies, explored further by John Henderson, and by Konrad Eisenbichler and Lorenzo Polizzotto and their *longue durée* studies of two Florentine youth confraternities that were particularly involved with theatrical performances.[31]

In the early 1970s, while I was leafing through handwritten catalogues of manuscripts in Italian libraries in search of Sienese comedies, I became dimly aware that D'Ancona's anthology, for all its merits, had one serious defect: it was based entirely on the printed texts that he found in the libraries of Florence and did not draw at all on the vast body of plays that existed only in manuscript. In 1983, when I published a group of these texts, I attempted to contextualize them in confraternal performances and the *edifici* of the processions for the feast of St. John the Baptist. I was able to draw some conclusions about significant differences between the plays of the third quarter of the fifteenth century, and those that we knew only in print from the last decade of the fifteenth century and the first two decades of the sixteenth. But it also became clear that more research was needed both to refine the chronology of the plays and to document the association between the *edifici*, the plays, and specific confraternities.

Even before the first publication of D'Ancona's *Origini*, theatre historians were aware that the *sacre rappresentazioni* had been performed by

---

[31] Henderson, *Piety*; Eisenbichler, *The Boys*; Polizzotto, *Children*.

youth confraternities,[32] but nobody had looked seriously at the documents contained in two important *fondi* of the Archivio di Stato of Florence. The first bears the title *Compagnie religiose soppresse da Pietro Leopoldo* and became the property of the state when the Austrian grand duke of Tuscany Pietro Leopoldo suppressed all but a handful of Florentine confraternities in 1785.[33] In 1983, guided initially by John Henderson, I began to work through the account books of the youth confraternity of the Purification, which had attracted my interest because they covered the years for which I hoped to find some records of a performance of a Purification play. My search was richly rewarded. In this confraternity, which Lorenzo Polizzotto has since shown to be closely entwined with Medici plans for San Marco and subsequently with Savonarola's reforms, we find the earliest documentary evidence of members of a youth confraternity staging plays.[34]

Cyrilla Barr and I then worked independently on the archive of an adult company, the Compagnia di Santa Maria delle Laude e di Sant'Agnese, part of an earlier group of companies that had been suppressed in 1752 and absorbed into one of Florence's most enduring charitable institutions, the Bigallo, before it too was suppressed in 1784. Here we found account books and inventories that document the performance of the Ascension *festa* in Santa Maria del Carmine from 1425 until its demise at the turn of the century. Subsequently I worked systematically through the documents relating to the Compagnia di Santa Maria delle Laude e dello Spirito Santo, responsible for the Pentecost play in Santo Spirito, and the very meagre documentary evidence relating to the Annunciation *festa* in San Felice, and published my findings in *Feste d'Oltrarno: Plays in Churches in Fifteenth-Century Florence* (1996).[35]

Further important work on the social milieu and function of plays in female communities, based on archival research and close reading of texts, has emerged around the works of Antonia Tanini, wife of Bernardo Pulci. Revising important early work by James Cook, Elissa Weaver has been able to reconstruct the life and corpus of this extraordinary lay woman and to trace

---

[32] Cionacci, "Sopra *Le rime sacre*," 13.

[33] The various archives were deposited with the hospital of Santa Maria Nuova and transferred to the State Archives in 1876; see Toccafondi, "L'archivio," 146; Evangelista, "L'attività spettacolare," 309–312.

[34] Newbigin, "The Word Made Flesh"; Polizzotto, *Children*. The Purification company is discussed in chapter 3 below.

[35] See also the studies of Barr, "A Renaissance Artist," and "Music and Spectacle."

the vigorous survival of the plays in female religious houses long after they had ceased to be performed publicly for lay audiences.[36]

Since the "New Art History" of the 1970s and 1980s, *sacre rappresentazioni* have been scoured by art historians for ideas about how figures from the Old and New Testament, from the *Golden Legend*, and the *Lives of the Desert Fathers* were visualized in action. There has been much discussion, informed and otherwise, about the relationship between art and painting, but in the absence of a detailed understanding of chronology of the plays and how they changed over time, such enterprises have been hazardous. Despite this new tangential interest, and occasional specific explorations of authors such as Feo Belcari, Lorenzo de' Medici, Castellano Castellani, and Antonia Pulci, there has been little interest in the genre as a whole. As a genre that emerges after Humanism, after the re-emergence of Plautus and Terence, and after the rediscovery of realistic representation and linear perspective in art, it sits uneasily in medieval drama sessions at the great medieval congresses of Kalamazoo and Leeds; while as a manifestation of late medieval lay piety, it is peripheral to the core business of the Renaissance Society of America.

At smaller, specialized conferences, such as those organized annually from 1976 to 2009 by Federico Doglio and the Centro Studi sul Teatro Medioevale e Rinascimentale in Viterbo, Anagni and Rome, the situation was different. On given subjects, such as saints and martyrs on stage (the theme of the 2000 conference), fifteen or twenty scholars from art history, musicology, history, and cultural studies, as well as literary and theatre historians from a range of backgrounds, interacted around the key issues of a selected play that was performed during the conference. The centre's director was the leading sponsor in Italy of explorations of medieval and early modern theatrical performance, and the list of productions of *sacre rappresentazioni* alone is impressive: Lorenzo de' Medici's *San Giovanni e Paulo* in the Teatro Valle, Rome, in 1987; Castellano Castellani's *Storia di sant'Onofrio* in the cloister of Sant'Onofrio al Gianicolo, Rome, in 1992; the *Rappresentazione di un miracolo di due pellegrini* and the *Rappresentazione di un miracolo di tre pellegrini* in Anagni in 1999; the *Rappresentazione di santo Alessio* in 2000; and the *Rappresentazione di Stella* in 2004.[37] There is significant resistance, however,

[36] Pulci, *Florentine Drama*, trans. Cook; Pulci, *Saints' Lives*, ed. Weaver, trans. Cook.

[37] Published proceedings, plays performed, and video-recordings from between 1976 and 2009, are held centrally in the Biblioteca Don Bosco of the Università Pontificia Salesiana, Rome. For performances, see http://evodrama.net; and also Perrone Capano, "Momenti," and "Regards." Other Italian productions include the *Rappresentazione del*

in Italian academic circles to any kind of historical reconstruction or even reinterpretation of medieval drama beyond the ever-enduring re-enactments of the Passion.[38]

The conferences of the Société Internationale pour l'Étude du Théâtre Médiéval (SITM), and those organized in Camerino by Sydney Higgins from 1996 to 1999, embody a different approach. Student companies from Holland, Germany, France, Spain, Italy, Great Britain, the United States, and Canada have regularly brought medieval texts to life for broad and appreciative audiences and have provided fora for discussion of the how and why both of the original performances and of the contemporary one. Like confraternal drama itself, student performances are a learning experience for teachers and students alike, while for scholars they are an indispensable tool for textual and performance analysis. The Camerino conference is no longer held, but its spirit survives in *European Medieval Drama* (1996–), the only specialist journal that encompasses continental medieval drama.

This volume draws together a century of scholarship on drama and social history, and almost fifty years of my own research in the archives and on manuscript and printed sources, to provide a coherent overview and a new perspective on the *sacre rappresentazioni* of fifteenth- and sixteenth-century Florence. Much of the evidence for the how and why of the *sacra rappresentazione* has been lost: to floods, to neglect, to changes in taste and public policy. Other sources, I am sure, have yet to be discovered. And more still lies just beyond the scope of this study, in the world of civic and religious processions and entries, marriages and funerals, *feste*, and ceremonies that are not based on the performance of a text.[39] I leave these aside with reluctance. They are germane to my subject, and the occasions were often enriched by plays, but — with the exception of the *rappresentazioni* for the St. John the Baptist and Magi processions — I must let them pass by.

The book begins, however, not with the plays in their performance spaces but with texts. Chapter 1, "The Manuscript Evidence of Florentine *sacre*

---

viaggio di Uliva in the Teatro Argentina in 1993; and the *Conversione di Maria Maddalena e la resurrezione di Lazzaro*, attributed to Castellani, in the Duomo of Piacenza in 1997; see Perrone Capano, "Momenti," 84.

[38] See *Sacre rappresentazioni: arte, etica, Vangelo delle comunità* (2010); and the Europassion network, online.

[39] For recent overviews, see doctoral dissertations by Chrétien, *The Festival of San Giovanni*; Rogers, "Art and Public Festival"; Dunlevie, "*Virginibus puerisque*"; Stallini, "*La sacra rappresentazione*"; Mori, "Lo spettacolo."

rappresentazioni," explores the genesis of the plays, the anthologies that were produced in confraternities and friaries, the copies that were made in personal *zibaldoni* (miscellanies of things to be remembered that are characteristic of Florentine families), and in presentation copies. Careful analysis allows us to date the plays with a greater degree of certainty and avoid the trap of consigning all *sacre rappresentazioni* to a timeless contemporaneity. With an increased clarity about names and dates, we can begin to reconstruct a network of relationships between play texts and individual confraternities — particularly the youth confraternity of the Purification — and between the confraternities themselves. Table 1 tabulates the result of this research. Sixty-five plays in manuscript have been identified, not all Florentine, but all with links to Florence. Underpinning the entire volume is an argument for the priority of the manuscript sources over the printed sources in the study of the plays.

Chapter 2, "Plays in Churches," draws on the rich archival resources and eyewitness accounts that have allowed us to trace the development of the spectacular Annunciation, Ascension, and Pentecost plays in the great conventual churches of Florence's Santo Spirito quarter. From the earliest indications around 1390, through to Vasari's exhumation of the machinery to perform the Annunciation in Santo Spirito in 1566, and his description of it in the second edition of his *Lives of the Artists* in 1568, these plays astounded viewers with a dazzling spectacle of revolving lights, hoisting machinery, music, and fireworks. Texts are not central to these early *feste*. They evolved in the hands of the *confratelli* (confraternity members, brethren) who owned every aspect of them, with little interference from the monks and friars who hosted them. They also enjoyed long-term public subsidies that enabled the artists and artisans of the three confraternities to invest extensively in structural alterations to the churches and improvements to machinery and lighting. Political interference, however, appears to have sapped the enthusiasm of the members and in the sixteenth century the plays became an instrument of Medici propaganda.

During his sojourns in Florence between 1434 and 1443 at the invitation of Cosimo de' Medici, Pope Eugenius IV approved statutes for a number of confraternities — called *compagnie* (companies) or *scuole* (schools) — for boys and young men, creating spaces in which they could socialize and follow the path of a Christian life, as well as practise the formal skills of discussion, decision-making, and record-keeping that were part of every Florentine male's education in preparation for participation in civic life. Chapter 3, "Youth Confraternities and Their Plays," examines the mid-century appearance, in the youth confraternity context, of *rappresentazioni* — scripted plays in *ottava rima*, introduced and closed by an Angel. Extensive documentation from the youth confraternity of the Purification, which flourished under direct Medici sponsorship, allows us to see the earliest plays emerge — Belcari's *Festa d'Abramo* (Play of Abraham), Muzi's *Vitel sagginato* (Fatted calf), and a *festa* of the Purification — while others are associated with the Vangelista and San Giorgio companies. The performance spaces in the cloister of San Marco, in the garden of Lorenzo, and on the hills of Fiesole suggest a close and continuing relationship between the Purification company and the Medici household. Most of the plays are anonymous, but they quickly acquire a thematic coherence, discussing notions of filial piety and generational conflict, humility and obedience (Isaac, Esau, Jacob, the Prodigal Son, St. Alexus); of *misericordia* and almsgiving as a duty toward God, even in the face of suffering (Tobias); and, later in the century, of virginity and steadfastness in the face of persecution (Queen Rosana and St. Cecilia). The widespread pedagogic view of the plays as instruction for the young is reformulated to see the young themselves as teachers, as the adolescent performers, like Daniel in the Susanna play, challenge their elders in the audience to higher standards of public and private morality. The chapter is a long one and discusses the plays in detail, to establish these common threads but also to highlight the varied texture of these early confraternity plays that are far more diverse than the modern anthologies would suggest.

From both adult and youth confraternities, scions of powerful families and minor guildsmen were conscripted into the devotions honouring the city's patron, St. John the Baptist, whose nativity was celebrated on 24 June. Chapter 4, "*Edifici* for the Feast of St. John the Baptist," deals with the procession of *edifici*, both before and after the reforms required by Archbishop Antoninus and implemented by, among others, Matteo Palmieri, who subsequently described them in his history of the city. The *edifici* were mobile platforms with elaborate superstructures that were carried in procession to the Piazza della Signoria, and on them "representations" were "done" recounting the history of Man's Salvation from the Creation to the Last Judgment. When the procession of lay confraternities was separated from the procession of professed religious in 1454, the verbal component of the *edifici* increased and the "representations" became more surely *rappresentazioni*. Among the earliest, we can identify plays of the Creation, the Annunciation, the Nativity with Octavian and the Sibyl and the Shepherds, a second Nativity with the Magi, the Last Judgment, and the Play of the Three Living Kings and the Three Dead Kings, each of these accompanied by a processional element. The presence of the Sibyls and Hermes Trismegistus in the procession of 1454 is a remarkable indicator of the *volgarizzamento* or translation into the vernacular of new humanistic interests. New research in the archives of the Innocenti, together with descriptions by the Camaldolese monk Agostino di Portico and the humanist historian Biondo Flavio, casts new light on the role of children in the procession. Like the plays in the Oltrarno churches, the plays performed on *edifici* succumbed to interference. Shut down after the Pazzi conspiracy of 1478, they did not return until 1488, when they were eclipsed by new allegorical triumphs controlled by a single man.

Chapter 5, "Playing Outdoors" turns to plays that were performed in large outdoor spaces and made use not only of the technical potential and the religious and political significance of those spaces, but also of the city's "festive kingdoms" that we find mentioned in the early chronicles. Most famous is the *festa de' Magi,* in which an adult confraternity, the predominantly Medicean company of the Magi, celebrated this most Medicean devotion with a procession that arrived from the festive kingdoms of India, Arabia, and Armenia and went to worship the Christ Child. Cavalcades and display were also an important part of the martyrdom of St. Bartholomew, performed on several occasions in Piazza Santa Croce. As Rab Hatfield has shown, the men of the Magi confraternity and those of the San Bartolomeo company used elaborate ceremonial language in communicating with each other. The feast day of the Beheading of St. John the Baptist on 29 August was celebrated in 1451 with a play performed to a huge audience outside the Porta al Prato della Giustizia, that is, in the place of public execution outside the city walls to the east of the city, and ended with the spectacular explosion that engulfed Herod's queen. In 1477 a great two-day play of St. Peter and St. Paul, saints who enjoyed increased prestige after Florence's victory at Anghiari on their feast day in 1440, was performed in the Piazza della Signoria, where the surrounding buildings made it possible to stage Simon Magus's flight and fall to great effect. No less spectacular was the two-day play of St. George (the second day has only recently been discovered), with the slaying of the dragon on Day 1, and battles between the armies from the exotic kingdoms of Persia, Ethiopia, and Armenia on Day 2. The discussion moves to other outdoor plays of St. James, as well as to Rome, where Florentine *festaiuoli* were summoned to perform for Eleanora of Aragon as she travelled from Naples to Ferrara to marry Duke Ercole I d'Este in 1473. Among those plays was the *Miracolo del Corpo di Cristo,* a Profanation of the Host play set in a Florentine reconfiguration of Paris. The long battle to establish Dominican 'ownership' of the feast of Corpus Domini is not discussed here, but the play allows the subject of Jewish oppression to be raised and explored.

For ten years after the Pazzi conspiracy of 1478 the great public spectacles lapsed, but in this period the *rappresentazioni* underwent the first stage of a generic transformation: they changed from being private texts, held by confraternities, or circulated among acquaintances, or copied in private *zibaldoni* as an act of personal devotion, to become public texts, seeking a wider reading audience through the medium of the printing press. Chapter 6, "Antonia Pulci, Antonio Miscomini, and the Transition to Print," considers the collection of thirteen plays printed by Antonio Miscomini in or very soon after 1483. Of these plays, three are identified as being by Antonia Pulci and one as being by her husband Bernardo, but when these plays are viewed along with other works by Luigi and Luca Pulci, by Poliziano, and by Bernardo Bellincioni that were printed by Miscomini at the same time, and in the light of contemptuous remarks by Bartolomeo Scala, it becomes apparent that these elegant volumes headlined by Antonia are part of a deliberate move to claim authorship and literary recognition for a very particular group of plays. Extending the examination to all the plays linked to Antonia Pulci and her family, we find an increased interest in female protagonists: wives like Esther and Vashti, and King Saul's unnamed wife who is brutally murdered; martyred virgins like Domitilla and Apollonia, and persecuted brides like Guglielma and Stella, whose patience is finally rewarded by restoration to their rightful place.

Chapter 7, "Defying Anonymity: Belcari, Poliziano, Bellincioni, and Lorenzo de' Medici," discusses the small group of male authors whose plays escape from the oblivion of anonymity. Belcari's name has appeared in several contexts, but here his *oeuvre* is examined as a whole. Poliziano and Bellincioni are discussed as Florentine authors who took the *rappresentazioni* of their youth and adapted them to other contexts: the court of Mantua in the case of Poliziano and the court of Milan, in the case of Bellincioni, with a set designed by Leonardo da Vinci. The first three poets certainly had literary ambitions, but Lorenzo's *San Giovanni e Paulo* (1490/1), is part of an elaborate rhetorical gesture of denouncing ambition and claiming weariness of the burdens of princely rule. The play is viewed in the context of a youth confraternity performance at a time when Lorenzo was making a final push to consolidate a Medicean dynasty in Florence. I argue, however, that it is little more than a gesture. Despite moments of elegant poetry, and the fact that having a named author has cemented the place of these plays in the literary canon, these plays are not *ipso facto* superior to any number of the anonymous plays preserved in manuscript and print.

The history of the plays is inseparable from the history of the material object, the booklets in which they were printed. Chapter 8, "Bartolomeo de' Libri, Antonio Miscomini, and the Illustrated Editions," examines both the new category of the printed book with illustrations, and its implications for the history of printing in Florence and for the theatrical genre. If the Miscomini plays were, indeed, the first plays to go into print, they were very quickly followed by a handsome edition of Feo Belcari's *Abramo* (ISTC ib00297250, c. 1485). From the early 1490s onwards the plays were transformed again into yet another genre. They became illustrated devotional tracts, printed in two columns of a smaller type, and illustrated with woodcuts: an angel and a scene specific to the play on the title page, and other woodcuts, often deriving from other sources, scattered throughout. Antonio Miscomini reprinted some of his earlier titles; Bartolomeo de' Libri, closely associated with the Dominicans in San Marco, printed the rest and many more. Even as Savonarola effectively shut down this rather joyful form of religious education and entertainment, his printers were making the plays available as reading material for a wider public in a format that shared aesthetic values with the editions of Savonarola's sermons. The groundwork of this chapter was laid by Paul Kristeller and Max Sander's studies of early Italian woodcuts, but an extraordinary document published by Gustavo Bertoli in 2001 brings us closer to understanding the relationship, proposed by Bernard Berenson in 1903, between the painter Bartolomeo di Giovanni, a follower of Domenico Ghirlandaio, and Bartolomeo de' Libri's illustrated editions. This chapter looks closely at the illustrations that accompanied the plays, some new and some recycled, and documents their close relationship with contemporary painting, rather than with performance practice.

The death of Savonarola in 1498 did not lead to an immediate return of the plays to their traditional venues. Even though Argentina Malaspina, wife of Piero Soderini who had been appointed *gonfaloniere* for life in 1502, may have sponsored performances, it was only with the return of the Medici in 1511 that the plays returned to the spotlight. A new surge of publication began, as the printers Antonio Tubini and Andrea Ghirlandi, working for Francesco Benvenuto, bookseller and 'publisher' at the Canto de' Bischeri, acquired Miscomini's old woodblocks — but not those of Bartolomeo de' Libri — and reissued Miscomini's titles as well as new ones by a new author, Castellano Castellani (1461–1519). Chapter 9, "Savonarola and Beyond:

Castellano Castellani," considers the plays of the new century. Castellano Castellani, member of a collateral branch of that same family that employed Luigi Pulci before he became an intimate of the Medici family circle in the early 1460s, is remarkable for his flexibility, moving his support from Savonarola to Soderini and then to the Medici in the nick of time. The sixteen titles associated with him are mostly plays of gruesomely martyred saints, plays about steadfast faith and cruel martyrdom, but there are also a *Passione* and a *Resurrezione* that seem rather to be high-brow Florentine responses to the enormously successful Passion and Resurrection of the Roman confraternity of the Gonfalone, written or at least reworked by the Florentine priest Giuliano Dati. Castellani became the *guardiano* of the flagellant confraternity of San Girolamo that met in the Ospedale di San Matteo in Piazza San Marco and maintained a close relationship with the Purification company, which continued to perform *rappresentazioni* into the second half of the sixteenth century. The simplicity of Belcari's *ottave* gives way to a higher literary ambition: grandiose verbosity, but also a virtuosity in lower registers of the vernacular that owes much to Luigi Pulci's epic poem *Morgante maggiore*. With the exception of his *San Venanzio* (1502), we have no record of any of Castellani's plays in performance, so it is sometimes difficult to see how the attempt to fuse the *rappresentazioni* with high culture worked on stage.

Even as Castellani was attempting to elevate the language and the tone of the *rappresentazioni*, theatrical taste was changing. The courts of Northern Italy, which had from time to time imported Florentine actors and technical expertise, forged two new kinds of vernacular theatre: the pastoral eclogue with nymphs and shepherds, and five-act comedies modelled on those of Plautus and Terence. Florence, without a noble court to fund this more expensive kind of theatre, had yielded its precedence in matters theatrical to the northern courts; only with the return of the Medici was any attempt made to reclaim it. Even so, the officially sponsored attempts by Jacopo Nardi and Eufrosino Bonini are theatrical failures, while Machiavelli's *Mandragola* and *Clizia*, marginalized from the mainstream, stand out for their extraordinary understanding of what was required to make a comedy work.

Chapter 10, "The Afterlife of the Plays," explores two aspects of the post-performance life of the plays. First, it examines how the *rappresentazioni* immediately became part of an antiquarian enterprise, as the Giunti, Florentine printers and publishing entrepreneurs who cooperated closely with the Florentine Academy and with the court of Duke Cosimo de' Medici. Their three omnibus collections (1555, 1560, and 1578) contained reprints of the *rappresentazioni* of the previous seventy years, illustrated with original or reproduction woodcuts, some from the 1490s, and were the first attempt to appreciate the *rappresentazioni* as a genre. In 1568, the Giunti also published the second edition of Vasari's *Lives of the Artists*, in which Vasari placed on record what was remembered of the *feste* of San Felice and of the Carmine, and what he had learned from his own attempt to resurrect the machinery in 1565–1566. The plays then adapted to find their place in a changed cultural space, and new models emerged of *rappresentazioni sacre*, oratorios, five-act comedies, spiritual tragicomedies, and a host of other forms to meet the needs of Counter-Reformation groups. The notion that the *sacra rappresentazione* was in some way replaced by the *commedia erudita* (five-act comedies) can be entirely discounted: the *sacra rappresentazione* and its successors continued side by side with the scripted *commedia erudita* and the improvised *commedia dell'arte* and each occupied a different social and cultural space.

Second, this final chapter examines the book collectors, starting with Hernando Colón, in whose hands the printed plays became collectors' items and the objects of study. Collected in Italy in the seventeenth century and prized more for the purity of their language than for their illustrations, the *rappresentazioni* found their way back into the book market when insolvency or political upheaval struck. Fabulous wealth from the British and French colonies made it possible for northern European collectors to form huge collections, with spectacular excesses of bibliomania that rivalled the tulip mania of the 1630s, and the South Sea Bubble of the 1720s. The end of such collections was often financial disaster, but this has made it possible to follow some of the choicest sets of plays from one sale catalogue to the next and eventually into the relative safety of public and university libraries. The *rappresentazioni* have also been listed and catalogued by antiquarian booksellers, play collectors, students of woodcuts, and students of devotional literature. Most recently they have been digitized and made freely available once more to a wide audience. They have been bound, unbound, washed, restored, and rebound, sometimes with the most exquisite bindings from the greatest craftsmen.

Illustrations form an important part of this study, so I am grateful to the publishers for their willingness to include images with the text. Broadly speaking, I do not argue that the plays influenced pictorial representation, but rather that plays measured themselves against the narrative detail of earlier painting. Painters were members of confraternities, which in turn used their services, and confraternities operated in spaces that were richly decorated with painting and sculpture. Many of the images are thus analogous rather than directly illustrative, but they provide yet another pathway into understanding the visual and devotional culture that informs the plays.

I have incorporated into my text as much as possible of the contemporary source material that underpins my argument, in translation in the text and in its original language in the footnotes, to allow the voices to speak for themselves and keep present the original terminology, which in translation may be ambiguous and risk misunderstanding. In this "dominion of the ear," to use Blake Wilson's fortunate phrase,[40] it is a delight to hear the voices that emanate from the texts themselves. The plays, which were so difficult to access when I began this study and are now freely available in digitized form, are cited with parallel metrical translations. This choice sacrifices the accuracy of word-for-word literal prose translation, which tends to sound dull and foolish, in favour of more vigorous and entertaining verse that engages with the writers' skill in handling dialogue. I have also edited a number of the plays, and in some cases translated them in full, in the hope that they will become more widely known.[41] I have attempted to deal with as many single plays as possible, assembling tools that will assist in understanding them in a broader context. My hope is that students and scholars from many disciplines will find a way of accessing plays that both stimulate and explore their own interests.

The picture that emerges from this study is one of a genre of performance that bloomed for a short and glorious season, c. 1450–1485, before transforming itself on the one hand into a new kind of printed devotional literature available to all and, on the other hand, into a form of cloistered and apologetic drama for the world of women and youths rather than for the adult male world of Florentine citizens. Some modern readers, especially those used to the ironic wit and pace of Ariosto's *ottava rima*, may find the *rappresentazioni* tedious beyond measure. That indeed was the opinion of an unnamed spectator at the Ascension *festa* in the 1390s, and it has been my own response to a modern production, where the *longueurs* of the second hour of a performance in unsympathetic acoustics allowed close examination of the architecture of a fifteenth-century cloister. But the plays do reward a closer reading with both *utile* and *piacere*.

---

[40] Wilson, "Dominion of the Ear," on the model of Marvin Trachtenberg's *Dominion of the Eye*.

[41] For details, see Table 1 and 2.

The different forms of theatre, performed at different times, in different spaces, and by different groups, were driven by a common desire to perform devotion, to be the actors and not just the spectators, and to enjoy the experience. They invite further consideration in the light of those social changes explored in Richard C. Trexler's seminal essay "Ritual in Florence: Adolescence and Salvation in Renaissance Florence" (1974): laicization and the full experience of devotion among the laity, the emergence of the young as the focus of religious and educational concern, secularization, which includes finding spiritual meaning in worldly activities, and the socialization of individuals through collective, public religion.[42] The richness of the theatrical experience, the generosity of the values, and the lightness of touch of some of our plays were not fully evident in the anthologies compiled by D'Ancona and his immediate successors. I hope that *Making a Play for God* will bring those playful qualities into clearer focus.

---

[42] See Weinstein, "Critical Issues," coda to Trexler, "Ritual in Florence."

CHAPTER 1

THE MANUSCRIPT EVIDENCE OF THE
FLORENTINE *SACRE RAPPRESENTAZIONI*

> This story, or rather festive representation of the blessed Patriarch Abraham has been copied by me, Marco di Francesco, for the contemplation of my son Francesco, that he may wish to copy it out in more beautiful letters when he knows how. Copied on the day of the Feast of the Holy Spirit in the year 1477.
>
> Marco di Francesco[1]

This chapter will not mire itself in the question of the origins of the *sacra rappresentazione* and whether it derived from the liturgical drama in Latin, the Umbrian *laude drammatiche*, or some intermediate stage of *devozione*. Earlier scholarship has wrestled with those questions. Instead, I will assert that before the middle of the fifteenth century, in Florence, the *ottava rima*, or eight-line stanza of verse narrative, was adapted to a new form of storytelling through dramatic representation. Boccaccio had established the ottava as a literary form with his *Teseida* (1340), and over the next century it became the standard vehicle for verse narrative.[2] It was used, alongside the *terza rima*, by the *canterini* or performance poets who versified current events, bawdy tales, lives of saints, and above all the chivalric romances, and recited them with prodigious feats of improvisation and memory in the public squares

---

[1] Siena, BCI, I.viii.37, fol. 160ᵛ: "Questa storia o vòi tu dire asenbramento di festa del santo patriarcha Abraam ò ritrata io, Marcho di Franciesco, a chontenprazione di Franciesco mio figluolo e perché gli venga voglia rasenprala in più bela forma di lètare quando per lui saprà. Fata ne· dì de la pasqua de lo Spirito Santo anni 1477." Other works copied by Marco di Francesco are listed in Dessì "La prophétie," 433–435.

[2] On the *ottava*, see Branca, *Il cantare trecentesco*, and Delcorno Branca, "Introduzione"; De Robertis "Cantari antichi"; Delcorno Branca, "Fra cantare e sacra rappresentazione"; Bendinelli Predelli, "The Textualization"; Barbiellini Amidei, "In margine"; on the forms of the *rappresentazione*, see Ventrone "Per una morfologia."

and private spaces of Italy. In Florence, the piazza in front of the church of San Martino del Vescovo, which would become the headquarters of Cosimo de' Medici's charitable group the Dodici Buonomini di San Martino, was the place where Florentines great and small could gather to listen to these tales, probably over and over again. Some listeners went home and recorded in their *zibaldoni* the poems they had heard or otherwise procured; others, like Benedetto Dei, could boast of the poems they knew by heart.[3]

In this most literate and literary city, there was no shortage of men skilled in improvising verse. There were performers who made it their living, like Antonio di Guido, summoned by Lorenzo de' Medici to Careggi to entertain the young Galeazzo Maria Sforza in 1459, and to Vallombrosa in 1473 to provide music for a sonnet.[4] But there were many for whom composition or improvisation in *ottava rima* was simply a sideline. Brian Richardson and Luca Degl'Innocenti have recently shown us that Niccolò Machiavelli was renowned among his contemporaries for his ability to extemporize in *ottava rima* from any text, while accompanying himself on the *viola da braccio*.[5] That is a late example, but Machiavelli, born in 1469 and an adolescent in Lorenzo's Florence, may conceivably have honed these skills in a youth confraternity. According to his anonymous biographer writing around 1540, Leonardo da Vinci was a skilled musician and improviser; Lorenzo de' Medici sent him to Milan in 1482 with Lorenzo's gift to Gian Galeazzo Sforza of an exquisitely crafted lyre in the form of a horse's head.[6] Of Lorenzo himself, we know that

---

[3] See, for example, the two *zibaldoni* of the Scarlatti brothers discussed later in this chapter; Dei, *La cronica*, 139–140.

[4] Letter from Galeazzo Maria to his father, in Becherini, "Un canta in panca," 243–244; letter from Lorenzo in Vallombrosa (ASF, MAP 29, doc. 575), in M. Martelli, *Studi laurenziani*, 122–124. On the *canterini*, see Villoresi, "Tra Andrea da Barberino e Luigi Pulci"; Wilson, "Dominion of the Ear," and now his *Singing to the Lyre*; L. Degl'Innocenti, *"Al suon di questa cetra"*; as well as the classic chapter in Flamini, *La lirica*, 148–299. On Antonio di Guido, also called Antonio della Viuola, see Böninger "Ricerche."

[5] Richardson, *Manuscript Culture*, 252–253; L. Degl'Innocenti, "Machiavelli."

[6] Frey, ed., *Il codice magliabechiano* (also called "l'Anonimo Gaddiano"), 110: "Et haueua 30 annj, che'l dal detto Magnifico Lorenzo fu mandato al duca di Milano insieme con Atalante Megliorottj a presentarlj una lira, che unico era in sonare tale extrumento" (He was thirty when he was sent by Lorenzo the Magnificent to the duke of Milan, together with Atalante Migliorotti, to give him a lyre, for he was incomparable in playing this instrument). Vasari says that it was 1494, when Leonardo would have been forty-two, and both Lorenzo and Gian Galeazzo Sforza were already dead; Vasari, *Le vite* (1568), 3.1:5, *Vita di Lionardo da Vinci pittore, et scultore fiorentino*; see also L. Degl'Innocenti, *"Al suon di questa cetra,"* 29.

he saw to it that his sons were instructed in the art of improvisation; in 1490, Poliziano reported on his son Piero's progress in acquiring the art.[7] It was in this milieu of improvised narratives in *ottava rima* that the plays were conceived, written, and performed. But plays are fundamentally different. Plays are written and learned by heart, rather than being improvised, and there is no evidence that the speakers were accompanied by the viola. They move a step closer to written culture and to literature.[8]

Because they are part of a written culture rather than an oral tradition, the material evidence of the earliest plays, from the 1440s through to the first printed editions in the 1480s, is in manuscripts copied for groups and for individuals and handed down within lay confraternities and religious houses as well as within families. Only very seldom are we told why they were copied, so we can only conjecture that it was for the pleasure of remembering and sharing, or for didactic and devotional purposes. What is clear, however, is that the corpus of *rappresentazioni* found in manuscript is far more varied in its subjects, its sources, and its social values than the printed *rappresentazioni* published in D'Ancona's *Sacre rappresentazioni dei secoli XIV, XV e XVI* (1872). The manuscript corpus is by no means complete, and we have no way of knowing what has been lost due to the wear and tear of re-use, to simple neglect, or to floods and other disasters. Later chapters will discuss what is *in* the plays, but this chapter will look at the various typologies of manuscript and their different modes of use.

The range of play-manuscript typologies for Florence is less complex than that which Graham Runnalls has described for France,[9] but the broad parameters are the same. A play text passes through various stages from composition and revision to fragmentation into roles and re-composition into a finished text. It may be preserved simply for posterity, or it may be intended for future re-use or adaptation by the original performance group, for sharing with another, as reading matter, or occasionally as a presentation copy. One thing is probably true of all the surviving texts: that they reflect only imperfectly a performance that has taken place. Very seldom can a documented performance be linked to a surviving text, nevertheless I take the existence of a play text as material evidence of a performance.

---

[7] Villoresi, "Panoramica," 18.

[8] On the question of whether the plays were sung or intoned like the *cantari*, see chapter 9 below.

[9] Runnalls, "Towards a Typology"; see also Riccò, "Testo per la scena."

When Florentines started to stage plays, for a liturgical feast day in a particular church, like the Ascension in Santa Maria del Carmine, or in the context of public celebrations like the feast of St. John the Baptist, or in private confraternal spaces like the company of the Purification, or at Carnival, celebrated universally with masks and costumes and entertainments, various possibilities were open to them. They could rework their existing annual *festa*, deciding which parts were to be performed, having some or all of the text overhauled, then copying and distributing roles to the actors. The great *feste* of the Annunciation, Ascension, and Pentecost, which will be discussed in the next chapter, existed long before the known play texts that appeared around the middle of the fifteenth century. For the Annunciation, Feo Belcari reduced the tedium of the prophets described by Abraham of Suzdal in 1439 and added an exquisite Dispute of the Virtues, while his Ascension text consists of only nine stanzas. The surviving Pentecost play, which must have replaced Belcari's 'play' of just three stanzas, was probably composed much later for the performance staged in Santa Maria del Carmine at the request of Piero di Lorenzo de' Medici in 1489.[10] We know that lines for a play of the Last Judgment were composed by Antonio di Matteo di Meglio, herald of the Signoria, between 1444 and 1448, and supplemented by Feo Belcari,[11] while Belcari's play of the childhood of St. John the Baptist had extra lines added to it by Tommaso Benci.[12]

Alternatively, and this is the case from the late 1440s onwards, the confraternity could commission an entirely new play. Many of the texts that we find in manuscript were written for the companies that performed them. Piero di Mariano Muzi was *guardiano* or leader of the youth confraternity of the Purification, and wrote for them *La festa del vitel sagginato* (The play of the fatted calf) (fig. 1.1).[13] Feo Belcari, aspiring humanist, tells us in the dedicatory sonnet, addressed to Giovanni di Cosimo de' Medici, that precedes his *Abramo* that he studied Genesis, Origen, and Nicholas of Lyra before

---

[10] For discussion, see chapter 2.

[11] See below, chapter 4.

[12] See below, chapter 7.

[13] This anthology of *laude* and *rime spirituali*, BAV, Chigi L.vii.266, was compiled by the Florentine merchant Filippo Benci between 1448 and 1464. It is the only source to attribute the play to Muzi. The attribution is further supported by the fact that the *lauda* that closes the play, "Deh, sappiatevi guardare," is attributed to him in the earliest edition of *Laude facte & composte da piu persone spirituali* (1485/6), fol. cxxiii^v. On Benci's ownership, see Tanturli, "I Benci copisti," 302–303. See below, chapter 3.

he composed his play, performed in 1449 by an unidentified group, almost certainly a youth confraternity (fig. 1.2).[14] Such statements of paternity, however, are rare. Other authors collaborated anonymously with confraternities or with their aristocratic patrons. The Pulci family, Bernardo and his wife Antonia Tanini, as well as his brother Luigi Pulci, never seems far away from the Florentine *feste*, and especially plays performed by the youths of the Purification in San Marco; some of their plays seem custom-made to reflect the devotional interests of Luigi's patron Lucrezia Tornabuoni and her extended family.

As later discussion of individual plays will show, the stories often came from a wide range of vernacular sources: not "the Bible" in Jerome's translation but the individual books of the Bible that circulated singly or in small groups and in a variety of *volgarizzamenti*; not the Latin text of Jacobus de Voragine's *Legenda Aurea* but the Tuscan *volgarizzamenti* of it and of a multitude of individual saints' lives; not the *Vitae Patrum* attributed to Jerome, but Domenico Cavalca's translation, the *Vite dei Santi Padri*; not to mention the *Fioretti di san Francesco*, various miracles of the Virgin, and the *Dialoghi* of St. Gregory, all taken from vernacular rather than Latin sources. And a *volgarizzamento* is not the same as a translation: the processes of rendering the Latin narrative in the vernacular often required the introduction of more homely elements, and close attention to the *volgarizzamento* that stands between the play and its biblical source has revealed numerous instances where the "emotional realism" found in the play is already present in the *volgarizzamento*, and is not an invention of the dramatist.[15]

Many of the texts that we find in manuscript must have been written expressly for the companies that performed them. Once the text was provided by the author, single parts were copied, sometimes by the performers themselves, or simply learned by heart in the rehearsal process.[16] The *frottole*

---

[14] This battered codex, BNCF, Magl. vii.744, is unique among the Florentine play manuscripts for the elaborate decoration of its title page. Testaverde and Evangelista, eds., *Sacre rappresentazioni*, 16, suggest that the fine portrait on the right, of a man with a very prominent hooked nose, is of Giovanni di Cosimo de' Medici, but it does not resemble Mino da Fiesole's straight-nosed portrait bust in the Bargello. It possibly represents Feo Belcari himself. See also fig. 7.1 below.

[15] Belcari's *Abramo* is an exception in its use of more than one source.

[16] See discussion below in this chapter, and n. 53. This fragmentation occasionally made it impossible to reconstitute the original; see the 1496 letter from Ercole d'Este to his son-in-law Francesco Gonzaga, cited in D'Ancona, *Origini*, 2:368–369.

or metatheatrical scenes that begin to frame the *rappresentazioni* at the beginning of the sixteenth century,[17] when a new theatrical aesthetic was coming into vogue, tell us more about the rehearsal process. From the *Frottola di tre suore*, we glean that the nuns owned copies of *Sant'Alesso* (St. Alexis) and of *Il re superbo* (The proud king), but the latter had "gone to Viterbo," presumably on loan to another religious house. Lines had been copied for each actor, but Sister Maria Maddalena was a slow learner and lost her lines, so they had to be copied out again:

Egli è stato una pena	It's really been a pain
a fargli torre e versi;	to make her learn her lines;
dipoi la gli ave' persi,	she lost them after that,
riscriver bisognòe.[18]	they had to be rewritten.

(lines 151–154)

The play texts that survived the performance process entered the next stage of transmission. Some were lost altogether. Others were recomposed, possibly from memory, and fair copies were made. Some survive only in manuscript, others in both manuscript and print, and others still only in print. Table 1 shows the wealth of material that has survived only in manuscript, with details of locations and modern editions. Some plays are grouped together in manuscript anthologies or copied into personal *zibaldoni* or commonplace books of popular poetry or devotional works. Some are contained in miscellaneous volumes, sometimes assembled with visible effort, but more often the result of a later binder's whim that has placed between a single set of covers works of similar size — but not always of similar age and content — not so much for ease of reading but for better conservation and appearance.[19] Anthologizing the manuscript plays probably determined their survival, since the anthology was subsequently treated with more respect.

Only one author operated outside these standard typologies. Feo Belcari, to whom I will return in various contexts, had his works copied in a scriptorium as *libri cortesi* (court-books)[20] and circulated them assiduously,

---

[17] See discussion below, chapter 9.

[18] Razzolini, "Frottola," 177.

[19] On compilations of popular texts, see D.V. Kent, *Cosimo de' Medici*, 69–93.

[20] On Petrucci's classification of medieval manuscripts, see Bendinelli Predelli, "The Textualization," 149–150. Belcari's scriptorium copies include BNCF, Magl. vii.690, vii.1115, vii.1163; BRF, Ricc. 2896/BNCF, Magl. vii.1114: BMLF, Redi 121; BACF, 131;

but he does not appear to have seized the opportunity to have his works printed with the same enthusiasm.

The conventions for copying these texts were already established in the fourteenth century, and came from liturgical texts rather than from classical theatre texts.[21] The words spoken by the characters were copied in black ink; the *didascalie* or instructions — we would now call them stage directions — were copied in red ink (figs. 1.3–1.6).[22] Whereas the spoken word, locked in place by rhyme and metre, remained relatively stable as the text passed through the hands of successive copyists, the stage directions displayed an extraordinary fluidity. They were usually inserted in a second phase of the copying, into spaces left by the copyist; for the same text they can offer variants that range from long and descriptive (or prescriptive) to simply the name of the speaker. They varied even within the one copy of a play, being sometimes in the present indicative ("Eustachio says …"), sometimes in the present subjunctive ("Let him go out of the house and say …"), and sometimes, echoing their prose narrative source, in the past tense ("Agabito who knew well that this was his brother, did not want to reveal himself yet but rather he wants to hear more about what happened to them, so he says …").[23] Occasionally they contained explicative material for the benefit of a reader and invisible to the viewer ("As his flesh struggles with his reason, Isaac replies …").[24] The length of the stage direction is as much a function of page design — sandwiching octaves of black between rubricated stage directions for aesthetic effect — as

BCoR, 43.D.3; BEUMo, Gamma.X.2.9 (formerly Càmpori 1277); and MLMNY, Ms. M.480; see Nosow, "Binchois's Songs," 222–225.

[21] Newbigin, "Rubrics."

[22] In *Abramo*, in BRF, Ricc. 1721, fols. 42ʳ–57ʳ, the copyist has not returned to add the rubrics. *Abramo* is preceded by Francesco Filelfo, *Vita di san Giovanni Battista*, which ends, fol. 41v: "Copiata per me scriptore Jacopo di Niccolò di Chocho Donati cittadino fiorentino, et finito questo dì ij di novembre MccccLiiij. Laus in altissimo deo" (Copied by me, Jacopo di Niccolò di Cocco Donati, *scriptor*, Florentine citizen, finished this day, 2 November 1454). Since *Abramo* is copied in the same hand, and probably at the same time, this may be the earliest dated manuscript.

[23] *La festa di sant'Eustachio*, stage directions after oct. 27: "Eustachio dice"; oct. 2: "Esca di casa e dica così"; oct. 79: "Agabito, che ben conosceva quello essere suo fratello non si volle ancora però scoprire ma vuole intendere più oltre che seguisse di loro, onde dice"

[24] Belcari, *Abramo*, stage direction after 26: "Isac, combattendo la sensualità con la ragione, piangendo risponde."

an attempt to shape some future performance. I do not believe that they were read aloud on stage.[25]

The earliest dated anthology, BNCF, Conv. Soppr. F.3.488, came into what is now the Biblioteca Nazionale Centrale in Florence with the Napoleonic suppression of the Camaldolese hermitage at Camaldoli in 1810.[26] It was copied by Lorenzo di ser Nicolaio di Diedi (fig. 1.7).[27] Lorenzo's father, Ser Niccolò (or Nicolaio) di Diedi, was the accountant and record keeper from 1438 to 1462 of the Opera di Santa Maria del Fiore, responsible for the construction of Florence's cathedral.[28] Lorenzo himself, like his brother Giovanni, was a member of the youth confraternity of the Purification. He was one of the two *sagrestani* in the period May–August 1465,[29] the very period, just before his exit from the company, when he finished copying his anthology, which is dated 17 February 1463/4 (fol. 65r), and 29 July 1465 (fol. 86v). In this codex Lorenzo included plays that we can associate with some certainty with youth confraternities, as well as others performed outdoors by adult companies. The volume contains twelve of the finest texts: the *Creazione*; the *Vitel sagginato* (Fatted calf) by Piero di Mariano Muzi; Feo Belcari's *Abramo*; *San Bartolomeo*; the play of the *I giudici che Iddio mostrò a un Romito*

---

[25] Corinna Salvadori Lonergan's statement that "the 'festaiuolo' (producer) was on stage all the time, somewhat apart from the actors, and he read the stage directions" does not have precedents in the documents I have examined before the 1530s; Salvadori Lonergan, "'A Lorenzo il Leon d'oro?,'" 35. The device was used, however, in the 2004 production of *Stella*, directed by Luciano Alberti; see Ulysse, "Donne perseguitate," and chapter 6 below.

[26] For a summary table of manuscripts and the plays they contain, and of the printed editions, see Table 1. For manuscripts of *rappresentazioni* in the BNCF, see Testaverde and Evangelista, eds., *Sacre rappresentazioni*, 3–31.

[27] BNCF, Conv. Soppr. F.3.488, inside cover and fol. 1r, fig. 1.7. The heading reads: "Al nome di Dio Amen. Questo libro è di Lorenzo di ser Nicholaio di Diedi il quale à scripto di sua propia mano nel quale sono scripte xij Rapresentatio[ni] le qual sono scripte qui di sotto" (In the name of God, Amen. This book belongs to Lorenzo, son of the notary Nicolaio di Diedi, who wrote it in his own hand. In it are written twelve *Rappresentazioni*, which are listed below).

[28] Florence, AOSMF, II 1 87–93. In January–February 1438/9 he was notary to the priors when Cosimo de' Medici was Gonfaloniere di Giustizia; and held that office again in September–October 1451; see Petriboni, *Priorista*, 287, 347).

[29] ASF, CRSPL 1654 (P.xxx.30), fols. 109r, 112v. In the same years Lorenzo, born on 15 March 1445/6, also copied Juvenal's *Satires* (BMLF, Conv. Soppr. 437) and three works by Cicero (BMLF, Conv. Soppr. 537). Like the BNCF codex, these manuscripts came from the hermitage at Camaldoli.

per uno Angelo (The judgments that God revealed to a Hermit by means of an Angel), later called *L'abataccio* (The bad abbot); Antonio the Herald and Feo Belcari's *Dì del Giudizio* (Judgment Day); *Ottaviano* (Octavian); the *Purificazione* (Purification); *San Giovanni Battista quando fu decollato* (The beheading of John the Baptist, henceforth *San Giovanni decollato*); *Susanna*; *L'ortolano elemosiniere* (The beneficent gardener); and *Il re superbo* (The proud king). No book of plays is listed in the company's later inventories, so this may have been copied for Lorenzo's own use.

The volume BRF, Ricc. 2893 is likewise an early compilation.[30] The manuscript is undated and the paper unwatermarked; it is copied in *littera antiqua*, an archaizing gothic hand, rather than a 'modern' humanist or mercantile hand. It contains eight plays: *San Giovanni decollato* (performed 1451); Belcari's *Abramo* (performed 1449); the Nativity play with Octavian and the Sibyl (first mentioned 1454); a play of the child Moses and his ordeal by fire; Belcari's *Annunciazione*, with the Dispute of the Virtues unencumbered by prophets and sibyls (1465, but conceivably earlier; fig. 1.8); a very early *Magi* play in the metre of the fourteenth-century Umbrian *ballata maggiore*, but with linguistic characteristics of northern Italy; a static *Natività*, in which Mary — who does not speak — is possibly a statue or a painting;[31] and finally Muzi's play of the *Vitel sagginato*. It is not possible to date the manuscript more precisely. The hand suggests a non-professional copyist and perhaps the cultural backwater of a convent; at the end a different hand has added, partly in Latin, partly in Italian: "This book belongs to Sister Arcangela, daughter of Domenico Alamanni. This book belongs to me, Arcangela."[32] The datable plays are all relatively early, before 1465.

---

[30] Castelli, ed., *Manoscritti teatrali*, a *catalogue raisonné* of theatrical manuscripts in the Biblioteca Riccardiana, describes Ricc. 2816 (see below) but omits Ricc. 1094, 1429, 1720, 1721, 2893, 2900, and 2971, all of which contain *rappresentazioni*.

[31] The *Natività*, beginning "Oda ciascun fedele," is found also in a Sienese manuscript, BCIS, I.ii.33, which contains the Magi play as well. In addition, and very remarkably, stanzas 1–2 and 5–6, together with prophets and sibyls from the Florentine Annunciation and Purification plays, also appear in a Nativity of Florentine origin that bears the date 1583, and the name of an owner, Pier Francesco Torrigiani; see BMVe, It. ix.93 (= 6861), fols. 1ᵛ–2ʳ. See Newbigin, "La longevità," 534–538.

[32] BRF, Ricc. 2893, fol. 89ᵛ: "Iste est liber sororis Archangele, figliola di Domenico Alamanni | Iste liber est mei Archagele." There is insufficient information to identify Domenico Alamanni, but in 1500 a person of that name sold a property outside the Porta San Gallo to Antonia Pulci, which became the convent she founded. Arcangela is not among her first companions; see Weaver, in Pulci, *Saints' Lives*, 27.

The miscellaneous volume BRF, Ricc. 2816, presents a different typology. This important codex, as it exists now, is made up of four sections copied in different hands but containing similar popular vernacular material, largely of a religious or moral nature. The first section is copied in an elegant humanist cursive, and each play ends with the Greek word *Telos* (The End) written in Greek letters.[33] The plays included are *Giuseppe, Giacobbe, e i fratelli* (Joseph, Jacob, and the brothers); a play of *Lazero risucitato* (The raising of Lazarus); *San Giovanni decollato* (fig. 1.9); a "play of St. Bernard," about *Uno signore che facea rubare le strade* (A baron who sent his men out as highway robbers), taken from the hugely popular *Miracoli della gloriosa vergine Maria*; Belcari's *San Panuzio*; and the play of the *Giudizio di Salamone* (Judgment of Solomon). Of these, only *San Giovanni decollato*, *San Panuzio*, and *Salamone* found their way into print. The second part of the volume, consisting of three sections, contains various spiritual and secular works including, quite remarkably, a copy of Lucrezia Tornabuoni's lives of St. John the Baptist and of Judith in *ottava rima*, as well as three plays: the *Vitel sagginato*, the *Festa del pellegrino* (The miracle of the pilgrim, that is, of the three pilgrims who visited St. James in Galizia), and Belcari's *Abramo*. *San Bernardo*, *San Panuzio*, and the narrative poems of Lucrezia Tornabuoni also occur together in BEUMo, Gamma.D.6.34 (formerly Càmpori 10). Tornabuoni's poems had very limited circulation, largely within her household, so this configuration suggests that the plays may have been seen as closely connected with her household.[34]

Similarly complex is the miscellany BRF, Ricc. 1720, that bears the name (or names) "Filipo Pauolo | Michele | de Matteo" on the original parchment cover. Copied in various hands and on different batches of paper, it contains the widely circulated late fourteenth-century *cantare* of the Passion, beginning "O increata maestà di Dio," attributed to Cicerchia; a good manuscript

---

[33] Pezzarossa, in Tornabuoni, *I poemetti*, 118, dates the Tornabuoni section to the beginning of the sixteenth century but, in line with the library's own date of "sec. XV," I would suggest 1460–1470; see Newbigin, ed., *Nuovo corpus*, xx–xxi. The *ciseaux* watermark of the first section containing most of the plays is similar to Briquet 3720 (1460s?). The watermark of the section containing the *Vitel sagginato* is a five-petalled flower (fols. 73 and 136), similar to Briquet 6372 (1473); and that of the section containing *Abramo* is a *chapeau*, similar to Briquet 3370–3374 (1470s). At the end of the codex, fol. 189ᵛ, the date mccccLxxviijᵒ (1478) appears, probably relating only to the last part of the volume, which contains Belcari's *Abramo*.

[34] On Tornabuoni manuscripts, see Pezzarossa, in Tornabuoni, *I poemetti*, 113–124.

of Belcari's *Abramo*; the *Purificazione* with twenty-two prophets and three sibyls[35]; a *cantare* of the Last Judgment, beginning "Quel vero Iddio, mente incarnata"; *La festa del pellegrino*; and finally the *cantare* of *Il lamento di Costantinopoli* (The lament for [the fall of] Constantinople). It is not possible to date the manuscript, but watermarks suggest that the individual parts were all copied in the third quarter of the fifteenth century. Bizarrely, there are two final folios for Belcari's *Abramo* in two different hands. The fascicule that originally occupied fols. 49–60 has been excised, taking all but the last leaf of *Abramo*, which is renumbered fol. 62; a new fascicule, fols. 49ʳ–61ᵛ, containing a new and possibly better *Abramo*, has been inserted.

Only one true *zibaldone* (commonplace book) contains *rappresentazioni*: BAMi, C 35 sup., copied by Giovanni d'Antonio di Scarlatto Scarlatti between 1470 and 1473. It contains poems, recipes, a list of tariffs charged at the gates of Florence, and other trivia, as well as the texts of ten plays: *Susanna*, *Lazzero ricco e Lazzero povero* (Dives and Pauper), *Il pellegrino*, *Il re superbo* (fig. 1.10), *Il glorioso san Giuliano* (The glorious St. Julian [the Hospitaller]), *San Jacopo Maggiore* ([The martyrdom of] St. James the Great), *L'ortolano elemosinario*, *San Piero e san Pagolo* (St. Peter and St. Paul), Belcari's *Abramo*, and his *Annunciazione*. The Ambrosiana *zibaldone* is closely related to one copied by Giovanni's brother Filippo, now BMLF, Acquisti e doni 759, which contains no plays at all. Both brothers appear to have been peculiarly obsessive in their copying, but Filippo the more so, claiming as his own works that were widely recognized as being by his contemporaries.[36]

BRF, Ricc. 2971, consists of three parts of matching size bound together at a later date. Part I is the *zibaldone* of a pious layman, containing twenty-four works including three plays — Belcari's *Abramo*, Muzi's *Vitel sagginato*, and the *Festa di san Jacopo* (The play of St. James, that is, *La festa del pellegrino*) — along with prayers, prophecies, sonnets and ballads, and saints' lives (fig. 1.11).

Other evidence of ownership of manuscripts comes from the inventories compiled by the Magistrato de' Pupilli on behalf of a testator's heirs. The inventory of the possessions of the late Francesco di Baldino Inghirami, prepared in 1471, includes "a book of *Plays of various saints*, on paper, with

---

[35] There are no sibyls in the earlier manuscript, BNCF, Conv. Soppr. F.3.488.

[36] Concari, *Nozze*; described in Jordan and Wool, *Inventory*; Emilio Pasquini, "Il codice," esp. 375–377.

wooden boards," as well as "a book of the *Play of Abraham*, with no cover."[37]
Many such volumes may be hidden behind less specific descriptions. The
inclusion of plays in private miscellanies and in personal "libraries" was not
for the purpose of performances. Copying them out for personal use was
a form of appropriation, a way of remembering — and perhaps learning by
heart — a performance that had made a strong impression. In turn, plays
like Belcari's *Abramo* and Muzi's *Vitel sagginato* became didactic texts in
the education of young children. When the Sienese wool merchant Marco
di Francesco copied Belcari's *Abramo e Isac* at Pentecost 1477, he wrote the
words cited at the beginning of this chapter, offering the play to his son both
as a behavioural model and as an expression of the aspiration that his son's
education will surpass his own.[38]

Of all our authors, Feo Belcari is the one person to have systematically
overseen the copying and circulations of his works, so they survive in greater
numbers than for any other known author.[39] They are copied, for the most
part, in a fine gothic book hand, *littera antiqua*, often on vellum, and are accompanied by dedicatory sonnets or letters. Some also contain Belcari's *laude*
and sonnets in addition to plays.[40]

Another manuscript, BNCF, Magl. vii.293, hints elusively at authorship.
Made up of a series of discrete *fascicoli* copied by several hands, it contains
fourteen of Luca Pulci's eighteen *Pistole* (fols. 1[r]–22[v]), Luigi Pulci's *Giostra
di Lorenzo de' Medici* (fols. 23[r]–42[v]), and Bernardo Pulci's *Passione* in *ottava
rima*, with its dedication addressed to his sister-in-law, Annalena de' Tanini
(fols. 43[r]–58[v]), along with a short *Passione* in *terzine* that ends with the Fifth
Word from the cross (fols. 67[r]–69[v]; fol. 70[r–v] blank); the second half of a play
of *San Giorgio* (St. George) (fols. 71[r]–86[v]) (see fig. 5.7); *Ciriffo Calvaneo*, the
short epic poem begun by Luca Pulci and completed by Luigi Pulci, but without Bernardo Giambullari's *aggiunta* (fols. 87[r]–168[v]);[41] and finally a second
rappresentazione, *Un bel miracolo di Nostra Donna* (A beautiful miracle of

---

[37] Bec, *Les livres*, 188: "un libro di *Rapresentazioni di più santi*, di charta banbagina,
choverto d'asse"; "un libro della *Rapresentazione d'Abram*, sanza coverta." On Francesco di
Baldino Inghirami (1441–1470), banker and manager of the Medici bank in Florence, see
U. Martelli, *Ricordanze*, 239, n. 2; Elisabetta Pasquini, *Libri di musica*, 122–124, 152–161.

[38] See above, n. 1.

[39] See below, in particular, chapter 8.

[40] For further discussion of Belcari manuscripts, see chapter 7 below.

[41] Bucchi, "Un poema," 167–168; Parretti, "*Ciriffo Calvaneo*," not seen. The *fascicoli* have been bound out of order: fols. 87[r]–155[v] contain i 103–vii 81; fol. 156[r–v] contains

Our Lady) (fols. 169ʳ–189ʳ). The volume is valuable for several reasons. The *Secondo dì di san Giorgio* (Second day of St. George) completes the St. George play printed in the 1490s, of which no manuscript remains. The first day takes us only up to the rescue of the princess from the dragon, while the second day recounts the saint's battles for the faith and his martyrdom. The *Bel miracolo* is an exquisite romantic fantasy that anticipates the persecuted brides of the last decade of the century.[42] The volume moreover provides us with an indication of the kind of copy text that the early printers were dealing with, since the deficiencies of the *Secondo dì* manuscript help to explain those of the printed *Primo dì.* The positioning of the two *rappresentazioni* among works securely attributed to the men of the Pulci household suggests that these works too may be associated with that family.

The copyist of Palatino 445 worked in a different fashion.[43] The whole codex was copied on paper by a single hand for "B(ar)t(olome)o di Giovanni Cha—," who stated his ownership in a different but contemporary hand on fol. 1ʳ and prepared the table of contents on fol. 1ᵛ.[44] The first quire contains the play of *Salamone*, which we know from Ricc. 2816 and Magl. vii.1201. It is copied twenty-two lines to the page, on watermarked paper. This quire became somewhat dog-eared on its own, but in the blank pages that remained, fols. 15–20, the copyist began to copy Feo Belcari's *Abramo*, using as his copy text the printed edition dated 24 October 1485, a year after the author's death. He needed more paper of the same size as the first, and the next quire is made up of paper that might date back to the middle of the fifteenth century. There, he finished *Abramo* and began the play of *Un monaco che andò al servizio di Dio* (A monk who went to serve God). From then on, he found other plays to add to his collection, acquiring more paper from different sources as he went. *Sant'Eufemia* (St. Euphemia; fig. 1.12) and the play that follows, *San Grisanto*

---

i 95–102; and fols. 157ʳ–168ᵛ contain the beginning of the work, i 1–94. Bucchi surmises that the manuscript is copied from the Miscomini edition, ISTC ip01108000, c. 1485.

[42] For details of *San Giorgio* and the *Bel miracolo,* see Table 1.

[43] Formerly in the collection of Gabriello Riccardi, with shelfmark V.i.1041; see *Bullettone Lami,* BRF, Ricc. 3824, fol. 101ʳ: "– Salomone, Abraam, S. Eufemia, Grisanto e Daria, Miracolo della Vergine, SS. Giovanni e Paolo, S. Eustachio. Codex chartaceus in 4°." The *Monaco che andò al servigio di Dio* is not mentioned.

[44] The family name has been overwritten. The clearly legible letters are *Cha* in the underwriting, and the final *nj* in the overwriting. Palermo, *I manoscritti,* 2 (1860): 297, reads "Berto di Giovanni ….."; Gentile, *I codici,* 593, reads "bartolomeo di giovanni Chalzini." The *Manoscritti datati* database transcribes it as Caiazi (http://www.manoscrittidatati.it). I have found no suitable "Bartolomeo di Giovanni Cha—."

e Daria (Saints Chrysanthus and Daria), are almost surely by Castellano Castellani (1461–1519?), who in the first decades of the sixteenth century renewed almost single-handedly the traditions of confraternal drama, writing plays in which martyrdom plays a central role.[45] *Sant'Eufemia* did not appear in print, and the version of *San Grisanto e Daria* that was printed in 1517 for Castellani's regular publisher, Francesco di Giovanni Benvenuto,[46] has been trimmed of some of its doctrinal preaching and is about two-thirds the length. The next play, *Uno miracolo di Nostra Donna* (A miracle of Our Lady), which we know was performed in Pistoia in 1517, remained unpublished until 1979 despite its charm and propriety.[47] The two works that complete the volume are Lorenzo de' Medici's *San Giovanni e Paulo,* written for the youth confraternity of the Vangelista in 1491, when his son was *Messere,* responsible for Carnival celebrations; and the *Sant'Eustachio,* a play that we know had been performed in the youth confraternity of the Purification during Carnival 1476/7, copied from a manuscript source that was much less polished than Miscomini's edition.[48]

At least one anthology was compiled for confraternal use outside Florence. In 1482, just before the *rappresentazioni* first went into print, a professional Bolognese copyist, Tommaso Leone, copied a collection of twenty-three plays for the men of the Bolognese confraternity of San Girolamo, which had been founded some time before 1417 and met in the Church of Sant'Anna.[49] The first play of the collection, now BNCR, VE 483,[50] is a major processional

---

[45] On Castellani, see chapter 9 below.

[46] Florence: [Antonio Tubini and Andrea Ghirlandi] for Francesco di Giovanni Benvenuto, 4 February 1516/17, CNCE 61693, that is, in the middle of Carnival; see below, chapter 9, n. 174.

[47] Lorch, ed., *La festa*; Vigo, *Una confraternita.*

[48] For further details, see chapter 3, and Table 1.

[49] The men of San Girolamo were also responsible for the *putti* (young boys) of the youth confraternity of San Girolamo ed Anna; Vittorio, *Origine*; Mesini, "La catechesi," 1981, 240–267. Pietro Delcorno has indicated his intention to prepare a full study of this group and its plays.

[50] M.A. Parenti, "Osservazioni"; De Bartholomaeis, *Le origini,* 427–433; Vecchi, "Le sacre rappresentazioni." The description provided on-line in *Manus,* CNMS\00000043380 requires updating. The following plays are unequivocally Bolognese in origin: the processional play from the Creation to the Last Judgment (i); the Transfiguration (x); Christ taking leave from his Mother (viiii; also in Bologna, Biblioteca Universitaria, Ms. 157; ed. in Vecchi, "Le sacre rappresentazioni," 307–324); the Last Supper (iv); the Instruments of the Passion (iva); the Passion (iii); the Resurrection in four parts: the Placing of the

play of the Creation, with patriarchs and sibyls, matriarchs, saints, martyrs, four Virtues, and an *edificio* of the Annunciation that owes much to the Florentine procession for the feast of St. John the Baptist, but is for the most part a Bolognese creation. Of the remaining plays, a group relating mostly to Holy Week are Bolognese in origin but follow Florentine models. Fifteen are clearly Florentine in origin, but here overlaid with a heavy linguistic patina of Bolognese. Seven of these are well-known plays that found their way into print in the fifteenth century, some in substantially different redactions: *Susanna* (fig. 1.13), Belcari's *Abramo*, *San Giovanni quando andò nel deserto* and *Dì del Giudicio*, Muzi's *Vitel sagginato*, *Santa Cecilia*, and the play of *Ottaviano*; five more have been edited in modern times: Belcari's *Annunciazione*, *Ascensione*, the St. James play of the *Festa del pellegrino*, the earlier of the two plays of *San Giuliano*, and *Sant'Andrea*; and three are only now being provided with modern editions: a play of *Piero Teodinario* ('Peter Godpenny') to which the play of the *Tre re vivi e morti* has been grafted incongruously, a play of the *Beato Giovanni Colombino*, and a *Magi* play.[51] So many of these plays are known only in this codex that we are forced again to confront the fact that a large number of our plays must be lost.

How were these various manuscript anthologies used? Of the ones that survived, we can surmise both from their physical condition and from their very survival that they were not used much. The only example we have of a working miscellany comes not from Florence but from Rome. The Confraternity of the Gonfalone reworked its Passion play in 1490 when it moved its performances to the Colosseum. Totally revised by the Florentine Giuliano Dati in the form of a Florentine *sacra rappresentazione* in *ottava rima* with an angelic prologue, it was then printed in about 1496. The title page suggests that the text was as it had always been, and the numerous reprints of that edition imply that it remained unchanged from then on, but the number of variant versions bound into the so-called *Mazzo XII* (1530s) of the confraternity's archive shows that revisions and reworking were an accepted part of the annual performance.[52] Once elements to be performed had been established by the overseers, the individual parts — *rôles* — were copied onto long strips

---

Guard, the Harrowing of Hell, Christ appearing to his Mother, the Maries at the tomb (xiiii); and *Come Cristo si turbò col mondo* (How Christ was angered by the world [and sent St. Francis and St. Dominic to set things to right]) (xiii), ed. in Vecchi, "Le sacre rappresentazioni," 293–304.

[51] For details see Table 1.

[52] See chapter 9 below, and discussion of Castellano Castellani's *Cena e Passione*.

of paper — *rotuli* or rolls — with cues consisting of the last line of the preceding speech. A number of these parts, for Judas, Caiaphas, and Pilate, were returned to the company and bound into the *Mazzo XII*; they are the only such parts to survive.[53]

We cannot confidently assert that a similar process existed in fifteenth-century Florence, but it seems probable that for the early plays of the Annunciation and the Purification, for example, there was considerable flexibility both in the number of prophets and sibyls and how they were summoned, and in the way the core event was presented. The *ottave* of the prophets and sibyls also had a separate existence, as part of a series of prints, but they were shuffled among speakers without regard to traditional sources.

The discovery of *rappresentazioni* in manuscript has been serendipitous. This project began to take shape as I became aware that the plays of the manuscript tradition had different characteristics from those of the plays in print, and that Alessandro D'Ancona's 1872 anthology to some extent misrepresented the genre by neglecting those plays that did not find their way into print. I searched the manuscript catalogues of libraries in Florence and beyond but found that they were not always sufficiently detailed for me to identify *rappresentazioni* and distinguish them from *cantari* on the same subject. In large libraries, meanwhile, there were so many separate *fondi* without a single unified catalogue that I have inevitably missed some. My most useful search tool in the times before electronic databases proved to be Paul Oscar Kristeller's *Iter Italicum* (1963–1996), which identifies manuscripts containing works by Feo Belcari. Thanks to his translation of Ambrogio Traversari's Latin version of Mosco's *Pratum Spirtuale*, Belcari met Kristeller's criteria for a 'humanist'; since Belcari's *Abramo* was almost unfailingly included in every anthology of plays, I was able to identify collections of *rappresentazioni* throughout Italy and beyond. This may, of course, be a false premise, and it is based on cataloguers recognizing the *Abramo* as the work of Belcari. I continue to identify new manuscripts thanks to new electronic resources: the French king François I's copy of Belcari's *Abramo* in BnF, Ms. italien 1085; a flood-damaged collection in the library of the Accademia della Crusca, Ms. 131; three plays by Belcari in a miscellany in the Archivio provinciale dei Cappuccini lombardi, Ms. A01; a play of the *Popolo d'Isdrael* dated 1499 in the Morgan Museum and Library in New York; and no doubt more to come.

---

[53] Now AAV, Arciconfraternita del Gonfalone 36; see Wisch and Newbigin, *Acting on Faith*, 328–333 and figs. 12.3–12.5.

The zeal of collectors of printed books and the distorting lens of D'Ancona's anthology bequeathed us a genre largely trapped in the Savonarolan moment of 1490–1520. A wider view that takes in the rich manuscript tradition of the plays reveals a richer corpus, one that reached its creative peak in the third quarter of the fifteenth century and reflects a far more varied and vigorous charitable and devotional culture than that suggested by the printed plays alone. It is to the earliest plays that we now turn.

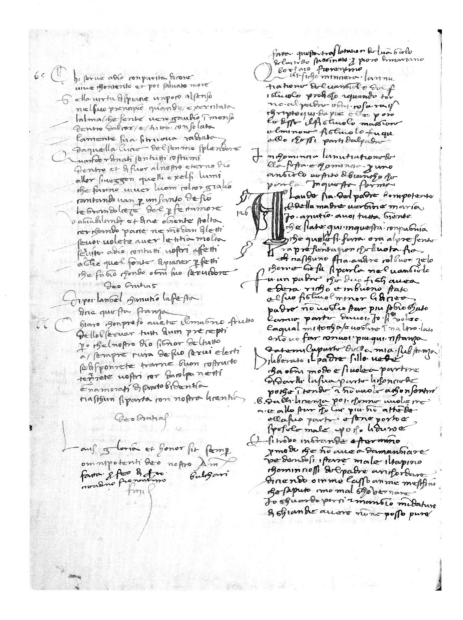

Figure 1.1. Piero di Mariano Muzi, *Qui si chomincierà l'annutiatione del Vangielo del figliuolo prodigho* (*La festa del vitel sagginato*). 1448–1464. Ink on paper. Copied by Filippo Benci. BAV, Chigi L.VII.266, fol. 62ᵛ, col. 2.

Figure 1.2. Feo Belcari, *Festa di Abramo*, dedicatory sonnet addressed to
Giovanni de' Medici. Before 1463. Ink, tempera, and gold leaf on vellum.
BNCF, Magl. VII.744, fol. 1ʳ. © By permission of MiBACT/BNCF.

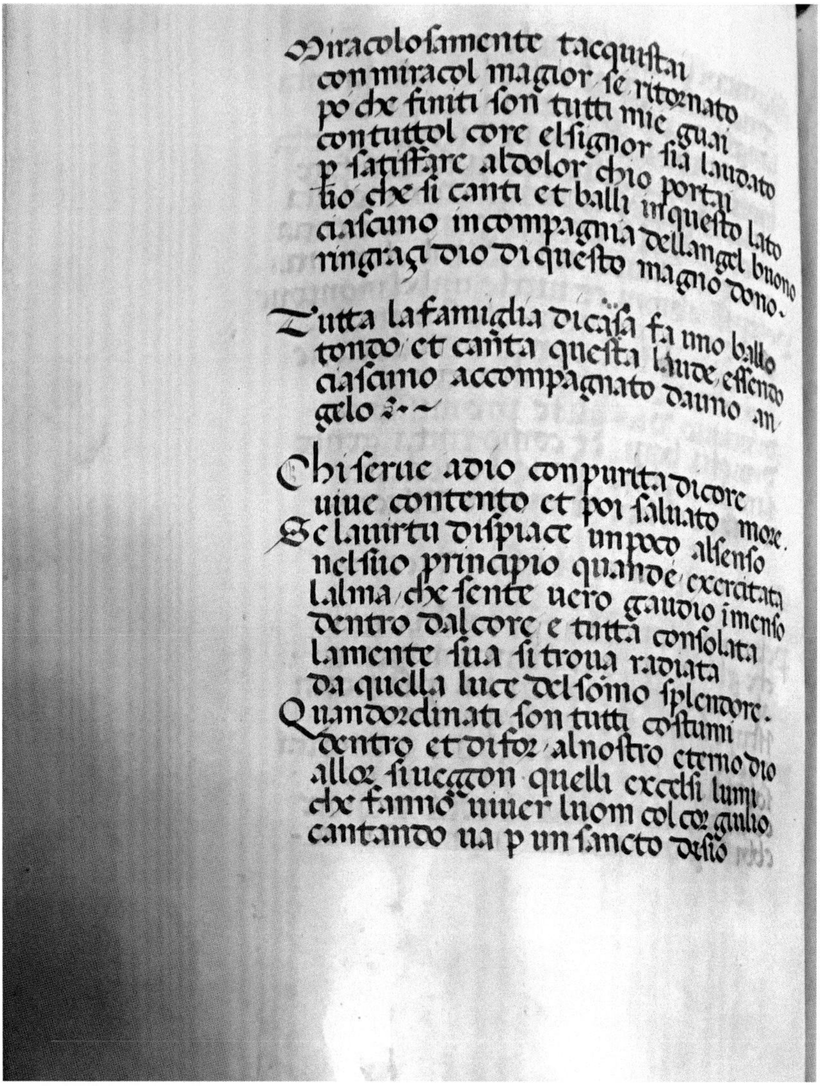

Figure 1.3. Feo Belcari, *Questa è la rapresentatione d'Abram quando volse fare sacrificio di Isac*, stage direction after octave 60. Before 1484. Black and red ink on vellum. Formerly owned by the author's son, Jacopo di Feo Belcari (fol. 173ᵛ); his grandson, Feo di Jacopo di Feo Belcari (guard leaf 2ʳ); and Giovanni di Pagolo Davanzati "che l'hebbe da Feo" (who got it from Feo; fol. 173ᵛ). Prov. Gaddi. BNCF, Magl. vii.690, fol. 118ᵛ. © By permission of MiBACT/BNCF. All rights reserved.

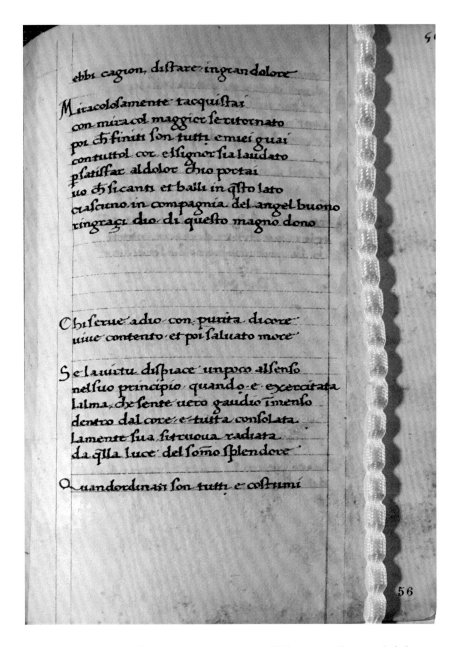

Figure 1.4. Feo Belcari, *Rappresentazione d'Abramo* with space left for rubricated stage directions. c. 1455. Black ink on paper. Copied by Jacopo di Niccolò di Cocco Donati. BRF, Ricc. 1721, fol. 56ʳ. © By permission of MiBACT/BRF. All rights reserved.

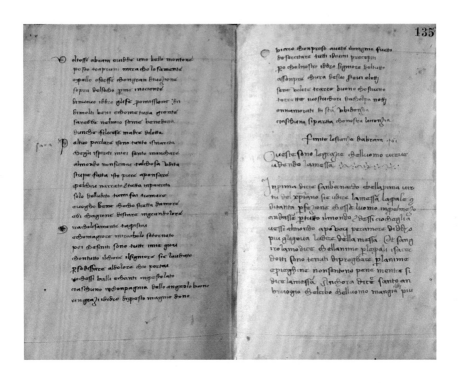

Figure 1.5. Feo Belcari, *Le stanze d'Abramo* without stage directions. 1461. Black and red ink on paper. BRF, Ricc. 1429, fols. 134ᵛ–135ʳ. © By permission of MiBACT/BRF. All rights reserved.

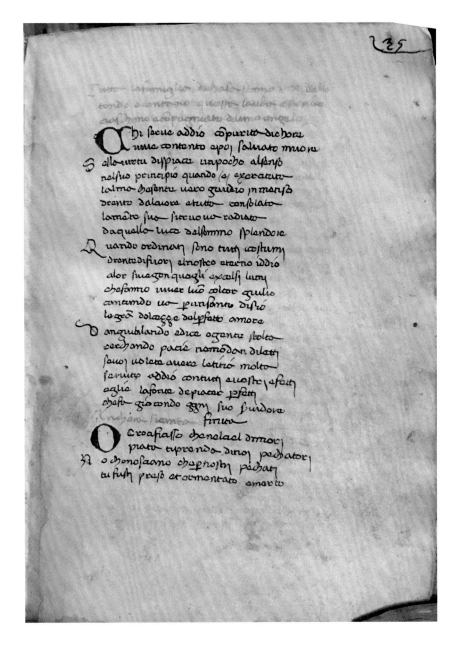

Figure 1.6. Feo Belcari, *La rapresentatione d'abram quando volle fare sacrificio d'Isac*. 1464–1465. Black, red, and blue ink on paper. Copied by Lorenzo di ser Nicolaio di Diedi. Prov. Camaldoli. BNCF, Conv. Soppr. F.3.488, fol. 35ʳ. © By permission of MiBACT/BNCF. All rights reserved.

Figure 1.7. *Rappresentazioni*, with first folio of *Una notabile rapresentatione chiamata la Creatione del mondo. 1464–1465*. Black, red, and blue ink on vellum and paper. Copied by Lorenzo di ser Nicolaio di Diedi. Prov. Camaldoli. BNCF, Conv. Soppr. F.3.488, inside cover and fol. 1ʳ.
© By permission of MiBACT/BNCF. All rights reserved.

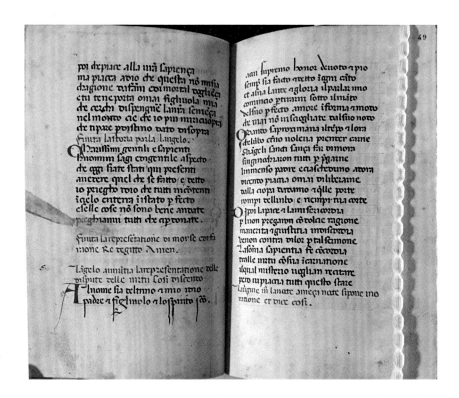

Figure 1.8. Feo Belcari, *La representatione delle dispute delle Virtù* (*La festa dell'Annunciazione*). 1450–1475. Ink and tempera on paper. Owned by Suor Arcangela, daughter of Domenico Alamanni. BRF, Ricc. 2893, fols. 48^v–49^r.

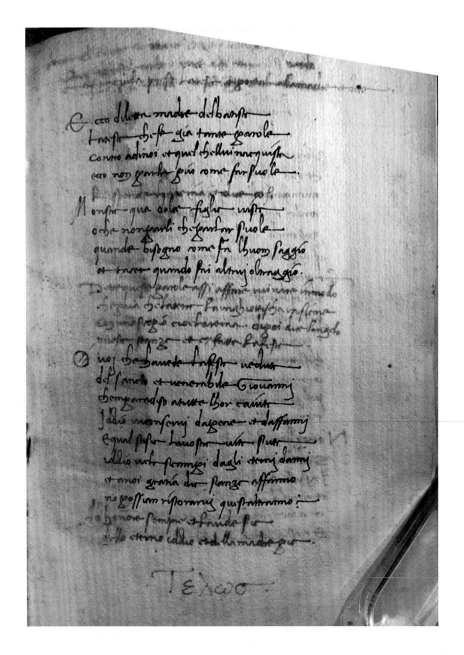

Figure 1.9. *La diuota Rapresentatione di Sancto G‹i›ovanBatista cioè quando
fue dicollato,* last page with word *Telos.* 1450–1475. Red and black ink on
paper. BRF, Ricc. 2816, fol. 44ʳ. © By permission of MiBACT/BRF.

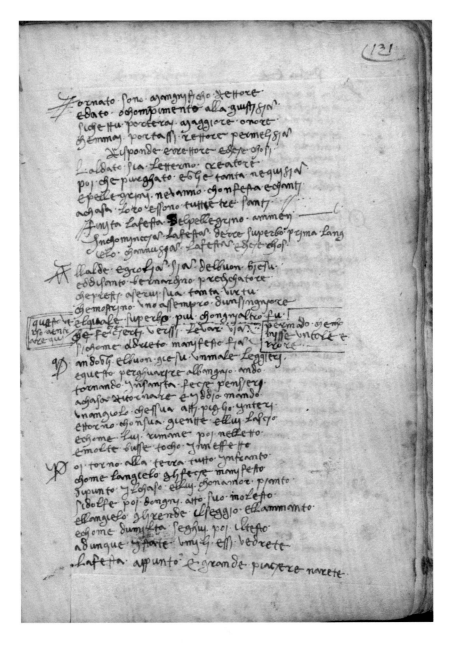

Figure 1.10. End of *La festa del pellegrino*, beginning of *La festa de·rre superbo*. Third quarter, fifteenth century. Red and black ink on paper, copied by Giovanni d'Antonio di Scarlatto Scarlatti. BAMi, C 35 sup., fol. 131[r].
© Veneranda Biblioteca Ambrosiana.

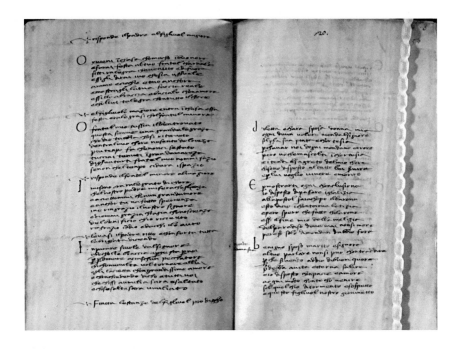

Figure 1.11. End of Piero di Mariano Muzi, *Le stanze del figliuol prodigho*
(*La festa del vitel sagginato*), and beginning of *La festa del pellegrino*. 1450–
1475. Ink on paper. BRF, Ricc. 2971/1, fols. 49ᵛ–50ʳ. © By permission of
MiBACT/BRF. All rights reserved.

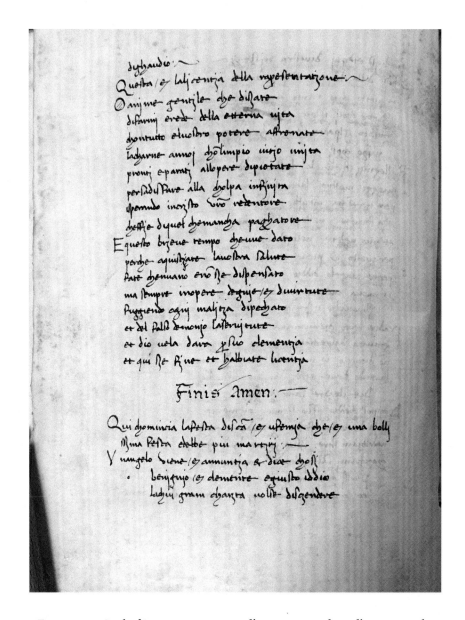

Figure 1.12. End of *La rapresentatione d'uno santo padre e d'uno monacho dove si dimostra quando il monacho andò al servigio d'Iddio e chome ebbe molte tentazioni et era buono servo d'Iddio*, and beginning of *La festa di sancta Eufemia che è una bellissima festa ed ebbe più martiri*. First quarter of sixteenth century. Ink on paper. Prov. Riccardi, Guadagni, Poggiali. BNCF, Pal. 445, fol. 39ᵛ. © By permission of MiBACT/BNCF. All rights reserved.

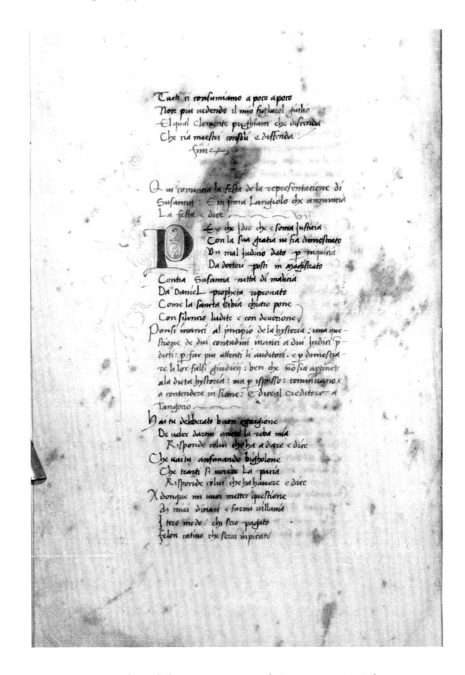

Figure 1.13. *La festa de la representatione di Susanna*. 1482. Ink on paper, with red and blue decorations. Copied by Tommaso Leone. BNCR, VE 483, fol. 67ᵛ. © By permission of MiBACT/BNCR. All rights reserved.

Chapter 2

Plays in Churches

Pavilioned in splendour,
And girded with praise.
Robert Grant[1]

The best known and most studied Florentine *rappresentazioni* are the Annunciation, Ascension, and Pentecost *feste* that were performed in the monastic and conventual churches of the Oltrarno from the end of the fourteenth century through to the middle of the sixteenth century.[2] Research since the 1980s has attempted to reshape our perceptions of these plays, but has been slow to overwrite misconceptions that have prevailed since the late nineteenth century.[3]

All three *feste* were staged by *laudesi* confraternities, adult devotional groups dedicated to Santa Maria delle Laude and their own particular devotion, who sang *laude* or hymns in the vernacular and contributed to the devotional life of their host church.[4] In return they were permitted to erect vast

---

[1] Robert Grant, "O worship the King," hymn based on Psalm 103 (104), first published in Bickersteth, ed., *Christian Psalmody*, 1833.

[2] These three *feste*, performed in San Felice, Santo Spirito, and Santa Maria del Carmine, were the subject of my *Feste d'Oltrarno: Plays in Churches in Fifteenth-Century Florence* (1996). Vol. 1 contains chapters on the three *feste*, with an epilogue on their sixteenth-century heritage; vol. 2 contains transcriptions from the surviving account books and inventories of the confraternities that mounted the *feste*. I returned to the question of the plays in 2007, in "Greasing the Wheels of Paradise," and again in 2017, in "Pavilioned in Splendour." This chapter draws heavily, but not exclusively, on that material.

[3] These will be dealt with in the course of the chapter, but I will state from the beginning: (a) the Annunciation was probably never performed in the Servite church of the Santissima Annunziata, as asserted by Wesselofsky, D'Ancona, Larson, Zorzi, Danilova, and others, or in San Marco as argued more recently by Ventrone, but was always the *festa* of San Felice in Piazza; (b) the *festa* was already well established when Belcari wrote his play (c. 1465); (c) the anonymous *Annunciazione* printed in D'Ancona's anthology is not by Belcari; and (d) we have no evidence of any performance of Belcari's text, in San Felice, in the San Giovanni procession, or elsewhere. Details will be given in notes that follow.

[4] On *laudesi* confraternities, see Barr, *The Monophonic Lauda*; Wilson, *Music and Merchants*. The surviving records are now held in the Florentine Archivio di Stato and

89

mechanical devices within the fabric of the church, which remained in place year-round. In 1565, when Vasari was preparing the second edition of his *Lives of the Artists*, he probably became involved in the processes of dismantling, cataloguing, and storing equipment that had been salvaged from San Felice in Piazza, once home of the Annunciation plays, and from Santa Maria del Carmine, site of the Ascension plays. He was responsible with Vincenzio Borghini for the restaging of the Annunciation in Brunelleschi's new Santo Spirito, which had replaced the church destroyed by the fire that arose from the unextinguished embers of the Pentecost play in 1471.[5] Vasari was acutely aware that memory of the plays was slipping away. On the basis of the equipment stored in the crypt of Santa Maria del Carmine and used again in 1566 in Santo Spirito, he attempted to describe the plays that had once flourished, tentatively attributing the machinery of the Annunciation to Brunelleschi, and that of the Ascension to Francesco d'Angelo, called *il Cecca*. There is no trace of any contribution by Francesco d'Angelo in the account books of the confraternity responsible for the Ascension.[6] For the Annunciation, no such books survive, but it is possible that the goldsmith called Pippo or Filippo di Baldo, responsible for the disappearing-light devices in the mandorla of the Ascension that are recalled in the notebooks of another engineer, Bonaccorso Ghiberti (figs. 2.1 and 2.2), merged in popular memory with the more famous Filippo di ser Brunellesco Brunelleschi, and that he was simply one

---

are catalogued as *Compagnia di S. Maria delle Laudi detta di S. Agnese* and *Compagnia di S. Maria delle Laudi e Spirito Santo detta del Piccione*, and not within the larger series of *Compagnie religiose soppresse da Pietro Leopoldo*. The archives of the San Felice company do not survive. Until the last circle of walls was completed in 1333, San Felice in Piazza stood just outside the southern gate, at the beginning of the Via Romana; it seems always to have celebrated the Virgin's particular relationship with Florence. The Carmelite friary of Santa Maria del Carmine, like the other mendicant friaries, lay completely outside the walls, and only the Augustinian friary, which enjoyed a privileged relationship with the Republic, lay within the walls. By the fifteenth century, all three were within the city walls.

[5] Newbigin, "Greasing the Wheels."

[6] Vasari, *Le vite* (1568), 1:301–326, *Vita di Filippo Bruneleschi scultore et architetto*, and 1:440–445, *Vita del Cecca ingegnere fiorentino*. For translations that relate the terms invented by Vasari to describe the machinery to the terms used by the *festaiuoli* themselves, see Newbigin, *Feste*, 1:22–24 and 64–65. It has long been acknowledged that *il Cecca* could not chronologically have been the "inventor" of the Ascension *festa*, but it is inconvenient to the narrative of art history to deny Brunelleschi the role of "inventor" of the Annunciation *festa*. I have avoided reproducing these two famous descriptions, which were not based on eye-witness accounts, in order to focus below on Vasari's first-hand experience of the machinery and the plays.

of a large group of talented and innovative artisans who have been called the *Brunelleschiani*.[7]

A second description of the same *feste* re-emerged toward the end of the nineteenth century. A Russian bishop, Abraham of Suzdal, who travelled to Florence for the Council of 1439 with Isidore, Metropolitan of Kiev, described the Annunciation and Ascension that he saw, providing the dimensions of the churches and details of the action and the pyrotechnics, and expressing amazement that the Angel of the Annunciation was "in all his appearance [...] like a painted image of an angel of God."[8] The discussion of the three *feste* that follows is based on a close reading of these first-hand accounts by participants and observers, and attempts to peel away some of the mythology that has grown around them.

The Ascension of Christ in Santa Maria del Carmine

Since the documentation of the Ascension *festa* in Santa Maria del Carmine is the most complete, and stretches from the 1390s to the removal of the

---

[7] Borsi, Morolli, and Quinterio, *Brunelleschiani*. In fig. 2.1, Ghiberti explains: "This tube is made of tinned iron attached to the throne and inside it there is a copper lamp that has a wire underneath, which, when a piece of string is pulled as you can see in the drawing, makes the light spring out of the tube, and one piece of string triggers six or eight, so that when the time comes they all come out at once" (Questo chanone è di fero istangniatto apichatto in sul ttrono che v'è denttro una luciernuza di rame che à uno filo di fero di sotto che ttiratto uno spagho chome vedi disengnatto fa ischizare fuori del chanone e· lume e uno ispagho ne pingne 6 o 8 i· modo che quando è ttenpo ttutte a un'otta venghano fuori). Thus the mandorla blazes into light as Christ, or an angel, or the soul of a martyred saint, steps into the *nugola* to be raised into heaven. The winch may also belong to this apparatus: "This handle [is made] of iron so that it turns faster because with the cross piece (capstan?) it would take too long" (Questo manicho di fero perché vadia più fortte ché cho la + porrebe ttropo). In fig. 2.2, Ghiberti shows the mechanism for the *nugola*, stabilized by two parallel, tensioned ropes that were anchored to beams in the roof and below the stage, and hoisted by a third, attached to the *nugola*.

[8] Wesselofsky, "Italienische Mysterien"; D'Ancona, *Origini*, 1:246–253; Larson, "Bishop Abraham"; Fabbri, Garbero Zorzi, and Petrioli Tofani, eds., *Il luogo teatrale*, 56–57, no. 1.6 (Elvira Garbero Zorzi), 60–61, no. 1.19 (Elvira Garbero Zorzi); Zorzi, "Introduzione," 9–13, reissued with notes as "Firenze: il teatro e la città," in his *Il teatro*, 63–76, 137–168; Zorzi, "La scenotecnica"; Ciseri, "Spiritualità e spettacolo," 452–455; Ventrone, "L'eccezione," "'Una visione,'" "La propaganda unionista," and *Teatro civile*, 123–124, 367–397; Signorini, "Le sacre rappresentazioni." English translation in Newbigin, *Feste*, 1:60–63; but for an important essay, with a literal translation, based on Prokofiev, *Russkie khozhdeniia*, see Dresvina, "The Unorthodox *Itinerary*," cited here, from p. 115.

machinery in 1554,[9] I shall begin there rather than dealing with the plays in calendrical order. The feast of the Ascension, on the Thursday that falls forty days after Easter, was a particular devotion of the Carmelites who linked their foundation to Mount Carmel — from which Elijah (Elias) was taken to heaven in a fiery chariot (4 Kings 2:11) — and thus to the traditional prefiguration of Christ's ascent into heaven. The earliest records of the confraternity of Santa Maria delle Laude e di Sant'Agnese required its members to sing *laude* for a range of feast days, but already by 1292, Ascension was their principal feast, celebrated with a supper.[10] Their great *laudario*, illuminated by Pacino di Bonaguida in the 1320s and by the Master of the Dominican Effigies in the 1340s, but now dismembered, shows the importance of this key feast day,[11] while Franco Sacchetti, author of witty short stories and *facetiae*, provides our earliest account (c. 1392) of a performance in the Carmine of Christ's ascent into heaven. Sacchetti was unimpressed by the speed and commented: "Unless he hurried up, he is still on his way."[12]

In 1422, Paolo Petriboni recorded in his *Priorista* that "a solemn and beautiful *festa*" (una solenne e bella *festa*) was performed.[13] The church was newly completed and consecrated. The nave had timber roof trusses and a masonry *tramezzo* (dividing wall), several metres thick and perforated by three archways, that divided the choir of the Carmelite friars from the space of the general congregation (see floor plan, fig. 2.4). Access to the roof was (and is still) via the stairs next to the sacristy, but in 1436, to facilitate preparations

---

[9] Newbigin, *Feste*, discussion, 1:45–155; documents, 2:283–657, with Newbigin, "Greasing the Wheels," 203–204.

[10] *Il libro degli ordinamenti*, 65, §45. No fifteenth-century statutes survive, but Florence, Archivio Arcivescovile, holds their statutes for 1505 (CR 06.42) and 1516 (CR 06.43), a declaration for 1543 (CR 06.40), and inventories and *memoria* for 1621 (CR 06.41); see Aranci, Bellacci, and Faldi, "La sezione," 18. On suppers in confraternities, see Newbigin, "*Cene* and *Cenacoli*"; Terpstra, "The Stripping of the Tables."

[11] For details of surviving leaves, see Boehm, "The Master," 58–80; Zimei, "New Light." On the *laudario* in its confraternal context, see Barr, "Music and Spectacle," 389–404.

[12] Sacchetti, *Il trecentonovelle*, 186–188, lxxii: "Se non andò più ratto, egli è ancor tra via."

[13] Petriboni, *Priorista*, 150–151. On the *tramezzo* in Florentine churches, see Hall, "The Tramezzo." A *Priorista* is a list of the men who served each term in the offices of *gonfaloniere della giustizia*, the priors, and their notary, from the foundation of the Republic in 1282 to its final demise in 1531. The list was often enhanced, like Petriboni's, with a description of the notable events of each period, in part copied and in part original. See Anselmi, Pezzarossa, and Avellini, *La "Memoria,"* for a list of 330 such volumes.

for its *festa*, the confraternity built its own spiral staircase from its oratory on the eastern side of the church, opening onto the *tramezzo* where the performance took place and continuing up to the roofline.[14] By 1467, when the painter Neri di Bicci made an inventory of the confraternity's possessions, the *castello* (castle) on the left of the *tramezzo* represented Jerusalem, and the *monte* (mount) on the right represented the Mount of Olives, from which Christ ascended diagonally to *Cielo* (Heaven) above the High Altar, hoisted by ropes and pulleys in an illuminated *nugola* (literally 'cloud,' but in reality a metal-framed mandorla, bearing Christ and two angels).[15] In Heaven, he was received by God the Father, surrounded by rotating wheels of lights and choirs of angels. At this point, *Paradiso* (Paradise), which was a different location from Heaven and home to a second God the Father, opened directly above the Mount of Olives, and two angels descended to comfort the apostles before returning to Paradise and the choirs of angels. The church was further illuminated by an enormous *stella* (star) suspended in a horizontal plane over the nave, with rotating spokes supporting lights and life-sized cherubim and seraphim moulded out of leather. All of these items remained in place, gathering dust, until activity began again the following year.

Preparation for this *festa*, performed on the vigil of the Ascension, began immediately after Easter Sunday. The confraternity of Sant'Agnese, which had its meeting rooms adjoining the eastern side of the church and patronage of two altars in close proximity to them,[16] appointed *festaiuoli*, who would take responsibility for organizing the *festa*. They ordered new keys, purchased brooms and rat poison, and set about cleaning up the space on top of the *tramezzo* and in the roof areas. They checked the costumes for Mary and Mary Magdalene, and for Christ and the apostles (for the most part old church vestments), as well as beards and wigs. For the angels, they frequently made new wings — from chicken feathers, paper of many different colours, or even ostrich feathers hired from a silk merchant, depending on resources. They checked the ropes, pulleys, and winches that raised and lowered the *nugole*, and devised new light-sources that would astonish the audiences; they hauled barrels of water into the roof as a fire-safety measure;

---

[14] Newbigin, *Feste*, 1:55–56; the staircase is visible from outside.

[15] The equipment for the *festa* is discussed extensively in Barr, "A Renaissance Artist," and "Music and Spectacle"; the full text of the inventory is in Newbigin, *Feste*, 1:67–79 (English translation), and 2:530–539. On the *nugole*, see Buccheri, *The Spectacle*; Mamone, "Le nuvole," online.

[16] Berti, ed., *La chiesa*, 145 and figs. 3–5.

and primed lamps and wicks with oil. They recruited musicians wherever they could be found. Finally, as a security measure, they issued colour-coded beads to identify those who were permitted to enter the different areas of the roof and the *tramezzo*.[17] The actors (although they do not yet have this name) were members of the confraternity; they received no reward at all, apart from the pleasure of socializing with their fellows and being fed throughout the process and at a large banquet after the performance. The angels who "went on the ropes" to accompany Christ to Heaven, and descended from Paradise to the apostles, were young boys recruited from the cathedral choir;[18] they received a gift of red hose, such as we see in Filippo Lippi's *Martelli Annunciation* in San Lorenzo (fig. 2.5).[19]

Two texts survive that may be associated with the Carmine *festa*. The first is a minimal *lauda drammatica*, "In ciel si fa gran festa" (In Heav'n there's great rejoicing), found in various forms and in a number of manuscripts. The earliest dates to about 1415, and another is recopied in a scriptorium manuscript of the plays and *laude* of Feo Belcari.[20] The Angel announces to Mary that Jesus has surely ascended to heaven and invites her and the apostles to join in heaven's rejoicing, for soon they will be "enflamed" with joy. Mary replies that this is the fulfilment of her Annunciation and, in the version contained in the Belcari manuscript, with a change of metre from *settenari* to

---

[17] Newbigin, *Feste*, 1:82.

[18] See, for example, Newbigin, *Feste*, 2:542, no. 13 (1467): "A Fazio merciaio al Chorno lire dua soldi dua chontanti, furono per libra una d'otone brillante per soldi 26 la libra e per dua bande di fero istagniato el quale otone togliemo per fare l'alia agli Agnioli di Paradiso che venghono giù pelle funi" (To Fazio the mercer at the sign of the Horn, £2 6s. in cash, for 1*lb* of polished brass at 26s./*lb*, and for two bands of tin-plated iron, and we got the brass to make the wings of the Angels in Paradise who come down on the ropes).

[19] Newbigin, *Feste*, 2:360. Christa Gardner von Teuffel drew my attention to Lippi's angels, so intent on displaying their stockinged feet (and also to the blue-stockinged feet of the angel of another Lippi *Annunciation* now in the Frick Museum, New York, Accession no. 1924.1.85); see Gardner von Teuffel and Castelli, "La tavola," 39. As a Carmelite friar in Santa Maria del Carmine, Lippi must have seen the angels who went on the ropes preparing for the Ascension play.

[20] BNCF, II.ix.58 (copied by Bernardo di Messer Niccolò da Rabatta, and dating to c. 1415, in six stanzas), fol. 12ʳ⁻ᵛ; Florence, Accademia della Crusca, Manoscritti letterari 131, fol. 105ᵛ. A modified version, beginning "Nel ciel si fa gran *festa*," with *cantasi come* (lit. 'to be sung to the tune of'), was published in *Laude uechie & nuoue* (after 1507), fol. LVIIʳ; see Wilson, *Singing Poetry*, 53. Text and translation: Newbigin online. It is found also in BNCF, Landau Finaly 249, fol. 48ʳ⁻ᵛ (which contains the *Vitel sagginato*, *Abramo*, and *Jacob ed Esaù*), without the last two stanzas present in BNCF, II.ix.58.

endecasillabi, she rejoices in the imminent return of his Love.[21] The seven (or eight) stanzas and a four-line refrain scarcely constitute a play, but the repetition of *festa* (in the first line of the refrain and the last line of each stanza) may tie this *lauda* to what the Sant'Agnese company always called "our *festa* of the Ascension" (la festa nostra della Scensione)

A second Ascension text survives, prepared by Feo Belcari (1411–1484) and accompanied by a sonnet, in the name of the *festaiuoli* of the Ascension, that is addressed to Cosimo de' Medici and asks for a gift of wine.[22] It is not possible to establish a date, but it is reasonable to imagine that this short text belongs to 1443, when Cosimo's son Piero gave a barrel of wine to the *festaiuoli*, who in turn did honour to the person who had rewritten the lines of Christ.[23] Medici patronage is significantly at arm's length: whatever role Piero's taste may have played in imposing a text on a play that might have been unruly and sometimes slow, the engagement between client and patron is a ritual one of supplication and reward. The *festa* was entirely in the hands of the confraternity, and Piero — whether in his own right or on behalf of his father — secured their goodwill by contributing to the feasting that accompanied the *festa*.

This text, too, is very short, just nine stanzas, and much is unsaid. The first stage direction, after the Angel's prologue, reads: "Then Christ, having supped with the Apostles, comes out of Jerusalem, and all the Apostles hold their emblems in their hands, and at the foot of the mount Christ says to them […]" (Dipoi Cristo, avendo mangiato con gli Apostoli, esce di Ierusalem, e tutti gli Apostoli hanno in mano i loro segni, ed a piè del monte Cristo dice a loro […]; stage direction after oct. 1). The implication is that Christ, his Mother, and his disciples were first visible around the table in the Upper Room, above the gate of Jerusalem. The shape and appearance of this Jerusalem — the *castello* — will become clear with our examination of the Pentecost play in Santo Spirito; in the meantime, here as in the visual arts, the focus of the action is the *monte*, as we see in Jacopo di Cione's *Ascension* panel in the National Gallery, London (fig. 2.6). They leave the city and make their way to the Mount of Olives where Christ bids farewell to his disciples and ascends to heaven. Two Angels descend to promise Christ's return, and the Virgin intercedes on behalf of the apostles, asking for the consolation of the Holy Spirit.

---

[21] The six-line stanza is related to the last octave of Belcari's *Ascensione*.

[22] For manuscripts and modern editions, see Table 1. On Belcari, see chapter 7 below.

[23] Newbigin, *Feste*, 1:98.

The words, however, were of lesser importance since the *significatio* of the *festa* was inscribed almost entirely in the visual spectacle. Just as Elijah, the legendary founder of the Carmelites, had ascended in a flaming chariot from Mount Carmel, so Christ ascended from the Mount of Olives. The *confratelli* strove to increase each year the honour and magnificence of their *festa*, the principal feast day of their church, "to the honour of God and for the greatness of the city," using elaborate machinery and lighting effects.[24]

The feast of the Ascension was not unchallenged. In 1440, the Carmelites' own Andrea Corsini, bishop of Fiesole, who had died in 1373 and was buried in the church, came to the aid of Florence in a moment of great crisis. As Milan threatened, Corsini miraculously emerged from his tomb and advised Florence to attack the Milanese on the plain below Anghiari on the feast day of St. Peter and St. Paul, 29 June. The Brancacci chapel, to the right of the high altar, already celebrated these two founders of the Church; now for their feast day, and in honour of their victory at Anghiari, the Commune inaugurated a new procession to the Carmine and an offering to the poor.[25] This new devotion was of relatively short duration, and did not disrupt the primacy of the Ascension *festa*, which continued to grow in ingenuity and magnificence until 1471 when, after the visit of the duke of Milan, it was transformed into the Assumption of the Virgin.[26]

Pentecost in Santo Spirito

From at least 1416 and until embers from Pentecostal tongues of fire destroyed the church in 1471, the Augustinian church of Santo Spirito was the scene of a Pentecost play.[27] Pentecost, fifty days after Easter, was the church's principal feast day and the dove of the Holy Ghost hovered over every part of the church's decoration. The *festa* had previously been the responsibility of the Frescobaldi family, patrons of the high altar, whose property and gardens in Via di Santo Spirito adjoined the northern end of the church. By 1419

---

[24] "A honore di Dio e a magnificentia di questa città." The justification is included in their application to the Commune for funding in 1445; see Newbigin, *Feste*, 2:420.

[25] Ciappelli, "A Trecento Bishop"; Newbigin, "Playing in the Piazza." Corsini was beatified in 1440, following his miraculous apparition.

[26] Newbigin, *Feste*, 1:134–137, and below in this chapter.

[27] The present church, to Brunelleschi's design, was already planned when the old church was destroyed; see Quinterio, "Un tempio." For descriptions of the fire, see Newbigin, *Feste*, 2:746–752.

the *festa* had passed to the confraternity of Santa Maria delle Laudi e dello Spirito Santo, called the *Piccione* or *Pippione* (Pigeon) for the dove of the Holy Ghost. Although less well-organized than their neighbours in the Carmine, they were no less enthusiastic. Their archive contains inventories and account books relating to their *festa*, and their fourteenth-century *laudario* is preserved in the Biblioteca Nazionale (fig. 2.7).[28]

The play would ultimately be performed over three locations: Heaven, with God the Father; a *castello*, which once again represented Jerusalem, as it did in the Ascension *festa*; and the rest of the world, represented by the space in front of the *castello*. A description of the *festa*, reproduced by the eighteenth-century Jesuit Giuseppe Richa, explains how the *castello* was used:

> In the middle of the church, above the choir, or rather the dividing wall, there was attached to the roof a Heaven full of angels, which moved mechanically, and there was an infinite array of lights that looked like stars, which could be uncovered and then concealed again in a flash. The angels were boys of about twelve, tied and belted on and secured to special bases, so that in spite of the swift movement they could not have fallen if they had wanted to. And besides moving, when the time came, they took one another by the hand and, as they swung their arms, they seemed to dance by means of a turning hemispherical dome. In this dome there were three garlands of lights that could not tip up, and all around there were ingenious clouds of cotton wool, on the highest point of which the Eternal Father sat, and with Christ to one side, both surrounded by angels who were likewise little boys of eight years old. In the middle a shining white Dove, symbolizing the Divine Spirit, spread its wings and sent down a shower of fire. And the Eternal Father, Christ, the Holy Spirit, the angels, the infinite number of lights, and the sweetest music truly represented Paradise. And below was a *cenaculum*, or rather a room illuminated by the tongues of fire shining above the heads

---

[28] The illuminated fourteenth-century *Laudario* of the Spirito Santo company is one of two listed in their 1444 inventory (Newbigin, *Feste*, 1:169). The opening illustration, probably repainted, shows the Pentecost scene in the upper room, with Mary, the Twelve, and the company's other patrons, St. Augustine on the left and, on the right, the Augustinian *beato*, St. Nicholas of Tolentino, not canonized until 1446. For the archives, see n. 4 above; Newbigin, *Feste*, discussion, 1:157–208; documents, 2:659–752.

of the apostles, who sat with the Mother of God, making the most
natural gestures that changed frequently. And finally, right below
on a stage, the *festa* was performed by fine actors, but it ended
in a most terrible tragedy, as has been mentioned: through the
carelessness of the attendants who were meant to extinguish the
vast number of lamps, one was left alight within a wooden tube,
and in the early hours of the night it caught alight and was the
spark of that terrible fire, from which only the wooden Crucifix
of the Bianchi survived unharmed.[29]

The *castello* was a two-storey structure representing the city gate of Jerusalem and the house of the Upper Room, closely reflecting the iconography
of fourteenth-century painting. It reverberated in the design both of commercial theatres in sixteenth-century England and of puppet booths, still called
'castles' to the present day.[30] The open upper floor represented the *cenacolo*,
the upper room of the Last Supper, which is the same upper room ("in eodem loco," Actus 2:1)[31] where the apostles gathered, after Christ's ascent into

---

[29] Richa, *Notizie*, 9 (1761): 15–16; see Appendix, doc. 1. Richa claims to be quot-
ing contemporary documents but does not give details. Wilson, *Music and Merchants*,
90, notes other *stelle*, like the Heaven described here, used in *laudesi* celebrations. The
description appears to owe something to Vasari's description of the Heaven in San Felice.
Richa's reference to a dividing wall (*ponte*) seems likewise to have been influenced by
Vasari. There may have been a wall around the choir, but confraternal documents make
no mention of *volte* (vaulted arches that were part of the *tramezzo*), such as we find in the
Carmine.

[30] See also Andrea di Bonaiuto's *Pentecost* in the Dominican chapter house (the
'Spanish Chapel') of Santa Maria Novella. From the fourteenth century onwards, the Upper Room, the city of Jerusalem, and the gates of the city are all represented in a single
structure which, in the play, becomes the *castello*. The Holy Spirit descends on the Twelve
in the Upper Room, and they emerge from the gates below to preach to the Gentiles,
whose otherness is expressed in skin colour, clothing, exotic headwear, and gesture. The
term *castello* has a long afterlife in theatre history. Johannes de Witt's sketch of the stage
of the Swan playhouse in London, c. 1596, preserved in Buchelius's *Adversaria* (Utrecht,
Universiteitsbibliotheek, Hs 7 E 3, fol. 132ʳ), shows that the basic configuration of upper
balcony with doors below was still exploited as the primary acting space. For a different
visualization of the *castello*, see Zorzi and Lisi's interpretive model of the *castello* for the
Ascension, in Fabbri, Garbero Zorzi, and Petrioli Tofani, eds., *Il luogo teatrale*, 59–60, no.
1.18.

[31] Acts of the Apostles 1:13–14, 21–26, 2:1. Modern exegesis reads *in eodem loco* as "in
one place." As this summary makes clear, the order of events in Acts 1:1–2:5 is rearranged,

heaven, to select Matthias as Judas's replacement, and where the Holy Ghost descended on them in tongues of fire (see Fra Angelico's *Pentecost* panel from the *Armadio degli Argenti* in the Museo di San Marco, fig. 2.8). The apostles assembled there with the Virgin Mary were not actors but wooden figures robed in ecclesiastical vestments. They were probably life-sized, since they moved like real people ("striking the most natural poses that changed often"). Animated sculptures like these were found in an extraordinary range of Deposition groups.[32] On their heads were golden *corone* (haloes or diadems) and, for the *festa*, those diadems were packed with fireworks. The action began when a plaster dove, powered by a rocket, sped from Heaven to the Upper Room in the middle of the church and ignited the fireworks. When they were finished, the curtains of the Upper Room were closed and live actors emerged from the door below, speaking in tongues. The conversions and baptisms they performed were represented by another shower of fireworks.

Richa's description is problematic, unsourced, and appears to be influenced by Vasari's account of a rotating Heaven with living children. The evidence of inventories and account books provides a slightly different picture, with Heaven above the high altar, a magnificent *stella* in the middle of the church, and a *castello* to one side. The angels on the *stella* are listed in the inventory of 1444 as life-size figures, not children: "twenty-four angels for the *stella* in the church, big, gilded, beautiful, each 2 *braccia* high," along with twenty-four seraphim and forty-eight doves.[33] There is no indication in the inventories of live angels on the *stella*.

Fireworks were both functional and spectacular. The dove that descended from Heaven was propelled by a rocket along a cord the length of

---

so that the selection of Matthias as replacement for Judas and the Descent of the Holy Ghost precede Christ's Ascension. The Virgin Mary, primary patron of the confraternity, is present throughout. Feo Belcari's text, in just three *ottave*, conflates the two events: after the Angel's prologue, Peter prays for a sign of which man to choose, and the fire descends on Matthias; see Belcari, *Le rappresentazioni*, 113–114; Newbigin, *Feste*, 2:256–257. For a far more elaborate Umbrian text, see *Il laudario perugino*, 1:447–464.

[32] Richa, *Notizie*, 9 (1761): 16: "facienti le più naturali attitudini, che spesso ancora variavansi." Kopania, "The Assumption," 50, n. 38, cites animated wooden sculptures of the apostles and Satan in the Assumption play in Rouen cathedral, suppressed in 1460.

[33] Newbigin, *Feste*, 1:170 and 2:708: "24 Agnioli per la Istela di chiessa, grandi, messi a oro, begli, di bracia 2 l'uno." In the Carmine, the *stella* had moulded *papier-mâché* puppets — twenty-four angels and twenty-three seraphim — presumably totally destroyed in the floods of 1557 when only timber and metal parts survived; Newbigin, *Feste*, 1:72 and 2:533. This may have led Vasari to believe that the angels were played by children.

the church to the *castello*. There it ignited the thirteen crowns of the thirteen wooden figures of Mary and the apostles, crowns that were fitted with little fire tubes packed with fireworks, and fitted with devices made by Domenico di Lorenzo the tinsmith in 1428 so that they exploded in tongues of fire.[34] By 1465, when a second inventory was compiled, the confraternity also had a baptismal font for the play, fitted with a *girandola*, or whirling firework device, that showered sparks on the newly-converted.

The two inventories allow us to glimpse another semi-dramatic ritual that this confraternity shared with the Carmine and possibly others. The *Piccione* company in Santo Spirito in fact owned two *castelli*, one for the Pentecost play and a second for displaying its life-size poseable wooden figures of the twelve apostles and the Virgin Mary, seated around a wooden table, throughout Holy Week.[35] The Sant'Agnese confraternity in the Carmine had a similar but smaller display: kneeling painted apostles with Christ and the Virgin, arranged in memory of the Last Supper on a table that they placed in front of their altar in the church on Maundy Thursday. There they received offerings when their *laudiere* — soloist and choir master — sang the *Stanze della passione*, and on Good Friday they distributed those offerings as bread for the poor.[36] I have not identified any wooden sculptures in modern collections that can be directly related to these figures of the apostles, but recent research on the incorporation of wooden figures into thirteenth- and fourteenth-century liturgies of the Annunciation and the Deposition shows how vibrantly dramatic these rituals were.[37]

---

[34] Newbigin, *Feste*, 1:176–179; 2:677, 706.

[35] Newbigin, *Feste*, 1:74; 2:535: "14 fighure di legniame, cioè 12 Apostoli e una Nostra Donna, tute ginochioni e dipinti e quali si ponghono in sul descho Giovedì Santo, e uno Domenedio" (Fourteen wooden figures, namely twelve Apostles and an Our Lady, all kneeling and painted which are placed on the desk on Maundy Thursday, and a Lord God [i.e. Christ]). The apostles spent the rest of the year on shelves in the oratory: "a cupboard made of boards, that the wooden Apostles stand on in our oratory" (uno armario d'asse dove istanno suso li Apostoli de legnio ne· luogo); Newbigin, *Feste*, 2:709. For a small maiolica set of such figures, seated rather than kneeling, see Boston, Museum of Fine Arts, Accession no. 1983.61, Faenza, sixteenth century; with thanks to Patricia Simons.

[36] Newbigin, *Feste*, 1:74, 79; 2:338–339, 410, 535. There is no indication that the Sant'Agnese company's statues moved.

[37] Bernardi, "La Deposizione"; Sapori and Toscano, eds., *La Deposizione lignea*; Flores d'Arcais, ed., *Il teatro delle statue*; Kopania, *Animated Sculptures,* 2017.

The Annunciation in San Felice in Piazza

Of the three great Oltrarno spectacles, the Annunciation *festa* in San Felice is the most famous, and the most misrepresented. From the time Alessandro D'Ancona published his translation of Wesselofksy's German translation of Abraham of Suzdal's Russian description of the performance of 1439, the play — known to its contemporaries as the *Festa di San Felice* — had been mislocated in the Servite church of the Santissima Annunziata rather than in San Felice in Piazza. On the basis of Vasari's very tentative attribution to Filippo Brunelleschi (1377–1446), authorship of the spectacular devices has unhesitatingly been ascribed to the great architect.[38] And it has been asserted that the *festa* was performed on 25 March, the feast of the Annunciation.

The *laude*se confraternity of Santa Maria delle Laude e della Santissima Annunziata (or della Nostra Donna) that met in San Felice in Piazza is first mentioned in 1277, when the church and monastery were occupied by the Benedictines of San Silvestro di Nonantola.[39] Around 1413, the monastery passed to Camaldolese monks,[40] and was closely linked to Florence's other Camaldolese monastery of Santa Maria degli Angeli, so that San Felice was in the orbit of the humanist monk Ambruogio Traversari, of the Medici, and, from the 1420s, of Filippo Brunelleschi as he planned their new church. The confraternity's archives do not survive. The earliest allusion to its *festa* in San Felice is found in the records of the *Piccione* company of Santo Spirito, which recorded on 16 March 1436/7 that their syndic Luigi di Matteo Biliotti was authorized to lend "to the Annunziata company one rope and one God the Father mask, taken by Papi di Pagnozzo Ridolfi, and he is responsible for returning it."[41] The *festa* was already established in San Felice before 1439.

Abraham of Suzdal's Description

The earliest description of the Annunciation *festa* is by the Russian bishop Abraham of Suzdal:

---

[38] See n. 6 above.

[39] In the *catasto* of 1431, it is called the "compagnia della Nostra Donna"; ASF, Catasto 425 (1431), fol. 10ʳ, cited in Henderson, *Piety*, 462–463.

[40] On the history of the church and its art, see Meoni, *San Felice*, esp. chapter 3.

[41] Newbigin, *Feste*, 2:697: "alla Chonpagnia della Nuziata un chanapo e una maschera di Dio Padre, èbella Papi di Pagniozo Ridoffi e egli n'è tenutto a rèndello." Henderson gives an earliest date for the company of 1435, but I have not been able to corroborate this.

In the city of Florence, a certain clever man, Italian by birth, has created a wonderful work of genius closely representing the descent from heaven of the Archangel Gabriel to the Virgin Mary in Nazareth to announce to her the conception of her only begotten Son, the Word of God. This is how it was done.

In a certain monastery of that city there is a sizable church dedicated to our purest mother of God,[42] above the main door and below the roof at a height of about 7 yards,[43] a square platform was constructed up against the front wall. It measures 1½ yards on all sides. Small, cleverly crafted steps lead up to it. The platform and the steps are both concealed by curtains. This platform is supposed to represent the heavenly spheres, from which the Archangel Gabriel was sent by God the Father to the Virgin. On this elevated platform is set a throne, on which a man of majestic appearance sits, in a chasuble and with a crown on his head. In every way he reflects the likeness of the Father; in his left hand, he holds the book of the Gospels.[44] Around him and at his feet is

---

[42] That is, San Felice in Piazza. In his description of the Ascension, Abraham is similarly mistaken, calling Santa Maria del Carmine "the church of the Ascension of our Lord and Saviour Jesus Christ"; see Newbigin, *Feste*, 1:60. I have amended the translation I provided there, now taking into account the new literal translation in Dresvina, "The Unorthodox *Itinerary*," 112–116. In an authoritative but still late manuscript (c. 1550; see Dresvina, 124), the church is identified as San Marco, and Paola Ventrone prefers this reading (*Teatro civile*, 377 n. 37). As Teubner showed, a *tramezzo* was indeed commissioned in San Marco in 1438 (and demolished by Vasari in the 1560s; Teubner, "San Marco," 247, fig. 8), but the church was a building site in 1439, and not reconsecrated until 6 January (Epiphany), 1442/3. See also Ferrara and Quinterio, *Michelozzo*, 185–196.

[43] The unit of measurement used in the Russian text is the *sazhen*, a unit equivalent to anything between 1.4 m and 2.8 m, but the unit is probably a misreading of an abbreviation not understood by the author or a later copyist. If he measured the church at all, it was probably pacing it out at ground-level. By calibrating Abraham's measurements of the Carmine with its actual measurements, I have calculated the unit that he uses as being approximately 0.9 m, that is, a pace or a yard, and I use the term yards in my translation. This interpretation has not found favour with other scholars, but it has the merit being coherent. See Stallini, *Le théâtre*, 156–159; Dresvina, "The Unorthodox *Itinerary*," 112 n. 76; Ventrone, *Teatro civile*, 377 n. 38. For earlier studies see Danilova, "La rappresentazione."

[44] The actor playing God the Father wore a large mask; see n. 41 above for one borrowed in 1437. The 1444 inventory lists "two masks, one for God the Father, and [the other for the] Son" (dua maschere, l'una per Idio Padre e [l'altra per il] Filiolo), Newbigin, *Feste*, 2:707; while the 1467 inventory of the Sant'Agnese company lists "one mask, that covers

a multitude of little children, suspended with an ingenious device and representing heavenly Powers. Around the throne and amid the children around the Father there are more than five hundred little lights, and this is a source of great wonder. And this is all up high, behind the curtain.

From the main door to the middle of the church is about 25 yards. There in the middle a stone platform runs from one side wall to the other, on stone pillars, 3 yards high and 1½ yards wide.[45] The platform is completely covered in beautiful cloth and upon these layers of cloth on the left side stands a bed, draped with the finest, richly worked cloths and covers. At the head of the bed is a chair adorned with the most wonderful and precious cushions. In this grand and wonderful chair a beautiful young man sits, dressed in sumptuous and wondrous maiden's garb,

---

the face of God the Father" (una maschera, tiene al viso Dio Padre) in Heaven, and also "one mask, that covers the face of God the Father when we do the *festa*" (una maschera tiene al viso Dio Padre quando si fa la festa), in Paradise; see Newbigin, *Feste*, 2:536, 537.

[45] No trace remains in San Felice of a stone dividing wall (called *volte, ponte* or *tramezzo*) or of its removal in the well-documented restructuring for the Dominican nuns after 1553; see Meoni, *San Felice*, 26–27. The front and the rear of the nave, however, are so different in their architecture that there may have been some kind of division between the two spaces even before the construction of the nuns' choir. Alternatively, the performance space may have been on temporary scaffolding: since it was completely covered by rich drapes, Abraham may have surmised that it was a stone *tramezzo* like that in the Carmine and in Santa Maria Novella, or even described as stone something that was painted wood, as he did with the "stone castle" of Jerusalem in the Carmine. The use of the *tramezzo* as a stage was described in a letter from Luigi Pulci to Lorenzo de' Medici early in 1472. He wrote from Foligno that "this last Sunday everybody was in San Domenico to hear the sermon of a friar that they are very fond of, and rightly so; and many people had climbed up on certain arches that span the church — or used to span it — like the ones in Santa Maria Novella, or where we make the stage for our *feste*. And these blessed arches, may they have God's benediction and mine, suddenly collapsed, and, what with everything, they buried perhaps 300 people" (domenica passata era qui tutto il popolo nella chiesa di San Domenico a udire predicare uno frate molto accepto a costoro, et meritamente; et molti erano saliti sopra certe volte che fanno ponte, overo facevano, come è a Sancta Maria Novella o dove noi faciamo il palchetto per le nostre feste. Queste sancte volte, che benedette sieno elle da Dio e da me, rovinorno a un tratto; e copersono in tutto tra ogni cosa forse 300 persone); Pulci, *Morgante e Lettere*, 976. He had earlier described a similar collapse in Camerino, 974–975, 6 January 1471/2. The description of the 1533 Annunciation in San Felice (see below) makes it clear that the "stage" is constructed across the middle of the church.

with a diadem on his head. In his hands he holds a book, from which he reads quietly. In everything he appears to be the most pure Virgin Mary.

And on the same platform there are four men in costume, wearing long beards and the hair of their heads flowing down over their shoulders. They wear small gilded haloes fastened over their hair. The robes about their shoulders are not elegantly made nor handsomely designed, but, rather like undershirts, they were long, white and flowing and tied at the waist. Each of them wears over his right shoulder a small red stole, not for ornament but to fasten their robes. They are dressed quite in the likeness of prophets.

All of these things [on the lower platform] are covered, like the upper platform of which we spoke before, with precious Italian woollen fabrics and exceedingly beautiful drapery. From the upper place that we have already mentioned, down through the stone platform, run five fine strong ropes, right to the altar.[46] Two of them however are close together and pass in front of the person who plays the part of the most pure Virgin. It is on these that the Angel sent by God descends, [lowered] by means of the fine rope, to give her the good tidings. Then in jubilation he returns to heaven again whence he came. These three cords pass right through the middle of the platform.

Later when the time comes for the spectacle, many people gather from everywhere for the great and wonderful event, in the hope of seeing it. And when the church is full of a great multitude of people, after a little while they fall silent, looking up in the direction of the platform constructed in the middle of the church. After a while the curtains and hangings are swept open and everybody can see the person dressed as the most pure Virgin Mary, sitting on the magnificent seat beside the bed. This is a beautiful and marvellous thing to contemplate, a source of moving and absolutely ineffable joy.

Then onto the platform come the four men of whom I spoke before, who are dressed to look like the prophets. They hold

---

[46] Two of the ropes, duly tensioned, supported the weight of the Archangel, while a third raised and lowered him. The remaining two must have been wrapped with the fireworks that exploded at the end of the play, but this is not explicit in the text.

in their hands various texts, that is, the ancient prophecies of Christ's descent from heaven and his Incarnation. They begin to stride backwards and forwards on the platform, each looking at his scroll, and each pointing with his right hand toward the upper platform, which is still enclosed, and saying to the other: "That's where Mankind's salvation will come from." And one says to the other looking at his scroll: "The Lord will come from the south" [Psalm 74:7 (75:6); Habakkuk 3:3]. They began to argue with each other, tearing up their scrolls and throwing them away for being false. But then they leap up and seize other scrolls and come forward to the edge of the platform, where they bow to each other and each one examines the other's scroll and points to it, hitting it with his hand and pointing here and there and arguing. One of them says: "That is where God will come from to seek his lost sheep" [Ezekiel 34:1–31], and another disagrees. So they keep arguing for about half an hour.

While they are arguing, the curtains covering the upper platform are swept back to a sound like cannon fire, in imitation of heavenly thunder. The prophets with their scrolls disappear in the flash. There on the upper platform, the venerable Father can be seen; around him, as we have described above, burn more than five hundred lights. These lights move endlessly to and fro, quickly weaving in and out, some going up and others going down. Little children in white robes surround him, representing heavenly Powers. Some of them are singing, others play the cymbals, others play the lute and pipes. In every respect it is a wonderfully joyous spectacle that no man can describe.

After some time, the Angel sent from on high by the Father comes down on the two ropes already mentioned to the Virgin to announce the conception of the Son of God. The Angel is played by a beautiful, curly-haired boy: his gown is snow-white and decorated all over with gold as is the angelic stole over his shoulders. He has gilded wings, and in all his appearance he is like a painted image of an angel of God. He comes down on the ropes singing softly and he stands before her sweetly, just like a [real] angel. In his hand he carries a branch like a palm of victory. His descent is accomplished in the following manner. Attached to his trousers in the middle of his back he has two small pulleys, invisible from below on account of the great distance. And by means of these two pulleys he is attached to the two ropes. Meanwhile the third and finest rope is hauled by people who are up high and out of sight, who lower the Angel and pull him back again. The machinery is amazingly wonderful, even to grown men. And everything is decorated in gold.

But to return to our account. The Angel comes down on the ropes in front of the Virgin, then he turns to face her, holding in his hand the beautiful branch of which we spoke before. He then addresses her with a sweet and gentle voice: "Rejoice Mary, you are blessed among women. You have found grace with God. Behold you will conceive in your womb a son, the Word of God, and you will bring him forth and call him Jesus. And he will free men from their sins." She rises up quickly in fright, and replies with quiet maiden modesty: "O young man, how dare you approach my threshold and enter here and say such unthinkable things to me? You said that God is with me and wants to be incarnate within my womb. I do not believe your words, for I partake not in matrimony and I have known no man. So take yourself off, young man, so that Joseph does not see you talking to me in my house and chop your head off with an axe. I implore you: be gone, or else he will turn me out of the house as well." Seeing her so terrified, he answers: "Fear not, Mary, I am the Archangel Gabriel, sent by God to announce to you the conception of the Son of God. Do not doubt my words: the conception is without seed, the Holy Ghost shall come upon you and the power of the Highest shall overshadow you."

Looking up, she sees the Father enthroned in great might and magnificence blessing her from above. When she sees him, she folds her hands on her breast and says to him humbly: "Behold the handmaiden of the Lord; be it unto me according to your word." The Angel gives her the beautiful branch that he had brought and returns on high. Having accepted the branch from the Angel, she stands and watches the Angel ascend.

While the Angel is going up, simultaneously there emerges from God the Father on high a loud and continuous thunderflash, that moves down the ropes to the middle of the platform where the prophets were; and the fireworks race up and down again, so that all the church is full of sparks. The Angel meanwhile continues up, rejoicing, waving his hands and moving his wings; it really looks as if he were flying. Fire pours from the upper platform and explodes all around the church with terrifying thunder, and unlit lamps all over the church are lit by the fireworks, but it does not scorch the clothes of the spectators nor harm them in any way. It is a spectacle both marvellous and terrifying.

When the Angel has gone back into the place from which he had come, the flames are extinguished, and all the curtains closed as they had been before.

This is the marvellous ingenious spectacle that we saw in the city of Florence. I have described it as well as my limited wit was able to understand it. It is not possible to describe it better because it was amazing and indescribable. Amen.[47]

The machinery evoked here, created by "a certain clever man," is quite different from the machinery described by Vasari a century later, and apart from the ingenious clockwork mechanisms that move the lights, and complexity of the ropes, pulleys, and winches, there is little here that we can identify as 'Brunelleschian.'[48] What distinguishes this play from the other two *feste* is the complexity of its action: "half an hour" of dramatic debate among four white-robed and bearded men, whom Bishop Abraham identified as prophets, followed by an extended interaction between Mary and the Archangel Gabriel. Leaving aside the problems of text and translation, we must assume that Abraham understood these characters correctly. They *were* prophets, and not bearded Daughters of God (see fig. 2.9) in some prototype of Belcari's *Annunciation*,[49] and this debate of the prophets has its origins in the *Ordo prophetarum* that belongs to the Christmas liturgy and will come to

---

[47] Translation adapted from Dresvina, "The Unorthodox *Itinerary*," 112–116.

[48] Ropes, sourced in the ports of Pisa and Genoa, were an integral part of the plays, as were the complex winches, pulleys, and tackle blocks that were used to hoist the machinery. Brunelleschi's notebooks do not survive, but the *Taccuino* of Bonaccorso Ghiberti and Leonardo da Vinci's *Codex Atlanticus* (dating 1478–1519) both contain drawings related to stage machinery; see Prager and Scaglia, *Brunelleschi*; Cordera, ed., *Codex Atlanticus 3*.

[49] There are no grounds for asserting that the play performed was Belcari's *Annunciazione*. Ragusa and Green discuss the pictorial models for this image: "The artist may have turned to the type of the *Aspiciens a longe*, where Christ (sometimes in a mandorla) appears above a group of Prophets who gesture towards him. [...] This correspondence may account for the representation of the virtues as men, for otherwise they are normally

mark the Florentine Annunciation and Purification plays, and the debate of the Pharisees that we find in the printed Florentine Nativity play.

It is also curious that, from where he stood, Abraham saw the Virgin's chamber on the left, which means that the standard — but not invariable — Italian iconography of the *Annunciation* with the Angel on the left and Mary on the right is reversed. Among the many examples cited by Denny, two panels, both indirectly associated with the Oltrarno plays, seem to share this alternative viewpoint: an *Annunciation* by Bicci di Lorenzo with Neri di Bicci, dated 1440 (fig. 2.10), and another by the Carmelite friar Filippo Lippi, dated variously between 1439 and 1458, show a similarly inverted scene.[50] These correlations do not by any means demonstrate a clear line of influence from art to drama or from drama to art; rather they are a reminder of what Michael Baxandall proposed so clearly: the "period eye," shared by painters and performers who operated in the same physical and cultural milieu.[51]

In 1445, when the play had been firmly established for many years ("iam multis annis elapsis") in San Felice in Piazza, the Annunciation company applied to the Commune for a directive that the Six Captains of the Merchants' Tribunal should include the Annunciation among the *feste* that received an offering from them.[52] It was duly decreed that the Merchants' Tribunal, together with the consuls of all twenty-one guilds, were to go in procession to San Felice when the *festa* was done on the Monday after Easter Sunday. The celebration of the Annunciation on Easter Monday requires explanation: the feast of the Annunciation, on 25 March, fell almost invariably during Lent, when restrictions on all forms of celebration precluded the festivity associated with the play, so the play was postponed until after Easter.

---

women (as also in the text)"; *Meditations*, 7 and 403–404. Flora, *The Devout Belief*, 76, sees it as the result of an ambiguous instruction to the illustrator.

[50] Denny, "The Annunciation from the Right." Neri di Bicci, the painter who will be most intimately associated with the Ascension *festa* in Santa Maria del Carmine, had his workshop, together with his father Bicci di Lorenzo, in the area called Camaldoli (now Piazza Torquato Tasso), just south of the Carmine. He represents Mary on the left, reading her book, and the Angel; the opulent fabrics, the bed, and the throne are all part of Abraham of Suzdal's description. The more 'modern' *Annunciation* by Filippo Lippi, now in the Palazzo Doria Pamphili in Rome, inv. FC 668, is not divided by a pillar but instead by a pitcher (the *orciuolo* of the confraternity's name) containing lilies.

[51] Baxandall, *Painting and Experience.*

[52] ASF, Provvisioni, Registri 135, fol. 162ᵛ; Newbigin, *Feste*, 2:270–271.

Revival in 1465: New Equipment, New Text?

The play lapsed, however, continuing only as an *edificio* in the St. John the Baptist procession.[53] We hear nothing of it until 1465, when the Annunziata company joined with the *Piccione* company to stage its play. Again, bare details emerge indirectly from the *Piccione*'s records: they had lent money to the company in San Felice against a pledge first of ropes, which broke, and then of "an iron frame for sending the Angel down on the ropes," with various decorations and pully blocks. But in May 1465 the San Felice company redeemed its pledge "because this year, on the third day of Pentecost, we did the *festa* of the Annunciation in San Felice."[54] The company from Santo Spirito joined forces with the company in San Felice to do their *festa*.

When Vasari linked the Annunciation *festa* to the name of Brunelleschi, he was more concerned with mechanisms than with forms and volumes, but the "umbrella-spoke dome" of heaven that he describes is unequivocally reminiscent of the Brunelleschi-designed cupolas that had taken shape around the city (see Zorzi's reconstruction in fig. 2.11).[55] When Brunelleschi died in 1446, only the cupola of the cathedral and the Old Sacristy of San Lorenzo had been completed. Michelozzo continued work on the Pazzi Chapel in Santa Croce; and the great dome of Santo Spirito would not be started until after the fire of 1471, and not completed until 1482. There is no documentation of the umbrella-spoke dome machinery from Brunelleschi's lifetime: all that had had been mentioned was a system of ropes and pulleys and, in the other *feste*, a *ferro* or mandorla in which the Angel could be lowered and raised.

In Milan, however, long the touchstone of taste and innovation if not of artistic genius, the new architectural umbrella-spoke dome was combined with the Annunciation to embody the new iconography. In the church of Sant'Eustorgio, Pigello Portinari, director of the Medici bank in Milan and banker to the duke of Milan, was building a chapel to house his own tomb

---

[53] See chapter 4 below.

[54] Newbigin, *Feste*, 2:731: "un fero da mandarvi sù l'Angnolo giù pelle funi [...] perché questo anno facemo el terzo dì dello Spirito Santo la festa della Nunziata in San Felice."

[55] Of the beguiling Annunciation and Ascension models created for the exhibition *Il luogo teatrale a Firenze: Brunelleschi, Vasari, Buontalenti, Parigi*, Florence, Palazzo Medici Riccardi, 31 May–31 October 1975, only the reconstruction of the Paradise of San Felice stands unchallenged by subsequent research. It conflates the descriptions of Abraham of Suzdal and Giorgio Vasari to show the dome of heaven, the umbrella-spoke dome within it, and the *nugola* on which Gabriel was lowered to Nazareth.

and the head of St. Peter Martyr.[56] Work began in about 1462, and is believed
to have been complete, with Vincenzo Foppa's decoration, when Portinari
was buried there late in 1468 (fig. 2.12).[57] The primary dedication of the
chapel is perforce to the relics of the martyr, and scenes of his life are depicted in the lunettes. But the chapel's Florentine patron also acknowledged
his city's special relationship with the Virgin. On the inside of the triumphal
arch before the altar, hidden from general view, is the Assumption. On the
outside is a divided scene of the Annunciation, while in elaborate perspective,
above and behind it, God the Father looks down from a balcony, with rotating
spheres behind him and angels around him. Inside the cupola in front of the
altar, overlapping coloured feathers, like angels' wings, fade from bright to
pale as they ascend. Around the opening of the dome dance terracotta angels,
originally granite-coloured, linked by garlands and bells of fruit and flowers.
The swing of the tunics and ribbons and the different positions of the bells of
fruit and flowers create the illusion that the dome is turning. The umbrella-
spoke dome, with its central *oculus* and alternating saints and *oculi* around
the lower edge, echoes not only Brunelleschi's architectural trademark but
also the machinery of Heaven in San Felice. The model is unquestionably
the Old Sacristy in San Lorenzo, which Giovanni di Averardo de' Medici, a
close associate of Pigello's father, had commissioned from Brunelleschi; the
Brescian painter Vincenzo Foppa brings extraordinary polychrome exuberance to Brunelleschi's original lines. It is not possible to place Foppa in Florence, but he had certainly imbibed Florentine influences. For Mauro Natale,
his work is dominated by the "masterly accomplishment" of Masaccio seen
on the walls of the Brancacci Chapel in the Carmine in Florence, and in Pisa,
while for Ferrara and Quinterio, the interior of the chapel is "an authentic at-
las of convergences, linguistic fusions assembled with that *mitteleuropäische*

---

[56] I note the doubts raised by Zanoboni concerning Portinari's role in the decoration
of chapel; Zanoboni, "'Et che … el dicto Pigello,'" 88–94. Trexler argued that the *festa dei
Magi* had its origins in Sant'Eustorgio and was transplanted to Florence by the Ubriachi
family; Trexler, "The Magi Enter Florence." On the Magi, see below, chapter 5.

[57] Parallels between the Portinari chapel and the *festa* were first observed by Fischel,
"Eine florentiner Theateraufführung" (1920), but his work has been largely overlooked.
On the Portinari chapel, restored in 1999, see Mattioli Rossi, ed., *Vincenzo Foppa*. The
construction of the chapel resulted from Portinari's vision in 1462, and a dating between
1462 and October 1468, the date of Portinari's death, is generally accepted; see also Scotti,
"Alcune ipotesi"; Ferrara and Quinterio, *Michelozzo*, 383–385; Newbigin, "Greasing the
Wheels," 230–231; Ventrone, *Teatro civile*, 78–79.

international eclecticism that has always characterized Milan."[58] Foppa may not have been an eyewitness of the *festa di San Felice*, but he could certainly have heard reports of it through his patron. It is also possible that the renewal of the play was stimulated by reports of this new and grandiose chapel being constructed for the Medici banker in Milan.

The earliest surviving text of a Florentine Annunciation play is Feo Belcari's *Rappresentazione quando la Nostra Donna Vergine Maria fu annunziata dall'Angelo Gabriello*, written before 1468 and dedicated to Piero di Cosimo de' Medici (d. 1469).[59] The play has four parts: a short and tightly controlled procession of prophets (an antidote, perhaps, to the half-hour of prophets arguing, described by Abraham of Suzdal); a long and elegant debate of the Four Virtues, Truth, Justice, Mercy, and Peace; Gabriel's descent to Limbo to announce the imminent redemption of the Old Testament Righteous, and his return to heaven; and Gabriel's descent to Nazareth where the scene of the Annunciation adheres closely to the narrative of Luke's Gospel. The Holy Ghost descends on Mary, and there is great rejoicing in heaven.

The Debate of the Four Daughters of God, or Dispute of the Virtues, is also found in the Umbrian *laudari*, but derives ultimately from the *Sermo I: In Festo Annuntiationis Beatae Mariae Virginis* of Bernard of Clairvaux (c. 1090–1153), which is developed elaborately in the *Meditations on the Life of Christ* (c. 1300).[60] As befits the celebration of the incarnation of the Word,

---

[58] Natale, "Gli affreschi," 45: "il magistero [...] un autentico atlante di convergenze, fusioni di linguaggi assemblati in quell'eclettismo internazionale 'mitteleuropeo' col quale Milano si è sempre distinta"; Ferrara and Quinterio, *Michelozzo*, 384.

[59] Belcari, *Le rappresentazioni*, 87–106; D'Ancona, ed., *Sacre rappresentazioni*, 1:181–189 (incomplete); Newbigin, *Feste*, 2:239–253; for English translation, see Newbigin online. See Table 1 for a list of manuscripts. Belcari's accompanying sonnet is dated 1468. The *Annunciazione* printed by Bartolomeo de' Libri at the end of the fifteenth century, and erroneously attributed to Belcari by Galletti, D'Ancona, ed., *Sacre rappresentazioni*, 1:167, and a legion of subsequent cataloguers and scholars, is quite different.

[60] Bernard of Clairvaux, *PL* 183 (1862): 383–390, glossing Psalm 84:10–11 (85:9–10); *Meditations*, 7–9, chapters 1–2. Although authorship of the *Meditations* is still hotly contested, early modern readers accepted them unquestioningly as the work of the Franciscan St. Bonaventure. For current debates on language and dating of the *Meditations*, see Tóth and Falvay, "New Light." For earlier semi-dramatic and dramatic Annunciations, see Jacopone, "L'omo fo creato vertüoso," in his *Laude*, 10–24; *Il laudario perugino*, 1:119–125 (De Bartholomaeis, ed., *Laude drammatiche*, 1:98–102); *Il Laudario assisano 36*, 5–14; and the Orvieto *Annunciazione*, which has stanzas for Adam in Limbo, Mercy, and Justice, in *Laudario orvietano*, 235–240. On the Dispute in drama, see Newbigin, "Between Prophecy and Redemption," as well as other essays in Chiabò, Doglio, and Maymone Siniscalchi,

Belcari's text is an exquisitely crafted piece of word-play, founded on Hebrew puns in Psalm 84:11 (85:10), translated in the Vulgate as: "misericordia et veritas obviaverunt sibi; justitia et pax osculatae sunt" (Mercy and Truth have met each other; Justice and Peace have kissed). Mercy has taken pity on Adam, who has been waiting in Limbo for five thousand years; Truth says that if he is released, she will be discredited:

LA MISERICORDIA *dice alla Verità*:
Se tal peccato mai non si dimette,
dunque mi truovo in Ciel sanza bisogno.

MERCY *says to Truth*:
If such a sin can never be forgiven
then I am here in Heaven needlessly.

LA VERITÀ *dice alla Misericordia*:
El nostro Padre la sentenza dette
ch'Adam morisse, e questo non è sogno.

TRUTH *says to Mercy*:
The sentence was delivered by our Father:
Adam must die, and this is not a dream.

LA MISERICORDIA *alla Verità*:
Un sogno sare' io se l'alme elette
non fussin salve come io agogno.

MERCY *to Truth*:
I'd be a dream, if these elected souls
were never saved, the way that I desire.

LA VERITÀ *dice alla Misericordia*:
Di' quel che vuoi, che non m'occiderai.

TRUTH *says to* MERCY:
Say what you will, I'll not be killed by you.

LA MISERICORDIA *risponde*:
Né tu sempre mai morta mi terrai.

MERCY *replies*:
Nor will you keep me here forever dead.
(oct. 28)

Justice replies that Adam's sin was such that this punishment is justly warranted; and Peace demands a resolution, or she will cease to exist. They seek the help of the Son who tells them that they must find someone who will "fare la morte buona," that is, die a good death and make death good. After searching on earth and in heaven they report that no such person can be found, and the Son resolves to take on this task himself. The play demonstrates that the primary beneficiaries of Christ's Incarnation are the Old Testament Righteous, waiting in Limbo; we are their fortunate successors.

---

eds. *Atti del IV Colloquio*; and also M. Martelli, "Firenze," 118–120, and his *Letteratura*, 29–31.

In addition to Nazareth, Belcari's play requires a large acting space in heaven, for the Virtues, as well as the new acting space of Limbo.[61] It also requires actors who can deliver their speeches clearly. Whereas earlier versions relied on spectacle, gesture, and memory of the Gospel's *Ave Maria* in their recreation of the "visible speech" (visibile parlar) of the scene, the debate of the Virtues relies for its effect on refined wordplay and complex theology, and the actors must have been able to handle the acoustics of the performance space to make this debate come alive.

There is absolutely no record of Belcari's play ever being performed, nor is there evidence that it belongs to the *festa* of San Felice rather than to some other context. The text was not influential; even though Poliziano works the Dispute of the Virtues into a vernacular sermon on the Passion,[62] it does not become part of the visual iconography of the Annunciation in Florence and does not seem to have derived from the play. The existence of twelve manuscripts (but no early printed edition) tells us more about Belcari's skill in self-promotion than about the popularity of the play. Nevertheless, it is not implausible that Feo Belcari, Medici client, pious Christian, minor humanist, and more than competent vernacular poet and translator, should have provided the confraternity with a text to elevate the *festa* when it was revived in 1465.[63] It was nearly two decades since the first fully-scripted plays had appeared: Antonio Araldo's *Dì del Giudizio* (1444–1448), Belcari's *Abramo* (1449), and Piero di Mariano Muzi's *Vitel sagginato* (Carnival 1449/50). Since then, plays had proliferated both in the youth confraternities and on the *edifici* of the San Giovanni procession. Belcari's new text, however, would have been a radical departure for the *festa* of San Felice. He appears to be disciplining

---

[61] Limbo in the Purification play was represented by Jonah's whale; for the Beheading of John the Baptist and in the Resurrection, both performed outdoors, Limbo was mounted on an *edificio*. There are no side chapels in San Felice to serve as Limbo, but a side door linked the church to the adjacent monastery.

[62] Poliziano, *Prose volgari*, 6–8, "Sermoni recitati in una compagnia di dottrina [1468–1478]," 2; M. Martelli, *Letteratura*, 26–27.

[63] For an acute analysis of Belcari's craft in this play, see M. Martelli, *Letteratura*, 20–31; useful for its insights, Phillips-Court, *The Perfect Genre*, 23–56; see also Phillips-Court, "Framing the Miracle"; Guccini, "Domande," and "Le quattro figlie." The Bolognese pageant that opens BNCR, VE 483 (copied in 1482; see De Bartholomaeis, ed., *Laude drammatiche*, 3:223–225), includes, as well as prophets, sibyls, and the four Virtues, "uno edifizio con l'Annunciata suso" (an *edificio* with the Annunciation on it), fols. 15ᵛ–16ᵛ, which recycles oct. 41–48 from Belcari's text. In addition, the complete Belcari text is reproduced in the same manuscript, fols. 59ʳ–66ʳ.

and simultaneously embellishing their *festa*: the half-hour of chaotic ranting by the prophets witnessed by the Russian bishop is replaced by three prophets and eight sibyls marshalled into just eight octaves, who lead into the witty wordplay of the Virtues.

Whether with Belcari's text or not, the confraternity revived its *festa* in 1465, and in 1470 succeeded in renewing its communal subsidy, but this renewal created problems with the Camaldolese monks in San Felice. In 1470, the Commune responded to a complaint about noise by moving the *festa* from the Tuesday after Easter to the following Sunday, Domenica in Albis or the Octave of Easter:

> Since [...] the people who have the job of building the platforms
> and stages and constructing the other equipment in the church
> for the *festa* have to work there right through Holy Week and on
> the Sunday and Monday of Easter, which is precisely that time
> when everybody attends more to matters of the soul than they
> do all the rest of the year, and since it happens that with that
> continual noise and banging they cause great tribulation in that
> period both to those who are reciting the office in the church and
> to those who go to hear it and to confess and take communion,
> and because they wish to ensure that the *festa* and its play and the
> equipment that is built for it in the church is prepared at a time
> that does not deprive anybody of devotion and the consolation of
> his soul, it is determined: that henceforth and whenever the *festa*
> is done in the future it be changed to the Sunday of the Octave of
> Easter, to be done in the morning and during the day, with the
> solemnities that were customary for the *festa* on the first Tues-
> day after Easter, and likewise that the offering that the Signori
> and the Six of the Merchants' Tribunal, and the Consuls of the
> Guilds were required to make on that Tuesday should no longer
> be made on the Tuesday after Easter, but should be changed to
> the morning of the Sunday of the Octave of Easter.[64]

[64] ASF, Provvisioni, Registri 161, fols. 134ᵛ–135ʳ, 16 October 1470; Newbigin, *Feste*, 275: "Considerato che [...] quegli che sono deputati a fare i palchi e palchetti et altri appa-rechi che si fanno in detta chiesa per detta festa lavorino in quella tutta la Settimana Sancta e la domenica e il lunedì della Pasqua, che è appunto quel tempo nel quale universalmente per ciaschuno s'attende più a' fatti dell'anima che non si fa poi in tutto il resto dell'anno, che si viene pure per quello strepito e busso che v'è del continovo in que' dì a dar gran

The following year, however, Lenten observances were disregarded when the young duke Galeazzo Maria Sforza (1444–1476), together with his new wife Bona of Savoy and a huge entourage, visited Florence. Galeazzo had visited the city as a sixteen-year-old and been taken at the end of his stay to the Ascension *festa* in the Carmine.[65] Now the Commune required all three Oltrarno confraternities to stage their *feste* during Lent for the benefit of the visitors. The *Libro di Ricordanze* of the Augustinian friary records the disaster that ensued:

> He went to the one in San Felice, but not to the Carmine's or to ours. The one in the Carmine was done at great risk to the lives of several people. Ours was done on 21 March [1470/1], late in the evening because they were still waiting for the duke. When the *festa* was over, the *festaiuoli* left without paying attention to the risk of fire and as a result five hours after dark fire took hold in the dome of the *castello* and, before anyone noticed, it spread so much that the flames took hold in the roof.[66]

---

noia, e a quegli che dicono l'uficio in quella chiesa, e a chi vi va per udirlo e per confessarsi e communicarsi, et però desiderando provedere per modo che la festa di detta rappresentatione e l'apparechio che si fa per quella in detta chiesa si faccia a tempo che non habbia a torre ad alchuna persona la divotione e consolatione sua dell'anima, si provede: Che da quinci innanzi per ogni tempo da venire la detta festa s'intenda essere et sia permutata a la domenicha dell'octava di detta Pasqua, facendola nel dì della detta domenica dell'octava la matina e il dì, con le solemnità usate farsi per detta festa il primo martedì drieto alla detta Pasqua, et così l'offerta che è ordinata che vi si faccia il detto martedì pe' Signori e pe' Sei della Mercatantia con le Capitudini non vi si possa fare più nel detto martedì drieto alla detta Pasqua, ma intendasi permutata a·ffarsi e possasi fare la mattina della detta domenica della octava di detta Pasqua."

[65] *Le onoranze fiorentine*, 114, lines 4603–4608.

[66] ASF, CRSGF 122 (Santo Spirito), 67, fol. 280ʳ: "Trovossi a quella di San Felice, ma al Carmine et alla nostra non si ritrovò. Fecesi quella del Carmine con gran pericolo di vita di più persone. Fecesi la nostra a dì 21 di marzo [1470/1], la sera al tardi pure aspettando il Duca. Fatto la festa i festaiuoli si partirno senza havere riguardo a' pericoli del fuoco e per che a hore 5 di notte nella cupola del castello degli apostoli s'appigliò il fuoco, et prima che niuno se n'avvedessi crebbe tanto la fiamma che s'appigliò al tetto della chiesa"; cited in Newbigin, *Feste*, 1:205; 2:749. For another fire caused by a play, see below, chapter 9, n. 39.

The destruction of the old church, its liturgical books, altarpieces, and vestments — including "twelve copes[67] in the *castello* and a deep blue cope of precious cloth" — was a catastrophe, and Machiavelli records the popular response that this was God's punishment for the excesses of the duke's visit during Lent.[68] On the other hand, the fire accelerated the construction of the new church, which had been designed by Brunelleschi some thirty-five years earlier and was proceeding at a snail's pace. The events leading up to the fire show that by 1471 Lorenzo de' Medici was increasingly influential in shaping the public *feste* of Florence. At the time of his grandfather Cosimo and father Piero, the *laudesi* confraternities of the Oltrarno had enjoyed autonomous ownership of their plays and received occasional assistance from the Commune or from the Medici across the river. Under Lorenzo, the balance shifted, imperceptibly at first, and then in a major way after the Pazzi conspiracy of 1478.[69]

After the Fire in Santo Spirito: The Assumption of Mary

The Pentecost play never returned to Santo Spirito, even after 1488 when the new church, constructed to Brunelleschi's design, was consecrated. We hear no more of the Annunciation play in San Felice until 1494, when it was performed — presumably at the behest of Piero di Lorenzo de' Medici but after

---

[67] ASF, CRSGF 122 (Santo Spirito), 67, fol. 280^r: "paliotti 12 sul castello et un peviale azzurro di drappo." *Paliotto* can be used for 'cope' as well as for 'altar frontal'; see also Neri di Bicci's inventory for the Ascension equipment: "12 fine cotton copes of different colours, with trim of all different colours, and a cope for Christ, which are used to dress the 12 Apostles when we do the *festa* of the Ascension" (12 paliotti di bochaccino di diversi cholori, frangiati tuti di diversi cholori, chontando uno paliotto per Cristo, e quali vestono e 12 Apostoli quando si fa la festa della Sensione); Newbigin, *Feste*, 2:533. *Boccaccino* (bocasin) is a fine buckram that has the appearance of taffeta.

[68] Machiavelli, *Istorie fiorentine*, 681–682, vii.28.5–6. Out-of-season performances were not unprecedented. In June 1451, the Signoria paid for the Ascension to be done a second time for the singers of Alfonso of Aragon, king of Naples, who had come to Florence to learn the Florentine techniques; in 1465, the Ascension was performed on 26 June, for Ippolita Sforza, who was travelling to Naples to marry the duke of Calabria, son of King Ferrante; Newbigin, *Feste*, 1:113 and 119.

[69] On Easter Sunday, 26 April 1478, members of the Pazzi family, in conspiracy with others, attempted to assassinate Lorenzo de' Medici and his brother Giuliano in Santa Maria del Fiore. Giuliano was killed but Lorenzo survived and immediately tightened his control of the government of the republic. See Martines, *April Blood*.

he had fled the city — in honour of Charles VIII of France. Only the plays in the Carmine continued to evolve. Their subsidy had been renewed in 1465 for the "honour and delight of all our people and of visitors,"[70] and new account books, kept lovingly by the painter Neri di Bicci, were begun in 1466. The Sant'Agnese confraternity rebuilt its equipment: heaven, the *nugola*, and the revolving planets. The *stella*, with the disappearing light device created by the goldsmith Pippo di Baldo, was taken back to him for overhaul, and the structure beneath it was decorated by the painter Pietro del Massaio and his assistant Bernaba.[71]

The duke's visit marked the beginning of a new regime for the Sant'Agnese company. In 1471, its subsidy was again renewed, and that year, instead of repeating the Ascension play, which had already been performed in Lent, the company performed — for the feast of the Ascension of Christ — the Assumption of Mary, with a new scenographic repertoire: a bed chamber, a tomb (*il Monumento*), lavish fireworks with sulphur, and eighteen flaming bird-dishes.[72] The renewed subsidy also heralded an influx of new members that included men of higher social standing than the old membership, as well as artists and artisans including Alessandro di Mariano Filipepi, better known as Botticelli.[73] The changes to membership must have caused alarm citywide, because in their wake old laws were reinvoked banning those who were eligible for high public office from becoming members of confraternities.[74]

Since no text of the new Assumption play survives, we cannot tell whether the play shared the serenity of Botticini's *Assumption* (fig. 2.13) or featured the violent attempt of the Jews to interrupt the funeral procession and overturn the Virgin's bier, as recounted in the *Legenda Aurea*, that is part of the Assumption *feste* in other parts of Europe.[75] Botticini's huge work, with an awe-inspiring dome of heaven, was commissioned by Matteo Palmieri for his chapel in San Piero Maggiore, and shows him and his wife, Niccolosa

---

[70] ASF, Prov. Reg. 156, fol. 255ᵛ: "honore et contentamento di tutto el popolo e de' forastieri"; see Newbigin, *Feste*, 2:511.

[71] Newbigin, *Feste*, 1:123.

[72] Newbigin, *Feste*, 2:622: "18 beveratoi da ucelini per le fiame del Sopracielo di Nostra Dona."

[73] Newbigin, *Feste*, 1:134n.

[74] Weissman, *Ritual Brotherhood*, 168–169; Newbigin, *Feste*, 1:135–136.

[75] Jacobus, *Legenda Aurea*, 2:870–871, cxv.93–06; see Massip, "Staging"; and on the great Assumption of Elx, Massip, *La Festa d'Elx*.

de' Serragli, daughter of a major Oltrarno family, in the foreground.[76] It was painted c. 1475–1476, when the Assumption *festa* was at its height, and shows the *monumento* or tomb, filled with flowers, on the *monte*, with the Virgin kneeling before Christ in heaven, surrounded by saints and angels.[77]

Throughout the 1470s, fully scripted *rappresentazioni* were performed all over Florence: in cloisters and gardens, in piazzas and churches. Florentine *festaiuoli* were summoned to or co-opted in Naples, Rome, Ferrara, and Milan to present their spectacles.[78] And in the Carmine, the Sant'Agnese company followed the trend. The company had always celebrated the feast of St. Agnes, on 24 January, in honour of their relic — the foot of St. Agnes, which survived the fire of 1771 and is still venerated in the church — and in honour of Cione Vernacci's widow Agnese, who had founded the church.[79] In January 1472/3, however, the confraternity's members celebrated the saint's feast day with a play, possibly of St. Agnes herself.[80] They subsequently returned to their traditional fare of the Ascension and Assumption, although some years it seems that the plays were not performed.

For Carnival 1483/4, they allowed the boys of the youth company of San Giorgio to perform the *festa* of Queen Rosana, using the machinery and performance space in the Carmine.[81] In 1488, they made the Florentine chancellor Bartolomeo Scala (1430–1497) an honorary member, exempt, like Lorenzo de' Medici, from all duties, dues, and age restrictions; on the same day, they resolved to apply again for a subsidy to do the Ascension. Four teams of *festaiuoli* — twenty-four men in all are named — were appointed with responsibility for Heaven, Paradise, the Mount, and Jerusalem, but it

---

[76] On Palmieri's role in the San Giovanni procession of 1454, see chapter 4 below.

[77] On Botticini's *Assumption* for the Palmieri Chapel in San Piero Maggiore, see Sliwka, *Visions of Paradise*. On the Assumption *festa* in Siena, see A. Campbell, "A Spectacular Celebration."

[78] On Florentines in Naples, 1443, 1476, 1477: Helas, *Lebende Bilder*, 71–88; in Rome 1473: Newbigin, *Feste*, 1:140–141; in Milan 1475: Corio, *Storia di Milano*, 2:1396; in Ferrara 1476: Ferrarini, *Memoriale*, 45; Lipani, "Lo spettacolo sacro."

[79] Newbigin, *Feste*, 1:47, and 54–55; Eckstein, "The Widows' Might," esp. 106–111.

[80] Newbigin, *Feste*, 1:145, 2:630. The surviving *Sant'Agnese* play, CNCE 75530, dates to c. 1515, but the woodcut, in which the name S. Agnes is reversed, is surely a copy of an earlier edition; there is nothing, however, to link it to the *festa* of 1472/3.

[81] Newbigin, *Feste*, 1:148–149; the youth confraternity of Sant'Antonio da Padova, which had its oratory on the Costa San Giorgio, is one of the groups discussed in the next chapter with the play of *Rosana*.

appears that the *festa* did not go ahead.[82] Other plays, however, did: the *edifici* returned to the San Giovanni procession after a hiatus of ten years, while Lorenzo launched himself into the huge program of cultural magnificence that would mark the final 'princely' years of his life.

The performance of 1489 was possibly the last for the Sant'Agnese company. Piero de' Medici, Lorenzo the Magnificent's seventeen-year-old son for whom the minimum age-limit had been waived so that he could hold office, asked for the Pentecost *festa* to be performed in the Carmine.[83] The new church of Santo Spirito had been completed the year before and it must have been clear immediately that the pristine lines of Brunelleschi's umbrella-spoke dome were incompatible with the old *feste* that descended from timber roof trusses. The surviving printed text of the *Festa del miracolo dello Spirito Santo* (fig. 8.28) is probably the text prepared on this occasion, employing the Carmine's resources of the Mount, Jerusalem, and Paradise to present the descent of the Holy Ghost from heaven.[84] The play has little to commend it: there is not enough in the gospel narrative to make a full play, and instead the dramatist has given us suspense, fervour, anxious waiting, and hymn-singing to pass the time. The Apostles come down the mountain "with their eyes and hands raised ardently to heaven" (levati gli occhi e le mani al cielo infiammati; stage direction before oct. 9), and they are described repeatedly as *ferventi*, *desiderosi*, and *infiammati* (fervent, filled with desire, and ardent).The descent of the Holy Ghost is represented as a direct response to the prayers of Mary and the Apostles. Tribaldo de' Rossi observed in his *Ricordanze* that "nobody, or almost nobody, liked it."[85] Something of the atmosphere of "irrational excitement" may be preserved in Botticelli's large panel of *The Descent of the Holy Ghost*, now in the Birmingham Museum and Art Gallery, where a muscular, middle-aged Mary with big hands sits among the twelve apostles,

---

[82] Newbigin, *Feste*, 1:152, 206; 2:650, 653. Pentecost fell on 31 May 1489.

[83] The thirteen-year-old Piero had attended the "festa del Carmino" with the priest Matteo Franco on 12 May 1485; see ASF, MAP 72, doc. 5, fol. 6ʳ; and also Franco, *Lettere*, 84. Santi Mattei notes that in this year, two people were killed as a result of an accident associated with the plays, and the church "was desecrated, and had to be reblessed" (fu profanata, e dové ribenedirsi); Mattei, *Ragionamento*, 15–16. I have not identified his source, but he implies that the cause was a fire.

[84] *La festa del miracolo dello spirito sancto* ([Florence: Bartolomeo de' Libri, not after 1495]), ISTC ir00029650; Cioni, *Bibliografia*, 278, xcvi.1; for modern edition and translation, see Table 2.

[85] BNCF, II.ii.357 (formerly Magl. xxvi.25), fol. 91ᵛ: "Non piaque a persona o a la maggior parte," correcting Tribaldo de' Rossi, *Ricordanze*, 23:276.

all with hands raised in prayer and amazement (figs. 2.14–2.15).[86] The painter names the apostles in their tooled haloes (Acts of the Apostles 1:13), including Mary and Matthias, even though at Pentecost he is not yet one of the twelve (Acts 1:23–26).[87]

In 1491 the Sant'Agnese company applied again for a public subvention for the Ascension *festa*, and again failed. The Commune chose, instead, to invest in Lorenzo's last and magnificent *festa* for the Feast of St. John the Baptist, with six of the old *edifici* and with fifteen new Triumphs of his own creation.[88] Following Lorenzo's death, the new Savonarolan republic closed the company completely from July 1494 to May 1497. When it reopened, the bustle of activity was to remove the equipment that had been constructed year by year in Santa Maria del Carmine. All the structures around Heaven, in the niche above the high altar, were removed: 370 lbs of iron, together with timber and winches; but in April 1498, just before the execution of Savonarola, the company was applying for a subsidy again. The office bearers of the confraternity took fright, however, at the prospect of staging a play that they could not afford and set strict limits on any future performance. Again, it did not go ahead.[89] Heaven above the high altar had been removed, but now Paradise was causing the roof above the *tramezzo* to collapse. In May 1500 major structural repairs were undertaken at the expense of the Carmelite friary, and Paradise was moved from the western end of the *volte* to the eastern end, where the *castello* had been. And there, it would seem, the plays came to an end.

---

[86] The painting (fig. 2.14) has been heavily restored and cropped top and bottom; a dove that formerly hovered above the scene has been removed. What remains, however, is a scene of "irrational excitement" that shares "the same highly charged atmosphere" as Botticelli's *Mystic Nativity* in London and suggests links also to the miniature tradition; Cannon-Brookes, "Botticelli's 'Pentecost,'" 274, 277. The drawing (fig. 2.16) almost certainly shows what Botticelli intended for the lower part of the Pentecost panel; see Waldman, "Botticelli." The painting may also be compared to the Pentecost scene of the Piccione company's own *laudario* (fig. 2.7) and reminds us that the archaic fourteenth-century iconography held a powerful grip over the subject, in painting as well as in the plays; see also Gardner von Teuffel, "Ikonographie."

[87] But see the comment on Belcari's stanzas for Pentecost, above, n. 31. In the later play, Mary Magdalene speaks but Matthias does not appear; compare Acts 1:14: "with the women, and Mary the mother of Jesus, and with his brethren."

[88] Tribaldo de' Rossi, *Ricordanze*, 23:270–271; Del Lungo, "Una lettera," 39; Newbigin, "Carried Away."

[89] Newbigin, *Feste*, 1:152–154.

The angels continued to dance in heaven in the memory of the artists who had been involved in the plays. Filippino Lippi, son of the Carmelite friar who was so taken by the angels' stockings, had only recently completed Masaccio's frescoes in the Carmine's Brancacci Chapel when he was summoned to Rome in 1488 to fresco the chapel of Cardinal Oliviero Carafa in Santa Maria sopra Minerva. Around an altar scene of the Annunciation with St. Thomas Aquinas and his patron Carafa (and a crystal jug that links the Virgin's purity and Carafa's own name), he frescoed a huge Assumption of the Virgin, with the Mount and Jerusalem in the distance. She is accompanied by nine angels, three supporting the cloud on which she ascends, the other six dancing around her with their musical instruments (fig. 2.16). Botticelli, too, remembered his time in the Carmine as a member of the Sant'Agnese company: like his *Coronation of the Virgin*, his *Mystic Nativity* looks up to the dome of heaven with angels in a circle around the opening (fig. 2.17).[90]

It is not, of course, possible to relate these images to the plays in any directly causal way. Spectacles and images were part of the shared visual culture of Florentine audiences, but two painters, Neri di Bicci and Pietro del Massaio, were the moving forces in the Ascension plays at their height, and the names of many other painters appear in their records. The *festaiuoli* sought constantly to make their *festa* even better than before, but careful examination of the texts and scenographic elements suggests that it was always with close attention to the 'old' iconography. Innovations in painting, when they come, are not based on developments in drama, but rather on changes in taste and technique.

Charles VIII, 1494

The Annunciation, the *festa di San Felice,* still had some time to run, as Florence identified more with Nazareth as the city of the Virgin Annunciate than

---

[90] Hatfield, in "Botticelli's Mystic Nativity," demonstrated the direct dependence of this painting on Savonarola's sermon delivered on Christmas Eve 1493, in which the preacher imagined a heavenly scene, using the words of Psalm 84:11–12 (85:10–11). The personified Virtues are part of the debate that precedes the incarnation in Belcari's *Annunciazione* (see above, n. 49), and there seem to be strong echoes also of the *festa di San Felice* in the angels dancing in the dome of heaven. In relating the *Mystic Nativity* to the *festa di san Felice,* Olson, "Brunelleschi's Machines," notes also the dancing angels in Fra Angelico's *Nativity* (1440–1450) in the Museo di San Domenico, Forlì.

with Savonarola's New Jerusalem.[91] Late in 1494, two years after the death of Lorenzo de' Medici, the army of Charles VIII of France (1470–1498) was moving down through the Italian peninsula to assert the French claim on the kingdom of Naples. Florence found herself undefended and, when Lorenzo's son Piero appeared to capitulate to French demands, the Florentines seized the opportunity to rebel against the Medici oligarchy. Piero was expelled on 9 November. The Dominican friar, Girolamo Savonarola, who now held Florence in his sway, had already been sent to greet Charles in Pisa, and welcomed him as the saviour of the Christian republic.[92] On 17 November, when Charles entered Florence in triumph through the Porta San Frediano, he was greeted with a series of elaborate spectacles, including a wagon with the *edificio* and *nugola* of the Annunciation, presumably the traditional San Giovanni *edificio*. It was displayed for him in Piazza Frescobaldi, at the southern end of Ponte Santa Trinita, since his entry route from Pisa did not pass by San Felice in Piazza.[93]

Charles remained in Florence until 28 November, negotiating the terms of his passage through Florentine territory, and enjoying his accommodation in the palace Piero had just vacated. On Sunday 23 November the *festa* of the Annunciation was performed in his honour in San Felice. Two accounts survive. Luca Landucci, apothecary and diarist, describes the tension between the French and the Florentines, and the citizens' sneering at the young French king when he was caught in a narrow alley. From there,

> He went through the Mercato Vecchio and over to San Felice in Piazza to see the *festa* of San Felice, which they were doing then in his honour, and when they got to the door he refused to go in; and they did it several times and he never went in. Many said that he was afraid and did not want to be enclosed, and this showed us that he was more afraid than we were.[94]

---

[91] On Nazareth and Florence, from Jerome and the *Legenda Aurea* to Brunetto Latini, Villani, and the ancient chronicles, see Del Popolo, *Tra sacro e profano*, 25–28. On Savonarola and Florence, see Weinstein, *Savonarola and Florence*; Dall'Aglio, *Savonarola*.

[92] On these events, see Najemy, *A History*, 375–380.

[93] Landucci, *Diario*, 79; P. Parenti, *Storia*, 1:134; Borsook, "Decor in Florence," 108; Plaisance, "L'entrée," 48–49.

[94] Landucci, *Diario*, 84: "andonne per Mercato vecchio, e andonne infino a San Felice in Piazza per vedere la festa di San Felice, che allora la facevano per suo conto, e giunti alla porta non vi volle entrare; e fecionla più volte e non vi entrò mai. Molti dissono che

The historian Jacopo Nardi records instead that after the king had rested for a few days, he was entertained:

> with the performance of some splendid and beautiful *feste*, like the most remarkable one of the Annunciation of the Virgin, which was represented with ingenious and marvellous artifice in the church of San Felice in Piazza: and he found it so pleasant and delightful, that having seen it once publicly, he wanted to see it several times more incognito and privately.[95]

The two accounts are not irreconcilable: they agree that the *festa* was done at least three times; they agree that the king went three times; but Landucci adds the information that whatever Charles saw, he saw from the door, and he saw enough without going in to want to go back again and again. This tells us that the platform above the entrance door was no longer central to the performance. Charles could stand at the entrance, and see all that there was to see, and we must assume that by 1494 this is, above all, the wonderful equipment that Vasari would later describe and attribute to Brunelleschi. The text cannot have been important: it is difficult to imagine that Charles was captivated by the play of the Annunciation, with its tedious procession of prophets. Instead, we must imagine him marvelling, three times over, at the doors that rolled back to reveal the dome of heaven, from which descended the umbrella-spoke frame with angels; from that frame, the mandorla bearing Gabriel with the other angels was lowered, and Gabriel delivered his message to the Virgin before returning to heaven.[96]

It is possible that the play was newly cobbled together from existing material for the 1494 performance for Charles VIII. Even though Belcari's play of the Annunciation circulated widely in manuscript, it was not printed. Meanwhile, the *Annunciazione* that *was* printed is unknown in manuscript.

---

egli aveva paura e non si voleva rinchiudere, e questo ci mostrava che egli aveva più paura di noi."

[95] Nardi, *Istorie*, 1:37: "con la rappresentazione d'alcune solenni e belle feste, come quella molto singulare della Vergine Annunziata, che si rappresentò con ingegnoso e maraviglioso artifizio nella chiesa di san Felice in Piazza: la quale tanto gli fu grata e dilettevole, che avendola veduta una volta publicamente, la volle rivedere altre volte sconosciuto e privatamente."

[96] I extrapolate from Vasari's account (see n. 6 above); Bishop Abraham described curtains.

La festa dell'annunziazione di Nostra Donna was published anonymously no later than 1495 by Bartolomeo de' Libri (fig. 2.18). It was reprinted by him around 1500, and then by Antonio Tubini and Andrea Ghirlandi for Maestro Giovanni di Benvenuto, before 1515 (figs. 8.15 and 8.16).[97] The first edition — or at least the earliest known — breaks the typographical convention, already established, of placing title, annunciating angel, and climactic scene on the title page. Instead, the first page contains a scene consciously recalling the play itself: the woodcut shows a schematic version of the dome of heaven, from which the Angel Gabriel descends in a *nugola*, accompanied by two smaller angels. Tubini and Ghirlandi did not normally reprint Bartolomeo's editions unless they added extra material; here it is in the form of two anonymous *ternali* that fill the remaining blank pages, further contaminating the textual tradition. Not having access to Bartolomeo's original woodblocks, they made the first of many copies.[98]

The text in broad outline follows the structure first noted by the Russian bishop in 1439: prophets, followed by the descent of the Angel, the Angel's return to heaven, and jubilation. Here, twenty prophets and ten sibyls are summoned by the Angel to sing their prophecy of the birth of Christ, in a text that has so long forgotten its origins that the Old Testament prophets Zephaniah, Micah, and Hosea have become female sibyls.[99] The angels that accompany Gabriel on the *nugola* sing a *lauda*;[100] Gabriel sings another to Mary; the mystery of the Annunciation is spoken entirely in Latin, and the angels return to heaven singing the *Magnificat*.[101] The disordered intermingling of vernacular

---

[97] *La festa della annuntiatione di nostra donna* ([Florence: Bartolomeo de' Libri, not after 1495]), ISTC ia00757400; Cioni, *Bibliografia*, 228, LXVIIB.1; for modern editions, see Table 2.

[98] *La Festa della annuntiatione di nostra Donna. Con una aggiunta di dua Capitoli* ([Florence: Antonio Tubini and Andrea Ghirlandi, not after 1515]), CNCE 62241; Cioni, *Bibliografia*, 228, LXVIIB.3. See also chapter 8 below, n. 25.

[99] For further discussion of the prophets and sibyls and their origin, see chapter 4. For a table of correspondences between the sources (biblical and other), Belcari's *Annunciazione*, and the play of the *Purification*, see Newbigin, "Feo Belcari, Baccio Baldini."

[100] "Laudate el sommo Dio" is to be sung to the same tune as Belcari's "Cristo ver huom e Dio," for which the musical setting is provided in Razzi, *Libro primo*, fols. 47ᵛ–48ᵛ; edited in Cummings, *The Politicized Muse*, 146–147.

[101] Tubini and Ghirlandi added two *ternali* ("Vergine santa immacolata e pia" and "Laudate il sommo Dio, angeli santi") to fill blank pages at the end of their edition. The final stage direction, "Now the Angels return to heaven and continue to sing this psalm" (Ora gli Angioli se ne tornano in cielo, e seguitano di cantare questo salmo), refers back

prophecies and Latin liturgy stands in contrast to Belcari's exquisitely structured *rappresentazione*. It may well be that the printed play preserves the skeletal remains of the original *festa*, with various accretions and distortions, but firmly rooted in the traditions of San Felice in Piazza — traditions that Belcari did not succeed in reforming.

Ducal and Grand-Ducal Florence

Marvin Becker rightly attributes the strength of lay piety in Renaissance Italy to the absence of courts, dynasties, and monastic centres of classical studies, which allowed lay culture to surface more easily since competing forces were weaker.[102] It is difficult to reconcile the confraternities' own view of Lorenzo de' Medici as their benefactor with their near-total demise as popular organizations of lay piety in the city under his control. Whereas Cosimo or his son Piero had once sent wine for the Ascension supper, and Piero had provided money to proud and independent *festaiuoli*, the 1480s saw the Sant'Agnese company grovelling to no avail. And under the Savonarolan regime, the *laudesi* confraternities were closed completely. With the return of the Medici in 1512 as dukes, and later grand-dukes, of Florence and then Tuscany, the initiative for the *feste* now came from above — and out of season — rather than from below. A letter from Florence dated 28 June 1514, copied by the Venetian Marin Sanudo into his great diary, noted that following the revival, in the presence of seven visiting cardinals, of all the old *feste* for the Baptist, "for Thursday they are preparing the *festa di San Felice*."[103] In 1518, when Duke Lorenzo de' Medici was preparing to marry the daughter of the count of Auvergne, orders went out that *armeggerie* or stylized displays of armed combat were to be organized by the plebian *potenze*, as well as "triumphs, firework whirligigs, *feste*, San Felice, the Carmine, Santo Spirito and more."[104] I have found no further evidence that these orders resulted in the *feste* being performed.

---

to the *Magnificat*, of which Mary has just spoken the first line, and not to the extraneous *ternali* that follow. This corrects D'Ancona (1:180), and the anthologies that follow him.

[102] Becker, "Aspects of Lay Piety," 182; for these observations, see "Epilogue: The Republican Heritage in Grand-ducal Florence," in Newbigin, *Feste*, 2:209–210.

[103] Sanuto, *I diarii*, 18 (1887), cols. 313–316 (316): "per Jovedì si prepara la festa di San Felice."

[104] Cerretani, *Ricordi*, 351: "trionfi, girandole e feste, San Felice, il Charmine, Santo Spirito e altro."

The Annunciation *festa* was resurrected in April 1533 for another Medici wedding, this time to celebrate the 'marriage' of the ten-year-old Margherita of Austria to Duke Alessandro de' Medici, just twice her age. Niccolò di Stefano Fabbrini provides a contemporary description, in the form of a dialogue between himself and an unidentified Giovanni, of the *ingegni* that Vasari attributed to Brunelleschi, and of the performance of a text that is probably the printed *Annunciazione*. Niccolò tells his companion:

The church of San Felice, both inside and out, is beautifully decorated, and in the middle of the church, across its width, is constructed a platform. At one end is the chamber of Our Lady, with curtains drawn so that nothing can be seen. At the other end are choir stalls with room for many actors and, when they appear at the beginning, they are empty. And when it is time to begin the *festa*, first of all, by means of fireworks, eight candelabra are lit, which last right through the *festa*, and an Angel comes and announces the *festa*, exhorting everybody to pay attention. Then one by one he calls a large number of Prophets and Sibyls, ordering each one to tell what he or she knows of the Incarnation of the Son of God. And they come before the Angel and in a single stanza each sings what he or she has prophesied of the birth of the Messiah and, when they have finished, they go and sit in the empty stalls described above, which is a beautiful spectacle. When these Prophets are done, Heaven opens with dancing, music, and celebration, and the Angel Gabriel is there in the midst of six angels, who are rejoicing and dancing, and God the Father gives him the message that he is to take to the Virgin. When he steps from the *nugola*, he greets the Virgin and says to her the words of the Gospel of St. Luke that begin *Missus est* [Luke 1:26], and then the Virgin replies, and the Angel. At the end the Virgin says *Ecce ancilla Domini* [Luke 1:38], and the Angel goes back to Heaven. The Virgin sings the canticle of the *Magnificat* [Luke 1:46–55], and the angels, continuing it, return to Heaven with other music and songs, and Heaven closes, and it is all over. And in this play there are thousands of beautiful details, especially — something I didn't say before — when she says *Ecce ancilla*, to represent the sending of the Holy Ghost, lots of lilies and other lights are lit up above the chamber of the Virgin, and likewise in the *nugola* of the Angel there are lots of lamps that are lit and extinguished as required, and lots of other secrets that can better be understood from seeing them at first hand than from any report. I have no more to add, except that the *festa* was done three times, on 19, 20, and 21 [April 1533], and once on each of these three days, so that as many people as possible might see it, and the Duchess went on Sunday, which was the 20th.[105]

There is no further mention of the *festa* in the chronicles until 1547, when an exceptional event caused it to be noticed again. According to an anonymous diarist, the play was once again performed three times over several days, starting on the octave of Easter Monday. Piazza San Felice was covered with a starry blue awning, and verdure tapestries, once the property of the assassinated Alessandro de' Medici, covered the walls around it. An arch, looking down Via Maggio, was decorated with a scene of Octavian and the Sibyl. Everything proceeded smoothly, until a halberdier from Duke Cosimo's German guard, who was keeping the doorway clear before the *festa* began, was rushed by the crowd as the duke arrived. He lowered his weapon to force the people back and wounded one of them seriously. "Everybody pulled back after this, and he was much praised by the duke."[106]

---

[105] The dialogue is dialogue is known through a seventeenth-century copy in BNCF, NA 982, fols. 161ʳ–173ʳ, mod. num.; see Appendix, doc. 2. The description is dated 28 April 1533, but the marriage itself was not celebrated until 18 January 1536. The play described corresponds closely to the anonymous printed *Annunciazione*. See also Fabbri, Garbero Zorzi, and Petrioli Tofani, eds., *Il luogo teatrale*, 67–68, no. 1.36 (Elvira Garbero Zorzi); Decroisette, "Fêtes"; Garbero Zorzi, "Le 'nozze' medicee"; and Cummings, *The Politicized Muse*, 140–147. When Giovanni asks who paid for the various spectacles in honour of the marriage, Niccolò indicates that the expense for the fifteen days of celebration was absorbed by private citizens, including the "festaiuoli di San Felice," fol. 173ʳ. Palermo indicated that he had seen the four opening speeches of this dialogue among Borghini's autograph papers, which suggests that it was among Borghini's resources when he was preparing the 1566 performance; Palermo, *I manoscritti palatini*, 2 (1860): 460.

[106] BNCF, II.iv.19, fols. 103ᵛ–104ʳ, mod. num.: "Visto questo, ognuno si tirò da canto, et haveva gran credito dal Duca." See also *Cronaca fiorentina*, 65. The copyist is Antonio di Orazio da San Gallo, formerly regarded as the author of the *Cronaca*. The Orciuolo did the *festa* in 1525, and the piazza outside was decorated, as was customary, with a most beautiful triumphal arch by the painter Jacone; see Vasari, *Le vite* (1568), 3.2:545, *Vita di Bastiano detto Aristotile da San Gallo pittore, e Architetto Fiorentino*. It is possible that the play continued to be performed annually without incident until the Camaldolese monks made way for the enclosed order of Dominican nuns in 1557. Mellini was presumably

By 1554, neither the Annunciation nor Ascension were still being done, and to the outrage of the officers of the Sant'Agnese company — who for some time had been finding it difficult to convene enough members to fulfil the obligations of their statutes — the Carmelite friars began to remove the last equipment in the decaying roof of the Carmine.[107] The officials petitioned Duke Cosimo to halt this destruction which, they argued, would "remove all trace and memory of such a *festa*," so that even if the duke wanted the *festa* to be done again, it would not be possible. The men claimed that their confraternity "was entrusted long ago by the Commune of Florence with the care and preservation of the machinery of Heaven." They now proposed to Cosimo that he should ensure that the machinery was placed somewhere for safekeeping, "in order that posterity should not lose all memory of such ingenious things, especially since what was in San Felice, now that it is to become a convent of nuns, will no longer be useable, and since, because they are similar, both of the *feste* could be done in the church of the Carmine."[108]

The demolition went ahead, and all the Ascension machinery — ropes, iron frames and winches, and timber — was rotting and rusting away when ten years later, in January 1563/4, the officers again petitioned Cosimo through the Captains of the Parte Guelfa, asking permission to sell it as scrap to raise funds for the refurbishment of their chapel.[109] They also pointed out to the duke that:

> the *ferri* and other pieces of machinery that were formerly used
> for the *festa* in San Felice in Piazza are in a room in the Carmine
> that has no proper storage and floods when the river rises, and
> they are deteriorating, and if these were refurbished, because

---

describing the *festa* of 1547, however, when he reported that Cosimo had the *festa di San Felice* staged five times over, "and it was many, many years since it had been done" (che per molti e molti anni non si era fatto); Mellini, *Ricordi*, 35.

[107] Newbigin, "Greasing the Wheels," 202–212.

[108] ASF, Capitani di Parte Guelfa, Numeri Neri 702, no. 59: "levar via ogni vestigio, et memoria di tal festa"; "fu anticamente dal Comune di Firenze constituta sopra la cura et preservazione dello edefizio del cielo fatto nella chiesa del Carmino"; "acciò che la posterità non perda la memoria del tutto di così artifiziose opere, stante maxime che quello che era in San Filice, per tornarvi un monasterio, non si potrà più esercitare, e che per essere simili, nella Chiesa del Carmino si potrebbe fare l'una et l'altra festa"; see also Newbigin, "Greasing the Wheels," 233–234.

[109] On the refurbishment, see Clover, "Documentation."

they are more modern, they could be used for the Carmine *festa* whenever it pleased Your Excellency that it should be done.[110]

The Captains of the Parte Guelfa, Cosimo's officers of public works, added that they had received their own report that the equipment was indeed in very bad condition. They recommended that the *ferri* of the Carmine, weighing in all 1500 lbs, should be sold, and explained that they had not been able to assess the San Felice equipment, which was half buried in mud. Neverthless:

> If Your Excellency pleases, the petitioners could be given permission to sell the Carmine equipment that they have under their control in order to refurbish their chapel, which will be an act of piety, and given care and custody of the other equipment, to clean off the mud and gather it together and register it in a book so that if it were necessary it could be found.[111]

The Last Annunciation, 1566

Such an occasion soon arose. In March 1564/5, just a year after this final petition, the marriage of Duke Cosimo's son Prince Francesco to Giovanna of Austria was announced.[112] Cosimo appointed the painter and art historian

---

[110] ASF, Capitani di Parte Guelfa, Numeri Neri 715, no. 139, Petition from the Captains of the Parte Guelfa, on behalf of the Captains and Officers of the Company of Santa Maria delle Laudi e di Sant'Agnese, to Duke Cosimo I, 12 January 1563/4: "li ferramenti et altri ordigni che servivano già per la festa di San Felice in Piazza sono in una stanza del Carmine sanza custodia dove entra la piena, et vanno male, et che rassettando questi per essere più moderni potrebbono servire alla festa del Carmine ogni volta che piacessi a Vostra Eccelenza che s'havessi a fare"; see Newbigin, "Greasing the Wheels," 234. The equipment in the Carmine had been largely refurbished and replaced in the 1460s and 1470. Since the equipment from San Felice was newer ("più moderni"), it is unlikely that it was designed by Brunelleschi.

[111] In the same document: "Piacendo a l'Eccellenza Vostra potrebbesi dar facultà a' detti supplicanti di possere vendere di quelli del Carmine che sono in loro potere per rassettare detta Cappella che sarà opera pia e delli altri darli la cura et custodia con farli nettare dalla mota e ridurli tutti insieme et notarli a un libro acciò che sempre quando occorressi si potessero ritrovare"; Newbigin, "Greasing the Wheels," 235.

[112] On the Annunciation of 1565/6, see Zorzi, *Il teatro*, 162–164, n. 29; Garbero Zorzi, "Le 'nozze' medicee"; Falletti, "Teatro subalterno"; Decroisette, "Fêtes"; Newbigin,

Giorgio Vasari, the genial polymath Vincenzio Borghini, and the accountant and administrator Giovanni Caccini as a committee of three to organize the city's celebrations. Having abandoned the idea of doing all three *feste*, they resolved, some time after June 1565, to do the *festa di San Felice* in Santo Spirito and draw on all three companies for whatever resources they could provide. Borghini minuted their decision:

> As far as the *festa di San Felice* is concerned, it seems that the first thing to do is to nominate the *festaiuoli* to the prince and to establish in advance how it is done and what the usual customs are. As I seem to remember, there are usually two kinds: the *festaiuoli* for inside and the ones for outside, or for Heaven and for Earth as they are called, and I think that this time I would create four or six more than usual for each part, because there are many things that have to be renewed and they have to get the whole business going again when it has fallen completely into disuse; and because the church is much bigger than the ones where these *feste* used to be done and has a different shape.
>
> It would also be good to get the Companies of the Orciuolo[113] and Sant'Agnese going again, and, if possible, the *Pippione*, and they could be entrusted to Luigi Gianfigliazzi who is one of the captains of Sant'Agnese. He could also take responsibility for the things needed for Heaven, since he has in his possession the equipment that is still in existence for this *festa*.
>
> I don't know what condition the affairs of these three companies are in. The *Pippione*, I think, has all but given up the ghost. But since the location of the *festa* is being changed, I would think that, just for the *festa* on this one occasion, they could come together just for this purpose, and in this one case make just one body, leaving each one as it was for all the rest of their income and their offices and their meeting places, at other times and apart from these *feste*. But as soon as we know exactly how they stand, and the state they are in today, we will easily be able to

---

"Greasing the Wheels," 213–228; Lepri, "Bartolomeo Traballesi," and *Le feste medicee*, 1:292. Lepri links Bartolomeo Traballesi's *Annunciation* formerly in Santissima Annunziata to the performance.

[113] See n. 50 above.

decide what is proper in this respect, and what can be done, and for my part I think that of these three only the Agnese company is still in existence and functioning.

As far as the *festa* is concerned, seeing that we are moving it, and since the time and the ways of doing things are so different, we could think of giving the thing to two or three people. One of them could be Messer Francesco Corteccia,[114] to consider the style of singing and also the matter of those Prophets and Sibyls who used to wear the audience down and they removed much grace from the beauty of the rest, so that perhaps they could be tempered in some way, and improved and made more refined with some worthwhile innovation suitable to the refinement of these times. As for Paradise and the *mazzo*,[115] these cannot be improved on, or not much, for they are what constitutes all the beauty of the *festa*. And for this purpose, perhaps Giovanni Bizzeri[116] would be good, as he has much experience of comedies, and good taste in the modern ones, and perhaps there are other people that I don't know.

But the officer of works must take measures before this commission is made public to establish clearly all the work that he needs done, and all the men and the timber and the other materials, because, as soon as the official announcement is made, the carpenters and the others will make a lot of trouble, and for this *festa* the seating in the church and the decorations outside will take tons of wood, and therefore I would like to have firm estimates and requisitions and supply of everything that is needed.

As for the timber for the seating, I know that there cannot be any shortage because there are some wholesale timber merchants that have plenty, and at the worst they will assume responsibility

---

[114] Chapel-master to the Medici court, Francesco Corteccia also provided the secular music for the third, fourth, and last *intermezzi* of the comedy, Francesco D'Ambra's *La cofanaria*, performed at Carnival; see Antolini, "Corteccia."

[115] *Mazzo*, usually translated as "nosegay of angels," is Vasari's term for the inner umbrella-spoke frame that was lowered from the *mezza palla tonda* or dome of heaven; see n. 6 above.

[116] Little is known of Giovanni Bizzeri. Letters in ASF, Mediceo del Principato, identify him as "provveditore del Monte di Pietà." Vasari's *Ricordanze* mention of a portrait of him; Arezzo, Museo di Casa Vasari, Carte Vasari 30, fol. 13r.

for building the seating, and then sell the seats for a price;[117] but in all this, the best way is to make sure beforehand of everything.

Remember, too, for these seats that have to be built in the church, that they should all be built to the same height and shape and dimensions, to avoid the infinite confusion and disorder that tend to arise. And all this is to be thought through and decided in advance, so that places are assigned in good order, for the court, the magistrates, the *festaiuoli*, and all the rest.[118]

A huge crew set to work to rebuild the old Heaven machinery from San Felice inside Brunelleschi's umbrella-spoke dome above the high altar in Santo Spirito. A new text was prepared that trimmed the thirty prophets and sibyls back to seventeen and provided psalms in the vernacular to be sung by the angels (fig. 2.19).[119] New music was composed to accompany them. On 8 March 1565/6, almost at the end of the wedding festivities, Borghini watched

---

[117] This is the only mention I have found of charging for seats at a performance of a *rappresentazione*. The revenue went to the timber merchants, not to the actors.

[118] BNCF, II.x.100, fols. 8^v-10^r; see Appendix, doc. 3, and also Palermo, *I manoscritti palatini*, 2 (1860): 457–459; Fabbri, Garbero Zorzi, and Petrioli Tofani, eds., *Il luogo teatrale*, 68–69, no. 1.39 (Elvira Garbero Zorzi); Newbigin, "Greasing the Wheels," 238–239.

[119] *La rapresentazione dell'annunziazione della gloriosa Vergine. Recitata in Firenze il di .x. di marzo 1565. Nella Chiesa di Santo Spirito* (Florence: [Heirs of Lorenzo Torrentino] for Alessandro Ceccherelli, 1565[/6]), CNCE 42745; Cioni, *Bibliografia*, 232, LXVIID.1; no modern edition. On Ceccherelli, see Bramanti, "Il 'cartolaio' Ceccherelli." The title and typographical details are inserted into the frame used for the 1550 edition of Vasari's *Vite*. At the top, *putti* point to the Medici *palle*, which sit between garlands of fruit. On either side caryatids of Pomona and Apollo support the pediment, while putti on the plinth below lift a curtain to reveal a view of Florence. It was printed 'con privilegio' and was not reprinted, as Giunti soon took over as the official grand-ducal printers. The author may have been Anton Francesco Grazzini. In his list of his works, compiled in September 1566, he includes under the heading *Rime spirituali*: "Stanzas, the *festa* of San Felice in Piazza, that is, the Annunciation of the Virgin" (Stanze, la festa di san Felice in Piazza, cioè l'Annunziazione della Vergine); Grazzini *Le rime*, CXXI. Grazzini referred again to the *festa* in his comedy *La spiritata* (1560/1), IV.3: "GIOVANGUALBERTO: What did you see? TRAVELA: Master, there's a blazing light in your room, with so many lamps it looked like the paradise in San Felice in Piazza" (GIOVANGUALBERTO: Che hai tu veduto? TRAVELA: Padrone, uno splendore è in camera vostra, e con tanti lumicini, ch'ella pare il paradiso di San Felice in Piazza); Grazzini, *La spiritata*, 38. Pignatti suggests the documented *feste* of 1533 or 1547 as the occasion of this composition; Pignatti, "Le poesie," 126.

a technical rehearsal for the *festa* that was to be performed two days later, on the second Sunday in Lent. He wrote to Vasari the next day:

> Yesterday the *festa* went well but, in my opinion, it needs the following:
>
> 1. More music in Heaven; but I don't know whether wind instruments will be right. Rather, I would reinforce the keyboards and strings.
>
> 2. Heaven should not lurch as it did yesterday evening. But it might have been that they weren't absolutely ready then.
>
> 3. I think that the music of the *mazzo* falls short in the sense that because they take longer to come and go than they did before, because everything has grown, they need to have more material on hand, even though yesterday they didn't sing the *Magnificat* right through; and I am sure that really they will do it better.
>
> 4. Lights, lights, lights! And keep your eye on that, because you couldn't see the *mazzo* at all. And I'm telling you, that however many you have, they will still seem too few. And the Angel who announces and summons the prophets, he also needs to be seen. And if the *ferro* came down at an angle and made him lean out, so that he could be seen the length of the church, it would be better. Come by and see me when you can, and God be with you.
>
> 9 March. Yours, Don Vincenzo.[120]

The speed of the *nugola*, noted by Sacchetti in the Ascension of the 1390s, continued to be a critical factor in the success of the spectacle.

Throughout the festivities, Vasari and Borghini had been working with Giovambattista Cini and Domenico Mellini to prepare an official description of them, which Vasari then appended to the new edition of his *Vite* (1568). Mellini described Vasari's solutions in the re-use of the machinery from San Felice:

> Then in the first holy days of Lent that followed, there was a performance of the most famous and once so celebrated *festa di San*

---

[120] Frey and Frey, eds., *Der literarische Nachlass*, 2 (1930): 221–222, letter DXXII, Vincenzio Borghini to Giorgio Vasari, 9 March 1565/6; see Appendix, doc. 4. See also Newbigin, "Greasing the Wheels," 226.

Felice, so called for the church where it used to be done, in the hope of pleasing the most religious bride, but to the very great satisfaction of all the entire population, who had been deprived of it for many years and thought it was never to be done again, since some pieces of this most ingenious machinery had gone missing. But this time, beyond what was desired by the most excellent Lords, and with the care and at the expense of four leading and very talented gentlemen of the city, it was performed in the church of Santo Spirito, which is more spacious and more beautiful, with elaborate preparation and with all the old machinery and no small number of new additions. As well as lots of Prophets and Sibyls, who sang in the simple traditional way and predicted the coming of our Lord Jesus Christ, what was even more remarkable, even though it was devised in those primitive ancient times, was Paradise, wonderful, stupendous, and beyond compare, that opened in a moment, full of the Hierarchies of Angels and Saints, and representing the various spheres with their different movements. Paradise lowered the divine Gabriel almost down to the ground, full of infinite splendours and surrounded by eight more little angels to bring the news to the glorious Virgin, who appeared humble and devout sitting in her room. And they were all lowered down and then raised up again, in the most marvellous way, from the highest part of the cupola of the church, where the Paradise I have described was represented, down to the stage with the Virgin's chamber, which was not very high from the ground, and all done with such sureness and in such a beautiful and simple and ingenious way that the human mind could scarcely surpass it. And with this, the *feste*, all prepared by the most excellent Lords for the most royal marriage, had their conclusion, not only splendid and famous, but also devout and religious, as well befitted true and Christian princes.[121]

Vasari had revived the Annunciation *festa* for the last time, and he followed it with one final gesture: he incorporated into the second edition

---

[121] Mellini, *Descrizione*, in Vasari, *Le vite* (1568), 3.2:979 (misnumbered 981); see Appendix, doc. 5. The Annunciation was performed three times, on 10, 14, and 18 March; see Lapini, *Diario*, 151. In addition to Mellini, see Settimanni, *Memorie*, ASF, Manoscritti 128, fol. 362[r–v].

of his *Vite* the understanding of the Annunciation and the Ascension *feste* that he had derived from examining their equipment and re-using it in Santo Spirito. To find space for his descriptions of the machinery, he had to attribute them to known artists. The Annunciation found its home in his life of Brunelleschi, and the Ascension *festa* in his life of Francesco d'Angelo, called *il Cecca* (1446–1488). Vasari warned his readers that the attribution was tentative, framing his description of the Annunciation with: "It is also said that the mechanical devices for Paradise in San Felice in Piazza in this city were invented by Filippo to do the play, or rather the *festa* of the Nunziata, in the way that it always used to be done in ancient times in that place in Florence"; and "These mechanical devices that I have described, and much more, were invented by Filippo; although other people insist that they had been invented long before. Whatever the truth, it has been good to discuss them, because they are now no longer in use at all."[122] In his life of *il Cecca*, having made his tentative attribution of the *nuvole* of San Giovanni to the engineer,[123] he goes on to describe the Ascension *festa*, concluding: "These mechanical devices and these inventions are said to have been made by *il Cecca*, because even if Filippo Brunelleschi had made similar ones long before, nevertheless many judicious additions were made to them by *il Cecca*. And from these he got the idea of creating the nuvole that processed through the city on the eve of San Giovanni, and the other beautiful things they did. And that was his

---

[122] Vasari, *Le vite* (1568), 1:321: "Dicesi ancora, che gl'ingegni del Paradiso di San Filice in piazza, nella detta Città, furono trovati da Filippo, per fare la Rappresentazione, o vero festa della Nunziata, in quel modo, che anticamente a Firenze in quel luogo si costumava di fare"; and 1:323: "Questi dunque così fatti ingegni, e molti altri furono trovati da Filippo, se bene alcuni altri affermano, che egli erano stati trovati molto prima. Comunche sia, è stato ben ragionarne, poi che in tutto se n'è dismesso l'uso." The description in the 1550 edition is one sentence: "It is said that the Paradise machinery in San Felice in Piazza in this city was invented by him to do a play: an industrious sight to behold a heaven full of living figures moving, and iron counterweights turning and moving, with covered lights that light up when they are uncovered; things which brought Filippo great praise" (Dicesi che gli ingegni del paradiso di Santo Felice in piazza in detta città furono trovati da lui per fare una rappresentazione; cosa industriosa a vedere muovere un Cielo pieno di figure vive; e i contrappesi di ferri girare e muovere e con lumi coperti e da scoprirsi s'accendono; cose che diedero a Filippo grandissima lode), Vasari, *Le vite* (1550), 1:327.

[123] Vasari, *Le vite* (1568), 1: 441: "Dicesi, che le nuvole, che andavano in Fiorenza, per la festa di S. Giovanni a processione cosa certo ingegnosissima, e bella, furono invenzione del Cecca, il quale allora, che la città usava di fare assai feste, era molto in simili cose adoperato."

responsibility, because, as we have said, he was a person who served the public."[124]

It is not necessary, however, to look for single authors for these *feste*, just as it is probably not useful to look for a high level of spiritual or artistic self-awareness in the motivations of the participating individuals. The evidence of the confraternal account books shows that these *feste* were a voluntary and autonomous expression of neighbourhood collectivity and rivalry. Each year, the men of the confraternity invested time and effort to work together to produce a *festa* that was bigger and better than the year before.[125] Their reward was the pleasure of collaboration, of achievement, of distraction from day-to-day business, of eating together beforehand and partying afterwards, and — we must assume — of basking in praise when all went well. The plays did not survive their loss of autonomy. Where Cosimo and Piero de' Medici had fostered the confraternities that mounted the plays, Lorenzo chose to control them and the plays and their machinery fell into disuse, to be revived and documented as a magnificent princely gesture by Duke Cosimo I.[126]

---

[124] Vasari, *Le vite* (1568), 1:442: "Questi ingegni dunque, e queste invenzioni si dice, che furono del Cecca: perché se bene molto prima Filippo Bruneleschi n'haveva fatto de' così fatti, vi furono nondimeno con molto giudizio molte cose aggiunte dal Ceccha. E da queste poi venne in pensiero al medesimo di fare le Nuvole, che andavano per la città a processione ogni anno la vigilia di San Giovanni; e l'altre cose, che bellissime si facevano. E ciò era cura di costui, per essere, come si è detto persona, che serviva il publico."

[125] On *meraviglia* as an aim of the *feste*, see Terry, *"Meraviglia."*

[126] For one more *Cielo* in Santo Spirito, for the marriage of Virginia de' Medici and Cesare d'Este in February 1585/6, see the life of Bernardo Buontalenti, in Baldinucci, *Notizie*, 2:509. When heaven was lowered and then opened, the singers of the motet "O benedetto giorno" were struck dumb in terror and only Giulio Caccini was able to continue, earning himself the life-long sobriquet of Benedetto Giorno. I do not believe that this was a performance of the *Annunciazione* or that a second edition of it was issued in 1586, but for a different view, see Fabbri, Garbero Zorzi, and Petrioli Tofani, eds., *Il luogo teatrale*, 69, no. 1.39 (Elvira Garbero Zorzi).

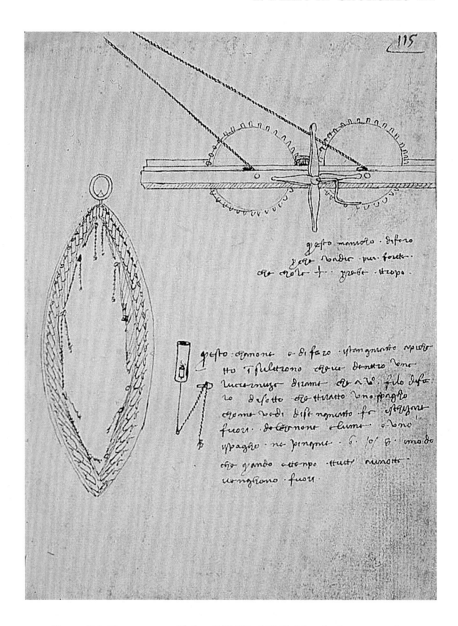

Figure 2.1. Bonaccorso Ghiberti (1451–1516), *Nugola*, incorporating disappearing-light device. Fifteenth century. BNCF, Banco Rari 228, fol. 115[r].

Figure 2.2. Bonaccorso Ghiberti (1451–1516), *Nugola*, with roof anchors and under-stage winch. Fifteenth century. BNCF, Banco Rari 228, fol. 115^v.

Figure 2.3. Pacino di Bonaguida, *Ascension*. Leaf from the dismembered
Laudario of the Compagnia di Santa Maria delle Laude e di Sant'Agnese,
originally fol. LXXVII^v. About 1340. Tempera and gold on parchment, 44.4 ×
31.8 cm. Los Angeles, The J. Paul Getty Museum, Ms. 80a (2005.26).
Open content.

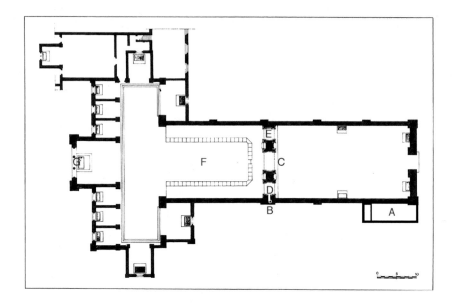

Figure 2.4. *Santa Maria del Carmine*, hypothetical reconstruction. Legend:
A. the oratorio of Santa Maria delle Laude e di Sant'Agnese; B. spiral
staircase onto the *tramezzo* and up into the roof; C. the *tramezzo*; D: the
castello; E: the *monte* with *Paradiso* above it; and F: the *Stella* above the
choir; G: *Cielo* in the wall above the high altar. Based on Fabbri, Garbero
Zorzi, and Petrioli Tofani, eds., *Il luogo teatrale*, 58, no. 1.18.

Figure 2.5. Filippo Lippi (1406–1469), *Martelli Annunciation*. About 1440. Tempera on panel, 175 cm × 183 cm. Florence, Basilica di San Lorenzo, Martelli Chapel. Wikimedia Commons / CC BY-SA-3.0. Photo Sailko.

Figure 2.6. Jacopo di Cione and Workshop, *Ascension*. 1370–1371. Tempera
on wood, 95.5 × 49 cm. Upper tier panel of the altarpiece from San Pier
Maggiore. London, National Gallery, NG577. Wikimedia Commons / CC
BY-SA-3.0. Photo: National Gallery.

Figure 2.7. Compagnia di Santa Maria delle Laude e dello Spirito Santo, detta del *Piccione, Laudario*. Fourteenth century (or later replacement folio?). Miniated scene with the Descent of the Holy Spirit on Mary and the Apostles, with St. Augustine and St. Nicholas of Tolentino. BNCF, Banco Rari 18 (formerly II.i.122), fol. 2ᵛ. © By permission of MiBACT/BNCF. All rights reserved.

Figure 2.8. Fra Angelico (Giovanni da Fiesole, 1395–1455), *Pentecost*. 1451–
1453. Tempera on wood; 38.5 × 37.5 mm. Panel from the *Armadio degli
Argenti*, formerly church of the Santissima Annunziata, Florence. Florence,
Museo Nazionale di San Marco, inv. 1890, no. 8502. Wikimedia Commons /
CC BY-SA-3.0. Photo: Sailko.

Figure 2.9. *Meditatione de la vita del nostro Signore Ihesu Christo.* The Virtues Justice, Truth, Mercy and Peace kneel before God. Fourteenth century. Ink and tempera on paper. Paris, BnF, Ms. italien 115, fol. 4ʳ. By courtesy of Bibliothèque nationale de France.

Figure 2.10. Bicci di Lorenzo (with Neri di Bicci), *Annunciation*. 1440.
Tempera on wood. From church of San Michele Arcangelo, Legnaia (FI).
Florence, Museo Diocesano di Santo Stefano al Ponte. By courtesy of the
Fondazione Zeri, inv. no. 33804. Photographer unknown.

Figure 2.11. Ludovico Zorzi and Cesare Lisi, *Hypothetical reconstruction of the "ingegno brunelleschiano" in San Felice in Piazza, c. 1430.* 1975. Wooden model. Florence, property of Regione Toscana; present location: Parco di Pratolino, Scuderia. Photo: Ugo Scaletti, Studio 72.

Figure 2.12. Vincenzo Foppa, *Dome with dancing angels, and scene of the Annunciation.* 1462–1468. Painted vault with terracotta angels; fresco. Milan, Basilica di Sant'Eustorgio, Portinari Chapel. Photo: by courtesy of Museo di Sant'Eustorgio.

Figure 2.13. Francesco Botticini, *The Assumption of the Virgin*. 1475–1476. Tempera on wood. 228.6 × 377.2 cm. London, National Gallery, Accession no. NG1126. Wikimedia Commons / CC BY-SA-3.0. Photo: Sailko.

Figure 2.14. Alessandro di Mariano Filipepi, called Sandro Botticelli (1445–
1510), *The Descent of the Holy Ghost*. 1495–1505. Oil on panel, 207.0 ×
229.8 cm (originally 8 × 5 *braccia*, or 466.9 × 291.8 cm). Birmingham, UK.
Birmingham Museum and Art Gallery, accession no. 1959P31. Wikimedia
Commons / CC BY-SA-3.0. Photo: Terminators.

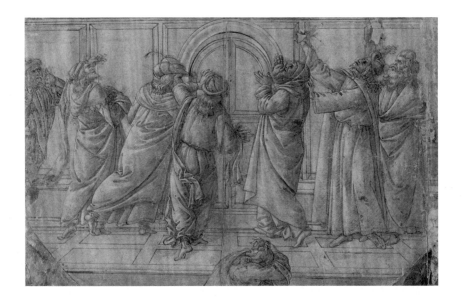

Figure 2.15. Alessandro di Mariano Filipepi, called Sandro Botticelli (1445–
1510), *Gentiles at the gate after Pentecost*. 1495–1505. Black chalk, pen,
and brown ink, brown wash with white gouache, on paper, 231 × 365 mm.
Darmstadt, Hessisches Landesmuseum, Accession no. AE.1285.
Photo: by courtesy of Hessisches Landesmuseum, Graphische Sammlung.

Figure 2.16. Filippino Lippi (1457–1504), *Assumption of the Virgin*, with *Annunciation* altarpiece. 1489. Fresco. Rome, Santa Maria Sopra Minerva, Carafa Chapel. Wikimedia Commons / CC BY-SA-3.0. Photo: Urnes.

Figure 2.17. Alessandro di Mariano Filipepi, called Botticelli (1445–1510), *Mystic Nativity*. 1500/1. Oil on canvas, 108.6 × 74.9 cm. London, National Gallery, Accession no. NG1034. Wikimedia Commons / CC BY-SA-3.0. Photo: Crisco 1492.

¶ La feſta della annuntiatione di noſtra donna

Qui cominciano leſtanze & larapreſenta
tione della feſta della anuntiatione di
noſtra dōna. Imprima uiene uno ange
lo & annuntia lafeſta & dice.

UOi excelenti & nobili auditori
che ſiate alla preſenza raghunati
per gratia uipreghiamo euoſtri cori
attenti ſtieno honeſti & coſtumati
a udire & uedere congrandi amori
emeſtier ſancti qui anuntiati

dello incarnar di dio & chi lha decto
fermando aqueſto tutto lontellecto
Io priego ladiuina prouidenza
che doni gratia allontellecto mio
chipoſſa anuntiar di queſta eſſenza
uerbo incarnato uer figluol di dio
ilqual fu pieno di ſomma ſapienza
& anuntiocci lauia del diſio
chi ha a riſponder parli con douere
epropheti diranno ellor parere

Figure 2.18. *La festa della annuntiatione di nostra donna* ([Florence:
Bartolomeo de' Libri, not after 1495]), fol. a1r. Rome, Biblioteca
Casanatense, Inc. 1670; ISTC ia00757400. BEIC / CC BY-SA-4.0.

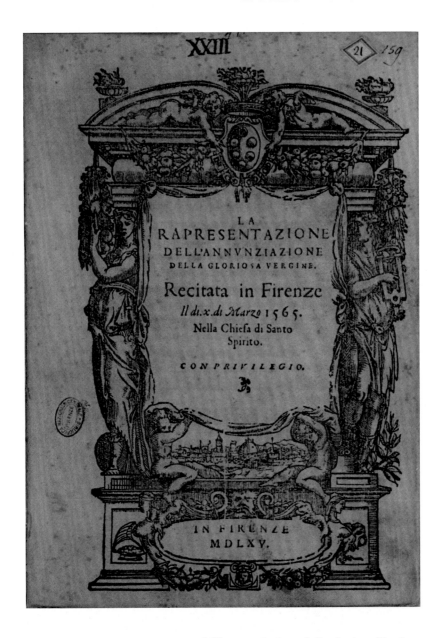

Figure 2.19. *La rapresentazione dell'annunziazione della gloriosa Vergine. Recitata in Firenze il di .x. di Marzo 1565. Nella Chiesa di Santo Spirito. Con Privilegio* (Florence: [Heirs of Lorenzo Torrentino] for Alessandro Ceccherelli, 1565[/6]), fol. a1ʳ. BNCF, Banco Rari 179.21; CNCE 42745.

CHAPTER 3

YOUTH CONFRATERNITIES
AND THEIR PLAYS

> Religious companies were not set up
> for ceremonies or for singing hymns,
> but rather to preserve and purge your souls
> of all the vices and of every fraud.
>
> Feo Belcari[1]

While the *laudesi* confraternities of the Oltrarno rejoiced in their autonomy, a new form of devotional grouping was being promoted in Florence to harness and direct the enthusiasm of boys and young men. In the second and third decades of the fifteenth century, four *compagnie di fanciulli* or youth confraternities were founded. The confraternity of the Archangel Raphael, known also as the Nativity and the Scala, was founded in 1411, and moved from Santissima Annunziata to various locations around Santa Maria Novella.[2] Its offspring, the confraternity of the Purification (1427), began in the hospital of San Matteo di Lemmo, or dell'Elmo, and moved with the support of Cosimo de' Medici to San Marco.[3] The confraternity of St. John the Evangelist, called simply the Vangelista, which met in Santa Trinita Vecchia, was founded the same year under the protection of the *buca* or men's flagellant company of San Paolo.[4] San Niccolò del Ceppo, founded in 1417, met "in the parish of San Jacopo tra' Fossi, next to the convent of the Poor Sisters, in the place called *il Ceppo*."[5] A fifth company, of Sant'Antonio da Padova,

---

[1] Feo Belcari, *Alquante stanze composte per Feo Belcari intermesse nella representatione del Giudicio*, BNCF, Magl. vii.690, fol. 141ʳ: "Le sante compagnie non fur trovate | per usar ceremonie o canti o laude, | ma per tener l'alme vostre purgate | da molti vizî e da ciascuna fraude," oct. 27.1–4.

[2] Eisenbichler, *The Boys*.

[3] Polizzotto, *Children*.

[4] On the Vangelista company, see below in this chapter. On the physical remains of these confraternities, see Sebregondi, "Tracce," and "La soppressione." On the San Paolo company, see Weissman, "Lorenzo."

[5] *Capitoli* in BNCF, Conv. Soppr. D.3.270 (recopied 1558), f. 6ᵛ: "nel popolo di San Jacopo tra' Fossi appresso al monasterio delle Poverine, luogo detto il Ceppo." See

founded in 1441 (although its statutes were not approved until 1453), met on the Costa San Giorgio. It, too, was the offspring of an adult flagellant company, the *buca* of San Girolamo in Costa San Giorgio. Sant'Antonio da Padova, also known as San Giorgio, constituted the only youth group in the Oltrarno.[6] Less is known about a sixth confraternity, of San Bernardino e Santa Caterina, known later as San Bernardino in Pinti, founded in 1461 and located first in Santa Maria degli Alberighi, and from 1490 in Santa Maria Maddalena in Cestello, in Borgo Pinti.[7] More groups would appear later, but it is in the context of these six youth confraternities that a new form of *sacra rappresentazione* emerged around the middle of the fifteenth century.[8] There has been vigorous and valuable recent scholarship on youth in Florence as well as institutional histories that chart the journey of the youth confraternities until their suppression by Grand Duke Pietro Leopoldo in 1785,[9] but my focus will be on the plays — the *rappresentazioni* and *feste* with texts rather than the ceremonial celebrations of feast days — and the social and spiritual values they embody. The chapter is long, examining most of the plays that can be linked to youth confraternities in the fifteenth century. Its concentration

---

Sebregondi Fiorentini, *La compagnia e l'oratorio*, 5. The members were separated into *fanciulli* (boys, from 12 to 17 years) and *giovani* (young men, from 18 to 24 years), a division not found elsewhere.

[6] *Capitoli* of the Compagnia di San Girolamo in Costa San Giorgio, ASF, CCRS 81, fol. 21v. See also Cancedda and Castelli, *Per una bibliografia*, 31–37. For more detailed discussion see below in this chapter, and also chapter 5.

[7] Their 1612 statutes, ASF, CCRSPL 839, provide faulty details about their foundation, but it appears certain that their original statutes were approved by Giovanni di Dietisalvi Neroni, archbishop of Florence 1462–1473 (fols. 2^v–3^r), and that in 1490 their organization was consolidated with that of the Vangelista, the Purification, the Archangel Raphael, and Sant'Antonio da Padova, under the administration of the prior of the Florentine Badia; see ASF, Notarile Antecosimiano 7670 (= F412 Jacopo di Marcantonio delle Fonti, 1487–1497), fol. 22^v, with further contracts on fols. 20^r and 23^r. See also Luchs, "Cestello," 60, 348; Sebregondi, *Tre confraternite*, 14; Eisenbichler, *The Boys*, 30–31, and "Cosa degna," 828.

[8] D'Ancona, *Origini*, 1:401–416.

[9] Trexler, "Ritual in Florence"; Weissman, *Ritual Brotherhood*; Henderson, *Piety*; Taddei, *Fanciulli*, "Attività spettacolare," "L'Encadrement," "Puerizia," and "Confraternite e giovani"; Aranci, "La catechesi"; Eisenbichler, *The Boys*, and numerous other fundamental studies which will be cited individually; Polizzotto "The Medici," and *Children*; Evangelista, "L'attività spettacolare"; Ventrone, "La sacra rappresentazione fiorentina, ovvero la predicazione," "The Influence," "I teatri delle confraternite" online, and *Teatro civile*. Aranci, Bellacci, and Faldi, "La sezione," 19, notes the presence of the confirmation of the statutes, 1465–66 in the Archivio Arcivescovile, CR 07.20.

on the plays of the Purification company is determined by the survival their account books where those of the other groups have been lost, but it also considers plays of the Vangelista and of San Giorgio, which benefited similarly from Medici intervention in their affairs.

It has long been recognized that the humanists of fifteenth-century Florence developed new thinking in relation to the education of children. The curriculum they developed both intuitively and systematically prepared boys and young men for public life at whatever level was appropriate to the birth and abilities of the individual.[10] Pedagogic theory was based on the fundamental premise that the child had potential that was to be nurtured and directed by various means, including socialization and instruction through well-chosen friends, good role models, and clear ethical guidelines. Giovanni Dominici's *Regola del governo di cura familiare* (Rule for the management of family care, 1401–1403) and Maffeo Vegio's *De educatione liberorum et eorum claris moribus* (The character and studies befitting free-born youth,1443), with their combination of moral, social, Christian, and educational principles, resonated with this new philosophy, offering a pedagogy not just for future princes but also for the sons of urban merchants aspiring to improve and consolidate their status.[11] In Florence, this awareness of children as an asset worthy of investment manifested itself in a special magistracy for orphans (the Magistrato dei Pupilli, instituted in 1393); the establishment of a spectacular foundling hospital (the Ospedale degli Innocenti, begun 1419); the appointment of schoolmasters to teach *grammatica* and *abacus* to the sons of an increasingly prosperous artisan class; and the preparation of tracts on child-rearing and on the spiritual education of youth. The new youth confraternities were part of this trend, appearing alongside the thirteenth- and fourteenth-century foundations of *disciplinati* and *laudesi* and welcoming young males who were old enough to reason but not yet old enough to take any part in civic life.

Like the adult confraternities, the youth groups had *capitoli*, or statutes, formulated on the model of monastic and communal statutes and

---

[10] Taddei, *Fanciulli*, 65–118; Garin, ed., *Il pensiero*; Eisenbichler, "Il ruolo."

[11] Extracts from Latin text, with Italian translation, in Garin, ed., *Il pensiero*, 170–197; Vegio, *De educatione*. Luisi, "Minima fiorentina," 82, citing Vegio, *De educatione*, notes that Vegio had been in Florence with Eugenius IV after 1434, and had associated with Bruni, Marsuppini, Traversari, and Palmieri; his treatise is dated in Rome, "nono Kal. ianuari 1444," that is, the end of 1443. On humanist pedagogy more broadly, see Woodward, *Vittorino da Feltre*, 179–250; Grafton and Jardine, *From Humanism*.

sumptuously copied to constitute an important ritual object (fig. 3.1).[12] After a preamble invoking the confraternity's divine patrons, statutes typically began with the words: "The Holy Spirit speaks through the mouth of David saying: Decline from evil and do good" (Psalm 36 (37):27).[13] They went on

---

[12] On the early statutes of the confraternities, see Polizzotto, *Children*, 22–38; Taddei, *Fanciulli*, 170–173.

[13] Bloomington, Lilly, MR 26, fol. 3[r]: "Lo Spirito Santo parla per la bocca del profeta David dicendo: *Declina a malo et fac bonum.*" The later copy of the Purification statutes in BCNF, Magl. VIII.1500 (11), has long been known. Lorenzo Polizzotto located the earlier illuminated copy, sold by Sotheby's in 1958 (formerly Dyson Perrins Ms. 62) and now in the Lilly Library of Indiana University (MS Medieval and Renaissance 26, hereafter Lilly, MR 26); Polizzotto, *Children*, 347–355; de Hamel, *Gilding the Lilly*, 136–137; Leader, "*Capitoli.*" The statutes of the Vangelista company (see n. 215 below) were drafted at the same time. The Purification statutes were revised in 1444, when Piero di Mariano Muzi was given full authority to make any necessary changes, but they were not approved by Antoninus until 24 April 1448. The date is given in cap. 1, fols. 3[v]–4[r]: "*Della rinouatione degli infrascritti capitoli, e in che modo ci possiamo ordinare a dDio. Capitolo primo.* Questi sono capitoli e constitutioni di nostra schuola, rinouati nell'anno del nostro Signore Giesù Cristo M°ccccxliiij° addì xxviiij° di giugno, cioè el dì di sancto Piero e sancto Paulo, e chosì ebbe piena licenza il nostro guardiano perla [*words anticipated from line below, omitted in* Magl. copy] da tutti e frategli di detta schuola unitamente. Io, sopradetto ghuardiano per la gratia di Dio, considerando la comessione a mme facta e rasghuardando gli antichi capitoli di detta schuola, i quali a' dì moderni non si confacieuano, per la gratia di Dio e per onore d'essi ne piglerò parte in diversi luoghi chome per inanzi si dirà che nne seghuà honore di Dio" (*Concerning the revision of these statutes, and how we can organize ourselves for God. Chapter 1.* These are the statutes of our school, renewed in the year of our Lord Jesus Christ 1444, on the 29th day of June, that is, on the feast of St. Peter and St. Paul. And to this end our warden was given complete authority by all the brothers of our school unanimously. I, the said warden by the grace of God, having considered the task given to me, and examining the old statutes of our school, which are not appropriate to modern times, with God's grace and in their honour shall take parts of them from various places, as will be explained further on, to the honour of God). The statutes were then copied in January 1447/8 by Fra Bartolomeo *iscrittore* (copyist) who was paid £5, and decorated by Battista *miniatore* (illuminator) who was paid £1 13s. on 14 April 1448; ASF, CRSPL 1654 (P.xxx.30), fol. 88[r-v]. On the illuminator Battista Sanguigni, see Dillon Bussi, "Battista miniatore," 44–51; de Hamel, *Gilding the Lilly*, 136–137. The statutes remained in force until July 1478, soon after the Pazzi conspiracy, when the constitutions of all the youth confraternities were revised to place them under much tighter control. Polizzotto refers to them as the 1444 *Capitoli*, to distinguish them from their copy in BNCF, Magl. VIII.1500 (11).

Polizzotto argues that the statutes contained in BMLF, Acquisti e Doni 336, are an early state of the Florentine Purification company's statutes (Polizzotto, "The Medici,"

to specify the office bearers of the organization and their duties: meetings to be held and documented, accounts to be kept and property administered; admission and investiture of members; prayers to be learned by heart and the frequency of confession and attendance at Mass; dues to be paid; the kind of mutual support that would be provided by the confraternity if a member fell on hard times; charitable causes; and prayers for the dead. The statutes also contained prohibitions and sanctions, listing a standard constellation of abominable sins: gambling; swearing; lying; visiting taverns, places where there is music, dancing, singing, jousting, and fighting, and other "places of ill-repute"; as well as the ever-threatening vice of sodomy.[14] Feo Belcari's additions to the *Rappresentazione del Dì del Giudizio* (Play of Judgement Day) dramatize the role of the confraternity in its constant struggle to control the behaviour of *fanciulli*:

Un Fanciullo *dal lato sinistro,*	A Boy *on the left side, when he sees St.*
vedendo che San Michele mena Traiano	*Michael taking Trajan to the right, entreats*
dal lato destro, sì lo prega dicendo:	*him, saying:*
O san Michel, gonfalonier di Dio,	St. Michael, standard-bearer before God,
abbi pietà della mia fanciullezza.	be merciful, for I am but a child.
Scusar mi debba il piccol tempo mio,	My tender years are surely an excuse
la gola e 'l giuoco e la carnal bruttezza.	for gluttony, gambling, and carnal filth.
Per ignoranza feci ogn'atto rio,	I did each wicked act in ignorance,
non castigato della mia sciochezza.	and unchastised for all my foolishness,
Se 'l padre mio m'avesse custodito,	for if my father had protected me,
di questi vizi non sarei vestito.	I'd not be clothed in vices such as these.

99–100; discussed further in Polizzotto, *Children*, 347–377), while Taddei, *Fanciulli*, 170–173, contends that the anomalies of that manuscript are too problematic to allow such attribution. In either case, the BMLF statutes would predate the introduction of plays into the confraternity's repertoire of devotions.

[14] Bloomington, Lilly, MR 26, fol. 18[r–v], cap. xv, "luoghi disonesti." On sodomy, see fols. 22[v]–23[r], cap. xviii: "Et se alchuno venisse in tanto errore, che non ci si viene se non per le chattive compagnie, che chomettesse lo sciellerato e orribile peccato di soddomia, saputo il ghuardiano la verità, sia tenuto a plubicarlo raso" (And if anyone should lapse into such sin — which only happens on account of bad company — that he committed the wicked and horrible sin of sodomy, once the warden has learned the truth he is obliged to declare him struck off).

SAN MICHEL *risponde*:

Non era il tempo tuo tanto piccino
che tu non conoscessi 'l mal dal bene,
ma per le ghiottornie e pel quattrino
tu non temesti vergogne né pene.
Fuggendo buoni stavi a capo chino
al tristo giuoco, donde ogni mal vene.
Ma quello ch'all'inferno più t'invia
è il brutto vizio della soddomia.

Allora QUEL FANCIULLO *si volge irato
contr'al padre che è quivi tra' dannati
e dice:*

Maladetto sia tu, padre cattivo,
Cristo ti mandi nella magior pena.
Per tua cagion del ciel mi veggio privo
e vo nel fuoco senz'aver mai lena.
Se battuto m'avessi quando givo
a giocar, non sarei in questa mena,
e così quando co' ribaldi andavo
tu stavi cheto perch'io ne cavavo.

UNO PADRE *buono dal lato destro dice
a uno suo Figliuolo:*

Figliuolo, or vedi il frutto delle busse
che già ti detti, quant'è salutifero.
Meglio sarebbe a quel nato non fusse
perché 'l vedrai nelle man del Lucifero.
El gastigarti a molti ben t'indusse
e fètti salvo d'ogni mal pestifero.
Oltra di questo la compagnia buona
ti farà in cielo aver magior corona.

EL FIGLIUOLO *così risponde:*

Io rendo laude a Iesù Cristo in prima
e a te, padre, del tuo custodirmi.
La disciplina, ch'è virtù sublima,
de' buon costumi tutto fe' vestirmi.
Ma' non credetti allor che tanta stima
fusse da far del tuo spesso ammonirmi
ed ancor quella santa compagnia
fu gran cagion della salute mia.

(Magl. VII.690, fols. 137ʳ–138ʳ)

ST. MICHAEL *replies:*

You weren't so very young you couldn't see
the difference between wrong acts and right,
but in your lust for money and for food
you feared no shame nor any punishment.
You fled good people, and instead sat bowed
over your sorry game, source of all ills.
But what sends you to hell, above all else,
is the obnoxious vice of sodomy.

Then THE BOY *turns angrily against his
father who is there among the damned and
says:*

O wicked father, may you now be cursed
and may Christ send you to the harshest pain.
Because of you, I am deprived of Heav'n,
and go forever down into the fire.
If you had beaten me whenever I
would go and gamble, I would not be here,
and likewise, when I hung out with the lads,
while I was making money, you kept quiet.

A GOOD FATHER *on the right-hand side
says to one of his sons:*

My son, you see the fruit of all those blows
I gave you, and how they saved you from sin.
Better for him if he had not been born,
for Lucifer will get him, as you'll see.
Chastisement led you to many good things
and rescued you from all corrupting sin.
Moreover, it is this good company
that guarantees your greater crown in heaven.

THE SON *replies as follows:*

I offer praise first to Lord Jesus Christ
and to you, father, for protecting me;
for discipline, a virtue so sublime
has clothed me in the very best of habits.
I never then believed that such regard
was to be placed in all your cautioning,
and all the time that holy company
was the great cause of my deliverance.

The Bad Boy has succumbed to the perils of gluttony, gambling, and carnal sin — and, worse than all, sodomy — and curses his father for not disciplining him. The Good Boy thanks his father for the necessary beatings that have clothed him in virtue, and — with a gentle pun on the two meanings of *compagnia* as both 'company' and 'confraternity' — for the good *compagnia* that has been the cause of his soul's salvation.[15]

Instead of engaging in forms of social behaviour that could easily imperil good order, safety, and salvation, such as stone fights, sword play, and contesting the territory of rival *potenze* or festive kingdoms, particularly at Carnival, the adolescents and young men of these confraternities, also called *compagnie* and *scuole*, developed life skills and virtues that would open the gates of heaven. Castellano Castellani makes this choice explicit in the last lines of his *Figliuolo prodigo* (before August 1515), "And so, fleeing from Carnival and stones | in these sweet games we'll find our nourishment" (Così fuggendo el carnasciale e ' sassi, | ci pascerem di questi dolci spassi; oct. 121.7–8).[16]

The statutes banned, in effect, all the aimless pleasures and entertainments that an adolescent male might wish to pursue and replaced them with continuous devotion. As he walked down the street, he received cues from every shrine on every corner to cross himself, and do prayerful reverence to the saints, to Christ crucified, and to the Virgin. The *fanciulli*, admitted at the age of thirteen and normally required to leave by the age of twenty-four, were enrolled in a group that would control their leisure time as effectively as their employer, apprentice master, or parent would control them the rest of the time. If there was any respite from this regime of discipline and devotion it was on feast days, prescribed by the confraternity and endorsed by the host church and by the city.

The early statutes were all revised and recopied in the 1440s at the behest of the Venetian Pope Eugenius IV, who spent long periods in Florence between May 1434 and his death in 1447. The first visit of Eugenius,

---

[15] On Florentine responses to the fear of sodomy, see Rocke, *Forbidden Friendships*. Despite being an all-male environment and engaging in theatricals (on which see Pandolfi, "Le spurie origini," XI–XIII), confraternities do not appear in the prosecution records for the offence of sodomy. This is in contrast to Latin masters who directed performances of Roman comedies and are found regularly among the prosecutions; Black, *Education*, 2:398–399. See also Eisenbichler, "How Bartolomeo," and below in this chapter. On other moral threats, see Eisenbichler, "Adolescence and Damnation."

[16] D'Ancona, ed. *Sacre rappresentazioni*, 1:389.

together with the return of Cosimo after his exile in 1434, coincided with a huge growth of numbers in the Purification company.[17] Eugenius developed a close interest in the first four youth confraternities, and in his bull of 24 June 1442 he took measures to avoid scandal by placing all four under the control of the Benedictine abbot of the Florentine Badia and the Dominican prior of San Marco, Friar Antoninus, who would become archbishop of Florence in 1446.[18] They in turn approved the nominations of *guardiani* or wardens for each confraternity, older men of impeccable rectitude who would guide the young. The *guardiani* were also required to meet with each other quarterly "in Cestello," that is, in the Cistercian monastery of Santa Maria Maddalena in Borgo Pinti. While all the lesser offices rotated among the members, who thus acquired experience in a wide range of administrative skills, the position of warden was a long-term one. A list compiled by Matteo Palmieri in 1454 allows us to identify the wardens of four of the confraternities: Ser Antonio di Mariano Muzi, a respected notary and civil servant, in the Archangel Raphael; his brother Piero di Mariano Muzi, a purse-maker, in the Purification; Jacopo di Biagio, a cloth-shearer and one of the first twelve procurators of the Buonomini di San Martino, in the Vangelista; and Onofrio di Filippo di Bartolomeo, a shoemaker, in Sant'Antonio da Padova.[19] Of these four, only Ser Antonio could claim rank in Florence: as principal coadjutant and deputy to Poggio Bracciolini in the Florentine chancery, he must also have had a reasonable level of humanistic culture. The others were artisans, immersed in the values of lay piety and vernacular culture that Cosimo, Antoninus, and Eugenius had set out to foster.[20]

---

[17] Polizzotto, *Children*, 39–42. On the Purification company and its art, Ahl, "'In corpo di compagnia'"; Matchette, "The Compagnia"; O'Malley, "Altarpieces."

[18] Aranci, "La catachesi," 82–83, *scheda* 4.9. On Antoninus (Antonino Pierozzi, 1389–1459, canonized 1523), see Sanesi, "Sant'Antonino"; Orlandi, *S. Antonino*; Cinello and Paoli, eds., *Antonino*; Ventrone, "Sant'Antonino."

[19] Palmieri, *Historia Florentina*, 172–174; and chapter 4 below.

[20] In the Chancery from 1433 as coadjutor to Carlo Marsuppini and to Poggio Bracciolini, Antonio Muzi was Second Chancellor of the Florentine Republic from 1457 to 1475, and again from 1480 until his death in 1494, with a five-year interval as the notary of the *Tratte*. He notarized the act by which the company of Sant'Antonio da Padova was approved; see Eisenbichler, *The Boys*, 98–99. Vespasiano da Bisticci joined Antonio's company on the recommendation of Cardinal Giuliano Cesarini; Vespasiano da Bisticci, *Vite*, 132; Del Migliore, *Firenze*, 256. Antonio's brother, Piero di Mariano Muzi, a *borsaio* or purse-maker, is described as a *laudese* or singer of hymns in BAV, Chigi L.vii.266, fol. 28r; see Nosow, "Binchois's Songs," 235. For further information, see Newbigin, ed., *Nuovo*

After various relocations, the company of the Purification came under the direct patronage of Cosimo de' Medici, who financed their new oratory behind the newly-expanded Dominican friary of San Marco.[21] The Purification company preserved the narrative of this foundation and in 1501 copied it once again as a record of its debt to him, incurred more than half a century earlier:

> To the praise and glory and honour of almighty God, Father, Son, and Holy Spirit, and of the glorious everlasting Virgin Mary mother of Jesus Christ, and of St. Zanobi our head and leader, and of the most blessed martyrs St. Cosimo and St. Damian, and of all the heavenly, triumphant court, and for the benefit and consolation and peace of all the devout brothers of this company called the company of the Purification and of the Virgin Mary and of St. Zanobi (and those are our principal feast days), which meets and operates at the friars of San Marco. And it was Cosimo di Giovanni di Bicci de' Medici who built or commissioned the building for us for this purpose and for the health of his soul, as appears in his Building book 9, and it lists all the expenses one by one that he took on for the company of Piero di Mariano, our present warden, and in the entrance to this oratory there is a chapel dedicated to St. Cosimo and St. Damian, and Cosimo gave us an altarpiece painted with these saints to be used on the altar of this chapel, and beyond this chapel is our oratory, dedicated to the Purification of the Virgin Mary and St. Zanobi, with sacristies and other rooms belonging to the oratory, and a courtyard and well and garden, and Cosimo gave us possession in the year of our Lord Jesus Christ 1444, on 29 June, that is the Feast of St. Peter and St. Paul, and there was a solemn procession with all the brethren of the company dressed in white, and we were given the keys to the oratory by Ser Alesso di Matteo on his behalf,[22] and this oratory

---

corpus, XXIX, n. 29. Jacopo di Biagio is named in the earliest statutes of the Buonomini di di San Martino: Archivio dei Buonomini di San Martino, 1.1.1.0.1, *Codice dei Capitoli*; and also beneath the lunette in the Chiostro di Sant'Antonino of San Marco by Michelangelo Cinganelli (1558–1635), *Saint Antoninus Founds the Company of Good Men at San Martino*; see Hughes-Johnson, "The Fresco Decoration," 89–90.

[21] Polizzotto, *Children*, 49–52.

[22] On Ser Alesso di Matteo Pelli, see D.V. Kent, "A Window."

was built with the permission of the friars of San Marco, and the friars granted him the land freely, in order to build the oratory, because they were certain that it was a worthy enterprise; and it is our intention to give praise to God there in our meetings, and to pray to God for Cosimo, asking Him to grant grace for this good deed that he has done for us, and to reward him in the life hereafter. And so may it be, for his piety and mercy.[23]

The patron provided materially for the confraternity, and the *confratelli* prayed for the soul of their patron. The Purification company remained closely aligned with Cosimo and his successors, and their devotional and charitable interests — *pietà* and *misericordia* — are reflected in every aspect of the Purification confraternity's activities.

La rappresentazione della Purificazione

Cosimo's role in the 'invention' of the *sacra rappresentazione* is more difficult to determine. For Paola Ventrone, the plays were part of a project developed by Antoninus and Cosimo de' Medici in the 1440s to educate young people as perfect Christians and citizens.[24] It is plausible, indeed, that Cosimo may have encouraged a Marian *festa* in the oratory of the Purification company, to complement (but certainly not to rival) the great *feste* across the Arno. And from this first experience, the warden of the confraternity may have moved on to experiment with his play of the Prodigal Son.

The Purification statutes were revised when the company moved to San Marco in 1444, but they were only approved by Antoninus, now archbishop of Florence, on 3 April 1448.[25] It is there that the first reference to a representation of the Purification appears. Chapter XXIII of the statutes reads as follows:

> *Concerning our feast day of the Purification of Our Lady and those of St. Zenobius and of Saints Cosmas and Damian.* To the praise and honour of the glorious Virgin Mary, mother of Jesus Christ, our advocate and guide, we ordain that every year on the day of

---

[23] ASF, CRSPL 1646 (P.xxx.7), fol. 240ʳ; see Appendix, doc. 6.

[24] Ventrone, *Teatro civile,* 140–142. See also Newbigin, "*Serio ludere.*"

[25] See n. 13 above.

her Purification a most solemn *festa* be celebrated with devotion
in our oratory, and in order to do this, our warden should adopt
the following procedure. He is to elect the number of brethren
that he deems sufficient to be the *festaiuoli* in charge of the *festa*,
and these *festaiuoli* will be diligent in adorning our oratory properly with laurel or myrtle, and bench-drapes, or other things, such
as are appropriate for our oratory, and are virtuous and devout.
And if it is possible to get enough priests to sing a high mass, then
let that be done in the name of God, otherwise let one or more
low masses be said, as our warden deems fit. The warden should
give orders for enough bread buns to be made to give one to each
fratello, and let them be blessed by the priest, and the priest who
says mass will hand them out himself and the brethren will take
them devoutly, and if it is possible to give a candle that has been
blessed along with the bun, then our warden should arrange for
them to be bought. And to save our confraternity expense and to
be able to hand out buns on that morning, we desire that in the
month of January every year each of the brethren be required to
give and to pay two *soldi di piccioli* and this money be collected
by the *camarlinghi* and they are to keep a record of it in an account book called the Subscription Book, and this money is to
be spent on making the bread and on buying wax and the other
things for the *festa* and the buns are each to weigh two ounces
and up to three and no more, and on the day of the Purification
of Our Lady, and afterwards at the supper, the brethren should
be assiduous in singing hymns and solemn [canticles].[26] Afterwards, the representation should be done of the Purification of
Our Lady, that is, when she took our Lord Jesus Christ to the
temple with her tiny offering.[27]

The addition of a *rappresentazione* among the regular embellishments
of a confraternal feast day is without precedent in this confraternity, although
it was already the norm in the adult *laudesi* confraternities across the Arno.
From their earliest surviving financial records, dating to 1434, the standard

---

[26] A word is omitted and a space left in both manuscripts; the formula of "laude e
cantiche" is found elsewhere.

[27] Bloomington, Lilly, MR 26, fols. 30ᵛ–32ʳ; see Appendix, doc. 7, and also Magl.
vιιι.1500.11, fol. 19ʳ⁻ᵛ.

payments for the feast of 2 February — known in Italian as the *festa della Purificazione* or *Candelora*, and in English as the Feast of the Purification of the Blessed Virgin Mary, or of the Presentation of Christ at the Temple, or as Candlemas — were for string and nails, for making bunches of fragrant laurel and myrtle leaves and attaching them to the walls of the oratory, for porters to bring in benches for the supper, and for bread rolls and candles, costing in all less than £1 each year.[28] On 2 February 1447/8, however, just after the new statutes had been ratified, their spending on the *festa*, combined with their spending on Carnival, leaped to £16 18s. 2d., a sum regrettably not itemized in their general accounts but transferred from the Subscription Book that had been required by the new statutes.[29] In that year, Candlemas fell in the last week of Carnival, and Piero di Mariano, the warden of the confraternity, ordered *berlingozzi* or sweet fried dough for the celebration. But, more importantly, I believe that he had found a way of diverting the *fanciulli* from the mischief of Carnival, with its masquing and *mummie*, into a new and wholesome form of activity: just as his new statutes stipulated, Piero di Mariano was staging a play.[30]

The expenses for the following February 1448/9 were incorporated into the general accounts, and the preparation process was now clearly visible. Money was spent on refurbishing things for the play, and on colours for painting the faces. Even though some of the items purchased the previous year must have been reused, the confraternity was still paying for the new wigs of the angels and prophets in March.[31] But it is the expenses for February

---

[28] See, for example, ASF, CRSPL 1654 (P.xxx.30), fol. 83ᵛ (1445): payments for "bread rolls, candles, tacks, and nails to decorate the *festa* [...] one quart of oil" (panellini [...] chandele [...] bullette e chiovi per achonciare la festa [...] 1° quarto d'olio).

[29] ASF, CRSPL 1654 (P.xxx.30), fol. 88ʳ, 1 February 1447/8: "Per più ispese fatte in dette feste ccioè di Santta Maria Chandelaia e di Charnacciale [...] lire 16 soldi 18 denari 2" (For various expenses for the said *feste*, that is, for Candlemas and Carnival [...] £16 18s. 2d).

[30] On Carnival in Florence, see Ciappelli, *Carnevale e Quaresima*, and especially 172–180. On diverting young men from the vanities of Carnival, Trexler, "Ritual in Florence," 219.

[31] ASF, CRSPL 1654 (P.xxx.30), fol. 88ᵛ: "per cholori a dì 17 di gennaio soldi 3" (for colours on 17 January, 3s.); fol. 89ʳ: "libre dua di chandele di segha per veder [*cancelled*: lume] achonciare le chase [chose?] della festa [...] tre libre d'auti soldi dodisci [...] ispagho da far filze [...] cholori per dipingnere i visi" (for 2 lbs of suet candles to see [*cancelled*: light] to fix up the houses [things?] for the festa, [...] three pounds of nails 12s., [...] for string to make garlands, [...] for colours for painting the faces); fol. 89ᵛ: "per dua libre

1449/50 that make it unequivocally clear that a play was being performed. In addition to the usual expenditure for greenery, nails, and string, they bought taffeta of various colours for the angels; large sheets of paper, and gold, to cover "Jonah's fish," which constituted a major scenic element; gold to put stars on the angels' robes, on Simeon's hat, and on three other hats; gold for the temple and for the steps in front of it; and nails for the construction of a *palchetto* (raised platform) and/or a *tramezzo* (dividing wall used as an acting space) in the oratory. The final expenses were for attendants to stand at the door and guard it, and for a bushel of bread rolls for the supper afterwards.[32] The play is without doubt a play of the Presentation of Christ at the Temple, as related in Luke 2:22–38, which was the primary devotion of the confraternity and which would later be incorporated into the predella of its altarpiece (fig. 3.2).[33] The cast included Simeon and Anna, Mary and Joseph, and angels, as we find in the pictorial tradition, but theatrical elements were added. The decorated leviathan, Jonah's 'fish,' must have represented Limbo, from which prophets could be called forth to prophesy the birth of the Messiah.[34]

Like the Annunciation *festa*, already well established in San Felice in Piazza, the Purification play began with prophets whose presence was probably inspired by the far older tradition of the *Ordo Prophetarum*. The Procession of Prophets was part of the medieval liturgy for Christmas, and based on the Pseudo-Augustinian *Sermo contra Judaeos, Paganos, et Arianos Sermo*

---

di chanapa pettinata per fare le chalpelliere algli angnoli e a' profeti soldi otto" (for two pounds of combed hemp to make the wigs for the angels and the prophets, 8s.).

[32] ASF, CRSPL 1654 (P.xxx.30), fol. 90ᵛ–91ᵛ. The expenses are discussed in Newbigin, "The Word Made Flesh."

[33] The scene is part of the predella of their altarpiece, commissioned from Benozzo Gozzoli in 1461. The central panel, *Virgin and Child Enthroned among Angels and Saints*, is in the National Gallery, London; the other surviving predella panels are in the collection of Her Majesty Queen Elizabeth (*The Fall of Simon Magus*, RCIN 403372, see fig. 5.12 below); the Pinacoteca di Brera, Milan (*St. Dominic restores Napoleone Orsini to life*, inv. 1221); the Gemäldegalerie, of the Staatliche Museen zu Berlin-Preussischer Kulturbesitz (*St. Zenobius resurrecting a child*, inv. 60c); and the National Gallery of Art, Washington D.C. (*The Feast of Herod and the Beheading of St. John the Baptist*, Kress 1952.2.3). While the last two can be seen as invoking protection for children, the first three may be related to the confraternity's public performances.

[34] The representation of Limbo as a leviathan's mouth, in depictions of the Harrowing of the Hell, is relatively rare in Central Italy (Worthen, "The Harrowing of Hell," 51), but common elsewhere. The 'teeth' that surround the mouth of Limbo in Andrea di Bonaiuto's *Harrowing of Hell* in the Sala Capitolare of Santa Maria Novella are a clear acknowledgement of this association; see also Guccini, "Le fauci."

de Symbolo.[35] In France the *Ordo* grew in the context of the cathedral schools and the *Libertas Decembris*, the days of licence preceding Christmas Day. In fourteenth-century Rouen, Beauvais, and Sens it had developed into the *Festum Asinorum* (Feast of the Ass), with twenty-eight prophets (including Virgil and the Sibyl), ending with the arrival of the comic figure of Balaam riding on his recalcitrant ass and a scene with Nebuchadnezzar and the fiery furnace.[36] Although we have no record of similar activities in Florence, the Pseudo-Augustinian *Sermo* was certainly well known there,[37] and the dramatization of prophets (but not sibyls) that we find in the earliest Purification text, dating to the early 1460s, has echoes of the summons and response recited in the *Sermo*. The 1449 play, like the text that survives of the *Play of the Purification, that is, when the Virgin Mary presented Jesus Christ in the Temple to Simeon,*[38] must have been similar in its structure and proportions to

---

[35] Young, "*Ordo Prophetarum,*" and *The Drama*, 2:125–171. The *Sermo* dates to the fifth or sixth century.

[36] By the eleventh or twelfth century, a version from the Monastery of St. Martial at Limoges is fully 'dramatized' in Latin verse set to music, while the thirteenth-century version from Laon contains a list of characters and details of their costumes: for example, "Isaiah: bearded, dressed in a dalmatic, with a red stole over his shoulders, hanging down front and back" (Ysaias: barbatus, dalmatica indutus, stola rubea per medium verticis ante et retro dependens); Young, *The Drama*, 2:145.

[37] See, for example, the two fifteenth-century manuscripts in BMLF, San Marco 620 (1375), and San Marco 673 (Sec. XII; *ex* Niccolò Niccoli). The *Sermo* is documented as part of the liturgy in sixteenth-century Salerno; see De Bartholomaeis, *Le origini*, 452, 496–498.

[38] BNCF, Conv. Soppr. F.3.488, fols. 87^r–96^v "Qui comincia la rapresentatione della purifichatione cioè quando la uergine Maria presentò Giesù Xpo nel tempio a Simione" (Here begins the play of the Purification, that is, when the Virgin Mary presented Jesus Christ in the temple to Simeon). It follows immediately after the Nativity with Octavian and the Sibyl, which Nicolaio had finished copying on 29 July 1465. The opening line of the *Purificazione*, "Dio vi salvi tutti, o frate miei" (God save you all, my brothers) bears a striking resemblance to the opening of Machiavelli's *Mandragola*, "Idio vi salvi, benigni auditori" (God save you, gentle listeners, Prologo, 1.1) — a comedy which in turn contains echoes of both Annunciation and Purification plays; see Newbigin, "Machiavelli, Pirandello." I have looked in vain for the name of Niccolò di messer Bernardo Machiavelli among the members of the company of the Purification, but from 1456 his father, Messer Bernardo di Niccolò Machiavelli, was a member of the parent company, Santa Maria della Pietà, called the Buca di San Girolamo, which met in the hospital of San Matteo next door to San Marco; see Henderson, "Le confraternite," 93; Black, *Machiavelli*, 9.

The sibyls appear for the first time in the miscellany BRF, Ricc. 1720, fols. 72^r–82^r, undated, but the watermark of *lunettes* (similar to Briquet 10624, 10626) suggests a date

the Annunciation. A weighty procession of prophets — probably augmented over time — introduced, in the *Purificazione*, a very short dramatization of the gospel narrative: the presentation of Christ at the Temple and Simeon's short canticle, the *Nunc dimittis* (Luke 2:22–39); and, in the *Annunciazione*, the angelic salutation followed by the *Magnificat* (Luke 1:26–55). The surviving prophecies in the various Annunciation texts, the Purification, and the single sheet engravings of the prophets and sibyls attributed to Baccio Baldini have a very complex relationship that I have explored elsewhere.[39]

Was the Purification company the first youth confraternity to stage a play? According to the seventeenth-century antiquary Ferdinando Leopoldo Del Migliore, Pope Eugenius IV, in the company of the entire Signoria of Florence, was present in 1430 when a Nativity play was performed in San Pancrazio by the youths of the confraternity of the Archangel Raphael, but the information appears spurious, and the date clearly not possible.[40] Instead,

---

between 1455 and 1478. The later printed Purification play incorporates both prophets (just Jacob, Daniel, and Malachai, who come to Simeon) and shepherds (who come again with gifts to Bethlehem) but contains no direct link with the manuscript tradition. See *Rappresentatione della purificatione di nostra Donna: Cioè la Festa di sancta Maria Candellaia* (Florence: [heirs of Bartolomeo de' Libri], for Bartolomeo di Matteo Castelli, c.1520–1525), CNCE 61924; Cioni, *Bibliografia*, 232, LXVIIII.1; for modern edition, see Table 2.

[39] See Newbigin, "Feo Belcari, Baccio Baldini"; and also Dempsey, *The Early Renaissance*.

[40] Del Migliore, *Registro*, BNCF, Magl. XXV.418, fol. 59ʳ: "L'anno 1430 per una rapresentazione della Natività del Signore, che alcuni di quei giovanetti recitavano in San Pancrazio alla presentia di Papa Eugenio 4° e di tutta la Signoria con aplauso grandissimo, se ne passarono col favore di quel Pontefice, a cui piacque grandemente la vivezza di quella gioventù veduta in quell'atto, ad abitare in una semplice chiesa dell'ospedale della Scala aprovando i *Capitoli*, ne' quali volse che la Compagnia militasse sotto nome della Natività del Signore et havesse per avocato l'Angiol Raffaello" (In the year 1430, on account of a play of the Nativity of the Lord that some of these boys performed to great applause in San Pancrazio in the presence of Pope Eugenius IV and all the Signoria, they moved with the support of the pope, who very much liked the vigour of these young people that he had seen in that play, to take up residence in a simple church belonging to the Ospedale della Scala, and he approved their statutes, in which he required that the Company should march under the banner of the Nativity of the Lord and that it should have as its advocate the Angel Raphael). See also Eisenbichler, *The Boys*, 30, and 352, n. 33. Eugenius was elected pope on 3 March 1430/1 and fled to Florence only in June 1434 (while Cosimo de' Medici was still in exile), taking up residence in Santa Maria Novella. With the exception of the period April 1436 to January 1438/9, Eugenius remained in Florence, returning to Rome only late in 1443. He died in Rome on 8 March 1446/7; see Pastor, *The History*, 1:303. Since other evidence cited by Eisenbichler, *The Boys*, 34–35, indicates that the

we can confidently assert that probably in February 1448/9 and certainly in February 1449/50, the Confraternity of the Purification produced a *festa* modelled on the liturgical *feste* of the adult *laudesi* confraternities across the Arno.

La festa del vitel sagginato

The lads of the confraternity had clearly developed a taste for theatricals, and six weeks later, for Carnival 1449/50 — with engagement in chaste and virtuous playmaking keeping them away from violent and lascivious entertainments — they prepared another play: the *Play of the Fatted Calf*. The entry in their account book records two payments: "on 19 February to Giovanni, messenger of the customs collectors, 2*s*. for the permit for the heifer of the *Play of the Fatted Calf*; and two days later: "to Bartolomeo d'Antonio the butcher for the flour for the *berlingozzi* that were made for the *Play of the Fatted Calf*, 3*s*. and 8*d*."[41]

Here for the first time, we have reference to an identifiable text: *La festa del Vitel sagginato*, written by Piero di Mariano Muzi, warden of the

confraternity already had rooms in the Ospedale della Scala in 1427, and that the links of the San Paolo company with San Pancrazio are fictitious, it is probably safer to discount Del Migliore's assertion. On the question of the Nativity and the Pope, see also Leuker, *Bausteine*, 71 and n. 26; Ventrone, *Teatro civile*, 142, n. 137, suggesting a date closer to 1442. On Del Migliore's notorious unreliability, see Del Lungo, "Le vicende," 12–13, who cites a contemporary's opinion of him as "a modern antiquary who makes great claims about everything and mistakes molehills for mountains" (un antiquario moderno che pretende sopra tutte le cose e piglia granchi come balene).

Eugenius and some of his cardinals contributed to the Ascension *festa* of 1442 (Newbigin, *Feste*, 2:398), while Aeneas Silvius Piccolomini, the future Pope Pius II, accompanied by the Signoria and the German Emperor Frederick III, may have witnessed a performance of the Resurrection in front of Santa Maria del Fiore on 2 February 1451/2 (Newbigin, "'Quasi insalutato ospite,'" 8 and 38), but I have found no other claims of papal patronage. As Pius II, Piccolomini may have seen a procession of *edifici* in April 1459, when he and the youthful Galeazzo Maria Sforza were guests in Florence; Benedetto Dei, *La cronica*, 68, lists "l'Agniolo Raffaello" among the companies that went in procession to honour the visitors with "a large number of floats and plays and devotions" (*edifici* and *rapresentazioni e divozioni assai*).

[41] ASF, CRSPL 1654 (P.xxx.30), fol. 91ᵛ, 19 and 21 February 1449/50: "a dì 19 di febraio a Giovanni messo della doghana soldi dua per la licenza della vitella della *Festa del vitel saginato* soldi 2"; "a Baltolommeo d'Antonio becchaio per la farina de' berlinghozi che si feciono per la *Festa del vitel saginato* soldi 3 danari 8." Ash Wednesday fell on 18 February.

confraternity, and known in eight manuscripts.[42] When Muzi's text was print-ed in the 1490s by Bartolomeo de' Libri, the woodcut of the title page showed the fatted calf, a stage prop rather than supper, at the banquet prepared for the Prodigal Son (fig. 3.3).[43] The play is quintessentially apt. Like the par-able of the Prodigal Son in Luke 15:11–32, it cautions boys and young men against the folly of disobeying their fathers, but promises them unconditional love, forgiveness, and delight when they return to a virtuous life and live in harmony with their brothers.[44] The play embodies the confraternities' broad-est moral, religious, and pedagogic ideals, teaching young men by example to turn away from sinful company and toward virtue, exercise free will, and accept that filial duty should overcome all sense of personal entitlement. Even so, it has its origins, like so many of the *rappresentazioni* that will follow, in a deeply rooted generational hostility that is here reconciled.

The action starts slowly as the Younger Son argues with his Father and his Father's steward, Free Will. The pace quickens as the Younger Son takes up with the *brigata* of Seven Deadly Sins, led by Pride himself, and heads off to indulge in riotous living (the Vulgate is explicit that this was whoring, *vivendo luxuriose*, Luke 15:13), while the Older Son is instructed by his Father to visit their rural landholdings and settle the accounts with tenant farmers, skills ab-solutely essential for owners of even the smallest farms outside the city walls. There are no scenes of pigsties and squalor; the Prodigal Son simply returns in tatters and is welcomed by his Father who summons the personifications of Hope, Prudence, and Joy to make him welcome. The aggrieved Older Son is reconciled with his Father, and musicians are summoned. A banquet is prepared, and the play ends with feasting — the confraternal feast is part of the play, and the *confratelli* are the invited guests — and dancing to a *lauda*

---

[42] The attribution to Muzi is found in BAV, Chigi L.vii.266, fol. 62ᵛ. For manuscripts, modern edition, and translation, see Table 1.

[43] *La festa del uitel sagginato* ([Florence: Bartolomeo de' Libri, not after 1495]), ISTC iv00305500; Cioni, *Bibliografia*, 303, cvii.1. No subsequent edition of the play is known, but the woodblock was reused in *Epistole & Euangelii* (1495), fol. xxxʳ, and copied in reverse for Castellano Castellani's *Figliuolo prodigo* (before 1515). That block was then re-used in Antonia Pulci's *Figliuol prodigo* (c. 1550). For a discussion of this play, and comparison with the two later versions of the parable, see Neri, "Studi," 9–16; Weaver, in Pulci, *Saints' Lives*, 47–54; Stallini, *Le théâtre*, 85–105 and 271–282; and Delcorno, *In the Mirror*, in particular 254–273. See also chapters 6 and 9 below.

[44] Dominici cites the stories of Cain and Abel, Isaac and Ishmael, and Esau and Jacob as key texts in teaching brothers to respect one another; Dominici, *Regola*, 148. The issue of brotherly rivalry is also taken up in the plays of Joseph and his brothers.

that shared a tune with a well-known popular song that cautioned young men to beware of taking a wife:

Deh! sappiatevi guardare	Be sure to keep yourselves from harm
dalle cattive compagnie,	and from bad company because
imperò ch'elle son rie	such friends are evil, and they lead
e fanno altrui malcapitare.	their fellows into sinfulness.

(*lauda* after oct. 54)[45]

The parable, beloved by dialectologists and perplexing to dutiful children, clearly provides problems for moralists. The comic charm of the "boon companions" who reveal themselves as Vices, and the luxury of the banquet, are clearly at odds with the ascetic virtue preached overall. One manuscript redaction goes out of its way to reduce our sympathy for the Older Son: he undertakes the duties imposed on him by his father, but the farmers come to complain that he is cheating them; another version, however, adds a stanza in which he too attempts to persuade his brother not to leave.[46] The moral, however, quite possibly relates to a particularly Florentine issue of laws of succession, which did not rely on primogeniture. The conflict of the play is resolved when the Older Son accepts his Father's instructions and greets his younger brother with the words: "I want you as my equal, | and everything I have is yours as well" (I' vo' che sia iguale | a me, e ciò ch'i' ho tu' è ancora; oct. 60.4–5).[47] The lessons are as much about the economics of family as about the need to avoid sin and bad company.

Muzi was a lesser poet than those who would follow. His syntactic units are seldom more than two lines of verse, linked paratactically rather than logically, and only rhyme holds the stanzas together. The vocabulary is repetitive. The rhymes are the simplest, relying extensively on infinitives and past

---

[45] The *cantasi come* is given in BAV, Chigi L.vii.266, fols. 258ᵛ–259ʳ (the play is copied earlier in the codex, fols. 62ᵛ–65ᵛ). The *canzone a ballo*, "Deh! sappiatevi guardare | O garzon, di non tôr moglie" (Be sure to keep yourself from harm, | my boy, and do not take a wife), is one of those that Benedetto Dei knew by heart, attributing it to "D. Arnolfi," otherwise unidentified; see Dei, *La cronica*, 183; Luisi, "Minima fiorentina," 89. The *lauda* was included in *Laude facte & composte* (1485/6), fol. cxxiiiiʳ⁻ᵛ, as the work of Piero di Mariano Muzi.

[46] The lines are added in BNCF, Conv. Soppr. F.3.488, fol. 18ʳ⁻ᵛ (after oct. 35), and in Siena, BCI, I.ii.33, fol. 5ʳ (after oct. 23).

[47] For what Florentines meant by 'substance' in the context of laws of succession, see Kuehn, *Heirs, Kin, and Creditors*.

participles. The play is the work of a fluent but ungifted improviser, writing in simple language for an unsophisticated audience. There are also some technical hesitations: Muzi is working in a new genre that is just establishing its conventions, and some of his terminology strikes us a strange. The play itself is called an 'annunciation' both at the beginning and at the end of the earliest manuscript.[48] The prologue is 'announced' by an Angel dressed in white, but a long rubric repeats in prose a paraphrase — not to be spoken aloud but for the benefit of the actors or readers — of what has just been announced in verse by the Angel. These technical uncertainties were quickly resolved, and later manuscripts adhered fully to the conventions of the *rappresentazioni* that became so firmly rooted that four decades later the *Angelo annunziatore* became the brand-identifier for the printed play.

The *feste* of Pentecost and Ascension on the other side of the Arno had established their own conventions of scenic space and could represent travel between Jerusalem and the Mount of Olives in the space of a stanza, but Muzi's set did not require such devices. He limited himself to a single space — outside the house of the Father — where the players sat, rising when they were to speak, in line with mid-fifteenth-century understanding of classical performance practice. Nevertheless, within that acting space there was room for a banquet with musicians and a *ballo tondo* or round dance where everybody — actors and audience — could join in singing, dancing, and, finally, feasting.

It is tempting to look for classical correlations in the unity of space observed in the *Vitel sagginato*. I am reluctant to see a direct link between the inexorable revival of interest in classical drama and the unity of place we might perceive here, but the protagonists of that revival were not far removed from the confraternity. Nicholas of Cusa, working as an agent for Poggio Bracciolini, had rediscovered an eleventh-century manuscript containing twelve lost plays of Plautus in 1427,[49] and Poggio spent several years claiming possession of it. Both Nicholas and Poggio had been in Florence in 1439. Piero

---

[48] BAV, Chig. L.vii.266, fols. 62v and 65v: "Qui si chomincierà l'annutiatione del Vangielo del Figliuolo prodigho e quando tornò al padre" (Here will begin the annunciation of the parable of the Prodigal Son and when he came back to his father); "Finita la nuziatione della festa, questa stanza si è del ringraziamento che aparicie l'angielo che à anuziata la festa e da licenza a tutti e dicie chosì …" (At the end of the annunciation of the *festa*, this stanza is by way of thanks, and the Angel who announced the *festa* bids everyone farewell and says …).

[49] Now BAV, Lat. 3870.

di Mariano Muzi's brother Antonio was, as we have seen, Poggio's coadjutor. The dividing line between humanistic passions and vernacular lay devotion was not impermeable, and it is possible that Muzi was influenced by classical practice in his use of space.[50]

La rappresentazione d'Abramo

At this very same moment, another play with a similar moral was being prepared: Feo Belcari's play of *Abramo*.[51] Known in manuscript and in the earliest editions as *La rappresentazione d'Abramo quando volse fare sacrificio di Isac* (The play of Abraham when he resolved to sacrifice Isaac), it was performed for the first time in 1449 — possibly at Easter, when Genesis 22:1–19 was the third reading for the Vigil of Easter — in the church of Santa Maria Maddalena in Cestello, the Cistercian monastery in Borgo Pinti where the confraternities' wardens were required to meet every three months.[52] The church had a large walled garden in front of the entrance (fig. 3.4),[53] which may have been used for the play in the same way that the Vangelista company's cloister would be used in 1491 for Lorenzo de' Medici's *San Giovanni e Paulo*.[54] It must have been there that it was seen by Roberto Caracciolo, the charismatic Franciscan preacher from Lecce, who recalled it in a sermon in Padua during Carnival 1451.[55] The preacher is discussing activities that

---

[50] On religious drama and the humanist tradition in sixteenth-century Germany, see Parente, *Religious Drama*. Ventrone, *Gli araldi della commedia*, deals with this intersection in fifteenth-century Florence.

[51] For manuscripts and printed editions, see chapter 7, and Tables 1 and 2.

[52] BNCF, Conv. Soppr. F.3.488, fol. 35v: "Finita la sopradetta *festa* e rappresentatione la quale si fece la prima volta in Firenze nella chiesa di Sancta Maria Madalena luogho detto Cestegli anno domini 1449 deo gratias amen" (The end of the above play and representation, which was done for the first time in Florence in the church of Santa Maria Maddalena, in the place called Cestello, in the year of our Lord 1449. Thanks be to God. Amen).

[53] The uncoloured sketch in Marco di Bartolomeo Rustici, *Codice Rustici*, fol. 19r, was added later than the other illustrations, but probably before Marco's death in 1457. Construction of the present cloister in front of the church was begun in 1491; see Luchs, "Cestello," 22–28.

[54] See chapter 7 and figs. 7.10 and fig. 7.11 below.

[55] Carracciolo's mention of the performance, in a sermon now dated to 1451, was recently brought to light by Pietro Delcorno: see Delcorno and Steenbrugge, "A Biblical Story," with an important discussion of the play and of this passage, on which I depend here.

are suitable for Carnival, and following Bonaventure and Antoninus, he cites spiritual plays and gives a specific example:

> In Florence such spectacles are performed very well. I saw the Ascension of Jesus Christ, done in such a way that it is unthinkable that the human heart would not be tenderly moved by it. It was truly an amazing performance. I remember that in the presence of some devout men the play was performed of the Obedience of Abraham, and there was much weeping.[56]

The play was hugely successful: at least thirty-seven manuscripts survive. Copies were made by lay and religious men and women;[57] it was reworked into prose[58] and into Abruzzese six-line stanzas;[59] and a number of presentation

---

[56] Caracciolo, *Quaresimale padovano, Sermo tripudii et quando licet tripudiare*, 98: "Florentie similia valde bene fiunt, vidi Assentionem Ihesu Christi fieri taliter quod non reputatum fuisset cor humanum quin se tenerime commovisset, profecto fuit stupenda devotio. Recordor quod inter quosdam devotos facta fuit representatio obedientie Abrae, ubi valde ploratum fuit." Caracciolo was in Florence for five months in 1448/9, from Lent onwards. For Antoninus's view, see below, chapter 4, nn. 101–102.

[57] BNCF, Magl. vii.367 seems to have been used in the Ridolfi family; Benedetta, wife of Piero d'Antonio Niccoli, copied *Abramo* in 1461, in BRF, Ricc. 1429, fol. 56ᵛ, 135ʳ; a father copied it for his son to copy again when he was older; see above, chapter 1, n. 1.

[58] BAnR, 2235 (sec. XV), fol. 48ʳ, in which Belcari's famous first *ottava* is paraphrased in prose as follows: "The eye, they say, is the first thing that the intellect understands and savours. The second, that's hearing with a clear voice, that makes our minds robust. So listen and you will hear a holy and pious story recited, but if you want to understand such a mystery, be devout and filled with desire to hear such a sweet and well-made story" (L'ogio se dicie che è la prima cossa la qualle lo inteletto vene a intendere e gustare la seconda e quello sie lo odire con voce scorta che fa la mente nostra essere robusta. Però intenditi e olderiti in sorta reciptare una storia sancta e pia ma se vollite intendere tale misterio stati divocti e con disiderio de oldire cossì fact'et dulcia istoria).

[59] BNCR, VE 361, fols. 54ʳ–64ᵛ, with a note on fol. 95ᵛ that reads: "The end. 1576, on the feast day of St. John the Baptist at Vespers. Pray to God for me, a wretched sinner, Maria Jacoba Fioria of Chieti, unworthy servant of the crucified Christ and of his mother Mary" (Finis 1576. Die sanctissimi Johannis Battista hora vesperis. Pregate Dio per me misera peccatrice Maria Jacoba Fioria teatina, indigna serva del Crucifixo et de sua matre Maria). On this codex from Chieti, see De Bartholomaeis and Rivera, eds., *Il teatro abruzzese*, 223–230 and 344–345; Nardecchia, "Per una nuova edizione." The manuscript opens with a *Rappresentazione di Rosana*, fols. 1ʳ–52ʳ, which is, however, unrelated to the Florentine *Rosana*, discussed later in this chapter.

copies were probably overseen by Feo himself.[60] The earliest surviving edition dates to c. 1485 (fig. 3.5), and none of the nine incunable editions survives in more than a single copy.[61]

Like the *Vitel sagginato,* Belcari's *Abramo* preaches the virtue of filial obedience: of Isaac to Abraham and of Abraham to God. By 1472, when Benedetto Dei (whose brother Miliano had married Feo Belcari's daughter Papera[62]) compiled his list of *feste* being performed annually in Florence, "the great *festa* of Abraham and Isaac and Sarah" was being done in San Giorgio, which I take to be the youth confraternity of Sant'Antonio da Padova that had its oratory on the Costa San Giorgio in the Oltrarno.[63]

Belcari already had a strong sense of the genre that he was creating and may already have had experience writing stanzas for the *edifici* that went in the San Giovanni procession. He commanded attention with an opening stanza that has become emblematic of the whole genre:

L'occhio si dice ch'è la prima porta	The eye is the first gateway, it is said
per la qual l'intelletto intende e gusta;	by which the mind can savour and perceive;
la seconda è l'udir con voce scorta	and hearing is the second, with clear voice,
che fa la vostra mente esser robusta.	that makes all of your minds to be robust.
Però vedrete ed udirete in sorta	You'll see, therefore, and hear in such a way
recitar una storia santa e giusta,	a just and holy story performed here,
ma se volete intender tal misterio,	but if you want to grasp this mystery,
state devoti e con buon desiderio.	watch it devoutly and with all good will.

(oct. 1)

---

[60] Belcari himself sent a copy of his plays to Barbara of Brandenburg, Marchioness of Mantua, after her daughter-in-law had praised some of his poems when she visited Florence (see his letter in Newbigin, *Feste,* 2:252–253), and addressed two sonnets to her, dated 13 April and 28 August 1468 (see Belcari, *Le rappresentazioni,* 171–173). On the relationship between the Belcari manuscripts, see Nosow, "Binchois's Songs," 222–225; Wilson, *Singing Poetry,* 57–62.

[61] ISTC ib00297200, ib00297250, ib00297300, ib00297350, ib00297400, ib00297500, ib00297600, ib00297700, ib00297800; see Newbigin, "Feo Belcari's *Rappresentazione*," and chapter 7 below.

[62] Di Crescenzo, "The Imagined Family."

[63] Dei, *La cronica,* 93: "fassì la gran festa d'Abran e d'Isah e di Sarra." On Belcari's *Abramo,* see Maier, "Due 'sacre rappresentazioni'"; Guccini, "Retoriche," and "Domande"; Newbigin, "Il testo e il contesto," and "'L'occhio si dice'"; Eisenbichler, "Per un nuovo approccio"; Ventrone, "La *Rappresentazione di Abraam*"; and D.V. Kent, "'La cara e buona immagine.'"

Although the vehicle of the *sacra rappresentazione* was the *ottava rima* of popular narrative, Belcari was fully aware that a new visual element had been introduced. The eye and the ear had to attend simultaneously to the *storia* in order to *intendere* — not just hear but understand and savour — the inner mystery.[64] The play is relentlessly didactic: the story is narrated by the Angel, enacted in the course of the play, and narrated again by Isaac to his mother, so there was no possibility of any audience member failing to know what was going on.[65] The play does not deviate greatly from the biblical account, but — as he told Giovanni di Cosimo de' Medici (1421–1463) in the dedicatory sonnet he attached to the play (fig. 1.2) — Belcari also drew on other sources. He could not use a scholastic method of exegesis, with multiple possibilities, refuted one by one; he had to make a coherent series of choices in his characterization.

For the emotions and the reasonings of the characters, his source is Josephus's *Jewish Antiquities*.[66] Josephus's Isaac, however, is twenty-five years old and makes no mention of his mother. For Belcari's purposes, despite the continuous evocation of Isaac as a prefiguration of Christ, a younger Isaac was important: he needed to be old enough to make his own rational decision, but young enough to be stripped bare and bound on the altar, to be a model of docility, and to engender pathos with his invocation of his mother.[67] Belcari developed this scenario from the biblical exegesis of the Franciscan Nicholas of Lyra (c. 1265–1349), whose exposition of the Bible was said to

---

[64] The starting point may be the Peripatetic axiom, "Nothing is in the intellect that was not first in the senses" (Nihil est in intellectu quod non sit prius in sensu), found in Thomas Aquinas, *De veritate*, q. 2 art. 3 arg. 19, deriving ultimately from Aristotle. On the opening stanzas of *cantari* and *rappresentazioni*, see Ventrone, "Per una morfologia," 206–213; Delcorno Branca, "Fra cantare e sacra rappresentazione," 100–101; on visual and verbal storytelling as the first basis of child-raising, see Dominici, *Regola*, 130–133; on the eye and ear in the plays, see Newbigin, "'L'occhio si dice'"; on the decorum of attention, see Gaston, "Attention."

[65] On the effect of the triple narrative, see Maier, "Due 'sacre rappresentazioni.'"

[66] Josephus, *Jewish Antiquities*, 1 (1930): 108–117, 1.4.222–236; for a discussion of the sources see Newbigin, "Il testo e il contesto," and for an alternative view Guccini, "Retoriche," final note. Caracciolo, cited above, n. 56, is exceptional in his recollection of the emotional response to this pathos.

[67] On contemporary theories of age and intellectual development, see Taddei, "Puerizia." For a discussion of the age of Isaac in English medieval drama, see Woolf, "The Effect of Typology," 813–814; on 'mother love' in the Abraham plays, Riggio, "The Terrible Mourning," 298–304; on other plot elements, see Elliott, "The Sacrifice."

have influenced Luther.[68] In his *postillae* to Genesis 22, Nicholas discusses Isaac's age — thirty-five [*sic*] "as in Josephus" (although twenty-five is the age more commonly found in texts of Josephus) — and the extent to which his obedience was rational and freely given.[69] Belcari works with both extremes to present an Isaac who is still a child (*puer, fanciullo*) but is nevertheless rationally obedient to his father and to God.

ISAC, *con la ragione superiore vincendo la inferiore e intendendo chiaro che doveva ancora resuscitare, dice*:	ISAAC, *his superior reason triumphing over his inferior reason,*[70] *and understanding clearly that he would rise again from the dead, says*:
O fedel padre mio, quantunque el senso pel tuo parlar riceva angoscia e doglia, pur sed e' piace al nostro Dio immenso ch'i' versi il sangue e arsa sia la spoglia in questo loco sopra 'l foco accenso, vo' star contento all'una e l'altra voglia, dico, di Dio e di te, dolce padre, perdendo tante cose alte e leggiadre.	O faithful father, even though I sense anguish and sorrow for these words of [yours, yet if it pleases our almighty God that I should shed my blood and then be [burned in this place, here upon the burning fire, I'll happily submit to both your wills, that is, to God's, sweet father, and to yours, although I forfeit great and lovely things. (oct. 31)

From Origen's *Selecta in Genesim*, which he must have read in Latin rather the Greek,[71] Belcari develops the parallels between Isaac and Christ. Glossing Genesis 22:6, for example, "And he took the wood for the holocaust, and laid it upon Isaac his son: and he himself carried in his hands fire and a sword. And [...] they two went on together," Origen pointed to the parallel between Isaac carrying the wood into the desert and Christ carrying the Cross out of Jerusalem. Belcari further creates distinct echoes of the Gospels, for

---

[68] This is according to the adage "Si Lyra non *Lyrasset*, Lutherus non *saltasset*" (Had the Lyre/Lyra not played, the Luthier/Luther would not have danced). For Nicholas's commentary I have used *Biblia latina cum postillis Nicolai de Lyra* (1481).

[69] Josephus, *Jewish Antiquities*, 1 (1930): 112–113, I.4.227.

[70] According to Thomas Aquinas, *Summa*, I.79.9.co., higher and lower reason are different functions of the intellect by which we know the eternal and the temporal respectively.

[71] Origen, *PG* 12 (1862):117–120, *Selecta in Genesim* 37–38; *PG* 12 (1862): 203–210, *In Genesim Homilia* VIII.

example with Isaac's words: "My soul is full of sorrow and of woe | for what you've said, and even unto death" (Tutt'è l'anima mia trista e dolente | per tal precetto e sono in agonia; oct. 29.1–2), which echo Christ's words in Matthew 26:38, "My soul is sorrowful even unto death" (Tristis est anima mea usque ad mortem). Belcari further reinforces the typological link between Isaac and Christ by representing Sarah with the attributes of Mary: grieving over her son's departure, comforted by her servants and even, in one important codex, by two *ancille* (handmaidens).[72]

Belcari takes command of his narrative and establishes the conventions of scenic space, journey, and time that will remain fixed for the genre. The grand *feste* of the *laudesi* confraternities superimposed one miraculous moment on the great everlasting narrative of heaven. In Belcari's play, there are no unities of time and place. The action ranges from the house of Abraham to the mount but seems to make nothing of the symbolic centrality of that mountain: Moriah, Zion, and later the Temple Mount. Instead, it represents 'far, far away,' a distant uninhabited Calvary on the other side of a wasteland, while Abraham's house represents the inhabited 'here.' The two-day journey into the desert, with Abraham, Isaac, two servants, and an ass, is accomplished in one stanza (oct. 15); the joyful journey down the mountain after the sacrifice takes two stanzas of song (oct. 50–51).

From the account books of the Sant'Agnese confraternity, we know that the mountain of the Ascension was made at various times of just three steps, or of a raised platform covered with painted hessian and decorated with trees in pots.[73] The Abraham and Isaac panels prepared by Brunelleschi and Ghiberti in 1401, as they competed for the commission to make the second set of Baptistery doors (figs. 3.6 and 3.7), show how the iconography can be reduced to a bare minimum and still tell the whole story.[74] The 'house' of Abraham, like the house of the Prodigal Son, is not described in any way, but here my impression — and it is only that — is of a tent, such as we see in Ghiberti's panel in the Porte del Paradiso (fig. 3.8). There is no attempt, such as we saw in the *Vitel sagginato*, to move the action indoors.

---

[72] BAV, Chigi L.vii.266, fols. 69ʳ–62ᵛ with addition on fol. 109ʳ. The stanzas are transcribed in Newbigin, "Il testo e il contesto," 35–36; for translation, see Newbigin online.

[73] Newbigin, *Feste*, 1:97; 2:392 (1442).

[74] According to Vasari, Brunelleschi gave his unsuccessful panel to Cosimo de' Medici, and it was later incorporated into the *dossale* of the altar in the Old Sacristy in San Lorenzo; Vasari, *Le vite* (1568), 1:305. This may have contributed to Giovanni di Cosimo de' Medici's particular affection for Abraham, noted by Belcari in his dedicatory sonnet; Belcari, *Le rappresentazioni*, 2.

As the prologue states, the ear is the second gateway to understanding, and Belcari's play has a particular aural texture. After the Angel's prologue, and the call of the second Angel, Abraham dominates the play, which is one-quarter done before Isaac first speaks in octave 17. Isaac's role grows, however, until he comes down the mountain singing a *lauda* so sweetly that Abraham's servants compliment him on it.[75] Isaac has found his voice: Abraham is too tired to speak when they return to Sarah, so it is the boy who tells his mother what has happened. She rejoices and orders singing and dancing, and the play concludes with a *lauda* that was destined to enjoy considerable fame. In the manuscripts (but not in the printed tradition) the rubric before octave 61 reads: "All the members of the household do a round-dance and they sing this *lauda*,[76] each one accompanied by an Angel" (Tutta la famiglia di casa fa uno ballo tondo et canta questa laude essendo ciascuno accompagnato da uno Angelo; see fig. 1.3), a scene that evokes Fra Angelico's *Last Judgment* panel, painted for the Camaldolese monastery of Santa Maria degli Angeli (fig. 3.9).[77]

Storia di Jacob ed Esaù

While Belcari's *Abramo* and Muzi's *Vitel sagginato* had considerable success, a third play, the *Storia di Jacob ed Esaù*, disappeared almost without trace. The *Story of Jacob and Esau* is known in a single undated manuscript that preserves no indication of its original owner or purpose (fig. 3.10).[78] The co-dex contains three *rappresentazioni* and a collection of *laude* and religious verse, largely anonymous. The first two are *Abramo* and the *Vitel sagginato*; *Jacob ed Esaù* is the third and belongs in all probability to the same period

---

[75] On these stanzas and their musical setting, See also below, chapter 9, n. 150.

[76] "Chi serve a dio con purità di core"; a polyphonic setting of the refrain only is in Wilson, *Singing Poetry*, 73. See also Osthoff, *Theatergesang*, 30–31.

[77] After the first printed edition, the stage direction becomes "Sarah and all the other members of the household except Abraham and those two Angels, the one who announced the *festa* and the other one who appeared to him on the mountain, they all do a dance together singing this hymn" (Sarra & tutti gli altri di casa excepto d'Abraam & quegli due angioli luno che annuntio la festa laltro che gli appari insul monte & tutti insieme fanno uno ballo cantando questa lauda), *Qui comincia larapresentatione da habram* ([Florence: Bartolomeo de' Libri], 24 October 1485), ISTC ib00297200, fol. a10ʳ.

[78] BNCF, Landau Finaly 249, fols. 32ʳ–44ʳ; see Lazzi and Rolih, eds., *I manoscritti Landau Finaly*, 2:242–427. The script is a fifteenth-century *gotica bastarda*, on paper with a horse watermark similar to Briquet 3561; for edition, see Table 1.

and the same milieu of youth confraternities. Like Belcari's *Abramo*, it has as its source the extraordinary poetry of Genesis, and the author has done little more than versify those parts of chapters 27–29 and 31–32 that he (or she) wished to retain.[79] If I am right in seeing this play as close in date to Belcari's *Abramo* and to Muzi's *Vitel sagginato*, then it too is roughly contemporary with the unveiling of Lorenzo Ghiberti's Doors of Paradise in the Florentine Baptistery in 1452 (fig. 3.11), and deals with the same ideas.[80] Discussing the Isaac panel, which layers seven exquisite episodes from the difficult birth of the twin boys to Isaac's blessing of Jacob, Paul Barolsky draws attention to the intense speaking and listening of the scene, and to the demands on the viewer to hear what is being said.[81] Like Belcari's *Abraham*, *Jacob ed Esaù* calls upon the eye and the ear.[82] The generic self-reflection of Belcari's first stanza is not repeated in the *Storia di Jacob ed Esaù* but the first line of the second stanza:

Nel Genesi appar distesamente	In Genesis, the story's told at length
che da Abramo Isacche discese...	of Isaac, Abraham's begotten son...
	(oct. 2.1–2)

is an evident echo of Belcari's second stanza:

Nel Genesi la santa Bibbia narra	In Genesis the Bible tells how God
che Dio volse provar l'ubidienzia	decided he would test if Abraham
del patriarca Abram, sposo di Sarra,	the patriarch, married to Sarah, would
un angel gli parlò in presenzia.	obey him, speaking to him through an angel.
	(oct. 2.1–4)

Our anonymous author shows here (and later, as I will discuss) a clear awareness of Belcari's model but is conscious of operating in a new genre and is still trying to find a way through its conventions. The play is not yet called a

---

[79] There may also be traces of an influence of Antoninus's *Summa Theologica*. For Antoninus, as for biblical commentators, Jacob prefigured Christ and Esau stood for hatred of Christ and the Christless wicked; Antoninus, *Summa*, 1:459C, I.vi.3 §1. See also oct. 4.7, where Jacob echoes Christ's words to the apostles as he gives bread to his brother: "Receive and eat my food" (Ricevi e mangia del mio companatico).

[80] Ghiberti's panel is the source of the Jacob and Esau prints in Colvin, ed., *A Florentine Picture-Chronicle*, Plates 12–13.

[81] Barolsky, "There's No Such Thing," online.

[82] Newbigin, "'L'occhio si dice.'"

rappresentazione (Muzi showed similar uncertainty in his *Vitel sagginato*); it is not introduced by an Angel (although there are other angels in the play); it is apologetic and unsure of its own merit. After octave 36, for example, more than two-thirds through the play, one of the *festaiuoli* makes an announcement to the audience:

UNO DE' FESTAIUOLI *anunzia agli auditori che s'abrevi la storia per meno di lor tedio e di lor tempo, dicendo così:*	ONE OF THE FESTAIUOLI *announces to the audience that the story is being abridged to minimize their tedium and take less time, saying:*
Per men tediar le vostre riverenzie qui della storia alquanto lascereno, ritraendo nel dir solo l'essenzie e pervenendo a quel che proponemo: d'Esaù e Jacobbe le presenzie congiugner quanto più breve potremo, di che crediam sarete consolati, s'attenderete in umiltà fondati.	Lest tedium overtake your reverences, we'll leave a good part of the story out, restricting to its essence what we say, and coming to the point that we proposed: Esau and Jacob will be brought into each other's presence, as soon as we can, and we believe that this will give you cheer if you watch closely in humility.

(oct. 37)

As a result of this abridgement, all discussion of Leah's fecundity, and of Rachel's barrenness and the two handmaidens who bear Jacob's children (Genesis 30), as well as of Jacob's skill in selective breeding from Laban's flock and herds (Genesis 31), is omitted. The action jumps to God telling Jacob that it is time to return home (Genesis 32), without any reference to Laban's justifiable displeasure; Jacob returns and is reconciled with Isaac.[83] The parts omitted may have been deemed unsuitable fare for chaste adolescent boys, or were genuinely too tedious, since the author had no strategies for speeding up the action other than by cutting it. The ending of the play is similarly apologetic. The last stanza reads:

---

[83] Also omitted is Jacob's all-night struggle on the eve of his reconciliation (Genesis 32:22–31).

Torna Esaù in Seir e Jacob va in su
quel luogo di Tabernaculi e passa nella
città di Saben Sicomor nelle parti di
Canam, tornante di Messopotamia
Siria, e abitò presso all'oppidio. E
qui più non mi stendo per brevità.
Scusomi nella mia ignoranza.

Esau returns to Seir and Jacob goes to the
place of Tabernacles and passes on to Saben,
city of the Sichemites, in the land of Canaan,
after he returned from Mesopotamia Syria,
and he dwelled near the city. And for the
sake of brevity I will not continue. I ask
forgiveness for my ignorance.

UN ANGELO conchiude la festa. Dice:
    Udito avete e veduto in parte
come il voler di Dio a noi si piega,
perché ciascuno hâ racôr le sarte
secondo l'operar s'asolve e lega.
Quest'operetta mostra com poc'arte
che l'aprendiate, da Dio vi si prega.
Però s'è fatta sol per una pruova:
chi ne vuol frutto e vizi suoi rimuova.

AN ANGEL brings the play to an end. He says:
    Now you have heard and also seen in part
just how the will of God affects us all;
for each must trim his sails according to
the way he's freed or bound by what he does.
This little work shows with as little skill
that you may learn, this we do ask from God.
It's done, therefore, as an experiment:
remove its defects and harvest its fruit.

(oct. 52)

The claim of "little skill" and the acknowledgement of defects are not simply rituals of modesty. The text of the play is not confident and the copy text from which it derives must have been almost illegible. Two sections have been lost altogether.[84] The final apology resonates with the one we find in the opening stanza of the play of *Santa Domitilla*:

O buon Iesù, per la tua gran potenza,
concedi grazia al mio basso intelletto
sì ch'io possa mostrar per tua clemenza
la sua storia devota e 'l gran concetto
di Domitilla [...] .

Good Jesus, by your great authority
grant to my lowly intellect the grace
that with your kindly mercy I may show
the holy legend and the high ideals
of Domitilla [...] .

(oct. 1.1–5)

The author in that case was Antonia Pulci (1452/4–1501), although her name disappeared from it after the first edition. Elissa Weaver has shown that her contemporaries believed her to have written many plays. Pulci's biographer Fra Dolciati wrote that she "also composed many beautiful and devout

---

[84] After oct. 31, Jacob's request for the hand of Rachel and Laban's agreement are missing, as well as oct. 44.3–8, which would have corresponded to Genesis 32:14–15.

plays, of Joseph, of David and Saul, of the Prodigal Son, and many others that I don't remember now, for it is now more than thirty-six years since I saw them."[85] *Jacob ed Esaù* is far less accomplished than the plays we recognize as part of Pulci's oeuvre, but it may have been hers, and she may simply have excluded it from publication for that very reason.

Like its models, Belcari's *Abramo* and Muzi's *Vitel sagginato*, *Jacob ed Esaù* is about the complexities of obedience, family, divine will, and what might now appear to modern sensibilities as outrageous injustices toward children. What did a Florentine youth make of such injunctions? That he should forgive the brother who squanders his patrimony and fails in his filial duty, obey the father who is willing to sacrifice him on a mountain, and make peace with the brother who steals his birthright? Beyond the universal aspects of family and inheritance, the play may have resonated with what Florentine youth confraternities knew in particular about their powerful patron, Cosimo de' Medici. Cosimo, like Esaù and Jacob, was a twin, and issues of patrimony and duty were seldom far from his mind.[86]

La rappresentazione di Moisè e Faraone re d'Egitto

One more play can plausibly be assigned to this first decade of confraternity plays, although it too is without a documented performance context. The *Play of Moses and Pharaoh King of Egypt* is contained in one of the oldest anthologies of *rappresentazioni*, BRF, Ricc. 2893 (fig. 3.12).[87] It has none of the uncertainty of genre found in the *Vitel sagginato* or *Jacob ed Esaù*, and already shows some of the exuberance of the plays of the 1460s and 1470s.

---

[85] Dolciati, *Pistola*, fol. 3ᵛ: "compose *etiam* molte belle e devote rappresentazioni, di *Joseph*, di *David e Saul*, del *Figliuolo prodigo* e assai altre delle quali ora non mi ricordo, emperoché sono più di trentasei anni non le ho vedute"; cited by Weaver, in Pulci, *Saints' Lives*, 24, n. 69.

[86] The claim that Cosimo was a surviving twin first appears in an eighteenth-century life of Cosimo. His recent biographer, Dale Kent, accepts the claim; see D.V. Kent, *Cosimo de' Medici*, 11, and 393, n. 24. Florentines must also have been aware of the questions that surrounded the patrimony of his brother Lorenzo, who had died in 1440, just as they were constantly struggling with their own difficulties in sharing and conserving family wealth. In passing, I note that I have found no play of Saints Cosmas and Damian, despite the legend's performability. Zanobi della Barba's *La istoria di san Cosimo & Damiano* ([Florence], 1558), CNCE 49481, was included in the *Terzo libro di feste*, 1578.

[87] BRF, Ricc. 2893, fols. 38ʳ–48ᵛ; for modern edition, see Table 1.

Moisè e Faraone recounts how the Pharaoh's daughter rescues Moses and then summons wet nurses to suckle him. Five are rejected before a Hebrew woman — Moses' natural mother — is found, and the child is raised. Pharaoh reluctantly admits the child to his court, but when the infant knocks the crown from his head, Pharaoh flies into a rage. On the advice of his sages, he tests the child. Moses is presented with a bowl of jewels and a bowl of burning coals, but he demonstrates his lack of worldly ambition by taking a coal and placing it in his mouth and is therefore allowed to live. The episode entered the Christian tradition by way of Josephus's *Jewish Antiquities* and Peter Comestor's *Historia Scholastica*,[88] but it may also have been known in the Florentine cultural tradition through the *Shemot Rabba*, the great commentary on Exodus.[89]

The most striking aspect of *Moisè e Faraone* is its theatricality. Where *Abramo* and the *Vitel sagginato* preached to their audiences, *Moisè e Faraone* manages to delight its public, possibly all male, with a cast of female characters: Pharaoh's daughter and her handmaidens, five wet nurses, and Moses's sister and mother, who effectively triumph over Pharaoh and his court. If the audience was male, as the epilogue suggests,[90] then the performers were male as well, youths dressed as women engaging in intrinsically female activities (not women who are made 'male' by virtue of study or eloquence). Men do not fare particularly well: when Pharaoh's crown is knocked from his head, his downfall is assured, despite his daughter's ironic promise to her father that her adopted child will not harm him. There is also an element of comic exaggeration, as the baby Moses (probably no more than a doll, since he does not speak) refuses the breast of not one but five wet nurses. There is implicit commentary here, which will return in the play of the *Rappresentazione di*

---

[88] Josephus, *Jewish Antiquities*, 1 (1930): 264–269, II.9.7; Peter Comestor, *Historia Libri Exodi*, cap. 5 in *PL* 198 (1855): 1143–1144.

[89] Lelli, "Christian and Jewish Iconographies," 227, argues that the creator of the "Florentine Picture-Chronicle" had direct knowledge of the Midrash.

[90] The epilogue is addressed to: "O dearest friends so noble and so wise, | men of sagacity and noble mien | who are assembled in our presence here | to see what we have done and what we've said" (Carissimi gentili sapïenti | uomini saggi e di gentile aspetto, | che oggi siate stati qui presenti, | a vedere quel che s'è fatto e detto; oct. 55.1–4). Other such epilogues are addressed specifically to mixed audiences of men and women, young and old.

Salamone, on the uncertainties of life and death in a time when newborn children were entrusted to wet nurses and on the social value of such women.[91]

The play disappeared almost without a trace.[92] There is only one manuscript, no record of performance, and only the barest trace of the subject in the visual arts. Benozzo Gozzoli included the scene of the trial of Moses in his Old Testament cycle in the Camposanto of Pisa (1468–1485) (3.13),[93] while the 1498 inventory of Lorenzo di Pierfrancesco de' Medici the Elder's villa at Trebbio records a Flemish painting on canvas of the "story of Moses when he took the crown from King Pharaoh's head."[94] The subject of refusal of royal power was certainly part of the civic narrative of republican Florence, but Moses was not a subject that was widely represented.

The 1460s

Following the death of Cosimo de' Medici in 1464, and his son's failure, due both to his ill health and to his character, to prevent the old divisions of Florentine politics from reappearing, Medicean ascendancy was challenged unsuccessfully by the anti-Medicean conspiracy of 1466. Over fifty years later,

---

[91] See Trexler, "The Foundlings"; Klapisch-Zuber, "Blood Parents"; Meneghin, "Nursing Infants." For Moses in the San Giovanni procession, see below, chapter 4; and for two further plays, see chapter 9.

[92] There are echoes, however, of its opening octave in the beginning of *San Giuliano*, VBAMi, C 35 sup., fol. 142ʳ.

[93] Gozzoli's fresco of the *Childhood of Moses* was almost completely destroyed by fire in 1944; see also Rossi, *Pitture a fresco*. An undated drawing by Filippino Lippi (1457–1504), now in the Národní Galerie in Prague, shows Moses being offered the bowl; see Bambach, "Technique," 21–28; Goldner and Bambach, *The Drawings*, 292–295; Zambrano and Nelson, *Filippino Lippi*, 503. Del Popolo, *Tra sacro e profano*, 179–181, draws attention to the woodcut in the illustrated Malermi Bible (Venice: Giovanni Ragazzo for Lucantonio Giunta, 1490), ISTC ib00644000, fol. d1ᵛ (Exodus 2); and to Giorgione's panel, *Moses Undergoes Trial by Fire*, and its pendant panel of *The Judgment of Solomon* (1502–1505), now in the Uffizi, inv. 1890, nos. 945 and 947; both are later than the play.

[94] Shearman, "The Collections," 25, no. 34: "Uno quadro, ch'è apichato in ditta camara sopra al camino, de lignamo con le cornice d'intorno misso d'oro finno, e d'intorno uno frigio misso d'azurro fino con lettere d'oro finno, e in ditto quadro è comisso l'istoria quando Moysè cavò la corona di capo al re Faraone, dipinta in panno lino in Fiandra — l. 60" (A picture that hangs in this chamber above the fireplace, made of wood with a frame decorated with gold leaf, and around it a frieze in fine blue, with gold leaf letters, and in this picture is the story of Moses when he took the crown from King Pharaoh's head, painted on linen canvas in Flanders, 60 *lire*).

Machiavelli looked back on the period and saw increased investment in public spectacle as Medicean propaganda and an attempt to contain dissent:

> As these troubles bubbled away throughout the city, some of the people who were disturbed by this civil discord thought it would be good to see whether it might be brought to an end by some new delight, because more often than not people without enough to do are tools in the hands of those who wish to overthrow the state. So to eliminate this idleness and to give men something to think about and turn their thoughts away from matters of government, since a year had passed since Cosimo's death, they seized the opportunity, seeing that it would be good to cheer the city up, and ordered two *feste* do be done with great ceremony like the others that are done in the city. One represented the Three Kings, when they came from the East following the star that pointed to the birth of Christ: it was so full of pomp and magnificence that its organization and performance kept the whole city busy for several months. The other was a tournament (for that is the name given to a spectacle that represents a battle between men on horseback), where the leading young men of the city tested themselves with the most renowned knights of Italy; and among the young Florentines the most renowned was Lorenzo, the firstborn son of Piero, who not by some special favour but on account of his own worth took the first prize. Once these spectacles had been celebrated, the same old thoughts returned to the citizens and, more diligently than ever, each pursued his opinions; and the result was disputes and great troubles, and these were greatly increased by two incidents.[95]

---

[95] Machiavelli, *Istorie fiorentine*, 649–650, VII.12.1–6: "Ribollendo adunque questi umori per la città, parve ad alcuno di quelli a' quali le civili discordie dispiacevano, che si vedesse se con qualche nuova allegrezza si potessero fermare, perchè il più delle volte i popoli oziosi sono instrumento a chi vuole alterare. Per tôrre via adunque questo ozio e dare che pensare agli uomini qualche cosa, che levassero i pensieri dello stato, sendo già passato lo anno che Cosimo era morto, presero occasione da che fusse bene rallegrare la città, e ordinorono due feste, secondo l'altre che in quella città si fanno solennissime. Una che rappresentava quando i tre re vennero di oriente dietro alla stella che dimostrava la natività di Cristo: la quale era di tanta pompa e sì magnifica, che in ordinarla e farla teneva più mesi occupata tutta la città; l'altra fu un torniamento (che così chiamano uno

Machiavelli pointed to just two public spectacles, but subsidies had been renewed for other spectacles as well. Across the spectrum of Florentine display, the 1460s are marked by an enormous increase in expenditure on *feste* — especially the civic *festa* of St. John the Baptist, the *festa* of the Magi, and the *feste* of the conventual churches in the Oltrarno. But they are also marked, I believe, by a shift in patronage. The plays and performances discussed in this chapter are an indication of increased activity in the youth confraternities that matched the increased expenditure on the 'civic' plays, and within these plays I detect signs that they were increasingly at the service of the Medici. The service was by no means servile: it was a symbiotic relationship, in which the Medici provided a venue and an occasion, and through their friends a text, and the *giovani* and *fanciulli* — including the scions of the illustrious family — were actors and crew for the entertainments that took place at San Marco, in the garden of their city palace, or possibly even at the villa built by Giovanni de' Medici in Fiesole.

In 1996 Mario Martelli reflected on the difficulty of writing history and the impossibility of finding a single rational thread that would lead him through the irrational tangle of factors that shaped literary production in the Florentine Renaissance, and coined the phrase "the filter of the 1460s," the point at which archaic forms were filtered out and new forms asserted themselves.[96] Through the 1460s, the *sacra rappresentazione*, like other forms of vernacular culture, served Medici interests as well as its traditional educative and devotional purposes. With the patronage of Cosimo de' Medici and the protection of Archbishop Antoninus, the Purification company flourished in

---

spettaculo che rappresenta una zuffa di uomini a cavallo) dove i primi giovani della città si esercitorono insieme con i più nomati cavallieri d'Italia. E intra i giovani fiorentini il più reputato fu Lorenzo, primogenito di Piero, il quale non per grazia, ma per proprio suo valore ne riportò il primo onore. Celebrati questi spettaculi, ritornorono ne' cittadini i medesimi pensieri, e ciascuno con più studio che mai la sua opinione seguitava. Di che dispareri e travagli grandi ne risultavano, i quali da duoi accidenti furono grandemente accresciuti." See also *Istorie fiorentine*, 782, VIII.36.10: "Tenne ancora, in questi tempi pacifici, sempre la patria sua in festa; dove spesso giostre e rappresentazioni di fatti e trionfi antichi si vedevono; e il fine suo era tenere la città abundante, unito il popolo, e la nobiltà onorata" (And in these times of peace he [Lorenzo] kept his city in a constant state of festivity, in which jousts and representations of ancient feats and triumphs were often mounted; and his aim was to keep the city prosperous, the people united, and the nobility honoured). For further discussion of the veracity of Machiavelli's recollection, in the context of the *Festa de' Magi*, see chapter 5 below.

[96] M. Martelli, *Letteratura*, 7–8: "il filtro degli anni Sessanta."

its new quarters in San Marco and performed plays that increasingly reflected the *pietà* and *misericordia* of its sponsors.

Following the success of the Purification *festa* and the *Vitel sagginato*, other plays followed. The second group of plays that I shall examine in this chapter come from the oldest and most important manuscript anthology, BNCF, Conv. Soppr. F.3.488, dated 17 February 1463/4 on fol. 65^r, and 29 July 1465 on fol. 86^v. It was copied, as described above in chapter 1, by Lorenzo di ser Nicolaio di Diedi, who was one of the two young *sagrestani* of the Purification company in the period May–August 1465 (fig. 1.7). It contains twelve plays. The *Creazione*, the *Natività* with Octavian and the Sibyl, and the *Dì del Giudizio* formed part of the John the Baptist cycle and will be discussed in the next chapter. The plays of *San Bartolomeo*, performed in Piazza Santa Croce by an adult confraternity that was in dialogue with the Compagnia dei Magi, and of *San Giovanni decollato* will be considered with outdoor plays in chapter 5. The *Purificazione*, Muzi's *Vitel sagginato*, and Belcari's *Abraham*, already discussed, can all be surely identified as youth confraternity plays. The four remaining plays — it is worth noting that the Oltrarno plays of the Annunciation, Ascension and Pentecost are not included in the codex — appear to belong to the intimate confines of the confraternity and will be examined here. Although they began life with much longer names, they are now known as *L'abataccio* (The bad abbot), *Susanna*, *L'ortolano elemosiniere* (The beneficent gardener), and *Il re superbo* (The proud king). The first eight plays of the collection can be dated quite surely to performances in the period 1448–1454; these four remaining plays date almost certainly to before 1465. Three of them, however, show that the *rappresentazioni* might have developed differently: *L'abataccio*, *Il re superbo*, and *L'ortolano elemosiniere*, which present neither Bible stories nor lives of saints, are all delightfully original, and incorporate humour and irony in a charming way. They are also polemical: the *fanciulli* performed plays in which the young and the powerless triumph over the old, rich, and powerful. And they performed plays for their elders — "fathers in age and in love" (padri per età e per amore; *Purificazione*, oct. 2.3) — that reproach the foolishness of the elders and exhort them to use their wealth and power for the common good. The much-discussed didactic element of the plays worked in two directions.

La rappresentazione de' giudici che Iddio mostrò a un romito per uno angelo

The *Play of the Judgments That God Revealed to a Hermit by Means of an Angel* is an undervalued jewel. It is found in BNCF, Conv. Soppr. F.3.488, fols. 51[r]–65[r], dated at its end 17 February 1463/4, that is, the first Friday of Lent. The earliest surviving printed edition, dated 1547 and with the more economical — but inappropriate — title of *L'abataccio* (The bad abbot), is probably not the first.[97] I shall focus my discussion on the manuscript version.

According to the Angel's prologue (oct. 4.1), the source of the play is to be found in the *Vita Padri*, that is, in the *Vitae Patrum* or *Vite dei Santi Padri*, the collection of legends concerning the Desert Fathers of the early Christian church, attributed to St. Jerome and translated into Italian by Domenico Cavalca around 1330. The tale is told, in Part iii, Chapter 122, of a solitary hermit in Egypt who asks to be shown God's judgments.[98] An Angel — disguised as a fellow hermit — appears and takes him on a journey: first to the cell of a third hermit, where the Angel steals a precious bowl and then deceives and subsequently kills the boy who is sent to retrieve it; and then to a hermitage, where the abbot refuses to admit paupers but a young boy shows them kindness, against the abbot's orders. The next morning, the Angel thanks the avaricious abbot and gives him the bowl. The hermit is increasingly scandalized by these gestures, but the Angel explains at the end that the beauty of the bowl had been distracting the first hermit they visited, and it was given to another who was already wicked, while the boy who was killed had been plotting to kill his master. The hermit of the title falls on his knees, recognizes his companion as an Angel, and acknowledges that God's judgment is true and just.

---

[97] *Rappresentatione del Abataccio* (Florence: for Lorenzo Peri, 1547), CNCE 61515; Cioni, *Bibliografia*, 63, i.1; for modern editions, see Table 1. Complete copy, BRF, N.A. O116, formerly in the collection of Horace Landau, ex Casanatense. The "Bad Abbot" is only one of a number of minor characters; it would be more appropriate to call the play *Il romito.*

[98] Cavalca, *Vite*, 2:1165–1169, iii.122, *De' giudicii di Dio mostrati ad uno monaco a ssuoi preghi*. The 1518 inventory of the Purification confraternity includes a large quarto printed *Vite dei Santi Padri*, bound in red leather with brass corners; see Matchette, "The Compagnia," 98, no. 173. On the continuity of the legend of the Angel and the Hermit, see Brémond, Le Goff, and Schmitt, *L'"Exemplum*," 85–107. About this play, I note Erario, "L'angelo," not seen.

That legend and its message, that God's wisdom far surpasses what mortal man can see and understand in this world, forms the basis of our play. The dramatist, however, has added further episodes to the two of the original (more scenes to involve more actors), and turns the genre of the *sacra rappresentazione*, as it has developed until now, quite on its head. Belcari had instructed his audience to look and listen: action and truth were absolutely co-extensive. This play, on the other hand, deliberately misleads us: it tells us that what we see and what we hear may be the opposite of the truth, and God's mysterious truth is only revealed by divine intervention.

The action begins at a spring in a sylvan setting, before moving into a desert landscape densely populated by hermits and reminiscent of the well-known scenes of eremitic life attributed to such artists as Fra Angelico and Paolo Uccello, which also go under the name of *Thebaid* (see fig. 3.14).[99] First a merchant, returning from Hungary, stops to rest but, when he departs, leaves behind a bag of gold coins. A second traveller finds the gold and takes it; a third traveller comes to the spring and is there when the merchant returns to look for his gold. When the traveller denies that he has taken it, the merchant cuts off his arm (oct. 8–22). The scene has been witnessed by the Hermit of the title, who doubts God's justice and resolves to leave the hermitage. He is joined immediately by an Angel in the form of a young man, who insists on accompanying the Hermit on his way to Alexandria. The Hermit accepts the angelic young man's guidance (oct. 23–31).

They stop first at the cell of a pious hermit, who welcomes them hospitably, and offers them food (oct. 32–33). While the Hermit and the Angel are eating with their host, the action cuts forward to the next location (a theatrical device that is unprecedented in the *rappresentazioni*), where we see two pilgrims arriving at an inn. The innkeeper instructs his son, Valletto, not to admit them because they have no money (oct. 34–36). Back at the hermit's

---

[99] Cosimo, Giovanni, Piero, and Lorenzo de' Medici all held a particular devotion to the Desert Fathers and the eremitic tradition as practised by the Hieronymite order; see Lillie, "Giovanni di Cosimo," 61. Malquori notes that the 1492 inventory of the Palazzo Medici records "in the corridor that leads to Piero's room off the *saletta*: a small wooden panel, measuring 4 *braccia* [2.36 m] long, by Fra Giovanni [da Fiesole called Fra Angelico], and in it are painted various stories of the Holy Fathers" (nell'andito che va alla camera di Piero in sulla *saletta*: una tavoletta di legname di *braccia* 4 in circha, di mano di fra Giovanni, dipintovi più storie dei santi padri), and she relates this panel to a part-panel by Angelico, now in the Szépművészeti Múzeum in Budapest; Malquori, "La *Tebaide*," 135, n. 49, citing Müntz, *Le collections*, 86. See also Callmann, "Thebaid Studies."

cell, the travellers leave, and the Angel steals a bowl from the hermit even as he thanks him in Christ's name. The Hermit reproaches him but is reminded of their pact (oct.37–40).

The Hermit and the Angel arrive at the inn that had previously turned away the pilgrims and are welcomed as paying guests and offered the best food and shelter (oct. 41–43). While they eat, the action cuts forward again, to a monastery where the Abbot instructs his Bursar to summon a poor tenant, Beco, at the same time as issuing instructions to his cook for his own lavish lunch. Beco arrives and is threatened with eviction and prison. As he leaves, Beco meets another tenant of the same Abbot, who laments similar brutal treatment (oct. 44–52).

The action returns to the Hermit and the Angel, who are bidding farewell to the innkeeper, and paying their bill. They ask for directions, and the innkeeper sends his son with them to the Danube. Without explanation, the Angel seizes the boy and drowns him (fig. 3.15), and the Hermit protests only to himself (oct. 53–55).[100] Now the Angel and the Hermit arrive at the monastery, where the Angel announces that they are poor pilgrims who cannot pay. The avaricious Abbot refuses to admit them, but the porter finds them room in the stables. The Angel asks for water and a light, which the Abbot refuses to send but the Porter brings in secret (oct. 56–64). In the morning, the Angel asks to see the Abbot in order to give him a gift. The Abbot greedily accepts the stolen cup and bids them farewell (oct. 65–69). The Hermit reproaches the Angel for all his wicked deeds, but the Angel reveals himself and explains God's will through all these actions. The merchant who lost the money had acquired it nefariously, the man who found the money was wise and generous with it, and the man who lost an arm had beaten his father. The stolen cup had been distracting the hermit and its removal saved his soul. The innkeeper had formerly given alms generously but he had desperately wanted a son and, when the son was granted to him, he became neglectful of his charitable duties; the son, moreover, was destined to wickedness and drowning him before his soul was damned was an act of mercy. Finally, the Abbot: although once good, he was now a master of wickedness. Presenting him with the stolen cup simply completed his damnation. With this the Angel vanishes (oct. 70–84).[101] The Hermit returns humbly to his hermitage (oct. 85–86), and

---

[100] For further discussion of the woodcut, see chapter 8 below, and fig. 8.5.

[101] In the printed edition of 1547, the explanation of the Angel is punctuated by stanzas of commentary by the Hermit.

the Angel of the prologue returns to bid farewell to the "fathers and brothers" (padri e frategli), cautioning them against curiosity:[102]

Nessun adunque sia presontuoso	Let no one be presumptuous and try
voler investigar quel che non lice	to look too closely at what's not allowed
e debbe all'intelletto esser nascoso	and must stay hidden from the human mind,
di noi mortali, come l'apostol dice.	as the Apostle says.[103] So let all men
Creda umilmente e non sia curioso,	be humble and uncurious in belief
se vuol fruir quella gloria felice	if they would reap the fruit of glory's bliss,
dove di giubilar mai non si resta	where there is never any end to joy
e questo è il fin della presente festa.	and that's the end of this our present play.
	(oct. 88)

The looping — almost cinematographic — pattern of the narrative and the sparseness of the stage directions make this a difficult play to read; it is not altogether surprising Toschi did not notice the absence of one third of the text he used for his facsimile edition.[104] In performance, however, each change of scene, which owed something to the practice of *entrelacement* in the chivalric romances, was clearly visible, and the audience would have had no difficulty identifying 'now' from 'next' in the action.

Who, then, made up the audience and what was the message to them? The "padri e frategli" may have been the fathers and brothers of the actors, but more probably they were the priests and friars of a convent, for whom the play was performed as a Carnival entertainment.[105] The presence of the play in a volume copied by a member of the confraternity of the Purification in San Marco prompts us to look for closer evidence of this being a play for the Dominican friars. The subject matter, with its injunction against curiosity,

---

[102] The Angel's farewell does not appear in the printed editions.

[103] The Apostle is Paul; see 1 Corinthians 2:7: "But we speak the wisdom of God in a mystery, a wisdom which is hidden."

[104] Toschi, ed., *Sacre rappresentazioni*, reproduces BNCF, Banco Rari 179.1, which lacks the central bifolio, fols. a³⁻⁴. A complete edition is held in BRF, N.A. O116.

[105] In the printed edition of 83 stanzas, the first episode of the merchant who loses his money, and the last two stanzas, which address the "padri e frategli," are absent (the play also has a totally different rustic interlude to show the avarice of the Abbot). The play of the youth confraternity of the Purification begins: "God save you, brothers, every one of you, | and you, our fathers both in age and love" (Dio vi salvi tutti, o frate miei | e padri per età e per amore; *Purificazione*, oct. 1.1–2). On audiences of confraternity plays, see Eisenbichler, "How Bartolomeo."

resonates with Antoninus's treatment of *curiositas* in his *Summa Theologica*, where 'curiosity' leads inevitably to 'scandal.'[106] The Florentine archbishop had already died in 1459, but his *Summa*, completed shortly before his death, remained enormously influential, not least in his former friary. Alternatively, the eremitic subject matter might suggest a performance in Santa Maria degli Angeli, the urban Camaldolese monastery that maintained its eremitic traditions, through study of the Greek sources of the *Vitae Patrum*, under Ambrogio Traversari (1386–1439).[107] The manuscript, after all, came to the library from Camaldoli, after the Napoleonic suppression of the monastery in 1810.

An even more curious proposition arises from studies by Amanda Lillie on Giovanni de' Medici's particular interest in the eremitic tradition and his association with the Hieronymite friary.[108] Between 1453 and 1459, Giovanni commissioned his villa on the steep slopes of Fiesole, a difficult site but one to which first Cosimo and then his son Giovanni were drawn by earlier family connections with the founder of the Hieronymite hermitage at Fiesole, Beato Carlo da Montegranelli (c. 1330–1417).[109] Lillie has shown that the villa project was tightly integrated from the start with the construction of a new friary of San Girolamo in the 1450s, and the two sites are linked by a monumental stairway from the villa up to the friary (figs. 3.16 and 3.17). When I come to the company of the Vangelista and the play of *San Romolo* at

---

[106] As Antoninus works down through the ramifications of sin, pride, curiosity, and scandal, he distinguishes five forms of *curiositas* that are sinful: desire to know the truth, which can lead accidentally to evil; *curiositas superstitiosa*, or the study of the occult and prophecy; an inordinate desire to learn the truth; seeking to know things that are known only to God; and seeking knowledge that does not lead to God; see Antoninus, *Summa*, 2:486C–489C, II.III.7 §2, following Thomas Aquinas, *Summa*, II.2.167.i. *Curiositas* is also crowding and disorder, wantonness, and aimless expenditure of energy; see Carruthers, *The Craft of Thought*, 82–101.

[107] The Purification company performed a St. Julian play at the monastery in 1493; see below.

[108] Lillie, "Giovanni di Cosimo," "The Patronage," and "Fiesole."

[109] Lillie, "Fiesole," 23, on Fiesole as a penitential landscape, a Thebaid wilderness. The Hieronymites, like the Camaldolese, were an eremitic order, focused on penitential prayer. At Giovanni's death, ownership of the villa reverted to Cosimo, who moved his Platonic Academy there from Careggi, but it was Lorenzo who later transformed it into an outdoor salon. The confraternity of Santa Maria della Pietà, called the Buca di San Girolamo, which had early oversight of the Purification company, held its first meeting in the Hieronymite friary in Fiesole in 1410; BMLF, Ashb. 969, fol. 4[r]; Sebregondi, *Tre confraternite*, 3, 14. The Purification company was released from their close guardianship in 1444; see Polizzotto, *Children*, 53–54.

the end of this chapter, I will be on surer ground, but I believe that this play of the *Giudìci che Iddio mostrò a un romito per uno angelo,* like the *Ortolano elemosiniere* discussed next, requires a garden performance in the presence of friars, and that it may be associated with Giovanni de' Medici, his devotion to the Hieronymites, and the festive and devotional life of his villa at Fiesole.

La rappresentazione dell'ortolano elemosiniere

The *Play of the Beneficent Gardener* "who stopped doing good and was struck down by a terrible illness, then repented and reformed and was freed" is known in two manuscripts.[110] Like the play just discussed of the *Abataccio,* the *Ortolano elemosiniere* is taken from a tale in the *Vitae Patrum.*[111] The Angel's prologue announces two morals to be drawn from the play: God's love of those who give alms to the poor, and his forgiveness of those who repent; the epilogue implies an audience consisting both of conventual friars and of citizens.[112]

The play begins with the worthy Gardener rising early, sending his servant to pick fruit and salad, and distributing alms to the poor at his gate. The poor perform for him: a pilgrim plays his rebec as he and his son sing — but only very briefly — the *cantare* of another pilgrim who went to the shrine of St. James in Galizia; a poor leper comes with bandaged legs and bells; a blind man sings the tale of St. Lucy of Syracuse; a blind man and a lame man together sing the *contrasto* of the Body and the Soul; and a *cornamusino* or

---

[110] "Comincia una rapresentatione d'uno ortolano limosinario il quale si ritrasse da tal bene e fu percosso di terribile infermitade e poi si penté e ravidesi e fu liberato," BNCF, Conv. Soppr. F.3.488, fols. 51ʳ–65ʳ, and the great *zibaldone* of Giovanni d'Antonio Scarlatti, VBAMi, C 35 sup., fols. 160ᵛ–168ᵛ; for a modern edition and translation, see Table 1.

[111] Cavalca, *Vite,* 2:1006–8, III.40, "D'un solitario li cui passi l'angelo innomerava e d'un ortolano infermo buon lemonsinieri, lo cui piede guasto fu miraculosamente sanato" (About a hermit whose steps were numbered by an Angel, and a frail gardener who was generous giving alms, whose injured foot was miraculously healed). The same miracle is found in Bonvesin da la Riva, *Vulgare de Elymosinis,* "De hortulano," in *Le opere,* 1:255–257, lines 473–540; and in a sermon of Bernardino da Siena, *Prediche volgari,* 2:1215. Cavalca appears to be the direct source; but see also Ventrone, "La sacra rappresentazione fiorentina, ovvero la predicazione," 264–267.

[112] "You who are in the service of our God [...] and you, devout, beloved citizens" (Voi, che siate a' servigi divini [...] e voi divoti e cari cittadini; oct. 52.1, 52.3).

bagpipe-player simply plays his instrument.[113] The Gardener gives alms to them all. But the next to arrive is the Devil, disguised as a pious hermit, who persuades the Gardener, with diabolical sophistry, that loving his neighbour as himself requires him first to love himself. His frugality, the diabolical hermit says, is excessive and displeasing to God, when he should be making provision for his old age. The steward of a local noble comes and buys his produce; the Gardener then hoards his coins and instructs his servant to send the poor on their way.

Next morning the Gardener wakes with a terrible pain in his foot and sends for a doctor. Three doctors arrive and squabble in Latin over the poultices to be applied, until gangrene sets in and the Gardener prepares himself to have his foot amputated.[114] Just in time, the Gardener repents his lack of faith. The Angel descends from heaven and asks him, with the "Ubi sunt" refrain:

Ove sono i denar ch'hai ragunati	Where is the money that you set aside
e la speranza che a essi ponesti?	and where is all the hope you placed in it?
Tu gli hai in medicine consumati	You've wasted it on medicines, and now
e ancor più che mai dolente resti.	you're left in pain far greater than before.
Raguarda un po' come gli hai dispensati	Just take a look at how you've spent it all
da poi che a' poveretti gli togliesti.	since you purloined it from the humble poor.
Tu' stato grado è ora afritto e tristo:	Your happy state is now just saddest woe:
vuoi far piatoso viver Iesù Cristo.	you're set on making Jesus live in pain.

(oct. 42)

The Angel heals the Gardener's foot and explains to the doctors that it is the work of the Lord. He is then joined by three Virtues: Faith in the World, Hope of Purgatory, and Charity from Heaven. A choir of angels arrives to sing two *laude*: two sing the verses and their fellow angels sing the refrain. Another Angel returns to sing the *congedo* in praise of almsgiving.

---

[113] The text just hints at their performances with one or two octaves for each; there is no indication of how they might have been expanded.

[114] For other doctors, and for the relationship between spiritual contrition and physical health, see the Dives and Pauper play, *La festa di Lazero rico e di Lazero povero*, discussed below, also found in VBAMi, C 35 sup., fols. 114ᵛ–121ʳ, and now published in Delcorno, "La Festa di Lazero rico," 111–135; see also his *Lazzaro e il ricco Epulone*, 108–116. For a discussion of the appearances of doctors, see D'Ancona, *Origini*, 1:581–587, and also Palermo, *I manoscritti palatini*, 2 (1860): 432–434; Ventrone, "Aspetti," 103–104. In *Sant'Agata*, St. Peter appears as a doctor in the cell of the saint and heals her.

For Banfi, the play was "flat and devoid of the least breath of life despite its completely realistic and everyday, even contemporary plot,"[115] whereas I find it full of wit and charm, with an eye to the confraternal sponsors. This musical *divertissement* brings together three Medicean preoccupations: wealth, charity, and illness. The familial gout of the Medici family was no laughing matter, but there is a humour in the parody of doctors and their opinions that reflects a keen sense of irony: the Medici, with all their wealth, could not heal themselves, and amputation — the miracle of the medical Medici saints Cosmas and Damian — might have seemed at times preferable to the pain they suffered.

Is it conceivable that this play could have been performed by a youth confraternity in a semi-private setting? Cosimo's family could command contributions to their celebration of feast days. Even before Giovanni's villa was completed, his wife Ginevra described to him an excursion to Fiesole in July 1455 to celebrate the feast of the city's patron, St. Romulus, with the assistance of civic resources:

> I have to tell you that we went up to Fiesole with Piero and Lucrezia and Agnolo della Stufa and the singers from the Baptistery of San Giovanni and they did a beautiful *festa*, and Ser Antonio's girls, don't ask [*cancelled*: danced], because they performed miracles and things that were out of this world, and drove everyone who was there wild; and we stayed and watched so long that it was two hours after dark before we got home to Florence.[116]

The family had access to all kinds of performers and did not hesitate to call on them to embellish family occasions. This garden-gate play may have been one of them.[117]

---

[115] Banfi, ed., *Sacre rappresentazioni*, 24: "piatta, priva del minimo soffio di vita pur nella sua vicenda completamente realistica e quotidiana: contemporanea, anzi."

[116] ASF, MAP 7, doc. 301ʳ, 8 July1455: "Avìsoti chome andamo a fFiesole, Piero et la Lucrezia [*cancelled*: el] e Angniolo della Stufa e ' chantori di San Giovanni, e ànno fato una bella festa; e le fanciulle di ser Antonio, non domandare [*cancelled*: ballato] che ànno fatto miracoli e chose dell'altro mondo, che 'mpazzava chiunche v'era; che stemo tanto a vedere che era du' ore di notte inanci tornassimo a Firenze"; cited in Lillie, "Giovanni di Cosimo," 196–197, 204, n. 59; Lillie, "Fiesole," 34, n. 73.

[117] See also *Sant'Eustachio*, performed "nel giardino di Lorenzo," discussed below.

La festa del re superbo

The *Play of the Proud King* is no less extraordinary. It is found in the same two early manuscripts, in a form that corresponds closely to that of the earliest printed edition of c. 1515 (fig. 3.18).[118] The play reworks an eastern legend that is retold as a story of King Solomon in the Talmud, in the play's form in Giovanni Sercambi's *Novelle*, and by Antoninus in his *Summa Theologica*.[119] In a fit of hubris, a king orders that the verse, "He hath put down the mighty from their seat, and hath exalted the humble" (Luke 1:52) be expunged from the *Magnificat*; he immediately falls ill. When he goes to the spa for a cure, his identity is usurped by an Angel, so that he is manhandled by his servants and finally forced to confront himself and acknowledge his pride. Freed of the straitjacket of a biblical text, the author creates recognizable contemporary characters: a newly promoted herald (oct. 4), a solicitous wife whom the king then sees claimed by his other self, doctors, an ill-treated innkeeper who takes his revenge. Their dialogue moves with extraordinary rapidity, with as many as six speakers in a single octave. The morning after the Angel has taken over the king's body, he sends one servant to wake the others. They reply:

UNO SERVO *che dorme dice*:	ONE OF THE SERVANTS, *who is asleep, says*:
Eccoci qui, noi non dormiam, bestione!	We're here, we're not asleep, you animal!
Che sempre sei comettitor di male?	Why do you always have to be the worst?

---

[118] BNCF, Conv. Soppr. F.3.488, fols. 131ʳ–146ᵛ; and VBAMi, C 35 sup., fols. 131ʳ–142ʳ (which contains a one-stanza *licenza* from the Angel); *Rappresentatione del Re superbo* ([Florence: Tubini and Ghirlandi, before 1515]), CNCE 62333; Cioni, *Bibliografia*, 259, LXXXVII.1; for modern editions, see Table 1. Periti, "Contributo," 185, R 37, dates this edition after 1516, but the Biblioteca Colombina's copy, 4.1.4(10), would allow a dating to 1515, the year of almost all his purchases of *rappresentazioni*, although it is heavily trimmed and thus without Colón's usual inscription. This was possibly not the first edition. Tubini and Ghirlandi's woodcut, often an indicator of an earlier Miscomini edition, shows one king addressing another — one of them is an impostor — in a court scene; Kristeller, *Early Florentine Woodcuts*, 139, notes no other use of this block, which may have been cut for an earlier Miscomini edition of this play.

[119] Rappoport, "The Dethroned King"; Sercambi, *Novelle*, Nov. LXI; Antoninus, *Summa*, 2:437D–438C, II.III.2 §4. For a French antecedent by Jehan de Condet, see Tobler, "*Le dit du Magnificat*," 93–104; see also Ventrone, *Lo spettacolo*, 214–216. For a consideration of the *beffa* that strips the foolish man of his identity in order to make him wiser, see discussion of *Il grasso legnaiuolo* in Rochon, "Une date importante."

EL SERVO *che chiama dice*:
Si' tu, cattivo, tristo, ribaldone,
che la persona tua nulla non vale.

THE SERVANT *who is waking them says*:
You are the one who's bad, wicked, and lazy,
you're just a useless waste of space round
[here.

[L'ANGELO *in forma d]el Signore dice loro
cosi*:
Voi siate tutta dua da far quistione,
e hovvi scorti per due gran cicale.

[THE ANGEL *in the form of*] the King
says to them:
The two of you are always arguing;
I've picked you for a pair of loudmouth
[twits.

EL SECONDO SERVO *dice*:
E cominciò egli.

THE SECOND SERVANT *says*:
He started it!

EL PRIMO SERVO:
        Cominciasti tu.

THE FIRST SERVANT:
                I did not! It was you!

Risponde [L'ANGELO *in forma d]el Signore*:
State cheti, non cicalate più.

[THE ANGEL *in the form of*] the King
replies:
Stop arguing and be quiet, both of you.
(oct. 45)

We see the wife greet her husband (the usurping Angel) warmly, even flirta-
tiously, and receive his assurance that he is in excellent condition:

Tu ben venuto sia, dolce mio sposo:
Come stai tu che sei di me colonna?
Come stai tu, compagno dilettoso.
[L'ANGELO *in forma d]el Signore dice*:
Io starò ben se altro mal non mi torna,
perch'io mi sento più che mai forzoso.

Sweet husband, I do bid you welcome here.
Dear column of my being, how fare you now?
How fare you, dear companion of delight?
[THE ANGEL *in the form of*] the King *says*:
Unless some ill returns, I'll be just fine
because I'm feeling stronger now than ever.
(oct. 48.2–6)

We do not see the outcome of this exchange because the action cuts immediately to the ill-tempered king, first berating his servants yet again when he is
not recognized at his own door, and then finding his wife with his other self:

EL POVER SIGNORE *vede la donna sua coll'Angelo che è el Signore e e' dice così*:	THE POOR KING *sees his wife with the Angel who is [disguised as] the King and he says:*
Omè, omè, quell'è la donna mia	Oh woe is me, that woman is my wife
e questo è il mio palagio alto et isnello,	and this is my *palazzo*, soaring high.
Omè, che cresce a me tutte mie pene,	Alas, my woes grow all around me here:
e perduto ho la donna e ogni bene.	I've lost my wife and all my worldly goods.
	(oct. 64.5–8)

Banfi, who revised D'Ancona's edition of the play in 1963, observed rightly that the play is charged with "a sharp ironic realism that sometimes seems to blunt some of its moral teaching."[120] When we read the play now, we cannot avoid seeing in the king, the owner of a great palace who repairs with his entourage, including two roundly satirized doctors, to the baths to treat his agonizing gout, some elements of Piero de' Medici, known as 'the Gouty.'[121] The king returns to his palace and learns from the Angel — his other self, or his conscience — what he must do. He instructs his herald:

Dunque, fa' che tu vada a' preti e [frati	Now you must go to all the priests and [friars
e di' di punto lor la mia intenzione,	and tell them just what I intend to do.
e voi, servi mia savii e pregiati,	And you, my wise and treasured servants all,
fate si scriva per l'abitazione	call people here to write throughout my house
e versi che eran prima via levati;	the verses that were taken out before.
mettete a or perch'i' v'ho devozione,	Write them in gold, for I do worship them
e appiccategli ora in mia presenza	and, in my presence, make sure they're affixed
pel gran palazzo e drento all'audienza.	throughout this mighty house and in the [Hall.
	(oct. 85)

No confraternity or friary could have dared to do a play with such an ironic edge against the wishes or without the knowledge of their principal patrons. We must assume therefore that it was done with the acquiescence — and

---

[120] Banfi, ed., *Sacre rappresentazioni*, 25: "un saporoso realismo ironico nel quale sembra a volte stemperarsi l'insegnamento morale."

[121] On spa life, see Portioli, *I Gonzaga*; on Lucrezia Tornabuoni's investment in the spa at Bagno a Morbo, P. Salvadori, "La gestione," 85–86.

perhaps even at the instigation — of Cosimo or his sons.[122] The invocation of "St. Bernardino the preacher" in the Angel's prologue[123] could suggest that the play was associated with the youth confraternity of San Bernardino e Santa Caterina, founded in 1461,[124] but its presence in Lorenzo di ser Nicolaio di Diedi's anthology is evidence of a relationship with the Purification company.

The only reference, however, to a performance of the *Re superbo* — and a fictional one at that — is in the undated *Frottola di tre suore* — published in the mid-nineteenth century without further details regarding its source.[125] In this extended 'curtain-raiser' for a performance of an unnamed *sacra rappresentazione*, nuns are bustling about preparing the stage but Suor Maria is so flustered that she doesn't even know which play she is setting up for. Her companion Giuditta says:

Elle volevon fare	They wanted to perform
quella del *Re Superbo*,	the one of the *Proud King*
ma l'è ita a Viterbo,	but it's gone to Viterbo,
e far non la possiamo.	and we can't do it here.
Risolute ci siamo	So we've resolved to do
di far quella d'*Alexo*.	the one of *St. Alexus*.[126]
È qui la scala presso.	The stairs are just right here.

(lines 122–129)

No date is provided. We have no other metatheatrical prologues before the *Popolo d'Isdrael* (1499),[127] and we do not have any documentation of plays in female communities in fifteenth-century Florence, but the mention of two early plays in this context suggests that the early plays continued to circulate well into the sixteenth century, and that we should be looking further for evidence of theatrical activities, both in Florentine convents and in sister houses in other cities.

---

[122] The play dates to after Bernardino's canonization in 1450; and no later than 1465, the date of BNCF, Conv. Soppr. F.3.488.

[123] "San Bernardin predicatore" (oct. 1.2.).

[124] See above, n. 7.

[125] Razzolini, "Frottola." Razzolini found the text in an unidentified *zibaldone* that he dated to the fourteenth century. I have sought his source unsuccessfully.

[126] On *Sant'Alesso*, another Purification company play, see below in this chapter.

[127] For the date of Lorenzo di Pierfrancesco de' Medici's *Invenzione della Croce*, assigned by Michel Plaisance to 1494, see below, chapter 7, n. 112.

La festa di Susanna

The last play I shall discuss from Lorenzo di ser Nicolaio's manuscript is the *Play of Susanna*, found in three manuscripts as well as in print.[128] The play is closely related to the vernacular prose *Leggenda di Susanna come Dio la campò di due falsi testimoni* (Legend of Susanna and how God saved her from two false witnesses), a fourteenth-century *volgarizzamento* of the deutero-canonical addition to the book of Daniel, the Old Testament reading for the Saturday after the Third Sunday of Lent.[129] The story of Susanna is a delight

---

[128] "Qui comincia la festa di Susanna quando ella fue achusata d'avolterio e poi fu condannata a morte e dipoi que' due vechioni che condannarono Susanna a morte furono poi lapidati" (Here begins the *festa* of Susanna when she was accused of adultery and then condemned to death, and afterwards those two old men who condemned Susanna to death were stoned), BNCF, Conv. Soppr. F.3.488, fols. 110^r–119^v; for other manuscripts and a modern edition, see Table 1. Printed edition: *Rappresentatione di Susanna* ([Florence: Antonio Tubini and Andrea Ghirlandi, not after 1515]), ISTC is00870700 and also CNCE 62391; Cioni, *Bibliografia*, 284–285, xcviii.1; Periti, "Contributo," 187, R 43. This edition survives in one copy, Venice, Cini, FOAN TES 842, *ex* De Marinis 232. For commentary, see Parducci, "La festa," "Intorno alla redazione," and "La Istoria di Susanna e Daniello"; Baskins, "La Festa di Susanna"; Simons, "Artemisia Gentileschi." For the Abruzzese *Devotione et festa de sancta Susanna*, BNCR, VE 349, fols. 75r–87v, not before 1478, see De Bartholomaeis and Rivera, eds., *Il teatro abruzzese*, 49–55, 334–344.

[129] For the fourteenth-century prose *volgarizzamento*, see BRF, Ricc. 1290, fols. 156^v–158^r; BNCF, II.iv.105, fols. 25^r–26^v, dated 1473–1474; BNCF, Magl. xxxviii.110, fols. 115^r–119^r; and with the title *Miracolo di Susanna* in an unidentified Ricasoli codex published by Razzolini, and in Yale University, Beinicke ms. 872, dated 1462, fols. 64^r–67^r. Octaves 51–53 of the play echo Daniel's cross-examination of the judges, which I cite from Razzolini, 663: "Disse Daniello all'uno: Invecchiato di mala vecchiezza, ora sono venute in palese le peccata tue, le quali tue ài fatte, judicando falsi judicij, e condennando le persone sanza colpa, e prosciogliendo quelle che sono colpevoli. Se tu vedesti Susanna commettere peccato con uno giovane, secondo che tu ài detto, dìe a noi sotto quale albero del giardino tue gli vedesti peccare insieme. Allora quegli rispuose e disse: Io gli vidi sotto il susino. E Daniello rispuose e disse: Tu hai mentito sopra 'l tuo capo. E fecelo menare via da parte; e fece venire l'altro dinanzi a sè, e dissegli: Oi, seme del Diavolo e non di Dio, la bellezza di Susanna t'ingannòe e reo desiderio pervertíe lo tuo cuore: túe credevi fare a Susanna secondo che tu eri usato di fare ad altre, le quali per paura della tua signoria facevano tutto ciò che tu volevi; ma Susanna non volle consentire alla tua iniquitate. Ora ti domando, che l'ài accusata che la vedesti commettere avolterio con uno giovane, sotto quale albero gli vedesti peccare? Egli rispuose: Sotto il pino." (Daniel said to one of them: You who have grown with evil old age, now your sins have come into the open, sins that you committed by delivering false judgments, and condemning guiltless people, and letting those who are guilty go free. If you did see Susanna sinning with a young man, as you have said, tell

of visual and verbal representation. Set in an enclosed garden, it combines the comely but chaste Susanna, the voyeurism of two lecherous and corrupt judges, and their forensic cross-examination by the *fanciullo* Daniel, who traps them by means of wordplay (fig. 3.19).[130]

There was originally no angelic prologue to this play. It was preceded instead by a rustic scene in which two *villani* or tenant farmers are having an argument. The stage direction in the oldest of our manuscripts is quite clear: "First an argument starts between two farmers and they go to settle it in court (that is, before those two Elders who condemned Susanna to death and then were stoned themselves) and they determined that the man who was owed money should have to pay the man from whom he was seeking it."[131] Lorenzo di Ser Nicolaio's version is only ten stanzas; Scarlatti inserts an additional seven stanzas at the beginning, lines that are also included in the slightly later Bolognese manuscript, dated 1482. This last adds a further, slightly paradoxical justification in the stage direction, for the benefit of the performer or reader only; without any other prologue, the putative Bolognese spectator is caught unaware and may not immediately realize the purpose of this scene:

Before the story begins, we have a dispute between two farmers
in front of these two judges, to make the audience more attentive and to reveal their false judgments, even though it does not

---

us under which tree in the garden you saw them sinning together. Then the man replied and said: I saw them under the plum tree. And Daniel replied and said: You have lied on your own head. And he had him taken away; and he had the other man brought before him and he said to him: O seed of the Devil and not of God, Susanna's beauty deceived you and wicked desire perverted your heart: you thought you could do to Susanna what you were accustomed to do to other women, who for fear of your power did everything you wanted; but Susanna refused to consent to your wickedness. Now I ask you, who have accused her saying that you saw her commit adultery with a young man, under which tree did you see them sin? He replied: Under the pine tree.) For Parducci, "La *Istoria*," 52, the phrase "Invecchiato di mala vecchiezza" was evidence that the play and the verse legend were known to each other, but in fact both echo this prose *volgarizzamento*. A much less animated translation (where the wordplay on trees is *cino* [*cynosbatos*, 'dog rose']/*pino*) is found in *Epistole & Euangelii* (1495), fols. xxiiii^v–xxxvi^r.

[130] The woodcut, showing the boy Daniel sitting in judgment over the two elders, is an inferior copy of the one created for *Epistole & Euangelii* (1495), fol. xxxiiii^v.

[131] BNCF, Conv. Soppr. F.3.488, fols. 110^r–111^v: "In prima comincia una questione che fanno due contadini e sì vanno a difinirla alla Ragione (cioè a que' due vecchioni che condannarono Susanna a morte e poi eglino furono lapidati), e sì giudicaro che quello avea avere abbi a dare a quello a chi egli addomandava."

strictly belong to this story, but is just for fun. They begin to argue and the Creditor says to Tangoccio ...[132]

Beco — already the stereotypical Tuscan *contadino*[133] — sues Tangoccio, who arrives in court with a basket of apples to bribe the judges:

[...] un panier di mele i' v'ho arrecate:	[...] here you are: a basketful of apples,
toglietele ché al porco i' l'arei date.	take them, for I'd have fed them to my pig.

(oct. 7.7–8)

The judges are easily corrupted, and Beco not only loses his ten *lire* but is ordered to pay another ten to Tangoccio. This rustic curtain-raiser reveals the corruption of the two elders before they even set eyes on Susanna. Their stoning at the end, a brutal *contrapasso* for their false accusation of adultery, gives the play an elegant symmetry.[134]

It is logical to ask whether there is any relationship between the 'rustic interludes' that we find in the *rappresentazioni* and the anti-peasant satire that pervades the farces of the Sienese Congrega dei Rozzi and their forebears.[135] The earliest known Sienese farces date to the early sixteenth century, while the Florentine interludes, of which the farmers at the beginning of *Susanna* were the first example, can be dated to the 1460s. They stand in sharp contrast to the pastoral dramas of the northern courts with their nymphs and lovesick shepherds, and there is an earthy realism in their situations and their language. In the rustic interludes, and in the scenes of gamblers, thieves, and cut-throats, Florentine authors delighted their audience by representing the colourful idioms, different speech patterns, and lexicon of the unlettered,

---

[132] BNCR, VE 483, fol. 67ᵛ: "Ponsi inanci al principio de la hystoria una questione de dui contadini inanci a' dui Iudici predicti: per far più attenti li auditori, e per dimostrare li lor falsi giudicii, benché non sia apertinente a la dicta hystoria: ma per ispasso. Cominciano a contendere insieme e dice il Creditore a Tangocio[...]".

[133] Beco had appeared as the exploited tenant farmer in the *Abataccio* discussed above. The name is a diminutive form of Domenico and synonymous with 'simple rustic'; Tangoccio is also an epithet used of someone who is comically fat.

[134] On stoning games in fifteenth- and sixteenth-century Florence, see Ciappelli, *Carnevale e Quaresima*, 123–126, 217–219.

[135] On anti-peasant satire generally, see Merlini, *Saggio*; Applauso, "Peasant Authors," 607–620; on the Rozzi, see Mazzi, *La Congrega*; for an edition and discussion of the Florentine *Sferza dei villani* (third quarter of the fifteenth century?), see Merlini, *Saggio*, 189–220.

not to vilify and brutalize their subjects but to express solidarity with them against the misuse of power. It is quite different from the vilification of the *contadino* in the Sienese farces. The language of the *contadini* in the *rappresentazioni* is not like that of the young Lorenzo de' Medici's *Nencia da Barberino* and Luigi Pulci's *Beca da Dicomano*, virtuoso performances that mock the amorous peasant whose grandiose language is a teasing exaggeration of what is appropriate. Rather, it is closer to the comic realism of Pulci in *Morgante maggiore.*

The plays discussed in this chapter show quite clearly that as Florentine *cittadini* extended their lives into the *contado*, they put the hardships of the *contadini* to their own uses. Much cited passages in Leon Battista Alberti's *Libri della famiglia* (1433–1440) are not reflected in the spirit of the plays. One of Alberti's interlocutors, Giannozzo, cautions his sons against the villainy and cunning of peasants: "It is unbelievable, the malice of these plowhands raised amid the clods! All they think of is deceiving you; they never let themselves be tricked in any matter; and their errors are only ever in their own favour."[136] He continues, however, that *contadini* teach you important life lessons:

> It is to your advantage to be able to handle such rustic wits so that you can suffer all the better city-folk who might have the same vile and spiteful customs and habits. Rustics teach you no small diligence; and provided you don't have traffic with hordes of labourers, their malice will not cause you grief, and if you are diligent in your affairs, your farm labourer will not be able to deceive you much, and privately you will find great delight in his little acts of malice, and you will laugh a great deal.[137]

---

[136] Alberti, *I libri della famiglia*, 208: "cosa da nolla credere, quanto in questi aratori cresciuti fra le zolle sia malvagità. Ogni loro studio sempre sta per ingannarti; mai a sé in *ragione* alcuna lasciano venire inganno; mai errano se non a suo utile." See also Ventrone, "Aspetti," 96.

[137] Alberti, *I libri della famiglia*, 208: "Molto giova trassinare tali ingegni villaneschi, per poi meglio sapere sofferire e' cittadini, quali forse abbiano simili costumi villani e dispettosi; e inségnanti e' rustici non poco essere diligente. E poi, dove tu non arai a conversare con troppa moltitudine di lavoratori, a te non sarà la loro malizia odiosa, e dove tu sarai diligente a' fatti tuoi, il tuo agricultore poco potrà ingannarti, e tu delle sue malizuole arai mille piaceri fra te stessi, molto e riderai."

Overall, as Cirese has observed, the century of Humanism is characterized by an openness toward the events of daily life, and a taste for the 'popular' in literature and music, in coexistence with the bucolic idylls that are their antithesis, finding a delicate equilibrium between cruel realism and sympathy.[138] Our authors are not, so far as we know, humanists themselves, but they too tread a delicate line between 'us' and 'them,' without being able to assert full belonging to either group.

The Bolognese copyist is probably not correct in his assertion that the scene is added for comic relief. The *contadini*, like the shepherds in Nativity plays and the beggars in the *Ortolano elemosiniere*, may have comic characteristics and entertain with their performances, but they are integral to the rational argument of the play. Nevertheless, the rustic intermezzo in *Susanna* took on a life of its own. It was adapted and printed as the *Comedia di due contadini intitolata Tangoccio* that survives in a single known copy dated some sixty years later,[139] and it could easily be mistaken for a simple satire of rural unsophistication, grafted onto the *Festa di Susanna*.

The two *contadini* of the play subsequently became part of the vernacular narrative of *Susanna*. In two pairs of *cassone* panels that depict the story of Susanna, the first scene shows the Judges in their corrupt court, in anticipation of the final scene of the naked bodies tied to the column where they are stoned.[140] Within this frame of corruption and punishment stands the Susanna story.

---

[138] Cirese, *Dislivelli*, 21–36.

[139] *Comedia di due contadini intitolata Tangoccio* ([Florence]: for Bartolomeo di Matteo Castelli, [ca. 1519–1525]), CNCE 76622; BNCF, E.6.7.58[II.14]; Periti, "Contributo," 61–62, C 56. Beco is here called Mechero; the *ragione* or *notaio* has become a *podestà*; Tangoccio sings a final *lauda* of triumph. On rustic interludes, see Mazzi, *La Congrega*, 2:8, 312; D'Ancona, *Origini*, 1:600–609.

[140] The panels appear to be closely related to the play. See two Susanna panels attributed to Domenico di Michelino, *Susanna*, Avignon, Musée du Petit Palais, M.I.533–M.I.534; and the dispersed *Susanna* panels (c. 1450) also attributed to Domenico di Michelino, now divided between Baltimore, Walters Art Gallery, 37.2503, and New Brunswick, NJ, Rutgers University Jane Vorhees Zimmerli Art Museum, no. 58.1.1, and Naples, Capodimonte, Fondo Mario de Ciccio, no. 935. See also a third pair, *Susanna and the Elders in the Garden, and the Trial of Susanna before the Elders*, c. 1500, and *Daniel Saving Susanna, the Judgment of Daniel, and the Execution of the Elders*, attributed to the Master of the Apollo and Daphne Legend, Chicago, The Art Institute, Inventory nos. 1933.1029 and 1933.1030. According to Callmann, focus shifts during the fifteenth century from Susanna to Daniel

The Susanna story proper is a dramatist's gift, but the play develops other themes that intertwine with the educative program of the youth confraternities. Daniel's innocent youth, his refusal to be co-opted into mob violence, his moral rectitude in the face of corruption, his intelligence, and his precocious eloquence make him an ideal role model for the young actors. And, like Daniel, the adolescents who perform the play challenge their elders in the audience to higher standards of public and private morality. Susanna's appeal is more ambiguous and dangerous. We see her both as a behavioural model in the privacy of the marriage chamber and, potentially, as an object of voyeuristic lust as her tale is recounted in public. For artists and poets, she has always provided an opportunity to represent chaste near-nakedness uncorrupted by the gaze of wicked men.[141]

The *Festa di Susanna* is, however, exceptional. Leaving aside the plays of the Annunciation and Purification of the Virgin, *Susanna* is the earliest *rappresentazione* with a female protagonist, almost two decade earlier than *Santa Cecilia*, copied in 1482, and Antonia Pulci's *Domitilla*, which bears the date 1483.[142] The prominence of the rustic interlude and of the figure of Daniel suggests that there is still some ambivalence concerning the propriety of making Susanna and her violation the centre of the action. Nonetheless, we know that her story also appealed to the Medici matriarch, Lucrezia Tornabuoni (1425–1482), who may already have written her own verse narrative in *terza rima* on Susanna.[143]

---

and the fate of the judges; see discussion in Callmann, "The Growing Threat," 86 and 91, n. 30; Baskins, "*La Festa di Susanna.*"

[141] Simons, *Susanna and the Elders*, in progress.

[142] See below, chapter 6.

[143] Parducci, "La *Ystoria*"; Tornabuoni, *La istoria della casta Susanna*; Tornabuoni de' Medici, *Sacred Narratives*, 54–71. Lucrezia's *Susanna* possibly dates to after the death of Piero on 2 December 1469, since the title in the only manuscript describes her as "wife of the late Magnificent Piero di Cosimo de' Medici" (donna fu del magnifico huomo Piero di Coximo de' Medici), BNCF, Magl. vii.338, fol. 84ʳ (in which case it would postdate the play), but the implied date may refer only to when it was copied. On Tornabuoni, see also Cionacci, "Sopra *Le rime sacre*," cols. 28–29; Pezzarossa, in Tornabuoni, *I poemetti*, 7–110; M. Martelli, "Lucrezia Tornabuoni"; Tomas, *The Medici Women*; Milligan, "Unlikely Heroines"; and Tornabuoni, *Poemetti biblici*, ed. Ardissino. Poliziano returned a copy of Lucrezia's "laude e sonetti e ternarii" (hymns, sonnets, and poems in *terza rima*) and reported that the ladies had enjoyed them and that her granddaughter had learned them all by heart, Poliziano, *Prose volgari*, 72, 18 July 1479; Tylus in Tornabuoni de' Medici, *Sacred Narratives*, 163–165, n. 5.

The only record of a performance of the Florentine Susanna play, complete with fountains, comes, however, from Rome. In summer 1473, Eleonora d'Aragona, daughter of the king of Naples, travelling to join her new husband in Ferrara, broke her journey in Rome. Pietro Riario, nephew of Sixtus IV and Cardinal of San Sisto, who had just been named Bishop of Florence, summoned *festaiuoli* from Florence to stage a series of dramatic entertainments for the bride in the piazza in front of Santissimi Apostoli. One was the play of *Susanna*, who has now become a 'saint':

> On this day [6 June] the cardinal of San Sisto, called Frate Pietro, had the whole of Piazza Santi Apostoli covered, and he built some stages around the square with tapestries and paintings like a loggia or corridor, and above the porch of the church he built another beautiful loggia, all ornate; and on those stages, the Florentine *festaiuoli* did the play of St. * *, and there were two fountains spraying water that came from very high up, I think, from the roof of Santi Apostoli.[144]

The name of the play is supplied by Bernardino Corio: "At midday, in the spaces just described, the play of Susanna was done by some Florentines with the most realistic gestures, and more fittingly than you could imagine."[145] The subject of wedding chests could also be a play for a bride."[146]

Rappresentazione di sant'Alesso

Close examination of the confraternity's account books allows us to glimpse some of the plays performed in the Purification company. There were probably

---

[144] Infessura, *Diario*, 77: "Lo cardinale di Santo Sixto ditto frate Pietro nel ditto tempo [6 giugno] fece coperire tutta la piazza di Santo Apostolo, e fece certi tavolati intorno alla ditta piazza con panni di razza e tavole a modo di una loia, et corritore, et anco sopra lo porticale della ditta ecclesia fece un'altra bella loia tutta ornata; et in quelli tavolati fo fatta per li Fiorentini festaioli la festa de santo * *, et stavanoci doi fontane che gittavano acqua, la quale veniva molto de alto, et credo dallo tetto di Santo Apostolo." See also Corvisieri, "Il trionfo romano," 647–648, 653; D'Ancona, *Origini*, 1:287–288. In addition see Ferroni, "Appunti," 46–65; and Cruciani, *Teatro*, 151–164.

[145] Corio, *Storia di Milano*, 2:1389, vi.2: "Il mezzo dì se fece ne le sale dimonstrate la representatione de Susanna per alchuni Fiorentini con li più veri acti e più aptamente che giudicar si potesse."

[146] See above, n. 140.

many more, concealed behind the generic term *festa*, which refers ambiguously both to the celebration of liturgical feast days and to plays, or not mentioned because they entailed no extraordinary expenditure unless something went wrong. Polizzotto argues that in the Purification records, *festa* always refers to a play,[147] but in many cases expenditure for candles and oil, nails and string documents only the illumination of the oratory and its decoration with greenery, and not the preparation of a play. Some plays are indicated clearly. The *Vitel sagginato* was done again for Carnival 1461/2; a play of St. Alexus in 1471/2; a play of Barlaam in late 1474; a play of St. Eustace (Sant'Eustachio or Santo Stagio) in Lorenzo's garden on 22 February 1476/7; a play of St. Julian the Hospitaller in Carnival 1492/3; and the 'comedy' of *Judìt* (Judith) for Carnival 1517/18.[148] I shall return to *Judìt* in chapter 9; the rest I shall discuss here.

The evidence for a performance of a St. Alexus play is brief: reimbursement of £2 6s. paid to the warden of the Purification, Domenico di Stefano, on 27 February 1471/2 (two weeks into Lent), "for various expenses incurred in doing the play of the *Festa di Santo Alesso*."[149]

The *vita* of St. Alexus (or Alexis) is found in the work that was one of the principal sources of saints' lives for our plays, namely the *Legenda Aurea* — the *Golden Legend* — of Jacobus de Voragine.[150] Compiled in Latin around 1260, this anthology of saints' lives was quickly translated into the European vernaculars and became a basic holding of conventual and monastic libraries. It was hugely popular, first in manuscript, with over one thousand manuscripts surviving, and then in print, with more than 150 editions before

---

[147] Polizzotto, *Children*, 81, n. 80.

[148] Newbigin, "The Word Made Flesh," 364–368; and Polizzotto, *Children*, 77–96; ASF, CRSPL 1646 (P.xxx.7), fol. 264[r–v].

[149] ASF, CRSPL 1654 (P.xxx.30), fol. 121[r]: "per più ispese fatte per la rapresentazione de la festa di santo Aleso."

[150] Jacobus, *Legenda Aurea*, 1:696–701, xc *De Sancto Alexio*; and Jacobus, *Leggenda aurea*, 2:780–786. Throughout this study, I cite the excellent annotated Latin text with Italian translation, edited by Giovanni Maggioni (Jacobus, *Legenda Aurea*, 2007). Only rarely is it necessary to cite Arrigo Levasti's unsatisfactory edition of the *volgarizzamento* in BRF, Ricc. 1254 (Jacobus, *Leggenda aurea*, 1924–1926), soon to be superseded by a new edition, described in LAI *Legenda Aurea in italiano*, online; see also Cerullo, *I volgarizzamenti*. Ryan's English translation (Jacobus, *The Golden Legend*, 1993) is based on Graesse's edition of 1845, which is accessible but does not accurately represent the corpus of lives circulating in fifteenth-century Florence; see, for example, the case of Apollonia in chapter 6 below. On the *Legenda Aurea* and *rappresentazioni*, see Testaverde, "La *Legenda aurea*."

1500, but it had almost disappeared from sight by the 1530s. The ever-growing database of the *Biblioteca Agiografica Italiana* (BAI) gives us insight into a second level of transmission of the individual legends, which were constantly given new autonomous vernacular translations and reconfigured into new, personalized anthologies for different audiences, including female convents, pious noble women, monks, and friars.[151] It has become clear in the course of preparing this volume and editing the texts that it is not sufficient to say that the plot comes from the *Legenda Aurea*. In many cases, there are intermediate versions, and it has been possible to identify texts much lower in the *stemma* and further from Jacobus's original. Often, the past tense of the prose narrative is carried over, sporadically rather than consistently, into the stage directions. Such descriptive rather than prescriptive rubrics are evidence not of a form of performance in which they were read out loud, but rather of a deliberate desire to preserve the link with the hagiographical source.[152]

No play of St. Alexus is known in manuscript, but the performance of 1471/2 is possibly related to the "Play of Sant'Alesso" that survives in print. No trace of a probable incunable edition has been found. The earliest extant edition is the *Rappresentatione di S. Alexo* (fig. 3.20) issued on 7 August 1517 by Tubini and Ghirlandi, who reprinted a large number of plays already published by Miscomini in the 1490s.[153]

After his birth, Alesso's noble Roman parents resolve to live in a pious and celibate marriage, caring for the poor. When Alesso reaches puberty, they marry him to the daughter of the Western Emperor Arcadio (and niece of the Eastern Emperor Onorio). As soon as the newly-married couple withdraw to

---

[151] *BAI* online lists eleven *volgarizzamenti* (Alessio di Edessa 10–11) and many more unclassified manuscripts; see *Vita di S. Alessio*; Golinelli, *La leggenda*. In the case of *Sant'Alesso*, we need to look beyond the Latin *vita* and its vernacular translation to one of the dozen or so other *volgarizzamenti* in verse and prose.

[152] See discussion of *San Giovanni decollato* in chapter 5 and of *Diecimila martiri* in chapter 9.

[153] *Rappresentatione di S. Alexo* ([Florence: Antonio Tubini and Andrea Ghirlandi], for Francesco di Giovanni Benvenuto, 7 August 1517), CNCE 61519; Cioni, *Bibliografia*, 81–82, vii.1; for modern edition, see Table 2. Marino Sanuto notes a performance in Venice on 13 February 1515, toward the end of Carnival: "In the evening, a play was done for the friars in the monastery of San Salvador; it was a very devout affair" (La sera fu fatto nel monastero di San Salvador una representatione per li frati, di santo Alexio; fo devota cosa); *I diarii*, 19 (1887): 433–434. The woodcuts both of *La storia e vita di santo Alexio Romano* ([Rome: Johann Besicken, after 1500]), ISTC ia00459000, and of the Florentine *Rappresentatione di S. Alexo*, CNCE 61519, appear to be copied from an earlier Florentine prototype.

their chamber, Alesso rejoices in her virginity, and announces his intention
to preserve it:

Però priego ed essorto grandemente	Therefore, I beg and pray most earnestly
che noi dobbiam fuggir carnalitade	that we should flee the pleasures of the flesh
e viver sempre al mondo castamente	and live forever chastely in this world,
col corpo netto e pien di puritade,	and keep our bodies fully pure and clean,
servendo a Dio col cor puro e fervente,	serving our God with pure and fervent hearts,
con devozione e pien di caritade.	filled with devotion and with charity.
Se in castità vivrem con pronto zelo	For if we live in zealous chastity
sarem per sempre possessor del Cielo.	we will possess forever Paradise.

(oct. 31)

His bride agrees joyfully, and Alesso steals away from Rome at once,
arriving in Edessa in Mesopotamia, where he gives away his wealth and
lives as a pauper, begging for alms. His mother and father send servants to
look for him, but the servants do not recognize him. Seventeen years later
Alesso returns to Rome and is taken in as a poor pilgrim to live under the
stairs of his father's house, enduring with Christ-like patience the mockery
of the household servants. Just before his death, seventeen more years later,
he writes down the story of his life, which is read aloud by the pope who
comes, together with both emperors, when he dies. Lamented by his father,
his mother, and his wife, he is buried in a richly adorned chapel.

St. Alexus is not a particularly Florentine devotion — I have found no
church or confraternity dedicated to him although the name Alesso/Alessio is
not uncommon — but his legend has lessons that are particularly apt for the
boys of the Purification company: that sexual chastity is the key to heaven,
and that spiritual blessings flow from giving alms, since the rags of a pauper
may conceal God's true saints.[154] The play may have offered the opportunity
to discuss the bones of historical narrative, and to explain the harmonious
simultaneous presence in Rome of two emperors and a pope, who are seated
on separate parts of the stage until it is their time to speak, but the surviving
text does not do so. Instead it follows the slightly surreal chronology and
geography of the *vita*, amplifying in particular the scenes of endless paupers
milling around the central characters, which provided nonspeaking parts for
all the young members of the confraternity. As indicated in the passage from

---

[154] Nerbano, "La storia di Sant'Alessio." The play was performed in Anagni in 2000
in conjunction with the 24th conference of the Centro Studi sul Teatro Medioevale e Rinascimentale.

the *Frottola di tre suore* cited above, the only scenery that the play required was a staircase.[155]

La rappresentazione di Barlaam e Iosafat

Between 1 September and 31 December 1474, the Purification company recorded an expense of "£3 paid to [the stationer, illuminator, and mosaicist] Monte [di Giovanni di Miniato], for part of the *festa* of Barlaam."[156] Since the Florentine festive calendar did not normally celebrate the feast day of Barlaam and Josaphat, the "festa di Barlaam" is not a feast day but almost certainly a play, and to be identified with the *Play of Barlaam and Josaphat* by Bernardo Pulci, published by Miscomini around 1484.[157] The story is a christianized Buddha tale, once, as in the prologue the play, attributed to John Damascene (c. 675–c. 749), but now ascribed to the Georgian scholar and philosopher, St. Euthymius of Athos (c. 955–1028). It was translated twice into Latin[158] and found enormous popularity in medieval Europe, with German and Old Norse translations following soon after. In the thirteenth century Vincent de Beauvais included it in the *Speculum Historiale*;[159] and at the end of the century Jacobus de Voragine added it as a kind of appendix to his *Legenda Aurea*.[160] In the Middle Ages the two were treated as Christian saints, and are found in the *Martyrologium Romanum* as Saints Barlaam and Josaphat, with their feast day on 27 November.[161]

---

[155] The relic of the staircase is preserved in the Basilica of San Bonifacio e Sant'Alessio in Aventino, which was one of the Forty Stations of Lent, visited by pilgrims to Rome from the Middle Ages.

[156] CRSPL 1654 (P.xxx.30), fol. 126[v]: "lire tre e quali ebe Monte per parte della festa di Barlaam"; Newbigin, "The Word Made Flesh," 368; Polizzotto, *Children*, 89–90.

[157] Bernardo Pulci, *Incomincia la rapresentatione di Barlaam et Iosafat composta per Bernardo Pulci* ([Florence: Antonio Miscomini, c. 1484]), ISTC ir00029680, fols. d–e[8] f[1]; Cioni, *Bibliografia*, 95, xiii.1; for modern editions and translation, see Table 2. Doglio, *Teatro in Europa*, 1:477, believed that it was performed in the company of the Evangelist. For commentary, see Ulysse, "Un couple"; Stallini, "Du religieux," 338–341; Cicali, "L'occultamento del principe." On Bernardo Pulci, see Flamini, "La vita"; and further information in Volpi, "Luigi Pulci," 1–28.

[158] *Hystoria Barlae et Iosaphat* (*BHL* 979); *Barlaam et Iosaphat* (*BHL* 979b).

[159] Vincent de Beauvais, *Speculum Historiale*, xvi, online.

[160] Jacobus, *Legenda Aurea*, 2:1390–1407, clxxvi *De Sanctis Barlaam et Iosaphat*.

[161] *Martyrologium Romanum* in *AASS*, Dec. *Propylaeum*, 68:548, 551–552, n. 8: "Apud Indos Persis finitimos sanctorum Barlaam et Iosaphat, quorum actus mirandos sanctus

The story of Barlaam burst back into the Italian scene in the early 1470s, with numerous printed editions of different versions of the tale. In 1473, the Duchess of Milan had to have a copy of it "at once";[162] and in 1474, it was judged appropriate for the boys of the Purification company. Pulci took a magical spiritual romance, and stripped out the magic, focusing attention on the son rather than on the father. Once again, it is a play about generational conflict: when Iosafat is born, one of the astrologers predicts that he will lead a good and virtuous life, "but he will differ greatly from his father" (ma molto discrepante dal suo padre; oct. 7.5), because he will bring Christianity to the realm (fig. 3.21).[163] The sages advise the king to lock the prince in the palace where thoughts of the future and of death cannot enter. The king calls at once for delights to distract the boy but fails to keep him from all knowledge of suffering. Barlaam comes to the gate disguised as a merchant, bearing a miraculous *gioia* (meaning both 'joy' and 'jewel') that can make the most ignorant man wise (oct. 26.1–3). Iosafat receives the 'jewel' — he is instructed in the joys of Christian faith — and is baptized (oct. 28–32), before Barlaam departs. The king renews his onslaught, arresting Anacor, who is Barlaam's double and has been sent to 'un-convert' the prince. An Angel alerts Iosafat, and Anacor is converted instead. A magician advises the king to send a host of dancing girls, who will fornicate with a malign spirit, sent by the magician, and incite Iosafat to lust:

Ioannes Damascenus conscripsit Novembris 27" (Among the Indians who border on Persia, Saints Barlaam and Josaphat, of whose wondrous deeds St. John Damascene wrote, 27 November).

[162] Galeazzo Maria Sforza in Pavia to Gallassio Gallassi, 29 October 1473: "when you receive this, you are to go to the female monastery of Sant'Agostino in Milan to borrow the *History and Legend of Josaphat*; and when you have it, send it at once to our Most Illustrious Consort who wants it" (Ricevuta questa, andaraj al monasterio de le donne de Sancto Augustino in Milano at domandare in prestito la historia e legenda di Josafat; & quella havuta, mandarla subito a la Illustrissima nostra Consorte che la vole); cited in *Questa si è la legenda de sancto Josaphat* 1982, 11. A large and beautiful manuscript of *La leggenda de sancto Josaphat*, Milan, Braidense, AC.XI.37⁹, with the coat of arms of Bona of Savoy, may have resulted from this request.

[163] The birth of St. Josaphat, in the manner of Ghirlandaio, was probably cut for this second edition, but the remaining cuts, of scenes scarcely related to the play, are taken from other works. See below, Chapter 8.

Fa' che di corte e baron sien levati	Get all the barons now to leave the court
e poste in cambio altretante donzelle	and fill it up instead with damsels fair:
ché tutti alla carne inclinati,	because we all can feel the lure of flesh,
massimamente delle cose belle;	particularly when it's beautiful;
e io un de' mia spiriti incantati	and I'll send one of my enchanted sprites
manderò insieme a fornicar con quelle	and he will fornicate with these fair maids,
e farenlo per forza ritornare.	and we will force him to revert again.

(oct. 62.1–7)

Not even this spectacle of depravity succeeds. Iosafat says to the damsels:

Fate fra voi, per Dio, quel che vi piace,	By God, do what you like among yourselves,
e non vogliate turbar la mia pace.	and make sure that you don't disturb my [peace.

(oct. 64.7–8)

Iosafat falls asleep, and when the king comes to them, the damsels admit defeat. The king then resolves to conquer Iosafat with kindness, and bestows on him half his kingdom, but he too is soon converted, as is Iosafat's baron, Barachia. Iosafat entrusts everything to Barachia and departs in search of Barlaam. He finds him living in the desert as a hermit, and the play ends with Barlaam's death and burial, and Iosafat's return to Barlaam's cell.

As D'Ancona observed, despite being the work of a Pulci — a family that included numerous able poets — this is a somewhat mediocre piece of writing.[164] The octave is often forced and the thoughts are disconnected, but the rich and lively action is a source of delight.[165] In the manner of a romance, it moves from palace to hermit's cell, from city to country, and makes humour of the failed seduction scene. From it, the *fanciulli* of the company could take

---

[164] D'Ancona, ed., *Sacre rappresentazioni*, 2:142. A second *rappresentazione* of the legend appeared toward the end of the century. The earliest surviving edition is: *La rappresentatione di Barlaam et Iosafat composta per il Socci Perrettano. Nuovamente Ristampata* (Florence: Alle Scalee di Badia, [1580?]), CNCE 79405. The author is probably 'from Pereta'; his name appears on *Rime et Ottave del Socio Peretano dun vecchio innamorato* (Florence: ad istanza del Socio Peretano, c. 1580); and *La istoria di Giudetta ebrea composta in ottava rima, per il Soci Peretano* (Florence: Baleni, 1583), both in the British Library; and *La guerra sabina* (1584), CNCE 76994.

[165] I note, for example, Gianni Cicali's student production, Devine Theater, Georgetown University, Washington DC, 17 April 2009.

the message once again that chastity is the key to heaven, and that good-living sons have power to influence even their fathers.

La festa di sant'Eustachio

We would know nothing of the circumstances of the performance of a play of St. Eustace were it not for an incident on 22 February 1476/7: a piece of baize was torn when the *Festa di santo Stagio* was done in the garden of Lorenzo, and the confraternity paid £1 2s. for it to be repaired; no other expenses were recorded.[166] The surviving text of the *Play of St. Eustace,* taken once again from the *Legenda Aurea,*[167] is a magnificent romp, a cross between the book of Job and *Candide.* Eustachio, a noble Roman, is converted when Christ appears to him on a cross between the antlers of a stag that he is hunting. When he and his family convert, he is rewarded with a succession of disasters, all borne with Job-like patience: the slaughter of his servants and his livestock, the theft of his property, the abduction of his wife by a sea captain as he attempts to flee to Egypt, and the loss of both sons to wild animals (fig. 3.22).[168] But when Rome needs his services he goes back and leads the army to a glorious victory. He is miraculously reunited with his sons (sent to enlist in his

---

[166] ASF, CRSPL 1654 (P.xxx.30), fol. 130ʳ: "A Giovanni del Raggio rimendatore lire 1 soldi 2 sono per rimendatura d'un panno rovescio si stracciò nel giardino di Lorenzo per la festa di Santo Stagio fecesi a dì 22 di febraio 1476" (To Giovanni del Raggio the mender, £1 2s. for mending of piece of baize that was torn in the garden of Lorenzo on the occasion of the *festa* of St. Eustace that we did on 22 February 1476/7); see Newbigin, "The Word Made Flesh," 368. 'Santo Stagio' is the Florentine form of 'Sant'Eustachio.' Giovanni del Raggio was also a minor poet, with one work in the Filippo Scarlatti *zibaldone,* BMLF, Acquisti e Doni 759 (formerly Venturi Ginori Lisci 3), fols. 303ᵛ–304ʳ; see Emilio Pasquini, "Il codice," 423. Elam identifies the garden as Lorenzo's sculpture garden on Piazza San Marco; Elam, "Lorenzo," 46.

[167] *Questa è la festa di sancto Eustachio* ([Florence: Antonio Miscomini, c. 1484]), ISTC ir00029700, fols. a–b⁸ c¹⁰; Cioni, *Bibliografia,* 134, xxviii.1; also copied later from a different and less polished manuscript source, in BNCF, Pal. 445, fols. 128ʳ–152ᵛ; for modern edition, see Table 2. Jacobus, *Legenda Aurea,* 2:1224–1233, clvii *De Sancto Eustachio.* On Sant'Eustachio, see Monteverdi, "La leggenda" and "I testi della leggenda"; and Donà, "Cervi," 27–35 with relevant bibliography.

[168] Eustachio, in the middle of the river, sees his younger son Teopista carried off by a lion, and his older son Agabito borne away by a wolf. Whereas the other woodcuts in this richly illustrated edition (see figs. 8.17–8.18) come from other sources and principally from Luigi Pulci, *Morgante maggiore* (1500/1), this block, with the characteristic arrowhead border, is unique and cut specifically for ISTC ie00130700.

army) and his wife (who recognizes her sons from an upstairs window of the enemy fortress). He returns to Rome with a full military triumph, but when he and his family refuse to bow down to the pagan gods they are sentenced to death. After lions refuse to devour them, they are placed in a fiery copper bull, to which a *nugola* descends and then raises their souls to heaven.

The number of animals is striking: a talking stag, the lion and the wolf that carry off the sons, and the lions that refuse to devour the reunited family. Animal masks have long been part of Carnival festivities, but here they are part of the Carnival play as well.[169] New elements have been added to the confraternity's scenic repertoire. Now, in addition to the basic mount and throne, there is a boat, a triumphal car drawn by two horses, a copper bull in which the family meets its glorious end, and a *nugola*, the mandorla frame in which the souls are whisked so quickly up to heaven. The confraternity has made a substantial investment in props that will allow them to do more, and more complex, plays.

Eustachio's military triumph is the first such triumph that I have found staged in Florence.[170] The stage direction reads:

Sia parato un carro trionfale in sul quale monti Eustachio e sia tirato[171] *da dua cavagli e inanzi vadino e suoni e poi e tesori acquistati, e poi i pregioni tutti legati apresso di lui seguita giù di sotto tutti e signori e cavalieri seguitino el carro appresso a lui e allato a lui la moglie e i figliuoli; il resto dello esercito seguiti il carro.* LO IMPERADORE, *quando gli vede venire, scende di sedia e viengli incontro e dice così a Placito quando è dismontato* [...]	*A triumphal car should be prepared for Eustachio to ride on, and it should be drawn by two horses and the musicians should go before it, and then the treasure that has been acquired, and the prisoners should follow in their bonds, on foot, and all the lords and knights should follow the car next to him and beside him his wife and sons; the rest of the army should follow the car. When the Emperor sees them coming, he comes down from his throne to meet them, and he says to Placido when he has dismounted* [...]
	(stage direction after oct. 98)

---

[169] Ser Giusto d'Anghiari records buying a mask for his children for Carnival 1450/1, Giusti, "I *Giornali*," 103.

[170] For further discussion, see Newbigin, "Carried Away."

[171] The manuscript adds "if possible" (se si può), as if this were the only difficulty.

In 1443 the Florentine community in Naples had staged a series of allegorical triumphs in honour of King Alfonso's victory over the barons the previous year (fig. 4.1); in 1459 the ten-year-old Lorenzo de' Medici had staged a Triumph of Love at his own expense in honour of Galeazzo Maria Sforza, the fifteen-year-old son of the duke of Milan; but these were allegorical triumphs, modelled on Petrarch's *Triumphus Cupidinis* and the iconography that sprang from it. Military triumphs, discussed at length in Biondo Flavio's *Roma Triumphans*, where the ancient triumphs are considered in relation to the *edifici* of the contemporary San Giovanni processions, did not become part of the vocabulary of public spectacle in Florence until the San Giovanni procession of 1491.[172] The fiction of a military triumph contained in the St. Eustace play, performed in the semiprivacy of Lorenzo's garden in the Carnival of 1476/7, is the first indication that Lorenzo is about to overstep the bounds of republican decorum.[173]

Caroline Elam points to a further lapse in decorum. Among the poems of Bernardo Bellincioni, published in Milan in 1493, is a sonnet that she has

---

[172] Biondo Flavio, *Roma Triumphans*, 1:214, Lib. x; see also below, chapter 4. On the *armeggeria* and Triumph of Love, mounted by Bartolomeo Benci in honour of Marietta, daughter of Palla Strozzi, celebrated in Carnival 1463/4, see Trexler, *Public Life,* 225–233.

[173] The play was possibly revived in Rome in 1490, when the anonymous viola-player "G.+.H" wrote to Ginevra de' Benci, wife of Luigi Niccolini, in Florence, describing the recent *San Giovanni Battista* celebrations, presumably among the Florentine community in Rome: "The feast day of St. John the Baptist was very beautiful here: there was a *palio* of gold brocade, *spiritelli*, male and female giants, the most beautiful firework whirligig, and it represented Pluto's rape of Persephone. There was even the cartload of fools, with a pair of organs and when the bellows were pumped, instead of producing a sound, the response came from a sack of piglets. Then there was the *festa* of Sant'Eustachio, and lots of things that are too irksome to recount. All our Florentine ladies triumphed, and madonna Teodorina [Cibo, sister of Franceschetto Cibo and daughter of Pope Innocent VIII] stayed in the house of the *papessa* in the evening, but during the day she was in the house of Francesco della Casa, and from there we watched the *festa*" (Il San Giovanni qua fu bellissimo: fucci il palio di brocchato, spiritelli, giuganti e giugantesse, la girandola bellissima, e fu la rapina di Plutone con Proserpina. Nè ancho ci manchò il carro de' matti, dove era un par d'organi che sonando e' mantici i·scambio del suono rispondeva un sacco di porchette. Poi ci fu la festa di Sancto Eustachio e molte cose che sono al dirlo rincrescevoli. Tutte le nostre fiorentine triomphavano, e madonna Theodorina stette in casa la papessa la sera, ma il giorno in casa Francesco della Casa e di lì vedevamo la festa); ASF, MAP 80, doc. 104ʳ, letter of 12 and 17 August 1490, edited in Carnesecchi, "Il ritratto," 294. Since the feast day of Sant'Eustachio was celebrated by Florentines on 20 May (*Calendario* in BNCF, Strozzi xxxvɪ.71, fol. 14ʳ), this *festa* in June seems to have been a play rather than a feast day.

very plausibly linked to the performance in Lorenzo's garden.[174] Although the sonnet is written in the obscene and allusive language of Burchiello, it is worth struggling to construe it, in order to understand the relationship between the young Lorenzo and the confraternity his grandfather had sponsored.

PER UNA CERTA FESTA SI FECE AL GIARDINO DI LORENZO DE' MEDICI D'UNA CERTA COMPAGNIA

I' ti mando un sonetto pien di risa
d'una nuova ghabbiata di pippioni
con certi nostri, e sai, pinzocheroni,
che fan del collo il campanil di Pisa.

Ma non intendo ben la lor divisa,
ch' e gonnellin conformin co'
[ciopponi;
et lodar rugginosi gli schidoni
et saper poi che cosa è la pernisa.

Però vieni a vedere costoro in tresca
ch'alla franciosa bacion l'Agnus Deo,
poi fanno a piè di Cristo la morescha.

El nome non vo' dir d'un ghabadeo,
che l'anima 'n un nocciuolo ha di
[pescha,
come 'n un forzarin l'ha proprio Feo.

Per non parer giudeo,
ti direi cosa d'un guancial sì bella
che rider ti faré più che 'l Gonnella.

FOR A CERTAIN *FESTA* THAT WAS DONE IN THE GARDEN OF LORENZO DE' MEDICI BY A CERTAIN COMPANY

I'm sending you a sonnet full of mirth
about a new cage full of fattened pigeons
and certain bigots of our own, you know,
whose heads are tilted like the tower of Pisa.

Their habit's quite beyond my under
[standing,
for underneath's the same as what's on top,
and blessèd be the spit that's left to rust,
so to know later what a partridge is.

So come and see them lead a merry dance
and give French kisses to the Agnus Dei,
and at Christ's feet perform their morris
[dance.

I won't reveal the pious fellow's name:
a peach stone's where the fellow keeps
[his soul,
the way that Feo keeps his in a box.

And lest you think me stingy,
I'll tell you of a pillow of a boy,
something to make you laugh more than
[Gonnella.

The tone is mocking at the expense of the boys: the youths putting on the play are plump pigeons, partridges, and pillows: objects of lust, ready to be skewered by Bellincioni and his friends. Their piety is scorned, their mock

---

[174] Bellincioni, *Rime* (1493), fol. n1^{r-v}; Bellincioni, *Rime*, ed. Fanfani, 2:64–65, sonnet LIX; noted by Elam, "Il Palazzo," 46 and 69, n. 48. According to the notes in Fanfani's gloss on the sonnet, the cage of plump pigeons in line 2 represents the youth confraternity, and Fanfani follows Salvini in glossing *guanciale* as 'fanciullo.' On Bellincioni, see below, chapter 7.

battles ridiculed as morris dances; but — and this is crucial — the second tercet seems to point toward Luigi Pulci as the author of the play.[175] Paolo Orvieto
relates this tercet to a polemic between Pulci and Ficino on the immortality of
the soul that had erupted in 1473 and continued until 1478. Pulci had written a
sonnet, beginning: "They're having such a battle all about | the soul and where
it comes from, where it goes, | and how it's like the kernel of a peach" (Costor
che fan sì gran disputazione | dell'anima ond'ell'entri o ond'ell'esca, | o come
il nocciuol si stia nella pèsca), for which he was much criticized; Feo Belcari
had written five sonnets in reply, which Benedetto Dei (whose brother Miliano
was married to Feo's daughter Papera) transcribed in his *Cronica*.[176] It is clear
from other sources that Pulci held various forms of religious superstition in
contempt, and in 1475 he ridiculed pilgrims travelling to Rome for Jubilee
indulgences, but since he is also the author of a solemn *Credo*, something of a
moralist in his *Morgante*, and close to the devout Lucrezia Tornabuoni, mother
of Lorenzo, his occasional contempt would not preclude him from also being
the author of *rappresentazioni*, like his brother and sister-in-law.

Bellincioni's sonnet brings into focus the ambiguities of the plays generally. They are a means of control, instructing the boys in the ideals of purity
and piety, virginity and obedience, and keeping them away from the moral
danger of Carnival. At the same time, as Konrad Eisenbichler has eloquently
explained, preadolescent and adolescent boys were exposed to various kinds
of moral danger within the confraternity: some, at least, were dressing as
women, while many were wearing costumes that exposed them in an unac-
customed and incongruous way to the lascivious and mocking gaze of older
men.[177] But, as I have already indicated, wardens of confraternities seem to
have eschewed the vices for which schoolmasters, particularly those with
theatrical interests, were often censured.

Having examined a dozen plays with identifiable links to confraternities, I now turn to plays that can be linked only on the basis of their publication history, content, or structure, and not on documentary evidence.

---

[175] The attribution of the five sonnets is in Orvieto, *Pulci medievale*, 213–243 (229);
Orvieto discusses Bellincioni's sonnet in detail but does not reproduce the coda.

[176] Dei, *La cronica*, 37–38; Frati believed that they were by Dei himself, "Cantari e
sonetti," 193–195; Orvieto, *Pulci medievale*, 229; Polcri, *Luigi Pulci*, 58–59.

[177] Eisenbichler, "How Bartolomeo."

La festa dell'Angiolo Raffaello e di Tobbia

The *Play of the Angel Raphael and Tobit*, sometimes attributed to Bernardo Pulci, is another play about keeping company with a wily and resourceful Angel.[178] There is no textual evidence to support the attribution to Bernardo: his name is not included in any of the surviving fifteenth- and sixteenth-century editions, and it seems to be a simple error that has spread from Cioni to the British Museum catalogue and to the Italian Catalogo Unico.[179] But while there is no textual evidence to link the play to Bernardo, there is contextual evidence that keeps the play firmly within the Pulci orbit.

The deuterocanonical book of Tobit tells the story of Tobit (in Italian, Tubbia), blinded as the result of burying the dead but dutifully constant in his acts of charity, who sends his son Tobias (in Italian, Tubbiuzzo, as in the play, or Tubbiolo) to recover a debt in distant Madia. Young Tobias is protected on his journey by the Archangel Raphael in disguise, makes a good marriage, and returns wealthy. There are multiple messages in the story: about acts of corporal mercy, faith in adversity, filial duty, chastity, blindness and insight, as well as angelic protection. The dramatist has not worked with Jerome's translation but with one of the *volgarizzamenti* that circulated from the fourteenth century.[180] The most likely source is the *volgarizzamento* transmitted by BNCF, Pal. 1, and BRF, Ricc. 683, but the prose text is supplemented by an important visual text: the scenes of the life of Tobit and Tobias in the residence of the Misericordia and Bigallo. One of Florence's public self-representations in the fifteenth century was in the antechamber to the *sala udienza* (meeting room) of the Compagnia della Misericordia, where two key images were on public

---

[178] *Incomincia la festa dellangiolo Raphaello et di Tobbia* ([Florence: Antonio Miscomini, c. 1484]), ISTC ir00029700, fols. g–h⁸ i¹⁰; Cioni, *Bibliografia*, 255, LXXXV.1; for modern editions, see Table 2. The signatures in the copy in the Getty collection (formerly Landau Finaly 9712) have been changed to a–b⁸ C¹⁰. See also Achenbach, "Iconography"; Gombrich, "Tobias"; Eisenbichler, "Devotion." The title may have been added by the printer. *Tobbia* (spelled *Tubbia* throughout) is the father, *Tobit*, while the son, Tobias is called Tubbiuz(z)o. The prologue makes it clear that this is the play of *Tobit* and the Angel.

[179] "Testo di Bernardo Pulci," Cioni, *Bibliografia*, 255, citing Colomb de Batines, *Bibliografia*, 38, where in fact Bernardo is not mentioned. D'Ancona does not refer to Bernardo in his edition.

[180] See for example the *Leggenda di Tobia e di Tobiolo*, based on BRF, Ricc. 683; *Il libro di Tobia*; and *Storia di Tobia*.

display.[181] On the right wall, a Daddi-esque monumental allegory of Miseri-cordia (1352), with the city of Florence and her citizens under her protective mantle, embodied the seven acts of corporal mercy that are named around her: *visito, poto, cibo, redimo, tegho, colligo* and *condo* (I visit, I give drink, I feed, I redeem, I cover, I bring together, I construct).[182] On the left wall a series of eighteen panels, dating to the mid-fourteenth century, narrated the story of Tobit and Tobias, as an exemplary and all-embracing account of the confraternity's charitable works.[183]

Various inscriptions tied together the two meanings of *misericordia*: the pain of heart that the sinner experiences in the face of the Man of Sorrows, and the corporal acts of mercy that he performs in expiation of those sins.[184] Florence had its penitential confraternities that focused on the suffering of the crucified Christ, but its public "Theatre of Mercy" (to use Carla Bino's phrase) was far more mercantile: a series of transactions that lead to salvation. In the play, where Tubbia sends Tubbiuzzo to perform these acts of mercy, I believe that we have an attempt to bring to life one of the defining narratives of Florence as a charitable and merciful city:

---

[181] The present Bigallo, facing the Bapistery, was originally home to the confrater-nity of the Misericordia. From 1425 to 1489, the Bigallo was forcibly amalgamated with the Misericordia on that site, and it remained there when the Misericordia moved to its present location in the sixteenth century. On the architectural history of the Bigallo, see Saalman, *The Bigallo*.

[182] These seven actions are particularly related to the Misericordia's activities, and not a simple translation of the six works of corporal mercy listed in Matthew 25:34–36, together with the seventh based on Tobit 1:17.

[183] The scenes were already "so blackened and ruined that there is no hope of man-aging to understand them" (così annerite, e guaste che non è sperabile l'arrivare ad in-tenderle) when Richa referred to them in his description of the Bigallo; Richa, *Notizie*, 7 (1758): 293–294; Palmeri, "Profilo." Six of them were lost to structural modifications in the seventeenth century; the remaining twelve have been detached and restored, but are still scarcely legible. Nevertheless, Federico Botana relates them very persuasively to the *volgarizzamento* of the Book of Tobit contained in BNCF, Pal. 1; Botana, *The Works of Mercy* and "The Frescoes." I thank Dr. Botana for his generosity in sharing his insights and access to the frescoes and their documentation.

[184] A range of recent works have led to these reflections: Tylus, in Tornabuoni de' Medici, *Sacred Narratives*; Bino, *Dal trionfo*; Botana's works cited in n. 183 above; Del-corno, "La *Festa di Lazero rico*." For a discussion of ways in which the plays shaped percep-tions of contemporary social problems, see Ventrone, "Politica."

Figliuol, to' questi fiaschi e questa [sporta	My son, pick up this basket and these [flasks
e portala a que' poveri prigioni.	and take them to those wretched prisoners.
Chi in questa vita e poveri conforta,	He who assists the poor in earthly life,
nell'altra poi arà gran guidardoni.	in life to come will gather great rewards.
Chi vuol che Dio gli apra del ciel la porta	He who wants God to open heaven's gate
e tutti e sua peccati gli perdoni,	and to forgive him all his trespasses
vesta gli ignudi e pasca gli affamati	should clothe the naked, give the hungry food,
e visiti gl'infermi e incarcerati.	and visit the infirm and those in jail.

(oct. 15)

The structure of the biblical narrative is difficult, and this difficulty is reflected in the play. The scene must be set in two places: in Nineveh, home of Tubbia, with a hill close by; and in a far country, Madia, home of his kinsman Raguello and Raguello's daughter Sarra. Such is the virtue of Tubbia and his wife Anna that God sends the Angelo Raffaello, disguised as the traveller Azaria, to accompany Tubbiuzzo on the journey to Madia to recover a old debt from Gabello, to whom Tobit had lent money years before. On the way, Tubbiuzzo is almost swallowed by a fish, but follows his companion's instructions to kill it and keep the gall bladder. Tubbiuzzo arrives at the house of his kinsman Raguello and is instructed by the Angel to ask for Sarra's hand in marriage. Sarra is chaste but accused by her maidservant of having caused the deaths on their marriage night of her seven lecherous husbands who failed in succession to respect the sanctity of marriage. Her father agrees to another marriage reluctantly, Tubbiuzzo marries her, and the two withdraw to the marriage chamber. The stage direction only hints at what happens next: "Now the Angel binds the devil and takes the fish gall and places it on the coals" (Ora l'Angiolo lega el diavolo e toglie del fiele del pesce e ponlo in su' carboni; stage direction after oct. 94.8).[185] We must imagine that a smoke screen of some kind conceals the marriage bed, while the action cuts briefly back to Tubbia in Nineveh, waiting anxiously for Tubbiuzzo to return. Five stanzas later, Sarra's maid reports to Raguello that both husband and wife have survived the consummation of their marriage. The Angel recovers the debt on Tubbiuzzo's behalf, and the bride and groom, with a huge retinue of servants, animals, and treasure, set out for home. Tubbiuzzo's dog runs ahead of the group. In the play, but not in its written sources, Tubbiuzzo's mother

---

[185] In *Tobit*, liver and heart are burned to ward off the demon (*Tobit* 6:8) and gall is rubbed on Tubit's eyes (*Tobit* 11:13).

scoops the dog up and carries it to Tubbia: "Anna, Tubbiuzzo's mother, goes for a walk on a mountain to see if Tubbiuzzo is returning, and seeing the dog, she runs to Tubbia with the dog in her arms and says [...]" (Anna, madre di Tubbiuzo, andando a spasso in su uno monte per vedere se Tubbiuzo torna, e vedendo il cane, corre a Tubbia col cane in collo e dice così [...]; stage direction before oct. 123). Only the Misericordia fresco reproduces the three parts of this exquisite moment (fig. 3.23), as the dog is picked up and carried down the mountain, then licks the face of blind Tubbia. Tubbiuzzo arrives, the blindness is cured (without further mention of fish gall), and the play ends with celebrations and thanks.

Raffaello e Tobbia shares its four opening stanzas with *Josef, figliuolo di Jacob* discussed below. The audience is once again exclusively male: "Fathers and brothers, dear and much beloved" (Cari e diletti padri e frate' nostri; oct. 1.1); and the actors are young, urged to model themselves on Tubbiuzzo. The performance is located "in these hills" (in questi poggi), and the time is presumably Carnival, when the youth should "flee all the crazy things they do today" (fuggir le pazie che si fanno oggi; oct. 1:7–8). There is no direct link to a youth confraternity, and while it is tempting to link the play of the Angel Raphael to the confraternity of the Archangel Raphael, there is insufficient evidence for us to do so with any confidence.[186]

The story of Tobias and the Angel also appealed to Lucrezia Tornabuoni, who composed a long narrative poem in *terza rima* adapting a *volgarizzamento* of the Vulgate.[187] The play fares better, in that it is based on a more attractive *volgarizzamento* that distinguishes clearly between the father and the son, and allows no confusion between the mother of Tubbiuzzo and the mother of Sarra, both named Anna. The play follows the line of the narrative exactly, but at every point introduces additional dialogue to make the narrative comprehensible.

---

[186] The adult confraternity of the Archangel Raphael, called Il Raffa, which met in Santo Spirito, celebrated the Archangel's feast day on 31 December; see ASF, CRSPL 149 (A.cxlvi.25): 1473 (fol. 65ʳ), 1474 (fol. 67ʳ), 1475 (fol. 69ʳ), 1476 (fol. 70ᵛ), 1477 (fol. 71ᵛ). The expenses for 1476 included "six fir-wood beams that Lorenzo Ridolfi acquired for the platform" (6 asse d'abete ebbe Lorenzo Ridolfi per lo palcho). The timing suggests that this platform could have been a stage for a play.

[187] In Tornabuoni, *Poemetti biblici*, ed. Ardissino; trans. in Tornabuoni de' Medici, *Sacred Narratives*, 72–117; Tylus's introduction is particularly useful.

The story of Tobit and Tobias continued to appeal well into the sixteenth century,[188] but at some stage in its history attention shifted from the charitable father and his son of marriageable age to the beautiful Archangel who accompanies the defenceless child on a journey. It becomes a tale of angelic protection and gives rise to an invocation and prayer to the Archangel that is carried as a talisman to invoke both cures for ailments and protection for travellers. One version from the early fourteenth century reads:

> *Verse*: Healing Raphael, be with me always.
> *Response*: And as you were with Tobias, stay with me always on the road. Let us pray.
> *Prayer*: God, who sent Raphael the Archangel to Tobias your servant as he hastened on his journey, and gave him protection along the way, grant that like him we may always receive assistance, in order that we may avoid the dangers of the present life and attain the joys of heaven. Through Christ our Lord.
> *Response*: Amen.[189]

The number of paintings of Tobias and the Angel, in which a prepubescent Tobias carries a implausibly fresh fish and is accompanied by an exquisitely beautiful Angel and a small dog, is testimony to the enormous versatility of the story.[190]

---

[188] See, for example, the *cassone* panels of *Scenes from the Life of Young Tobias* in the Staatliche Museen, Gemäldegalerie, Berlin, cat. nos. 142, 149 (each 58 × 157 cm), attributed to Francesco Granacci. Helas, "'Nicht aus reiner Lust,'" reads the *cassone* panels as commentary on exile, marriage, and financial considerations.

[189] Cited in Bocci, "Gli *Offici*," 211: "*V*. Raphael medicinalis | mecum sis perpetualis. *R*. Et sicut fuisti cum Tobya | mecum semper sis in via. | Oremus. *Oratio*: Deus qui Raphaelem archangelum tuum Thobie famulo tuo properanti per viam direxisti et inter vie discrimina donasti custodem, da ut eius semper protegamur auxilio quatenus et vite presentis vitemus pericula et ad gaudia valeamus pervenire celestia. Per Christum Dominum nostrum. *R*. Amen." The *versus* also appears on a scroll at the foot of the panel of *Tobias and the Angel* by Giovanni di Piamonte (1467), San Giovanni Valdarno FI, church of Santa Maria delle Grazie; and in another attributed to Benozzo Gozzoli, private collection; see Argenziano, "I compagni." On prayers to St. Julian, St. Mary Magdalene, and the Archangel Raphael that are carried for efficacy, see Rudy, "Kissing Images," online. See also *Oratione del Angiol Raphaello* (without typographical details but early-sixteenth-century), CNCE 79460; BL, C.20.a.31 (11).

[190] See comments by Achenbach, "Iconography"; Eisenbichler, "Nativity," 255; see also D.V. Kent, *Friendship*, 50.

La rappresentazione di Josef, figliuolo di Jacob

A third play from the Miscomini anthology, the *Play of Joseph, Son of Jacob*, also ties in with the activities of the youth confraternities.[191] This Joseph play in 148 octaves, also beginning "Cari diletti padri e frate' nostri," may plausibly be attributed to Antonia Pulci, as the *Joseph* play recalled by Friar Antonio Dolciati.[192] Pulci's *Figliuol prodigo*, which first appeared in print in about 1550, is a reworking of Muzi's earlier *Vitel sagginato*. The Joseph and Jacob play in question may similarly be a new version by Pulci to replace the earlier Joseph play, *La rappresentazione di Josef, di Jacob e de' fratelli*, in 88 octaves and beginning "A laude de l'immenso eterno Dio" (In praise of our immense, eternal God) that is found in BRF, Ricc. 2816, along with other early *rappresentazioni* and two of Lucrezia Tornabuoni's narrative poems.[193] Like its predecessor, *Josef, figliuolo di Jacob* follows closely the narrative of Genesis 37:1–44:9,[194] but with interpolations to assist the viewer: two *contadini* who recall Jacob as a boy (oct. 12–13); a change of order in setting Reuben's discovery of the empty cistern before Jacob's despair at Joseph's reported death; and an expansion of Joseph's downfall at the hands of Potiphar's wife (oct. 37–48) to include discussion of the nature of love and passion.

Sophie Stallini categorically rejects the proposition that the play is by Antonia Pulci on the grounds of structure (it lacks her characteristic

---

[191] *Incomincia la rapresentatione di Ioseph figliuolo di Iacob* ([Florence: Antonio Miscomini, c. 1484]), ISTC ir00029680, fols. k–l[8] m[10]; Cioni, *Bibliografia*, 201–202, LVI.1; for modern editions, see Table 2. A complete manuscript is in BNCF, Magl. VII.47, fols. 1[r]–22[v]. A fragment, with an alternative prologue and epilogue consisting of a macaronic debate between two philosophers, Diagora and Democrito, on the merits of the play, is in BMVe, It.XI.66, fols. 35[r]–36[v]; see Cristofari, *Il codice marciano*, 16; and Newbigin, texts online. On the two Joseph plays, see Stallini, "La *sacra rappresentazione*," 345–366. For Pandolfo Collenuccio's later play, *Comedia di Iacob e Ioseph*, see Curti, "'Per vostra utilitade.'"

[192] See above, n. 85.

[193] BRF, Ricc. 2816, fols. 1[r]–20[r]; Tornabuoni, *San Giovanni Battista*, fols. 73[r]–93[v], and *Giuditta*, fols. 94[v]–115[v]. See also chapter 1 above. For an edition of the earlier Joseph play, see Newbigin, ed., *Nuovo corpus*, 219–249.

[194] The story circulated both in Jerome's Latin translation of Genesis and in the vernacular retelling contained in the *Fiore* or *Fioretti della Bibbia* (see for example BRF, Ricc. 1265, 1266, 1279). The printed version, *Fiore novello estratto dalla Bibbia* (Venice: Alvise da Sale, 1 May 1473, and another fourteen editions up to 1500), is substantially different from the manuscript tradition. The earlier play follows the biblical narrative, which is itself very 'dramatic,' without interpolation.

invocation of the Lord), and themes (it deals with redemption, but not with violence, gambling, charity, men's wickedness, and the opposition of heaven and earth); it does not contain prayers and it barely hints at psychological motivations; and finally the lexicon does not overlap with that of other plays certainly by Antonia.[195] She proposes instead that the author is Antonia's husband Bernardo, noting the play's insistence on mercantile family values and its occasional recourse to Petrarch and Boccaccio for high style.[196] Finally, she points to the fact that it shares four opening stanzas with *Raffaello e Tobbia*, which she accepts without question as the work of Bernardo.[197]

It is worth examining those opening stanzas, which I transcribe exactly from the Miscomini volumes, italicizing the parts in the *Raffaello* prologue that differ:

INCOMINCIA LARAPRESENTATIO NE DI IOSEPH FIGLIVOLO DI IACOB. ET PRIMA LANGIO LO ANNUNTIA.	INCOMINCIA LAFESTA DELLANGIO LO RAPHAELLO ET DI TOBBIA. ET PRIMA LANGIOLO ANNVNTIA.
c Hari dilecti padri e frate nostri	c *Ari* & dilecti padri e frate nostri
noi uipreghiam p(er) lamor del [signore	noi uipreghiam p(er) lamor del [signore
poi che siate adunati in questi chiostri	poi che siate adunati in questi chiostri
state diuoti & non fate romore	state diuoti: & non fate romore
le fatiche son nostre epiacer uostri	*le*fatiche son nostre */* epiacer uostri
& ogni cosa cifa far lamore	& ogni cosa cifa far lamore
no uabbiam ragunati in questi poggi	noi uabbian ragunati in questi poggi
per fuggir lepazie che sifanno oggi	per fuggir lepazie che sifanno oggi
Noi uifarem uedere una figura	Noi uifaremo *una storia uedere*
molto gentil del testamento uechio	mol*ta* gentil del testamento uecchio
chi uuol intendere lasancta scriptura	chi uuole *lasancta scriptura sapere*
attento alnostro dir ponga lorechio	attento alnostro udir ponga lorechio
& questo fia lastoria bella & pura	*chi uuole iluero gaudio elgran piacere*
di ioseph gentile ilquale fu specchio	*uiua come tubbia: elqual fu specchio*
di fede di speranza & caritade	*damore charita speranza & fede*
giusto prudente & uaso dhonestade	*e tutta lasua robba a poueri diede*

---

[195] Stallini, "La *sacra rappresentazione*," 354.

[196] Oct. 30.1–5 recalls *Canzoniere* 84; oct. 31.1–5 recalls *Ninfale fiesolano*, oct. 273; see Stallini, "La *sacra rappresentazione*," 355–356. On echoes of Petrarch in the *rappresentazioni*, see also Villoresi, *Sacrosante parole*, 121–142.

[197] Stallini, "La *sacra rappresentazione*," 366.

Elqual fu poi da suo frate uenduto
  trenta danari aque di pharaone
  & una donna hauendolo ueduto
  si lorichiese di fornicatione
  e ricusando alsuo cuor dissoluto
  fu accusato: & poi messo in prigione
  dove dua anni elgiouane giulio
  con patientia sempre laudo iddio
Elgrande idio qual e/somma giustitia
  & mai non abandona eserui suoi
  in gaudio conuerti lasua tristitia
  per certi segni che dio fece poi
  chi uuol dilecto & lauera letitia
  cerchila in dio chella non e/tra uoi
  hor dogni cosa cauate buon fructi
  che in cielo citrouiamo insieme tutti
                (oct. 1–4, fol. k1ʳ⁻ᵛ)

Prima uedrete come efu menato
  nella cipta di niniue prigione
  essendo poi daquel Re liberato
  apoueri hauea gran compassione
  & ogni cosa hauendo perdio dato
  gliuenne una maggior tribolatione
  pouero e uecchio un giorno egliaciecoe
  e dogni cosa idio sempre lodoe
Elgrande idio qual e/somma giustitia
  e mai non abandona eserui suoi
  in gaudio conuerti lasua tristitia
  che langiol raphael glimando poi
  chi uuol dilecto & lauera letitia
  cerchila in dio chella non e/ *fra noi*
  hor dogni cosa cauate buon fructi
  siche in ciel citrouiamo insieme tutti
               (oct. 1–4, fol. g1ʳ⁻ᵛ)[198]

---

[198] Dearly beloved fathers and dear brethren, | we do beseech you in the Lord's dear love, | now that you're here assembled in these cloisters, | to be devout and make no noise at all: | the efforts are all ours, the pleasures yours, | and Love's what guides us as we do all this. | We've gathered you together in these hills | in order to escape today's misrule. || We'll set before your eyes a parable [*a story*] | from the Old Testament, and anyone | who wants to understand [*know*] the Holy Writ | should listen most intently to our words. | And this will be the story, sweet and pure | of noble Joseph, who was as a mirror | of faith and hope and charity, both just | and prudent, and the vessel of all honour. [*You who seek true joy and great delight | should live just like Tobit, who was as a mirror | of love and charity and hope and faith | and gave all his belongings to the poor.*] || And later, by his brothers, he was sold | for thirty pence to people from the Pharaoh | and then a woman who'd caught sight of him | demanded that he fornicate with her. | When he refused her dissolute desire | he was accused and then thrown into jail | where for two years this blithe young man remained | and with long patience always praised the Lord. [*First you will see how he was taken as | a prisoner to Nineveh and then | when he was later set free by the King | he cared with great compassion for the poor, | and, having given all his worldly goods | for God, he suffered greater tribulation. | When he was poor and old he lost his sight | and always praised the Lord for everything.*] || And God who is almighty righteousness | and never leaves his servants on their own | transformed his wretchedness into great joy | by means of certain signs that God revealed [*and sent the Angel Raphael to him*]. | And if you want delight and truest joy, | seek it in God, and not among yourselves [*among ourselves*]. | Now hear and learn from what we offer now | so we all meet again in heaven's realm.

The two prologues are certainly written on the same template. It is not possible to say which came first, but perhaps the rhythms of *Raffaello* are slightly forced as they try to fit new words to the existing stanza, an impression that is confirmed by two further stanzas at the end of each play that correspond:

Giunti che sono inanzi aIoseph
Iacob dice.

Chi potre mai render gratie alsignore
di tanto beneficio e tanto dono
dolce figliuolo conforto del mio core
tanto felice in questo mondo sono
non ha guardato a me uil peccatore
idio del ciel troppo pietoso & buono
poi chi tho ritrouato figliuol mio
faccia hor dime cio che gli piacie idio

Risponde Ioseph & dice.

Con mille lingue dir non sapre mai
il gaudio ella legreza che hor sento
padre che tanto tempo pianto mhai
oggi pon fine adogni tuo lamento
elresto che nel mondo uiuerai
dolcie mie padre tu sara contento
ristoreratti iddio per suo clemenza
ueduta latuo lunga patienza.

(oct. 147–148, fol. m10ᵛ)

Rispo(n)de Tubbia ralluminato
& dice cosi.

Chi potre mai render *laude* alsignore
di tanto beneficio e tanto dono
dolce figliuol conforto del mio cuore
quanto felice in questo *giorno* sono
non ha guardato a *questo* peccatore
idio del ciel troppo pietoso e buono
perdonami signore giusto & uerace
& fa del seruo tuo cioche ti piace

Risponde Tubbiuzo alpadre.

Con mille lingue dir non *potre* mai
el gaudio ella *letitia sento drento*
padre che *tanta pena portato* hai
oggi *e / lafine dogni tuo tormento*
elresto che nel mondo uiuerai
dolce mio padre tu sarai contento
ristoreratti idio per sua clemenza
ueduta la tua *buona* patienza

(oct. 134–135, fol. i7ᵛ)[199]

---

[199] When they stand before Joseph, Jacob says [*Tobit regains his sight and says as follows*]: Who could ever give thanks [*praise*] to our Lord | for such beneficence and such a gift? | Sweet son, the comfort of my very heart. | I am so happy just to be alive. [*How happy I am upon this day.*] | God in heaven, most merciful and good | has not looked down on me a [*down at this*] wretched sinner. | Now that I've found, dearest son of mine, | do with me what is pleasing to the Lord [*Forgive me, Lord, just and dependable.* | *Do with your servant anything you wish*]. || Joseph replies and says [*Tobias replies to his father*]: Not even with a thousand tongues could I | express the joy and happiness I feel [*and bliss I feel within*]. | Father, who shed your tears for me so long, | today you must put an end to your laments [*the end has come to all your torment*]. | And all the time you have left in the world, | my sweetest father, you shall be content. | God in his mercy will restore you in his clemency, | for he has seen your long-enduring [*good*] patience.

The same formulae appear yet again in the final stanza of *Griselda*: "Con mille lingue dire non potre' mai | el gaudio e l'allegrezza ch'oggi sento. | Ringratiato sie Iddio! S'i'

It is not possible to make a firm attribution of either play, but there is another point of correspondence between the two. Just as the action of *Raffaello* cuts back and forth between two places, Nineveh, the land of Tobit, and distant Media, the land of Raguello, so too *Josef* moves between two locations, Canaan and the house of Jacob, and Egypt with the court of Pharaoh. In both plays, the places are dictated by the sources, but they must have required similar solutions on stage, and the temporal linearity of the action takes the viewer back and forth without any confusion. A pair of *spalliera* panels by Biagio d'Antonio, roughly contemporary with the publication of the play (figs. 3.24 and 3.25), likewise divides the action geographically rather than chronologically, and the viewer is required to reassemble the narrative in chronological order, with the assistance only of labels.[200]

Joseph's chastity in the face of the wanton wife of Potiphar is a model for the youths of the confraternity and a caution against the wiles of predatory women, but it is the story of Joseph, and his good governance that allowed the state to feed those in its care, that intertwined with the Florentine civic narrative. Long before Duke Cosimo I commissioned the Jacob tapestries for the Sala dei Duecento,[201] Joseph was represented in the mosaics of the cupola of the Baptistery, completed between 1225 and 1330. In addition to the Last Judgment, which occupies three-eighths of the cupola, the mosaics of the Baptistery represent the angelic hierarchies, the stories of Genesis from the Creation to the Flood, the stories of Joseph, the stories of Mary and Christ, and the stories of St. John the Baptist; these spread over the five registers that descend through the remaining five-eighths of the cupola.[202] The story

---

piansi mai, | oggi è la fine d'ogni mie tormento. | Or priego te, dolce marito mio, | che 'nsieme rendian laude e gratie a dDio" (Not even with a thousand tongues could I | express the joy and happiness I feel | today. Thanks be to God! And if I wept | today all of my torment's at an end. | I now beseech you, sweetest husband mine | that we give praise as one and thanks to God; oct. 100.3–8); *Griselda*, in Morabito, *Una sacra rappresentazione*, 48. For further discussion of *Griselda*, see below, chapter 6.

[200] The Getty panel shows events that take place in Canaan, the land of Joseph's birth where Jacob dwells, while the Met panel shows events that take place in Egypt. Two panels in the Fitzwilliam Museum, Cambridge UK, dating to 1487, are less detailed, but see below, chapter 8, n. 34.

[201] For the tapestries woven by Johan Rost and Nicolas Karcher to designs by Bronzino, Pontormo, and Salviati, reunited for the 2015–2016 exhibition in Rome, Florence, and Milan, see Godart, ed., *Il principe dei sogni*.

[202] On the Joseph mosaics see Boskovits, *The Mosaics*, 267–278. Boskovits casts doubt on the presumed dependence of the Baptistery mosaics on Roman models in St. Peter's

of Joseph is told in fifteen panels that have escaped the worst excesses of restoration and are still completely legible. They are a reminder of what can be
achieved by a citizen who is upright, resilient in the face of derision and cal-
umny, granted special insight by God, and eloquent. They are also about good
and providential government, and about controlled forgiveness of those who
do you wrong. They embody the values of republican government in a fac-
tious society where *scandalo* — indignation leading to insurrection — could
strike at any moment. The story is germane not just to Duke Cosimo I; it had,
I believe, been one of the key narratives of the Florentine Republic.

Stallini makes a further important point. In 1473–1475, 1476–1477,
and again in 1483–1484, Florence and its *contado* were struck by famine. The
Ufficiali dell'Abbondanza acted to protect grain supplies while Lorenzo de'
Medici intervened to release grain at a reduced price so that the poor would
not starve.[203] "On Wednesday 22 [December 1473] in Florence, because grain
was becoming increasingly expensive and it had already gone up to 40s. a
staio, the *magnifico* Lorenzo di Piero di Cosimo de' Medici sent 25 bushels to
the piazza to be sold; and where others were asking 40s., he had his offered
for 30s. a *staio*: for which he was much commended."[204] Lorenzo's foresight
and magnanimity continued the traditions of Joseph — humble citizen — in
the court of the Pharaoh.

The printed Joseph play enjoyed popular editions into the nineteenth
century (fig. 3.26).[205] The continued success of Tim Rice and Andrew Lloyd
Webber's *Joseph and the Amazing Technicolor Dreamcoat* for high school
productions attests to the 'suitability' of this story in an educational setting.[206]

---

and San Paolo fuori le mura (276–277).

[203] Stallini, "La *sacra rappresentazione*," 359–360, citing P. Salvadori, *Dominio*, 90, and
contemporary chroniclers including Benedetto Dei, Giusto Giusti d'Anghiari, and Luca
Landucci.

[204] Giusti, "I *Giornali*," 173: "Mercordì a dì 22 detto [dicembre 1473] in Firenze, perché il grano rincarava e già era ito a soldi 40 lo staio, il magnifico Lorenzo di Piero di
Cosimo de' Medici ne fece arrecare del suo 25 moggia in piazza a venderlo; e dove l'altro
si chiedeva 40 dello staio, egli fece dare il suo a soldi 30 lo staio: che molto ne fu com-
mendato."

[205] Adriano Salani published many hundreds of theatrical *libretti*. This version contains three additional stanzas at the end, already added after "Il fine" in the Lucca 1782
edition, exhorting the viewer to forgive, like Joseph, those who have done them grievous
wrong.

[206] "Nearly 20,000 schools and local theatres, involving 700,000 performers of all ages,
and with an audience in excess of nine million. Today [29 June 2007] there are nearly 500

La rappresentazione di san Bernardo d'uno signore che facea rubare le strade

The *Play of St. Bernard, of a Baron Who Sent His Men Out as Highway Robbers*, is a beautifully constructed youth confraternity play about a brigand, in the thrall of the Devil but nevertheless reciting the Ave Maria each day, who is saved by St. Bernard at the Virgin's request.[207] The play, shaped in part by St. Bernard's oft-cited abhorrence of dirt,[208] derives from the second miracle of the *Miracoli della Vergine Maria* (fig. 3.27), an ever-changing Tuscan collection of prose legends that circulated widely and enjoyed thirty-five printed editions before 1500.[209]

The play begins with a normal day's work in the life of an honest and hardworking robber baron. His highway-robbing servants bring in a series of deserving victims — muleteers, merchants, and later hoarding peasants — who are relieved of their possessions and sent on their way. But when a group of four musicians are brought in, the baron reminds his companions that their kind should not be mistreated and asks the musicians to entertain him before they go. After a musical interlude, the cook appears before the baron with a lad who is asking to be taken on as a scullery hand.

Fifteen years pass. In a nearby forest, the Virgin appears to St. Bernard to tell him that the baron has in his employ a Fallen Angel, driven out of

---

school and amateur productions each year in the UK," according to the website of the copyright holders, http://www.reallyuseful.com/, consulted 12 October 2016.

[207] *La rappresentazione di san Bernardo d'uno signore che facea rubare le strade*, BRF, Ricc. 2816, fols. 44ᵛ–55ᵛ, and also in BEUMo, Gamma D.6.34 (formerly Càmpori 10), fols. 1ʳ–12ᵛ, which, like Ricc. 2816, also contains Belcari's *San Panuzio*, fols. 12ᵛ–16ᵛ; for edition, see Table 1. The actors are young, "questi giovinetti" (these young boys; oct. 66.6).

[208] Jacobus, *Legenda Aurea*, 2:904, cxvi.74 *De Sancto Bernardo*: "In uestibus ei semper paupertas placuit, sordes nunquam" (In his dress he always liked poverty, but never dirt). Wrestling with the Devil is a key ingredient of St. Bernard's *vita*.

[209] *Miracoli della gloriosa vergine Maria* (1500), fols. a3ʳ–a4ʳ, cap. ii *Come fu uno signore lo quale tenendo in casa lo demonio fu liberato dalla gloriosa Vergine Maria* (How there was a baron who was keeping the Devil in his house but was liberated by the glorious Virgin Mary). The legend begins with the arrival of a "holy man" who is not named. For a fourteenth-century manuscript version of the legend, see for example Ricc. 1675, fols. 42ʳ–43ʳ, lxvi; for an overview of manuscripts of the *Miracoli*, see Delcorno, "Corruzione," 285, n. 45. Giovan Maria Cecchi's *farsa, I malandrini* (1580–1587), derives from the same legend. D'Ancona notes versions in Sercambi, Bonvesin da la Riva, and in a *cantare* in ottava rima, *Istoria nuova e verissima del Cavalier d'Olanda*; D'Ancona, *Origini*, 2:157, n. 2.

heaven for the sin of pride, but that because the baron has kneeled and recited three Ave Marias every morning all his life, he and his men are to be saved from eternal damnation. St. Bernard sets out for the castle but is captured by the baron's henchmen on the way and brought as a prisoner before him. St. Bernard promises the baron riches and to save him from the Devil — the Fallen Angel in his employ — on account of the three Ave Marias. The baron sends his men to find this "Devil incarnate" but all they can find is the 'faithful' scullery hand who has been with him for fifteen years. At first the scullion refuses to come because of his shabby clothes but the baron insists. St. Bernard steps forward and challenges the man. He whinges and complains of mistreatment and recalls the fine position he once had, but finally he admits his diabolical identity and departs, leaving on the ground the greasy body that he has inhabited. There are no stage directions, but the legend suggests how it might be done: "immediately the Devil, with a great rushing of wind and noise disappeared like a puff of smoke."[210] The baron and his men go to join St. Bernard in his abbey.

Part of the charm of this play is that its subject allows for comic irony and ambiguity about wealth and appearances: none of the baron's victims has acquired his wealth honestly, and the baron is simply redistributing it. There is a stark message about the impermanence of earthly goods and the futility of trying to amass them. And the Devil, the Deceiver, is never what he seems. He is dangerous precisely because his lies are so convincing (the scullion's name here is Falserone or 'Forger'). The audience must know immediately from his name and his ungodly filth — but perhaps also from a glimpse of horns or a cloven hoof or scaly tail — that the scullery hand is the Devil, but there is still delight in revealing him to the baron.

La rappresentazione di Salamone

As well as the earlier Joseph play and the St. Bernard play, BRF, Ricc. 2816 contains two further plays that I shall discuss here: *La rappresentazione di Salamone*, which was printed at the end of the century by Antonio Miscomini (fig. 3.28),[211] and *Quando Gesù resucitò Lazero*. The *Play of Solomon* derives

---

[210] *Miracoli della gloriosa vergine Maria* (1500), fol. a4[r]: "Et lo Demonio incontinente con grande tempesta e romore disparve come fummo."

[211] BRF, Ricc. 2816, fols. 60[r]–68[v] (with a prologue of eight octaves, which — as in Belcari's *Abramo* — summarize the action); also in BNCF, Pal. 445, fols. 1[r]–12[r]; and Magl. VII.2101, fols. 31[r]–40[r] (both with a prologue of four octaves, introducing the play and its

directly from 1 Kings 3:16–28 and presents the Judgment of Solomon, in
which two mothers — both prostitutes — claim the same living child after
another child has been smothered by his mother as she slept. When Solomon
orders that the surviving child be cut in two, the Good Woman (and the true
mother) renounces her claim. Solomon orders that the child be given to her,
and the Bad Woman is punished for her false claim. The play is short, with
only fifty-seven octaves and very few speaking parts; it goes beyond the parameters of the biblical story only in ordering the punishment of the harlot
responsible for the death of the child. The stated moral is blunt and uncom-
plicated — even if it is not particularly relevant to boys and young men:

State in silenzio e con la mente unita,	Be quiet and focus all your thoughts on this:
pensando il mal che segue a chi nel letto	think of the harm that comes to her who
tien il suo figlio quando dorme al petto.	[keeps
	her babe at breast when she's asleep in bed.
	(oct. 8.6–8)

Nevertheless, King Solomon's youthfulness — "I am still but a child, and ignorant" (io sono ancor fanciullo ed ignorante; oct. 6.2) — like Daniel's, makes
him an ideal model for the members of a youth confraternity. Although we
have nothing to link this play with any specific group, the stage directions do
give us some remarkable information about the staging. The play appears to
use the increasingly standard set of Paradise or Heaven with God the Father,
a mountain, and a throne to represent a court. The stage direction after the
prologue reads:

---

moral). In the Magliabechi manuscript, a later hand follows the play with poems by Niccolò Cieco (fol. 40ᵛ), as if to suggest that the play is also by him, but the poet had probably
died around 1440. For printed editions, see *La rapresentatione di Salamone* ([Florence:
Antonio Miscomini, 1494–1495]), ISTC is00093800; Cioni, *Bibliografia*, 271, xcii; for
the date, see Tura, *Edizioni fiorentine*, 101, no. 86. The modern edition in Newbigin, ed.,
Nuovo corpus, 291–312, was based on Miscomini's edition, but Magl. vii.2101 (not known
to me in 1983) offers various more plausible readings.

Nel principio, tutti e vestiti di Salamone,	*In the beginning, all the servants of*
giunti al palco, si fermino giù al basso	*Solomon's court, having reached the stage,*
e faccino coro, e faccino reverenza a	*should stop below it and sing in chorus,*
Salamone passando pel mezzo di loro	*and bow to Solomon as he passes through*
per andare a fare il sacrificio; e fatto	*their midst to go and make his sacrifice.*
Salamone il sacrificio e tornato in sedia,	*And when Solomon has made his sacrifice*
tutti gli altri vadino a sedere. Salamone	*and returned to his seat, all the others*
va in sul monte e fa sacrificio a Dio con	*go and sit down. Solomon goes onto the*
mille agnelli e incenso sopra l'altare; e	*mountain and makes his sacrifice to God*
dipoi s'addormenta e Dio *gli parla in*	*with a thousand sheep and incense upon*
sogno.	*the altar, and then he falls asleep and*
	God *speaks to him in a dream.*

(stage direction after oct. 4)

Only the Angel, God, Solomon, the Good Woman, and the Bad Woman have speaking parts, but the crowd scene at the beginning brings every member of the confraternity onto the stage in costume, and they remain there for the duration of the play as actors and spectators. The composition of the rest of the audience is not clear. The *licenza* of the Angel is different in each of the three manuscripts: "O citizens, whose prudence does abound" (O popol magno di santa prudenza) in Ricc. 2816; "O citizens of great intelligence" (O popolo di magna intelligenza) in Pal. 445; and "My lords, assembled here to hear and see | the play we have presented up to now" (Signori stati a udire e vedere | infino a qui la rapresentazione) in Magl. VII.1201, lines which also introduce the two stanzas that are found at the conclusion of the *Creazione*.[212]

In Carnival 1490/1, the young monks of Santa Maria degli Angeli staged a Judgment of Solomon in Latin in the presence of the sixteen-year-old cardinal Giovanni de' Medici (future Pope Leo X) and other noble and learned men.[213] Pietro Delfin, general of the Camaldolese order, initially praised their skill at learning their lines, their pronunciation, and their movements and

---

[212] *Creazione*, oct. 75.1–2, in Newbigin, ed., *Nuovo corpus*, 27. On the Creation as the first and second *edifici* of the San Giovanni procession, see below, chapter 4. Around the middle of the century, the orphans of Florence and their wet nurses led the procession. There is no suggestion that *Salamone* was ever part of the San Giovanni procession.

[213] Delfin, *Epistolarum volumen*, fols. g3ʳ–g6ʳ, Lib. II, Ep. LXXIII, LXXVII; Schnitzer, *Peter Delfin*, 84–85 and 414, n. 46; Trexler, "Florentine Theatre" (revised 2002), 243; Black, "The Scuola," 360. In Carnival 1491/2, again in Latin and in the presence of Giovanni de' Medici, they performed an unidentified "Miracle of the Virgin," in which all the characters were monks, fols. i7ʳ–i8ʳ, Lib. III, Ep. XXV; Schnitzer, *Peter Delfin*, 85.

gestures, but three weeks later, having learned that others had taken offence at the lasciviousness of the performance, he reproached the prior for risking scandal. The confraternity incurred no such opprobrium. The women are described in the prologue as harlots, but their wanton behaviour is limited to abuse of each other as they stand before Solomon, reminiscent of the squabbling wet nurses in the *Rappresentazione della Natività di Cristo.*

The Company of St. John the Evangelist

Few fifteenth-century records survive of the youth confraternity of St. John the Evangelist, the Vangelista, which met in the Medici neighbourhood of the Leon d'Oro. From 1427, their oratory was in Santa Trinita dei Gesuati, or Santa Trinita Vecchia, in Via dell'Acqua (now the unoccupied Istituto di Sant'Agnese, Via Guelfa 79) in the parish of San Lorenzo, space that they shared with the adult company of San Paolo.[214] Two early versions of their statutes survive (figs. 3.29 and 3.30), but unlike the Purification company's statutes, they seem to contain no reference to plays.[215] The company can,

[214] For an eighteenth-century summary of part of their history, see the *Ricordi* of the Compagnia della Disciplina di Notte di San Pagolo, BMoF, Palagi 114, fols. 5ʳ–7ʳ; and also Evangelista, "L'attività spettacolare." See also Masi, *Ricordanze,* 15–16, §63, discussed in chapter 7 below; D'Ancona, *Origini,* 1:411–412; Del Lungo, *Florentia,* 194–196; Plaisance, "*L'exaltation*"; Carew-Reid, *Les fêtes florentines,* 235–237; Sebregondi, "I luoghi teatrali" and "Istituto di Santa Agnesa"; Eisenbichler, "Spazi e luoghi." By the end of the seventeenth century, the company hosted (or had effectively become) the Accademia degli Aquilotti; two of their plays are in the Archivio dell'Ospedale degli Innocenti, Florence, along with other documentation. See also Cancedda and Castelli, *Per una bibliografia,* 59–61.

[215] An early version of the Vangelista *Capitoli,* in thirteen chapters and dating to 1427, is in BNCF, Magl. xxxi.11; see Aranci, "La catachesi," 84–85. Their illuminated *Capitoli,* confirmed in 1451, were formerly in the collection of Major J.R. Abbey; see Alexander and De la Mare, *The Italian Manuscripts,* 32–35. The codex was sold by Sotheby's in 1989 and is now in a private European collection; see Abbey, *Catalogue,* lot 3020. I thank Christopher de Hamel for his assistance, but I have not been able to examine the text in full. On fol. 1ʳ, the larger image of the Holy Trinity acknowledges the confraternity's host church of Santa Trinita Vecchia. The illuminated N contains St. John the Evangelist and his emblem, the eagle. In the foliage around the left and upper borders are angels, while on the right and lower borders are the boys and young men of the confraternity, in their white robes with chaplets of greenery around their heads. The lettering on the first folio was entirely finished in gold leaf, now much abraded, applied over red bole lettering. The original binding, of dark brown goatskin over wooden boards, with metal corners and clasps, was adorned with a small painting, in the style of Benozzo Gozzoli, tempera on vellum, set under horn,

however, be linked to Lorenzo de' Medici's *Rappresentazione di san Giovanni e Paulo*, which will be discussed in Chapter 7. They were also probably responsible for the *Rappresentazione quando Gesù resucitò Lazero* from the 1470s, for three plays found in the Bolognese anthology BNCR, VE 483, *Beato Giovanni Colombino*, *Santa Cecilia*, and *Piero Teodinario de Costantinopoli*, and for two plays known only in print, *San Romolo* and *Sant'Agata*.

La rappresentazione quando Gesù resucitò Lazero

The *Play of the Raising of Lazarus*, found in BRF, Ricc. 2816, fols. 20^v-29^r, is short, simple, and a little dull. It is a reworking of John 11:1–45, the gospel reading for Lazarus or Passion Sunday, the Fifth Sunday in Lent. The Angel introduces the play with an invocation and a retelling of the gospel story of the death of Lazarus, including Christ's enigmatic words about life, walking in the light, death, sleeping, and resurrection. The prologue concludes:

Le cose a voi al presente narrate	The things that we have just narrated now
per rapresentazion mostrar vogliamo,	we want to show and represent as well,
e perché comprenderle possiate	and so that you can understand them all
tutti sicuramente v'esortiamo	with certainty, we do implore you now
vi piaccia far silenzio e ben gustate	to sit in silence and to savour well
le cose del Maestro, ché diciamo	the things the Master teaches, for we say
esser lo specchio della vita nostra	that in the holy works that Jesus did
l'opere sante che Gesù dimostra.	we find the mirror that will guide our lives.
	(oct. 7)

The passage from narration to representation is essential for understanding; and both seeing and listening in silence are required in order to savour the message. The play then enacts the full narrative of the Gospel, until Lazarus's shroud is removed and Christ invites Martha, Mary, and Lazarus to follow God. Where St. John's Gospel positions the raising of Lazarus as the trigger event for the Pharisees' plot against Jesus, the play ends with the miracle of Lazarus's resurrection. In bidding farewell to the audience, the Angel rejoices in the willing conversion of many of the Jews who were present that day and enjoins all Christians to love Jesus. Here, the tone is a conciliatory one, in contrast to the Easter plays of the Roman confraternity of the Gonfalone,

---

showing St. John the Evangelist with his eagle presenting the Gospel to a *confratello* and laying his right hand on his head.

where the Lazarus play ended with the stoning of Christ and was called the *Lapidazione*.[216] No printed edition of *Quando Gesù resucitò Lazero* survives, and I find no direct trace of it in the *Rappresentatione di S. Maria Maddalena* attributed to Castellano Castellani, or in the later play *La rapresentatione della conversione di santa Maria Maddalena*,[217] although that elaborate and sentimental play contains the episode. The Roman and Florentine plays have no more in common than their biblical source.

When I edited *Lazero* in 1983, I speculated that it may have come from the Vangelista company. The second octave reads:

Noi piglieremo una divota storia	We'll take a holy story to recite
secondo San Giovanni in un Vangelo,	according to the Gospel of St. John,
del qual vogliàn rinovellar memoria,	whose memory we wish to celebrate,
dove dimostra con divoto zelo	where he sets forth, with ardour and with zeal,
del nostro buon Maestro, Re di gloria,	about our loving Master, King of Glory,
quanto è per menar l'alma all'alto cielo,	and how he'll take our souls to highest heaven,
e farci in tutto creduli e fedeli	and give us faith and trust in everything,
con santi e prezïosi suoi Vangeli.	with his most holy and beloved Gospels.

(oct. 2)

The reference is not explicitly to the youth confraternity of the Vangelista, but as with the play of St. Agata discussed below, the lines seem to dwell on the Evangelist as the particular intermediary between the teaching of Christ and the faithful.

La rappresentazione del beato Giovanni Colombino

Feo Belcari's prose life of Giovanni Colombini (1304–1367), founder of the Jesuate order, is rightly regarded as one of the masterpieces of fifteenth-century vernacular hagiography.[218] Written in 1448 on commission from the Jesuates and dedicated to Giovanni di Cosimo de' Medici, the *vita* is based — as Belcari explains in his dedicatory letter — on three sources: Giovanni Tavelli da Tossignano's Latin *vita*, a life that does not survive by Cristofano di Gano

---

[216] See Wisch and Newbigin, *Acting on Faith*, 273; transcription in Luisi, "'Vedrete recitar'"; and in Newbigin online (Gonfalone) with other Gonfalone texts.

[217] On the two Mary Magdalene plays, see below, chapter 9.

[218] Belcari, *La vita del beato Giovanni Colombini*; Chiarini, *Feo Belcari*; on Colombini, see Piazzoni, "Colombini"; Gagliardi, "La trasmissione," in particular 239–250.

Guidini (better known for his role in preserving the letters of St. Catherine of Siena), and various "carte di pubblici notari," archival documents that must have been in the possessions of the Jesuates in Florence or Siena.[219] In Belcari's hands, the story of Colombini's conversion in 1355 — which may still have been part of oral history within the former Jesuate friary in Via dell'Acqua — becomes an extraordinary performance of penitence and charity, acted out in the theatre of the city. The play of the Blessed Giovanni's conversion and good works takes that theatricality a step further.

The *Play of the Blessed Giovanni Colombino* is transmitted by a single source, the anthology copied by Tommaso Leone for the Bolognese confraternity of San Girolamo in 1482,[220] where it is followed immediately by the *Santa Cecilia* play, which we know was performed by the company of the Vangelista (fig. 3.31). The Angel's epilogue suggests strongly an audience of adult males — Jesuates, perhaps, or else members of the adult company of San Paolo whose oratory the Vangelista company shared — in a confraternal performance space:

Finita è la festa del beato Zoanni Colombino. E questa stancia è quella che se dice, fatta la festa:	*The play of the Blessed Giovanni Colombino is done. And this is the stanza to be said at the end of the play.*
A vui tutti devoti che qui siete	To all of you devout men who are here
si rende laude, grazie e reverenza.	let us give praise and thanks and reverence,
Per vostra umanità degnato avete	for you have deigned, in your humanity,
venirci a visitar con pazïenza.	to come and visit us so patiently.
Quel che è mancato ci soportarete,	In all our failings we hope you'll forebear,
come omini discreti e di prudenza,	as men of prudence and discretion too;
e col nome di Dio licenciam voi;	and in God's name we bid you now farewell;
Cristo Iesù ve l' meriti per noi.	may Jesus Christ reward you on our part.
	(oct. 101)

---

[219] Tavelli, *Breve compendio*; Pardi, "Della vita," and "La *rappresentazione*." The 1501 inventory of the Purification company, ASF, CRSPL 1646 (P.xxx.7), fol. 212ᵛ, includes: "one small manuscript volume of the life of the Blessed Giovanni Colombino" (1° libretto in penna della vita del beato Giovanni Cholonbino).

[220] *La representatione del beato Ziovanni Colombino*, BNCR, VE 483, fols. 95ᵛ–110ʳ; for editions, see Table 1.

Despite the Bolognese patina applied by the copyist, I believe that the play came to Bologna from Florence along with at least fourteen others in the collection, and that it may originally have come from Siena.[221]

The play begins with a series of poor people arriving at the door of Giovanni, a wealthy Sienese merchant, to beg for alms. Some are simply unfortunate while others, like Galgano the gambler, have brought disaster upon themselves. They have rustic names, locating their origins in the Sienese *contado*, and all speak in a colourful language appropriate to their station. Moreover, each serves to reveal Giovanni's character, insensitive to suffering and willing to exploit even the most wretched to his own advantage.[222]

Only in octave 35 of the play do we arrive at Belcari's starting point. In a scene that was already luminous in Belcari's *vita*, we are introduced to Giovanni's long-suffering wife. Here, Belcari's two words, "replying kindly" (benignamente rispondendo), are elaborated into an episode of conjugal life:

ZOANE *se parte in fretta dal fondico, e va per manzare e dice a la donna e al fante*:

> Orsù, trovate ch'i' vo' disenare
> ch'i' voglio prestamente tirar via.
> El mi bisogna al fondaco tornare
> e par che vui dormiate tutta via.
> La mensa s'ha ancor a apparechiare!
> Per dispetto lo fate, in fede mia,
> che per mangiar in fretta i' son tornato
> e qui ancor non è nulla ordinato.

GIOVANNI *hurries out of the warehouse and goes to have lunch, and he says to his wife and to the manservant*:

> Be quick and find me something for my
> [lunch
> because I want to be right on my way.
> I really have to get back to the shop
> and here it seems that you're still half asleep.
> The table isn't even set for lunch.
> You do it just to spite me, I believe.
> I'm back because I want lunch in a rush,
> and here I find there's nothing ready yet.

---

[221] See chapter 1 above. On its possible Sienese origins, see Pardi, "La *rappresentazione*," 431–432.

[222] See also Ventrone, "Aspetti," 93–99; for other scenes with poor and/or exploited *contadini*, see *Susanna, Abataccio, Natività, Sant'Onofrio*; for the evils of gambling on cards, dice, and dominoes, see *Sant'Alesso, Miracolo del Corpo di Cristo*, Antonia Pulci's *Figliuol prodigo*, the *Questione di due fattori* at the end of *Uno pellegrino che andò a Santo Jacopo di Galizia*, and the later plays of *Sant'Onofrio (frottola)*, attributed to Castellano Castellani, and *Sant'Ippolito*. For the realities of gambling, see Pitti, *Ricordi*, 440 and passim.

Dice LA DONNA *a Zoanni:*
Che ti bisogna tanta fretta fare
e nella robba por tanta speranza?
Tanta tu n'hai che ti puo' riposare!
Tu hai de' tanti bien grande abundanza!
Tanta avarizia, deh!, lassala andare
e con lo mondo non far tal fidanza.
Egli è fallace ‹e› rio e non riesce:
tal pregio el crede aver che di man gli esce.

LA DONNA *dice:*
Non dubitare, che poco starai
che le vivande sono in perfezione.
Or piglia questo libro e ligerai
e certo n'arai gran consolazione.

ZOANNI *zetta el libro in terra:*
Altra facenda che leger non hai?
Non sono adesso per far lezïone.
Bisognami spazar perché ne vada:
costei mi crede qui tenere a bada.

Ma se gustasse la facenda mia
non tardaristi tanto quanto fai.
I' non ho nulla riposo che sia
e non c'è a dir se n'ho pensier assai
per poter ben tener la casa mia
e vivere ad onor come tu sai,
ma tu stampi sì spesso i paternostri
el giorno, e quisti sono i fatti vostri.

*Zoanni piglia lo libro mentre che la
donna apparechia perché la coscienza gli
morde e comincia legere e* LA DONNA
dice:
Zoanni, egli è in punto che tu pòi
a tuo piacer ogni volta mangiare.
Abi per iscusati alquanto noi
se t'avessimo fatto soprastare.

THE WIFE *says to Giovanni:*
Why do you have to be in such a rush?
And why is all you hope for just more stuff?
You have so much that you could just relax,
A great abundance of the things you own!
It's so much avarice! Just let it go
and do not put such faith in worldly things.
The world is false and wicked, and it fails:
the prize you think you've won just slips away.

THE WOMAN *says:*
Don't worry, you will only need to wait
a moment and your food will be just right.
Here, take this book and read it to yourself,
I'm sure you'll find it very comforting.

GIOVANNI *throws the book on the floor:*
Don't you have other things to do than read?
I'm not about to start my lessons now.
(I have to hurry up and make her go:
that woman thinks that she can keep me
[here.)

But if you knew just what my work is like
you wouldn't be as tardy as you are.
I never get a minute's rest at all
and there's no question, I have problems too
in trying to maintain my household well
and live with honour, as indeed you know,
but you recite your beads so many times
each day, and that is how things are with you.

*Giovanni picks up the book while his wife
prepares the table because his conscience is
biting him and he begins to read and* HIS
WIFE *says:*
Giovanni, things are ready now and you
can eat at any time just as you wish.
And do excuse us if by any chance
we've caused you some avoidable delay.

ZOANNI *a la donna*:
O io ho tanto aspettato voi
che un po' me vui potete aspettare,
tanto che questa legenda legh'io
puo' manzaremo col nome di Dio.

ZOANNI *lege e la donna lo vede così*
fisamente legere e dice così ginochioni:
    O dolce Iesù mio, da te procede
ogni suavità e ogni riposo.
Tu, vera pace, sì come si vede,
prestali tanta grazia al caro sposo
e lume d'intelletto e vera fede
che per tuo amor el sia largo e pietoso
e dia a' poveri per tuo santo amore
e sempre sia tuo fedel servitore.

GIOVANNI *to his wife*:
You kept me waiting long enough, now you
can wait a while for me, just so that I
can finish reading the life of this saint,
and then we'll eat together in God's name.

GIOVANNI *reads and his wife sees him*
reading so intently and kneels and says:
    O sweetest Jesus, from you doth proceed
all soothing sweetness and tranquillity.
You are true peace, as we can plainly see:
grant to my dearest husband all the grace,
enlightenment of mind and truest faith,
that for your love he may be merciful,
and for your holy love give to the poor
and so forever serve you faithfully.

(oct. 35–40)

The wife's prayers are answered. Giovanni returns to the office, countermands orders he has already given to his agent, and begins to dispense alms. He informs Mona Biagia his wife that they must "renounce | all carnal pleasure of our bodies" (lassar andare | d'i corpi nostri ogni carnal diletto; oct. 54.2–3). He recruits his brother Francesco and together they scandalize the citizens of Siena with their spectacle of penitence and almsgiving. In secret Giovanni wraps himself in a blanket and heads for a paupers' hospice, where the woman in charge delights him with pennyroyal tea. His wife and his brother persuade him to come home. Soon afterwards, his only son dies and, while his wife grieves, Giovanni rejoices that he is now free to give everything away. He asks his wife to release him from their marriage, but she categorically refuses. Next Giovanni and his brother find a leper at the door of the church. Giovanni carries him home on his shoulders and, over his wife's protests, puts the man in their marriage bed and drinks from the bathwater in which he has bathed him. Giovanni and his brother leave the man in her care and go to mass.

Pricked by remorse that she has done nothing for the leper, the wife opens the door and breathes the sweetest smell. When Giovanni and Francesco go to look, they find the bed empty and realize that the leper was Christ himself. The play ends with Mona Biagia, releasing Giovanni from marriage, allowing him to be united with the Paraclete. The final stanza already cited bids farewell to the men — friars perhaps, or members of the adult confraternity — who have come to watch the play.

As in so many of our plays, the central message — to the audience, as much as to the actors themselves — is that only through the practice of unconfined almsgiving can Christians draw close to Christ. Mona Biagia had urged restraint, "In great abundance you can dispense alms | but let it also be with temperance" (Lemosin tu pòi fare in abundanza, | ma vuolsi far con qualche temperanza; oct. 76.7–8), but Giovanni finds perfect joy in excess. The play has no interest in the rest of Colombini's life, and his travails in the founding of his new Jesuate order: it simply delights in the authentic representation of Giovanni's grotesque behaviour and his long-suffering wife's acceptance of it.

La rappresentazione di santa Cecilia

The *Play of St. Cecilia* also deals with marriage: Cecilia and Valeriano's chaste marriage, and their martyrdom. It is known in two substantially different redactions. The manuscript version, in 175 octaves, was copied by the Bolognese copyist Tommaso Leone in 1482,[223] while the printed version, in 110 octaves, the *Rappresentazione di santa Cecilia vergine e martire*, was issued by Antonio Tubini and Andrea Ghirlandi for Maestro Francesco di Giovanni Benvenuto around 1510. It bears the colophon: "Performed by the company of the Vangelista" (Recitata per la compagnia del Vangelista) on the last page (figs. 3.32 and 3.33).[224] The two versions have 90 octaves more or less in common.

---

[223] *La representatione di sancta Cicilia*, BNCR, VE 483, fols. 110ʳ–134ᵛ; for edition, see Table 1.

[224] *La rappresentatione di Sancta Cecilia uergine & martyre* ([Florence: Antonio Tubini and Andrea Ghirlandi, 1510?]), ISTC ic00363500, CNCE 54152 (type 86R); Cioni, *Bibliografia*, 104, xvi.1; Periti, "Contributo," 177, R 16. The statement that the play was performed by the Company of the Evangelist does not appear in subsequent editions. The copy of this edition in Yale University's Beinecke Library, Rare Book Room Hd7 330, lacks fols. a4–5, and a8, and has been so brutally trimmed that it has lost the title on fol. aiʳ. The present fol. a8, blank on the *recto* and bearing the printer's mark of Filippo Giunta on the *verso*, has been supplied from an unidentified and unrelated edition. There is, thus, no "Giunta edition." The edition now in the Biblioteca Colombina, 6-3-27(19) (type 88R, 6 fols.; Periti, "Contributo," 177, R 17), purchased in Rome in December 1515 for two *quatrines*, is different: the title is in gothic type and there is no broad frame around the woodcut of the saint, which is a copy of the cut in the first edition, but with a different border; it has no CNCE number. It was quickly followed by a third edition: Florence, for Francesco di Giovanni Benvenuto, 19 December 1517, CNCE 61539; Cioni, *Bibliografia*, 104, xvi.2; Periti, "Contributo," 177–178, R 18.

Both versions derive from a single Florentine archetype, which is in turn based on the life of the saint in the *Legenda Aurea*.[225] The manuscript follows the *vita* closely, but with the interpolation of a catechistic section, oct. 57–71 of the manuscript, in which Cecilia instructs Tiburzio in the history of Man's Salvation. The leaden clumsiness of these stanzas, which goes beyond the untheatricality of the subject, suggests a different author from the rest of the text. The version in print is much tighter and more theatrical, and probably dates to the period after the return of the Medici in 1512, when youth confraternities resumed their theatrical activities.[226] There are important differences. In the manuscript, as in the *vita*, we do not meet Cecilia before her marriage, so that her prayer to Christ to preserve her virginity, just before Valeriano comes to the marriage chamber, is as much a surprise to the audience as it will be to Valeriano. In the printed version, we know of this intention before her marriage, and the marriage itself is a much grander Florentine affair, with a traditional *serraglio*, in which the bridegroom's friends attempt to disrupt Cecilia's path to her marriage until her maidservant gives them ten ducats for their party. The preparations for the marriage, and Cecilia's announcement of her secret to Valeriano, are quite different:

[Manuscript]	[Printed edition]
Cicilia *risponde*:	
I' son contenta a te manifestare	
questo secreto, sì mi sta' âscoltare.	Cecilia *a Valeriano dice*:
Valariano, i' ho l'angel de Dio	Sappi che gli è più tempo io fui sposata
che ama me con molta gilosia	da uno sposo che, se saperrebbe
e con gran zel conserva il corpo mio,	che carnalmente m'avessi toccata
e se vedesse che con mente ria	subitamente lui t'ucciderebbe
tu t'acostassi a me con atto rio,	perché la sua progenie è sì pregiata
volendo tôrmi quel ch'i' non voria,	che niun riparo con lui non sarebbe,
quest'angel santo ti percoterebbe,	e questo sappi che è l'angiol di Dio
di poi la vita ancor sì ti torebbe.	che è con meco, e guarda el corpo mio.

---

[225] Jacobus, *Legenda Aurea*, 2:1322–1331, clxv *De Sancta Cecilia*.

[226] The first printed edition has no *licenza* at the end; the text of the play fills 8 leaves, and it would appear that the printer sacrificed the final stanza or two, rather than extend his text to 10 leaves by adding additional woodcuts throughout the text or *laude* at the end to fill the space.

Ma se vedrà che con sincero amore
tu ame me, come amar si debbe,
diventerà di puo' tuo defensore,
ché altramente facendo sarebbe
de tua felice vita destruttore,
ed ogni mal sopra di te verebbe.
Se tu amarai me con casto core
ci mostrarà sua gloria e suo dolciore.

VALARIANO *risponde*:
    Se tu vuoi ch'io ti creda, o dolce
        [amore,
dimostrami quest'angel che m'hai
        [detto,
e io prometto a te con tutto il core
di crederti di poi, quest'è l'effetto.
Ma s'i' vedrò che con carnal amore
tu ami o sara' amata a mio dispetto,
che s'io vi troverò in cotal sorte
certo amedui i' vi darò la morte.

(oct. 19.7–22.8, fol. 113ʳ)

E perderesti la tua giovineza
la qual da tanti è sì desiderata;
e se vedrà che m'ami con dolceza
e con sincero amor l'alma adornata,
amerà te come la mia belleza
e vedrai lui e sua gloria beata.

VALERIANO *dice*:
Creder non voglio alla parola tua
se io non vego lui in faccia sua.

E s'io vedrò che sia l'angel che hai detto,
io farò quanto allor tu mi dirai;
e se uomo sarà e tuo difetto,
e te e lui uccider mi vedrai.

(oct. 17–19.4, fol. a2ᵛ)

Ms: CECILIA *replies*: I'm happy that I can reveal to you | this secret, so be still and listen well. || 20. Valerian, God's Angel is with me | and loves me with immense suspiciousness | and with great zeal he keeps my body safe. | And if he saw that with a wicked thought | or wicked deed you brought yourself to me, | wanting to take from me what I'd not wish, | this holy Angel would first strike you down | and then would take your life and leave you dead. || 21. But if he sees that with sincerest love | you love me, as one is required to love, | he'll then become your own defender too, | for if you were to act another way, | he'd bring destruction on your happy life | and every woe would fall upon your head. | But if you love me with a pure, chaste heart, | he'll show his sweetest glory to us both. || VALARIANO *replies*: 22. If you want me to trust you, o sweet love, | show me this Angel that you've told me of | and I give you my promise, from my heart, | that I'll believe you: that's the sum of it. | But if I see that you've conceived a love | that's carnal, or that someone else loves you | in spite of me, and if I catch you out | then certainly I'll put you both to death.

Printed edition: Cecilia *says to Valeriano*: | 17. The fact is that some time ago I wed | a husband, who if he should ever learn | that you had touched me with carnal intent | he'd kill you there and then, without delay, | because his children are so precious that | no hiding place would keep you safe from him. | He is God's Angel, this you have to know | and he's with me, and guards me bodily. || 18. And you would lose the flower of your youth | that is by many people so desired; | and if he sees you sweetly loving me | and sees your soul adorned with sincere love, | he'll love you as he loves my beauty too, | and you will see him in his glory bless'd. | Valeriano *says*: I won't believe a word of what you say | unless I can behold him face to face. || 19. And if I see the Angel you describe, | I'll do whatever you will tell me to; || and if he is a man and you have sinned, | you'll see me come and kill both him and you.)

Valeriano receives baptism and he and Cecilia are each crowned with a wreath of flowers, invisible, according to the manuscript, to all but virgins (oct. 40.1–2). While the most entertaining part of the play is more lively in the printed edition, the differences in the rest of the play — the conversion of Valeriano's brother Tiburzio, their work among the poor and burying the dead, and the martyrdom of all three at the hands of Almachio until finally heaven opens and angels come for the soul of Cecilia — are minimal.

Whereas Giovanni Colombini's Mona Biagia, wife and mother, had been unwilling to untie the bonds of holy matrimony, Cecilia, virgin and bride, proposes a totally different version of marriage: a marriage that respects the bride's previous commitment to her heavenly spouse, and the presence of an Angel to defend her from any carnal threat from her husband. The legend had enormous traction with women, for whom marriage could often be short and brutal.[227] But here it is being offered as a model for boys: virginity and chastity in marriage are aspirations for young men as well as young women.[228]

---

[227] For some statistics on the duration of marriages, see Klapisch-Zuber, "La fécondité," esp. table 6, p. 48. The average duration was decreased above all by the age discrepancy between women and their older husbands, but also by the toll of plague, disease and childbirth. On the perils and disappointments of marriage, see *La rappresentazione di santa Domitilla*, oct. 17–22, in Antonia Pulci, *Saints' Lives*, 80–85.

[228] The Purification statutes required members to "practise chastity, and anyone who had a wife should practise matrimony as the Holy Church commands" (oservare chastità e chi avessi donna oservi il matrimonio chome comanda la sancta chiesa), Bloomington, Lilly, MR 26, fol. 22ᵛ, cap. xviii.

Various elements suggest that the play was being performed at Carnival by the time of the performance marked by the printed edition, but without the magnificent apparatus of Heaven, where God and his angels receive the soul of Cecilia in the manuscript version.[229] The prologue, absent in the manuscript, seems to allude to a Carnival performance by boys and young men for friars in their convent, an activity that fulfils the injunction of the confraternal statutes to turn away from evil and do good, which became most pressing during Carnival:

Oggi la santa madre Discrezione,	Today, Discretion, our most holy mother,
padri, sì ci ha condotti in questo loco	has brought us, fathers, here within this place
perché e giovani stieno in devozione,	so that young men may pass their time
levandogli da' vizi e tristo gioco	[devoutly,
vivendo la cristiana religione.	removed from vices and from sinful games,
	to live a Christian and religious life.
	(oct. 1.1–5.)

Nevertheless, the introduction of the *serraglio* (oct. 10–11 of the printed version) and the riot of *poveri* at the end who come to collect the alms that are being dispensed (oct. 107.7–8) suggest that the festive elements of misrule could be harnessed for spiritual purposes.

La istoria de Piero Teodinario di Costantinopoli

The same Bolognese manuscript contains the *Story of Peter Godpenny of Constantinople*,[230] based on a story told in the first *vita* of the fourth part of Domenico Cavalca's translation of the *Vite dei Santi Padri*.[231] Within the thirty-four chapters of the life of the seventh-century saint St. John the Almoner, patriarch of Alexandria, also called St. John the Merciful, is embedded

---

[229] In the printed edition, she is greeted by a choir of angels rather than by God himself. D'Ancona, *Origini*, 1:192, notes the use of the term *luogo deputato* in the printed edition to indicate a part of the stage; the manuscript makes it clear, however, that Paradise is above the acting space, as it was in Santa Maria del Carmine. The term, meaning 'appointed place,' appears first in the Umbrian plays and belongs to a scenography where multiple 'places' are present simultaneously on a single set, but are rendered invisible, either by convention or by a curtain, when not in use.

[230] *La hystoria de Piero Theodinario de Costantinopoli*, Rome, BNC, VE 483, fols. 31ʳ–42ᵛ; Pietro Delcorno's edition is forthcoming.

[231] Cavalca, *Vite*, 2:1266–1273, IV, 14.

a second life, of Peter the Tax Collector, recited by the patriarch as one of his "most edifying exemplars, especially of mercy and pity."[232] When Cavalca and his Pisan brothers in the Dominican friary of Santa Caterina came to translate the Latin *vita*, they found it necessary to gloss the epithet that traditionally accompanies Peter's name: "Concerning Peter Theolonarios, that is the avaricious banker or tax collector, and how he became so merciful that he even sold himself as an act of mercy."[233] The Latin word *thelonarios* is simply Italianized to *teolonario*, but the author of this play transformed the unfamiliar word a step further into *theodinario*, combining θεός (God) and *denarius* (penny) and from this conjunction he crafted a charming short play that, once again, reminds its audience of the charitable obligations that accompany wealth.

Peter Theolonarios's legend has two parts: his miserly and usurious life up to his conversion through a vision of being saved from hell by a single involuntary act of charity, namely throwing a loaf of bread at a hungry pauper; and his life after conversion, when he has himself sold into slavery and the money given to the poor. Only the first part is treated in the play (to oct. 48), but it is elaborated with enormous verve. The play begins with Piero (as he is called, in the Florentine form, throughout the play) giving orders to his *cassiere* (accountant) to think only of profit, and never to lend without collateral. A pauper who comes to beg for relief from his taxes is brutally dismissed. But Piero meets his match in a newly arrived *zaratano* (charlatan or mountebank), who is hungry, in the manner of itinerant actors, and consults two local *zaratani* for advice. They tell him that he will find food and wine almost anywhere, except from Piero Teodinario. The *zaratano* wagers that he will succeed where others have failed and puts on a performance of abject poverty and illness to extract charity from Piero. He meets with abuse and more, because Piero seizes a loaf of bread from a passing baker's boy and hurls it at him. The *zaratano* returns to his new friends, claiming that Piero has given him the bread freely and for the love of God (oct. 21.5–8). Meanwhile, Piero's rage causes him to fall ill. He consoles himself by gloating over his treasure and appears to die as he embraces it. An Angel and a Demon

---

[232] Cavalca, *Vite*, 2:1266–1273, IV, 14 [2]: "exempli di grande edificattione, maximamente exempli di missericordia e di pietade." The story is also remembered in *Il novellino* (XVII), along with other legends that are taken up by *rappresentazioni*, including Barlaam and Josaphat (XIV) and the charity of San Paolino Vescovo (XVI).

[233] Cavalca, *Vite*, 2:1266, IV, 14 [1]: "Di Petro teolonario, cioè banchieri uvero gabellieri avaro, come diventó sì pietoso ch'etandio si vendette per pietade."

battle fiercely for his soul until Christ intervenes. They gather together Piero's good and bad deeds and weigh them:

Come l'Angelo e il Demonio di presente	*The Angel and the Demon then place*
metteno el bene e il male de Piero in su la	*Peter's good and bad deeds on the scales,*
bilanza, e come el male avanza el bene, e	*and since the bad deeds outweigh the*
L'ANGELO *dica a Cristo*:	*good,* THE ANGEL *says to Christ*:
Ricordati, Signore onnipotente,	I beg you to recall, almighty Lord,
de la infinita tua gran caritade.	your charity, both great and infinite.
Se costui ha peccato mortalmente,	If he has now committed mortal sin,
se l'ha peccato per fragilitade.	that sin is the result of frailty.
Quanto che 'l pan non sia sufficiente,	And if that loaf of bread is not enough,
adopra in lui, Signor, la tua pietade.	then exercise your mercy, Lord, on him.
Fa' che ritorni al mondo con clemenza	Use clemency and let him now return
intanto che lui faza penitenza.	to the world just to do his penance there.

(oct. 33)

Piero awakes from what proves to have been a vision and resolves to return all his pledges to their owners and give away all his property. He is visited by three gentlemen who marvel at this conversion.

The second part of the play, from oct. 39, moves to a different legend altogether. It presents the story of the *Three Living Kings and the Three Dead Kings*, which is just as interesting, both for magic of its own and for the way it supplements our knowledge of the *edifici* of St. John the Baptist.[234] The three gentlemen, two young and one old, having failed to dissuade Piero from giving away all his money to the poor, leave him and set out to hunt. They meet a Hermit, who is guided by an Angel to reveal to them what their future holds after death. The Hermit leads the three gentlemen to the tombs of the three dead men, all surprised by death as they frittered their lives away in wealth and vanities, without time to repent. In the most tenuous way, the play links back to its first part as the three gentlemen resolve to follow Piero's lead and dedicate themselves to an ascetic life: "Let's leave the sin and dangers of the world | and give ourselves in full to serving God" (Lassiamo el mondo periglioso e rio | e dianci tutti al servicio de Dio; oct. 85.7–8).

The two parts are very different in tone and ethical thrust: the first continues the theme of Christian responsibility to dispense charity to the poor

---

[234] The two narratives are interwoven, oct. 39–49. See further discussion in chapter 4 below.

and God's infinite mercy to the charitable; the second part reveals a vengeful God, and the eternal punishment of those whose lives were consumed by vanity. Both appear to be Florentine in origin, but rhymes betray other influences.[235] In both parts the dialogue is exclusively in whole octaves with no attempt at all to divide the octave among several speakers, just as we find, for example, in those parts of the *Dì del Giudizio* that are by the Herald, Antonio di Matteo di Meglio.[236] Nevertheless the stage directions reveal a careful attention to performability. Both the play of Last Judgment and the play of the Living and the Dead were the responsibility, according to Benedetto Dei, of Santissima Annunziata. I shall return to these *edifici* and their iconography in the next chapter.

La festa di sant'Agata virgine e martire

Like the play of St. Cecilia, *The Play of the Virgin Martyr St. Agatha* presents virginity as an invincible and unflinching defence in the face of persecution. No manuscript survives, and the earliest edition was printed in Florence by Bartolomeo de' Libri, no later than 1495 (fig. 3.34).[237] The play begins with a prologue in praise of virginity spoken by one of the *fanciulli*:

---

[235] Examples of imperfect rhymes include: *villano | danno* | malanno, oct. 6, suggesting a north Italian origin; *zaratano | pano* (for *pane*), oct. 9, suggesting *zaratàn | pan* in the original; a merging of *o* and *u* in *vui | lui | vui*, oct. 13; and of *e* and *i* in *molesto | Cristo | tristo*, oct. 17; and recourse to assonance rather than rhyme: *conforto | corpo | morto*, oct. 73. It could be that these are stylistic tics of a less skilful versifier; certainly, the palette of rhymes is limited, with some combination of the rhyme *Dio | pio | rio | mio | io* recurring in twenty of the ninety octaves.

[236] Delcorno Branca, "Fra cantare e sacra rappresentazione," argues that whole-stanza speeches are characteristic of earlier plays. With a larger sample and more nuanced dating of the plays, I do not think that this view is entirely valid, but the two hands at work in the *Dì del Giudizio* (before 1448) are evidence of vastly different practice and ability. On Antonio di Matteo di Meglio, see below, chapter 4.

[237] *La festa di sancta Agata uirgine & martyre* ([Florence: Bartolomeo de' Libri, not after 1495]), ISTC ia00157450; Cioni, *Bibliografia*, 74, v.1; for modern editions, see Table 2. See also Raimondi, "Note sulla fortuna"; Del Popolo, *Tra sacro e profano*, 169–172. For the source, see Jacobus, *Legenda Aurea*, 1:296–301, XXXIX *De Sancta Agatha*; or one of the *volgarizzamenti* of the *Legenda Aurea*.

La virginità santa è un bel fiore	Holy virginity is a fair flower
come un candido giglio puro e netto	lily-like, pure, unblemished, snowy white,
dove Gesù riceve sempre odore.	whose perfume reaches Jesus ever more.
Di Vergin nacque il suo corpo perfetto:	His perfect body was of Virgin born:
per questo amò Giovanni e con amore	for this he cherished John and with love gave
lo die' alla Madre per figliuol perfetto;	him to his Mother as a perfect son;
per questa par lo Vaso di elezione	for this, it seems, the Chosen Vessel, Saul,
meritò aver la sua conversione.	was worthy of conversion to St. Paul.

(oct. 1)

Invoking St. John the Evangelist, as well as St. Paul's injunctions on virginity, marriage, and widowhood in 1 Corinthians 7, the opening stanza suggests that once again the confraternity responsible is the Vangelista, which shared premises with the adult confraternity or *buca* of San Paolo in Via dell'Acqua.[238]

Reports of fair young Agata's Christianity have aroused Quinziano, who sends his men to bring her to him by force. When Agata refuses to sacrifice to his gods, he sends for Madam Anfrodessa, who takes her away "among the young girls" (fra le figliuole; stage direction after oct. 25.8) and attempts to persuade her to be compliant. The other girls attempt to warn her of her fate if she disobeys and to lure her with music and dancing, but Anfrodessa returns to Quinziano to admit defeat. Quinziano turns to violence, first displayed, then actuated:

Deh! muta tuo pensiero, o meschinella	Come, change your mind, foolish little girl,
che vedi qui preparati i coltelli,	now you can see the knives laid out for you,
mantaco, fuoco, fun, carboni e taglie	bellows, fire, rope, coals, and pulley blocks,
ed arrotate son ben le tanaglie.	and the pincers have been sharpened well.

(oct. 43.5–8)

Agata is beaten, struck in the mouth (which, as with so many tortured virgins, only makes her more eloquent), and returned to her cell. She is still defiant when she appears before Quinziano again, and he orders the executioner, Maestro Piero, to take his pincers and tear off her breasts.[239] The text gives us

---

[238] Later, in her cell, Agata asks Christ to help her just as he consoled the Virgin by giving her the Evangelist as her son, oct. 51.6–8.

[239] As in Lorenzo de' Medici's *San Giovanni e Paulo* (oct. 131.7–8), *Santa Caterina vergine e martire* (oct. 76.4, 106.2, 122.1), *Reina Ester* (oct. 60.5), and *Santa Felicita* (oct. 50.1), the executioner's name is Maestro Piero, which Cionacci, "Sopra *Le rime sacre*," col. 20, speculated was the name of a contemporary Florentine executioner. In *Sant'Eustachio*,

the slightest hint of how it was done. The torturer is now the focus of attention and faces the audience. Agata turns away from the viewer to face him:

EL MAESTRO *a santa Agata*:
Volgiti in qua ch'i' ti farò provare
quel ch'è spregiare il nostro imperadore.
Chiam'or Gesù che ti venga ' aiutare,
paza, che se tu non rivolgi il core
agl'idoli, t'arò presto a spiccare
le tuo mammelle con molto dolore;
ma se ancora rinieghi il tuo Idio
troverrai Quinzïano esserti pio.

SANTA AGATA *al Manigoldo*:
Prima mi lascerò tutta tagliare
le membra a pezi, non che le
[mammelle,
e dalle fiere tutta divorare
e star nel fuoco o fra tagli e coltelle
ch'i' voglia il mie Signor Gesù negare.
Pon qui silenzio e le parole felle.
Fa' pur l'ufficio tuo sanza mercede
ch'i' vo' pur forte star nella mia fede.

EL MANIGOLDO *a santa Agata*:
Or oltre, porgi qua presto il tuo
[petto.

AGATA *al Manigoldo*:
Volentier perché questo è 'l mio tesoro.

EL MANIGOLDO *apicca le tanaglie*:
I' ti punirò or del tuo difetto.

SANTA AGATA *alza gli ochi al cielo e dice*:
O dolce mie Gesù, perdona loro
e me fa' forte nel tuo amor perfetto
in questo crudo e rigido martoro.
Gesù, Gesù, Gesù, dolceza mia,
dammi forteza in questa pena ria.

MASTER [PIERO] *to St. Agatha*:
Turn and face me, and I'll let you feel
just what it means to slight our emperor.
Now call on Jesus to come to your aid,
you fool! If you don't have a change of heart
and worship idols, I will have to hack
your breasts off, with no little pain for you;
but if you will deny your God, you'll find
that Quinziano will be good to you.

ST. AGATHA *to the Executioner*:
I'd rather let my very limbs be hacked
to tiny pieces, and not just my breasts,
and be devoured completely by wild beasts,
left in the fire or sliced by blades and
[knives,
before I would deny Jesus my Lord.
Let silence reign and wicked words be still.
Do what you must and use no mercy here
for I will yet stand firm within my faith.

THE EXECUTIONER *to St. Agatha*:
Come on and show me readily your
[breast.

ST. AGATA *to the Executioner*:
Most willingly: this is my treasure here.

THE EXECUTIONER *attaches the pincers*:
Now here's the punishment for your misdeed.

ST. AGATA *raises her eyes to heaven and says*:
O sweetest Jesus, pray forgive their sins
and fortify me with your perfect love
in this most cruel and wretched martyrdom.
O Jesus, Jesus, Jesus, sweetest love,
give strength to me in this most wicked pain.

---

which preserves the Romanitas of the legend, he is called Petrone (oct. 112.3). Del Popolo, *Tra sacro e profano*, 164, sees the name in counterpoint to St. Peter the apostle, who appears as a perfect doctor in *Sant'Agata* (oct. 68).

Tagliato le mammelle, SANTA AGATA *dice a Quinziano*:	*When her breasts have been cut off*, ST. AGATHA *says to Quinziano*:
O perfido, crudel, tristo tiranno,	O cruel oppressor, treacherous and base,
ché non ti se', ribaldo, vergognato	how, you low varlet, can you feel no shame
d'aver tagliato quel che più d'un anno	at having hacked away the place where you
alla tuo madre avesti già poppato?	suckled your mother's milk more than a year?
Ma sappi ch'i' non ho di questo affanno	But know, this causes not one whit of pain
ch'i' n'ho mille nell'anima apiccato	because I keep a thousand more within
colle qual mi notrisco et nutricai	my soul to nourish and to nurture me
quando sposa a Gesù mi consecrai.	since I became Christ's consecrated bride.
	(oct. 61–64)

Bloodied and mutilated, Agata is returned to prison, where she is visited by St. Peter the Apostle. He comes disguised as a doctor, accompanied by a young boy, and announces himself as "a perfect doctor" (un medico perfetto; oct. 68.1). When she protests that she has never been treated by a man, and that she would trust only God to heal her breast, St. Peter assures her: "And He it is who's sent me here to you | and verily I'm Peter, his apostle" (E Lui è quello il quale a te mi manda: | i' son Piero suo apostol veramente; oct. 70.1–2). Agata is immediately whole again. The play is following its narrative source, but audiences in Medicean Florence must have enjoyed St. Peter's parody of medical hubris as much as modern ones.

Agata is brought again before Quinziano and more torments are prepared, but they are forestalled by an earthquake. The people rise up against Quinziano and he flees to the top of the mount, where he falls. Devils seize him. Agata dies in prison and her soul is accompanied to heaven by angels. The ending — with devils and angels — strays from the *Legenda Aurea* only to use the scenic resources that the confraternities now had at their disposal: the mountain and heaven allowed for glorious effects. The play ends with two *laude* in praise of St. Agata, sung by angels as they carry her to heaven, and a third *lauda*,[240] in which the actors bid farewell to the audience rather than leaving this task to the Angel.

---

[240] An octave, sung to the tune of "Perché l'amor di Dio [tanto mi tira]" by Francesco degli Albizzi; see Wilson, *Singing Poetry*, database.

La rappresentazione di santo Romolo martire, vescovo di Fiesole

The earliest edition of Mariano Bellandini's *Play of St. Romulus the Martyr, Bishop of Fiesole* was printed by Tubini and Ghirlandi before August 1515 (fig. 3.35),[241] but the play almost certainly dates to several years earlier and marks the return to activity of the company of the Vangelista. The prologue, spoken by a *fanciullo* on behalf of his fellow actors, rather than by an Angel, makes this clear:

L'Aquila s'è alquanto un po' posata	Our Eagle has been resting for a while
per la fortuna e tempesta di mare,	away from fortune's woes and storms at sea,
ma ora, essendo alquanto umiliata,	but now, having been laid low for some time,
vorrebbe pur cominciare a volare.	she is ready to start flying high again.
Però ti priega, come l'è usata,	Therefore, she begs you, in her usual way,
che con silenzio la vogli ascoltare.	to pay attention to her silently.
Spera di darti pur consolazione:	It is her hope that she'll give you delight,
sta' ad udirla e abbi discrezione.	so sit and listen, and judge for yourself.
Tu vedrai qui l'apostol tuo San Piero,	Here you will see St. Peter, your apostle,
Romolo santo da lui battezzare.	and Romolo, the saint baptized by him.
In Gesù pose tanto desidero	His love for Jesus was so very great
che vescovo di Fiesol lo fe' fare.	that Peter made him bishop of Fiesole.
Tanto il suo cuore fu puro e sincero	His heart was so sincere and free from sin
che niuna pena volle ricusare.	that he would never turn away from pain.
Lui e ' compagni furono straziati	He and his followers were martyred there,
giù per quel poggio, e quivi collocati.	dragged down that hill and buried there [below.

---

[241] Mariano Bellandini, *La rappresentatione di Sancto Romolo martyre Vescouo di Fiesole* ([Florence: Antonio Tubini and Andrea Ghirlandi, before 8 August 1515]), CNCE 4861; Cioni, *Bibliografia*, 263, LXXXVIII.1; for modern edition, see Table 2. The *lauda* in honour of St. Romulus, which fills the space left on fol. 4ᵛ, is followed by the words "Composta per Mariano Bellandini," probably referring to the whole play. He may be related to Friar Serafino Bellandini of the Dominican friary of San Marco, who welcomed the Purification company into their new quarters in 1506; see Polizzotto, *Children*, 137. The "Aquila" (Eagle) of oct. 1.1 was the symbol of both the Evangelist and of the company dedicated to him.

Questi fanciul da ben son preparati	These boys, all of good family, have
di volertela un po' rappresentare	[prepared
perché fuggieno e tristi lor peccati.	the play they want to represent for you,
El guardiano gli consente così fare	in order to find refuge from their sins;
che, essendo in buona opera occupati,	Their Warden has consented to the play
el cattivo ozio non gli può esaltare.	because, if they're engaged in wholesome
Se la consolazione non sarà molta,	[work,
noi ti ristoreremo un'altra volta.	base idleness can't triumph over them.
	If consolation is but limited,
	we'll compensate for it another time.
	(oct. 1–3)

San Romolo was not simply a model of faith in the face of persecution. As Christiane Klapisch-Zuber has shown, St. Romulus was credited with remarkable efficacy against epilepsy, and the name Romolo became enormously popular in the last decade of the fifteenth century, to protect newborn infants from this terrible illness.[242] His power is praised in the last stanza of the *lauda* that closes the play of his life and martyrdom:

Tanta virtù ha questo nome	In this name such virtue lies,
e questo sì si è veduto.	and this truly has been seen.
Chi con fede al figliuol pone	A son given this name in faith
di mal mal non è caduto,	never falls down with *grand mal*,
tanto è grande il suo aiuto.	such great succour does he bring.
È in chi io ho fede e spero:	He's the one I trust and hope in:
el discepol di san Piero,	the disciple of St. Peter,
Santo Romolo benedetto.	blessèd saint, San Romolo.
	(*lauda* after oct. 125)

The feast day of St. Romulus, bishop of Fiesole, and his followers was 6 July.[243] The play may have been performed on his feast day, perhaps even near the very *poggio* (hilltop) where tradition holds that he and his followers

---

[242] Klapisch-Zuber, "San Romolo."

[243] See *AASS*, Jul. II, 29:253–262: "De Sancto Romulo Episcopo, ejusque sociis Marchitiano, Crescentio, Dulcissimo et Carissimo, martyribus, Faesulis ac Volaterris in Etruria" (Concerning St. Romulus the Bishop and his followers Marchitianus, Crescentius, Dulcissimus and Carissimus, martyrs in Fiesole and Volterra in Etruria).

were martyred (fig. 3.36),[244] below the Hieronymite friary, overlooking the Via Vecchia Fiesolana, and opposite the gates of the Villa Medici (fig. 3.17).

There is circumstantial evidence that after the Medici returned to Florence in 1512, Fiesole again became the scene of plays.[245] A later sixteenth-century reworking of the *Vita* of Savonarola attributed to Pacifico Burlamacchi, in its discussion of the Friar's reform of youth morality, interpolates among activities that boys could engage in "with decent modesty, humility, and reverence for things divine" on feast days, "excursions, for example to Fiesole and San Gaggio, for plays and other *feste*," even though such activities are not mentioned in earlier manuscripts of the *Vita*, and *rappresentazioni* are not mentioned at all in the Savonarolan text that is distantly echoed here.[246] The interpolation and favourable opinion of plays probably reflects practices that were current at the time this version of the *Vita* was compiled.

The paratheatrical *frottola* (a play-outside-the-play in a different metre) that frames and comments on a later Vangelista play of *Abramo e Agar* also leads us out of Florence and up to Fiesole. In it, the father asks his son Antonio what he wants, and on learning that the boy hankers after fashionable new clothes, he rails against modern youth. His virtuous son, Benedetto, however, wants nothing more than to spend this summer's day in Fiesole, watching a new play by the Vangelista company:

Vo' che indietro torniamo	I want us to go back
e vo' che noi andiamo	and take ourselves up to
a' fiesolani poggi,	the hills of Fiesole
ch'io mi ricordo ch'oggi	for, I recall, today
una festa non vista	the Vangelista boys
mai più el Vangelista	are doing a new play
vi fa e rappresenta.	that's not been seen before.

(lines 337–343)

---

[244] See oct. 2.8. The verse inscription on the roadside plaque reads: "Sopra di questo Sasso | Per man delle crudel fesulee genti | Spettacolo di morte orrendo e tristo | Qual vittime innocenti | Cadero esangui i gran campion di Cristo" (Upon this very rock, at the hands of the cruel Fiesolani, horrendous, wicked spectacle of death, the great champions of Christ fell lifeless as innocent victims).

[245] See discussion of the *Abataccio*, *Raffaello e Tobbia*, and *Josef, figliuolo di Jacob* above.

[246] Ginori Conti, ed., *La vita*, 122: "con honesta modestia, mansuetudine et reverentia alle cose divine"; "gite, come a Fiesole, a Santo Gaggio, a far qualche rappresentatione o altre feste"; for textual problems, see below, chapter 9, n. 14.

The boys of the Vangelista performed a play for their peers and their fathers, who were just like Antonio and Benedetto and their father. I shall return to this new framing device and its implications, as well as to Savonarola's attitude to plays, in chapter 9.

The Company of Sant'Antonio da Padova, or of San Giorgio

In the decade after the Pazzi conspiracy of April 1478, there were very few public performances of any kind. The *edifici* and their plays in the great public procession on the eve of the Nativity of St. John the Baptist ceased; we have no record of plays being performed in other public spaces like Piazza della Signoria or Piazza Santa Croce; there is a hiatus in *laudesi* company plays in the conventual churches of the Oltrarno; there are no jousts; and only the horse races appear to have continued without interruption. A revision of the Purification statutes in 1478 (and probably those of the other youth confraternities too) specified that when the five wardens met together on the first Sunday of every month, a boy from one of the companies should be chosen to preach a sermon.[247] Moreover,

> Our feast days and holidays henceforth shall not be celebrated except with most beautiful vespers, *laude*, prayers, wall-hangings, lights, and greenery, lest by wanting to adorn the walls we sully the inner man. ¶ In this way and at this time it seems sufficient that we should just meet together, lest by wasting time we should waste and fritter away the spiritual love and fraternal charity among us. Nobody should engage in other gatherings neither in the country nor in Florence, unless the guardian father is present at such spiritual recreation. Any person who wishes to meet with any of his spiritual brothers in any place and for any reason must seek permission from his warden, and he will be granted it kindly in reasonable cases, so that everything is done in the sight of God, with his blessing and reward.[248]

---

[247] *Capitoli*, Bloomington, Lilly, MR 26, fol. 40^r, addition dated 16 July 1478 (fol. 42^r). A similar paragraph was added to the Vangelista *Capitoli*; see Alexander and De la Mare 1969, 33.

[248] Bloomington, Lilly, MR 26, fol. 40^v: "le […] nostre feste et natali, da quinci innanzi più non si solempnizino sennone con bellissimi vesperi, laude, exhortationi, spaliere, lumi e verzure, aciò che volendo molto ornare le mura non lasciamo imbratato assai l'uhomo

The political situation may not have been the only reason for this change in rules. In Carnival 1475/6 Giorgio Antonio Vespucci had the boys in his school perform Terence's *Andria*, which is the first documented performance of a classical comedy. The following August, Piero Domizi, master of the cathedral school in Santa Maria del Fiore, had his pupils perform his *Licinia* (now lost) in the church of Ognissanti and in the presence of Lorenzo himself.[249] Not only was this the first sign in Florence that the theatrical tastes of the elite were changing, but it was also a harbinger of the fact that the boys who performed in them were in moral danger at the hands of the men who guided them.[250] Among the offenders were two key figures in the revival of classical theatre: Piero Domizi, who was accused of improper conduct in 1474, 1476, 1486, 1491, and 1498, and Paolo di Giovanni Comparini, who was censured in 1494.[251] As Robert Black documents, "fear of improper relations" between the youthful clerks and the clergy was a constant preoccupation. He cites a prohibition in San Lorenzo dated 1485 against youths entering the cloister and living area of the clergy even "for any honest reason";[252] a similar amendment is found in the 1491 statutes of the San Girolamo company in Costa San Giorgio, ensuring that "nobody from the said youth confraternity [of Sant'Antonio da Padova] can ever be sent or introduced into the areas that are reserved for your use, that is, the vestry, sacristy, and above all the entrance to the staircase that goes to your dormitories."[253] In an activity

---

interiore. ⁋ In questa forma et in questo tempo ci pare sia a soficientia el ritrovarci insieme, perché consumandosi el tempo non manchi né consumisi tra noi l'amore spirituale et fraterna charità. Altri ragunamenti per ciascheduno non si facci, né in villa né in Firenze, se già nonn è in tale spirituale recreatione presente il padre guardiano. Adunche colui el quale si volesse ritrovare con alcuni de' sua spirituali frategli in alcuno luogho et per qualunque cosa chiegha costui licentia al proprio guardiano, la quale nelle cose ragionevole benignamente riceverà, aciò che ogni cosa apresso di Dio si facerà con merito et benedictione."

[249] Del Lungo, *Florentia*, 379–387; Staüble, *La commedia umanistica*, 101–106; Trexler, "Ritual in Florence," 229–231; Ventrone, *Gli araldi della commedia*, 23–26; "La pedagogia."

[250] Viti, "Per una ricerca," 185–187.

[251] Black, "The Scuola," 359–360; Domizi enjoyed the protection of Lucrezia Tornabuoni and continued to teach until his death in 1518.

[252] Black, "The Scuola," 358.

[253] ASF, *Capitoli* di Compagnie Religiose Soppresse 81 (San Girolamo nel Monte di S. Giorgio), fols. 19ᵛ–20ʳ: "mai nessuno di detta Compagnia de' Fanciugli [di Sant'Antonio da Padova] possa essere messo né introdocto ne' luoghi vostri segreti a vostro uso, cioè spogliatoio, sagrestia e massime dentro all'uscio della schala che va ne' vostri dormentori."

that involved cross-dressing, impersonation of lascivious characters, and a degree of licence, constant vigilance was required. The wardens of the youth confraternities, under the close supervision of the abbot of the Badia and the prior of San Marco, appear to have avoided such *scandalo*.[254]

The performances might have ceased, but printing was about to ensure the dissemination of the plays in a more permanent form, and the publication of Miscomini's two-volume anthology of plays around 1484, within the orbit of the Medici, may have re-awakened interest in the youth confraternities and their plays.[255] In Carnival 1483/4, the adult *laudese* company of Sant'Agnese, traditionally responsible for staging the Ascension of Christ, and more recently the Assumption of the Virgin, in Santa Maria del Carmine, received a request from the youth confraternity of San Giorgio to use the Sant'Agnese meeting rooms as dressing rooms for an unnamed play they were doing in the church. The Sant'Agnese minutes recorded:

> Likewise, the said Captains solemnly resolved and determined by four votes in favour that the meeting rooms of our confraternity can and should be lent to accommodate the youths of the company of San Giorgio to do a certain play that they want to do in the church of Santa Maria del Carmine in Florence, on this condition: that they take care of the meeting place and room so that they may have it on another occasion.[256]

We know little about the San Giorgio company in the fifteenth century. I believe that it is the same as the company of Sant'Antonio da Padova, offspring of the adult flagellant confraternity of San Girolamo, and it came to be called San Giorgio because it met on the Costa San Giorgio.[257] Also known

---

If the warden needed to use the sacristy for *feste* or some other legitimate reason, he was permitted to do so, but it was to be locked again immediately.

[254] See above, n. 18.

[255] On the Miscomini volumes, see below, chapter 6.

[256] ASF, Compagnia di S. Maria delle laudi detta di S. Agnese 4, fol. 3ᵛ: "Item e prefati Capitani per loro solenne partito e per quattro fave nere vinsono e ottennono che el luogo della nostra Compagnia si possa e debbasi prestare e commodare a' fanciugli della compagnia di San Giorgio per fare certa rapresentatione vogl*i*ono fare nella chiesa di Sancta Maria del Carmino di Firenze con questo: debbino conservare e mantenere decto luogo e stanza in modo possono haverlo altra volta"; see Newbigin, *Feste*, 1:147–148, 2:647.

[257] See n. 6 above. The little that remains of its archives in ASF, CRSPL, 134–137, has the double title of Compagnia di Sant'Antonio da Padova detta di San Giorgio.

as the company "of the Jackdaw, or else of the Magpie" (della Cornacchia, o vuo' dire Gazza),[258] it was founded in 1441, although its statutes were not approved until 1453. It constituted the only youth confraternity in the Oltrarno. According to Benedetto Dei, the company of San Giorgio was responsible for the annual performance of an *Abraham and Isaac and Sarah* play.[259] Anton Francesco Grazzini (1503–1584) later mocked the San Giorgio company as a group of amateur players whose principal activity was "sending the dragon out every year in the procession."[260]

Rappresentazione di Rosana

All must have gone well, for the following year, the Sant'Agnese company again lent its meeting rooms and all its properties for a performance in Carnival of *La festa di santa Rosana*:

> Likewise, this day, 2 February 1484[/5], the said Captains, with Lorenzo Martelli absent, solemnly resolved with all votes in favour that Guido di Maestro Antonio can use the meeting rooms of our company and likewise all its costumes and properties to do the play of St. Rosana this Carnival, which it is to be done here in the church of the Carmine. On this understanding: that the said Guido is bound to account for all the properties and to return them in good order and condition and to indemnify the

---

[258] Benedetto Dei, BMoF, Moreniano 103, fol. 66ʳ.

[259] Dei, *La cronica*, 93; see n. 63 above. The founders were "Friars Paolo Bellincioni and Mariotto Montanelli, under the banner of the Annunziata and St. Anthony of Padua" (frati Pagolo Billincioni and Mariotto Montanelli [...] sotto il titolo della Nuntiata et Santo Antonio da Padova), ASF, CCRSPL 81, fols. 18ᵛ–20ᵛ. By the early eighteenth century, its *Capitoli* gave its full title as "Compagnia di S. Giorgio e S. Antonio di Padova, sotto la protezione di Maria Vergine Santissima Annunziata su la Costa a S. Giorgio," ASF, CCRSPL 730, fol. 1ʳ (see Florence, Archivio Arcivescovile, Compagnie Religiose — *Capitoli* 04.29 for a complete set of these statutes). The 1501 statutes of the confraternity, BRF, Ricc. 1748, make no reference to *rappresentazioni*.

[260] *Madrigalessa* xv, in Grazzini, *Le rime*, 321, cited in full below, chapter 5, n. 8; see also *Sonetto* cxxiv, pp. 99–100. For a parody of this company's statutes, see Morpurgo, "La Compagnia della Gazza." On its transformation in 1586 into the Accademia degli Infiammati, see Sebregondi, *I luoghi teatrali*, 337–338.

company against all damage both of the meeting rooms and of the said properties.[261]

This *Play of St. Rosana* most probably corresponds to the *Rappresentazione di Rosana*, printed in an illustrated edition by Antonio Miscomini in the last decade of the fifteenth century (fig. 8.26) and reissued throughout the sixteenth and seventeenth centuries and again in the twentieth century.[262] D'Ancona, in his edition of it, observes:

> The content of the play is purely secular, even though the author has added 'Saint' to the heroine's name and has mixed in a small

---

[261] ASF, Compagnia di S. Maria delle laudi detta di S. Agnese 4, fols. 4ᵛ–5ʳ: "Item e prefati Capitani oggi questo dì 2 di febraio 1484, absente Lorenzo Martelli, ottennono per loro solenne partito e per tucte fave nere che Guido di maestro Antonio possa usare el luogo della nostra Compagnia et similmente tutte le masseritie di quella per fare la festa di Sancta Rosana in questo Carnasciale che s'à a ffare qui nella chiesa del Carmine. Con questo inteso che decto Guido sia tenuto rendere conto di tucte decte masseritie e quelle rendere conservate et intere, altrimenti conservare la Compagnia d'ogni danno così del luogo come di decte masseritie"; see Newbigin, *Feste*, 1:148–149, 2:647–648. Guido is probably the son of Maestro Antonio di Guido, *cantore in panca*, with whom Feo Belcari exchanged sonnets; see Belcari, *Le rappresentazioni*, 185–187, 189–190; also Flamini, *La lirica*, 152–177, and *passim*. He was part of Lorenzo's *brigata*, a friend of Luigi Pulci, and his inspiration for Margutte; see L. Degl'Innocenti, "Il poeta," 147–148. Luca Landucci looked back to the famous men of Lorenzo's time and praised him as "Master Antonio di Guido, singer of improvised song, who has surpassed everyone in that art" (maestro Antonio di Guido, cantatore inproviso, che ha passato ognuno in quell'arte), Landucci, *Diario*, 2–3. See also Becherini, "*Un canta in panca*"; Lanza, ed., *Lirici toscani*, 1:680–681; Luisi, "Minima fiorentina."

[262] *Larapresentatione di Rosana* ([Florence: Antonio Miscomini, 1492–1494]), ISTC ir00338300; Cioni, *Bibliografia*, 264, LXXXVIIII.1; for modern editions, see Table 2. See also D'Ancona, *Origini*, 1:437; and De Bartholomaeis, *Le origini*, 342–351. For the prose legend, included in various "Books of Virgins," such as, for example, BNCF, II.iv.105, fols. 113ʳ–125ᵛ (1474), see D'Ancona, ed., *La legenda della reina Rosana*. According to Minucci, *Rosana* and Antonio Pucci's *Regina d'Oriente* are "two very well-known legends or plays, because they are sung every day by every simple woman" (due Leggende o Rappresentazioni notissime, per esser cantate giornalmente da ogni donnicciuola), Zipoli, *Il Malmantile*, 178. An unrelated Abruzzese play of the same legend, *Storia della regina Rosana e di Rosana sua figlia*, is contained in a manuscript dated 1576–1577, BNCR, VE 361, fols. 1ʳ–52ʳ, edited in De Bartholomaeis and Rivera, eds., *Il teatro abruzzese*, 231–261, and reissued by Giuseppe Tavani, *Storia della regina Rosana*. Miscomini's edition was copiously illustrated but none of the woodcuts were made specifically for *Rosana*.

religious element. In the tale that forms the plot of *Rosana*, we can easily recognize a shortened and modified version, perhaps as it circulated in traditional folk tales, of the event that forms the plot of Boccaccio's *Filocolo*, which derives as we know, from the French romance of *Floire and Blanchefleur*.[263]

In 212 octaves, the play is longer than the two contemporary plays with which it tends to be considered, Antonia Pulci's *Santa Guglielma* and the anonymous *Stella*, but not as long as the much later *Sant'Uliva*. It is to be performed over two days, with forty-nine speaking parts, male and female, as well as crowd scenes. The king and queen of Rome convert to Christianity and embark on a pilgrimage to the Holy Land in the hope of having a child. As they pass through the kingdom of Cesaria, the king and his retinue are killed, and his queen, Rosana, now pregnant, is taken to the court of the king of Cesaria where she gives birth to a daughter, also called Rosana, at the same time as the queen of Cesaria gives birth to a son, Ulimento. Three days later, Queen Rosana dies too, and the two infants are sent together to be raised by a wet nurse. Day 2 begins fifteen years later.[264] Prince Ulimento and Rosana return to the palace, clearly in love. Attempting to avoid the inevitable, the queen resolves that her son must be sent away to Paris to study, and after Rosana has baptized him he dutifully leaves. The queen further resolves that Rosana must be dispatched, but rather than kill her, the king sells her to merchants who plan to sell her on to the Sultan. Ulimento's friend witnesses Rosana's abduction and sends for him. Ulimento, with the help of an innkeeper and his wife, tracks Rosana to the Sultan's harem, releases her, and brings her home. The king and queen, forgiven and baptized, abdicate, and Ulimento and Rosana take their place. The play ends with Ulimento's invitation to all present to join the dancing and rejoicing.

---

[263] D'Ancona, ed., *Sacre rappresentazioni*, 3:362: "Il contenuto della Rappresentazione è puramente profano, sebbene l'autore abbia dato alla sua eroina l'aggiunto di Santa, e vi abbia meschiato un poco di elemento religioso. Nella favola che forma argomento alla *Rosana*, facilmente si riconosce una versione abbreviata e modificata, forse quale correva fra il popolo nei racconti tradizionali, del fatto che forma argomento al *Filocopo* del Boccaccio, tratto, come è noto, dal romanzo francese di *Floire et Blanchefleur*." For the Tuscan *volgarizzamento* of the prose legend, see BNCF, Panciatichi 75 and Magl. IV.105.

[264] The first octave of day 2 of *Rosana* is found also as the first octave of day 2 of *Santa Felicita ebrea*, discussed below, chapter 8.

The *Rappresentazione di Rosana* is a lively 'school play' with so many speaking parts that everybody has a role, but inevitably, as boys dressed up as maidens in the Sultan's harem, there must have been a hint of indecorum. The boys and young men of the San Giorgio company must have had access to costumes and properties beyond those that they borrowed from the Sant'Agnese company. Even if the *castello* on the masonry choir screen served as one palace, say, as the palace of the king of Rome, then one for the king of Cesaria and another for the Sultan were still required, along with an inn. And the play makes only limited use of the machinery in the roof of the Carmine: an Angel comes to forewarn the queen of her death, but nothing more. Perhaps it was already falling into disrepair and more elaborate usage was unsafe.

La festa di San Giuliano

It is only in February 1487/8 that we find evidence of a revival of the Purification play in San Marco.[265] Savonarola now had most of Florence under his sway, but, as I will argue in chapter 9, the Purification company as a group took little notice of the Friar's initiatives. In 1492/3, after the election of a new warden, the company staged a play of St. Julian at Santa Maria degli Angeli, the Camaldolese monastery that was at the heart of humanistic culture.[266] This is certainly not the first time a St. Julian play was performed — we have two earlier manuscript plays of the life of this Oedipal saint: the *Play of St. Julian* dating to 1464/5 and the *Play of the Glorious St. Julian* dating to about

---

[265] ASF, CRSPL, 1654 (P.xxx.31), fol. 105ᵛ: "A dì 20 di febraio 1487 lire quattro portò ser Zacheria di Domenicho di Stefano, aveva speso nella festa della Purificatione et in catene et fune sono rimaste alla chonpagnia" (On 20 February 1487/8, taken by Ser Zacheria di Domenico di Stefano, 4 *lire* that he had spent on the *festa* of the Purification and on chains and ropes that remained with the company); fol. 106ᵛ (1 January 1488/9): "A ser Zacheria di Domenicho di Steffano lire tre e soldi 5 sono per parte de' chamici di tafettà fati pella chonpagnia" (To Ser Zacheria di Domenico di Stefano, £3 5s., toward the cost of taffeta surplices made for the company).

[266] ASF, CRSPL, 1654 (P.xxx.31), fol. 111ʳ: "E a dì xxiii di febraio per seghatura di tre fagi per fare la festa di sa· Giuliano negli Agnioli, lire 5 soldi 8 danari 8" (on 23 February [1492/3], for sawing three beech logs to do the *festa* of St. Julian at [Santa Maria degli] Angeli); correcting Polizzotto, *Children*, 126. In May, fol. 111ᵛ, they finally paid £18 for: "una nugola e altre cose apartenente alla festa" (a *nugola* and other things relating to the *festa*). This is just two years after the performance of the Judgment of Solomon "in sermone latino" in the presence of Giovanni de' Medici; see above in this chapter.

1470.[267] According to the earlier and more luminous version, soothsayers predict at Giuliano's birth that he will cause the death of his parents, and his father wishes to slay the newborn child at once. As we also see in the first of the predella panels painted in 1485 by Pietro di Antonio Dei, called Bartolomeo della Gatta (1448–1502), for the *pieve* or parish church of San Giuliano in Castiglion Fiorentino (fig. 3.37),[268] his mother resists and undertakes to nurse him herself, and he is spared. On his eighteenth birthday, Giuliano learns the cause of his mother's weeping, and spares his parents further pain by leaving home (panel 1). In another land, Giuliano marries well. While he is out hunting, his parents arrive, in search of the son they have not seen for many years. They are greeted by his wife, who invites them to rest in her bed. Giuliano meanwhile is told by the Devil that his wife is in bed with her lover (panel 2) He rides home and races to his chamber and runs his sword through the couple he finds in his bed (panel 3) When his wife tells him that his parents are (now were) resting in his bed, he is overwhelmed by remorse, but his wife counsels active penance. She does not appear again. He will build bridges and hostels for pilgrims, but among the pilgrims who come to stay is the Devil, once again in disguise, who wreaks havoc on the bedding. Giuliano resolves to cease sheltering poor pilgrims and sends the next one away. The pilgrim, who is Christ in disguise, asks him to take care of his pilgrim's staff, which sticks to Giuliano's hand. Giuliano knows instantly that this pilgrim is Christ and, in his mercy, Christ promises him heaven at his death (panel 4).

Of all the versions of St. Julian's *vita*, only this earlier Florentine play contains all the elements depicted in the predella panels. There are perhaps

---

[267] *La festa di san Giuliano*, in BNCF, Panciatichi 25, fols. 8^r–33^r, copied in 1464/5 by Antonio d'Ubaldino d'Antonio del Rosso, a *corazzaio* (maker of cuirasses) and father of the painter Baldino Baldini; see Milanesi, in Vasari, *Le vite* (1878–1885), 3:277; and in BNCR, VE 483, fols. 206^v–222^r, copied in 1482; and *La festa del grolioso Santo Giuliano*, in VBAMi, C 35 sup., fols. 142^r–154^r, copied in the 1470s. For editions, see Table 1; for sources, see Jacobus, *Legenda Aurea*, 1:246–249, xxx De Sancti Juliani, where St. Julian Hospitaller is the fourth of the five Julians presented. For a *cantare* of San Giuliano, see *Historia di san Giuliano*, beginning "Al nome sia de l'alto Dio verace," ([Bologna: Nani, c. 1494]), ISTC ij00496500.

[268] By 1909, the four panels were displayed on little hooks — in the order 2, 1, 3, 4 — in the sacristy of the Collegiate church which had replaced the Pieve in 1820. In 1910, panels 2 and 3 were stolen and have not been recovered. For a description of the display, see G. Mancini, *Cortona*, 150–152. The restored altarpiece is now in the Collegiata; the two surviving panels are in the Pinacoteca Comunale. The panels were included in Berti, ed., *Nel raggio di Piero* 1992, 159–161, no. 29 (Laura Speranza); and discussed in Gatta and others, *Attorno a Piero*.

links with an earlier predella by Masolino, of which only one panel survives, but it is not implausible that the painter also witnessed the play as a young man, before he entered the Camaldolese community around 1468. We have no record of Giuliano de' Medici, younger and wilder brother of Lorenzo, being a member of the Purification company, but it is possible that Medici patronage of the confraternity and also of the monastery of Santa Maria degli Angeli influenced the choice of subject.[269]

As Pietro Delcorno points out, in the later dramatization of the legend — which contains echoes of the earlier version and must have had some knowledge of it[270] — the role of the wife in the salvation of San Giuliano is amplified. She, like Giovanni Colombini's wife, knows that wealth is for doing good works, through which sin can be expunged:

Primo non se' che 'l Dimon traditore	You're not the first the Devil has betrayed
con suo malizie ha saputo ingannare.	with all his wiles, and cunningly deceived.
No' pregheremo Iddio a tutte l'ore,	We'll offer prayers to God all times of day,
e gran ricchezze ci è da poter fare	and we have riches such that we can build
ponti, ispedali e degli altri ben tanto	bridges and hospitals and more besides
che per grazia d'Iddio tu sarai santo.	so that by grace of God you'll be a saint.

(oct. 93.3–8)

In the later text she works harder to lift Giuliano out of his gloom. She commissions the hospitals and bridges herself (although the servant reports back to Giuliano; oct. 67–68), and they go together to the hospital to care for pilgrims. Both versions develop the theme that we must see as central to the *rappresentazioni*: that of *misericordia* or acts of charity by which we find salvation and in which women are powerful agents, and both make it clear that the acts of mercy are not easy, that charity is not a soft option, because those in need can be very difficult in every way.

---

[269] Anna Laura Saso's *DBI* entry on Antonia Tanini Pulci (mistakenly called Antonia Giannotti), refers to a play of San Giuliano attributed to Antonia Pulci (Saso, "Giannotti"), but Giuliano appears to be a *lapsus* for Guglielma, copied repeatedly from the mid-nineteenth century onwards.

[270] Delcorno, "Dare credito," 232–241, and particularly 233, n. 66.

Some Preliminary Conclusions

With the exception of those of the Purification company, the fifteenth-century archives of youth confraternities do not survive, and evidence of performances is found in the salutations and epilogues of the plays themselves, greeting members of an enclosed audience and excusing the inexperience of the actors. The corpus of youth confraternity plays now invites the questions of why and for whom? I am disinclined to adopt the view that sees the principal purpose of plays as didactic, although this has been argued cogently by Paola Ventrone, Lorenzo Polizzotto, and most recently by Pietro Delcorno.[271] In an article of 2014, Delcorno takes as a starting point the suggestion of the Dominican Giovanni Dominici, in his *Regola del governo di cura familiare* (1401–1403) of a preaching game, whereby very young children imitated religious practices. This approach tends to see the boys as tools in an adult program of control and indoctrination, with little autonomy of thought and action. In this context, the *message* of the play is everything: it teaches the stories, it embodies moral instruction, it shapes argument.

But such a view of the *rappresentazioni* tends to overlook the *medium*. In the course of this study the medium of the *rappresentazioni* will shift from performance to book, but for now, we are dealing with plays that existed primarily as performance. And these plays were indeed a form of play, and that chaste pleasure was a primary purpose. That pleasure — as those who have been involved in amateur theatricals know — involves engagement with a group, collective effort, creativity, dressing up, showing off, late nights, and parties. All of these activities — except perhaps showing off — are documented in the confraternal account books, and through them the youths and young men of the confraternity were kept away from antisocial and irreligious activities at Carnival and during the summer.

Pleasure, however, must be combined with utility, so the plays embody a moral or theological principle, but after the earliest period and as the corpus grew, I believe that the performers 'owned' the plays, rather than being owned and directed by them. They are the agents of the performance, rather than the spectators, and they are the primary beneficiaries. There are further practical benefits: the youthful actors learn to memorize, to speak in public, to move,

---

[271] Dominici, *Regola*, 146–147, cited in Garin, ed., *Il pensiero*, 77–79; see Ventrone, "La sacra rappresentazione fiorentina, ovvero la predicazione," "The Influence"; Polizzotto, *Children*, 82–83; Delcorno, "'We have made it for learning.'"

aspects of physical deportment that will serve them in civic life for which this and, more importantly, their future guild membership will qualify them.

The subjects of the plays, at least after the earliest plays of *Abramo* and the *Vitel sagginato*, are chosen not just for their moral precepts but also for their potential to delight in performance, providing challenging roles for everybody involved in the production. They are selected from favourite stories, well-told tales, the wealth of saints' lives that are loved as much for their colour and movement as for their spiritual value. The contained rapture of St. Agatha, holding her breasts on a plate, that we find in gold-ground paintings, explodes joyfully into a representation of her martyrdom and birth into eternal life.

The moral themes, moreover, are not limited to those appropriate to the sons of respectable minor artisans. There are important civic themes — the responsibility of officials to be honest and fair, the responsibility of all to dispense alms to the poor — that will barely touch on the daily lives of the confraternity members but are central to the ethical framework of their ecclesiastical and political sponsors in the audience. Foremost among those sponsors are the Medici household that could have a play of St. Eustachio performed in its garden, and probably — given its patronage of various youth confraternities — wherever it wished; not, I would argue, as a means of controlling and directing youth, but more importantly for its own enjoyment and prestige.

There is no doubt that this moral, social, and civic zeal was part of a wider movement that found its highest expression, as David Peterson writes, in Archbishop Antoninus: "More than his patrician and curial predecessors in the archbishopric, this son of a Florentine notary epitomized the impulse of his humbler social peers to use religious institutions to impose controls and religious discipline on the social orders above as well as below them."[272] From Eugenius's reform of the youth confraternities, first implemented by Cosimo and Antoninus, through to the death of Lorenzo in 1492, we find play-making flourishing as one of the social enterprises that shaped the city as well as its future citizens.

---

[272] Peterson, "San Lorenzo," 88; see also Peterson, "Chiesa e città."

Figure 3.1. Compagnia della Purificazione della Gloriosa Vergine Maria e di San Zanobi. *Libro di Statuti*, fol. 1ʳ. February1447/8–April 1448. Manuscript on parchment, copied by Fra Bartolomeo, and decorated by Battista di Biagio Sanguigni. Bloomington, Indiana University, Lilly Library, Ms. Medieval and Renaissance 26. By courtesy of the Lilly Library.

Figure 3.2. Benozzo Gozzoli, *Presentation of Christ at the Temple and Purification of the Virgin.* 1461–1462. Predella panel, tempera and gold on wood, 24.8 × 36.5 cm. Philadelphia Museum of Art, Cat. 38. Wikimedia Commons / CC BY-SA-3.0. Photo: Sailko.

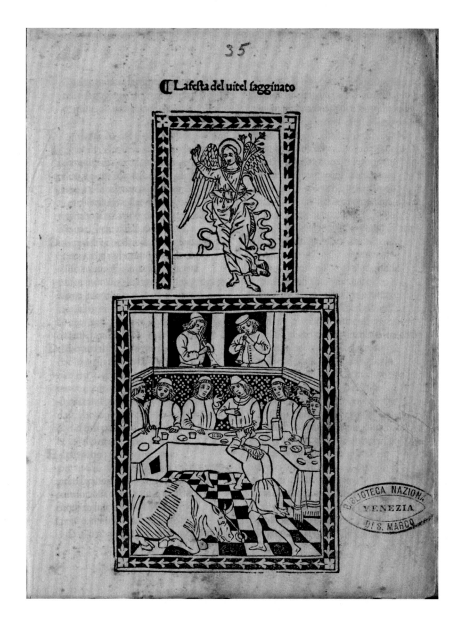

Figure 3.3. Piero di Mariano Muzi, *La festa del uitel sagginato* ([Florence: Bartolomeo de' Libri, not after 1495]), fol. a1ʳ. BMVe, Rari 501.35; ISTC iv00305500. BEIC / CC BY-SA-4.0.

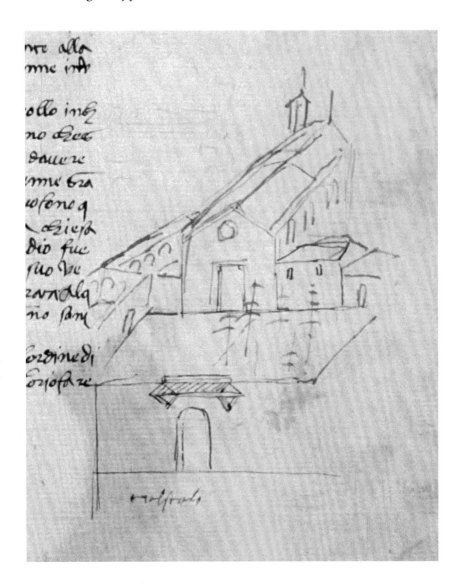

Figure 3.4. *Church and cloister of Santa Maria Maddalena in Cestello in Borgo Pinti.* Marco di Bartolomeo Rustici, *Codice Rustici: Dimostrazione*, fol. 19ʳ. Before 1459. Ink on paper. Florence, Seminario Maggiore Arcivescovile. By kind permission of the librarian, Dott. Elena Gurrieri.

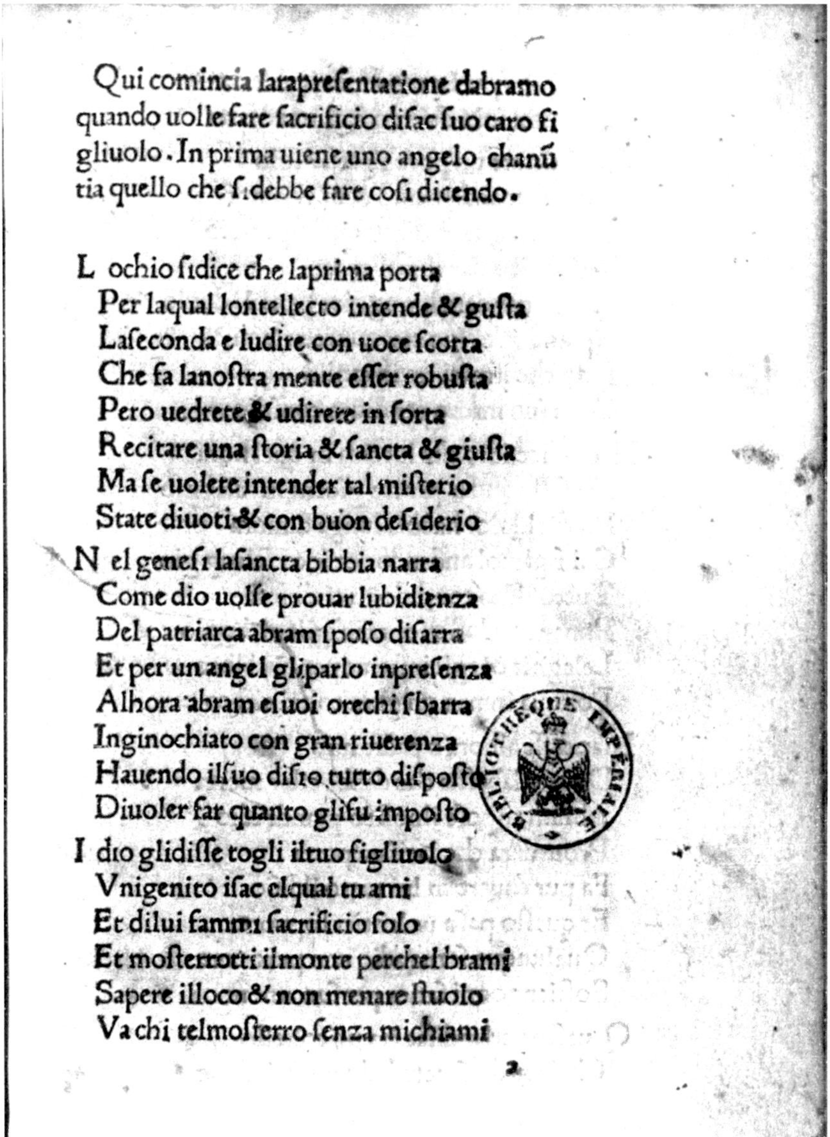

Qui comincia larapreſentatione dabramo
quando uolle fare ſacrificio diſac ſuo caro fi
gliuolo. In prima uiene uno angelo chanū
tia quello che ſi debbe fare coſi dicendo.

L ochio ſidice che laprima porta
  Per laqual lontellecto intende & guſta
  Laſeconda e ludire con uoce ſcorta
  Che fa lanoſtra mente eſſer robuſta
  Pero uedrete & udirete in ſorta
  Recitare una ſtoria & ſancta & giuſta
  Ma ſe uolete intender tal miſterio
  State diuoti & con buon deſiderio
N el geneſi laſancta bibbia narra
  Come dio uolſe prouar lubidienza
  Del patriarca abram ſpoſo diſarra
  Et per un angel gliparlo inpreſenza
  Alhora abram eſuoi orechi ſbarra
  Inginochiato con gran riuerenza
  Hauendo ilſuo diſio tutto diſpoſto
  Diuoler far quanto glifu impoſto
I dio glidiſſe togli iltuo figliuolo
  Vnigenito iſac elqual tu ami
  Et dilui fammi ſacrificio ſolo
  Et moſterrotti ilmonte perchel brami
  Sapere illoco & non menare ſtuolo
  Va chi telmoſterro ſenza michiami

Figure 3.5. Feo Belcari, *Qui comincia la rapresentatione dabramo quando uolle fare sacrificio disac suo caro figliuolo* (Florence: Maestro Franco [Cenni, c. 1485]), fol. a1ʳ. Paris, BnF, RES–YD–520; ISTC ib00297250. By courtesy of Bibliothèque nationale de France.

Figure 3.6. Filippo Brunelleschi, *Abraham and Isaac*. 1401. Competition panel, gilded bronze, 45 × 38 cm Florence, Museo Nazionale del Bargello. Wikimedia Commons / CC BY-SA-3.0. Photo: Sailko.

Figure 3.7. Lorenzo Ghiberti, *Abraham and Isaac*. 1401. Competition panel, gilded bronze, 45 × 38 cm. Florence, Museo Nazionale del Bargello. Wikimedia Commons / CC BY-SA-3.0. Photo: Sailko.

Figure 3.8. Lorenzo Ghiberti, *Abraham and Isaac*. 1425–1452. Gilded bronze quatrefoil panel, 79 × 79 cm. Florence, Museo dell'Opera del Duomo, Porta del Paradiso of the Battistero di San Giovanni Battista. Wikimedia Commons / CC BY-SA-3.0. Photo: Sailko.

Figure 3.9. Fra Angelico, *Last Judgment*, detail of the Blessed in Paradise. 1432–35. Tempera on wood. Full panel 105 × 210 cm. Florence, Museo di San Marco. Formerly Santa Maria degli Angeli. Wikimedia Commons / CC BY-SA-3.0. Photo: WGA.

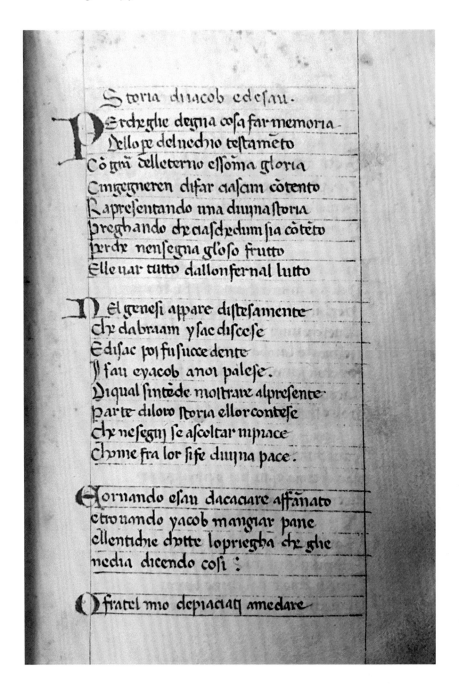

Storia di iacob ed esau.

Perche glie degna cosa far memoria
Dello pe del vechio testameto
Co gra delleterno essoma gloria
Cin gegneren difar ciascam cotento
Raprefentando una divina storia
preghando che ciaschedum sia coteto
perche nensegna gloso frutto
Elle uar tutto dallonfernal lutto

Nel genesi appare distesamente
Che dabraam ysac discese
Edisac poi fusuccedente
Isau eyacob anoi palese.
Diqual sintede mostrare alpresente
parte diloro storia ellor contese
Che nesegni se ascoltar mipiace
Chome fra lor sife divina pace.

Tornando esau dacaciare affanato
etrouando yacob mangiar pane
ellentidie dotte lopriegha che glie
nedia dicendo cosi :

O fratel mio depiaciati amedare

3.10. *Storia di Iacob ed Esaù*. Manuscript on paper. BNCF, Landau Finaly 249, fol. 32[r]. © By permission of MiBACT/BNCF. All rights reserved.

Figure 3.11. Lorenzo Ghiberti, *Jacob and Esau*. 1425–1452. Gilded bronze quatrefoil panel, 79 × 79 cm. Florence, Museo dell'Opera del Duomo, Porta del Paradiso of the Battistero di San Giovanni Battista. Wikimedia Commons / CC BY-SA-3.0. Photo: Sailko.

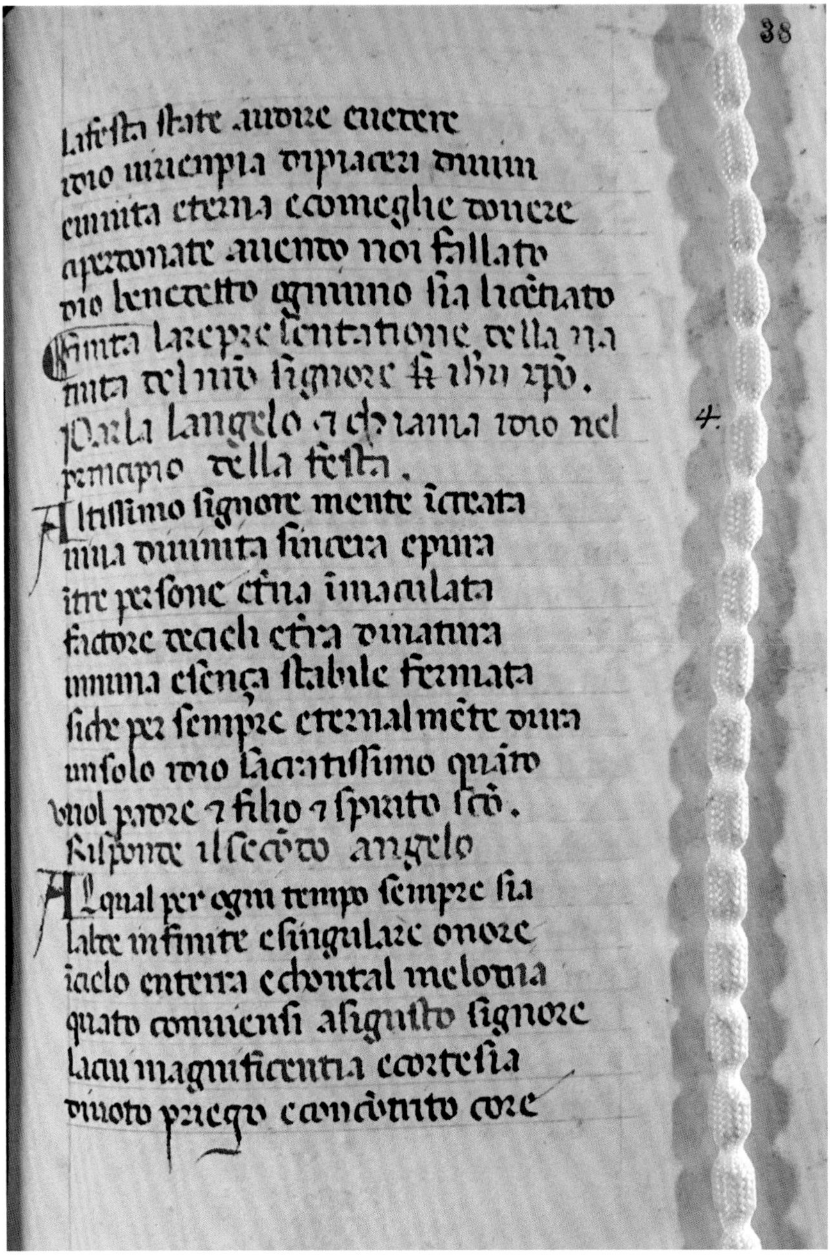

Figure 3.12. *La representatione di Moisè e di Faraone re d'Egitto* (title from *explicit*, fol. 48v). Black, red, and blue ink on paper. BRF, Ricc. 2893, fol. 38ʳ.

Figure 3.13. Benozzo Gozzoli, *Childhood of Moses* (detail). Fresco. Pisa, Camposanto, 1468–1484. Archivi Alinari, Florence. Photo: Brogi.

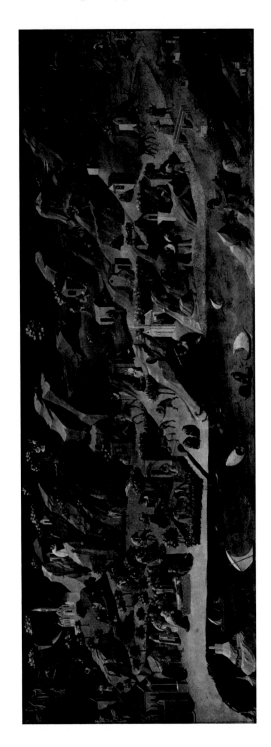

Figure 3.14. Beato Angelico (1395–1455), *Thebaid*. About 1420. Tempera on wood, 73.5 × 208 cm. Florence, Galleria degli Uffizi, inv. 1890, no. 447. Wikimedia Commons / CC BY-SA-3.0.

Figure 3.15. *Rapresentatione dell'Abbataccio* (Florence: Jacopo Chiti, 1572), fol. a1ʳ. BNCF, Pal. E.6.5.1^{I.1}; CNCE 53491. © By permission of MiBACT/ BNCF. All rights reserved.

Figure 3.16. Domenico Ghirlandaio, *Death and Assumption of the Virgin Santa*, detail showing the Convento di San Girolamo. 1490. Fresco. Florence, Santa Maria Novella, Tornabuoni Chapel. Wikimedia Commons / CC BY-SA-3.0. Photo: Sailko.

Figure 3.17. Giuseppe Zocchi, designer, and Petro Monaco, engraver. *Villa Medici and the Convento di San Girolamo. Villa della luna delli SS. Mar. Guadagni*, detail. 1744. Copperplate engraving on paper.

Figure 3.18. *Rappresentatione del Re superbo* ([Florence: Antonio Tubini and Andrea Ghirlandi] for Francesco di Giovanni Benvenuto, [c. 1515]), fol. a1ʳ. BNCF, Palat. E.6.5.1ⱽ·¹; CNCE 62333. © By permission of MiBACT/BNCF. All rights reserved.

Figure 3.19. *La rappresentatione di Susanna* ([Florence: Antonio Tubini and Andrea Ghirlandi, before 8 August, 1515]), fol. a1ʳ. Venice, Biblioteca della Fondazione Cini, FOAN TES 842; CNCE 62391. By kind permission of the Fondazione Cini.

Figure 3.20. *Rappresentatione di S. Alexo* (Florence: [Antonio Tubini and Andrea Ghirlandi] for Francesco di Giovanni Benvenuto, 7 August 1517), fol. a1ʳ. BNCF, Banco Rari 179.15; CNCE 61519. © By permission of MiBACT/BNCF. All rights reserved.

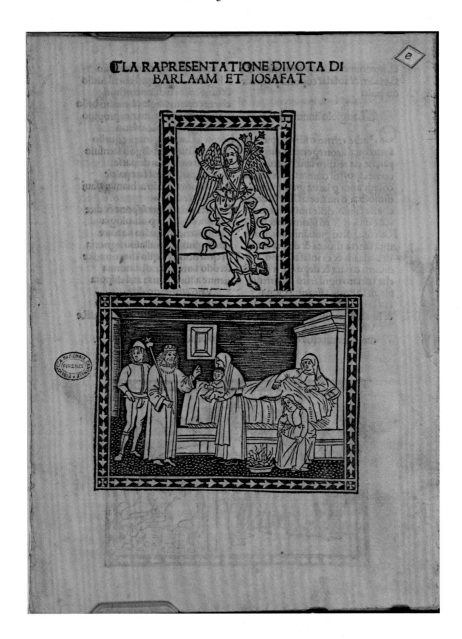

Figure 3.21. Bernardo Pulci, *La rapresentatione divota di Barlaam et Iosafat* ([Florence: Antonio Miscomini, 1492–1494]), fol. a1ʳ. BNCF, Banco Rari 189.e; ISTC ip01105500. © By permission of MiBACT/BNCF. All rights reserved.

Risponde ilfigluolo
No sian pur giuti q̃ gratia alsignore
torna idrieto pel mio fratel minore
Ritorna eustachio pelminore et
quãdo e̓nelmezo del fiume ue
de che e portato da uno leone el
fanciullo grida forte iuerso ilpa
dre quãdo uide illeone
Ome presto soccorri o padre mio
eltuo figluol el q̃l tu tãto amaui
daquesto fier leone tu uedi chio
assalito son mentre che tornaui
affretta ilpasso tuo opadre pio
aiuta me nelqual tanto speraui
o sõmo idio platua grã clementia
libera me da questa pestilentia
Vedẽdo eustachio come elleone
neporta uia Theopista i tal mo
do siduole & dice cosi
Ome crudel fortuna iniquo sato
o cielo o terra o mare ame contrario

ben hai almio dolore accumulato
dogni infelicita lostato uario
ogni dilecto i tristitia ha mutato
& hor qui mhai pur facto solitario
figluol dapoi chi nõ tiposso atare
tipotessi io almãco umpo toccare
Ritorni Eustachio idrieto per
passare laltro figluolo & quan
do siuolta uede che era portato
da un lupo/ & Aghabito dica
questa stanza quãdo illupo ua
uerso lui
Tornati idrieto o padre torna p̃sto
aiuta aiuta me che morto sono
un lupo uiẽ uerso me molto isesto
corre ueloce che par quasi un tono
misero ame chio nõ sperauo q̃sto
far qui della mia uita cotal dono
ma poi che te ipiacere o sõmo idio
tiraccomãdo lospirito mio

Figure 3.22. *La Diuota Rapresentatione Di Sancto Eustachio* ([Florence: Antonio Miscomini, 1492–1494]), fol. a4ᵛ. BNCF, Banco Rari 189.k; ISTC ie00130700. © By permission of MiBACT/BNCF. All rights reserved.

Figure 3.23. The Tobit Master, *The Story of Tobit and Tobias.* Detail of Tobias's mother with the dog. 1350s. Detached fresco panel. Florence, Museo del Bigallo. Photo: Author.

Figure 3.24. Biagio d'Antonio (1446–1516), *The Story of Joseph*. About 1485. *Spalliera* panel, tempera and gold leaf on panel, 66.7 × 149.2 cm. Los Angeles, J. Paul Getty Museum, Object Number 70.PB.41. Open Content.

Figure 3.25. Biagio d'Antonio (1446–1516), *The Story of Joseph*. About 1482. *Spalliera* panel, tempera and gold leaf on panel, 68.6 × 149.9 cm. New York, Metropolitan Museum of Art, Accession no. 32.100.69. Public Domain.

Figure 3.26. *Giuseppe figliuolo di Giacobbe* (Florence: Salani, 1888). Back and front cover, each 145 × 100 mm. BNCF, C.10.54.210.bis. © By permission of MiBACT/BNCF. All rights reserved.

cto huomo per quello camino incontinente edecti rubatori si lora
borno & fpoglorno: Dife in quella fiata eldecto fancto huomo aore
gli peffimi huomini: priegoui che miuogliate menare aluoftro figno
re perche gliuoglio dire alcune cofe molto utile perfe. Et effendo que
fto fancto huomo menato alfignore figli diffe. Priegoui che ragu-
niate tucta lauoftra famiglia pero che hoggi in quefto di fono mandato da dio per la uoftra falute:& cofi quello fignore incontinete gli
fece chiamare tutti inanzi alla fua prefentia : Et effendo quiui ragu-
nati diffe quello feruo di dio Vno della corte cimancha che non ei ue
nuto Allora uno grido & diffe: Elnoftro canouaio non par che cifia
Rifpofe el fancto huomo: Tu di iluero: Onde elfignore mando pre
ftamente per lui & effendo uenuto incomincio tucto a tremare & fta
ua tucto fpauentato: Elfancto huomo diffe allora alcanouaio Io tico
mando & fcogiuro daparte di dio che tu timanifefti & debbi dire chi
tu fe: Et quello rifpofe cofi Io fono eldimonio & non huomo elqua-
le prefi quefta forma fi come uoi uedete & fono ftato in quefta corte
dodici anni perche elnoftro principe lucifero mimando acio che i q
lunque di quefto fignore con chi io fono ftato non falutaffe lamadre

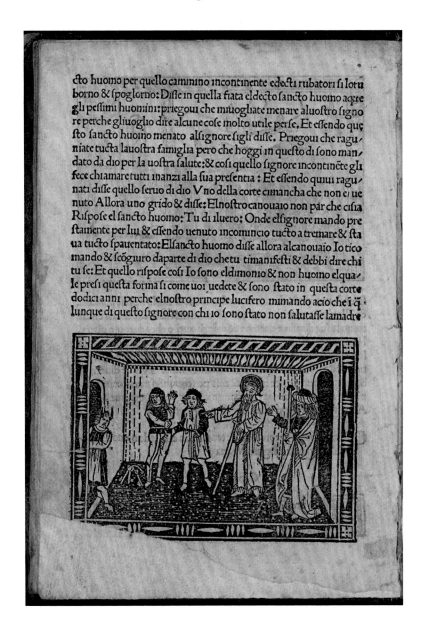

Figure 3.27. *Miracoli della gloriosa vergine Maria* ([Florence: Bartolomeo de'
Libri] for Piero Pacini, 15 June 1500), fol. a3ᵛ, cap. ii *Come fu uno signore
lo quale tenendo in casa lo demonio fu liberato dalla gloriosa Vergine Maria.*
BNCF, Magl. L.7.46. ISTC im00619600. © By permission of MiBACT/BNCF.
All rights reserved.

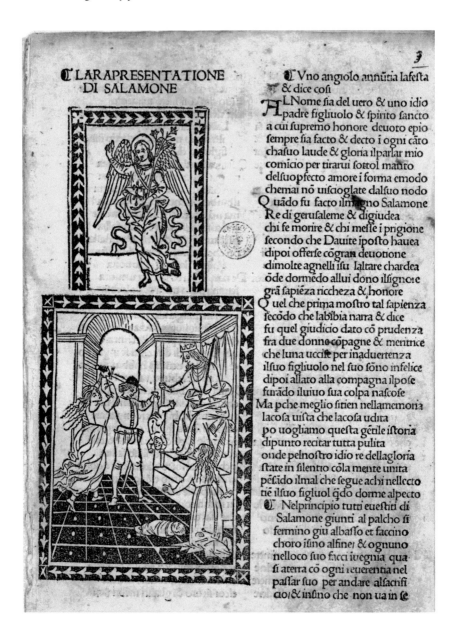

Figure 3.28. *La rappresentatione di Salamone* ([Florence: Antonio Miscomini, 1492–1494]), fol. a1ʳ. Milan, Archivio Storico Civico e Biblioteca Trivulziana, Rar. H 423. ISTC is00093800. © Comune di Milano. All rights reserved.

Figure 3.29. *Capitoli* of the youth confraternity of San Giovanni Evangelista, fol. a1ʳ. c. 1440. Tempera and gold leaf on vellum. 25 × 18.5 cm. Attributed to Battista di Biagio Sanguigni (1392/3–1451). Private collection. Photo by courtesy of Sotheby's.

Figure 3.30. *Capitoli* of the youth confraternity of San Giovanni Evangelista,
back cover. c. 1440. Brown goatskin over wooden boards. 25 × 18.5 cm.
Private collection. Photo by courtesy of Sotheby's.

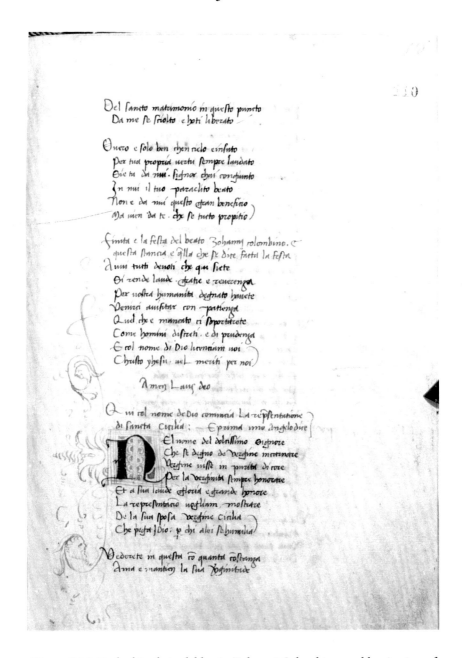

Figure 3.31. End of *La festa del beato Zohanni Colombino*, and beginning of *La representatione di sancta Cicilia*. 1482. Ink on paper, with red and blue decorations. Copied by Tommaso Leone. BNCR, VE 483, fol. 110ʳ.

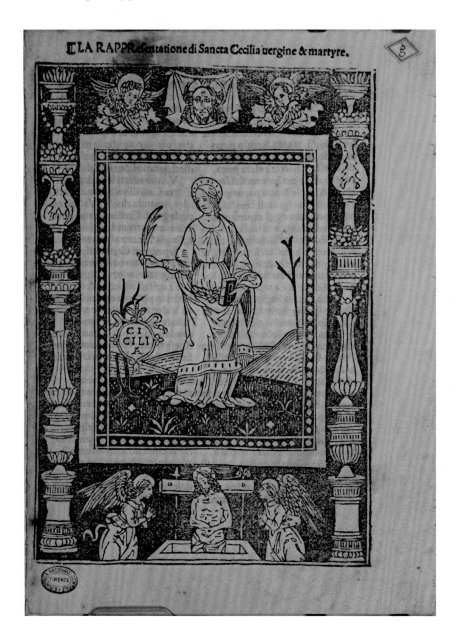

Figure 3.32. *La rappresentatione di Sancta Cecilia uergine & martyre*
([Florence: Antonio Tubini and Andrea Ghirlandi, c. 1510]), fol. a1ʳ. BNCF,
Banco Rari 189.g; CNCE 54152. © By permission of MiBACT/BNCF. All
rights reserved.

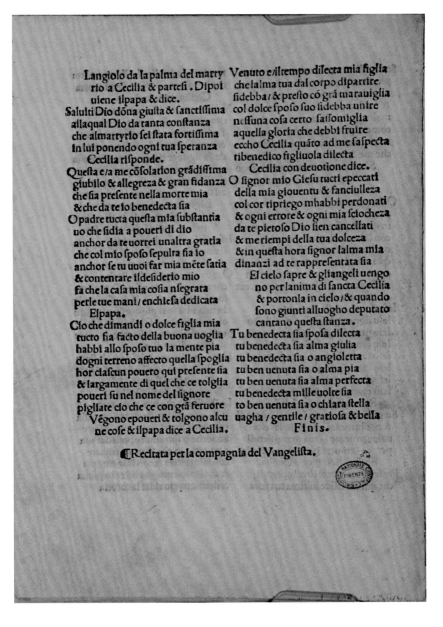

Langiolo da la palma del martyrio a Cecilia & partefi. Dipoi uiene ilpapa & dice.

Salulti Dio dóna giulta & fanctiffima allaqual Dio da tanta conftanza che almartyrio fei ftata fortiffima in lui ponendo ogni tua fperanza

Cecilia rifponde.

Quefta e/a me côfolation gràdiffima giubilo & allegreza & gran fidanza che fia prefente nella morte mia & che da te io benedecta fia

O padre tucta quefta mia fubftantia uo che fidia a poueri di dio anchor da te uorrei unaltra gratia che col mio fpofo fepulra fia io anchor fe tu uuoi far mia méte fatia & contentare ildefiderio mio fa che la cafa mia cofia nfegrata perle tue mani/ enchiefa dedicata

Elpapa.

Cio che dimandi o dolce figlia mia tucto fia facto della buona uoglia habbi allo fpofo tuo la mente pia dogni terreno affecto quella fpoglia hor ciafcun pouero qui prefente fia & largamente di quel che ce tolglia poueri fu nel nome del fignore pigliate cio che ce con grà feruore

Végono epoueri & tolgono alcu ne cofe & ilpapa dice a Cecilia.

Venuto e/iltempo dilecta mia figlia che lalma tua dal corpo dipartire fidebba/ & prefto có grà marauiglia col dolce fpofo fuo fidebba unire neffuna cofa certo faffomiglia aquella gloria che debbi fruire eccho Cecilia quáto ad me fafpecta tibenedico figliuola dilecta

Cecilia con deuotione dice.

O fignor mio Giefu tucti epeccati della mia giouentu & fanciulleza col cor tipriego mhabbi perdonati & ogni errore & ogni mia fciocheza da te pietofo Dio fien cancellati & me riempi della tua dolceza &in quefta hora fignor lalma mia dinanzi ad te rapprefentata fia

El cielo fapre & gliangeli uengo no per lanima di fancta Cecilia & portonla in cielo/& quando fono giunti alluogho deputato cantano quefta ftanza.

Tu benedecta fia fpofa dilecta tu benedecta fia alma giulia tu benedecta fia o angioletta tu ben uenuta fia o alma pia tu ben uenuta fia alma perfecta tu benedecta mille uolte fia to ben uenuta fia o chiara ftella uagha / gentile / gratiofa & bella

Finis.

⊂Recitata per la compagnia del Vangelifta.

Figure 3.33. *La rappresentatione di Sancta Cecilia uergine & martyre* ([Florence: Antonio Tubini and Andrea Ghirlandi, c. 1510]), fol. a8ᵛ. BNCF, Banco Rari 189.g; CNCE 54152. © By permission of MiBACT/BNCF. All rights reserved.

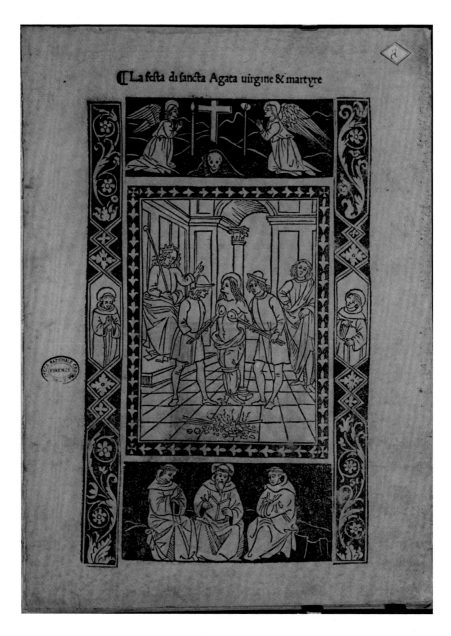

Figure 3.34. *La festa di sancta Agata uirgine & martyre* ([Florence:
Bartolomeo de' Libri, not after 1495]), fol. a1ʳ. BNCF, Banco Rari 189.a;
ISTC ia00157450. © By permission of MiBACT/BNCF. All rights reserved.

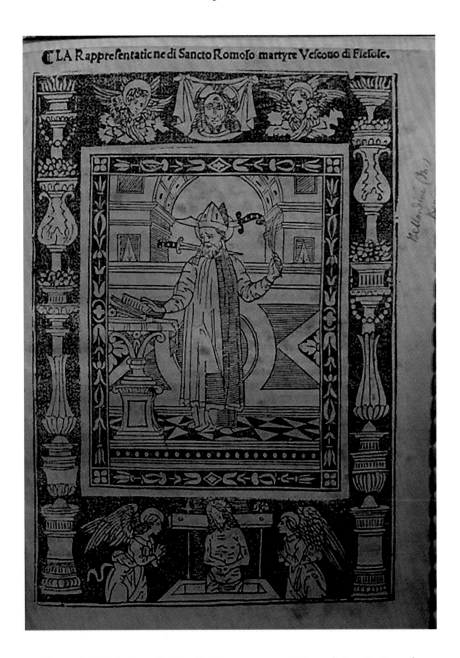

Figure 3.35. Mariano Bellandini, *La rappresentatione di Sancto Romolo martyre Vescouo di Fiesole* ([Florence: Antonio Tubini and Andrea Ghirlandi, before 8 August 1515]), fol. a1ʳ. London, British Library, 11426. dd.6; CNCE 4861. © The British Library Board.

Figure 3.36. *Traditional site of the Martyrdom of St. Romulus.* Fiesole, Via Vecchia Fiesolana, opposite Villa Medici. Photo: Author.

Figure 3.37. Pietro d'Antonio Dei, called Bartolomeo della Gatta, *Four Scenes from the Life of St. Julian the Hospitaller*, as displayed in 1909, in the order 2, 1, 3, 4. About 1485. Tempera on panel, each 22 × 58 cm. Panels 1 and 4: Castiglion Fiorentino, Pinacoteca Comunale. Panels 2 and 3: whereabouts unknown since 1909. By courtesy of the Fondazione Zeri, inventory number 47147. Photographer unknown.

CHAPTER 4

EDIFICI FOR THE FEAST OF
ST. JOHN THE BAPTIST

In our time, many new, great, and wonderful
things are seen and heard [...] not to mention the hymns, Gospels, and lamentations
in verse that are sung year-round to their
melodies, and especially during the holy
Lenten season, with great sweetness and devotion, and the many *rappresentazioni* that
are performed year-round and especially
for the feast of San Giovanni Battista, more
beautifully than at any other time.

Giovanni Rucellai, c. 1457[1]

Since the time of the Florentine chronicler and diarist Gregorio Dati (1362–
1435), descriptions of the celebrations in honour of the birth of Florence's
patron saint have been enshrined in a particular kind of laudatory narrative
designed to represent the city as prosperous, magnificent, harmonious, and
revelling in divine favour.[2] While the feast day itself, of the Nativity of St. John
the Baptist, was marked by tribute to the city from the Republic's territories,
and tribute to the saint and his Baptistery from the civic authorities, the eve of
the feast saw a procession of lay and professed religious groups to the piazza
in front of the palace of the Signoria, bearing the city's holiest talismans of

---

[1] Rucellai, *Zibaldone* (c. 1457), 182: "In questa età si sono vedute e intese più cose
nuove e grande e maravigliose. [...] Non dico nulla delle laulde, vangieli, lamenti in rima,
che si chantano tutto l'anno con ragione di chanto, e massime la santa quaresima con
grande dolcieza e divozione, e di molte rappresentagione, che si fanno tutto l'anno e massime per la festa di santo Giovanni Battista, più belle ch'a niun altro tenpo."

[2] Gregorio Dati, *Istoria*, 84–86; Mannucci, BNCF, Conv. Soppr. B.4.1579; Cambiagi,
Memorie; Guasti, *Le feste*; Gori, *Le feste*, vol. 1; Trexler, *Public Life*, in particular 240–263;
Pastori, "Le feste patronali"; Ventrone, "La festa di San Giovanni" online, and her *Teatro
civile*, 47–56, 192–204, 258–272, 347–361. In this chapter, the "feast day of St. John the
Baptist," "San Giovanni," and "San Giovanni Battista" are used interchangeably.

crosses, banners, and relics, all accompanied by stilt-walkers and a diabolical dragon. In the course of the fifteenth century, the *edifici*, or platforms with scaffolding bearing the relics, became more and more ornate, and the narrative component became stronger and more coherent. In 1454, the lay groups were separated from the professed religious, and the performances on the *edifici* became unequivocally theatre, with actors, costumes, gestures, impersonation and, most importantly, scripts.

As a saint, St. John the Baptist is an intriguing amalgam. He has two feast days: his Nativity on 24 June, and his Beheading on 29 August.[3] The Baptist's birth was celebrated at the summer solstice, in apposition to that of his cousin, Jesus, at the winter solstice. It was a fire festival, celebrated with huge offerings of wax, fireworks, and much more. The men of the city and its territories honoured the saint in a succession of different configurations: by *gonfalone* or local district, by guild, by religious order and lay confraternity, by hierarchical office, and by festive brigade. This chapter focuses exclusively on the *edifici* of the religious procession, originally paraded on 23 June, the eve of the feast day, and from 1454 moved a day earlier to 22 June; it frames the *edifici* in the historiography of the *festa* and of Florentine civic life.[4]

The Florentine 'temple' dedicated to the Baptist, the city's octagonal Baptistery that faced the city's cathedral, was believed to have been a temple of Mars. In the minds of Florentine chroniclers, it had been built in the reign of the Emperor Octavian, around the time of Christ's birth.[5] Before the reconsecration of the Duomo in 1436 as Santa Maria del Fiore, the Baptistery was the most important church in the city, with choir and clergy supported by the Arte di Calimala or cloth merchants' guild. The saint thus presided both over Florentine citizenship of the City of God and over the gold *fiorino*, which bore the Florentine lily on one side and the hirsute figure of the Baptist on the other.

The Baptistery and its patron remained the principal focus of the city's festive devotions. The original 1338 statutes of the Opera di San Giovanni, instituted by the Calimala, required its members to lobby those responsible for the drafting (or perhaps redrafting) of the communal statutes for elaborate cross-subsidization from the high offices of the Republic.[6] The Calimala

---

[3] For suggestions concerning the significance of the Baptist in Florentine civic and religious life, see Trexler, *Public Life*, 333, n. 3.

[4] Newbigin, ed., *Nuovo corpus*, XXV–L; Newbigin, "Rewriting John the Baptist."

[5] See for example, Rustici, *Codice Rustici: Dimostrazione*, 2:110, cap. 9.

[6] ASF, Arte di Calimala 5, fols. 46ʳ–47ʳ, "Delgli officiali a provedere dell'offerte di San Giovanni viij."

looked beyond the economic self-interest of the merchants; it undertook to honour the city and its patron saint by maintaining and embellishing the church dedicated to him, and by ensuring that others did the same, exacting tribute from citizens and subjects alike. The guild collected and registered the offerings of wax and of *palii* or banners of precious cloth, converting some to cash to be directed toward the building and maintenance program.

Giovanni Villani provides the earliest set-piece *laudatio* in praise of the St. John the Baptist celebrations. His mid-fourteenth-century chronicle looks back to the *festa* of 1283, in which the *brigate*, banquets, jesters, musicians, and dancing all constituted evidence of the good government of the Priors.[7] The first detailed description is the *canzone dialogata* (dialogue poem) copied, if not composed, by Zanobi Perini in February 1407/8, in which one Florentine, arriving in an unnamed foreign place from his native city, describes the *festa* to another, fresh from Paris.[8] The narrator's eye falls above all on the *mostra*, the display of merchandise and treasure, but moves to the offerings of the citizens and of the subject territories, the *palio*,[9] and above all to the beautifully dressed men and women who take part. The devotional pretext is all but eclipsed by a nostalgic desire to list and memorialize the riot of gold and brocades: it is above all the merchants' festival, described for the benefit of a merchant, and there is no reference to a procession of clergy and confraternities.

Praise of the *festa* returns in Gregorio Dati's *Istoria di Firenze*, composed by the Florentine silk merchant around 1409.[10] The work is not a standard chronicle in the style of Villani, but rather a dialogue, a series of leading questions and answers, in which Florentine liberty is glorified above Visconti tyranny. The festive interlude in Book 6 expresses Dati's sense of Florentine civic and social superiority. His interlocutor reflects on God's vengeance visited upon wicked cities like Sodom and Gomorrah, Padua and Milan, and men's failure to take note.[11] The panegyrist agrees and glides into a lyrical description of preparation for the feast of the Baptist as a rite of spring:

---

[7] Villani, *Nuova cronica,* 1:547–548, viii.89.

[8] Perini, "La festa"; for translation, see Newbigin online.

[9] The term *palio* indicates both the horse race and the rich cloth awarded as its prize. In contrast to the modern Sienese palio, this was a contest of individuals and their horses; it was also an occasion for significant gambling. On the Laurentian period, see Mallett, "Horse-Racing." I will italicize the term when it refers to the righ cloth and leave it in roman when it refers to the horse race.

[10] For date, see Viti, "Dati."

[11] Gregorio Dati, *Istoria,* 84.

When springtime comes and makes all the world rejoice, every Florentine begins to think of celebrating the feast of San Giovanni, which comes later in midsummer; and in good time they prepare their clothes and adornments and jewels. Anybody who has to arrange a wedding banquet or some other celebration postpones it until then, to honour the feast day.[12]

There is no trace in the description that follows of the vocabulary of sumptuary containment that we find in the fourteenth-century statutes and in preachers like the Franciscan friar Bernardino of Siena, who will roar into the pulpit in the next decade. Here, as in contemporary painters like Lorenzo Monaco or Gentile da Fabriano, we find gold and colours and gorgeous fabrics all on display. The elements described by Dati at the beginning of the century continue throughout its history.

The religious procession on 23 June was not mentioned by Perini, but in Dati's account it makes its way around the city and back, continuing the sumptuous display of the *mostra*:

Then, all around the city, at Terce [that is, three hours after sunrise], they have a solemn procession of all the clerks, priests, monks, and friars from a great number of religious orders, with so many saints' relics that it is endless and enormously devout, not to mention marvellously opulent in their adornments, for they wear the richest vestments in the world, robes of gold and silk with figures embroidered on them; and with many lay confraternities, each of which precedes the order of the church where that confraternity meets, dressed as angels, with music and instruments of every kind and marvellous singing; and they do beautiful representations of those saints and those relics that they are honouring. They set out from Santa Maria del Fiore, they go around the city, and they return to their starting place.[13]

---

[12] Gregorio Dati, *Istoria*, 84–85: "Quando ne viene il tempo della primavera, che tutto il mondo rallegra, ogni fiorentino comincia a pensare di fare bella festa di San Giovanni, che è poi a mezza la state, e di vestimenti, e d'adornamenti, e di gioie ciascuno si mette in ordine a buon'otta; chiunque ha a fare conviti di nozze, o altra festa s'indugia a quel tempo per fare onore alla festa."

[13] Gregorio Dati, *Istoria*, 85–86: "Appresso per la Terra in sull'ora della Terza si fa una solenne pricissione di tutti i cherici, preti, monaci e frati, che sono grande numero

There was still no performative element apparent in the lay confraternities' 'representations' of the saints.[14] The saint and his or her 'story' were determined by the devotions or relics of the religious order; and each religious order's position in the procession was dictated by a conventional hierarchy. Proximity to the end of the procession was defended at all costs.

Gregorio Dati would have us believe that the organization of the *festa* was somehow collective and voluntary, but we have very little evidence regarding how the religious procession was organized or financed. To some extent expenses must have devolved to the participants. We know, for example, that representatives of the Opera di Santa Maria del Fiore carried the relic of the Baptist's finger in the procession on the eve of the feast day, and paid for the offering of candles and for trumpeters, eight porters to carry torches, and a supper for all of those who accompanied the relic.[15] To this early period, before 1425, belong two splendid *cassoni*, one in the Bargello showing the *offerta* of the Guilds at the Baptistery, the other in the Cleveland Art Museum showing the horse race in the saint's honour.[16]

By the middle of the fifteenth century, the *festa* was increasingly regulated by the city's Priors, who appointed the organizing committee of *festaiuoli*

---

di regole, con tante reliquie di santi, che è una cosa infinita, e di grandissima divozione, oltre alla maravigliosa ricchezza di loro adornamenti, con ricchissimi paramenti addosso, quanti n'abbia il mondo, di veste d'oro, e di seta, e di figure ricamate, e con molte compagnie d'uomini secolari, che vanno ciascuno innanzi alla regola, dove tale Compagnia si raguna, con abito d'Angioli, e suoni, e stromenti d'ogni ragione, e canti maravigliosi, facendo bellissime rappresentazioni di que' santi, e di quelle reliquie, a cui onore la fanno. Partonsi da Santa Maria del Fiore, e vanno per la Terra, e quivi ritornano." On his description, see Pirolo, "Tre momenti."

[14] Trexler, "Florentine Theatre" (rev. 2002), 234, believed that these were "(sacred) representations." This may be true in a very broad representational sense, but they were not yet plays; see also Trexler, *Public Life*, 254–255. Trexler is correct in saying that the floats appeared in a very short space of time, but I think it was later. When Giovanni Rucellai worked Dati's account into his own *zibaldone*, he removed reference to the starting and ending point; Rucellai, *Zibaldone*, 476.

[15] Florence, Archivio dell'Opera di Santa Maria del Fiore, online, II 1 70, fol. 26ʳ (30 June 1417); II 1 73, fol. 25ᵛ (23 June 1418); II 4 8, fol. 24ᵛ (30 June 1418); II 4 8, fol. 47ᵛ (23 June 1419); II 1 77, fols. 70ᵛ–71ᵛ (28 June 1420); II 4 8, fol. 116ʳ (1–2 July 1421).

[16] Giovanni di Francesco Toscani, *Offering of the Standards of the Subject Territories to St. John the Baptist*, Florence, Museo Nazionale del Bargello, inv. no. Bargello Mobili n. 161; and Giovanni di Francesco Toscani, *The Horse Race for the Palio at San Giovanni*, Cleveland, Ohio, The Cleveland Museum of Art, Holden Collection 1916.801. See De Nicola, "Notes."

and disbursed, through the Camera dell'Arme, a sum of about £2000 each year — while at the same time trying to curtail the expense.[17] The eight-man committee of 1451, appointed on 16 May and including Baccio di Filippo Valori and Benedetto Dei, was allocated £2800 and 150 lbs of gunpowder for the *festa*.[18] It had authority to ask the *podestà* and the *capitano del popolo* to requisition whatever was needed, and presumably did so.

---

[17] For only one occasion, in 1461, have I found indication that the main funding came from elsewhere. On 14 May that year, Vitale, a moneylender from Montalcino, was arrested for practising his profession not in accordance with Florentine rules. Vitale the Jew, son of the late Dattero (or Dattilo) of Montalcino, was found to have in his possession a very large sum of money in various gold and silver coins, and another 4000 florins banked with other Jews of the city, including one named Andrea di Cristoforo. The Commune decreed that he owed it 22,000 florins, and immediately seized all the money he was holding, of which 1400 gold florins went directly to pay for the upcoming *festa*; of the remainder, 1000 went to building works in the Palazzo dei Signori, 600 to flood mitigation works on the Arno, and 100 each to the informants, Giovan Francesco the Jew and Andrea di Cristoforo the second-hand clothes dealer, who investigated the moneylender's paperwork. See ASF, Signori e Collegi, Deliberazioni in forza di speciale autorità 32, fols. 48ᵛ–50ᵛ (50ʳ): "Florenos mille quatragentos auri qui dari et solui per ipsum capserium [...] possint et debeant provisori camere armorum pro dando et solvendo illi vel illis cui seu quibus stantiatum fuint in una vice vel pluribus pro festaiuolo in festa Sancti Johanis Baptiste proximo futuri pro expensis processionis et edificiorum et aliorum opportunorum ad dictum festum" (1400 gold florins which may and must be given and paid by the *camarlengo* [...] to the *provveditore* of the Camera dell'Arme to be given and paid to the person or persons to whom payment is made on one or more occasions on behalf of the *festaiuolo* of the *festa* of San Giovanni Battista for the expenses of the procession and the *edifici* and other things necessary for the *festa*). Vitale was subsequently given four years to pay, rather than the original two, and the matter was notarized by Ser Johannes Francisci Neri Cecchi, notary of the Otto, on 21 May 1461, but I have not located the notarized record. In that same year, the Priors made an exceptional charitable donation of £600 at San Giovanni; see ASF, Miscellanea Repubblicana, Busta 1, Inserto 37, fol. 315ʳ, 21 June 1461: "pro erogando amore dei religiosis et piis locis in hoc festo Sancti Iohannis" (to be paid for the love of God to the religious orders and charitable institutions at the coming feast of San Giovanni). On Vitale, see Cassuto, *Gli ebrei a Firenze*, 73. As Rab Hatfield has shown, as late as 1456 and possibly beyond, Jews in Florence paid a turnover tax of 4 *denari* in the *lira* (4/240ᵗʰˢ) to fund the *festa dei Magi*; Hatfield, "The Compagnia," 114.

[18] ASF, Signori e Collegi, Deliberazioni in forza di ordinaria autorità 72, fol. 10ᵛ: "Electio festaiolorum Sancti Iohannis Baptiste" (Election of *festaiuoli* for St. John the Baptist); fol. 38ʳ: "det et solvat festaiuolis Sancti Johannis Baptiste pro festo Sancti Joannis fiendo Lire 2800" (give and pay to the *festaiuoli* of St. John the Baptist for the *festa* of St. John the Baptist £2800); fol. 39ᵛ: "libras 150 pulveris a bombarde pro festo Sancti Iohannis presente anno fiendo" (150 lbs of cannon powder for doing the *festa* of St. John this

The celebrations described by Dati began as usual with the *mostra* at dawn on 23 June. This is traditionally interpreted as a display of devotion and wealth, but the Florentines were probably pragmatic about its commercial value.[19] The focus of the various narratives tends to highlight a glorious ornate display of gold and silk, but we know from an incident in 1588 that the shopkeepers wished and expected to have their precious merchandise packed away before the heat of midday brought flies and dust to spoil their wares. In a parallel reality, the place of real rather than symbolic commerce was the St. John the Baptist market held on the Prato di Ognissanti, the area now known as the Cascine; and the proclamation of the market was always accompanied by the declaration of an amnesty, or *securitas*, as well as suspension of sumptuary laws. The feast of the Baptist gave Florentines who had been convicted of crimes or banished the possibility of returning to city and family without risk of being arrested; it brought a temporary freedom from fear.[20]

Petriboni, 1428: The Magi and the Prophet David

In 1428, the priests and clerks and relics were joined in the procession of 23 June by the company of the Magi on horseback, magnificently arrayed:

> On 23 June, in the morning, they had the procession, as is customary on the eve of the feast of San Giovanni. And notable and beautiful things and parts there were in it, not least on account of the great and worthy and devout procession, adorned with relics

year). Benedetto Dei records proudly that he was *festaiuolo* for San Giovanni in 1451 and 1452; see Dei, *La cronica*, 125. Valori does not mention it in his *ricordanze*; Polizzotto and Kovesi, *Memorie*, 64–78.

[19] Trexler, *Public Life*, 247–249. Giusto Giusti noted in 1473 that the *mostra* was postponed until the arrival of Eleonora d'Aragona, en route to her marriage in Ferrara, so that she and her court "would see all the goods on display, for the greater honour of the city and perhaps to increase profit" (vedessino le robbe della mostra per più onore della terra e forse per più utile); Giusti, "I Giornali," 176.

[20] Trexler, *Public Life*, 3, n. 7; 76, n. 152. Markets were held four times a year: Ash Wednesday (moveable feast), San Giovanni (24 June), St. Simon and St. Jude (28 October), and St. Martin (9 November). The June *securitas* began eight days before San Giovanni and ended eight days after. For the exemplary case of Leonardo, alias Bobo, who sought an amnesty for San Giovanni 1466, despite a fourteen-year record of theft, breaking and entering, and stealing, see ASF, Provvisioni, Registri 157, fols. 89ᵛ–92ʳ. His case was decided on 19 June, and he was released by a vote of 222 to 163, in light of the amnesty.

and with priests and choirboys. And among the other beautiful and marvellous things, the company of the Magi from San Marco made a great and rich contribution to the ceremony. And among the other beautiful, noteworthy, and delightful things there was a display of eight horses, caparisoned in silk, with eight pages dressed in silk, and with pearls, and decorations of special devices, and with shields, and their angelic faces, riding one behind the other in livery. And behind them, on a beautiful big horse, came a man of great age with a white beard, dressed in crimson, brocaded with gold, and a pointed crimson hat, covered with big pearls and other adornments of great value, like a king, such that no man in Christendom, if he wanted to adorn himself, whatever his rank, could surpass him in richness of adornment. And behind this king there was, in the middle of a *nimbus*, a boy about three years old, swaddled and with his hands free: and on one [he held] a live goldfinch, and with the other he made spontaneous natural gestures, such that a man of forty could not have done better. God seemed to be in the body of that boy, Francesco d'Andruccio de' Ricasoli.[21]

The procession was still just a procession, rich and magnificent but without a narrative element. Petriboni does not here identify the "man of great age" with an entourage of angelic pages, but in his description of the Magi procession of January 1428/9, which will be discussed in the next chapter, the figure who followed the Magi, standing aloft on a wagon, was clearly identified as David "who slew the giant with a slingshot," accompanied by three giants and a wild man.[22] It is not immediately clear why David is presented here as the ancient king and bearded prophet of Christ, and not as the David (*puer* or *adulescens*) who slew Goliath.[23] In Agostino di Portico's description of c. 1451–1453 discussed below, the prophet David is similarly singled out, riding on his horse and surrounded by pages. Already a civic symbol but not the republican symbol that Michelangelo's *gigante* will be, David is, here in the patronal feast day, located magnificently between the Magi and the

---

[21] Petriboni, *Priorista*, 212; see Appendix, doc. 8; also Hatfield, "The Compagnia," 111–112, 146.

[22] Petriboni, *Priorista*, 216: "che uccise il giughante colla fronbola"; see chapter 5, n. 17 below.

[23] 1 Samuel 17:33, 42, 55, 56, 58.

Nativity.[24] Following the prophet of Christ in Petriboni's description was the Christ Child himself in a *nugola* or *nimbus*, identified by the live goldfinch in his hand, with its bright patch of red above its beak.[25] Here the child is named and comes from an ancient aristocratic family, but later children will come from the city's orphanages.

Biondo Flavio and the nugole

The *nugole* would be described in great detail a century and a half later by Vasari in his life of *il Cecca*, but a description closer in time can be found at the very end of Biondo Flavio's *Roma Triumphans*, written between 1454 and 1459.[26] Biondo accompanied Pope Eugenius IV into exile in Florence in 1434. He returned to the city with Pius II in 1459 and must have seen and discussed the patronal festivities.[27] He concludes his monumental work on Rome's greatness with a consideration of triumphs, and his description of the

---

[24] See Hatfield, "The Compagnia," 112, n. 27; David is the third of Belcari's three prophets in his *Annunciazione*, oct. 6; his octave derives from Psalms 131 (132):11. A century later, in 1549, David and Goliath were revived as a trionfo, performed by the youth confraternity of the Archangel Raphael; see BNCF, II.iv.19, fols. 130v–131r, mod. num.: "L'antivigilia di san Giovanni Batista, advocato della nostra città, si fece una bella processione, et di molte belle cose. Tra esse fu una Compagnia che si chiama l'Angiol Raffaello, che fece l'abbattimento di David con Golia et David era sopra a un trionfo et recitò e sotto[scritti] versi avanti la porta del palazzo di sua Eccellenza, et così lui stava a udire a una finestra del palazzo, e sentiva benissimo" (Two days before the feast of St. John the Baptist, advocate of our city, there was a beautiful procession with lots of beautiful things. Among them was a company called the Angel Raphael, that did the battle between David and Goliath, and David was on a triumph and recited the lines [copied] below, in front of the door of His Excellency's palazzo, and he stood and listened at a window of the palazzo and he could hear very well). See also *Cronaca fiorentina*, 106–107, where the verse is reproduced.

[25] Friedmann, *The Symbolic Goldfinch*, 1–35 and, for examples in Florentine painting, 65–73 and plates 33–71. The goldfinch, easily tamed and tethered, presaged Christ's passion and death. It could be argued that the goldfinch was 'lifelike' rather than 'living.'

[26] Cruciani, "Dietro le origini," 15–16.

[27] Biondo's name appears on the papal bull of 8 Kalends July (that is, 24 June) 1442, approving the four youth confraternities; bull transcribed in Puccinelli, *Istoria*, 310–311; reproduced in Rolfi, Sebregondi, and Viti, eds., *La Chiesa e la città*, 82, and discussed there in Aranci, "La catachesi," 82–84. The bull refers to the risk of trouble among the confraternities if their proliferation is unchecked, which suggests that there may have been difficulties in the lead-up to the patronal feast day. For the procession of *edifici* mounted for Pius II in 1459, see above, chapter 3, n. 40, and below, n. 88.

Florentine *edifici* is a short *excursus* to illustrate pageant wagons, particularly those bearing children in 'nests' at great heights:

> The feast day of John the Baptist, celebrated every year in the city of Florence, is very famous. In it, machines of various kinds are carried in procession, and various spectacles are done with such subtle skill that they are in no way inferior to those of ancient time. The floats they use are of especially remarkable beauty, the sort too that our Hebrew [Josephus] so admired, that rose three storeys high. But if the more knowledgeable will pardon me, at this point I shall explain to the inexperienced the nature of these floats. Each consisted of a solid floor made of boards and measuring ten feet on each side, and from the centre of this base there rose a straight wooden pole, twenty feet high, to which were attached wrought iron branches that branched three and three again, and were covered in a great quantity of dense gold and silver foliage. And among them were positioned birds' nests, as it were, made of leather and strips of hide of various colours, as cribs for small children of two or three years at the most. Some of them had just their heads out, and some showed their whole bodies, and it was charming and funny to hear what they babbled according to the suggestion of their prompter, hidden in the foliage. This massive construction was carried about by a strong crowd of slaves, dressed, not in patchwork rags as happens in Florence now, but in crimson and gold. Though the floats in the triumph were many and varied, they were by no means carried one after the other, but other machines were interposed, borne on similar litters by slaves similarly got up.[28]

There is an awkward ambiguity here. Biondo appears to be describing the floats of antiquity — he cites Josephus and uses the past tense — but no classical source has been found, and it must be the Florentine *edifici* that he is

---

[28] Biondo Flavio, *Roma Triumphans*, 1:214 (end book x); see Appendix, doc. 9. The "Hebrew" is Flavius Josephus, who describes the triumph of Titus in *The Jewish War*, 505–507, vii.5, but not floats such as these. Newbigin, "Carried Away," 121–123. Patricia Simons has drawn my attention to a pen and ink drawing now in the Saray Museum, Istanbul, possibly the gift of Benedetto Dei to the Sultan Mehmed II, showing nests in scrolling foliage, holding babies and *phalloi*; see Landau and Parshall, *The Renaissance Print*, 91–94.

describing. This is further confirmed by the descriptions of Agostino di Portico and Vasari that will be discussed below, and by a run of expenses incurred by the *laudese* confraternity of San Zanobi in 1435.[29] In that first San Giovanni *festa* after Cosimo de' Medici's return from exile in 1434, the men of San Zanobi reimbursed £67 8s. 2d. *di piccioli* to the well-to-do merchant Gianozzo di Giovanni Strozzi and his companions, who had served as the company's *festaiuoli* for the San Giovanni procession that year. They had paid out:

> £10 12s. 2d. *piccioli* for timber for the litter for San Zanobi, and £1 4s. 6d. for ironmongery for the *edificio* on the litter,[30] and £5 1s. 8d. for nails, cotton wool, and wire, 9 groats for hiring three pairs of wings for the angels, and £1 19s. 4d. for taffeta for the canopy, and 4 groats for straps and stirrups, and £4 8s. to the craftsman who helped to build the *edificio*, for three days' work, and £4 8s. for colours, paper, and eggs for the *edificio*, and £4 to give to Benvenuto the painter, and £9 11s. to the men who carried the litter of the *edificio*, and £11 11s. for food and drink for the people who helped to make the *edificio*.[31]

The pattern was thus established: the confraternity constructed a platform to be carried on the shoulders of a great number of porters. On it was a painted structure, a silken canopy, and at least three angels, together with a reliquary or a representation of San Zanobi, the first bishop of Florence, to whom the confraternity was dedicated. The *edificio* is not yet a play, with dialogue and gesture, but rather the structure on the litter.

---

[29] See Henderson, *Piety*, 95, n. 107. For more on the confraternity, see Wilson, *Music and Merchants*.

[30] The term *barella* (barrow, bier, litter) is also used in the accounts of the *laudese* confraternity of San Zanobi in 1435, and by Matteo Palmieri in 1454. It indicates the wooden platform carried by porters, bearing the *edificio* or superstructure with its *rappresentazione*.

[31] CRSPL 2181 (Z.i.33), fol. 164[sin.]: "£10 s.12 d.2 per legname per la barella di San Zanobi, e £12 s.4 d.6 per ferramenti per lo dificio de la barella, e £5 s.1 d.8 per aguti, banbagia e fili di ferro, e grossi 9 per achattatura di tre paia d'alie per gli agnoli, e £1 s.19 d.4 per tafettà per l'onbrella, e grossi 4 per soatto e calcagnini, e £4 s.8 al maestro aiutò fare el dificio per 3 dì, e £4 s.8 per colori, cartta, e huova pel dificio, e £4 per dare a Benvenuto dipintore, e £9 s.11 a coloro portorono la barella del dificio, e £11 s.11 per mangiare e bere ebbono quegli aiutorono fare el dificio." Earlier and later expenses are less informative: in 1433, fol. 121[sin.], £26 16s. to "onorare la testa di San Zenobi" (honour the head of St. Zenobius); in 1436, fol. 178[sin.], £20 lump sum for the *festaiuoli* for 1436.

A Greek Response in 1439

A less than laudatory description of the procession of clergy and relics is provided by an outsider, an unnamed Greek participant in the Council of Florence in 1439. Almost overwhelmed by what he saw, he jumbles the constituent parts, beginning with the Last Judgment:

> On 23 June they hold a great procession and a great public *festa*, in which they do marvellous things, almost miracles, or representations of miracles. In fact, they cause the dead to rise again; St. Michael tramples demons; they crucify a man playing the part of Christ; they represent the Resurrection of Christ; they have men play the parts of the Magi; and men perform the birth of Christ with the shepherds, the star, the animals, and the manger. Then they go in procession with statues and saints' relics, images, and venerated crosses; they are always preceded by trumpets and other musical instruments. What can I say about the monk that they had performing the part of St. Augustine? They put him 25 *braccia* up and there he walked back and forth preaching. They also had actors playing the parts of bearded hermits, walking atop wooden stilts, which was a terrifying spectacle. We also saw statues, some of them very big, others very high up, that moved with enormous effort. What can I say about St. George, performing the miracle of the dragon?[32]

The Greek visitor recoiled from the *edifici* with their representations of the Fall of the Angels, St. George and the Dragon, the Nativity with Magi and Shepherds, the Crucifixion, the Resurrection, and the Last Judgment — the bare bones of the history of Man's salvation, which, with the exception of the Crucifixion, will remain the staple fare of the Baptist's procession. As Anna Pontani has pointed out, the Greek theologian, Symeon, archbishop of Thessalonica (d. 1429), had earlier expressed his dismay at the way the Latin Church represented divine truths by means of real actors and plays rather

---

[32] Greek text with Latin translation in Pasini, *Codices Manuscripti*, 1:271–272, now superseded by Pontani, "Firenze," 798–805, with new Greek text and Italian translation; see also Ventrone, "Sulle feste," 92–93.

than through icons, which are *images* of the divine truth.[33] It also offended him that because the Latins shaved, they had to wear false beards when they did their plays, and that they used bladders of animal blood to make a false Christ bleed from his wounds. The short-lived Union between the Greek and Roman church celebrated in Florence in 1439 did not address other divides that separated the two, particularly concerning theatre. For the Byzantine church, as Andrew Walker White puts it, "mimes, who had adopted hypocrisy as a profession, celebrated their own materiality on stage and in doing so distracted themselves and their audiences from spiritual matters."[34]

Benedetto Dei, Giusto Giusti, and the edifici

In 1451, Ser Giusto Giusti, who had been keeping a diary since 1437, recorded the next elements in his *Giornale*:

> Wednesday 23 [June 1451] was the eve of San Giovanni in Florence. During the day they did a beautiful procession with many beautiful *essempli* and *edifici*. On Thursday 24 they held a beautiful *festa*, and there were lots of foreign visitors. The *palio* was very beautiful and cost 500 florins or thereabouts. It was won by one of the racehorses of the Marquis of Ferrara.[35]

The words *essempli* and *edifici* again catch our attention. Paola Ventrone observed that this is the first occurrence of the term *edifici* in a description of the procession,[36] but as we have just seen, the *laudese* company of San Zanobi was already using the term in its 1435 accounts. What is new here is the term *essempli* (literally, 'examples'), which seems to designate *tableaux vivants* or

---

[33] See discussion, Pontani, "Firenze," 788–797; and translation of Simeon di Tessalonica, *Dialogus contra haereses,* Cap. xxiii: *Bisogna rappresentare le verità divine con rispetto e devozione, secondo la consuetudine stabilita* (from *PG* 155 (1866): 112A–116D), in Pontani, "Firenze," 806–812.

[34] White, *Performing Orthodox Ritual*, 84–85, reminding us that the Greek word for actor is ὑποκριτής (hypokrites).

[35] Giusti, "I *Giornali*," 104: "Mercordì a dì 23 detto [di giugno 1451] in Firenze fu la vigilia di San Giovanni. Fecesi il dì una bella processione con molti belli essempli ed edifici. | Giovedì a dì 24 detto in Firenze fecesi bellissima festa, e furonci molti forestieri. Fu il palio molto bello di costo di fiorini 500 o circa. Ebbelo un corsieri del marchese di Ferrara."

[36] Ventrone, "Sulle feste," 90, n. 4. Giusto Giusti notes *edifici* for St. John the Baptist in both 1451 and 1452; Giusti, "I *Giornali*," 104 and 107.

short dramatic scenes exemplifying the life of a saint whose relic was being carried, while *edifici* still designates the structures or scaffolding mounted on platforms or litters and borne by porters, which could be rested on trestles for a scene to be acted out. Only later, by extension, does the term include the play.

The year 1451 was Benedetto Dei's first year as one of the *festaiuoli*,[37] and he later boasted in his unpublished *Memorie*: "I was there [in Florence] in the time of the *edifici* that are created anew for San Giovanni, and to every visitor they would seem to have been created by magic."[38] This is a period of transition and innovation.

Agostino di Portico: *The Children of the Foundling Hospitals and the* edificio *of San Rossore*

An extended description of the procession by Agostino di Portico, a Camaldolese monk who witnessed it some time between 1451 and 1453, was unknown until published by Daniela Delcorno Branca in 2003.[39] The starting point of the procession is not specified but its final destination was the Piazza della Signoria. It was led by the least powerful: the orphans and wet nurses of the city's three orphanages of San Gallo, the Scala, and the Innocenti:

> The first thing was the three [foundling] hospitals, and each one had its cross and banner: the first was San Gallo, and the second was the Scala, and the third was the Innocenti. First came the cross, then many loads of tiny children in big baskets covered all over with flowers and they all had garlands on their heads. Each of these hospitals had many baskets and behind them, two by two, came all the wet nurses, and it was a devout and moving sight. Behind them followed the friars of each hospital with their rectors and priests and relics and other adornments. Then many hermits and confraternities with their humble crosses and adornments.[40]

---

[37] See above, n. 18.

[38] BMLF, Ashb. 644, fol. 11r: "sono stato [a Firenze] al tempo de' difici che si fanno di nuovo per San Giovanni, che a ogni forestiero parrebbono fatto per arte magica"; noted in Helas, "Alphonsis Regis Triumphus," 199. For manuscripts of Dei's *Cronica* and the related but unpublished *Memorie*, see Barducci, "Dei," 255.

[39] Delcorno Branca, "Un camaldolese."

[40] Delcorno Branca, "Un camaldolese," 9: "La prima cosa furono tre spedali ch'ognuno aveva la sua croce e stendardo: e l'uno fu San Gallo e l'altro la Scala e l'altro gli Innocenti. Prima andava la croce, di poi molte some di fanciulli piccolini in ceste grandi coperte di

We know from other lists that youth and *disciplinati* confraternities joined the procession, but not the *laudesi* companies.[41] They were followed by the regular clergy in ascending order of importance: Jesuates, Third Order Franciscans, Dominicans, Servites, Carmelites, Augustinians, and then the Humiliati of Ognissanti. The Humiliati, custodians of the relic of San Rossore that the Florentines had acquired from Pisa in 1422,[42] carried it on:

> a wonderful *edificio*, twenty *braccia* [11.6 metres] high with much adornment, full of living children who looked like angels with wings, who sang and played fiddles and cymbals and turned around as if they were dancing; and they were so high up I was amazed that they were not afraid. [...] This *edificio* was carried by sixty men or more, it was so big. When it arrived in front of the *palazzo* it stopped and there they sang and played.[43]

The presence of children on an *edificio*, together with the participation of the city's orphanages in the procession, suggests that the two were related. Lucia Ricciardi, archivist at the Ospedale degli Innocenti, has drawn my attention to records there that confirm not only the participation of the Innocenti

---

sopra con fiori e tutti avevano le grilande in capo. Ognuno di questi spedali aveva molte some e drieto a coppia a coppia andavano tutte le balie e era cosa devota e piatosa. Dietro seguitava gli frati di ciascun spedale con gli loro rettori e sacerdoti e reliquie e altri ornamenti. Di poi molti romiti e compagnie con loro humili croci e ornamenti."

[41] According to the list in ASF, Carte di corredo 45, fols. 18ᵛ and 49ʳ and dating probably to 1454, they did not process with the religious orders and other confraternities on 23 June, even though the youth confraternities processed both with the *edifici* in the new procession of 22 June and with the religious orders on 23 June. See also Ventrone, "Sulle feste."

[42] Petriboni, *Priorista*, 151. Donatello's reliquary of San Rossore, in the form of a silver and gilt bust, is now in the Museo Nazionale di San Matteo in Pisa; see Paolozzi Strozzi and Bormand, eds., *La primavera*, 338 (Marc Bormand). The text by Don Battista di Brunelleschi, *La rappresentatione di san Rossore martire. Nuouamente mandata in luce* (Florence: n.p., 1559), CNCE 7649, which was included in the *Secondo libro di feste* but composed decades earlier, is not related to the San Giovanni procession. See Solin and Tuomisto, "Appunti."

[43] Delcorno Branca, "Un camaldolese," 10: "uno mirabile edifitio alto braccia vinti di grande ornamento, pieno di fanciulli vivi che parevano angeletti con l'ali e che cantavano e sonavano ghigh'e ciembali e volgevansi intorno come balassero; e essendo tanto alti maravigliavami come non temevano. [...] Questo edifitio era portato da sesanta huomini o più, tanto era grande. Quando giunse dinanzi al palazzo si fermò e quivi cantorono e sonorono."

in the feast of St. John from at least 1448, but also their investment in *edifici* and *barelle* that were used in the procession. In 1448 the Ospedale nominated Nofri d'Agnolo Buonamici, *tessitore di drappi* (brocade weaver) and one of the original Twelve Good Men of San Martino appointed by Antoninus in 1442, as their *festaiuolo*. He was responsible for the "expenses incurred on behalf of the hospital for *edifici* and litters and other things we made for the *festa*," and was later reimbursed a total of £86 when a subsidy was received from the *festaiuoli di San Giovanni* appointed by the Commune.[44] Assistance was also provided by the hospital's sponsor, the Wool Guild, whose *famiglio*, or factotum, called *il Forte*, hired a carthorse "when we sent him out to [fetch] the wet nurses and their husbands for the feast of San Giovanni;"[45] beds were hired for them to sleep in before they returned to the country: "£4 15s., taken by Antonio di Domenico, who works for the linen merchant Giovanni di Bernardo and company, for the loan of several beds lent to us by Giovanni di Zacheria for the feast of San Giovanni for the wet nurses and their husbands."[46]

Money was spent on the construction of *edifici*. Payments were made to Lando di ser Jacopo the ropemaker in August 1448 for ropes and "other things borrowed for the feast of San Giovanni," while a final account of £5 7s. with Antonio di Piero the blacksmith was not settled until February 1448/9:

---

[44] Florence, Archivio dell'Ospedale degli Innocenti (AOIF) 4783 [2646] (s. 122, n. 2), fols. 3r (21 August 1448): "spese si fece pello spedale inn edifidici [*sic*] e in barelle e altre chose facemo per detta festa"; and fols. 108ʳ: "A Nofri d'Angniolo tessitore di drapi lire cinquantanove ebe contanti in più volte per la festa di San Giovanni per far festa" (To Nofri d'Agnolo brocade weaver £59 which he received in cash on various occasions for the feast of San Giovanni for the celebrations); and 110r (August 1448): "A Nofri d'Angniolo festa-iuolo lire venzette ebbe chontanti del mese di gungnio 1448 da' festaiuoli di Santo Giovani fatti pel Chumone [*sic*] di Firenze, i quali danari ce dettero per aiuto dil dificio facemo per la festa di Sancto Giovanni" (To Nofri d'Agnolo *festaiuolo*, £27 which he received in cash in June 1448 from the *festaiuoli* of San Giovanni created by the Commune of Florence, which was money they gave us to help with the *edificio* we made for the feast of San Giovanni). Also among those first Buonomini were Jacopo di Biagio, the cloth-shearer and *guardiano* of the youth confraternity of Vangelista (see chapter 3 above), and Ser Alesso Pelli, Cosi-mo's secretary, whose names have recurred in this account of the *feste*. On Nofri d'Agnolo Buonamici as a patron of Masaccio, see A. Cecchi, "Nuovi contributi," esp. 30 and 68–70.

[45] AOIF 4783 [2646] (s. 122, n. 2), fol. 101ᵛ (22 June 1448): "quando el mandamo fuori a' bagli pella festa di San Giovanni." The term *bagli* (for *bali*) is inclusive of both the women and their husbands.

[46] AOIF 4783 [2646] (s. 122, n. 2), fol. 106ᵛ (13 July 1448): "lire quatro soldi 15, portò Antonio di Domenicho istà con Giovani di Bernardo linaiuolo e chonpangni, per prestat-ura di più letta ci prestò Giovani di Zacheria per la festa di San Giovani pe' bali."

"as the balance due for ironmongery he lent when he made six [?] *edifici* for the feast of San Giovanni to carry children."[47] This final entry confirms that, in addition to the infants carried by their carers, there were children on *edifici*.

The twenty-four *guarnelli* (loose overdresses) sewn by Mona Agnola di Cristofano on 22 June 1448[48] may have been a regular renewal of clothing, but in June 1451 we find the institution paying £11 for "eight shirts and eight pairs of angels' wings for the choirboys of the house, and Francesco, called Stocky, the rag merchant, was the broker."[49]

Regular expenses are recorded "for keeping the children clothed and shod,"[50] particularly at the Quarter days of Christmas, Annunciation, St. John the Baptist, and Michelmas when dependants traditionally received new clothing. But in June 1452 there were additional expenses for *guarnelli* and *giornee* (overtunics) decorated almost extravagantly with brass buttons.[51]

The Innocenti hospital had taken its first foundling on 25 January 1444/5, and the children had soon been incorporated into the *festa*. In conjunction with the descriptions, these payments confirm that from 1448 at least the children, with the men and women who cared for them, went in procession at least until 1453, after which I have not located any such payments.[52] And they borrowed *ferramenta* — in all probability *nugole* — for their *edificio*. While Trexler emphasizes the pathos of these "interned" children whose innocence is exploited in times of crisis and whose innocent prayers are

---

[47] AOIF 4783 [2646] (s. 122, n. 2), fol. 108ʳ (9 August 1448): "altre chose avute pella festa di San Giovanni in prestanza"; fol. 107ᵛ (3 August 1448): £12, without further details; and fol. 127r (1 February 1448/9): £5 7s., "per resto di ragione di feramenti ci prestò che ci fe' di se' [?] difici pella festa di santo Giovanni per portare fanciugli." For Antonio di Piero's work building equipment for the Sant'Agnese confraternity in the years 1437–1443, see Newbigin, *Feste*, 2:338–339, 341, 344, 352–353, 356–358, 374, 382, 397, 400, 402.

[48] AOIF 4783 [2646] (s. 122, n. 2), fol. 102ʳ: "A spese di chasa £2 s.8 piccioli demo a mona Angniola di Cristofano per resto di chucitura di 24 guarnegli" (From household expenses we paid £2 8s. *di piccioli* to Mona Agnola di Cristofano for the rest of the sewing of 24 overdresses).

[49] AOIF 4786 [2653] (s. 126, n. 3), fol. 69ᵛ (4 June 1451): "otto chamiciette e otto paia d'ale da angnolietti [...] pe' cherici di chasa e funne mezane Francescho chiamato il Tozzo righattiere."

[50] See, for example, AOIF 4784 [2651] (s. 122, n. 4), fol. 90ᵛ (27 March 1452): "a vestire e chalzare e fanciugli [...] £10 s.16 picioli per loro," with expenses continuing to fol. 91r.

[51] AOIF 4784 [2651] (s. 122, n. 4), fol. 99ʳ (20 June 1452): "per chucitura e fornitura, e bottoni d'ottone di 6 guarnegli da fanciulle grandi" (for sewing and supplying and for brass buttons for six tunics for the older girls).

[52] The practice may have ceased with the reforms of 1454; see below.

vital to the salvation of the city,[53] I would point rather more prosaically to the excitement and pleasure such diversionary activities were likely to bring, not to mention the new clothes and extra food.[54] Moreover, this short period between the opening of the Innocenti in February 1444/5 and 1454 was one of relative optimism for the hospital, during which the children might have been judged fortunate.[55]

Agostino di Portico: David, the Dragon, the Annunciation

In second position in the procession came the Camaldolese monks with their *edificio* of the Annunciation, which was introduced by:

> The prophet David on horseback and many prophets and pages in livery and lots of people dressed up in the latest fashion, and live *spiritelli*, and besides this, ahead of these prophets, there was a great and terrible basilisk that had the body of a rooster but a very long tail like a serpent.[56]

The basilisk — the dragon of other descriptions — needs further explanation. It must here represent the forces of evil, like the asp and the basilisk of Psalm 90 (91):13: "Thou shalt walk upon the asp and the basilisk: and thou shalt trample underfoot the lion and the dragon."[57] The incarnation of Christ

---

[53] Trexler, *Public Life*, 368–369; also Trexler, "The Foundlings." Trexler identified only one procession, in 1422, in which the foundlings participated, but there were probably many more.

[54] For example, £7 10*s*. for "Pistoiese cheese we got for the hospital for the feast of San Giovanni" (*cacio pistolese toglemo per in casa pella festa di sancto Giovanni*), AOIF, 4783 [2646] (s. 122, n. 2), fol. 100ᵛ; and £4 10*s*. "for 400 eggs that *il Grassino* bought for the feast of San Giovanni" (*per quatrocento vuova chonperò il Grasino per la festa di San Giovani*), fol. 107v.

[55] Trexler, "The Foundlings," 275.

[56] Delcorno Branca, "Un camaldolese," 10: "David propheta a cavallo con molti propheti e scudieri ornati e aveano gente contrafatta di nuova fiorgia e spiritelli vivi e oltra a questo inanzi a questi propheti, andava un basilisco grandissimo e terribile ch'avea forma di gallo, ma avea la coda grandissima come serpente." Agostino interrupts his description of the Annunciation *edificio* to go back and describe the procession that preceded it.

[57] "Super aspidem et basiliscum ambulabis et conculcabis leonem et draconem." The "Basilisk" of the Vulgate and the Douay Rheims bibles is replaced by "adder" in KJV. See also Isaiah 14:29.

at the Annunciation, foretold by the prophets, will bring victory over the beast. But Agostino's basilisk is also also related to another mythic dragon. In his *Summa de Ecclesiasticis Officiis*, the Parisian theologian Jean Beleth (died c. 1185) discussed the rituals celebrated on the feast of the Nativity of the Baptist.[58] There are various versions of the text, but they all refer to the custom of collecting and burning dragon bones and carrying the embers in procession to produce smoke, because in this season dragons become aroused by the heat and fly through the air and inseminate wells and fountains, which will lead to a bad year, but burning the bones will ward them off.[59] There is no evidence of a conscious recollection of this belief in the Florentine procession,[60] but the dragon continued to make an appearance into the sixteenth century, almost always in the company of St. George, as in the 1439 procession described above.[61] Belcari's undated four-stanza text of *San Giorgio* probably belongs to

---

[58] Though hugely popular, Beleth's *Summa* was largely superseded as the standard exegesis of the Christian ritual by the *Prochiron, vulgo Rationale divinorum officiorum* of Guillaume Durand (c. 1230–1286).

[59] Beleth, *Summa*, 267–268, §137.17–33: "Antiquitus enim dracones in hoc tempore excitabantur ad libidinem propter calorem et uolando per aera frequenter spermatizabant puteos et fontes, ex quo inficiebantur aque, et tunc erat annus letalis, quia quicumque inde bibebant, aut moriebantur aut gravem morbum patiebantur. Quod attendentes philosophi iusserunt fieri ignem frequenter et passim circa puteos et fontes et inmunda ibi cremari et quecumque immundum redderent fumum" (For in ancient times dragons were incited to lust, on account of the heat of the season, and flying through the air they often sowed their seed in wells and springs, and the waters were tainted, and it was a deadly year, because whoever drank there either died or suffered grievous illness. In response to this, philosophers ordered fires to be lit all around wells and springs, and unclean things to be burned, and whatever was unclean would go up in smoke).

[60] In the feast of San Giovanni in 1478, already postponed to 5 July, the *girandola* fireworks failed to explode: "it did not work and the event did not take place in the space and the way and at the time and at the level of quality that they promised — to the grave shame and detriment of the Florentine people" (illud non perfecerunt et eis res non successit locis modis et temporibus et qualitatibus ut promiserunt — in eorum et populi florentini grave dedecus et damnum). The three craftsmen, Riccio the goldsmith, Bertoldo [di Giovanni, the sculptor], and a second goldsmith, Banco [di Filippo in Calimala], were sued by the *festaiuoli* and sent to prison; see Del Badia, "Girandola," 63; Landucci, *Diario*, 23; Draper, "Andrea vocato El Riccio." Fireworks are still used for prognostication in the annual Easter ritual of the *Scoppio del Carro*, although Gulino, *Il rito*, 125, notes that the use of the plaster dove as an incendiary device is first observed in the sixteenth century.

[61] It was still a significant part in 1577; see "Ordine della cavalleria fatta per la Compagnia di San Giorgio nella Processione di San Giovanni, L'Anno 1577," in *Descrizzione de i trionfi*, fol. 3ʳ⁻ᵛ, where the princess was followed by the seven Gifts of the Holy Spirit, each

this element of the procession, dealing simply with the saint's conquest of the dragon.[62] Conveniently, Belcari's dragon does not fall dead. As in the *Legenda Aurea*, the saint orders the damsel to tie her girdle around the dragon's neck and lead it away.[63]

When the Annunciation *edificio* appeared, it was:

> carried by seventy men or more. And this *edificio* was very high, and there were lots of little angels who sang and played and danced, and above them there was a Virgin Annunciate, a living person, and the Angel: and she was so beautiful and her clothes were so fine that she looked just like her, and the Angel likewise was a living person and had wings. [...] When it arrived in front of the Signoria it stopped; the Angel and Our Lady were on two great fronds of pinks. The Angel kneeled and said *Ave Maria!* (Hail Mary!) and everything that follows in the Gospel; and our Lady replied and made all those gestures of *Et quomodo fiet* (How can that be?), etc. At the end she said *Ecce ancilla domini* (Behold the handmaiden of the Lord), and at once a live dove flew out and descended upon her. This was so devout that it brought tears to the eyes and made me weep.[64]

leading the Deadly Sin she had vanquished, and finally St. George, followed by Fame and a triumph of Glory, accompanied by Praise, Honour, and Contentment.

[62] Belcari, *Le rappresentazioni*, 115–116, where Galletti mistakenly numbers the octaves 4–7. Another play, performed over two days, represented the entire legend of St. George from his conversion to his martyrdom; see *Il primo e il secondo dì di San Giorgio*, in Newbigin, "Dieci sacre rappresentazioni," 132–199, and discussion below, chapter 5.

[63] Jacobus, *Legenda Aurea*, 1:442–443, lvi.58–60 *De Sancto Georgio*: "Dixitque puelle: 'Proice zonam tuam in collum dracons nihil dubitans, filia!' Quod cum fecisset, sequebatur eam uelut mansuetissimus canis" (He said to the damsel: 'Throw your girdle around the dragon's neck and do not be afraid, my daughter. When she did this, it followed her as meekly as a dog). This detail is found in Uccello's *St. George* (c. 1470) in London, National Gallery, inv. no. NG6294; but not in his earlier *St. George* (1458–1460), now Paris, Musée Jacquemart-André, Acc. no. NG6294.

[64] Delcorno Branca, "Un camaldolese," 10: "portato da huomini settanta o più. E questo edifitio era altissimo, dove erano molti angeletti che cantavano e sonavano e ballavano, sopra ' quali era una Annuntiata viva e l'angelo: e era tanto bella e sì ben vestita che pareva essa, e l'angelo similmente era vivo co l'ali. [...] Quando fu dinanzi alla signoria sì ssi posò. L'angelo e la donna erano in su dua rami di viuole grandissimi. L'angelo sì ss'inginocchiò e disse "*Ave Maria*" e tutto come seguita il Vangelio; e la donna rispondeva e faceva tutti que' gesti "*et quomodo fiet* etc." Alla fine disse "*ecce ancila domini*" e di subbito una colomba

The Annunciation had long been performed in the Camaldolese church of San Felice in Piazza,[65] but this is the earliest and indeed the only documented link between the Camaldolese monastery of San Felice in Piazza and the representation of the Annunciation play in the procession; and, since his own order is involved, Agostino gives it particular attention. The *edificio* here was a litter that was carried on the shoulders of seventy men, in the same way as the Florentine community of Naples carried their allegorical litter in Alfonso's triumph of 1443 (fig. 4.1),[66] and as the *macchina di Santa Rosa* is still carried through Viterbo (fig. 4.2).[67] The *edificio* must have come to a stop and been placed on trestles.[68] On the *edificio*, live actors performed a scene, if not a whole play, with gesture and dialogue, taken directly from Luke 1:26–38.[69] We need not imagine that the monks themselves prepared the *edificio*, performed the play, or acted as porters. As we have seen, the *laudesi* confraternities did not go in the procession under their own banners, so it is plausible that they were the actors on the *edificio* of their host order, as Dati described, and that

---

viva uscì di sopra e venne sopra lei. Questa cosa fu tanto devota che extorse lagrime da gli occhi e fece me lagrimare." The dove, unlike the goldfinch of 1428, is probably 'alive' only in a fictive sense.

[65] Newbigin, *Feste*, 1:1–13; see above, chapter 2.

[66] This panel, and its pendant piece depicting *The Siege of Naples*, now in the John and Mable Ringling Museum of Art, Sarasota, are dated variously to 1452, 1463, and 1465. Documentary sources describe the contribution of the Florentines to the procession. Allegorical contributions representing Justice on the left and Fortune on the right flank an impersonation of Caesar, standing on an orb. The feet of the porters can be seen below their concealing brocade, which is decorated with heraldic devices; Brilliant, "The Triumphal Entry," 152, and "The Siege of Naples." See also Helas, *Lebende Bilder*, 71–74, and her "Alphonsis Regis Triumphus," and "Der Triumph"; Alisio, Bertelli, and Pinelli, *Arte e politica*. On Alfonso's attention to Florentine practices, see Newbigin, "Carried Away," 120–121.

[67] The illuminated *macchina* is carried by one hundred porters through the streets of Viterbo on the feast day of the saint, 3 September, and comes to rest in front of the Sanctuary di Santa Rosa. It is over 30 m high and is redesigned and rebuilt every five years or so. *La Gloria* (Glory), constructed in 2015, is almost three times the height of the Florentine *edifici*, and built of modern light-weight materials, but it creates a similar sense of wonder in the public.

[68] This is clear in the 1454 description (see below); there is no evidence that the play was performed in more than one location in the city, and no indication of its processional route.

[69] The lines quoted are from Luke 1:28, 1:34, and 1:38. There are no grounds for attributing the text, in this year or in any other, to Feo Belcari.

local workers lent muscle to the enterprise. Nevertheless, the surviving account books of the Oltrarno *laudesi* confraternities make no suggestion that they paid for the *edificio*.[70]

Agostino di Portico: *The Resurrection and Limbo*

Agostino's description moves directly from the Annunciation to the Resurrection, with no mention at all of any procession of Magi, nor of a Nativity *edificio*, nor of the Passion, which does not appear in the surviving descriptions after 1439. The Nativity *edifici* will be discussed in the context of the 1454 reforms in the next section.

The Resurrection and Limbo *edifici*, like the Annunciation, were accompanied by their host order, in this case, the 'black monks' of San Basilio:

> Among other things there was a great *edificio* with the Sepulchre and armed men who guarded it. Suddenly there was a great explosion and the cover fell to the ground and Christ came out with his banner. Two Angels appeared there, as it says in the Gospel, and they sat on the Sepulchre, and Christ went at once to Limbo, which was on another *edificio*, with flames pouring out, and there were lots of demons and they did not want to open up. Christ opened up the gates and those demons fled; and he brought forth Adam and Eve and all the great men and women of old, and with lots of angels he went off to Paradise. And these things were done so well that they were quite stupendous.[71]

---

[70] The Annunciation was also brought out on other occasions. For Charles VIII in 1494, the *edificio* of the Nunziata was mounted on a pageant wagon, stationed by Ponte Santa Trinita in Piazza Frescobaldi: "a wagon with an *edificio* and lots of fireworks when the Angel came to Our Lady" (uno carro con uno edificio con molti razi quando fo annonciata Nostra Donna); see Sanuto, *La spedizione,* 135; cited in Borsook, "Decor in Florence," 108; Plaisance "L'entrée," 48–50.

[71] Delcorno Branca, "Un camaldolese," 10: "Fra ll'altre cose venne uno edifitio grandissimo dove era il sepolcro e huomini armati che 'l guardavano. Di subbito venne uno grande scoppio e 'l coperchio andò a terra e Cristo uscì fuori con la bandiera. Quivi apparieno dua angeli come si dice nel Vangelio, e sedevano in sul sepolcro e Cristo andava di subbito al Limbo ch'era in su un altro edifitio donde usciva fuoco e quivi v'erano molti demoni e non volevano aprire. Cristo levò via le porti e que' demoni fugivano; e trasse fuore Adamo e Eva e molti barbassori antichi e con molti angeli andava al Paradiso. E

The performers on this trio of *edifici* were the confraternity of the Resurrection, known also as the company of the Armenians and the company of the Sepulchre, which derived, as its statutes tried to say, from the Kingdom of the Canto alla Macine (Millstone Corner).[72] Trexler argues that its activities were more festive than pious, and the person responsible for organizing the *edifici* was a 'king' as in the festive kingdoms.[73] Their statutes, revised in 1485, describe the responsibilities of the king, which were to be kept quite apart from those of the confraternity:

And we desire that, when we do the *festa* of San Giovanni in the future, if we are doing *edifici*, then the king can and must undertake to do the *edifici* for the company, and not for anyone else and not on his own behalf. And all earnings that derive from them are and must be the property of the company. And therefore, if through some accident of fire or anything else there is any loss, then the company is liable. And any king who goes against what has been said above concerning *edifici* will be deposed and struck off at once and a new king will be created. And the company will not give or lend anything that belongs to the *edifici* when other people are doing them, unless it has been carried in the body of the company by four fifths of the black beans [in favour], they cannot be lent to anybody at all. And any Captains who act against this will incur a fine of ten soldi each.[74]

---

queste cose si fece con tanto ordine che pareva cosa stupenda." In 1454, Earthly Paradise is a third *edificio*; see below.

[72] ASF, CCRSPL 100, fol. 8ᵛ: "Avendo considerato gli edificatori di questa sancta e divota conpagnia che essendo derivata dal Re di Macina deliberorono senpre dovergli fare honore, e però ordinorono che el Re dovessi essere a sedere nel seggio de' capitani, tra e capitani e' consiglieri e deba tenere silentio al desco ma rispondere quando sarà chiamato" (The founders of this holy and devout company, having regard for the fact that it derived from the king of the Millstone, resolved that they should do him honour, and they ordered that the king should sit in the Captains' pew, between the Captains and the Counsellors, and he is to remain silent at the bench but reply when he is asked). On the Medicean youths of the Canto alla Macine who supported Lorenzo in 1478, see D.V. Kent and F.W. Kent, "Two Vignettes," 252–260. For the company's names, see n. 75 below.

[73] Trexler, *Public Life*, 406–408, discusses these statutes, seeing them as an attempt to transform an ancient 'festive kingdom' into a confraternity, but they are clearly already a *compagnia di stendardo* with their own traditions.

[74] ASF, CCRSPL 100, fol. 9ᵛ: "E vogliamo el re, che per li tenpi saranno quando si farà festa di Sancto Giovanni, faccendosi edifici, possa e debba pigliare a fare edifici per

The Resurrection at least had been judged worthy of the Holy Roman Emperor. At Candlemas in February 1451/2, when Frederick III visited Florence on the way to his coronation in Rome, Cosimo de' Medici's factotum, Ser Alesso Pelli, who was also the notary to the organizing committee, arranged for the company to do its *rappresentazione* of the *Monumento* in the Duomo, complete with fireworks.[75] The three *edifici* of the Sepulchre, Limbo, and the Earthly Paradise required only a minimum of dialogue. It is likely that spectacle was even more important than words: fireworks to accompany Christ's Resurrection from the *Monumento* (tomb), devils playing around the fire-spewing hell-mouth, and angels to greet the Righteous in the Earthly Paradise.[76]

la conpagnia, e non per altri né sopra di sé. E ogni ghadagno che se ne facesse sia e essere debba della conpagnia, e così se per disgratia di fuoco o d'altro vi fussi perdita, la conpagnia ne sia tenuta. E qualunque re controfacesse a quanto è detto di sopra d'*edifici* sia disposto e raso di fatto, e faccisi nuovo re. E lla compagnia dare né prestare alcuna cosa apartenente a' difici quando gli facessi altri; se non si vince in corpo di conpagnia per quatro quinti delle fave nere, non si possino concedere a persona alcuna. E ' capitani che contra a cciò facessino, cagino in pena di soldi dieci per uno." This chapter (fols. 8ᵛ–10ʳ) was, however, struck out by the archbishop in a final addendum to his approval (fol. 29ᵛ): "Nevertheless we delete the fifth chapter entitled *Chapter concerning the King*, because we cannot confirm or approve this chapter, for good, just, and rational reasons" (Excipimus tamen quintum capitulum ubi dicitur Capitulum Regis, quod capitulum bonis & iustis ac rationabilibus causis animum nostrum moventibus nullo modo confirmamus nec approbamus), probably because it set the king and his barony outside the authority of the confraternity. Moreover, the *edifici* remained suspended from 1478, just after the Pazzi conspiracy, until their return in 1488.

[75] The "compagnia degli Ormeni," that is the confraternity of the 'Armenian' church of San Basilio at the Canto alla Macine (the intersection of Via San Gallo and the present Via Guelfa, and now the Seventh Day Adventist church), did the "the *festa* of the Entombment at Santa Reparata (the Cathedral) in front of the Emperor" (festa del Sipolchro a Santa Liperata inanzi allo 'nperadore), ASF, Camera dell'Arme–Repubblicana 51, fols. 47ᵛ–48ʳ; on the fireworks, fols. 39ᵛ–40ʳ; and Newbigin, "'Quasi insalutato ospite.'" On fol. 58r they are called the "the company of the Sepulchre" (compagnia del Sipolchro). The *edificio* of Limbo was possibly used in other contexts as well: when John the Baptist visits the Old Testament Righteous with news of Christ's imminent arrival, in the play of *San Giovanni decollato* (c. 1451); and when Gabriel visits Limbo in Belcari's *Annunciazione* (c. 1465).

[76] A similar *Resurrezione* was performed in Milan in 1457. Like the Florentine Resurrection, it required three wagons that represented the Sepulchre, Limbo with Hell, and the Earthly Paradise. It was described in rich detail by Giorgio Valagussa in a letter to Andrea Simonetta; see Resta, *Giorgio Valagussa,* 125–129; and also Tissoni Benvenuti and Mussini Sacchi, eds., *Teatro del Quattrocento,* 334–335. See also a Resurrection performed

We do not have an early Florentine text of the Resurrection and Harrowing of Hell, although a longer version, which in part follows the Florentine *rappresentazione* model, is to be found, like the play of the *Tre re vivi e morti*, in the Bolognese anthology of 1482.[77]

Agostino di Portico: Judgment Day

The second-to-last *edificio* presented Judgment Day. It is customary to begin an account of the drama of late medieval Florence with the Judgment Day disaster of 1304, and it is possible that this is the oldest of the pageants represented for the feast of the Baptist. Giovanni Villani, whose chronicle of Florence shaped the way Florentines perceived themselves and their forebears, records the event. After much civil discord, peace had finally been established between Guelfs and Ghibellines, and to celebrate both peace and the traditional spring festival of Calendimaggio,[78] the people of Borgo San Frediano, the district around Santa Maria del Carmine on the southern and poorer side of the Arno, sent criers about to announce that:

> whosoever desired news of the other world should be on the Ponte alla Carraia or along the Arno on May Day. And on the Arno, on boats and barges, they constructed stages and a set representing hell with fire and other pains and torments, and men disguised as demons, terrible to behold, and others who looked like naked souls and looked like people, and they set them in those different torments with much wailing and lamentation and raging, which was dreadful and terrifying to hear and behold; and many people were drawn to watch by this novel entertainment; and the Ponte alla Carraia, which at that time was built of wood between the pylons, was so crowded with people that it gave way in several places, and collapsed with the people who

---

"by some Florentines" (per alchuni Fiorentini) before more than eighty thousand people in the enclosed forecourt in front of San Francesco Grande in Milan (now demolished) at Easter 1475; Corio, *Storia di Milano*, 2:1396.

[77] BNCR, VE 483, fols. 141ʳ–157ʳ: *Qui comincia la rexurectione de Yhesu Xpisto.* The Bolognese text contains the Resurrection, the Harrowing of Hell, and the Maries at the tomb. See chapter 8 below for discussion of this text, and Castellano Castellani's *Resurrezione*.

[78] On Mayday festivities see Ciappelli, *Carnevale e Quaresima*, 148–149.

were on it; and many people were killed and drowned, and many were injured, so that the joke became reality, and just as the crier had announced, many died to have news of the other world, to the great weeping and sorrow of all the city.[79]

Villani's source for this narrative is a probable eyewitness, Paolino Pieri, who furnishes a range of additional details: the masquerade on the Arno was one of many, and organized by the Lord of the Kingdom of San Frediano, one of the plebeian festive kingdoms whose shadowy and largely undocumented history runs through into the sixteenth century when they are conscripted into the ducal propaganda machine.[80] The invitation was to anyone "who was desirous of news of the other world, or of being young again," and the occasion was already special even before the bridge collapsed, because the Kingdom had the services of "a true and most authentic skilled craftsman" whose name is not given.[81] Pieri alone gives statistics: 2000 people were on the bridge when it collapsed, 100 were killed in the accident, and many saved by the boats that were staging the pageant below.

Details of the event were repeated over and over again in copies of the *Priorista* that would be made in the centuries that followed, as well as in the

---

[79] Villani, *Nuova cronica*, 2:131–132, ix.70: "chiunque volesse sapere novelle dell'altro mondo dovesse essere il dì di calen di maggio in su 'l ponte alla Carraia, e d'intorno a l'Arno; e ordinarono in Arno sopra barche e navicelle palchi, e fecionvi la somiglianza e figura dello 'nferno con fuochi e altre pene e martori, e uomini contrafatti a demonia, orriboli a vedere, e altri i quali aveano figure d'anime ignude, che pareano persone, e mettevangli in quegli diversi tormenti con grandissime grida, e strida, e tempesta, la quale parea idiosa e spaventevole a udire e a vedere; e per lo nuovo giuoco vi trassono a vedere molti cittadini; e 'l ponte alla Carraia, il quale era allora di legname da pila a pila, si caricò sì di gente che rovinò in più parti, e cadde colla gente che v'era suso; onde molte genti vi morirono e annegarono, e molti se ne guastarono le persone, sì che il giuoco da beffe avenne col vero, e com'era ito il bando, molti n'andarono per morte a sapere novelle dell'altro mondo con grande pianto e dolore a tutta la cittade." See also D'Ancona, *Origini*, 1:95. Vasari repeats the story that Buffalmacco, painter of the scenes of Death in the Camposanto of Pisa, friend of Boccaccio, and prankster, was responsible for the spectacle, with his companions from the workshop of Maso del Saggio; Vasari, *Le vite* (1568), 1:159, *Vita di Buonamico Buffalmacco pittore fiorentino*. See also Meier, "The Afterlives."

[80] See Rosenthal, *Kings of the Street*.

[81] P. Pieri, *Cronica*, 78: "che volesse sapere le novelle dell'altro mondo, o volesse ringiovanire […] un buono e molto verace Maestro." The *Priorista* in ASF, Manoscritti 224, fol. 14v, provides one further element: that the name of the *maestro* was Gello, whence the expression, not otherwise recorded: "you're behaving like Gello" (tu fai gli atti di Gello).

numerous histories of Florence. There are slight variations. The invitation of the town crier was more or less fixed by Villani's time; the punchline, to the effect that people saw more of the other world than they expected, is delivered with varying degrees of wit. But the accounts are consistent in reporting that the event on the river was still a novelty in 1304, which makes it probable that the 'devil pageant' described by Dante in *Inferno* 21–23 was based on some kind of pageant that he had witnessed in person before his exile in 1301/2.[82] Villani's chapter concludes with a 'moral' that is a lingering topos in the chronicles of Florence (and elsewhere), that the *festa* was a portent of bad times that followed: "this was a sign of the future disaster that would soon befall our city on account of the surfeit of sins of its citizens."[83] We find it in Giovanni di Carlo's description of the *festa de' Magi* discussed in chapter 5, and in Machiavelli's account in his *Istorie fiorentine* of the fire in Santo Spirito in 1471, discussed in chapter 2.[84]

Agostino does not identify the group performing the Judgment Day play, but he does direct us toward a text:

> And then came another *edificio* of Judgment Day, and Christ was in the air and below there were lots of tombs. As soon as the trumpet sounded, lots of people emerged from them all, and did all the words and gestures as they are written, and it was a piteous thing, even though it made people laugh, because there were some who did not want to enter into hell, and there was a big battle.[85]

A text — "the words and gestures as they are written" — of the *Rappresentazione del Dì del Giudizio* was certainly in existence by the time Agostino saw the play, and the iconography of the scene was well established in the

---

[82] On the longevity of Dante's devils, and their comic value, see also chapter 5 below.

[83] Villani, *Nuova cronica*, 2:132, ix.70: "fu questo segno del futuro danno che in corto tempo dovea venire a la nostra cittade per lo soperchio delle peccata de' cittadini." On the topos see Green, *Chronicle*, esp. 24–25.

[84] Giovanni di Carlo, in Schena, "Frate Giovanni," 2:44–54; Machiavelli, *Istorie fiorentine,* 681–682, vii.28.5–6.

[85] Delcorno Branca, "Un camaldolese," 10: "Dipoi venne un altro *edificio* del Giudicio e stava Cristo in aria e di sotto erano molti sepolcri. Di subbito che sonò la tromba di ttutti uscirono fuore molta gente e così facea tutte quelle parole e atti che si scrivano, e fu cosa da piangiere, ben che facesse rìdare la brigata perché v'erano alcuni che non volevano intrare in Inferno e quivi fu grande battaglia."

visual arts. "Messer Antonio araldo," that is, Antonio di Matteo di Meglio (1384–1448), "cantor de cantionibus moralibus" (singer of moral songs) of the Signoria from 1417 until his death,[86] is named by Feo Belcari as the author of sixty-seven stanzas of the *Dì del Giudizio*, to which Feo himself subsequently added a *capitolo*, "Dei segni innanzi al Finale Giudicio" (Signs before the Last Judgment), and a further thirty-seven stanzas of the separation of the saved and the damned, where saints and sinners are no longer the Herald's lifeless allegories but recognizable contemporary Florentines.[87]

Agostino di Portico does not identify the performers, but Benedetto Dei tells us that in 1472 both the Last Judgment and the Quick and the Dead were the responsibility of Santa Maria dei Servi (better known as Santissima Annunziata). I surmise that they may have been the responsibility of the associated flagellant company that met in the crypt of the adjacent Spedale degli Innocenti.[88] The images of flagellants, bearing the banner *Agite peni-*

---

[86] BNCF, Magl. vii.690, fol. 136[r]. The herald is called both Antonio di Meglio and Antonio di Matteo di (or del) Meglio; Di (or Del) Meglio is almost certainly a family name rather than a patronymic. The official title of Herald did not exist before the mid-1450s, when it was granted to Francesco Filarete; see Trexler, ed., *The Libro Cerimoniale*, 39–40. On Antonio *araldo*, see also Flamini, *La lirica*, 204–206, 223–226; Bessi, "Politica," and "Eugenio IV"; Branciforte, "Antonio di Meglio"; Pallini, "Dieci canzoni"; Ventrone, "La sacra rappresentazione" (1993), 75–80, and *Lo spettacolo*, 150–154. Filippo Scarlatti called him "Antonio di Meglio buffone"; Emilio Pasquini, "Il codice," 434. Trexler traces Antonio's career and shows that from 1442 he was too ill to carry out his duties, some of which were ceded to Anselmo Calderoni. Calderoni, however, predeceased him in May 1446, and his duties passed to Antonio's son, Messer Gregorio d'Antonio. Antonio nevertheless kept his title until his death at some time before 24 July 1448. On the importance of heralds in the development of theatre in Florence, see Ventrone, *Gli araldi della commedia*, 137–162, and "'Civic Performance.'"

[87] For discussion of Belcari's text, see chapter 7.

[88] Dei, *La cronica*, 93; Henderson, *Piety*, 445; Sebregondi, "La 'Compagnia della Nunziata,'" 43–48. Dei, p. 68, gives a list of those involved in the procession of *edifici* and *rappresentazioni* mounted in April 1459, on the occasion of the visit of the fifteen-year-old Galeazzo Maria Sforza and Pope Pius II: "And then another *festa* was organized for the Pope, and this was a solemn and worthy procession of *edifici* and *rappresentazioni*, with great devotion. There were 46 processions of flagellants, making 2518 citizens in all. There was the Crocetta [the *laudese* company of Sant'Egidio]; the Zampillo [the company of San Giovanni Gualberto, in Santa Trinita]; San Bartolomeo [in Santa Croce]; lo Spirito Santo [the *laudese* company in Santo Spirito, responsible for the Pentecost play]; the *Nicchio* [San Jacopo]; San Niccolò da Tolentino [the young men of San Niccolò del Ceppo, in the parish of San Jacopo tra' Fossi]; l'Agnolo Raffaello [called *il Raffa*]; la *Capannuccia* [the youth confraternity of the Archangel Raphael, responsible for the Nativity]; San

tentiam, that decorated the supporting pillars of their confraternal space, are well known. The other faces of the pillars, however, are decorated with extraordinary skeletal figures that may link this confraternity to the play of the Living and the Dead.

The Judgment play, too, had a separate performance tradition. A scheduled performance of the *Dì del Giudizio* at San Miniato al Monte on the Octave of Easter 1454, forbidden by the Signoria, was allowed to proceed on the other side of the city, outside the Porta San Gallo, two days later, but no additional information allows us to contextualize that performance in two locations remote from each other and both outside the city walls.[89]

Agostino di Portico: Three Living Kings and Three Dead Kings

The final *edificio* of the "three living kings and three dead kings" is a strange dampener on the celebrations:

Rossore [in the Humiliati church of Ognissanti, who carried the relic of the saint's head]; the *Trinità*; the Gesù; the Magi [the adult company of the Magi in San Marco]; the *Crocifisso*; San Lorenzo; the Magpie [Sant'Antonio da Padova in Costa San Giorgio, also called the *Cornacchioni* or jackdaws, offspring of the company of San Girolamo]; San Sebastiano [the youth confraternity of San Jacopo sopr'Arno]; the Armenians [the company of the Resurrection in San Basilio, responsible for the Entombment, Descent into Limbo, and Resurrection]; the Camaldolese monks [who oversaw the Annunciation]; the *Freccia*; the Living and the Dead; and St. George, and a great many more that I cannot count, but all in all in Florence there was never a *festa* like it, nor similar processions, nor similar plays, nothing as great as this one that was done for Pope Pius and Galeazzo Maria Sforza, son of the duke of Milan, and afterwards there was a joust [...]" (E ordinossi dappoi un'altra festa pel Papa, e questa fu una solenne e degnia prociessione, edifici e rapresentazioni e divozioni assai, chon quaranzei prociessioni di battuti, che ffurono cittadini 2518, cioè la Chrocietta, el Zanpilli, San Bartolomeo, lo Spirito Santo, el Nichio, Sa· Nicholò da tTolentino, l'Agniolo Raffaello, la Chapanuccia, Sa· Rossoro, la *Trinità*, el Gesù, i Magi, el Chrocifisso e Sa· lLorenzo e lla Ghaza e San Bastiano e gli Ermini e Chamaldoli e la *Freccia* e· Vivo e 'l Mortto e San Giorgio e altri assa' ch'io non chonto. Ma tanto in Firenze non si fe' mai simile festa, né simile prociessioni, né simile rapresentazioni quanto fu questa, la qual si fe' al papa Pio e Ghaliazo Maria figlio del duca di Milano. E dappoi si fe' una giostra [...]). Another list, in BMoF, Moreniano 103, fol. 66[r-v] (also in BRF, Ricc. 1853, fols. 48[r]–49[r]), names thirty-three flagellant companies in 1466. The anonymous poems describing the visit do not mention a procession of *edifici* being assembled in honour of Pius II; see *Ricordi di Firenze*; *Le onoranze fiorentine*.

[89] ASF, Signori e Collegi, Deliberazioni in forza di ordinaria autorità 76, fols. 28[v] and 33[r]; see also Newbigin, "Quattro postille." The documents provide no reasons for the short-lived suppression or the location of both performances outside the walls.

Then the Righteous went to Paradise and St. Peter opened up. Behind them came three kings on horseback, richly adorned with great retinues, and the queens, all adorned in the latest fashions, and behind them came an *edificio*, on which there were three dead kings and a hermit in his cell; and those dead kings talked to the living ones and they were converted, and it was a beautiful thing. And I derived much pleasure from all these things and if I had not seen it I would not have imagined it for they seem quite incredible. It was a great multitude, I tell you, so many and so beautifully arrayed! A great crowd and finely decked out.[90]

Lists of the *edifici* are rare, but the procession regularly concluded with the *edificio* of the Living and the Dead. Matteo Palmieri describes it in 1454 as a "Cavalcade with the three kings and queens, damsels and maidens, with dogs and other appurtenances of the Living and the Dead."[91] In 1983, I proposed that Jacopone da Todi's "Quando t'alegri omo d'altura" (before 1306) might have formed the basis of this *edificio*, but Daniela Delcorno Branca correctly links the *edificio* to the Legend of the Three Kings.[92]

No freestanding play of the Three Living and Three Dead Kings survives, but we find it instead as the second, somewhat disarticulated part of the play of *San Piero Teodinario* found only in the Bolognese anthology of 1482, where it is part of a cogent discourse around almsgiving and the duties and frailties of kingship.[93] After Piero's conversion, three friends leave him to go riding in the forest. A hermit guided by an Angel brings them to the graves of three kings, who rise up to remind them of their duty to God. Where Piero had failed the dead kings succeed and the three men return home to a godly life.

---

[90] Delcorno Branca, "Un camaldolese," 10–11: "Di poi andavano gli giusti in Paradiso e San Piero apriva. Drieto venne tre re a cavallo molto ornati con gran gente, e con le reine molto ornate e avevano nuove forgie, e drieto loro venne uno edifitio che v'erano su tre re morti e uno romito che stava in una cella; e que' morti parlarono ad vivi e convertironsi e fu cosa bella. Di tutte queste cose io n'ebbi molta consolazione e se non l'avesse veduto non l'arei immaginato che paiano cose incredibili. Grande moltitudine diroti quante e belle, e paramenti. Grande popolo e molto ornato."

[91] Palmieri, *Historia Florentina*, 173: "Cavalleria di ‹t›re re e reine, damigelle e ninfe con cani e altre apartenenze al Vivo e Morto."

[92] Delcorno Branca, "Un camaldolese," 18–20.

[93] See above, chapter 3.

The legend had appeared in France toward the end of the thirteenth century,[94] but by the middle of the fourteenth century the figure of the Hermit had entered the narrative as a *meneur de jeu*, drawing the two sides into discussion and reflection. The scene was well-known through images and through pious readings. In Buffalmacco's fresco in the Camposanto of Pisa (before 1340), as in the illustration to Castellano Castellani's *Meditatione della Morte* (fig. 4.3),[95] the three skeletal figures are a *memento mori* to the living, an embodiment of the Roman epitaph, "As you are, so once was I; as I am, so you will be."[96]

The Dead returned as a performance group in Carnival 1506/7, this time in a wagon rather than on an *edificio*. Castellano Castellani composed *La canzona de' morti*, beginning "Dolor, pianto e penitentia" (Pain and tears and penitence), to accompany the *Carro dei morti*, shown in a woodcut on the title page (fig. 4.4). Eleven men on horseback accompanied the wagon, on which the Dead rose from their tombs, singing the *Canzona de' morti*. Three hundred people dressed as the Dead walked behind the wagon chanting the "*Miserere* psalmo di Davit."[97] The procession of the Living and the Dead that had been a fixture of the San Giovanni procession, in emblematic contrast to the magnificence of the Magi, now became one of the most memorable *carri* of the post-Savonarolan Florentine Carnival, in a grotesque parody of the illustrations to Petrarch's *Trionfo della Morte*.

---

[94] See also Settis Frugoni, "Il tema"; Bolzoni, *La rete*; Belcari, *Lettere*; Piccat, "Mixed Encounters." For Palmieri, see below in this chapter.

[95] Castellano Castellani, *Meditatione della morte* ([Florence: Antonio Tubini and Andrea Ghirlandi, before 8 August 1515]), CNCE 9923. The work, dedicated to Leonardo Buonafede (d. 1545), *spedalingo* of Florence's main hospital, Santa Maria Nuova, does not retell the legend of the Three Living and Three Dead Kings, but rather invites the living to look on the horrors of death. The woodcut probably comes from an earlier work. For a manuscript, see also BRF, Ricc. 1258, fols. 100^r–102^r.

[96] "Fui quod es, eris quod sum." See also the distich on the tomb below Masaccio's *Trinità* in Santa Maria Novella: "Io fu' già quel che voi sete, e quel ch'i' son voi anco sarete."

[97] Castellano Castellani, *La Canzona de Morti* ([Florence: Bartolomeo de' Libri or Giovanni Stefano di Carlo, before 30 October 1518]), CNCE 9918; see Prizer, "The Creation." The *carro* is described in detail in Vasari's life of the painter Piero di Cosimo: Vasari, *Le vite* (1568), 3.1: 22–24. Psalm 50 (51) may have been chanted in Latin, or it may have been "El psalmo *Miserere* in tertia rima" in the vernacular, which was included to fill fol. b8^{r-v} of *Santa Maria Magdalena*, CNCE 61586, and was — like the play — probably the work of Castellano Castellani. See below, chapter 9.

Reform

After the feast of the Baptist in 1452, the second year of Benedetto Dei's tenure,[98] new provisions were passed in an attempt to contain spiralling costs. The size of the organizing committee was reduced and its activities were carefully scrutinized; it was limited to one year's tenure and no budget was guaranteed.[99] Sometime in this period — perhaps after the *festa* of 1453 — the Dominican archbishop of Florence, Antonio Pierozzi, stepped in and reformed the *festa*:

> Inasmuch as to honour the feast day of the glorious Baptist it has long been the practice, and will continue to be, to observe the morning of the vigil of his most holy feast and nativity by holding solemn processions of all the clerics and religious from inside the city and from close outside, with all the trappings of vestments and relics of saints, to lead the people to devotion; and since, for some time, intermingled with that observance, there have been vanities and worldly spectacles that would ill adorn Carnival, let alone a procession, we therefore order, on pain of excommunication, that among the clerics and religious there should be no member of any confraternity, or any other people with any devices or contrivances or *rappresentazioni* or spectacles with people on foot or on horseback, so that the procession can be done more devoutly, and without interruption, and for the salvation of souls, and not their perdition. Otherwise the procession

---

[98] See n. 18 above. Again, Ser Giusto remarks on the magnificence of the celebration: "On Saturday 24 [1452] it was the *festa* of San Giovanni in Florence. They did a beautiful *festa* with lots of *edifici* and beautiful processions" (Sabato a dì 24 [1452] detto fu la festa di San Giovanni in Firenze. Si fece bella festa con molti edifici e belle processioni); Giusti, "I *Giornali*," 107.

[99] ASF, Provvisioni, Registri 143, fol. 221[r-v], 4 September 1452. Each of the Priors and the Gonfaloniere della Giustizia could nominate two people eligible for office; any member of the colleges could nominate one; all names were to be voted on, and then scrutinized, and one major guild member was to be elected for each quarter, together with a fifth from the minor guilds to represent the whole city. If one had to renounce his office, they were to take the next on the list. If anyone refused, he was to pay a fine of 20 gold florins. Nobody from a *consorteria* was eligible; nor could any office holder or his close relative be a *festaiuolo*.

will not be allowed to take place. And anyone who wishes to do a *rappresentazione* should do it in some other time and place.[100]

In the space of forty years, between Dati and Antoninus, both the *festa* and the rhetoric around it had changed. Spectacle had been supplemented by text and extended impersonation. The *ottava rima*, long the medium of the *canterini* or marketplace poets, was now employed in the youth confraternities to enact rather than recount lives of saints and biblical narratives. Soon the adult confraternities of the *Oltrarno*, the area of Florence south of the river, would add a textual element to the *feste* in their churches, and the narratives would include romance and adventure. There is here a confluence of several factors: the existence of accomplished vernacular poets like Feo Belcari, who were able to work the religious narratives into effortless vernacular octaves; a new taste for linguistic and visual 'realism,' for making scenes come to life; and a level of economic prosperity that permitted the expenditure of time and money on recreational activities. But the result was that what were formerly "bellissime rappresentazioni" were now perceived as possibly leading to sin. In his *Summa*, Antoninus articulates this new mistrust even more clearly: "And since the representations of spiritual things that they do today are intermingled with many jests and pranks and the wearing of masks, it is not appropriate to perform them in church, and even outside the church clergy cannot decorously take part."[101] Watching spectacles of any kind brought with

---

[100] BMLF, Antinori 18, fol. 6[r-v]: "Item con ciò sia cosa che a onorare la festa dil glorioso Baptista, ab anticho sia ordinato, e che ssi observi di continuo la matina della vigilia della sua santissima festa e natività, di fare sollempni processioni di tutti i cherici e religiosi della terra e di fuori vicini, con sollempne apparato di paramenti e reliquie di sancti, a inducere il popolo ad divotione; e da certo tempo in qua vi siano stato mescolato molto cose di vanità e mondani spettacoli che starebono male per carnasciale, non che nella processione; pertanto comandiamo sotto pena di scomunica, che fra i cherici e religiosi non vadino alcuno di compangnia o d'altra gente, con alchuni artificii, o ordingni, o rapresentationi, o altri spettacoli con gente, ad piè o ad cavallo, acciò che la detta processione si possa fare più divotamente, e continuamento, e per la salute dell'anime e non perdictione d'esse. Altrimenti la processione non si permetterà che vada. E chi pur vuole fare rapresentatione, la faccia in altro luogo e tempo." Edited in Trexler, "The Episcopal Constitutions," 265, §32. Trexler points out (p. 246) that this text of Antoninus's *Constitutiones* is an imperfect vernacular translation of what must have been a Latin original.

[101] Antoninus, *Summa*, 3:322C, III.viii.4 §12: "Et quia repræsentationes, quæ fiunt hodie de rebus spiritualibus, miscentur cum multis joculationibus et trufis et larvis; ideo non congruit eas in ecclesiis fieri, nec per clericos, extra."

it the risk of ocular lust, *concupiscentia oculorum*, which could lead to *scandalum* and to perdition. Antoninus concludes, citing the authority of Albertus Magnus, that "among the laity they are to be tolerated, provided it is not in a period when they are forbidden or in a holy place, and all the more they are to be tolerated the fewer there are."[102] Antoninus distinguished between the representation of pious subjects like the Adoration of the Magi, the Slaughter of the Innocents, the Passion of Christ, the Ascension, Pentecost, and the like, which in themselves were permissible, and the risks that accompanied them when they were done at the wrong time and with inappropriate interpolations.

The archbishop's edict was given *legal* effect by the Priors, who took the opportunity to enhance the role of their own procession of civic and guild officials in the celebrations.[103] The procession of *edifici* and their entertainments were now separated from the religious procession and moved to the morning of 22 June. Conscious that in the past the civic offering was made so early on 23 June that too few people turned up, the Priors moved this secular procession to the afternoon of 22 June — prime time, as it were — and required the attendance of all the major offices: Priors and Gonfalonier of Justice as well as forty other groups whose order was specified.[104] The confraternities and regular and secular clergy processed on 23 June, and the offerings and the horse race continued on 24 June in the traditional way.

The archbishop's ban was given *practical* effect by the *festaiuoli* of 1454: Giuliano Ridolfi, a merchant banker and later galley owner; Giovanni Serristori; Giovanni Battista Rustichi; and Matteo Palmieri (1406–1475), the humanist, chronicler, and apothecary. With Francesco del Nero as their secretary and administrator, they reorganized the *festa* and separated the *edifici* from the religious orders and confraternities, requiring them to process a day earlier, on the morning of 22 June.[105] Whether Antoninus intended it or

---

[102] Antoninus, *Summa*, 2:493B–494A, II.iii.7 §5: "in personis sæcularibus sunt toleranda exercitia eorum, dummodo non fiant tempore interdicto, vel loco sacro; ergo multo magis inspectio hujusmodi est toleranda, quum minus sit."

[103] While Trexler, "The Episcopal Constitutions," 253–256, sees this as a mark of Antoninus's extraordinary authority in the city, Casini, *I gesti*, 123–124, sees it as an initiative of the Commune to enhance its prestige. See also Carew-Reid, "Feste e politica," 32.

[104] ASF, Provvisioni, Registri 145, fols. 75ᵛ–76ᵛ, 6 June 1454; Trexler, "The Episcopal Constitutions," 252. Ser Alesso Pelli, Cosimo's secretary, was notary to the Priors for the period; Petriboni, *Priorista*, 405.

[105] For the list of *festaiuoli*, see ASF, Notarile antecosimiano 6246 (=D100, Ser Domenico di Francesco di Paolo), 26 June 1454, fol. 430ʳ: "Julianus Nicoli de Ridolfis,

not, the procession of *edifici* immediately became even more elaborate. Matteo Palmieri describes the new format in a vernacular section of his *Historia Florentina*: it was the history of Man's salvation, from the Creation to the Last Judgment, recounted in twelve *edifici* and their accompanying processions, with actors who clearly delivered extended dialogue. The list itself is already well-known, but bears repeating:

> For the feast of San Giovanni in 1454, they changed the order of events. Instead of having the display of wealth on 22 June, the procession of religious companies, friars, priests, and *edifici* on the morning of 23 June, with the dedication of the *gonfaloni* in the evening, and then on the feast day of San Giovanni itself the offerings in the morning and then the horse race during the day, they changed it as follows. On the 21st they would have the display of wealth, and the morning of the 22nd the procession of all the *edifici*, which in that year were the following, and proceeded as I shall now describe.
> 1.   At the head went the Cross of Santa Maria del Fiore with all the clergy and little boys, and behind them, six singers.
> 2.   The confraternities of Jacopo the cloth-shearer and Nofri the shoemaker, with about thirty little boys dressed in white as angels.[106]
> 3.   The *edificio* of St. Michael the Angel, over which God the Father was suspended in a *nimbus*, and in the square opposite the Palazzo della Signoria they did their *rappresentazione* of the battle of the angels, when Lucifer was chased from heaven with his angels that were damned.
> 4.   The confraternities of Antonio and Piero, sons of Mariano, with about thirty little boys dressed in white as angels.
> 5.   The *edificio* of Adam, that did its *rappresentazione* of when God created Adam and then Eve, and gave them the commandment, and their disobedience until he chased them out of

---

Johannes Antonii Salvestri Serristori, Johannes Baptista Rustichi, Mattheus Antonii Palmieri, Franciscus del Nero *proveditor* [?]."

[106] Their white processional habits, expressing the purity of their intentions, had been prescribed by Eugenius IV's bull of 1442; see Aranci, "La catachesi," 82–83, *scheda* 4.9, and below, n. 109. Here, and in no. 4, the words "e agnoletti" are added by the same hand, at a later time.

paradise, with the temptation beforehand of the serpent, and other appurtenances.

6.   A Moses on horseback, with a great cavalcade of the leaders of the people of Israel and others.

7.   The *edificio* of Moses, that did his *rappresentazione* in the square of when God gave him the Law.

8.   Various prophets and sibyls with Hermes Trismegistus and others who prophesied the Incarnation of Christ.

9.   The *edificio* of the Annunciation of the Virgin, that did her *rappresentazione*.

10.   The Emperor Octavian [Augustus Caesar] with a great cavalcade and with the Sibyl, to do its play, when the Sibyl predicted to him that Christ was to be born and showed him the Virgin in the sky with Christ in her arms.

11.   The *Templum Pacis* with the *edificio* of the Nativity to do its *rappresentazione*.

The Arrival of the Madman

And it happened that, when the *edificio* was in front of the Signoria, and Octavian had dismounted and gone up onto the *edificio*, under, or rather, into the temple, to begin his *rappresentazione*, there arrived a mad German, wearing just a thin shirt, and at the foot of the *edificio* he asked: "Where is the king of Aragon?" Somebody answered him: "There he is," and pointed to Octavian. The German got up onto the *edificio*, and lots of people thought he was one of the people who had a part in the *festa*, so nobody stopped him. First of all he took the idol that was in the temple and hurled it into the square, then he turned to Octavian who was dressed in a very rich robe of purple velvet embroidered with gold, and took hold of him and tossed him head over heels onto the people in the square, then he climbed up a column of the temple to get up to some small boys who were standing on the top of the temple dressed as angels, and when he did so, bystanders reached him with the maces they had in their hands, and by striking him heavily, with great difficulty they brought him to the ground, but he got up again, and tried to climb up again until, struck repeatedly by the maces from above and below, he was finally overcome.

12. A magnificent and triumphal temple for the *edificio* of the Magi, in which was concealed another octagonal temple, adorned with the Seven Virtues, and in the east the Virgin and the Christ Child, and Herod did his *rappresentazione* around this first temple.

13. Three Magi, with a cavalcade of more than two hundred horses, decorated with great magnificence, and they came with presents for the Christ Child.

The Passion and Entombment was left out, because it seemed that it was not suitable for a *festa*, and it continued:

14. A cavalcade of Pilate's cavalry, sent to guard the Sepulchre.

15. The *edificio* of the Sepulchre, from which Christ rose again.

16. The *edificio* of Limbo, from which he led the Old Testament Righteous.

17. The *edificio* of Paradise, where he put the Old Testament Righteous.

18. The Apostles and the Maries who were present at the Assumption [*here read*: Ascension].

19. The *edificio* of the Assumption of Christ, that is, when he ascended into heaven.

20. A cavalcade of Three Kings and Queens, maidens and nymphs, with dogs and other appurtenances of the Living and the Dead.

21. The *edificio* of the Living and the Dead.

22. The *edificio* of the [Last] Judgment, with litters for the Sepulchres, and Heaven, and Hell, with its *rappresentazione*, as we believe in faith it will be at the end of time.

All the above *edifici* did their *rappresentazioni* in the square in front of the Signoria and they lasted until midday.

On the evening of the 22nd all the people who are appointed to city offices in the palace went to make their offering, and there were forty-two offices and a total of 288 citizens. And after them came the Six of the Merchants' Tribunal with their captains.

On the 23rd there was the procession of all the youth and flagellant confraternities, and then the regular friars and priests with their standards and their litters with their relics and with an enormous array of vestments, richer than anyone ever remembered.

In the evening the offering of the Signoria, and then the xvi
standard-bearers with their companies in the usual fashion.

On the 24th in the morning the usual offerings, namely: First,
the Parte [Guelfa], and this year it was much more numerous
with more than 730 citizens. 2. The banners. 3. The great wooden
torches. 4. The great wax tapers, alight. 5. The [wagon of the]
Mint. 6. The Prisoners. 7. The racehorses. And behind them the
palio for San Giovanni and Sant'Eligio. And last, our Signori.

In the evening, they raced for the rich brocade *palio* in the usual
fashion.

And this year, the celebrations for Corpus Domini came in the
middle of this feast, and these were Corpus Domini on the 20th,
and on the 25th, the feast of Sant'Eligio, the *festa* for the miracle
of Sant'Ambrogio, which is celebrated by the Notaries' Guild.[107]

The first *edificio* to come into the piazza[108] was that of St. Michael the
Archangel, which was accompanied by sixty *fanciulli* of the four youth confraternities — the Vangelista, Sant'Antonio da Padua, the Arcangelo Raffaello,
and the Purificazione — dressed as angels.[109] The figure in the *nuvola* on the
edificio was God the Father, and the action below him was the battle of the
angels, when Lucifer and his followers were thrown out of heaven. The Fall
of the Angels was followed by the Creation of the World with Adam and Eve,
along with the Serpent and "other appurtenances." It seems likely that this
first *rappresentazione* was a fully scripted play, *La creazione del mondo*, found
in two early manuscripts.[110] A cavalcade of Old Testament figures — the de-
scendants of Adam — accompanied the third *edificio*, of Moses receiving the

---

[107] BNCF, Magl. xxv.511, fols. 50ᵛ–51ᵛ, mod. num.; see Appendix, doc. 10; edited with
omissions in Palmieri, *Historia Florentina*, 172–175; Newbigin, ed., *Nuovo corpus*, xxviii–
xxx. On Palmieri, see Valeri, "Palmieri."

[108] The unequivocal language of Agostino's description, "This *edificio* was carried
by sixty men or more" (Questo edifitio era portato da sesanta huomini o più; Delcorno
Branca, "Un camaldolese," 10) has given way to less specific language. It would seem however that the *edificio* both moved and stopped to perform.

[109] For identification of the youth confraternities and their leaders, see above, p. 164.
Trexler, "Ritual in Florence," 214–215, n. 4.

[110] See Table 1 for manuscripts and modern edition. No early printed edition survives
of the *Creazione*, but oct. 55–74 and 76, together with seventeen interpolated stanzas,
were printed as *La rappresentatione di Abel & di Caino: Nuouamente uenuta in Luce* (Florence: [Giunti?], February 1554/5), CNCE 52870, and collected into the *Primo Libro* of the

Law. We must imagine again a *nuvola* with God the Father on a mountain, and Moses on the platform of the *edificio* with the Children of Israel gathered around.[111] Next, prophets and sibyls together with Hermes Trismegistus announced the fourth *edificio*, of the Annunciation.

The fifth *edificio* was particularly complex, consisting of the Temple of Peace (which will fall when a virgin gives birth) and the Nativity. In the slightly later "Florentine Picture-Chronicle," Baccio Baldini depicts the "Templum in Pacem" as a round open structure with a domed roof supported by eight columns, and this *edificio* must have had the same basic appearance.[112] It arrived in the piazza accompanied by a cavalcade with the Emperor Octavian (Augustus Caesar) and the Sibyl.[113] The Emperor went up onto the *edificio* to make a sacrifice before an idol, only to be attacked by a "mad German" who mistook him for the king of Aragon and threw the idol and Octavian into the square before trying to climb up one of the columns to harass the child angels on the roof. He was eventually overpowered by bystanders who had at first thought he was one of the performers, an incident that provides clear evidence that the *edifici* were now plays and not just *tableaux vivants*.[114] According to the contemporary *Festa di Ottaviano* text, the Sibyl reveals

---

Giunti anthology with the letter O; Cioni, *Bibliografia*, 63, II.1; for modern edition, see Table 2.

[111] Trexler, "Florentine Theatre" (rev. 2002), 237–238, understood this to be "a cavalcade of the Florentine Jewish community," but I believe that it is more simply a procession of citizens dressed as prophets.

[112] Images of the Delphic Sibyl and the Temple of Peace (London, British Museum, Museum nos. 1889,0527.34 and 1889,0527.35) face each other in the "Florentine Picture-Chronicle"; see Colvin, ed., *A Florentine Picture-Chronicle*, plates XXXVI and XXXVII. The drawings are currently dated to 1470–1475 and were previously attributed to Maso Finiguerra. Patrizia Ceccarelli links the representation of Hermes Trismegistus, prophets, sibyls, and the Temple of Peace in the procession to the images of Hermes Trismegistus, Zoroaster, Moses, and other figures in the "Florentine Picture-Chronicle" as well as to Ficino's growing interest in Plato; P. Ceccarelli, "Le feste fiorentine," 96–97.

[113] Here, and in the *Festa di Ottaviano* (see n. 115 below), the Sibyl is not named, but is usually identified as the Tiburtine sibyl; here the artist has called her the Delphic sibyl and drawn her facing the Temple of Peace. The image bears no likeness to the Templum Pacis in Rome but is possibly indebted to the Temple of Hercules Victor in the Forum Boarium (formerly believed to be a Temple of Vesta). The two together may recollect the staging of the first of the two Nativity plays.

[114] I am indebted to the late Thomas Worthen for this insight some forty years ago, which changed the way I understood Palmieri's description. *Tedesco*, in this context, probably means 'from north of the Alps.'

to Octavian a vision of the Virgin and Child, after which the temple disappears — as predicted by the sages — in a splendid *coup de scène* to reveal a representation of Bethlehem and the Holy Family.[115]

The sixth *edificio*, of the Magi, was similarly complex: "a magnificent and triumphal temple": that is, a roof supported by columns that disappeared to reveal a second octangular temple (an echo of the Florentine Baptistery) adorned with the seven Virtues, and within it the Virgin and Child. This *edificio* was accompanied by the Magi and their cavalcade of 200 horsemen. Their business with Herod took place around the outer temple, which represented his palace in Jerusalem; their adoration of the Child took place in the inner, more ornate, temple, which stood for Bethlehem.

Even though the Crucifixion had been part of the 1439 procession, it was already absent from Agostino di Portico's description and was now deliberately omitted as unsuitable for the feast of the Baptist. I do not find this sense of festive decorum articulated elsewhere, but it may be that the criticisms of Greek visitors to the Council of 1439 gained more currency in Florence than they could have known. The appeal to the passions and the emotions along with the incitement to hostility against the Jews, which are intrinsic to Passion plays, have no place in the Baptist's celebrations.[116]

The next three *edifici*, here as in Agostino's earlier description, came as a group with a representation of the Harrowing of Hell, requiring the Sepulchre, Limbo, and the Earthly Paradise. They were followed by a procession of the apostles, Mary Magdalene, and the Virgin, who accompanied Christ to the Mount of Olives, and the tenth *edificio*, of the Ascension, presumably the responsibility of the Sant'Agnese confraternity from Santa Maria del Carmine, whose *festa* was discussed in chapter 2. The eleventh and twelfth *edifici* arrived together: the Living and the Dead, accompanied by the Three Kings and Queens; and the Last Judgment, with litters for the tombs, and heaven and hell, all bringing the procession to a visually impressive end.

The separation of activities between the various parties involved was probably not clear-cut. The youth confraternities were required to participate on both days, for the *edifici* of the Creation on 22 June and for the procession of religious orders and confraternities on 23 June; and presumably the

---

[115] *La rappresentazione della natività del nostro Signore Gesù Cristo* (known in print also as *La festa* or *Le stanze di Ottaviano imperadore*); for manuscripts and printed editions, see Tables 1 and 2; and Newbigin, "Il piede di Ottaviano."

[116] White, *Performing Orthodox Ritual*, 1–2.

religious orders and their *laudesi* confraternities continued to be involved to some extent with their *edifici*.

The *festaiuoli* had difficulty enforcing the new regulations. They came back to the council for increased authority to enforce the participation of the religious orders in doing honour to the patron saint. Immediately after the *festa* they made a notarized denunciation of the recalcitrant groups, and as a result, the Innocenti, the friars of Sant'Antonio, and several other institutions were denied their annual *oblatio*, or offering, from the Commune.[117]

Obligations worked both ways. Just as the faithful were required to honour the saint, so saints were responsible for conferring prestige on their supplicants, directly and indirectly. The official narratives of the *festa* tend to focus on devotion to the city and its patron, but in many of the contexts where money was spent, much of it went to the aggrandizement of the spenders and their hangers-on. In 1455, in addition to voting £2000 to the *festaiuoli*, the Priors spent £700 on themselves "for preparing the banquet for the Priors on the feast day and for gratuities for the pipers, trumpeters, heralds, and others coming to the *festa*, as is customary."[118] For the Priors, the guilds, the friaries, and for private families, the feast of the Baptist was a time of both giving and receiving, all finely calibrated according to social, civic, and religious considerations.[119]

The Prophets and Sibyls

As the only affirmed humanist among the *festaiuoli* of 1454, Matteo Palmieri was in all probability also the 'creative director'; and when it was all over, he

---

[117] See n. 105 above.

[118] ASF, Camera del Comune, Notaio di Camera Uscita Generale 7 (Campione Giallo, 1454–1457), fols. 406ᵛ–407ʳ: "pro dando et expendendo pro prandio faciendo per dominos priores in decto festo e per beveraggiis dandis pifferis tronbettis araldis et alijs venientibus ad dictum festum prout est consuetus."

[119] In a note tucked into the Opera's accounts for June 1454 is a payment of £58 4s. for 29 pairs of chamois gloves at 30s. a pair; 24 pairs of lambskin gloves at 38s. a dozen; and 4 pairs of men's gloves at 54s. a dozen; AOSMF, VIII 1 22, Quaderno di cassa e Riscontro di cassa di Niccolò d'Andrea Giugni (January 1453/4 to June 1454), fol. 79Aʳ. The gloves were given as a gratuity to individuals and groups who had participated in the *festa*. For a confraternity receiving glovesas compensation for participation in a *festa* and reselling them, see below, chapter 8, n. 85. The Statutes of the Arte di Calimala set out in close detail the order of seating at that banquet and the order of processing from the banquet to San Giovanni on the feast day; ASF, Arte di Calimala 5, fol. 212ʳ.

made a record of the new order that had been established for the procession of *edifici* and showed his pride in his innovations by including it — at disproportionate length — in his *Historia Florentina*. In Agostino di Portico's account, the order of the procession was determined by rules of precedence long established and jealously guarded among the religious orders of the city; the confraternities attached to each order processed with their church's relics, and there is no overarching 'narrative' apparent within the procession. Palmieri and his fellow *festaiuoli* changed that. They transformed the procession into a history of Man's salvation from the Creation to the Last Judgment, and the old *edifici*, borne on the shoulders of porters, became, I believe, more substantial acting spaces, on which short plays could be performed. Just as scripted plays had started to appear in the youth confraternities a few years earlier, so they were added to the San Giovanni *edifici*.

Between the *edifici* there were groups of 'extras': *fanciulli* from the youth confraternities, who then had parts in *La creazione del mondo* representing the nine choirs of angels, of whom some would fall with Lucifer; Old Testament figures, who constituted the 'children of Israel' in the play of Moses receiving the law; "various prophets and sibyls with Hermes Trismegistus and others who prophesied the incarnation of Christ," who preceded the play of the Annunciation; the Magi and their cavalcade, before the Nativity plays; a procession of armed soldiers, to guard the Sepulchre; and finally a procession of men, women, children, and hunting dogs, for the Last Judgment and the Three Living and Three Dead Kings.

In the old procession of *edifici*, the piazza had been filled with the colour and movement of the religious orders, confraternities, and the *sottoposti* who acted as porters, the giant and the giantess, *spiritelli* on stilts, the wild man, and a dragon.[120] In the 'new' procession, the 'new' social groups that Cosimo de' Medici had been fostering and supporting financially, as well as the long-established *laudesi* confraternities, stepped up to provide a huge swirling canvas of activity. And into this mix Palmieri and his committee brought humanistic 'high culture': Hermes Trismegistus and the sibyls achieved new prominence among the prophets of Christ.

---

[120] On the dragon, see above; on giants, fauns ('wild men'), and *spiritelli*, see Cennini's description below, and n. 138; Vasari, *Le vite* (1568), 1:444. In 1516 they were made by Nunziatino, and cost £70; Guasti, *Le feste*, 51. I am not aware of studies of the giants and wild men in the Florentine context, but they are found throughout Europe in various guises.

In his Berenson Lectures delivered at Villa I Tatti in the spring of 2008, Charles Dempsey focused on the importance of vernacular culture in spreading the new ideas and themes of the Renaissance.[121] He adduced, as an example, the way in which the *sacre rappresentazioni*, particularly the plays of the Annunciation and the Purification of Mary, incorporated prophets and sibyls in a configuration that must have derived ultimately from the sibyls painted around 1430 by Masolino in the villa of Giordano Orsini in Montegiordano just outside Rome. Dempsey hypothesized that the Latin prophecies of those sibyls had been rendered in vernacular octaves by Feo Belcari, which were then recycled in an ongoing series of *rappresentazioni* until the end of the century. While I do not think that it is possible to tie the octaves to Belcari — in fact, I think his contribution was to limit their tedium in his *Annunciazione* — I am convinced by the proposition that Hermes Trismegistus and the sibyls trace their origins directly back to Orsini's villa. Orsini did not enjoy his creation for long. In 1434 he followed his close friend and ally Eugenius IV into exile from Rome and spent much of the time until his death in 1438 with Eugenius in Florence and Bologna.[122] His villa continued to attract visitors, including Giovanni Rucellai in 1450,[123] but it was destroyed by his enemies, the Colonna, in the 1480s.[124]

Orsini was inordinately proud of his program of decoration, and it would appear that a complete transcription of the figures represented on the walls of both rooms soon circulated in humanist circles; numerous manuscripts have been identified that contain copies of both sets of figures and their identifying captions.[125] In 1454 Poggio Bracciolini, then Florentine chancellor, advised Roberto Valturio of Rimini as he was preparing the decorative program for the Tempio Malatestiano:

---

[121] Dempsey, *The Early Renaissance*, 117–206, with bibliography.

[122] Mode, "The Monte Giordano Famous Men Cycle," 18. Orsini is also remembered as the hapless patron of Nicholas of Cusa, who discovered the manuscript containing twelve lost plays of Plautus but let him wait many years to enjoy the fruits of his patronage.

[123] Rucellai, *Zibaldone*, 126.

[124] Mode, "The Monte Giordano Famous Men Cycle," 34–35.

[125] For a list of manuscripts, see Raybould, *The Sibyl Series*, 93–113. The Orsinian prophecies were circulating in Florence in at least two vernacular translations, as evidenced by BRF, Ricc. 1271, fols. 70ᵛ–71ᵛ, and Rustici, *Codice Rustici: Dimostrazione*, 2:209–210, cap. 57.

Cardinal Orsini, of dear memory, who died in the time of Eugenius, in a room of his palace called the Robing Chamber had all
the sibyls painted, with great care, with the inscriptions of what
each in her time prophesied Christ. So you should write to Rome,
and ask some learned gentleman to make a note of the form of
the paintings and the names of the sibyls and their epigrams, and
send it to you. For nowhere will you find what you are looking
for done more exquisitely, and you will spare yourself tedious
effort.[126]

The advice may have been taken: around 1454 the iconography and
the texts would seem to have found their way into Italian vernacular culture.
Dempsey argues that the Latin prophecies of the Orsini villa were translated
into vernacular octaves by Feo Belcari for the 1454 procession, and that those
octaves were incorporated into the drawings and engravings of prophets and
sibyls, once attributed to Maso Finiguerra and now securely ascribed to Baccio Baldini, that were printed in the 1470s.[127] As noted earlier, however, I do
not believe that Dempsey's initial attribution to Belcari can be sustained, but
there is no doubt that 1454 is the point at which the sibyls became important
in the context of Florentine vernacular culture.[128]

---

[126] Poggio Bracciolini, *Epistolae*, 3 (1840): 118–119, Lib. xi, Epist. 41: "Bonae memo-
riae cardinalis de Ursinis, qui tempore Eugenii defunctus est, in aula palatii sui, quae *paramenti camera* appellatur, sybillas omnes summa cum diligentia pingi fecit cum inscrip-
tione eorum quae suis temporibus, quaeque de Christo praedixit. Quare scribas Romam
licet, ut et formam picturae, et nomina Sybillarum, et epigrammata notentur ab homine
erudito, tibique mittantur. Nam nullo in loco reperies quod quaeris exquisitius, et simul
effugies molestium laborum." Hélin, "Un texte," 353, citing Pastor, *The History*; Simpson,
"Cardinal Giordano Orsini," 138, n. 13, citing Poggio; Mode, "The Monte Giordano Famous Men Cycle," 31.

[127] Colvin, ed., *A Florentine Picture-Chronicle*; Zucker, "Early Italian Masters."

[128] See Newbigin, "Feo Belcari, Baccio Baldini." I summarize my conclusions as follows. Feo Belcari had access to the version copied by Rustici (see n. 125 above), and echoed
it in his versified prophecies for eight sibyls that he used, with the Dispute of the Virtues, as
a prologue to his Annunciation play, beginning "Nel nome dell'immenso eterno Dio," dedicated to Piero di Cosimo de' Medici and thus dating to before his death on 2 December
1469. The anonymous author of the *Purificazione* (before 1464) began with a procession of
prophets but without any sibyls. When three sibyls were added in a later version (1470s),
they were taken from Belcari's *Annunciazione*. Later in the 1470s, when Baccio Baldini was
gathering texts for his series of twenty-four prophets and twelve sibyls, he drew from the
prophecies in Belcari's *Annunciazione* and from a source as yet unidentified, which had

After Palmieri

Between 1454 and 1478, the procession of *edifici* grew and thrived. It was staged out of season for the visit of Pope Pius II and Galeazzo Maria Sforza in April 1459,[129] and in 1461, when considerable supplementary funding was suddenly available,[130] some new *edifici* were constructed in the Sapienza by Giuliano da Maiano, working with Neri di Bicci and his assistant. Neri makes a careful record of his work on "shaping three dolphins on one *edificio*" and on "four large symbols of the Evangelists made of *papier mâché*, all painted."[131] In 1465, just after the death of Cosimo, the procession of *edifici* was staged for the visit of Ippolita Sforza, who was travelling from Milan with a vast retinue of nobles to marry Alfonso d'Aragona, duke of Calabria. Her arrival was delayed, and Marco Parenti subsequently looked forward to "the beautiful *festa* with the *edifici*" on 25 June.[132] In 1470, Giusto d'Anghiari records that

already been used by the authors of the *Purificazione* and would subsequently be used by the compilers of the printed *Annunciazione*. Many prophecies were reassigned, and a small number of new octaves were composed. By repurposing old octaves, and transforming prophets into sibyls, the compilers avoided the necessity of creating any new ones, except for the Sibilla Pontica. Belcari cannot be regarded as the author of this printed *Annunciazione*: it is unthinkable that the aspiring humanist who prefaced his *Abramo* with a list of references ("I've read Josephus, the historian, | and Nicholas of Lyra, learned doctor, | and Origen where he's not being sophistic") could ever have mistaken Zephaniah, Hosea and Michea for sibyls. But he certainly did start the process of versifying the Orsinian prophecies, on the basis of a prose translation very close to the one transmitted by Rustici.

[129] Dei, *La cronica*, 68. In 1434, Eugenius IV arrived in Florence on 23 June, and the procession was postponed until 25 June; Boninsegni, *Storie*, 50.

[130] See above, n. 17.

[131] Neri di Bicci, *Le ricordanze*, 163–164: "profilare 3 dolfini grandi ch'erano in sun uno 'dificio"; "quatro segni de' Vangelisti grandi che erano di charta inpastata, choloriti a punto." Neri was paid by Giuliano da Maiano, but for Giovanni's labour he accepted a pair of red stockings, the value of which was then deducted from Giovanni's salary. Giovanni d'Antonio di Jacopo ("Giovanni-istà-mecho") also assisted with the new *nugola* for the Ascension play in the Carmine in 1467; Newbigin, *Feste*, 1:127. On the use of the Sapienza, located between San Marco and Santissima Annunziata, for the preparation of *feste*, see Ferretti, "La Sapienza," 111–112, online; and also *Le onoranze fiorentine*, 107 and 109, lines 4291–4293 and 4369–4372.

[132] Strozzi, *Lettere*, 425: "la festa bella degli edifici." Ippolita's itinerary had been negotiated to allow five days in Florence; Magnani, *Relazioni private*, XXVIII–XXX. Marco Parenti reported that the visitors enjoyed the Ascension *festa* in the Carmine far more: "The lion hunt shamed us, because a bull chased them all back into their pens like sheep. Then they went to see the *festa* in the Carmine, which they found marvellously satisfying,

there were "many representations of saints done with beautiful and laudable decorum, and they were called *edifici* and there were nine of them. It was a long affair and lasted until midday. They did it in Piazza de' Signori. Lots of people came to watch."[133]

Early in May 1472 Luigi Pulci wrote playfully to Lorenzo de' Medici from Rome that he was anxious to be back in Florence:

> You need some of us there for the feast of San Giovanni, in which we are a major part of an *edificio*; because I know that it will be ill-done without us. And let it suffice that I hope, when I return, if the *festaiuoli* have been appointed in the usual way, to have a word in the ear of one of them that will make him weak with joy; and I'm a bit surprised at you, that you have backed away from this *festa* as much as you have, when you are a citizen and fond of the city of which the Baptist is protector, and we must do him honour. And if by mischance we were not to arrive in time, you would see what could be done without us. Now be wise and listen and believe somebody who has a good eye and is accustomed to telling the truth and no more.[134]

---

far more than the *festa di San Giovanni*" (La caccia de' lioni ci vituperò; ché un toro li rincacciò tutti dentro alle stalle come pecore. Andorono poi a vedere la festa del Carmino: e questa sodisfè loro maravigliosamente, più assai che la festa di Sam Giovanni), letter to his brother Filippo, 22–27 June 1465, in Strozzi, *Lettere*, 432–433.

[133] Giusti, "I *Giornali*," 160: "molte rappresentazioni di santi col bello e laudabile ordine; e chiamaronsi 'edifici,' che furono nove. Fu lunga faccenda: durò sino a ore 16. Feciarsi in su la piazza de' Signori. Fucci molta gente a vedere."

[134] Luigi Pulci, *Morgante e Lettere*, 979, letter xxviii: "Havete costì bisogno d'alcuno di noi per la festa di San Giovanni, della quale noi siamo gran parte a uno dificio; ché io so che male si può fare sanza noi. Et basti che ho speranza, al tornare, se saranno all'usato creati festaiuoli, dire a uno di loro nell'orecchio cosa che io lo farò tutto sollucherare d'allegrezza; et maravigliomi un poco di te che tu la sfornissi tanto quanto hai fatta la detta festa, sendo pure ciptadino et affectionato alla patria, della quale è pure proteptore il Batista, et noi dobbiamo farli honore. E se noi non vi fussimo per disgratia a tempo, vedresti come potessi fare sanza noi. Hor sia savio e 'ntendi, et credi a chi ha buono occhio et suole dire il vero e non più." On this letter, see Trexler, *Public Life*, 409. Ventrone propone quite plausibly that Pulci is referring to his participation in the *edificio* of the Magi; Ventrone, *Gli araldi della commedia*, 39–40. On Lorenzo's celebration of San Giovanni, see also Ventrone, *Teatro civile*, 258–272.

Ser Giusto put his seal of approval on the whole event: Florence had just taken Volterra, and on 23 June "they did various representations with beautiful *edifici* to honour the feast of San Giovanni."[135]

In 1473, Eleonora d'Aragona (now sister-in-law of Ippolita Sforza) timed her visit to Florence to coincide with the patronal feast day as she travelled with her retinue to Ferrara for her marriage with another of Florence's strategic allies, Ercole d'Este. Once again, Ser Giusto noted: "On Wednesday 23 in Florence they did the procession of *edifici* with various representations. Madama, the new bride who is going to her wedding, was there, and lots of lords and courtiers who were accompanying her."[136] Eleonora herself described them to her mentor Diomede Carafa back in Naples:

> On Wednesday morning we went to see the triumphs that these Florentines do on this day, and when I had arrived at the dais prepared for us in the piazza, first of all there came four giants, two male and two female. Next came seven *rappresentazioni*. The first, when our Lord God gave the Law to Moses. The second of the Annunciation of our Lady. The third of the Nativity of our Lord. The fourth of the Baptism. The fifth of the Resurrection and Descent into Limbo and the Liberation of the Holy Fathers. The sixth of Pentecost. The seventh of the Assumption of our Lady. In truth, beautiful things to see and skilfully done.[137]

---

[135] Giusti, "I *Giornali*," 173: "si feciano più representazioni di belli edifici per onorar la festa di San Giovanni."

[136] Giusti, "I *Giornali*," 176–177: "Mercordì a dì 23 detto in Firenze si fece la processione degli edifici di più rappresentazioni. Eraci a vedere quella madama donna novella che andava a marito, e molti signori e cortigiani che l'accompagnavano."

[137] Corvisieri, "Il trionfo romano," 655, letter of 25 June, 1473: "Mercurdì matino andammo ad vedere li triumphi faceano questi fiorentini in tal dì, et arrivata al talamo preparato per nuy in piacza vennero prima quactro giganti duy mascoli et duy femmene. Adpresso vennero sette rappresentationi. La prima quanno lu N. S. Dio donò la legge ad Moysex. La seconda della annunctiatione della nostra donna. La terza della nativitate de N. S. La quarta dello baptismo. La quinta della resurrectione et descensione al limo e liberatione delli sancti patri. La sexta della Penthecosta. La septima della assumptione della nostra dompna. In verità belle cose ad vedere et actamente facte." For further discussion of Eleonora's journey and the plays she saw in Rome, see below, chapter 3 (*Susanna*) and chapter 5 (*Miracolo del Corpo di Cristo* and *San Jacopo*).

This is the first year that we find Pentecost and the Assumption of the Virgin among the *edifici*, reflecting major changes in the *Oltrarno* confraternities of the Spirito Santo and Sant'Agnese. In 1471, as discussed in chapter 2, a fire in the *castello* had destroyed the basilica of Santo Spirito, and the play was no longer being performed, while in Santa Maria del Carmine, the Assumption had taken over from the Ascension as the *festa*. The two plays, as well as the Baptism of Christ, were now given their own *edificio* in the procession.

The Jubilee year of 1475 must have brought a steady stream of pilgrims travelling to and from Rome. I have found no mention of the *festa* for that year, but a global description of it in Latin, written in September 1475 by the Florentine humanist Piero Cennini, tells us more about the procession of *edifici*.

So the next day, 22 June, they perform holy plays from morning to noon: the Annunciation of the Virgin Mary, the Last Judgment, the Resurrection of Christ and the Descent into Hell and many other things of this kind are brought out on portable stages or in fictive trees. And make-believe giants and fauns stroll through the city, and centaurs. And boys that they call *spiritelli* walk around on stilts that are strapped to their thighs: a spectacle that is both marvellous to behold and delightful. [Masks for] giants of both sexes are fashioned out of *papier mâché*, and they look absolutely real. Each one is worn by a young man skilled in stilt-walking and the weight is supported on straps over his shoulders; and when the young men are enclosed inside they can look through an opening in the chest of the figure and see where they are going; and they strike a certain terror into the heart as they go along, for their roars are amplified in the hollow space. And there are also shaggy fauns with caprine feet, and centaurs that appear to be half horse. And whatever is lacking in their animated appearance is supplied by *papier mâché*. The *spiritelli* are not all of one kind. One is dressed as a nymph and carries a bow and arrows or spear. Another dressed as an angel wears a shining halo on his head and spreads the wings that hang from both shoulders. Another in full armour carries a naked sword and a make-believe severed head. Another, almost completely naked has wings on his shoulders and winged sandals attached to his feet. The tallest of all moves around with his feet eight *braccia* from the ground. Such is their daring and such is their skill in these things that they can stand without any assistance, and they can gesture and leap about on their stilts by themselves, and they do not fall.[138]

The vanities and worldly spectacles abhorred by Archbishop Antoninus had clearly returned to the Precursor's feast day and were a major part of its appeal.

In 1476, fear of the plague caused the *edifici* to be cancelled, but the *palio* went ahead, as it always did.[139] In 1477 there is no mention of *edifici* on 22 June; instead, on 29 June, the Feast of St. Peter and St. Paul, "On the Loggia de' Signori they did the *festa* of the *Rappresentazione della morte di san Piero e di san Pagolo*. There was a great crowd of people to see it."[140]

In 1478, not even the calamity of the Pazzi conspiracy was enough to curb enthusiasm for the feast of the Baptist but everything was delayed. The procession was held on 22 June, but it was "not as fine," because they postponed the *festa* until 29 June, to wait for the French Ambassadors who in fact did not come until 2 July, and only on 5 July were the *rappresentazioni* and the *palio* finally held. Giusto Giusti reported:

> And on the same day in Florence they did the *feste* of *rappresentazioni* of some saints that are called *nuvole*, as they were customarily done for the feast of San Giovanni. They had postponed doing them so that the Ambassador of the king of France could see them, and he had arrived and he was there to see these beautiful performances.[141]

Giusti chose his words carefully: these were not the *edifici* of the history of Man's salvation. They were the most ancient *nuvole*, bearing saints and their

---

[138] Edited in G. Mancini, "Il bel S. Giovanni," 224; see Appendix, doc. 11.

[139] Giusti, "I *Giornali*," 189.

[140] Giusti, "I *Giornali*," 194: "fecesi in su la loggia de' Signori la festa della *Rappresentazione della morte di San Piero e di San Pagolo*. Fucci gran moltitudine di popolo a vederla"; see chapter 5 below.

[141] Giusti, "I *Giornali*," 202: "non così bella"; "*Item* detto dì in Firenze si feciono certe feste di rappresentazioni d'alcuni santi che le chiamano 'le nuvole,' come si solevano fare per la festa di San Giovanni, che s'era sopratenuto a farle perché le vedesse l'ambasciadore del re di Francia ch'era venuto; e fu a vedere quelle belle cerimonie."

relics, such as had been described in the earliest accounts. The *edifici* with the plays have gone, and after plague again prevented their appearance in 1479, they disappeared for the next decade; it is possible that the plays never returned.[142]

Revival

The whole *festa* was revived and refurbished in 1488, when Lorenzo began to make a concerted effort to consolidate his family as rulers of Florence. Lorenzo's health was failing, and he was in a hurry to make arrangements for his children. In 1487, his daughter Maddalena was married to Francesco (called Franceschetto) Cibo, son of Pope Innocent VIII, from whom Lorenzo then obtained in 1489, at huge expense, a cardinal's hat for his son Giovanni, still only thirteen years old and thus raised *in pectore* (although the secret was widely known). After much prevarication, Franceschetto arrived in Florence on 21 June 1488. Once again it is the inveterate *festa*-watcher Benedetto Dei who describes the preparations:

> For this feast of San Giovanni, they are preparing a beautiful *festa* of *nugole* and *spiritelli* and wagons and other festive *edifici* and contraptions that are popular for passing the time, and with all the other festive devices that were customary in other times: and it is all being done on account of Messer Franceschetto, and because our people are in good and cheerful spirits.[143]

Five days later, Piero de' Medici's secretary, Ser Piero Bibbiena, wrote to Giovanni Lanfredini, the Florentine ambassador at the papal court, evaluating every aspect of Franceschetto's behaviour and reception.

---

[142] The suspension of the plays in 1479 was probably due as much to crippling taxes as to the plague that raged that summer; see also the *Ricordanze* of the Augustinian friary in Santo Spirito, ASF, CRSGF 122 (Santo Spirito), 67, fol. 126ʳ.

[143] Letter of 21 June 1488, in ASF, CRSGF 78 (Badia di Firenze), 316, without folio number: "In questo Sangiovanni s'apparecchia una bella festa e di nugole e di spiritelli e carri et altri festivi edificii et ingegni populari da passar tempo, e con tutte l'altre cose festive ordinarie altre volte: e tutto si fa per cagione di messer Franceschetto, e perché il popolo nostro si trova in buona disposizione e letizia"; cited in Del Lungo, "Una lettera," 39.

I don't want to forget to say that it's more than ten years that there have been no *edifici* and triumphs and in these days and for love of his Lordship they did six of them, which he found marvellous and divine.[144]

On 24 June 1488, wind and rain intervened to shred the blue *tende* or awnings that covered Piazza San Giovanni for the solemnities of the other days.[145] Ordinary Florentines, with nostalgia for the old *feste*, may even have been losing faith in their ability to do them to the old standard. On 19 June 1489, Francesco Sassetti in Lyon wrote to Benedetto Dei in Florence about the play that he had just seen there: "Here they've done a *festa* of the story of St. Dionysius and St. Paul, that lasted five days, which was very beautiful and well organized; because they act and speak very realistically and appropriately, as in real life, better than we do."[146]

In the years that follow, two reports allow us to glimpse a shift in the preparation of the *edifici*. On the one hand they are being prepared for Franceschetto (a grown man of thirty-eight, despite his diminutive name), on the other they are being done with popular enthusiasm, but this good will was precarious, and lapsed when they were not well done. We have no record of the *festa* in 1489 and 1490, but in 1491, for his last celebration of the Baptist before his death, Lorenzo abandoned all respect for popular traditions and for the devotional groups that had fostered them. Tribaldo de' Rossi described them in his *Ricordanze*:

> For the feast of San Giovanni, when Lorenzo de' Medici ordered those fifteen triumphs of Paulus Æmilius, the finest thing ever. They never did anything like it before nor anything so very beautiful

---

[144] ASF, MAP 59, doc. 179, fol. 189ᵛ, 26 June 1488: "Non voglio dimenticare di dire, che più di dieci anni sono non si feciono edifici et trionfi in questi tali dì et per amore della sua Signoria se ne sono facti da sei, che gli sono paruti maravigliosi e opera divina"; cited in Fabroni, *Laurentii Medicis*, 2:386–388 (388).

[145] Landucci, *Diario*, 55.

[146] Letter of 19 June, 1489, in ASF, CRSGF 78 (Badia di Firenze), 316: "Qui si è fatto una festa della storia di San Dionigi e di San Pagolo, che ha durato cinque giorni, molto bella e bene ordinata; perché costoro fanno gli atti e le parole vive e bene a proposito, tratte al naturale, meglio che non facciamo noi"; cited without folio reference in *Zibaldone* 1 (1888): 133; see also Runnalls, "Un siècle."

I record that on this day the 24th [of June 1491], the feast of San Giovanni, that is to say, on the eve, the *edifici* processed in the morning, and they did it very badly, except for the Nunziata, which they did very well, and they did the Sepulchre well and Limbo no, and three other *edifici* that processed they did badly and it was a great shame, because there were lots of visitors there. And that day, from late afternoon onwards, having ordered the construction of a most realistic fiction, Lorenzo de' Medici arranged for the Company of the Star to do — and it was his invention — fifteen triumphs of when Paulus Æmilius triumphed in Rome, when he returned from a city with so much treasure that Rome went on for forty or fifty years and the people did not have to pay any taxes because he had taken so much treasure as booty. The first triumph was when the stone obelisk came to Rome: nothing more beautiful was ever done in Florence, in everybody's opinion. They all came into the piazza in the early evening. There were fifteen triumphs, all highly decorated, of how Paulus Æmilius came with all his booty in the time of Augustus Caesar. Lorenzo de' Medici arranged for five teams of battle horses to come with the triumphs, all in fine order, he had them brought from their stables. And forty or fifty pairs of oxen pulled the triumphs, and it was reported to be the finest thing that ever processed for San Giovanni.

They didn't run the palio on the feast of San Giovanni
On the feast of San Giovanni, before the Signoria left the steps in front of the Palazzo, when the banners and the *ceri* and the offerings of wax had already moved off, it began to rain. Two young men were performing on the ropes in the piazza. They had only done a few tricks when it began to pour down. The Signoria and dignitaries went into the palace on account of the rain. It rained until late afternoon, with more downpours. Half the *girandola* was ruined, and it was only half finished. They didn't run the San Giovanni *palio* either, they kept it until the next Sunday. San Giovanni was on Friday. And the rain started again mid-evening and it poured down for almost an hour.

When they ran the palio for San Giovanni
They didn't race on Sunday. Fifteen barbary racehorses went to the start and when the Avemaria sounded[147] the people were waiting for it to be run. They could never agree on the start, and it wasn't run. Everybody was outraged. It was run the following day, Monday 27, and it was won by Lorenzo de' Medici. The St. Victor's Day *palio* is held over, to be run on St. Peter [and St. Paul, 29 June]. They had the *girandola* on Sunday evening, the Signoria had it lit with a great torch; it was three hours after sunset.[148]

Tribaldo's account tells us much about Lorenzo's takeover of public *feste* in Florence. The universal themes of the procession of *edifici* were eclipsed by the political themes of the triumphs the next day. As Lorenzo was systematically enriching himself and his family at public expense, he devised a pageant representing a general who seized so much booty that the citizens of Rome did not need to pay taxes for "forty or fifty years." Where his grandfather Cosimo had been scrupulously respectful of republican traditions, lay devotion, and above all collectivity, Lorenzo's support of the public *feste* reveals a willingness to exploit and manipulate public opinion. From the *armeggeria* of the Triumph of Love that he created in 1459, as a ten-year-old and "from his own allowance,"[149] to the Triumph of Paulus Æmilius in 1491, Lorenzo controlled the spectacles that he supported, rather than sustaining the groups that were their lifeblood. And with the expulsion of the Medici in 1494, the *edifici* disappear temporarily from the record.

Writing of the death in 1492 of "the evil tyrant" Lorenzo de' Medici, his hostile contemporary Filippo Rinuccini saw him as destroying the *feste* by a stealthy process of diverting festive expenses to his own self-aggrandizement and suppressing the old-fashioned and collectively based activities. He observed that Lorenzo never denied anyone anything,

as long as he believed he would speak well of him; and anything he granted was not from his own but from the public purse,

---

[147] At sundown; on the sequence of bells for the *Ave Maria*, see Atkinson, *The Noisy Renaissance*, 132–137.

[148] BNCF, II.ii.357 (formerly Magl. xxvi.25), fol. 67ᵛ; see Appendix, doc. 12. The syntax and punctuation are problematic, and the transcription in Tribaldo de' Rossi, *Ricordanze*, 23:270–272, is unsatisfactory.

[149] *Le onoranze fiorentine*, 113, line 4551: "a spese della sua mongioia."

without any rhyme nor reason, because wherever he had to spend his own money, he tended more readily, and not with restraint, to avarice than to liberality, with the exception of some vainglorious gestures, in which many things that were done at the expense of others were topped up by him in some small way and he took all the credit. And besides these, all the things that in olden times brought grace and reputation to the city, like weddings, dances, *feste*, and splendid clothes, all these he damned, and by his example and with his words he did away with them.[150]

Others saw Savonarola as the malign force responsible for the demise of the *feste*. In 1495, he preached against the *palio*, and the fact that San Giovanni had been reduced to "fire wheels, stilt walkers, and a thousand other frivolities." He urged the faithful "that for this feast day there should no longer be fireworks, or horse races, or such things, because otherwise God would turn his anger against you."[151] After the Friar's final sermon on Ascension Day 1497, Francesco Altoviti delivered an impassioned defence of the Republic, its magistrates, and its ancient ceremonies, and an attack on Savonarola as a schismatic cult leader. Among the Friar's crimes was his hostility to the *feste*:

He speaks ill of the ceremonies and festivals of our most flourishing city and of our ancient customs in relation to divine cult and to the salve of honest living, and just as he, with his superstitions, has introduced and spread civil discord, by saying that those who believe him will enter his Ark and the others will not, so he wants to prevent our sacred annual ceremonies and triumphs and festivals and the applause and light that rises right to the feet

---

[150] Rinuccini, *Ricordi*, cxlviii: "purché credesse che dicesse bene di lui; e quello gli concedeva non del suo ma del pubblico, sanza modo o misura alcuna; perché dove avea a spendere di suo, più presto pendeva, e non poco, nella avarizia che nella liberalità, eccetto alcune borie, delle quali molte cose fatte alle spese d'altri, con qualche piccola aggiunta rivolgeva a se tutte. Oltre a queste, tutte le cose che anticamente davano grazia e riputazione ai cittadini, come nozze, balli e feste e ornato di vestiri tutte dannava, e con esemplo e con parole levò via."

[151] Savonarola, *Prediche sopra Amos e Zaccaria*, 2 (1971): 23, *Predica* xviii, 1495/6: "girandole, e spiritelli e mille altre lascivie"; "per quella festa non si faccia più girandole, né correr palii o simili cose, perché altrimenti Dio si adirerebbe con voi." See also chapter 9 below.

and the threshold of our glorious God. And he wants our patron and benefactor St. John the Baptist and the other saints, in the absence of their customary honours, to take righteous offence against us and bring on the ruin and the destruction that Friar Girolamo and his army threaten against this city and all those who do not wish to enter his Ark. God demands and requires from men the customary triumphant ceremonies, in every degree and order of spiritual or temporal life. And with sacrifice, vows, and with the solemn joyfulness and the adornment of his people, our most joyful God becomes our gentle friend and benefactor of great cities. And if the ceremonies of the Florentine people bring no pleasure to Friar Girolamo, they have always pleased God and his saints and all mankind. Because all the other nationalities have come to Tuscany for the divine ceremonies and for the decent way men live. Fra Girolamo sins greatly in impiety when he offends Divine Majesty.[152]

Even allowing for hyperbole, Altoviti is claiming the centrality of the festivities honouring the Baptist to Florentine identity: an attack on the *feste* is an attack on the state and on God. And Savonarola's punishment was to be hanged and burned in the very square where those festivities had been staged. Just one month after the death of Savonarola in May 1498, the *girandola* returned — a reminder that this is a midsummer fire festival — but not the *edifici*.

The Edifici *after Lorenzo*

In the course of rehearsing this history of the *edifici* in the procession for St. John the Baptist, I have wrestled with the problem of just what they were. Were the 'representations' that were 'done' on the *edifici* plays as we understand them, with characters and scripts? Or were they *lebende Bilder*, to use the title of Philine Helas's important study, living pictures, a dumb show of beautifully costumed and kitted people who did largely static representations of mysteries and miracles? The only sure evidence that action and dialogue were part of the representations comes from 1454, with the advent of the unfortunate "mad German," and I am not sure that Palmieri's enthusiasm for this dramatic aspect was maintained for long after that year. Colour and movement remained

---

[152] Altoviti, *In defensione*, fol. A5^{r-v}; see Appendix, doc. 13.

important — giants and giantesses, *spiritelli*, devils, and fireworks — but the coherent narrative of Man's salvation gradually diminished.

Nevertheless, a description of the procession mounted by the Florentine community in Rome in the summer of 1492, just after Lorenzo's death, gives us a final glimpse of the combination of wagons that are 'drawn' by harpies and 'carried' (or perhaps 'brought') by men, and representations that are first static and then performed:

> The Florentines used boards and cloth to construct a beautiful, decorated church near Monte dell'Oro; they covered both sides of the street at Monte with tapestries; they put some beautiful fountains along the streets and they set up a great *girandola* in the middle of the piazza in front of San Celso. In the morning, Franceschetto Cibo, the count of Pitigliano, the Florentine ambassador, and the Florentine merchants went in procession with the *palio* from San Celso to the church; they were preceded by the giantess, all decked out, and she was followed by a giant. Then came two people with two soldiers' lances attached to their feet [*i.e.* on stilts], that they call *spiritelli*, and they came up to the height of the windows of the houses. Then came a wagon drawn by two harpies, and on it was a representation of the Baptist in the desert. Behind it came a second wagon, carried by men, with the Resurrection of Christ; and a third, also carried by men, with hell, and Satan on top of a fortress with four towers, inside them were the Old Testament Righteous. Behind them came lots of trumpeters and pipers from the Castello [Sant'Angelo?], preceding a fourth wagon pulled by two white horses ridden by two young Moors who were guiding them, and in it was the *palio* brocaded in gold. The people mentioned brought up the rear of the cortege. Mass was celebrated in the church and after lunch the representations that had been on the wagons were performed as plays, that is St. John the Baptist, and the Descent of Christ to Limbo. Then the *palio* was run, from Campo de' Fiori to Ponte Sant'Angelo. After supper, when it was quite late, they set fire to the *girandola*, which went for a long time.[153]

---

[153] Paschini, *Roma*, 445; see Appendix, doc. 7. I have not identified Paschini's source, and I have modified part of his first sentence, which Paschini cites as: "presso 'Monte

With the return of the Medici in 1512 came the return of the *festa di San Giovanni*, but the chroniclers' descriptions for 1513 indicate that it was marred by disaster and scandal: as a mock battle raged out of control, one of the stands collapsed, killing four spectators; an animal 'hunt' in the piazza ended with three escaped bulls being chased through the streets and killed.[154] Giovanni Cambi reports that in the evening, they watched:

> the *girandola*, which represented Sodom and Gomorrah and was a brutish *festa*, and they omitted the spiritual *feste* that they used to do for San Giovanni, namely four or six *edifici* well-appointed with representations of saints, with the result that San Giovanni was dishonoured and not honoured. May God help the City and reawaken her observance of her lost laws.[155]

---

dell'Oro'; coprirono con arazzi da ambo le parti le strade del Monte [Giordano]." Piazza dell'Oro was already the heart of the Florentine "nation" in Rome, and their church of San Giovanni de' Fiorentini would be constructed there in 1518.

There had been earlier Florentine celebrations in Rome. In 1473, after the departure of Eleonora d'Aragona for Florence, the Florentine community staged cut-down festivities of John the Baptist on the feast day of the Roman patrons St. Peter and St. Paul. This was all at the expense of Pietro Riario, who was about to be named archbishop of Florence (20 July 1473) and had summoned Florentine *festaiuoli* to perform plays to entertain Eleonora; see Infessura, *Diario*, 78: "Fece un'altra representatione nobilissima, et fo lo tributo, lo quale veniva alli Romani quando signoriavano lo mondo, dove stettero sessanta muli carichi tutti, copertati colla coperta di panno con l'arma soa, et fu corso lo pallio de' Fiorentini da porta dello Popolo fino ad Santo Apostolo; et hebbelo lo cavallo di Francesco Santa Croce; et dinanzi a queste fece certe altre representationi della natività di Iesu Christo con li Mai et della resurrettione di Christo quando spogliò lo inferno; et fece nello suo tempo godere, et trionfare ogno huomo tanto noto, quanto ignoto" (He arranged for another most noble representation to be done, of the Tribute that came to the Romans when they ruled the world, and in it there were sixty fully-laden mules each covered with a cloth bearing his arms, and they ran the palio of the Florentines, from Porta del Popolo to Santi Apostoli; and it was won by Francesco Santa Croce's horse; and before these he arranged for certain other representations, of the Nativity of Jesus Christ with the Magi, and of the resurrection of Christ when he harrowed Hell; and in his time he offered hospitality and rejoicing to all, both notable and unknown). In 1490, the Florentine community in Rome celebrated St. John the Baptist's day with just the three *edifici* of the Resurrection, Limbo, and the Earthly Paradise; see ASF, MAP 60, doc. 42ʳ, Geri Valdambrini to Bernardo Dovizi, secretary to Lorenzo de' Medici, 28 June 1490; published in *Zibaldone* 1 (1888), 134–135; Cruciani, *Teatro*, 209.

[154] Landucci, *Diario*, 340–341.

[155] Cambi, *Istorie* 22 (1786): 24–25: "la girandola, cheffù una finzione di Sodoma, et Ghamurra, cheffù una festa tutta bestiale, et lasciorono stare le feste spirituale, che ssi

Cambi continues, with sorry indignation, that a platform over the door of the Bargello had been constructed to allow two prostitutes to view the mock battle, and its collapse crushed two brothers, a notary and a priest, who were standing below, "which was God's judgment, and the Devil took his share; so the Devil took seven-eighths of the *festa* for himself because San Giovanni didn't want it."[156]

The following year, 1514, Giuliano de' Medici, duke of Nemours and proxy ruler of Florence on behalf of his brother Leo X, received advice on restoring order to the *festa di San Giovanni*, in a document entitled *Ordine e modo da tenersi nella solennità di San Giovanni, piacendo a Vostra Magnificenza* (Order and procedures for the San Giovanni ceremony, as Your Lordship pleases). The tone of this draft program was deprecating of the *edifici* and patronizing toward those who prepared them. It proposed:

> On the 22nd, in the morning, ten *edifici* and no more, so as not to bore the bystanders; and hand them over to *laudese* or flagellant confraternities,[157] to bring greater credit and honour to the Office; because they will be realized with less expense and greater love, and everybody will want the honour.
> 1. the Fall of Lucifer with his followers
> 2. the Creation of Adam with his story
> 3. the Annunciation of Our Lady with her mysteries
> 4. the Nativity of St. John the Baptist
> 5. the Nativity of Christ with his story
> 6. when St. John baptized Christ
> 7. the Sepulchre, that is, the Resurrection of Christ
> 8. the Assumption of Christ
> 9. the Assumption of Our Lady
> 10. the Living and the Dead.[158]

---

solevano fare per S. Gio. cherano 4. o 6. edificj bene a hordine di raprexentatione di Santi, in modo, che S. Gio. era disonorato, et none honorato. Iddio sia quello, che aiuti la Ciptà, e rialumini a hoservare la sua leggie chè persa."

[156] Cambi, *Istorie* 22 (1786): 25: "cheffù giudizio di Dio, el diavol ne portò la parte sua; sicchè di detta festa, il Diavolo la tolse e' 7/8 per se, perchè a San Gio non piaque."

[157] On the meaning of 'di stendardo' in the early sixteenth century, see Varchi, *Storia fiorentina*, 2:108; Henderson, *Piety*, 438–439.

[158] ASF, Carte Strozziane, Ser. i, 361 (d), formerly 1396: "Addì 22, la mattina, dieci edifizii e non più, per non tediare e circunstanti; e quelli dare a governo di Compagnie

In all probability, the writer had not seen a procession of *edifici* for over twenty years, if at all. There is no direct mention of the Magi (the company had been disbanded in 1494) or of the Last Judgment, but the Nativity of the Baptist is a proposed addition. The inclusion of "with her mysteries" and "with his story" suggests that some *edifici* may have had more dialogue and action than others, but the writer certainly has no taste for them and counteracts them with a proposed afternoon entertainment of four triumphs, of Julius Caesar, Pompey, Octavian, and Trajan, with cavalcade.

An eyewitness, perhaps a Venetian ambassador, sent an enthusiastic report of the procession, and the hour-long *moresca* that preceded it, and the seventeen *carri* of the triumphs of Camillo that followed, to Venice where Marin Sanudo copied it into his diary:

> The next morning, which was Friday 23 [June], in accordance with ancient custom, they did the *nuvole* or *edifici*,[159] representing first of all when God banished Lucifer and his followers from heaven; then the Annunciation of Our Lady; next when St. John baptized the Lord; and the *madia* was not left out, or rather the Sepulchre, when Christ rose again and led the Holy Fathers from Limbo. Next came another mystery, of when Our Lady went up to heaven and left her girdle for St. Thomas; and last the Living and the Dead. I would go on too long if I related every detail, for truly everything was done honourably and in good order.[160]

di standardo o disciplina, per utilità et onore dello Ufizio; perché saranno messi in opera con manco spesa e più amore, et ognuno cercherà di avere onore. Li edifizii che altre volte sono soliti andare, e il meglio, sono questi, cioè: p.º la Ruina di Lucifero con sua seguaci. 2.º la Creazione d'Adamo con sua istoria. 3.º la Annunziazione di nostra Donna con sua misterii. 4.º la Natività di San Giovanni Batista. 5.º la Natività di Cristo con sua istoria. 6.º quando San Giovanni battezzò Cristo. 7.º il monumento, cioè la Resurressione di Cristo. 8.º l'Assunzione di Cristo. 9.º l'Assunzione di nostra Donna. 10.º il Vivo e 'l Morto"; another copy in ASF, Manoscritti 739, no. 18, is cited in Guasti, *Le feste*, 25–28. Giuliano is not named in the document. D'Ancona believed it was addressed to Lorenzo de' Medici; *Origini*, 1:255. See Cummings, *The Politicized Muse*, 88.

[159] The two terms may be equivalent in the ambassador's mind, or *hedificii* may be a correction to a more accurate term than nuvole.

[160] Sanuto, *I diarii*, 18 (1887): cols. 313–316 (313): "La matina seguente, che fu Venerdì, a dì 23, secondo l'antico costume furon fate le nuvole overo *hedificii*, rapresentando prima quando Dio cazò Luzifero e soi seguazi dal cielo; di po' l'Anonciatione di Nostra Dona; apresso quando San Giovanni batizò el Signore, e la madia non vi manchò over

A second description, bearing the publication date of the "vii kalen. Iulii" (that is, 24 June) 1514, glorifies the *festa* in seventy pompous octaves.[161] Not only are the *edifici* reduced to six but they are preceded by a "fusta di macti" (ship of fools).[162] The Medici restoration after 1512 shifted the ownership of the *festa* from the communal organizations so lauded by Dati to the Medici rulers themselves.

Vasari's Description

A process of recovery and documentation began. The first to go back in search of things lost was Giorgio Vasari. In the second edition of his *Vite*, he attempted systematically to understand as much about the old *feste* as possible. He had probably been involved in the disposal of the old Ascension machinery in the Carmine, and in the salvaging, storing, and cataloguing of the Annunciation apparatus, subsequently reused in 1565/6. Furthermore, he wrote a description of this equipment into the lives of Brunelleschi and Francesco d'Agnolo (1446–1488), called *il Cecca* — possibly with erroneous attributions in both cases.[163] In his life of *il Cecca* Vasari also discussed at some length the old *edifici* of the John the Baptist procession, recording what was still alive in public memory almost a century after their heyday. He took his readers back to a time when the plays were performed, calling them *nuvole* rather than *edifici*:

---

munimento, sussitando Christo estrasse e Santi Padri del nymbo. Seguì di poi un altro misterio, quando Nostra Donna salì in cielo e lassò la cyntura a San Thomaso; e per l'ultimo el vivo e 'l morto; che troppo mi estenderei a voler narare ogni particulare, che veramente ogni cossa passò honorevolmente e ben ordinata." Sanudo does not mention the Ascension and the Ship of Fools (see n. 161 below).

[161] *Pompe et cerimonie celebrate nella inclita ciptà di Firenze nella festività del Precursore Iohanni Baptista l'anno M. D. XIIII* (Florence: Antonio Tubini, 1514); CNCE 60574. The narrator in the person of "Cynthia" addresses the work to "Carlo mio."

[162] Guasti, *Le feste*, 33. The Fools in the San Giovanni procession of 1493 were already traditional: "the wagon or triumph of the Fools, according to the common design" (carrum sive trionfo de' buffoni, secundum disignum comunis), ASF, Monte Comune o delle Graticole, Parte 2, no. 2088, fol. 5ʳ, cited in Prizer, "The Creation," 101, n. 14. On the Ship of Fools of 1514, see Minio-Paluello, La *"fusta dei matti."* The jousting prowess of "Lauro" (Lorenzo di Piero de' Medici, nephew of Giuliano) is praised at length from oct. 39 to the end.

[163] Vasari, *Le vite* (1568), 1:301–326, 1:440–445; see Newbigin, "Greasing the Wheels." On *il Cecca*, see Quinterio "Francesco d'Angelo."

The *nuvole*, which were made in different ways by the confraternities and with different devices, were generally done in this fashion. They made a square *telaio*[164] of planks, about two *braccia* [1.16 m] high, and at the ends it had four stout supports, constructed like table-trestles and fastened together like the shafts of a cart. On top of this frame two planks, each one *braccio* [0.58 m] wide, were placed in a cross, and in the middle they had a hole half a *braccio* wide, through which was placed a long pole on which was mounted a *mandorla*. Inside the *mandorla*, which was all covered in cotton wool, cherubim, lights, and other ornaments, on a metal crosspiece, a person either sat or stood, according to the requirements, representing the Saint who was the principal devotion, or advocate, or protector, of the confraternity; or a figure of Christ, or the Madonna, or St. John, or such. The costume of the figure covered the frame so that it couldn't be seen. On this same pole, other iron pieces were mounted that rotated below the *mandorla*, making four or so branches, like tree branches, that had other frames at the tips, and each of these held a small boy dressed as an angel. And these, as required, rotated on the frame where their feet rested, which was on an axle. And sometimes two or three orders of angels or saints were suspended from these branches, depending on who was being represented. And all this machine and the pole and the iron frames, which sometimes made a lily, sometimes a tree, and often a *nuvola* or something similar, were covered with cotton wool, and, as I have said, with cherubim and seraphim, gold stars, and other such ornaments. And inside there were porters or country boys who carried it on their shoulders. They placed themselves all around this platform, which we have called the *telaio*. Leather cushions stuffed with feathers or cotton wool, or with something else that would yield and be soft, were nailed to what I have called the *telaio*, beneath all the places where the weight rested on their shoulders. And all the devices and the ladders and other things were covered as we have said with cotton wool, which was a beautiful spectacle, and these machines were called *nuvole*; behind came their cavalcades of men and their foot soldiers of various kinds, according to the

---

[164] Lit. 'weaver's loom'; here, a strong wooden frame.

story that was being performed, just as these days they follow the wagons or the other things they do instead of the *nuvole*; and in my book of drawings, I have some very well-executed drawings by *il Cecca*'s hand, beautifully done and very ingenious, and full of beautiful devices. With *il Cecca*'s inventions they did several Saints that were carried in procession, either dead or tormented in various ways: some seemed to be transfixed by a lance or by a sword; others had a dagger in their throat and other such things about their bodies. I won't go into this kind of thing, which is well known these days, and is done with a broken sword, lance, or dagger, held tightly in place and aligned by means of a metal strap on each side, with the part that is to appear to be plunged into the victim, carefully measured and removed. Let it suffice that it is generally believed that they were the invention of *il Cecca*.[165]

In the decades after Vasari, the pomp returned to San Giovanni. The Parte Guelfa, given a new lease of life as the overseers of the grand duke's public works, directed the celebrations, and the Monarchies or plebeian festive groups that ranged over the city — also called *potenze* — received a grand-ducal subsidy to embellish the patronal *festa* with their *carri*. The histories of Benedetto Varchi (not published until 1721) and Scipione Ammirato (published in 1600, a year before his death), both acknowledge the centrality of the *festa* while exploring the complex detail of its celebration. Antiquaries of the seventeenth and eighteenth century set about recovering that detail and enacting it, until, in the first half of twentieth century, the *festa* of San Giovanni, like so much else, became once again part of the propaganda machine of the state.[166]

---

[165] Vasari, *Le vite* (1568), 1:443–444; see Appendix, doc. 15. The drawings that Vasari owned have not been identified; on his now dispersed books of drawings, see Ragghianti Collobi, *Il Libro.*

[166] Lasansky, *The Renaissance Perfected.*

Figure 4.1. Anonymous, *The Triumphal Entry of Alfonso of Aragon into Naples, 1443*. Third quarter, fifteenth century. *Cassone* panel, tempera and gold on wood, 43.2 × 167.7 cm. Naples, private collection. Photo: Author.

Figure 4.2. Porters carrying the Macchina di Santa Rosa called *La Gloria*.
Viterbo 2015. Photo: Acistampa.

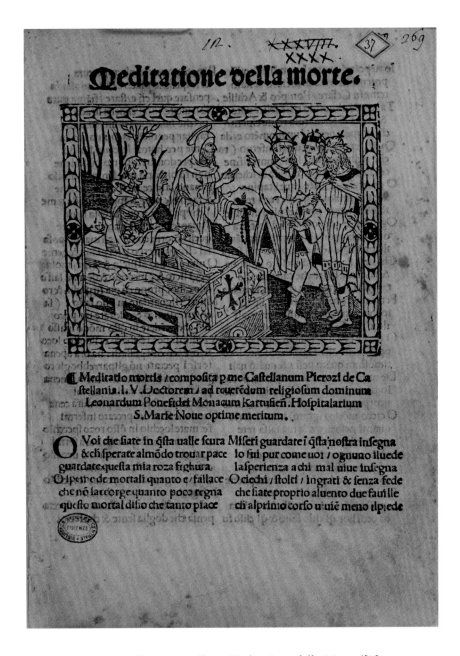

Figure 4.3. Castellano Castellani, *Meditatione della Morte* ([Florence: Antonio Tubini and Andrea Ghirlandi, before 8 August 1515]), fol. a1[r]. BNCF, Banco Rari 182.37; CNCE 9923. © By permission of MiBACT/BNCF. All rights reserved.

ℭ La Canzona de Morti

O Olor / pianto & penitétia
citormenta tucta uia
quefta morta compagnia
ua gridando penitentia
Fumo gia come uoi fete
uoi farete come noi
morti fian come uedete
cofi morti uedren uoi

& dila non gioua poi
doppo elmal far penitentia
Anche noi per Carnouale
noftri amori gimo cantanc
& cofi di male in male
uenauan multiplicando
hor pel modo andia gridac
penitentia / penitentia.

Figure 4.4. Castellano Castellani, *La Canzona de Morti* ([Florence: Bartolomeo de' Libri or Giovanni Stefano di Carlo, before 30 October 1518]), fol. a1ʳ. BNCF, Pal. E.6.6.154[I.15]; CNCE 9918. © By permission of MiBACT/BNCF. All rights reserved.

CHAPTER 5

PLAYING OUTDOORS

To the honour of God and his apostles and for the pleasure of the people who delight in spectacles of this kind.

Funding request, 1489[1]

In addition to the *feste* of the *laudesi* companies of the Oltrarno and the *edifici* for the eve of San Giovanni with their increasingly dramatic element, we find from the middle of the fifteenth century a small group of plays being performed outdoors and — with one notable exception — in the summer months. The evidence is tantalizingly small, and there is no guarantee that the texts that survive relate to the performances that have been documented in passing, but circumstantial evidence for conflating text and performance points to an interesting group of plays that take advantage of the spaces provided by the city.[2] The plays discussed in this chapter are the Magi *festa*, already studied in depth by Rab Hatfield;[3] *San Bartolomeo* (1452, 1471 and 1489); *San Giovanni Battista quando fu decollato* (1451); *San Giorgio*; various plays in honour of St. James the Great; the *Miracolo del Corpo di Cristo* (1473, 1477, 1502); and *San Pietro e Pagolo* (1477). Some are barely differentiated in their dramaturgy from the plays performed within the youth confraternities' cloisters. Others are striking not only for their scale but for the way in which they appear to draw in the old festive kingdoms of the city — India, Arabia, Armenia, Medea, Sheba, Persia, Ethiopia, and Nubia — to provide cavalcades and armies for the plays. The magnificence of the plays is an expression of the magnificence of the city.

---

[1] ASF, Provvisioni, Registri 180, fol. 25ᵛ, 26 May 1489: "In honorem dei et suorum apostolorum et in consolationem populi qui huiusmodi delectatur spectaculis."

[2] On the use of public spaces for spectacle, see, as a starting point, the essays in Hanawalt and Reyerson, eds., *City and Spectacle*; Emerson, Tudor and Longtin, eds., *Performance, Drama and Spectacle*; Milner, "The Florentine Piazza"; and most recently Presciutti, ed., *Space, Place, and Motion*.

[3] Hatfield, "Three Kings," vol. 1, part I, 39–61; Hatfield, "The Compagnia."

The Festa de' Magi

Of all these plays, the earliest and the best known is the *Festa de' Magi*, introduced into Florence, Richard Trexler argued, in the 1390s and co-opted (if usurped is too harsh a term) by Cosimo de' Medici and his family, who forged an association between themselves and the *Re Magi*, the Wise Men of the East.[4]

According to the dominant legend, the Magi relics went to Constantinople with St. Helena and were removed to Milan by Bishop Eustorgio, where they rested in the church bearing his name. In 1164 the relics were lost to Cologne, but the cult of the Magi reappeared spontaneously in 1336, in the hands of the Milanese Dominicans of Sant'Eustorgio. Galvano Fiamma — alone among the chroniclers and in only this one year — describes a Milanese pageant in which the Kings processed across the city to the church of Sant'Eustorgio, which housed for the occasion the stable where the Christ Child was born.[5] From Milan, the cult of the Kings — Balthasar, Melchior, and Gaspar — appears to have been introduced to Florence in the 1340s when Turino Baldesi founded a nunnery dedicated to San Baldassarre, in honour of his father Baldese Baldesi. This may have been a cue for Baldassarre Ubriachi, another prosperous Florentine merchant who had interests throughout Italy, to engage in a similar form of self-commemoration. On his return to Florence in the 1370s, Baldassarre began preparing for death with a series of endowments to Santa Maria Novella, in particular for a chapel in the Chiostro Grande, completed in 1378 and dedicated to the Magi, of whom his namesake, Balthasar, was his personal Magus. Baldassarre's fortunes waned, and he was no longer in Florence when the first documented Magi procession was held there in 1390.[6] It is described in a contemporary anonymous chronicle:

---

[4] Trexler, "The Magi Enter Florence," *Public Life*, "Les mages" online, "Triumph and Mourning," and *The Journey of the Magi*; Trexler and Lewis, "Two Captains and Three Kings." The *Adoration of the Magi* decorated Cosimo's cell in the Dominican friary of San Marco (Fra Angelico, 1441–1442) and the private chapel of the Palazzo Medici (Benozzo Gozzoli, 1459).

[5] Galvano Fiamma's description of the 1336 procession (Fiamma, *De rebus*, 1017–1018) is discussed in Trexler, *The Journey of the Magi*, 88–92, on which I draw here. See also Cardini, *I Re Magi*, 123–126.

[6] Even so, his former house outside Porta San Frediano, where Eugenius IV stayed before he entered Florence in 1434, could still be identified as the house "where the Magi are,

How they did the solemn festa of the Magi [...]
On 6 January [1389/90], they did a great and solemn *festa* in
Florence, at San Marco, the church of the [Sylvestrine] friars, of
the holy Magi and the Star. The Magi rode all around the city,
dressed very honourably, on horseback, and with great retinue
and with many new things. King Herod was at San Giovanni on a
very finely decorated stage with his court. And as they passed [the
Baptistery of] San Giovanni they went up onto the stage where
Herod was and they debated about the child that they were going to worship, promising to come back to Herod. And when the
Magi had made their offering to the child and had not come back
to Herod, Herod pursued them and had lots of children, made
to look like real children, killed in the arms of their mothers and
wet nurses, and with this the *festa* ended in the evening, an hour
before sundown.[7]

The *festa* had both spectacular and dramatic elements. The Magi rode
around on horseback with great retinues, and there was little to distinguish
them from visiting cardinals, emperors, or ambassadors.[8] But there was also
an element of theatre, with impersonation and dialogue. There were sages
who debated with the Magi the identity of the King who was to be born;
there were discussions between the Magi and Herod; and, at least on the
occasion just cited, there was an attempt to make a realistic representation

above the door" (dove sono i magi, sopra la porta); Corazzini, "*Diario*," 285; Trexler, "The
Magi Enter Florence," 193–194. A comparable lintel relief of the Magi is still displayed in
the Ubriachi chapel of Santa Maria Novella.

[7] *Alle bocche della piazza*, 89: "*Chome si fe' solenne festa de' Magi* [...] A dì vi di genaio
si fe' in Firenze una solenne e magnia festa alla chiesa de' frati di Sancto Marcho, de' santi
Magi e della stella. I Magi andorono per tutta la città, molto orevolemente vestiti e chon
chavagli e cho·molta conpagnia e co·molte novità. I·re 'Rode istette a Santo Giovanni i·sun
uno palcho molto bene adornato, chon sua gente. E passando da Sancto Giovanni, sali-
rono i·su·palcho dov'era Erode e quivi disputorono del fanciullo che andavano ad adorare
e promettendo di tornare a Erode. E fatta l'oferta i Magi al banbino e non tornando ad
Erode, Erode gli perseghuitò e fe' ucidere molti fanciulli contrafatti in braccio alle madri
e balie, e chon questo finì la sera la festa alle 23 ore"; see also Hatfield, "The Compagnia,"
144. Despite the cult's earlier association with the Dominican friary of Santa Maria Novella, the friary of San Marco, not yet in the hands of the Dominicans, became the destination of the procession.

[8] For the rituals of receiving visitors, see Trexler, ed., *The Libro cerimoniale*.

of the Slaughter of the Innocents. This performance of the *festa* of the Magi may have been directly inspired by a memory of the Milanese *festa*, but it was roughly contemporary with the Ascension performance in the Carmine, derided by Sacchetti.[9] It belongs to the very earliest attempts in Florence to develop a new kind of public devotional spectacle that involved the citizenry on a magnificent scale.

I will come shortly to the ways in which different members of the Medici family appropriated the *festa dei Magi* to make the *festa* an expression of their aspirations, but first it is necessary to recall the festive geography of Florence. A reading of late medieval chronicles, *Priorista* volumes, and *ricordanze* allows us to glimpse how the *quartieri* (quarters) of Florence and the four *gonfaloni* (districts) within each of those quarters constituted the civic units of the city, as distinct from the spiritual units constituted by parish and confraternity, and other groupings according to guild, commercial activity, and family strongholds.[10] But there were also spontaneous or ephemeral groupings, when young men gathered at the corner of their block, like the Canto alla Macine. The *garzoni* (lads) organized various forms of often agonistic entertainment: battles over territory or bonfires, football games, dances, costumed parades, even spectacles like the Last Judgment of 1304. They elected leaders and gave themselves grandiose names: *Re della Macine* (King of the Millstone) and *Imperatore della Città Rossa* (Emperor of the Red City; see fig. 5.1). They enjoyed the patronage of the magnate families of the district, offering them in return support when they were threatened by insurrection.[11] The surviving evidence of the festive kingdoms is fragmentary and spread over several centuries; even so, it gives the impression that such *brigate* had a very long tradition. It is from these festive 'kingdoms' — of India, Arabia, and Armenia (almost always called Ermenìa) — that our three kings arrive in Bethlehem.[12]

I can find no explanation for San Marco's claim to the Feast of Epiphany, but like Sant'Eustorgio in Milan it became Bethlehem and received offerings from the Magi and the civic authorities on 6 January.[13] In 1416/17, the Magi

---

[9] See above, chapter 2, n. 12.

[10] See broad discussions in Trexler, *Public Life*, and Mantini, *Lo spazio sacro*.

[11] D.V. Kent and F.W. Kent, "Two Vignettes."

[12] Very little evidence of the monarchies survives from the period before the Medici dukes. For the later period, see Rosenthal, *Kings of the Street*.

[13] See Hatfield, "The Compagnia," 109, and 144–145, doc. 2 (1408). By 1460, their only official offering from the Signoria was on the feast day of St. Mark, 25 April; ASF,

company made a submission to the Priors for a subvention for the *festa*, done until that point every three years "to the glory of God and for the reputation of the city at their own expense"[14] and they were now granted a subsidy to be funded out of a fourpence-in-the-pound increase in the turnover tax paid by Jewish moneylenders.[15] The rationale of this levy, which made the Jews themselves responsible for revealing to the gentiles the coming of the Messiah, is acted out in the play text discussed below. When the Magi arrive at the court of Herod, he consults his sages, who leave to consult their scrolls and come back not to debate with the Magi (as we read in the 1390 description) but to confirm the Magi's reading of the star through the words of their own prophets.

The *festa* lapsed again, but on the day after Epiphany, 7 January 1427/8, the company of the Magi applied once more to the Commune for funds. The minute reads:

> Recalling to memory the representation of the ceremonies of the
> Three Kings bringing gifts, which used to be done in the city of

---

Signori e Collegi, Deliberazioni in forza di speciale autorità 32, fols. 40ʳ–43ʳ (Oblationes, 1460). On Sant'Eustorgio in Milan and Pigello Portinari's chapel, see above, chapter 2.

[14] ASF, Provvisioni, Registri 106, fols. 327ᵛ–328ᵛ, 25 February 1416/17: "ad honorem Dei et famam civitatis propriis expensis"; see also Hatfield, "The Compagnia," 145, doc. 3. The submission refers to triennial performances. I have extended Hatfield's list of performances in 1389/90, 1416/7, 1428/9, 1435/6, 1438/9, 1446/7, 1447/8, 1450/1, 1468/9, and 1497/8 by only two: 1419/20 and 1422/3. On 19 December 1419, the Opera del Duomo ordered their carpenters to construct: "a dais for the officials of the Opera in Piazza San Giovanni for the feast of the Epiphany etc" (quod fiat per magistros Operis unus palchettus super platea Sancti Iohannis in festo Epifanie etc..), AOSMF, II 1 76, fol. 36ᵛ. On 30 December 1422, the Opera agreed to lend to the *festaiuoli* of the Magi "certain old timber" (quedam lignamina vetera), AOSMF, II 1 81, fol. 36ᵛ; and on 10 December 1428, they agreed to lend a room in the papal apartments of Santa Maria Novella "as a dressing room for certain men at the time of the *festa* and also [...] the timber that they requested for the *festa*" (pro induendo certos homines tempore festi ac etiam [...] illa lignamina que ipsi peterent pro dicto festo), AOSMF, II 2 1, fol. 97ᵛ — notices indicating that the *festa* was mounted in 1420 and 1423, and providing further confirmation of the *festa* in 1429. Hatfield, "The Compagnia," 113, records that in 1447, the interval is declared to be five years, but I note that from 1448, the intervals are still in multiples of three, and that there may have been un-remarked performances in the intervening years.

[15] For other instance of Jews being obliged to fund public Christian *feste*, see the fine imposed on Vitale da Montalcino, chapter 4, n. 17 above; for the requirements that Roman Jews should participate in honouring the papal *Possesso*, see Linder, "'The Jews too'"; and for Carnival, see Stow, *Taxation, Community.*

Florence on the solemn feast of the Epiphany of Our Lord Jesus
Christ at the church of San Marco in Florence, by a large group of
citizens of the city who are said to belong to a particular confraternity that is accustomed to meet in that church, which bestowed
no small magnificence on the city, and aware that the said *rappresentazione* lapsed some years ago and the feast day has ceased
to be celebrated, because, it is said, these gentlemen citizens and
persons of the said Company no longer meet in the usual way in
or rather at the said church; and desiring that something which
used to be done for the magnificence of the Florentine people
should not cease on account of the negligence of the city, and
wishing to offer some remedy to this situation, they order that
they should have access to the church of San Marco and that they
should do the *rappresentazione* every year.[16]

In June 1428, the chronicler Paolo di Matteo Petriboni recorded in his
Priorista the Magi company's magnificent participation in the procession of
the Eve of St. John the Baptist, discussed in the previous chapter. Six months
later, at Epiphany 1428/9, he described the *festa dei Magi*, the first to be done
since the reopening of confraternities after a period of suppression:

On Thursday 6 January 1428[/9], they did the *festa* of the Magi
and it was an honourable and beautiful *festa*. In Piazza de' Signori they built a platform next to San Romolo, and on it stood the
tableau[17] of King Herod, richly dressed as a king, and with a large
retinue, and with a credenza displaying silver of great value. The
festa began in the morning and lasted until sunset the same day,
not counting the day before. And in the morning twenty men,
in friars' habits, passed through the square with a tableau of Our
Lady and her Son, and it went onto the stage in Piazza San Marco.
And after lunch about seven hundred men in costume rode in on

---

[16] ASF, Carte Strozziane, Ser. ii, 77, p. 100, correcting Fabriczy, "Michelozzo," 93. The
register from which Strozzi copied this information, Signori e Collegi, Deliberazioni in
forza di ordinaria autorità for January–February 1427/8, is now missing. I have updated
the superseded shelfmarks provided by Fabriczy.

[17] Literally 'signification, meaning,' *significato* here seems to mean 'signifier,' possibly
in the form of 'a person dressed as,' an 'image or statue or figure representing,' or simply a
'tableau.' The Christ Child was almost certainly a doll.

horseback, among whom were the three Magi and their companions, honourably dressed. And among the beautiful things they had with them were three giants and a wild man, and on a wagon a tableau of David who slew the giant with a slingshot. And the person who played the part of David stood aloft and very skilfully on the wagon. And along the Via Larga, from the Canto di San Giovanni to Piazza San Marco, on both sides of the street, there were platforms and benches decorated with bench-covers and rugs and *spalliere* (wall-hangings). And it was a beautiful thing to see that decoration along that street.[18]

There is a play text that can plausibly be linked to this description: the Magi play in BRF, Ricc. 2893 — a codex containing some of the earliest *rappresentazioni* — which, like the performance of 1428/9, focuses on Herod's court (thirty of its forty-seven stanzas) and does not include the Slaughter of the Innocents.[19] The text is of non-Florentine origin. Rather than the octaves of the plays discussed to this point, the verse form here is the *ballata maggiore*, found also in the great *laudari* from Perugia and Assisi compiled around 1400, where it is termed the *modo pasquale* or joyful mode, in contrast to the *modo passionale*.[20] Our Magi play, however, contains no linguistic elements to suggest that it arrived in Florence from Umbria; instead its patterns of rhymes indicate that it originated north of the Po, and possibly in Milan, and it may indeed have arrived in Florence with the Magi cult at the end of the fourteenth century.

---

[18] Petriboni, *Priorista*, 216, discussed in Hatfield, "The Compagnia," 112; see Appendix, doc. 17. On David in the John the Baptist procession, see chapter 4 above.

[19] Edition in Newbigin, ed., *Nuovo corpus*, 183–203. On the date of Ricc. 2893, see discussion of *Moisè e Faraone* in chapter 3 above. A different redaction is found in BCIS, I.ii.33; see De Bartholomaeis, "Di un codice senese," 306–308; and edition in De Bartholomaeis, ed., *Laude drammatiche*, 2:203–208. See also Hatfield, "The Compagnia," 112 n. 28, and Trexler, "Les Mages" online and "Triumph and Mourning." Although their feast day is 28 December, the Innocents were often part of the Epiphany play in Latin liturgical drama. Another Magi play of Florentine origin, a fifteen-octave 'tableau' play, is copied along with the *Festa di Ottaviano* at the end of BNCR, VE 483, fols. 228^v–230^r (that is, after the date of 1482 on fol. 222^r, and in a different hand).

[20] The *modo pasquale* consisted of eight alternating seven- and eleven-syllable lines, rhyming aBaBbCcX; the *modo passionale* consisted of six eight-syllable lines, rhyming ababcc. See *Il laudario perugino*, and *Il Laudario assisano 36*.

The identification of the Kings as Balthasar of Arabia, Melchior of Persia, and Gaspar of India comes from the Armenian tradition. The Kings however are fully acclimatized: they come from the Florentine festive kingdoms of Arabia, Ermenìa (Armenia), and India Maggiore, which Trexler identified respectively as the areas around Sant'Ambrogio, where the marker of the Città Rossa is still visible (fig. 5.1); around the Armenian church of San Basilio at Canto alla Macine; and around San Tommaso in the Mercato Vecchio.[21] At some point, the festive kingdoms of the city were co-opted into the celebrations of Epiphany on 6 January and brought under the auspices of the company of the Magi, an adult confraternity based in the Sylvestrine monastery of San Marco. When Cosimo de' Medici returned from exile in 1434, he worked with Pope Eugenius IV to bring Observant Dominicans from Fiesole to replace the Sylvestrines, providing funds for renovation of the complex. He also took responsibility for the confraternities, including the youth confraternity of the Purification and the adult confraternity of the Magi, for which he provided homes in the friary. No confraternal archive of the Magi survives, so it is impossible to reconstruct their devotional activities; it may be that in this early period they were active only when they were preparing a *festa*, and only later did they become a regular devotional confraternity, in which members delivered sermons to each other.[22]

A tailed sonnet by Niccolò Cieco suggests that the *festa* was due to be staged in 1435/6, but that the Captains of the company were dithering. He urges them to stop arguing and let those who know what they are doing get on with the job:

Sonetto del detto maestro Niccolò Cieco da Firenze fatto a' capitani della festa de' Magi a dì 6 di novembre 1435, perché s'aparecchiavano a fare la festa	Sonnet by Maestro Niccolò the Blind of Florence written to the captains of the festa of the Magi on 6 November 1435, as they were getting themselves organized to do the festa

---

[21] Arabia Rossa was one of the three parts of Arabia. Trexler, *Public Life*, 402. On Armenia and the kingdom of the Millstone, see chapter 4 above; also Marco di Bartolomeo Rustici's sketch of the church and the millstone in Rustici, *Codice Rustici: Dimostrazione*, 1, fol. 12ᵛ. India received Christianity from the apostle Thomas, whence the possible association with San Tommaso in the Mercato Vecchio, now demolished. India was also the scene of St. Bartholomew's martyrdom, performed in front of Santa Croce.

[22] For a selection from these sermons, see Hatfield, "The Compagnia," 153–161; for a list of confraternal sermons, Bandini, *Specimen*, 2:160–163.

Agli alti essordî e vaghi parlamenti	High-minded introductions and vague talk,
silenzio date, signor capitani;	must end, Lord Captains, and let agile brains
gl'ingegni, el senno e le frequente mani	and common sense and more experienced hands
piglino in cura i magni ordinamenti.	take care of organizing the great day.
E piena fé sie data agl'intendenti,	And let full trust be placed in those who know,
né si rapelli i lor consigli sani.	don't hesitate to take their sound advice.
Tanti begli atti suttil, varî e strani	Your views are holding back so many fine,
si tiran dietro i vostri intendimenti.	varied and clever and astounding acts.
L'opere son nemiche de' sermoni;	Deeds are the foes of sermons without end;
nelle 'mportanze la ragion promette	in things important, reason's what it takes
seguir gli effetti e le conclusioni.	to carry through to outcomes and conclusions.
Ché, se la cosa in pratica si mette,	For if this thing is put into effect
porrebbe partorir confusïoni	it could engender confusion, unless
ma 'l buon sollecitar vinca le frette.	good, careful effort triumphs over haste.
Non s'aspettin le strette;	Do not wait to be goaded:
ché, se l'onor fiorisce e non ne spica,	if honour forms a bud and cannot bloom,
tardi vi scuserà spesa o fatica.[23]	expense or effort won't excuse you later.

The Captains appear to have exerted some control over the *monarchie*. In June 1439, as the city prepared for San Giovanni in the presence of visitors attending the Council of Florence,[24] Lorenzo di Giovanni de' Medici wrote to his brother Cosimo with a request that Ser Alesso Pelli, Cosimo's secretary and household *factotum*, should dress up one of their farm workers, Beco, and send him as an ambassador from the King of Ermenìa (the Medicean territory of Canto alla Macine) to the Emperor (presumably of the Città Rossa, or Arabia), in order to find out what was going on.[25] Presumably, it was the responsibility of the 'king' to dress his retinue for the Magi procession, just as

---

[23] Lanza, ed., *Lirici toscani*, 2:211.

[24] For the chronology, see Gill, *The Council*, 180–181. I have found no record of the *festa de' Magi* during the Council, but the Three Kings were part of the San Giovanni procession on 24 June, described by the anonymous Greek visitor; see chapter 4 above.

[25] ASF, MAP 11, doc. 268[r–v], 13 June 1439, Lorenzo de' Medici to Cosimo de' Medici: "Voi, ser Alesso, achattate una cioppa alla ghreca a Bechone et mandatelo per imbasciadore allo 'mperadore per parte del re d'Ermenia, et guardate s'abbi aviso dacciò" (You, Ser Alesso, borrow a fancy Greek cloak for Bechone and send him as an ambassador to the Emperor on behalf of the king of Armenia, and see if you find anything out with that); see also D.V. Kent, *Cosimo de' Medici*, 314.

the *signori* did for *armeggerie*, and jousters and knights did for their pages.[26] It is just such a branded procession that was represented two decades later by Benozzo Gozzoli in the private family chapel of the Palazzo Medici in the Via Larga.[27]

In 1445, as confraternities reopened after their temporary closure the previous year, the *laudesi* confraternities of the Oltrarno received renewed subsidies to support their *feste*. In November 1446, we find the first unequivocal indication of Medicean involvement in the Magi *festa*. The reconstituted Magi company turned to the Commune for funds to do the *festa* on a five-yearly basis, "in reverence for the worship of God and to do honour to the people of Florence and for the exaltation of the city,"[28] and the city responded with a subsidy funded by an impost on the tax collectors at the city gates, probably supplemented from the tax still levied on the Jews.[29] On 29 November, the company elected ten *festaiuoli*, among them Giovanni di Cosimo de' Medici and the goldsmith-architect Michelozzo Michelozzi,[30] and submitted

---

[26] On lending clothes for plays, see also the letter from Contessina de' Bardi, wife of Cosimo de' Medici, to her son Giovanni, 18 December 1450, informing him that Messer Rosello Roselli of Arezzo "has brought Cosimo a beautiful flannel cloak with marten and sable, and a pair of gloves, and a fish tooth (rostrum?) a *braccio* long; and if the *festa de' Magi* is to be done again, these things will give some respite to my cloth of gold" (ha arrecato a Cosimo una bella ciopa a la polana di martore e zibelini e i° paio di guanti e un dente di pesce, è lungo un braccio; che abiendosi a fare più la festa de' Magi, queste cose darano un po' di risquitto al mio drapo a oro); ASF, MAP, 8, doc. 140ʳ. See also clothes lent by Francesco Castellani for the play of San Lorenzo in 1460, chapter 6 below.

[27] On Gozzoli's *Magi*, and the way in which the pageantry of Franco-Flemish tapestry and Milanese and Mantuan frescoes are reworked in Florentine realities, see Ahl, *Benozzo Gozzoli*, 111–112. See also Domenico Veneziano's *Adoration of the Magi*, Berlin, Gemälde-galerie der Staatlichen Museen, Ident. Nr. 95A; and Wohl, *The Paintings*, 70–72, 120–127.

[28] ASF, Signori e Collegi, Deliberazioni in forza di ordinaria autorità 65, November–December 1446. fol. 7ᵛ mod. num., 12 November 1446: "ad reverentiam cultus dei et ad honorificentiam populi florentini et exaltationem eiusdem civitatis"; also cited in Fabriczy, "Michelozzo," 93–94. On the earlier closure, see Henderson, *Piety*, 63.

[29] Hatfield, "The Compagnia," 114, n. 38. The *festaiuoli* themselves were also expected to contribute funds. On 7 March 1451/2, the priors nominated the eight Consuls of the Magi (including Cosimo's nephew Pierfrancesco di Lorenzo de' Medici) and sixteen advisers, and promptly levied from them a contribution toward the newly installed city clock; ASF, Signori e Collegi, Deliberazioni in forza di ordinaria autorità 74, fol. 6ᵛ, 7 March 1451/2.

[30] I have not identified the letter from Rosello Roselli to the barber-poet Burchiello (1404–1449), also dated 29 November 1446, relaying messages from Giovanni di Cosimo de' Medici, and urging him to involve Michelozzo in the construction of the float, noted

their names to the Commune. The fact that these names needed to be ratified with an assertion of their "laudable intelligence and expertise,"[31] in order that members of the society should give them the respect that was due to them, suggests that the nominations were contested in some way.

These Florentine Magi were a perfect fit with the Medici 'brand': royal but popular, they democratized authority and preserved Florentine republican *Libertas*, basing their 'kingdoms' in and on existing popular structures; they were guided by a star whose meaning they alone fully understood; and they led the city to an intimate encounter with the Holy Family. The Magi were a metaphor, as Dale Kent documents, for the search for salvation by a family that was wealthy and wise.[32] Cosmas and Damian had been useful medical saints for the Medici and continued to enjoy some favour, but the Magi offered the "Wise Men" of the family a bigger ceremonial stage on which to work. The Medici took a leading role in this great demonstration of civic magnificence while at the same time they represented themselves as true republicans.[33]

Giusto d'Anghiari records in his diary: "Friday 6 January [1446/7] in Florence was the feast of Epiphany. They did the *festa* of the Magi in Florence. It was a beautiful *festa* and it would have been more beautiful if the wind had not spoiled it."[34] Ser Giusto's very next entry concerns a joust:

---

in D.V. Kent, *Cosimo de' Medici*, 314. There is, however, an undated sonnet by Burchiello, addressed to Rosello, "Non pregato d'alcun, Rosel, ma sponte," CXVII, which concludes: "I remind you, get everything | ready for the *festa de' Magi* | since Michelino [that is, Michelozzo] wants you on the wagon" (Nototi che t'ammanni | Per la festa de' Magi, in punto omnino, | Che ti vuole in sul carro Michelino).

[31] "Cognita laudabili intelligentia et solertia predictorum festaiuolorum, et ut omnes de dicta sotietate erga illos debitam reverentiam habeant," ASF, Signori e Collegi, Deliberazioni in forza di ordinaria autorità 65, November–December 1446. fol. 23ᵛ mod. num., 29 November 1446; also cited in Fabriczy, "Michelozzo," 94. The *festaiuoli* were: Filippo d'Antonio del Vigna, Andrea di Lotteringo Dalla Stufa, Piermatteo di Forese Sacchetti, Larione di Cante Compagni, Giannozzo di Giovanni Strozzi, Giovanni di Cosimo de' Medici, Albertaccio di Agnolo Carducci, Niccolò di Lorenzo di Gino Capponi, Michelozzo di Bartolomeo [Michelozzi], goldsmith, and Simone d'Andrea di Guerriante, butcher.

[32] D.V. Kent, *Cosimo de' Medici*, 305–328, 374.

[33] For a thoughtful exploration of Medicean *dimostrazione* and *rappresentazione*, see Brown, "De-masking."

[34] Giusti, "I *Giornali*," 91: "Venerdì a dì 6 di gennaio [1446/7] in Firenze fu pasqua di Befana. Fecesi in Firenze la festa de' Magi. Fu bella festa e saria stata più bella se 'l vento non l'avesse guasta."

On Monday 23 [January 1446/7] in Florence they did a beautiful and magnificent joust with swords and shields, and there were thirteen jousters in the lists, and most of them came into the lists very honourably, with banners and silk tunics decorated with silver and pearls. They jousted for two prizes, namely a helmet and a banner. The first prize was won by a man-at-arms who had been sent in by Giovanni di Cosimo de' Medici, and the second prize was won by a man-at-arms equipped by Luca Pitti. There was a very large crowd, and a young man from the Alberti household died from a blow in the joust; he was called *il Gobbo*.[35]

I have reported both these events because the pattern is repeated in an emblematic and politicized description of a joust and a Magi procession included by the Dominican theologian Giovanni di Carlo in his *Libri de temporibus suis* (previously titled *Libri Cosmianarum rerum*), composed between 1480 and 1482.[36] In Book 2, having recounted Piero's triumph over the threatened banking collapse following Cosimo's death in 1464, Giovanni di Carlo describes two magnificent *feste*, organized by Piero to lift the spirits of the citizens. The first is quite unequivocally Lorenzo's joust of 1469, here reported in lavish detail (fols. 68ᵛ–71ᵛ).[37] The second is a *festa de' Magi* (fols. 71ᵛ–76ʳ), for which the Dominican describes the assembly of the Magi in Piazza della Signoria, the visit of their emissaries to the Signoria, their procession with the Signoria down the Via Larga and past the Palazzo Medici, accompanied by huge quantities of baggage, exotic animals, and gifts (the image conjured is of Gozzoli's procession), and finally their arrival at Herod's magnificent palace

---

[35] Giusti, "I *Giornali*," 91: "Lunedì a dì 23 [gennaio 1446/7] detto in Firenze si fece una bella e magnifica giostra a brocci e scudi, e furonci in campo tredici giostranti, e la maggior parte entrarono in campo molto orrevolmente con bandiere, e sopraveste di seta e arienti e perle. Giostraronsi due onori, ciò è un elmetto e una bandiera. Ebbe il primo onore un uomo d'arme el quale aveva messo in campo Giovannino di Cosimo de' Medici, e il secondo onore ebbe un uomo d'arme il quale aveva messo in punto Luca Pitti. Fucci moltissimo popolo, e per colpo di giostra morì un giovane degli Alberti che giostrava, che era chiamato il Gobbo."

[36] The first two books are edited in Pieraccioni, "Frate Giovanni," and Schena, "Frate Giovanni," respectively. Frate Giovanni di Carlo is also called Giovanni Caroli, a misconstruing of the Latin form of his name, Johannes Caroli. I thank Dr Schena for making her edition available to me.

[37] For a contemporary prose catalogue of the elements of the joust, see BNCF, Magl. vɪɪɪ.1503, published in Fanfani, ed., *Ricordo di una giostra;* see also Luigi Pulci, *La giostra.*

at San Marco, where the young emissaries, in masks and costumes that make them look like their fathers,[38] make brief speeches to Herod, present him with gifts, and return whence they came.

> And another spectacle was presented at almost the same time with the same organization and for the same reason. A society of young men decided to revive it in men's memories by performing the *festa* of the Magi who brought gifts to the Christ Child, to be done as a dramatic representation, an ancient custom of the city. Even though it had not been done for many years, they decided to stage it with remarkable effort, so that from its former magnificence people might learn how excellent its future fame might be. And this is the way it was done.
>
> They conceived this city in the likeness of Jerusalem where Herod reigned. They placed the three Kings who came in three parts of the city. In the fourth was Herod. It is amazing how each strove to increase the magnificence of his King, lest any other part exceed it in expense and magnificence. And Herod's station at the church of San Marco, in the square that adjoins the church,[39] was constructed in this fashion. They built a rectangular stage constructed in wood to look like columns. It was fifteen *braccia* high and forty *braccia* long and twelve *braccia* wide [9 × 25 × 30 m].
>
> It was adorned in this fashion. The walls of the palace were covered with what are called *arazzi*, tapestries worked with amazing skill. Above, *spalliere* hangings, woven with the same rare skill, decorated the whole palace, and were a sublime crowning glory. The rods at the top and bottom of the *spalliere* were adorned with ivy and laurel, all intertwined with golden garlands,

---

[38] On sons dressing as their fathers in antiquity, see Trexler, "Ritual in Florence," 226, n. 1; Garin, ed., *L'educazione*, 64.

[39] The open space stretched from the Ospedale degli Innocenti to the Via Larga. Paola Ventrone locates Herod's palace in the Medici garden, to the west of San Marco; the Latin, however, "Herodis autem statio ad sancti Marci edem, in eo qui tempio adjacet campo, hac erat arte constructa," does not readily allow this interpretation, since *campo* refers to the open space in front of the church, rather than to Lorenzo's garden, which was acquired between 1472 and 1475; see Elam, "Lorenzo," 47; Ventrone, *Lo spettacolo*, 79; Hatfield, "The Compagnia," 149; Newbigin, "Carried Away," 124. In the same text, Lorenzo's joust is described as taking place in the "the square adjoining the church of Santa Croce" (camp[o], qui Sanctae Crucis adiacebat templo), fol. 69[r]; Schena, "Frate Giovanni," 2:37.

that adorned the front beautifully. In the middle of the *spalliere* hung splendid shields bearing various coats of arms, which were surrounded by balls of myrtle and woven with similar garlands that emitted sweet perfumes. The shields seemed to hang from lions' heads and seemed to be held up by rings that they held in their mouths. And from those rings, garlands hung down between the orbs like arches, and they were woven together so that they were thin and delicate at the ends and thicker in the middle. Some were made of pine, others of cypress, some fir, others of myrtle or olive branches, woven together, and draped all around. And this was the appearance of the facade. The roof of the whole building was made of an airy cloth, which was supported by a network of ropes that attached to the highest part, and it was full of stars, like the heavens, and of lilies. In the corners there were orbs of greenery, in which various emblems had been arranged, and garlands floated around them, holding the orb in their midst, and in the orb the royal symbols were appropriately displayed.

The side that faced the Via Larga was quite open to the outside; it was supported by columns that were covered in festive greenery. From the base of the columns there was an elevated stage, with latticework covered with myrtle and laurel, which served as the acting space [*deambulatorium*] in front of the king's bedchamber, and it seemed to represent a throne-room. For there were elevated seats set within it, royal thrones, silk cloth glittering with great quantities of gold, which gave great delight to those who saw it. Every floor of the place was covered with great carpets and everything else was arranged with great skill and effort. So that the place would not be dark, they left windows to allow the spectators to see into the palace. Facing onto this space which we called the acting space, there were three chambers, arranged with amazing skill, in one of which was the royal bed, covered in magnificent purple cloth and decorated with silk curtains that were marvellously beautiful and very costly. It contained the royal thrones and beds and various pieces of furniture and all the other things that one finds in a royal chamber. Everything was placed there in perfect order. Likewise, in the other two, which might well be called antechambers, in which officials and courtiers slept, girdles, cups, silver vessels, wine-bowls, saucers, drinking-vessels, and various pieces of clothing and whatever might seem useful for ministerial duties were laid out there in a most excellently prudent fashion. In the corner on the right-hand side of the stage as you entered there were various pieces of furniture. In the middle chamber, the person playing Herod was sitting with a great crowd of officials around him, wearing a purple robe glittering with gold and jewels and a diamond and gold crown.

Around the king were his prefects and his nobles and a multitude of servants and courtiers were all milling around everywhere. Some were grandly dressed, as if it were the king's birthday, or as if the king wanted to show off his royal magnificence. Those who played his ministers came and went continually, seeming to be very busy providing whatever was necessary for those who were about to arrive. The set prepared for each of the Kings whose role was to come to Herod was as follows. There was a tent erected for each King in a different part of the city, and their royal majesty was evident in their mode of travel as much as in their splendid apparel. For just like those who might stop to rest somewhere, you would have seen horses, knights, and a not insignificant number of servants around their tents; in addition, enormous numbers of pack horses and mules moved their provisions about, carrying their luggage and baggage and much other impedimenta. They had arranged among themselves the time at which they were all to gather at the Palazzo Pubblico, as if they were to call upon the Signoria, not in person, since that would seem undignified for such royal personages, but through ambassadors whom they proposed to send to Herod. Therefore, when the time came, with everybody in attendance, they arrived in the city square. And they had dressed people up as all leading men from the optimate families of the city, as if Herod was sending them to do honour to the ambassadors and to bring them before the king; and these representations of the citizens were so close to the real citizens that it was scarcely believable. For their appearance and faces had been so fashioned by masks that they were barely distinguishable from the real people, and indeed their clothes had been taken by their very own sons and then worn by them, and they had mastered all their gestures and could imitate every act and gesture admirably. It was beautiful for the real citizens who had assembled at the Palazzo Pubblico to see themselves impersonated with such dignity and such processional pomp as the royal magnificence and great senate of the city that they represented so excellently. As they assembled, the ambassadors of the Kings gathered and entered the Palazzo and having paid homage to the Signoria and delivered an oration, shortly afterwards they joined all the citizens in costume and went forth to Herod the king. This was the order of the procession. First of all came the people carrying the supplies and a train of people carrying things necessary for the journey. These were followed by the gifts that were being sent by the Kings to King Herod and others with whom the ambassadors expected to break their journey. They also brought many wild animals and beasts of many kinds, some of them stuffed animals, that appeared to be asleep on the pack animals, and others real, for a show of magnificence. There were dogs as well, best suited for hawking and hunting, and birds skilled at hunting game. Then came the entire household of the Signoria, many of whom had been impersonated with great art, as well as courtiers and bodyguards, some of whom protected them with great care, and some of whom were to go with the ambassadors on account of their singular magnificence. They were followed by a huge band of slaves in exotic garb with different gestures and turbans and most remarkable headwear. They seemed so well-trained in barbarian manners and accustomed to their gesticulations that they seemed surely to have been born and raised among those people. They preceded the ambassadors, and played their instruments, they made sweet harmonies with their horns and flutes, and their cymbals clashed with such sweet music, that their harmony and rhythms delighted the spectators hardly less than their appearance. These were followed by a beautiful vanguard of young men, ornately dressed and glittering with gold, silver, and precious stones, with caps on their heads with precious stones glistening on their brows, of such beauty and value that their price would be set at many thousands of gold coins. The courtiers that we said were servants surrounded this squadron of Cupbearers in the most excellent order. In last place came the ambassadors of the Kings, clothed in exotic robes and distinguished by their gold and silver and great sumptuousness and pomp. They were surrounded by the bodyguards already mentioned, who used their silver maces to repel the threat of all those who jostled and bumped them, so that nobody could approach the ambassadors or manhandle them in their desire to see them. The appearance of the ambassadors was such that they differed not at all from real heathens, in their movements and gestures and dress and appearance. Some of the Signoria, like royal officials, surrounded them and escorted them, and they were followed by the whole multitude of citizens in costumes that we have mentioned. The organization of this procession was amazing, in that they observed both the dignity of men's rank and reverence for their age, and they marched exultantly, showing their great magnanimity as they walked along. Thus, the whole populace, spread out all along the route they followed, was filled with a great and avid desire to see these things, and they left no empty spaces. Some crowded the streets, others placed themselves at windows, the rest took over the rooftops, and the multitude of people who ran along beside them competing desperately for a view was incredible. When this procession came to Herod's palace, the other officials who had remained with Herod came forth from the chambers there in a long and pomp-filled procession. When the whole palace had been filled with music, then at last Herod himself came forth, wearing his royal crown and his purple robes, adorned with jewels and gold, and was set on his throne to receive the ambassadors with great and gracious kindness. When they had entered and been received most humanely as decorum dictated, one of them recited a short oration in which he set out the reason for their coming and in addition gave them messages from the Kings. Herod praised them kindly and sent them on their way with many gifts. They bade farewell to the king and left and returned to their tents by the same route.

Thus was the manner and the end of this spectacle, surely the most excellent of all that were staged in these times. Oftentimes as I think about these things, it does not appear as a *festa* but more a certain portent of the times that were to come, in which, on account of civil wars and the great evils that were perpetrated, not just Florentine citizens but even their images and shadows have been totally erased. For they prevail neither in prudence nor in great wealth, nor does their high reputation remain among foreign peoples, but I would say, forgive me, they are like ghosts, like men of straw, and we see them exposed in turn to the mockery and the deception of all. The things that we will shortly relate will demonstrate clearly that this is the case. Therefore, with the *feste* now ceased, by which the spirits of the citizens were soothed for a little while, they soon returned to their activities of old, of cruelly tearing each other apart. Nor indeed were the spirits of the mighty engaged by these pleasures, so that they were restrained from doing and saying many of the things that we described before. It was opposed by the greater part of the citizens most obstinately.[40]

The passage was identified and published by Hatfield, who noted that it was the source of Machiavelli's claim that Piero turned to public entertainments to consolidate his power after Cosimo's death.[41] But Hatfield also pointed out that Giovanni di Carlo had manipulated the dates: Cosimo died in August 1464, the banking crisis was 1466, and Lorenzo's joust was not until 12 February (Carnival) 1468/9, so the sequence of events cannot be as Giovanni describes. No other diarist mentions a *festa de' Magi* in the second half of the 1460s. Furthermore, Giovanni di Carlo was exiled to the friary of San Romano in Lucca in 1461 and it is not clear that he returned to Santa Maria Novella before the end of the decade.[42]

---

[40] Text in Hatfield, "The Compagnia," 148–158, doc. 9b, but here taken from Schena, "Frate Giovanni," 2:44–54; see Appendix, doc. 18. I have also consulted the English translation by David Armstrong in Rogers, "Art and Public Festival," 659–663, and I thank Frances Muecke for her assistance.

[41] Machiavelli, *Istorie fiorentine*, 649–650, vii.12.1–6; see chapter 3 above.

[42] V. Marchetti, "Caroli," 524. The events described in the following letter of 11 May 1465, ASF, MAP 20, doc. 152ʳ, from Piero in Florence to Lorenzo in Milan, may be at the origins of this 'misremembering': "Get your business done [there in Milan] so that you return here in good time. Here we are preparing, for the visit of the Lords [of Milan], to stage a beautiful *festa* for St. John the Baptist and so we are looking for a different way of doing them great honour. Our Giuliano has got himself up, fitted out by Baccio Benci and by others, and they would like to joust, but do it more magnificently than usual. The Signoria wants them to do it. I'm not happy about it; I will try to get out of it if I can. I would rather not have so much trouble at once, and I'm amazed at Giovanni de' Pazzi: having done it once he wants to do it again a second time. You'll find out what happens"

Chronology is not the only problem. Despite verisimilitude in many details, the structure of the *festa* is implausible. It is not conceivable that the Magi could have made their journey in order to present gifts to Herod in Jerusalem and depart without visiting the Christ Child.[43] And Piero, who ten years earlier had commissioned Gozzoli to paint the exotic cavalcade of the Magi in the household chapel, could scarcely have sponsored a procession that did not bring the Magi to the presence of the Child. Nor can Friar Giovanni di Carlo's apparent enthusiasm for the spectacle be reconciled with the caution of his mentor Antoninus, who included the *festa dei Magi* among spectacles that could be watched without risk of mortal sin, but framed it in a series of injunctions against *concupiscentia oculorum, curiositas*, and *scandalum* (eye-lust, curiosity, and scandal):

> If, however, other vain and delightful things are represented for pleasure, but nevertheless do no harm to the Church or the clergy, or religion, of itself it does not appear to be a mortal sin, neither performing nor watching, nor making masks, dragons, kings, and the like. Likewise, watching dancers, tumblers, footracers, people wrestling or jousting or playing other games does not in itself seem to be mortal sin even though it is vanity and a waste of time.[44]

Did the pageant have a parodic or allegorical element, and what might it be? We know that Giovanni di Carlo, as prior of the Conventual Dominicans

---

(Atendete voi acciò che ritorniate qua in buono ordine. Qui s'aparecchia, per la venuta di cotesti Signori, fare una bella festa per San Giovanni et così si cerca per altra via fare loro grandiximo honore. Èssi levato su Giuliano nostro, messo al punto da Baccio Benci, et da altri, et vorrebbono armeggiare, ma farla altrimenti magnifica che non s'è usato. La Signoria vuole che faccino. Io non me ne contento. Vedrò di sgabellarmene se potrò. Non vorrei tante noie a uno tracto, et maraviglomi di Giovanni de' Pazzi che havendo facto una volta ci si rimetta la seconda. Che seguirà, saprai). The procession of *edifici* for San Giovanni presumably had a component with the Magi.

[43] Cardini and Frale, *La congiura*, online, section 1.6, posit a continuation the next day with the Adoration of the Child, but there is no hint of it in Giovanni di Carlo's text.

[44] Antoninus, *Summa*, 2:493E, II.III.7 §5, *De spectaculis*: "Si autem alia vana, et solatiosa repræsent'entur ob solatium, quod tamen non sit in opprobrium ecclesiæ, vel cleri, vel religionis, de se non videtur mortale nec exercitatio, nec aspectio, ut facere larvas, dracones, reges, et hujusmodi; similiter aspicere chorizantes, saltantes, currentes ab bravium, in palestra se exercentes, vel hastiludiis, vel aliis ludis de se non videtur mortale, quamvis vanitas sit, et amissio temporis."

at Santa Maria Novella, was at loggerheads with the Observant Dominicans at San Marco (and would later be in open conflict with Savonarola and his followers).[45] Was he using this commentary on the banking crisis to say that Christ no longer resided at San Marco; that it was inhabited by a tyrant of immeasurable wealth, surrounded by satraps, scribes, and pharisees? This would have been an implicit reproach of the cultural policies of Piero di Cosimo, which Friar Giovanni had in fact supported, but by the time he was writing, Piero was long dead and Lorenzo was recovering from the shock of the Pazzi conspiracy.

Like so many of our plays, the Magi procession lapsed after the Pazzi conspiracy of 1478, and it was not among the public *feste* that were revived in Lorenzo's desperate flurry of activity after 1488. Nevertheless, at his death in 1492, the men of the Magi company accompanied Lorenzo's body from San Marco to burial in San Lorenzo.[46] And no sooner had the Medici left Florence in 1494 than the friars of San Marco took possession of the space that had been occupied by the Magi confraternity.[47] The Signoria resumed (or continued) its annual offering to the friary, and on 6 January 1497/8, to the amazement of Savonarola's friends and foes alike, went to San Marco and "kissed the hand of Friar Girolamo at the altar" (baciorono la mano a frate Girolamo all'altare).[48] The following Sunday, within the octave of Epiphany, Savonarola, already excommunicated and just months away from his execution, revived the *festa* behind the closed doors of San Marco. The *Vita di Savonarola*, attributed to his follower Fra Pacifico Burlamacchi, describes the event.[49] Although there is no record of use of the *Quem queritis* tropes of the Latin liturgical 'drama' in the Florentine Church, the friars of San Marco stripped away the

---

[45] Edelheit, "Humanism," esp. 274–280.

[46] Del Lungo, *Florentia*, 194; Trexler and Lewis, "Two Captains and Three Kings."

[47] ASF, Signori e collegi, Deliberazioni in forza di ordinaria autorità 96, fol. 100ᵛ mod. num., 1 December 1494: "locus societatis de' Magi restituatur fratribus sancti Marci de Florentia prout antiquitus erat et quod de bonis mobilibus dictae societatis fiat inventarium et per eosdem fratres retineantur dicta bona ad istantiam dictorum dominorum" (the oratory of the company of the Magi is to be returned to the friars of San Marco in Florence, as it was in former times, and an inventory is to be made of the goods and chattels of the said company, and the said goods are to be retained by the friars, by order of the Priors); also cited in Fabriczy, "Michelozzo," 94.

[48] Landucci, *Diario*, 161, cit. Hatfield, "The Compagnia," 140.

[49] Ginori Conti, ed., *La vita,* 117. For an earlier version of this fluid text, see Burlamacchi, *Vita*, 102–103.

magnificence of the Medicean procession to return to the roots of the Magi play within the liturgy of the Epiphany Mass.[50] The Kings were played by three priests "with the most beautiful copes of silk, decorated with gold and jewels, of which the first was God's servant Friar Girolamo [Savonarola], the second Friar Francesco Salviati, prior of San Marco, and the third Friar Domenico da Pescia, prior of Fiesole."[51] Led by a novice, Friar Jacopo Gucci, dressed as an angel, carrying a star on a pole, the procession was made up of the other friars in their most ornate feast day vestments. The dialogue in Latin was taken from the Vulgate text of St. Matthew's Gospel: *Ubi est qui natus est rex Iudeorum? Vidimus enim stellam eius in oriente* (Where is the King of the Jews who has been born? We have seen his star in the East; Matthew 2:2). To which the friars replied, *In Bethlehem Iude, sic enim scriptum est per prophetam* (In Bethlehem in Judea, as is written in the prophets; Matthew 2:5). After the Introit, *Ecce dominator quem vos queritis et angelus testamenti quem vos vultis* (Behold the Lord whom you seek and the Angel of the testament whom you desire; Malachi 3:1), and the Response: *Deus meus, Deus meus es tu* (My God, you are my God; Psalm 117 (118):28), the Christ Child, represented by a doll, was placed on a portable altar in the middle of the church, and the first Magus — that is, Savonarola himself — picked it up and gave it to each friar who kissed its feet to the erotically charged antiphon, *Dilectus meus candidus et rubicundus, electus ex millibus* (My beloved is white and ruddy, chosen out of thousands; Song of Songs 5:10). The friars replied, *Dominus meus et Deus meus* (My Lord and my God; John 20:28). Vernacular *laude* followed, then the second Magus handed the doll to each friar who kissed its hands, singing the antiphon, *Fasciculus myrrhe dilectus meus mihi, inter ubera mea commorabitur* (A bundle of myrrh is my beloved to me, he shall abide between my breasts; Song of Songs 1:12). Finally, in the choir, the third Magus handed the doll to each friar who kissed it on the mouth, to the antiphon *Obsculetur me obsculo oris sui* (Let him kiss me with the kiss of his mouth; Song of Songs 1:1).[52]

---

[50] For the Latin *Officium Stellae* and the more elaborate *Ordo ad Representandum Herodum* and the *Interfectio puerorum*, see Young, *The Drama,* 2:29–124; Wyndham, *The Fleury Playbook,* 2.

[51] Ginori Conti, ed., *La vita,* 117; see also Trexler, *Public Life,* 189–190.

[52] Ginori Conti, ed., *La vita,* 117–118. For these Marian antiphons, see *Cantus* online.

The friars then processed into the refectory for supper, carrying lighted candles and red crosses. One of them preached a sermon while the others ate, and the laity, and Savonarola's enemies, spied through the cracks in the door:

> So fervent and joyful were the friars in those days that their hearts burned with love of Jesus; and the laity, even their enemies, ran to peer through the cracks of the doors of the church, and as they watched they were amazed by such fervour.[53]

The outward display of the old *festa* was replaced by intimate devotional fervour and the *festa* slipped from view for five centuries. In 1997 it was revived by the Chapter and the Opera of Santa Maria del Fiore to mark the seventh centenary of the foundation of the cathedral, and is repeated annually. As in the time of Lorenzo, the principal participants are dressed in lavish costumes, ride beautifully caparisoned horses, and are accompanied by their retinues, including including *sbandieratori* and a group performing Renaissance dances, with a nod to exotic modern multiculturalism through the presence of Asian and African schoolchildren. They go in procession from the Palazzo Pitti to the Palazzo Vecchio, where they are joined by the city's *corteo storico*,[54] then move on to Santa Maria del Fiore where they make their offering at the *presepe vivente*, the Nativity scene constructed by the cathedral steps. The event ends with a gospel reading, a greeting from the archbishop, and various speeches. The experience is both exhilarating and disquieting. The willing participation of so many volunteers in lovingly crafted costumes does honour to the city and brings visitors and revenue to its merchants, but there is also tension — as there must always have been — between commercialism and devotion, between the opulence of the Magi and the wretchedness of the refugee family in the stable.

---

[53] Ginori Conti, ed., *La vita*, 118: "Tanto era il fervore et allegrezza de' frati in quelli giorni che gli lor cuori ardevono d'amore di Iesu; et li secolari, et[iam] degli adversarii, correvano a vedere a' fessi delle porte della chiesa et riguardando restavano admirati di simil fervore."

[54] Florence's *corteo storico* (re-enactment procession), now under the aegis of the Commune of Florence, was originally formed by the Associazione Viva Fiorenza in 1930. Its members dress in costumes reflecting the styles of 1530 to represent the civil, military, and guild authorities of Florence, the four quarters, the sixteen *gonfaloni* or districts, heralds, trumpeters, drummers, flag carriers, pages, and the "madonne fiorentine."

La rappresentazione del martirio del glorioso apostolo san Bartolomeo

Among the documents published by Rab Hatfield in 1970 is one that relates to communication between the company of the Magi and the festive company of San Bartolomeo.[55] According to Vasari, the San Bartolomeo company was responsible for one of the "four most solemn *feste* that were done publicly almost every year, one for each quarter, except for San Giovanni, whose *festa* was celebrated with a very solemn procession [...]: Santa Maria Novella did the *festa* of St. Ignatius; Santa Croce that of St. Bartholomew, called San Baccio; Santo Spirito did the *festa* of the Holy Spirit, the Carmine did the Ascension of our Lord and the Assumption of the Virgin Mary."[56] Leaving aside the absence of any evidence of an annual St. Ignatius play and the failure to mention the Annunciation *festa* of San Felice, this is a valuable recollection of an important *festa* that disappeared almost without a trace in the sixteenth century. The single surviving text of a St. Bartholomew play was copied by Lorenzo di ser Nicolaio di Diedi before February 1463/4.[57] The actors were not the *fanciulli* of a youth confraternity but rather the *giovani* of an adult group. The earliest mention of it is in Ser Giusto d'Anghiari's diaries:

> Thursday 24 [August 1452] was the *festa* of St. Bartolomeo in Florence. They did a beautiful *festa* and representation of the martyrdom of St. Bartholomew. There were lots of people.[58]

---

[55] Hatfield, "The Compagnia," 148, doc. 9a.

[56] Vasari, *Le vite* (1568), 1:441, *Vita del Cecca ingegnere fiorentino* (passage not in the first edition of 1550): "quattro solennissime, e publiche [*feste* che] si facevano quasi ogni anno, cioè una per ciascun quartiere eccetto San Giovanni, per la festa del quale si faceva una solennissima processione [...]: Santa Maria Novella quella di Santo Ignazio, Santa Croce quella di San Bartolomeo, detto San Baccio, Santo Spirito quella dello Spirito Santo, e il Carmine quella dell'Ascensione del Signore, e quella dell'Assunzione di Nostra Donna." Vasari makes no mention here of the Annunciation in San Felice, nor any at all of the Magi *festa*, despite its close relationship with his Medici patrons.

[57] BNCF, Conv. Soppr. F.3.488, fols. 36ʳ–5ᵛ; see Molinari, "La *Rappresentazione*." Molinari believed that the play was performed over two days (p. 260), but other evidence suggests that there were processions around town on the first day, and the performance on the second.

[58] Giusti, "I *Giornali*," 108–109: "Giovedì a dì 24 detto fu la festa di San Bartolomeo in Firenze. Si fece bella festa e rassembrazione della passione di San Bartolomeo. Fucci molta gente." The San Bartolomeo company also participated in the procession of "edifici

Richer documentation from almost twenty years later gives a better idea of the way in which it was organized.[59] As Richa first noted, the confraternity applied to the Commune in 1471 for a subsidy, which was duly granted on the grounds that other groups received a similar subsidy:

> The magnificent and excellent Priors, being reminded by several citizens that this year the play of the *festa* of the glorious apostle St. Bartholomew is to be done, as is traditional from time to time, in the city of Florence in Piazza Santa Croce, and that this *festa* is very costly, and that the Commune has been accustomed in other times to grant a subsidy to the *operai* or *festaiuoli* appointed to organize this *festa*, by means of the citizens who are appointed to the gates, and judging that it would be good to offer them some similar subsidy so that they can bring their *festa* to a perfection that brings dignity to the city and pleasure to all the citizens, and since it is customary to provide assistance not only in this *festa* but also in many other similar *feste* from the public purse, and wishing to provide part of what is necessary for this *festa*, they resolve as follows: that by virtue of the present provision, the drawing of lots to send citizens to the city gates and to the mills should be suspended for two months, beginning on 1 July next, and for these two months no citizen shall be selected to go to the gates and mills, but citizens will continue to be sent to each gate and mill as at present, and they are to be sent by the said *operai* or *festaiuoli* for the *festa* of St. Bartholomew or their representative of the men of the opera or others agreed by them.[60]

Regular selections to these positions were suspended for two months, and instead the *festaiuoli* provided the manpower to collect the taxes, with authority to retain up to 300 florins for the *festa*. The names of the six *operai* and thirty other approved members were listed in a notarized document

---

e rappresentazioni e divozioni assai" (*edifici* and *rappresentazioni* and acts of devotion), staged for Pius II and Galeazzo Maria Sforza in 1459; see Dei, *La cronica*, 68; and above, chapter 3, n. 40.

[59] Giusti, "I *Giornali*," 168.

[60] ASF, Provvisioni, Registri 162, fols. 61ʳ–62ᵛ, 11 June 1471; see Appendix, doc. 19, and also Hatfield, "The Compagnia," 120–121, 148; Trexler, *Public Life*, 396–398, 401–403, and Richa, *Notizie*, 1 (1754): 47.

identified by Richard Trexler, who then established age and place of residence of about two-thirds of them. Like the *laudesi* confraternities responsible for the *feste* across the Arno, San Bartolomeo players were predominantly local, from the *gonfaloni* of the Leon Nero and Bue in the Santa Croce quarter. They ranged in age from fourteen to fifty, with a mean of twenty-seven-and-a-half, but as a cohort, they were from a higher social class than the *laudesi* members. Almost all have family names, and none is listed with an occupation: as people eligible for public office, they would normally be excluded from confraternity membership by the 1455 legislation, and on this occasion they are simply a group that has come together just for the *festa*, here called the "opera festivitatis," rather than members of the San Bartolomeo confraternity in Santa Croce.[61] Little is known about the San Bartolomeo confraternity. Its altar in the Cerchi chapel, which also held the remains of the blessed Umiliana de' Cerchi, was surmounted by an imposing majolica dossal, attributed to Andrea della Robbia, representing Bartholomew, with St. Francis and the Archangel Raphael and Tobias as its secondary patrons (fig. 5.2); its meeting rooms were in the Franciscan friary.[62] In 1564, some of its *masserizie* (belongings, confraternal items) passed to the youth confraternity of the Arcangelo Raffaello, but not the archives of the confraternity of San Bartolomeo which had been lost in the flood of 1557.[63]

An undated letter of exaggerated formality, identified by Rab Hatfield, probably relates to the performance of 1471.[64] The kings of San Bartolomeo have evidently asked the Magi to lend them costumes and properties, and the Magi reply:

> Gaspar, Balthasar, and Melchior, etc. By the grace of almighty God, in the East, to their loyal Principalities, and deputies, etc.

---

[61] On the regulations of 1455, see Henderson, *Piety*, 63. The names of those subsequently approved for this task (six syndics and thirty members, all with family names) are notarized in ASF, Notarile antecosimiano 11679 (= L 139 [1470–1476], Bartolommeo di Gabriello Lioni), fol. 51r; see Trexler, *Public Life*, 397–398.

[62] See 1489 document cited below, n. 67.

[63] ASF, CRSPL 160.7/8, fol. 14r–v, discussed by Eisenbichler, *The Boys*, 74. See also Henderson, *Piety*, 450; Hall, *Renovation*, 164; Moisè, *Santa Croce*, 174–175, 426. The presence of Tobias and the Angel together with St. Bartholomew in the majolica altarpiece suggests that the association between the two confraternities was older.

[64] For the problems of dating, see Hatfield, "The Compagnia," 120, n. 51, who assigns it to 1466, 1467, or 1468, while Trexler, *Public Life*, 401, n. 161, proposes 1471.

To the most devoted and worthy princes, governors and protectors of the most excellent university dedicated to the holy college which convenes under the glorious name of the apostle Bartholomew in the Italic parts of the splendid city of Florence, greetings in Christ.

Between the vigils of human necessity, one must attend principally to spending one's days, which fly faster than an arrow, under the ensign of virtue, always engaged in praiseworthy actions and works that bring fame; and thus memory becomes eternal and immortal, for nothing is more blessed than this and nothing should be desired more by mortal men. And because the ears of our majesties have heard tell that Your Excellencies have chosen and continue to follow the true way to reach these heights, undertaking intolerable effort and most copious expense, and that Your Magnanimities, to ensure your outcome with the aid of Hope, mistress of all things, are preparing to stage in the near future a new *festa* and triumph, which will be memorable above all others, we therefore advise Your Illustrious Lordships that, in the sight of the Thrones of our Dominions, your works are acceptable and most pleasing, and that much benevolence is stirred within us toward [Y]our Clemencies, which must engender gracious effects in the future toward Your Enlightenednesses. We would like to have been able to attend such solemnity in person, but we find ourselves busy in reforming our kingdoms — and above all Egypt, Ethiopia and Nubia, Arabia, Sheba, India, Medea, and both the Armenias — for which we find it impossible to be absent. We are therefore sending our servant, Sheba the tall, bearing gifts, to present our apologies for this, and to give notice, with these gifts, of our incomparable intentions toward Your Most Magnificent Lordships. We shall send you in the near future a solemn embassy by which you will understand our enthusiasm more fully, and you will receive messages of infinite consolation. We entrust ourselves to Your Most Excellent Lordships and inform you that we may fail to do all the things that would be pleasing in your sight, but we are not lacking in good will.

From eastern parts, where they border on the equinox, in the
year 5110 since the flood of waters.[65]

The Magi did not join the *festa* as themselves, but they sent their moral
support and gifts, and promised to send an embassy — costumed riders to
take part in the cavalcades, perhaps — in the near future. Like their richer
and more influential friends the Magi, the oriental kings of the Bartholomew
play harnessed the resources of the festive kingdoms of their quarter, and
their activities were sufficiently harmonized for them to be able to discuss an
exchange of costumes and props.

And so we come to a description of the cavalcade. On Thursday 22 August 1471 in Florence, in Piazza Santa Croce, the young men were building
the stages and the great sets to do the *festa* of St. Bartholomew. Again, it is the
inveterate observer, Ser Giusto Giusti of Anghiari, who describes the events:

> On Thursday 22 [August 1471], in Piazza Santa Croce, they
> continued to build the stages and great sets to do the *festa* of San
> Bartolomeo. [...]
>
> On Saturday 24 the *festaiuoli* who were doing the *festa* of
> the martyrdom of St. Bartholomew continued to build the very
> beautiful set: stages all highly adorned with columns that looked
> like marble, and canopies with lots of compartments skilfully
> worked and a great set; and during the day they sent a cavalcade
> all around Florence, and they had two kings, a Black King and a
> White King, with lots of beautiful costumes made to look real,
> and some real ones of great value. It was judged to be a fine thing;
> and this was all set up in Piazza Santa Croce.
>
> On Sunday [25 August] in Florence, the *festa* of St. Bartho-
> lomew continued with those ceremonies and those beautiful
> sets and the representation of miracles, even though the rain

---

[65] BNCF, II.iv.128, a *zibaldone* copied by Giovanni Pigli, fols. 37ᵛ–38ʳ; see Appendix, doc. 20. See also Hatfield, "The Compagnia," 120–121 and 148, doc. 9a; Flamini, *La
lirica*, 184–185, and, importantly, Trexler, *Public Life*, 401–403. The list of kingdoms owes
something to Psalm 71 (72):10: "The kings of Tharsis and the islands shall offer presents:
the kings of the Arabians and of Saba shall bring gifts"; and to Isaiah 60:6: "The multitude
of camels shall cover thee, the dromedaries of Madian and Epha: all they from Saba shall
come, bringing gold and frankincense: and shewing forth praise to the Lord"; see Hatfield,
"Three Kings," Introduction, 14.

interfered, because it rained very heavily for an hour before midday and then stopped. The *festa* lasted until evening.[66]

Two decades later, in Lorenzo's final burst of magnificence that began
with the wedding of his daughter to Franceschetto Cibo in 1488, the play was
revived again. The young men of the confraternity of San Bartolomeo, now
specifically named, again applied successfully for a communal subsidy:

> The magnificent and excellent lords, the Lord Priors of Liberty
> and the Standard Bearer of Justice of the Florentine people, hav-
> ing heard how a large number of Florentine citizens, and young
> men in particular, who meet in the friary of Santa Croce under
> the name of the Society of St. Bartholomew the Apostle, wish to
> celebrate this present year in the city of Florence the feast day
> of the said apostle, by representing his martyrdom and miracles.
> This was last done in the year 1471, but on account of the great
> expense for the set and other essential things, they would desire
> to be assisted in some part from the public purse, just as was
> done in 1471. And having heard their requests and entreaties
> and believing that it would not be inappropriate to assist in this
> work which is to the honour of God and his apostles and for the

---

[66] Giusti, "I *Giornali*," 168: "Giovedì a dì 22 detto [di agosto 1471] in Firenze in su la piazza di Santa Croce si seguitò il fare i palchetti e grandi apparecchi per far la festa di San Bartolomeo. [...] | Sabato a dì 24 detto i festaiuoli che facevano la festa della Rappresentazione della passione di San Bartolomeo seguitarono in fare molto bello apparecchio di palchetti molto adornati di colonne a vista di marmo e con sopracieli con molti compassi di gran dimostrazione e grand'apparecchio, e mandarono il dì per tutto Firenze gran cavalleria, che feciano fussino due re, un nero e un bianco, con molte belle veste contrafatte, e delle vere e di valuta. Fu tenuta bella cosa; ed era detto apparato in su la piazza di Santa Croce. | Domenica a dì 25 detto in Firenze si seguitò il far la festa di San Bartolomeo con quelle solennità e con que' begli apparecchi e con dimostrazione di miracoli, benché l'acqua la turbasse, ché piovve tra le 15 ore e le 16 una grossa acqua, e poi restette. Durò detta festa sino a ore 22." See also Lionardo Morelli, *Chroniche*, 188: "On 25 [August 1471] they did the festa of St. Bartholomew very beautifully in Piazza Santa Croce" (Addì xxv detto si fece la festa di S. Bartolomeo in su la piazza di Santa ✠ molto bella). The same wording is found in Ridolfi, *Priorista*, ASF, Manoscritti 225, fol. 181r.

entertainment of the people who take delight in spectacles of this kind.[67]

The formulaic coupling of *honor* and *consolatio* — honour and entertainment — is frequent in the justification of spectacle. In this context, *consolatio* is no longer the alleviation of distress but the active experience of pleasure, entertainment, and recreation.

Once again, a play text is preserved and, like the surviving Magi text, it is in the Umbrian *ballata maggiore* form rather than *ottava rima*, although there is nothing in the language to suggest other than a Florentine origin.[68] It was copied by Lorenzo di ser Nicolaio — as indicated in chapter 1, a member of the youth company of the Purification — into an anthology compiled largely before 1465, and even though it may have been revised and adapted for earlier and later performances, this text probably provides the basic structure of the piece.

Whereas the performance space of the Magi representation ranged across the whole city, the Bartholomew play, after the 'advertising' cavalcades of the first day, was contained within Piazza Santa Croce. We do not know exactly where the "stages and great sets" described by Ser Giusto were located or how they were configured, but it seems probable that, like the stage in front of San Marco described by Giovanni di Carlo, they were elevated on the steps in front of the church, and consisted of a series of colonnaded rooms, covered by a cloth canopy, with an acting space in front of them. The piazza in front of the Franciscan church was indeed constructed with preachers and audience

---

[67] ASF, Provvisioni, Registri 180, fols. 26ᵛ–27ʳ, 26 May 1489: "Habentes notitiam magnifici et excelsi Domini, domini Priores libertatis et vexillifer iustitiæ populi florentini, quemadmodum multi cives florentini, iuvenes admodum, qui congregantur in locis habitationum fratrum Sanctae Crucis sub nomine Societatis Sancti Bartholomæi apostoli, cuperent hoc presenti anno celebrare in civitate Florentiæ festum dicti apostoli, eius passionem et miracula representando, quod ultimo factum fuit in anno M cccc Lxxi. Sed quia sumptus magnus in apparatu et reliquis necessariis fit, cuperent ex publico iuvari in aliqua parte prout etiam in dicto anno M cccc Lxxi factum fuit. Et auditis ipsorum postulationibus nec non etiam supplicationibus, et credentes non esse inconveniens eisdem aliquod præstari auxilium in hoc opere quod cedit in honorem dei et suorum apostolorum et in consolationem populi qui delectatur spectaculis."

[68] See above, n. 57. The source is an unidentified non-Tuscan translation of the vita of San Bartolomeo in the *Legenda Aurea*; Jacobus, *Legenda Aurea*, 2:922–933, cxix *De Sancto Bartholomeo.*

in mind, and it is this kind of frontal performance that was enacted here, rather than the spectacle in the round represented by jousts.

The saint's story is not complex and plays symmetrically on the binary opposition, described by Ser Giusto, of the Black King and the White King. The scene is India, "at the end of the world" according to the *Legenda Aurea*,[69] where Bartolomeo went after the Resurrection and where he lives as a pilgrim in a temple. There are two temples, five miles apart, inhabited by two incompetent demonic pagan gods, Astarotto and Berit, while hordes of hapless paupers shuttle between them until they are saved by Bartolomeo. There are two kings, Polymius and his brother Astyages of Armenia according to the *Vita*, but only Astagio is named here. The first king is converted, after his daughter is saved from demonic possession by the saint, while the second king, Astagio, orders Bartolomeo's crucifixion, flaying, and eventual beheading.

For the play, the central space of the stage is occupied by *palchetti* (raised platforms, stages) with columns of fictive marble and canopies, like the ones for the *festa* of the Magi described by Giovanni di Carlo. The temples are at either end of the stage. The martyrdom of the saint is handled enthusiastically, but the audience's horror is mitigated by clear markers that his suffering is not real. After much business of ensuring that the blade is sharp enough to skin an elephant (stanza 74:6), the executioner sets to work and removes Bartholomew's skin. Then, with his skin slung over his shoulder, and his body "battered and bleeding" (guasta e sanguinante; stanza 81:2), the actor impersonating the saint continues, unimpaired, to proselytize and baptize until the pagan king orders his beheading. Bartholomew's soul is then carried off to heaven.[70]

Rappresentazione di santo Giovanni quando fu decollato

Earlier than the Bartholomew performances and unrelated to the festive kingdoms, but still performed in the open air, is the *Play of St. John when he was beheaded*. On 29 August 1451, on the feast day of the Beheading of St. John the Baptist, just two weeks after the proclamation of a league between Florence and Milan that cemented Cosimo's alliance with Francesco Sforza and his weakening interest in Venice, Florence witnessed an unprecedented spectacle. Ser Giusto Giusti is the only chronicler to mention it:

---

[69] Jacobus, *Legenda Aurea*, 2:922, CXIX.11: "que est in fine orbis."

[70] See also discussion of the departure of the Baptist's soul, below.

On Sunday 29 August [1451] they did a beautiful *festa* on the meadow outside the Porta alla Giustizia of the *Play of the Beheading of St. John the Baptist*. There were lots of people. It was estimated that there were more than fifty thousand people.[71]

Until it was moved in 1531, Florence's place of public execution was just outside the Porta San Francesco, in the space that is now Piazza Piave, on the northern bank of the Arno (fig. 5.3).[72] Florentines were used to the spectacle of justice: the sight of condemned criminals being sent around the city in a cart, dressed in ignominious costumes, or of *confratelli* in their hooded black robes accompanying condemned men to the gallows, urging them to think only on Christ in that time between their absolution and death.[73] In the early part of the century, a tableau of the Crucifixion of Christ had been part of the procession for the feast of the Nativity of St. John the Baptist, but this is the first time, I believe, that the Florentines saw a full-scale outdoor fiction of execution, and the horror of that bloody execution is much attenuated.

The *Rappresentazione di San Giovanni quando fu decollato* is found in six manuscripts and in print, but did not find its way into D'Ancona's anthology,[74] possibly because the text of the printed editions was extremely corrupt (fig.

---

[71] Giusti, "I *Giornali*," 105: "Domenica a dì 29 d'agosto in Firenze si fece una bella festa in sul prato della Porta alla Giustizia della rapresentazione della Decapitazione di San Giovanni Batista. Fuvi molta gente. Stimossi vi fussino più di cinquanta migliaia d'anime." The number is spelled out in full; this corrects Trexler's reading of "5000" in Trexler, "Florentine Theatre" (rev. 2002), 237. According to the *Estimo* of 1431, the total population of Florence was 123,796 *bocche* (mouths); BNCF, II.i.394, *Ricordi 1400–1475*, fol. 86ᵛ. Fifty thousand may be an over-estimation, but the crowd must have been very large.

[72] This remained the 'performance' space of the comforting confraternity of Santa Maria della Croce al Tempio, also known as the Congrega de' Neri, into the sixteenth century. Their statutes prescribed, ASF, CCRSPL 202, §37 (1586), that for the feast of the Beheading of St. John the Baptist they should "go in procession in the evening to the meadow of Justice, say the Nocturn of the Dead, and make a bonfire of logs" (la sera, sempre in processione, recarsi al pratello della Giustizia, dire il notturno dei Morti, bruciare i ceppi). The detail of the Florentine chain map shows the scaffold outside the city walls. The play of *San Giovanni decollato* was performed in this area in 1451 and may have made use of the scaffold for the performance.

[73] Edgerton, *Pictures*; Falvey, "An Investigation"; Eisenbichler, "Il ruolo"; and more broadly Mills, *Suspended Animation*.

[74] *La rappresentatione di sancto Giouanni dicollato* ([Florence: Bartolomeo de' Libri, not after 1495]), ISTC ij00254700; Cioni, *Bibliografia*, 189, LI.1; for manuscripts and edition, see Table 1.

5.4). The dramatist's source is not the gospel account of the Baptist's death in Matthew 14:1–10, but rather the enormously popular Italian prose *Vita di san Giovambatista* dating to the fourteenth century,[75] which furnishes the apocryphal scene of the Baptist's arrival in Limbo and the final procession. The same *Vita* served Lucrezia Tornabuoni for her verse *Vita di Sancto Giovanni Baptista* (Life of St. John the Baptist) and Feo Belcari for his play of *San Giovanni quando fu visitato da Cristo nel diserto,* in which San Giovannino, the child Baptist, is visited in the desert by the Holy Family as they returned from Egypt.[76]

The author is fortunate in his source. The *Vita*, modelled closely on the *Meditations on the Life of Christ,* directs the reader's mental gaze to the most vivid and emotive scenes in the Baptist's life and invents them where they did not previously exist. The dramatist changes the order of some events but keeps the *Vita* so close at hand that the rubricated stage directions frequently echo the chapter headings in the manuscript *Vita* — headings that are regrettably not reproduced in the printed edition cited. The stage directions swing from the present indicative or subjunctive to the *passato remoto*, but the dramatist is constantly aware of the exigencies of performance: how to get actors from one location to the next. As the action moves from place to place, the speeches are timed to allow movement. The places required are the River Jordan, the desert where the Baptist preaches, a mount representing heaven, Herod's Palace and dining hall where the Daughter dances, the Queen's Chamber, Limbo with the Old Testament Righteous, the Prison where John the Baptist is held, and finally, the stage with a trapdoor for the Queen's disappearance in an explosion. The final stage direction, for a scene of the dramatist's own invention, reads: "When the Queen has spoken these words, she is to be destroyed and there has to be an explosion, and the one has to coincide with the other, and the earth opens and swallows the Queen. Then the Angel says this stanza and bids farewell to everyone" (Dette queste parole, hàssi a fare ruinare la Reina e fare uno scoppio che s'accordi l'uno coll'altro e la terra s'apre ed inghiottisce la Reina. Dipoi dice l'Angelo questa stanza e licenzia ognuno; stage direction after oct. 74.8). We know that the *laudesi* companies across the Arno and the 'Armenians' who staged the Resurrection of Christ were skilled in devising

---

[75] *Vita di S. Giovambatista.* For manuscripts, see *BAI.*

[76] Tornabuoni, *I poemetti,* 88–89 and text, 151–200. For Belcari's play, see chapter 7 below.

pyrotechnic effects, but there is something heartfelt in this injunction that suggests the *coup de scène* was not always entirely successful.

The *festaiuoli* were experimenting with a new acting space. Until the sixteenth century, the terrain sloped down to the river, but there is no indication of whether the action was staged in the middle of that space, or against the wall or the city gate. The acoustics of the place must have presented a challenge. Even though there are reports of the eighteenth-century English preacher George Whitefield addressing and being heard by an attentive congregation of 20,000–80,000,[77] we cannot assume that the audience was able to hear as well as see every part of the play. The audience may have stood or sat spellbound but it is also possible that there were hawkers and hecklers and the usual buzz of the crowd to make hearing difficult. The opening stanzas, where the Baptist preaches in the desert before the action of the play begins, serve to some extent as a crowd-settling device.[78] If the crowd could not get close enough, the story of the city's patron saint was sufficiently broad-featured and well-known that no action would be unrecognized, while the character of the Baptist, sermonizing in the desert, was played by an actor with a voice strong enough to declare: "In water I baptize, I trust in Christ, | and through the wilderness I shout my way" (Battezzo in acqua ed in Cristo mi fido | e con gran boce pel diserto grido; oct. 13.7–8).[79]

There is no indication of the group responsible for this performance, but a clue may lie in the appearance once again of Limbo, which together with the Sepulchre belonged to the Armenians or the company of the Resurrection that met at the church of San Basilio at Canto alla Macine. It is possible that the same wagon or *edificio* was used for the Baptist play, and that the confraternity contributed to or was wholly responsible for it.

The author introduces a further level of experimentation in his treatment of Christ as a character on stage. With its scene of Christ and the Precursor in the Precursor's cell, this is the first of the Florentine plays to invent uncanonical lines for Christ. Jesus appears first on the mount with God the

---

[77] Boren and Roginska, "Analysis of Noise Sources."

[78] On performance in the round and audibility in the English morality play *The Castle of Perseverance* (c. 1440), see Johnston, "The Parliament," 376–377.

[79] A whole stanza of the Baptist's sermon (oct. 8) is based (without irony) on Ulisse's speech to his men in *Inferno* 26.118–20; a similar easy recycling of Dante is found in the Emperor's speech in the *Festa di Ottaviano*: "How can it be that I should be adored | when I was born, eat, drink, and put on clothes" (Come esser può ch'io sia adorato, | che nacqui, mangio, beo e vesto panni; oct. 15.1–2), recalling *Inferno* 30.141.

Father, who may well have been represented by a mask as in the Oltrarno *feste*, rather than by an actor, since he does not speak. The Holy Ghost that descends on Christ after his Baptism is represented by a dove and a hidden voice, but when Christ comes to comfort the Baptist in his prison cell, he is taking on a new role that goes beyond the biblical or liturgical text.

For the visual arts, the most emblematic part of the Baptist's life is the dance of Herod's stepdaughter, which tends to shrink chronologically into a single event combined with the beheading of the Baptist and the servant's return with his head on a salver.[80] The play stretches this moment out and attempts a level of psychological exploration that is scarcely compatible with the size of the performance space. Herod's dismay appears genuine when he is trapped into granting his stepdaughter the Baptist's head. The fine reasoning might escape the audience, but the emotion is evident.

In the prose *Vita*, the beheading of the Baptist is described in gory detail, before the action moves back to the banquet. In the play, the immediate departure of the Soul for Limbo instantly erases the horror of the beheading: the audience must realize at once that it is a dummy, a San Giovanni *contraffatto*, that appears at the door of the prison and is beheaded.[81] The prose *Vita* surrounds the soul with defending angels and riotous devil play,[82] which are not mentioned in the play but are not necessarily absent. The next chapter of the *Vita* begins:

> *How the disciples carried away the body of John the Baptist.* And they carried away that precious body wrapped in a wretched cloak that had been taken from that most blessed body that was

---

[80] Gozzoli's Purification altarpiece of the *Virgin and Child Enthroned among Angels and Saints*, incorporates the scene in its predella; see above, chapter 3, n. 33.

[81] The dummy is not specifically mentioned, but a similar device is used in the play of *Santa Cristina*: "Lo Scalco, mentre che s'ha a scambiare el contrafatto, dice" (The Steward says, while they swap over the dummy [...]; stage direction after oct. 79.2); and in *Sant'Apollonia*: "Hora alquante donne piangono sopra Sancta Apollonia e uno di loro la piglia sotto il mantello, e un altro ne pone quivi una contrafatta che assomigli a santa Apollonia e il manigoldo dice a quelle donne" (Now several women weep over St. Apollonia and one of the men takes her under his mantle and another places a dummy in her place that looks like St. Apollonia and the executioner says to those women [...]; stage direction before oct. 128).

[82] *Vita di S. Giovambatista*, 258–259.

so mangled, without its head, and all bloodied, so that it dripped on the ground.[83]

In the play, the mortuary procession is foreshadowed in the prologue, but it is not mentioned again, presumably because there is no dialogue to accompany it. The *Vita* is the only source of details. As the "fifty thousand" members of the audience dispersed, some at least may have accompanied the 'dead' Baptist back to some confraternal lying in state.

La rappresentazione di san Giorgio martire

There is at least one more play that employs the resources of the festive kingdoms. It is a splendid two-day *Play of St. George the Martyr*, totalling some 232 octaves, of which I have found no record of performance.[84] St. George with the Dragon was an integral part of the San Giovani procession, in continuation of medieval traditions discussed in chapter 4. We know too that members of the youth confraternity of Sant'Antonio da Padova, with their oratory in Costa San Giorgio, were known as San Giorgini both for their location and because they did the San Giorgio play, discussed in chapter 3. In the sixteenth century they were known also as the Compagnia della Gazza (the Magpie Company) and seem to have been transformed to some extent into a festive kingdom with links to the Canto alla Macine,[85] but with insufficient expertise to protect themselves from the patronizing satire of Anton Francesco Grazzini (1503–1584), who charges the San Giorgini with over-reaching:

---

[83] BRF, Ricc. 1408: "*Come i discepoli ne portarono il corpo di Giovanni Batista. E portòronsene quel corpo prezioso rinvolto in uno vile mantelluccio che s'avevano levato da dosso quello beatissimo corpo così smozicato senza la testa e molto insanguinato tanto che gocciolava insino a terra.*"

[84] Day 1: *La rapresentatione di sancto Giorgio martyre* ([Florence: Bartolomeo de' Libri, not after 1495]), ISTC ig00146500; Cioni, *Bibliografia*, 182, xlvi.1. Day 2: BNCF, Magl. vii.293, fols. 71ʳ–86ᵛ. For modern edition, see Table 1. As a two-day play, it is too long to have been part of the procession for St. John the Baptist.

[85] Morpurgo, "La Compagnia della Gazza," 97.

Trovar mai non potete,	You're never going to find
voi san Giorgin, più bella invenzione,	a finer plot, you lovers of Saint George,
da poi che 'l drago avete	because you get to take
ogni anno da mandare a pricissione:	the dragon in procession every year:
dunque per che cagione	so why then do you seek
scioccamente volete,	to show your foolishness
con altre invenzion goffe e sgarbate,	with other crude and foolish frippery,
con musicacce ladre e sgangherate,	with music plagiarized and out of key,
allungar e guastar la pricissione?	to prolong and to spoil the cavalcade?
Ma, se dalle persone,	But if you yearn to find
gloria e onor pure acquistar bramate,	glory and honour with your audience
a tutte l'altre imprese date il volo:	send all your other projects on their way
ed attendete solo	and concentrate on this:
a far più spaventoso il vostro drago,	on making your great dragon scarier,
e più fiero e più vago	and your Saint George more proud
san Giorgio, e la donzella	and handsome, and the Maid
trovar più che potete onesta e bella,	as chaste and beautiful as she can be,
e vestito ed adorno ognun di quella	and have each one of them dressed and adorned
maniera, che conviensi riccamente.	in finery, as custom would dictate.
E stievi ancora a mente	And keep this in your mind:
che la lor compagnia	that all their entourage
bene a cavallo e ben guernita sia:	should ride in well-accoutred cavalcade.
e colla fantasia	And keep your grand ideas
non cercate di far più degne prove:	in check and do not try to overreach;
e l'imprese lasciate altere e nuove	so that all men are pleased and satisfied,
(da contentare e piacere ad ogni uomo)	leave the attempts to do what's brave and new
fare alla compagnia del nostro Como.	to our good Comus and his company.[86]

In the San Giovanni procession the dragon was little more than an accessory, but in the play it has a full role and even its own *luogo deputato* (stage directions after I, oct. 36.3 and 36.8), from which it appears with pyrotechnic effects to consume its victims. It is probably larger in relation to the saint than the one portrayed in the woodcut in Bartolomeo de' Libri's illustrated

---

[86] Grazzini, *Le rime*, 321. The Sangiorgini are invoked also in the *Questione di dua fattori* (Argument between two farmers), the *frottola* appended to the *Rappresentatione d'uno peregrino che andando a santo Jacopo, el diavolo lo ingannò* (Play of a pilgrim who was tricked by the devil on his way to the shrine of St. James); see n. 104 below, and D'Ancona, ed., *Sacre rappresentazioni*, 3:415–433 (431).

edition of c. 1490 (fig. 5.5), and it is later led away from its *luogo deputato* by the Princess Lucilla and taken into town to be slain by St. George's lance.[87]

The play goes far beyond the dragon-leading of the St. John the Baptist procession. Based closely on the account in Jacobus de Voragine's *vita* of St. George, it deals with the more heroic and pathetic aspects of his life on Day 1, and with his military exploits and martyrdom on Day 2. On Day 1, the kingdom of Silena, a city of the island of Libia, is besieged by the dragon that kills King Sileno's finest knights. Citizens are ordered to bring their children, whose names are then drawn by lot for sacrifice to the monster. We watch Massimino being led to his death, then Deidamata, and finally Lucilla, daughter of the king. She is of course saved by the saint, summoned just in time by an Angel, half-way through Day 1 (I, oct. 66). San Giorgio wounds the dragon and the princess leads it back to the city with her girdle. The king and his people are converted, but a disgruntled citizen denounces them all to the emperor Diocliziano in Rome. As Day 1 draws to a close, the emperor prepares for war against Libya and King Sileno, and Daziano king of Persia and the kings of Ethiopia and Ermenìa converge on Rome with their armies. In the final stanza, the emperor says:

Per Giove onnipotente e sommo dio,	By Jupiter, almighty and supreme,
ch'i' non ebbi ma' più tanta allegrezza	I never had more joy than I find here,
quant'or veggendo nel cospetto mio	now that I see before me in my sight
el senno di tre regni e la fortezza:	the wisdom of three kingdoms and their strength:
onde son certo, e più non dubit'io	wherefore I'm certain, and I have no doubt
non ottener di Libia la grandezza:	that I will conquer Libya's great might.
per che, incliti re, pe' mie palagi,	So go, most noble kings, and take your ease
tanto ch'i' parta, prendete vostr'agi.	within my palaces as I depart.
Finita la [prima parte della] festa di santo Giorgio martire.	*End of [the first part of] the play of Saint George the Martyr.*

(I, oct. 111)

The processions of exotic kings appear to exploit resources similar to those of the *festa de' Magi*, and there is a certain regal choreography as the kings sweep into the palaces and as the Roman emperor departs.

---

[87] The woodcut, incorporating the weeping princess, her castle, the knight, and the dragon into a very confined space, has echoes of the miniature tradition. The turrets of the castle in the background certainly suggest a northern European model, represented on a larger scale by Rogier van der Weyden's *Saint George and the Dragon*, now in the National Gallery of Art, Washington DC, inv. 1966.1.1.

Only Day 1 went into print. Day 2 remained unnoticed in a manuscript volume of works largely by members of the Pulci family, BNCF, Magl. VII. 293,[88] where it bears the title of *Il secondo dì di San Giorgio* and continues on directly from the end of the printed edition (figs. 5.6 and 5.7). Day 2 introduces themes that will become increasingly popular in the last quarter of the century: the struggle between paganism and Christianity, between authority and faith; the representation of conversion and glorious martyrdom; the mobilization of huge armies — or representations of them, like those that will return in Lorenzo de' Medici's *San Giovanni e Paulo* — to entertain with mock battles.[89] The emperor and the three kings set out from Rome with their armies to attack King Sileno, but San Giorgio prays for divine intervention, "And going into battle, St. George routs the enemy" (E facendo fatti d'arme, san Giorgio rompe i nimici; stage direction after II, oct. 22). The armies return home to Persia, Ethiopia, and Armenia. An Angel sends San Giorgio to convert Daziano in Persia and the saint takes his leave of Sileno. Even before he arrives, Daziano orders his arrest, and when his torments do the saint no harm, Daziano is convinced that San Giorgio is protected by necromancy. He sends for his own necromancer, Simon Mago, and a poison-drinking contest between San Giorgio and Simon Mago follows, in which the Magus is converted and promptly executed. The saint is to be subjected to a further series of torments, but at every point divine intervention thwarts Daziano's intentions: the wheel shatters, lead cools, fire divides. San Giorgio then feigns submission to the pagan gods, but when the time comes to sacrifice to them, he prays to God and the temple falls in ruins. Daziano is intransigent, but his wife is converted, to which he responds by hanging her by her hair. After a final miracle, the saint is beheaded. Daziano, convinced that he has triumphed, addresses his people, warning them against the folly of serving Christ, before the Angel returns to invoke Christ's blessing and St. George's assistance in the pursuit of divine peace.

Although no record of performance survives, the play is immensely theatrical and draws on a wide range of special effects: pyrotechnics for the dragon, battles, a collapsing temple, torture, and beheading. But, like all of our plays, it is careful to let us see the tricks of verisimilitude. The story is one of Christian steadfastness, but the delight for the audience is a rollicking story, well told.

---

[88] See above, chapter 1.

[89] On armies in plays, see Newbigin, "Armies of God." The battles may have been stylized *armeggerie* or even *moresche* (morris dances).

San Jacopo

Another festive group emerges from the pages of Ser Giusto's diary in the performances of a play or plays of St. James the Great in 1467 and 1473. On the first occasion, while the twenty-three-year-old Galeazzo Maria Sforza was a guest in the house of Piero di Cosimo de' Medici (because he did not like the apartments in Santa Maria Novella), the feast of St. James was celebrated by a play at San Jacopo tra le Fosse. Ser Giusto records:

> Saturday 25 [July 1467] was the feast of St. James [the Great] in Florence. They did a beautiful performance at San Jacopo tra le Fosse of the play of the martyrdom of St. James.[90]

A similar note six years later offers slightly more context:

> Sunday 1 August [1473], in Florence, in front of the church of San Jacopo tra le Fosse they did a performance of the play of St. James. It was done by some young men of the company. The set was beautiful, and well-devised.[91]

The same location, this time called the "canto degli Alberti," was used again in August 1482, when Andrea di Piero de' Medici and Zanobi di Nicola Salvetti borrowed "beech-wood or fir-wood planks in the number needed" from the Operai del Duomo "for setting up and finishing the stages that are to be erected at the Canto degli Alberti for the purpose of staging or performing there the play of St. James, commonly called *the Play of the Pilgrim*."[92] I shall return to this second St. James play presently.

---

[90] Giusti, "I *Giornali*," 152: "Sabato a dì 25 detto [di luglio 1467] fu la festa di San Iacomo in Firenze. Si fece una bella festa a San Iacomo tra le Fosse della rappresentazione del martorio di San Iacomo."

[91] Giusti, "I *Giornali*," 177: "Domenica a dì primo d'agosto [1473] in Firenze dinanzi alla chiesa di San Iacopo tra le Fosse si fece una festa della rappresentazione di San Iacopo. Fecerla certi giovani della compagnia. Fu bello apparato e bene ordinato."

[92] AOSMF, II 2 6, Deliberazioni, 1482–1486, fol. 33v (4 August 1482): "assium fagum et seu abietum usque ad numerum oportunum [...] pro aptando et perficiendo pulpita erigenda iuxta angulum de Albertis in civitate Florentie pro demostrando et seu representantum festum ibidem sancti Jacobi, quod festum a vulgaribus dicitur la festa del Pellegrino"; see G. Poggi, *Il Duomo*, 2:204, no. 2405.

The piazza in front of San Jacopo tra le Fosse, now the Chiesa Evangelica or Methodist Church of Florence, is tiny when compared to the larger areas of Piazza Santa Croce and Piazza San Marco, and it sits on a major thoroughfare from Ponte alle Grazie.[93] The "young men of the company" may well have been members of the youth confraternity of San Niccolò del Ceppo, founded in 1417, whose oratory was "in the parish of San Jacopo tra' Fossi."[94] As we shall see, the intimacy of the acting space, with more favourable acoustics, encouraged an increased interest in words and argument over spectacle and visual effects.

Rappresentazione di San Jacopo Maggiore

A play of the martyrdom of St. James the Great is found in the miscellany copied between 1470 and 1473 by Giovanni di Antonio Scarlatti.[95] Following the saint's life as it is told in the *Legenda Aurea*,[96] the play begins with the sorcerer Ermogene who sends Fileto to spy on the preaching of the saint. Fileto returns converted and tells Ermogene that his books will be the cause of his damnation. Ermogene calls on Satan, who sends a devil to immobilize Fileto, but Fileto manages to send word to San Jacopo, who responds with a kerchief by which Fileto is freed. In a spectacle of impotent rage, Ermogene summons up a legion of devils:

O Belzabù, prencipe de' dimoni,	O prince of all the demons, Beelzebub,
che se' di sotto a tutta la Caina,	submerged beneath the bottom of Cain's ice,
piaciati d'assaldir le mie orazioni.	I pray to you to grant me what I ask.
Mandami Sïataca e Calcabrina,	Send to me Calcabrina and Siataca,
Farferello, Ciriatto, Scarmiglioni,	Farfarel, Ciriatto and Scarmigliòn,
e Barbericcia colla sua decina,	and Barbericcia with his troop of ten,
e venga Rubicante e Draghinazzo,	and Rubicante and Draghinazzo too,
e Graffiacan, Libicocco e Cagnazzo.	Graffiacan, Libicocco and Cagnazzo.

(oct. 19)

---

[93] Marco di Bartolomeo Rustici links the church to James the Less; *Codice Rustici: Dimostrazione*, 2:136, cap. 78.

[94] See chapter 3, n. 5.

[95] VBAMi, C 35 sup., fols. 154ʳ–160ᵛ, 48 octaves; for edition, see Table 1.

[96] Jacobus, *Legenda Aurea*, 1:726–739, xcv *De Iacobo Apostolo*.

The lineage of these comic devils can be traced back to Dante's *Malebranche* (Evil Claws) in the *bolgia* (ditch) of the thieves, *Inferno* 21–23, where for more than 200 lines the poet offers his own version of a devil pageant, recalling the one of 1304 that caused the collapse of Ponte alla Carraia.[97] We do not know where Dante's names came from, but we have here a clear incorporation of his poem into popular culture, an appropriation that leads to an exploration of diabolical magic. As in the St. George play already examined, and the Peter and Paul play discussed below, we witness a magic contest between the saint and the sorcerer that provides the comic core of the *rappresentazione* and invites the use of charming stage gimmicks. Ermogene sends the devils to fetch Jacopo but the saint, protected by an Angel, fights them off. Cowardly and comic, they beg his mercy. Jacopo issues a counter-order: that they should go and fetch Ermogene. The sorcerer gathers up his pagan books, lamenting:

O falsi libri, o scienza mondana,	O lying books, O knowledge of this world,
che se' cagion di tanti danni e mali!	you are the cause of so much harm and woe.
O poesia, o filosafia vana,	O poetry, O vain philosophy,
la tua superbia è velen de' mortali!	your pride is poison to all mortal men.
Più seppe e 'ntese la Sammaritana	The woman of Samaria understood
che non fanno e filosafi bestiali!	and knew more than the brute philosophers.
Gli uomin dotti e superbi son dannati,	The men of pride and learning are all damned,
e ' semplici e gli umili in Ciel beati.	the simple and the humble bless'd in Heaven.

---

[97] See above, chapter 4, n. 79. Dante's Alichino (*Inferno* 21.118, a distant antecedent of Harlequin of the *commedia dell'arte*) is missing from this list; but he reappears in the legion of devils that comes for the soul of the Rich Man in the Dives and Pauper play, *Festa di Lazero ricco e Lazero povero*, oct. 37.1, transmitted by the same manuscript, fols. 114ᵛ–121ʳ; see Delcorno, "La *Festa di Lazero rico*," 129. We also find Malacoda and Libicocco in the *Rappresentazione d'uno miracolo di Nostra Donna che per mezzo d'uno peregrino risuscitò el figliuolo d'uno Re che cascava di quel mal male* (Play of a miracle of Our Lady who, through a pilgrim, raised from the dead a king's son who suffered from the falling sickness), oct. 7–8, 45, 48, 91. Calcabrino and Farfalletto appear in *Teofilo che si dette al diavolo* (Theophilus who gave himself to the devil), oct. 21, 30. See also Del Popolo, *Tra sacro e profano*, 31.

Che vale ormai la gran filosofia	What use now is the great philosophy
d'Aristotile, Socrate o Platone?	of Aristotle, Socrates, or Plato?
Che vale al Mantovan la poesia,	What use is poetry to the Mantuan,
Omero, Orazio, Lucano o Nansone?	to Homer, Horace, Lucan, or to Ovid?
Che vale a Tolomeo l'astrologia?	What use astrology to Ptolemy?
Che giova e libri che fe' Cecerone?	What use lies in the books of Cicero?
De' negromanti e libri son più rei,	More evil are these books than necromancers,
però arder vo' tutti e libri miei.	and for this reason I'll burn all my books.

(oct. 27–28)

The names of the pagan authors whose works are to be destroyed are the dramatist's addition to the *vita*, but the scene hints at misgivings about classical learning and its connections with forbidden arcana long before Savonarola's intrusion onto the Florentine stage. Ermogene gives them to Jacopo to burn, but Jacopo orders him to cast them to the bottom of the sea, distribute his treasure to the poor, and accept baptism. Jacopo is denounced to the High Priest and condemned to death. On the way to his execution, he heals Josia, who resolves to die with him, and baptizes him, promising:

oggi vedremo in Ciel, compagno mio,	today in heav'n, my friend, we'll surely see
Gesù, figliuol d'Iddio, nostro Signore,	Jesus our Lord who is the son of God,
in compagnia degli angeli e santi	accompanied by angels and by saints
che ci faranno festa tutti quanti.	who will rejoice together with us all.

(oct. 47.5–8)

According to tradition, St. James's body was borne on a boat to Galicia, but there is no stage direction to that effect. The play ends not with an Angel but with the saint's invocation of the Lord's mercy on those who pray to him in the saint's name (oct. 48).

La festa del pellegrino

A second play, called *The Play of the Pilgrim* in the manuscript tradition and *The Three Pilgrims who went to St. James in Galicia* in the printed tradition, presents a miracle of St. James the Great. It enjoyed wide popularity and is known in five manuscripts of its first redaction, and in two further printed redactions under various titles.[98] In all its versions it tells of three pilgrims, mother, father, and son, who go on a pilgrimage to the shrine of St. James at Compostela. On the way, an innkeeper's wanton daughter attempts to seduce the son and, when she is scorned, she secretes a silver cup in his scrip and has him arrested and hanged. The grieving parents continue to Compostela, but on their return journey they find that their son has been supported on the gallows by St. James himself and that he is still alive. The news is reported to the governor of the place, who is banqueting. He declares that it is more likely that the roasted fowl on his table should stand up and crow than that their son should be alive — at which point the hen and the rooster come to life. The innkeeper and his wife are hanged, the daughter Fiammetta is consumed in a bonfire, and the pilgrims return home singing and rejoicing.[99]

Stefano Infessura tells us that "a representation of St. James" was performed in Rome by Florentine *festaiuoli* for the Neapolitan princess Eleonora of Aragon as she travelled to Ferrara in 1473.[100] We have no way of knowing whether it was this play or another, but three years later yet another version of the play was performed in Ferrara. It was described by Girolamo Ferrarini:

> *Festa done and performed about a man who could not have children.*
> On Sunday 16 June [1476] a Florentine, together with other men from our city, having had a long stage and scenery set up along

---

[98] For manuscripts and editions, see Tables 1 and 2, St. James the Great. For Text A, see *Rappresentatione duno mracolo di tre Peregrini che andauono a sancto Iacopo di Galitia* ([Florence: Tubini e Ghirlandi, not after 1515]), CNCE 62082, beginning "Devoti, honesti e magni cittadini"; ending "Voi peregrini, andate a vostra via"; Cioni, *Bibliografia*, 178–179, xlv.1 (see also 2, 3, 6); for Text B, see *La rappresentatione di tre pellegrini che andorno allo Apostolo San Jacopo di Galitia* ([Florence: n.p., after 1550]), CNCE 53315, beginning "Benigni aspettatori, al cui cospetto"; ending "questa historia è finita al vostro onore"; Cioni, *Bibliografia*, 179–180, xlv.4, 7, 9, 10, 11, 16 (others not seen). This second printed redaction, of which there is no modern edition, does not stage the execution of the innkeeper and his daughter.

[99] The miracle of the cock and the hen is associated with Santo Domingo de la Calzada but passed to St. James of Compostela. The narrative elements of the play, with the addition of a vow to the saint by the childless couple that is fulfilled in the journey, are also found in an anonymous *cantare* of twenty-nine octaves, *Miracolo dei tre pellegrini a Sant'Iacopo di Gallizia* (Miracle of the three pilgrims to St. James in Galicia); in *Miracolo*, ed. Menghini; Battelli, ed., *Le più belle leggende*, 169–177.

[100] Infessura, *Diario*, 78: "una rappresentazione di santo Jacovo." Other accounts do not mention this play.

the side of the tax collectors' offices in our city of Ferrara, did a play about a man who could not have children and made a vow to St. James that if he did have one, he would go and visit his shrine. And so, as a result of the vow, his wife became pregnant and they had a son. Then, on their journey to St. James, this son was hanged because the innkeeper said he had stolen a cup; and his daughter, who was enamored of him, had put it in his purse, and how this became public. The *festa* began four hours before sunset and lasted two hours. I stood and watched it from the second balcony on the piazza, with Messer Sigismondo and Gurone d'Este.[101]

It seems plausible that the St. James play performed by the Florentine *festaiuoli* in Rome for Eleonora in June 1473 is the same as the one that was performed in Florence less than two months later and again in Ferrara in June 1476 just before the birth of Eleonora's first son. Sergio Costola notes that the printed texts (like the manuscripts) do not refer to a vow, but nothing precludes a new prologue that makes this connection.[102]

Miraculous survival of hanging is a recurrent theme in late medieval miracle collections.[103] A version of this miracle is recounted in the life of St. James the Great in the *Legenda Aurea*, but without the innkeeper's daughter or the miraculous poultry. The play's charm lies in its domesticity, as Jacobus

---

[101] Ferrarini, *Memoriale*, 45: "*Festa facta et representatione de uno che non poteva haver filioli.* A dì domenega 16 zugno [1476] uno fiorentino, inseme cum altri dela città nostra, havendo facto fare et parare uno tribunale lungo dal lato dele bolete dela città nostra di Ferrara, fece una representacione de uno el quale non poteva haver fioli, qual fece vodo a sancto Iacobo se ne haveva de andare a visitare la giesia sua. Et così per il voto la dona sua se impregnò et ne hebe uno. Qual filiolo poi andagando a Sancto Iacobo fu apichato perché lo hosto diceva che ge haveva robata la taza, et la fiola sua, innamorata di epso, l'aveva mesa in le sue tasche, como de questo se fe' publice. Comenzò dicta festa ad hore 20 et ad hore 22 fu finita. Io steti a vedere tal cosa suso il segondo pozollo de piaza, sopra il qual era messer Sigismondo et Gurone da Este." I amend "se sa' publice" to "se fe' publice." See also Coppo, "Spettacoli," 43. Zambotti, *Diario*, 1:11, specifies that the stage was erected "in front of the customs collector's office, opposite the bishop's palace" (denanti a l'officio de le bolette, aprovo la cha' del vescho).

[102] Costola, "Storia," 214; Costola, 209–210, proposes the *cantare* (see n. 99 above) as the source of the play. On the Ferrarese performance, see also Calore, *Pubblico e spettacolo*, 28; Lipani, "*Con sanctissima pompa*" and "Lo spettacolo sacro."

[103] See, for example, *Miracoli della gloriosa Vergine Maria* (1500), fols. 23ʳ–24ʳ, cap. XXIII *D'uno huomo molto diuoto della madre di Christo Iesù il quale contro a ragione fu iustitiato & come fu aiutato da llei.*

de Voragine's German father and son are transformed into a quintessentially Florentine nuclear family; and in the theatrical illusions required by these miracles: the saint who supports the dummy representing the hanged son (figs. 5.8 and 5.9);[104] the dancing fowls; and the carefully constructed bonfire in which the dummy of the innkeeper's daughter is burned. Although fireworks are a regular feature of plays in churches, it is likely that the outdoor location of all these performances allowed a full-scale bonfire that was so much part of street celebrations. The action moves briskly — even comically — to Compostela and back, and the moral message appears to be that chaste and obedient sons will always enjoy divine protection, even when it appears to have been lost. In the second printed redaction, this is further underscored when the son is invited to avoid punishment by marrying the innkeeper's daughter but refuses because he has taken a vow of chastity.

Florentine festaiuoli *in Rome, 1473*

The fame of the Florentine *rappresentazioni* led to an exceptional event in the summer of 1473. As the Neapolitan princess Eleonora of Aragon travelled to Ferrara with her entourage for her marriage to Ercole d'Este, she stopped in Rome, where she was entertained lavishly with banquets, gifts, and a series of *rappresentazioni* performed by Florentine *festaiuoli* at the behest of Pietro Riario. Cardinal of San Sisto and nephew of Pope Sixtus IV, Riario would be named archbishop of Florence on 20 July, but it seems that he could already call on Florentine resources. We do not know, however, whether large numbers of actors travelled from Florence for the occasion, or whether the actors were drawn from the large Florentine community in Rome that centred around the church of San Giovanni dei Fiorentini.[105]

---

[104] Two other plays of miracles of St James, with woodcuts by the same hand, were issued at the same time: *Rappresentatione duno peregrino, che andando a sancto Iacopo, el diauolo lo inganno* ([Florence: Antonio Tubini and Andrea Ghirlandi] for Zanobi dalla Barba, [1510–1515]), CNCE 62046; and *Rappresentatione duno miracolo di duo peregrini che andorono a sancto Iacopo di Galitia* ([Florence: Antonio Tubini and Andrea Ghirlandi, before 8 August 1515]), ISTC ir00029625 and CNCE 62048; for editions, see Table 2. The woodcut in fig. 5.9 may relate to a miracle of St. Nicholas of Tolentino; see, for example, Zanobi Machiavelli, *St. Nicholas of Tolentino Saving a Hanged Man*, 1470, Amsterdam, Rijksmuseum, inv. SK-A03442; and also Newbigin, "Le rappresentazioni fiorentine."

[105] D'Ancona, *Origini*, 1:287–288; Ferroni, "Appunti"; and documents republished with an important introduction in Cruciani, *Teatro*, 151–164. Riario had been appointed cardinal of San Sisto on 15 December 1471, and of Santi Apostoli in November 1472, and

Stefano Infessura, who would later himself be involved in the Gonfalone confraternity's Passion plays in the Colosseum, recorded in his diary a brief description of the stage and loggia around the square.[106] Further details are supplied by Bernardo Corio:

> They arrived at Santi Apostoli, where the Cardinal of San Sisto (who could really be called the supreme pontiff) had ordered the whole piazza to be covered with awnings, and along the side of the piazza there were three new open rooms, done in the antique style, with columns covered with greenery and flowers, and above there was a frieze, which was very rich and beautiful, with the arms of the Pope, the cardinal of San Sisto, the king of Naples, the duke of Milan, and Duke Hercules of Ferrara. One room was very long, and all set up for the banquet and to watch the games that were to be played, and the other rooms were for performing certain plays.[107]

The next day, which was Pentecost, 6 June, "at midday the play of Susanna was performed in the rooms just described, by some Florentines, with the most natural gestures, and with more skill than one can imagine."[108] The play was

---

would be archbishop of Florence for less than six months, from 20 July 1473 until his death on 5 January 1474; see also Farenga, "*Monumenta*."

[106] Infessura, *Diario*, 77; see also Corvisieri, "Il trionfo romano," 643–644.

[107] Corio, *Storia*, 2:1385–1386, citing Teofilo Calcagnini, letter to Ercole d'Este, Rome, 7 June 1473, now Padua, Biblioteca Universitaria, Ms. 342, fols. 54ᵛ–59ʳ: "Giunti a Sancto Apostolo, dove il prefato cardinale de San Sixto, *qui vere dici poterat summus pontifex*, havea facto coprire tutta quella piaza de velle e da lato de la piaza tre sale aperte, nuove, facte a la fogia antiqua con colonne coperte a fogliami e fiori et uno friso sopra richissimo e bello con le arme dil papa, dil cardinale San Sixto, del re di Napoli, dil duca de Milano e del duca Hercule de Ferrara. L'una sala era molto lunga, apparata per fare il convito e per spectare li giochi se havevano a fare, e le altre sale erano per fare certe rapresentatione." For the identification of Corio's source, see Cruciani, *Teatro*, 154–155.

[108] Corio, *Storia di Milano*, 2:1389: "il mezo dì se fece ne le sale demonstrate la rapresentatione de Susanna per alchuni Fiorentini con li più veri acti e più aptamente se puotesse existimare." I have amended "apertamente" to "aptamente," as in the 1503 edition, fol. O3ʳ. Eleonora herself describes it: "At Vespers, the cardinal of San Sisto [Pietro Riario] arranged for a play of the *Story of Susanna* to be staged, truly a very beautiful thing and worth watching" (In so lo vespero lu cardinale de san Sixto fe' fare una rapresentatione de la storia de Susanna, cosa veramente multa bella et dingna ad vedere); letter to Diomede

almost certainly the *Festa di Susanna*, copied as early as 1465 and always a suitable subject for wedding chests and for brides.

On Monday, Eleonora was entertained with a spectacular banquet that framed a series of mythological representations of grimmer aspects of love and marriage: Heracles and Deianira, Jason and Medea, Theseus and Phaedra, Bacchus and Ariadne,[109] but on Tuesday the entertainments were once again sacred, if violent. "On Tuesday they did the play about that Jew who roasted the body of Christ; and on Wednesday they did the one of St. John the Baptist when he was beheaded."[110] Infessura adds a play of St. James ("di santo Iacovo"), and tells us further that on 29 June, the feast day of Sts. Peter and Paul, Riario sponsored what was in effect a transposed *festa di San Giovanni Battista*, in honour of the patron saints of Rome.

La rappresentazione d'uno miracolo del Corpo di Cristo

Of the plays performed by Florentines for Eleonora in Rome, the *Miracle of the Body of Christ* stands out. In Florence, the annual procession for the feast of Corpus Domini is documented only from 1425 and was hotly contested for decades between the Dominican friars of Santa Maria Novella and the canons of Santa Maria del Fiore. It began, I have argued elsewhere, partly as a response to what was seen as the figurative cult of the Holy Name of Jesus that was preached by the Franciscan friar Bernardino of Siena.[111] A truce was reached in 1461, when the friars and the canons combined in a single procession and celebration, and by 1472, according to Benedetto Dei, the feast was celebrated every year in Santa Maria Novella: "They do the great *festa* of Corpus Domini in the same month [June] in Santa Maria [Novella]."[112] Around that year, a play was grafted to the Corpus Domini solemnities in Florence,

---

Carafa, June 1473, cited in Corvisieri, "Il trionfo romano," 647–648. On Susanna, see chapter 3 above.

[109] Deianira accidentally killed her husband Hercules with a poisoned shirt; Medea murdered Jason's children and his new wife; Phaedra betrayed Theseus with Hippolytus, then accused Hippolytus of rape; Ariadne, abandoned by Theseus, was consoled by Bacchus.

[110] Corio, *Storia di Milano*, 2:1392: "Il martedì fu facta la representatione di quello iudeo che rostì il corpo de Christo; et il mercoledì se fece quella di sancto Ioanne Baptista secundo che fo decapitato."

[111] Newbigin, "Imposing Presence."

[112] Dei, *La cronica*, 93: "Fàssi la gran festa del Chorpo di Christo, in detto mese [di giugno], a Santa Maria [Novella]." This, rather than a *festa* of St. Ignatius as proposed by

and in 1473 Florentine *festaiuoli* performed it or a similar play in Rome. In 1477, Ser Giusto Giusti recorded in his diary: "Thursday 5 [June] was the feast of Corpus Domini in Florence. The feast day was beautiful, with beautiful processions, and at Santa Maria Novella they did the play of the *Festa del Corpo di Cristo*."[113] In 1502 it was done again, on the Sunday after Corpus Domini, with lavish expenditure, along with a new play by a new author, the *Rappresentazione di san Venanzio* by Castellano Castellani, on the steps in front of the ornate facade that had been completed in 1470:

> On 29 May 1502 they did the *Play of a Miracle of the Body of Christ*, and then the *Play of San Venanzio*; it was a beautiful *festa*, with a stage that went right across the steps of the church, for the full width of Piazza Santa Maria Novella at that end, and the *festa* cost the men of the confraternity of St. Thomas Aquinas 150 gold *scudi larghi* from their own purses.[114]

The *Representation of a Miracle of the Body of Christ*, as it survives in print (fig. 5.10),[115] is based on what is essentially a Parisian story set in the year 1290 that had been retold by Villani in his *Nuova cronaca* and had thus become part also of Florence's history.[116] A Jew has lent money to a woman against the pledge of her cloak. When she wants her cloak back for Easter Day, he proposes that she redeem it with a consecrated host, which he then places in a pan over the fire. His sacrilege is betrayed by the blood that flows from it;

Vasari, was the responsibility of the quarter of Santa Maria Novella. See Fineschi, *Della festa*; Borsook, "Cults and Imagery"; Newbigin, "Imposing Presence."

[113] Giusti, "I *Giornali*," 193: "Giovedì a dì 5 detto [di giugno] fu la festa del Corpo di Cristo in Firenze. Si fece bella festa e belle processioni, e fecesi a Santa Maria Novella la rappresentazione di detta festa del Corpo di Cristo. Fucci gran popolo."

[114] Cambi, *Istorie* 21 (1785): 176–177: "Addì 29 di Maggio 1502 si fiece la rapresentatione d'un miracholo del Chorpo di Christo, e dipoi la rappresentatione di San Venantio Martire, bellissima festa, che ffu un palcho, che teneva tutte le schalee della Chiesa, e quanto era lassù larga la piazza di Santa Maria Novella, e chostò detta festa scudi 150 larghi d'oro agli uomini della Chonpagnia dell'Aquino, e di borsa loro." I amend "scudi 150 l'anno d'oro" to "scudi 150 larghi d'oro." See also D'Ancona, *Origini*, 1:333. See further discussion in chapter 9 below.

[115] *Larapresentatione d'uno miracolo del corpo di Christo* ([Florence: Bartolomeo de' Libri, not after 1495]), ISTC ir00029550; Cioni, *Bibliografia*, 171, XLII.1; for modern edition, see Table 2.

[116] Villani, *Nuova cronica*, 1:616–617, VIII.143.

he is seized and burned, and a church is built to sanctify the site. In the hands of the Florentine dramatist, the story is framed within the Miracle of Bolsena and the foundation of the feast of Corpus Domini, and ranges from the court of the king of France to the cells of the Dominican friar Thomas Aquinas and the Franciscan friar Bonaventura. It focuses on the inn where Guglielmo Giambelcari loses his money, the pawnbroking shop of Manuel the Jew where he pawns his wife's cloak, and his house. The woman's plight is caused by her feckless, gambling husband, and at the end she is saved from execution by the intervention of St. Thomas Aquinas, who appears in a dream to the king of France. The Jews are summoned by name and are beaten by the soldiers.[117]

We do not know the circumstances of the earlier Florentine performances, but it is possible to contrast the Roman performance of 1473 and the Florentine revival of 1502. In Rome, the play was appropriated by Franciscan interests. Sixtus IV and his cardinal-nephew Pietro Riario were Franciscans and dedicated to the advancement both of their order and of the Monte di Pietà, the new Christian lending fund that was promoted heavily in other centres as a means of freeing poor Christians from the clutches of 'perfidious' Jewish moneylenders. The play is part of a long tradition of propaganda against usury, which was considered the dire fate that awaited those who gambled. The cardinal's choice of *this* play, performed in the square in front of Santissimi Apostoli, is far less appropriate to the occasion than the *Susanna* of the previous day. If this has any message for the bride, it is that salvation is possible even when one is married to a boozing, gambling, blaspheming, and devious husband. Given the relatively narrow dimensions of the piazza — though it was larger then than it is now — it is not clear that any more than the princess's immediate entourage could have been in the square. The Roman performance was not to instruct the *popolo* but rather to impress and entertain the royal guest. The princess herself was part of the spectacle, along with the credenza of silverware. The awnings that covered the square, the 'rooms' that accommodated the banqueting princess on one side, and, opposite her, the stage and the performers made this a private affair.

In Florence, the play remained closely affiliated to Dominican interests. The Dominicans of Santa Maria Novella, who maintained their distance from Savonarola and his followers in San Marco, had long struggled against the Canons of the Cathedral for 'ownership' of the Corpus Domini procession,

---

[117] Rubin, *Gentile Tales*; R.L.A. Clark, "Host Desecration"; Delcorno, "Dare credito," in particular 214–225; Delcorno, "'E i miei denari.'"

and now, on the Monday after Trinity Sunday, just three months before Soderini's election as *gonfaloniere a vita*, they restated their claim with a play
about a Jewish moneylender. The play thus occupied a very public space that
was designed for sermons,[118] and enacted a subject — the real Presence of
Christ in the Host — that had been central to the Dominican claim to the
feast.

In Florence as in Rome, the Franciscans were engaged from mid-century in an escalating program of preaching against the Jews.[119] In 1437 Jewish
moneylenders had been given a *condotta* or licence to operate by the state,
as part of a scheme to limit the power of the Arte del Cambio or Bankers'
Guild.[120] Four decades later, the aim of the mendicant orders was to disestab-
lish Jewish pawnbroking and allow the expulsion of the moneylenders, but
the Medici succeeded in keeping both the preachers and the Monte at bay
until their exile in 1494. The Monte di Pietà, first mooted in Florence in 1473,
was finally established there in 1495, between the expulsion of the Medici in
1494 and the death of Savonarola in 1498. The return of the play in 1502 once
more justifies that victory.

It has been customary to link the play and its woodcut to Paolo Uccello's predella panels (1467–1468) for the *Corpus Domini* altarpiece painted
for the Urbino confraternity of the Sacrament, but it is more closely related to
a predella panel (one of a possible three or four) for an unknown altarpiece
attributed to Bartolomeo della Gatta (fig. 5.11). This panel has been dated to
around 1485, but nothing is known of its original destination. If the dating
is correct, the creator of the woodcut may have drawn on the arrangement
of figures in Bartolomeo's painting. The panel shows on the left the errant
husband gambling in the inn and on the right his wife redeeming her cloak,
while the pawnbroker and his son stab the Host as it cooks over the flames.[121]
Paris in 1290 has become a generic Tuscan scene of the late fifteenth century.

----

[118] For the enlargement of the piazza in front of Santa Maria Novella to accommodate
the sermons of St. Peter Martyr, see Meersseman, ed., *Dossier*, 191–192.

[119] Owen-Hughes, "Distinguishing Signs"; Mormando, *The Preacher's Demons*,
164–218.

[120] Fubini "Prestito ebraico," 119–120; Delcorno, "The Roles of Jews," 254–260.

[121] See Lavin, "The Altar"; Goukovskj, "A Representation"; C. Martelli, *Bartolomeo
della Gatta*, 191–195; 327–328. A second panel from the same altarpiece, formerly in the
Hirsch Collection in Basel, was sold by Sotheby's, London, 20–21 June 1978; reproduced
in Martelli, 192.

Rappresentazione di san Pietro e san Pagolo

The last open-air play I shall examine is the *Play of St. Peter and St. Paul.*
Giusto Giusti once again provides the only record of a performance:

> Sunday 29 June [1477] in Florence was the feast day of St. Peter.
> On the Loggia de' Signori they did the *festa* of *Play of St. Peter
> and St. Paul.* There was a great crowd of people to see it and in
> the evening they set fire to the *girandola*, which they hadn't done
> on the feast day of San Giovanni. And it went well and was a
> great display of the skill of the person who made it.[122]

The play came at the height of the summer holy-day season, but possibly at the expense of the procession of *edifici*. After the processions of Corpus
Domini (on 5 June), the palio of Sant'Onofrio (12 June), the vigil and feast-
day processions for the Nativity of St. John the Baptist (23–24 June), and the
horse races for St. John the Baptist and San Lò (St. Aloysius or Eligius) on 24
and 25 June, the feast day of the founders of the Roman church was celebrated
on 29 June. The addition of a Peter and Paul play to the midsummer festivities
seems excessive, but in 1477 the traditional communal festivities were at their
absolute peak.

The single surviving Florentine Peter and Paul play text is probably slightly earlier than 1477. It is contained in the *zibaldone* of Giovanni
d'Antonio Scarlatti, bearing dates that range between 1470 and 1473, so the
performance in 1477 may not have been the first.[123] Devotion to St. Peter
and St. Paul seems to have been centred in the Oltrarno.[124] Florentine victory
in the Battle of Anghiari, fought on their feast day of 29 June 1440, was the

---

[122] Giusti, "I *Giornali*," 194: "Domenica a dì 29 giugno in Firenze fu la festa di San
Piero. Fecesi in su la loggia de' Signori la festa della Rappresentazione della morte di San
Piero e di San Pagolo. Fucci gran moltitudine di popolo a vederla; e la sera si diede fuoco
alla girandola, ché non s'era fatto il dì di San Giovanni. E fece bene e gran dimostrazione
d'ingegno di chi l'aveva fatta." The last sentence probably refers to the *girandola* or firework
apparatus, rather than the play.

[123] *Qui inchomincia la rapresentazione di san Piero e di san Pagholo appostoli*, VBAMi,
C 35 sup., fols. 169ʳ–187ʳ. For edition, see Table 1. For a detailed discussion of the play in
relation to the Brancacci Chapel, see Newbigin, "Playing in the Piazza."

[124] I note however that the youth confraternity of the Vangelista, under the control of
the men's flagellant company of San Paolo, paid annual tribute on the feast of the Conversion of St. Paul, BMoF, Palagi 114, fols. 10ᵛ, 77ʳ⁻ᵛ.

result of a miraculous vision in Santa Maria del Carmine granted through the intervention of the Carmelite *beato* Andrea Corsini. Subsequently, the Commune made an annual oblation to the friars on that day and, as the fresco decoration of the Brancacci chapel was completed by Filippino Lippi, the friars ensured that the *vita* of St. Paul was incorporated coherently into the life of St. Peter already painted by Masaccio.[125]

The play must have lasted anywhere from one to three hours depending on the amount of stage business the actors provided. The Angel's prologue sets out the play's three parts, which correspond to elements taken from Peter's three feast days as they are commemorated in the *Legenda Aurea*: the raising of Gamaliel, son of Teofilo, who has been dead for fifteen years (from the Chair of St. Peter, 22 February); St. Peter's liberation from prison (from St. Peter in Chains, 1 August); and the battle between Peter — that is, Simon who was called Peter — and his antagonist Simon Magus (from St. Peter and St. Paul, 29 June).[126] The death of Simon Magus leads directly to the deaths of the two saints, Paul elsewhere, and Peter — or rather a dummy representing him — in full view of the spectators.

The play's narrative does not derive directly from the lives of the saints as they are partitioned in the *Legenda Aurea*, but rather it weaves them freely together to create a contrast between the true miracles worked by Christ through Simon Peter and the false miracles of his antagonist Simon Magus. This contrast is the pretext for a series of grandiose *coups de théâtre* enacted between the *ringhiera* (ceremonial steps) of the Palazzo de' Signori and the other natural stage of the Loggia de' Lanzi.[127] Each effect is carefully crafted not through the stage directions but through the dialogue itself.

The play rejoices in its special effects: when the father demands a miracle, Peter drives out the demon that inhabits the pagan idol and casts it to the ground; when he demands a further miracle, Peter agrees and is led to

---

[125] See Eckstein, *Painted Glories*.

[126] Jacobus, *Legenda Aurea*, 1:316–323, XLIV *De cathedra Sancti Petri*; 1:626–643, LXXXIV *De Sancto Petro*; 1:784–793, CVI *De Sancto Petro ad Vincula*; see also 1:644–667, LXXXV *De Sancto Paolo*; and 1:232–235, XXVIII *De conversione Sancti Paoli*; together with Acts of the Apostles 12. In the fourteenth-century vernacular book of legends, BMLF, Ashb. 395, fols. 27ʳ–38ᵛ, for example, the three chapters on St. Peter and the two of St. Paul, fols. 38ᵛ–45ʳ, are brought together into one sequence; see *Le Vite di Santi del codice Magliabechiano*, 253–255.

[127] For further discussion of the Loggia dei Lanzi as stage, see Strocchia, "Theatres," 67.

the tomb where the son's bones lie. St. Peter prays, and the son is wondrously restored, from pile of bones to naked youth. The king sends at once for rich clothes, and father and son are baptized, while Peter is given a royal throne. When Simon Magus flies with the help of demons, Simon Peter shoots him down with a prayer, upon which Nero orders his execution (fig. 5.12).[128] The young actors — who apologize in the *licenza* for their lack of experience — are clearly well-equipped to deliver the play (oct. 138.4–5).

The Costs of Festive Magnificence

The large public plays like the *Magi* and *San Bartolomeo* involved the participation of huge numbers of citizens, but none have left descriptions of how they viewed their roles. What does survive, however, is a solid body of evidence that documents the way in which plays inhabited public spaces: preaching spaces in front of churches, a civic space like the Piazza della Signoria, and a space beyond the walls, like the Prato della Giustizia. In contrast to confraternal spaces and private gardens, these spaces were subject to external controls and limitations on the way they were used, but with the exception of the Judgment play, moved in 1454 from San Miniato al Monte to outside Porta San Gallo,[129] I have found no communal interventions in the location of the plays, and no evidence of external censorship or self-censorship beyond the constant reworking of favourite themes like the Prodigal Son, Joseph the Patriarch, and the Nativity. Only in the celebrations of St. John the Baptist, of which the city as a whole claimed ownership, were the individual performance groups regularly subjected to external control, that is, until Lorenzo's return to festive politics in 1488.

---

[128] Benozzo Gozzoli painted this scene twice, once for the Purification Altarpiece (1461; see above, chapter 3, n. 33), and again for the Alessandri Polyptych (1442–1444? or after 1461?, New York, Metropolitan Museum of Art, 15.106.1). In both cases the 'scenography' appears to anticipate the episode in the *Rappresentazione di San Piero e San Pagolo*. In both versions, the emperor Nero is seated on a throne positioned on a raised podium (which is the standard iconography for scenes of command and judgment from Giotto onwards, and in the woodcuts of the printed *rappresentazioni*), while Simon Magus, who appears twice in the picture, launches himself from a trestle and is held aloft by demons until he crashes in the foreground, brought down by St. Peter's prayer. See Ahl, *Benozzo Gozzoli*, 112–119, 224–226, 235–236.

[129] See above, chapter 4, n. 89.

Many of the public plays received communal subsidies, and for this reason too the confraternities were subject to scrutiny and promised continuous improvement. An anonymous and obsequiously pro-Medici description of the festivities for the visit to Florence in 1459 of the fifteen-year-old Galeazzo Maria Sforza and Pope Pius II would have us believe that every Florentine was glad to be involved in the effort and expense of public magnificence:

Non duol lo spendio e non nuoce [l'affanno	Expense is painless, effort does no harm, and everyone is fired with such delight:
ma in tanta allegrezza ognun s'accende	the more he spends the less it seems to hurt.
che quanto più si spende par men danno.	Spending brings joy, for joyfully he spends,
Chi spende gode perché allegro spende	and those who sell their labour find great [joy,
e chi lavora a prezzo molto gode	
e gode quel che la sua merce vende.	as does the man who sells his merchandise.[130]

The sense that financial profit as well as pleasure flowed naturally from financial investment in *feste* continued to the end of the century. Around 1497, Francesco Altoviti accused Savonarola of being an enemy of the poor because "he did not want the rich to spend money on *feste*, or brides, or respectable family banquets, so that poor artisans would have no income, and he nurtured hunger little by little in this city."[131]

It is customary to seek doctrinal reasons for the decline of the *rappresentazioni* but I believe that the reasons may have been more banal. In the fifteenth century, the plays were wholly the responsibility of confraternities that increasingly had to seek assistance with the costs. In 1491, when Lorenzo turned away from the old *rappresentazioni* in favour of his triumph of Paulus Æmilius, the confraternities were left largely without communal support. The plays simply became too costly to stage. After the *Miracolo del Corpo di Cristo* and *San Venanzio* were performed in 1502 at the personal expense of the members, the plays returned to cloistered confraternal hands and slipped into relative oblivion. By the time that Vasari was designing the sixteenth-century decorative program of the Palazzo Vecchio and facilitating the inclusion of

---

[130] *Le onoranze fiorentine*, 62, lines 2014–2019.

[131] Altoviti, *In defensione*, c. 1497, fol. a8ʳ: "non ha voluto che li richi spendano in *feste*, spose o conviti parentevoli et honesti, acciochè li poveri artigiani non abino alcun guadagno, et ha nutricata la fame a poco a poco a questa città."

Giovanni Stradano's *feste* in the Sala della Gualdrada (1561–1562),[132] neither the *edifici* for San Giovanni nor the *rappresentazioni* performed publicly at other times of the year were included. Vasari expressed no interest in any texts that may have been performed in any of the *feste* he described.

Figure 5.1. Boundary marker: Città Rossa Florence, Church of Sant'Ambrogio, south-west corner on Borgo La Croce. Lower stone, before 1486; upper stone, 1577. Wikimedia Commons / CC BY-SA-3.0. Photo: Sailko.

---

[132] Van Veen, *Cosimo I*, 39–48. The Sala della Gualdrada was occupied by the ladies-in-waiting of Eleonora of Toledo. The *feste* shown in the friezes were the principal occasions when Eleonora's ladies were allowed out of the palace, under strict rules of decorum; see Edelstein, "Ladies-in-waiting," 146–155. For the *edifici* in the Florentine merchants' contribution to Alfonso's triumph, see chapter 4, n. 66 above and fig. 4.1.

Figure 5.2. Andrea della Robbia (attr.), St. Bartholomew, *St. Francis receiving the Stigmata with Brother Leo, and Tobias and the Angel*; below: "Holy Father Bartholomew, pray for us" with two hooded *confratelli*. About 1475. Altar dossal with central ciborium, in glazed polychrome terracotta, from the altar of the Compagnia di San Bartolomeo, Santa Croce. Florence, Museo dell'Opera di Santa Croce, Room 3. Wikimedia Commons / CC BY-SA-3.0. Photo: Sailko.

Figure 5.3. Francesco di Lorenzo Rosselli (designer), Lucantonio degli
Uberti (engraver), *Pianta della catena* (c. 1472), detail of Porta al Prato della
Giustizia. 1500–1510. Woodcut on paper, eight sheets, 57.8 × 131.6 cm.
Wikimedia Commons / CC BY-SA-3.0. Photo: Sailko.

Figure 5.4. *La rapresentatione di sancto Giouanni dicollato* ([Florence: Bartolomeo de' Libri, not after 1495]), fol. a1ʳ. BNCF, Banco Rari 189.o; ISTC ij00254700. © By permission of MiBACT/BNCF. All rights reserved.

Figure 5.5. *La rapresentatione di sancto Giorgio martyre* ([Florence:
Bartolomeo de' Libri, not after 1495]), fol. a1ʳ. Rome, Biblioteca
Casanatense, Vol. Inc. 1671; ISTC ig00146500. BEIC / CC BY-SA-4.0.

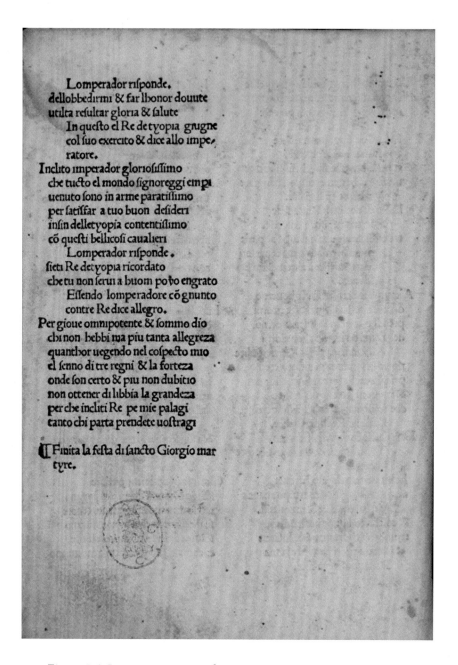

Lomperador rifponde.
dellobbedirmi & far lbonor douute
utilta refultar gloria & falute
    In quefto el Re de tyopia giugne
    col fuo exercito & dice allo impe,
    ratore.
Inclito imperador gloriofiffimo
    che tucto el mondo fignoreggi em pa
    uenuto fono in arme paratiffimo
    per fatiffar a tuo buon defideri
    infin delletyopia contentiffimo
    cō quefti bellicofi caualieri
        Lomperador rifponde.
    fieti Re detyopia ricordato
    che tu non ferui a buom poto engrato
    Effendo lomperadore cō gnunto
        contre Re dice allegro.
Per gioue omnipotente & fommo dio
    chi non hebbi ma piu tanta allegreza
    quanthor uegendo nel cofpecto mio
    el fenno di tre regni & la forteza
    onde fon certo & piu non dubitio
    non ottener di libbia la grandeza
    per che incliti Re pe mie palagi
    tanto chi parta prendete uoftragi

¶ Finita la fefta di fancto Giorgio mar
    tyre.

Figure 5.6. *La rapresentatione di sancto Giorgio martyre* ([Florence:
Bartolomeo de' Libri, not after 1495]), fol. b4ᵛ. Rome, Biblioteca
Casanatense, Vol. Inc. 1671; ISTC ig00146500. BEIC / CC BY-SA-4.0.

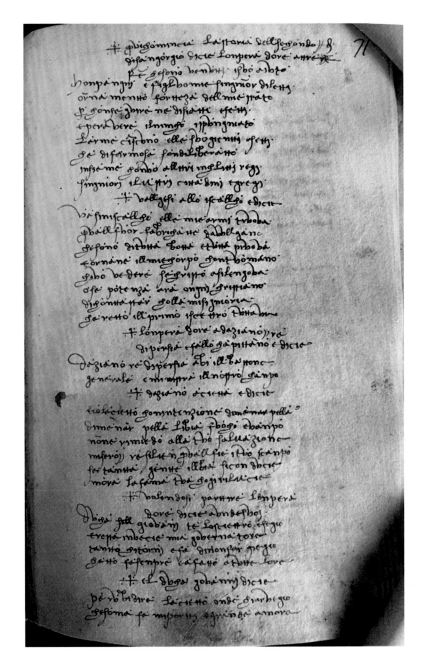

Figure 5.7. *Il secondo dì di San Giorgio:* "+ quivi chomincia la storia dell
sechondo dì di san Giorgio." BNCF, Magl. vii.293, fol. 71ʳ. © By permission
of MiBACT/BNCF. All rights reserved.

XXV.

CRAPPRESENTATIONE ¡DVNO MRACOLO DI TRE

Peregrini che andauono a fancto Iacopo di Galitia.

C Langelo annuntia la fefta.

O Euoti/ honefti & magni cittadini
in carita noi uiuogliam p̄gare
che ftiate in pace grādi & picholini
che uederete qui rapprefentare
un bel miracol di tre peregrini
dequali loftiera elgiouin fe fpiccare
& perche facio fu fenza ragione
lo libero fan Iacopo barone
Eperegrini fipartono dalla citta
per andare a fancto Iacopo di Ga

litia / & caminato che hanno al
quāto / moftrādo deffere ftrac/
chi / elperegrino uechio pofan
dofi un poco/dice alla moglie.
El camin lungo & la uia fangofa
el noftro figlio ha facto ftanchare
& anchor noi dolce donna & fpofa
onde laibergo io uorrei trouare
doue poteffimo prefto far ripofa
che poi porremo meglio caminare
pche ilbuon lecto elcibo uantagiato
conforta molto ilcorpo affaticato

Figure 5.8. *Rappresentatione duno mracolo di tre Peregrini che andauono a sancto Iacopo di Galitia* ([Florence: Antonio Tubini and Andrea Ghirlandi, not after 1515]), fol. a1ʳ. BNCF, Banco Rari 183.22; CNCE 62082. © By permission of MiBACT/BNCF. All rights reserved.

Et uoltafi alla famiglia &dice,
hor fu brigata oltre ui auuiate
El caualier mena el pelle grino al
la iuftitia,& quando hanno co
minciato a falire le fcale delle
forche la madre dice.
Sie benedetto o dolce mio figliuolo
Idio ti faccia forte nel paffare
fare io nõ poffo che nõ mi fia duolo
uederti attorto cofi tormentate
o impia gente,& ocr u dele ftuolo

come lafciate il giufto condemnare,
far douerrefti per fua innocentia
indrieto ritornar quefta fententia
El figliuolo rifponde.
O madre mia che tanta pena porti
qfta mia morte omai de porta in pace
chio non riceuo folo fimil torto
piacer debbe a te poi che a Dio piace
molti ne fono ftati al mondo morti
fenza lor colpa o difetto uerace
non pianger piu o dolce madre mia

fe uuoi che nel morir conftante fia
El manigoldo hauendo menato
el peregrino in fulle forche, &
cominciandolo a legare el pa;
dre dice.
Io non credetti o dolce figliuol mio
perderti in quefto luogho ome tapino
o cafo ftrano uergognofo & rio
nel qual ti uegho miftro e mefchino

io raccõmando all'Apoftol di Dio,
percui tu eri fatto peregrino
che lui t'aiuti al paffo del morire
&me ancor che mi fento finire
El figliuolo rifponde.
Padre mio charo habbi patienza
non ti dar e na della morte mia
che conofcendo idio la mia innocenza
a liberami credo prefto fia,

Figure 5.9. *La rapresentatione d'uno miracolo di Tre Pellegrini che andauano a .S. Iacopo di Galitia* (Florence: n.p., 1555), fol. a4[r]. BNCF, Pal. E.6.5.1[IV.38]; CNCE 61839. © By permission of MiBACT/BNCF. All rights reserved.

Figure 5.10. *Larapresentatione duno miracolo del corpo di Christo* ([Florence: Bartolomeo de' Libri, not after 1495]), fol. a1ʳ. London, British Library, IA.27488. ISTC ir00029550. © The British Library Board.

Figure 5.11. Bartolomeo della Gatta (attr.), *Miracle of the Profanation of the Host*. About 1485. Predella panel, tempera on wood, 15 × 35 cm. St. Petersburg, The Hermitage State Museum, inv. ГЭ 7657. Photograph © The State Hermitage Museum. Photography by Pavel Demidov.

Figure 5.12. Benozzo Gozzoli, *St. Peter and the Fall of Simon Magus*. 1461. Predella panel, tempera on wood, 24.3 × 34.5 cm. Formerly, oratory of the Company of the Purification. London, Hampton Court, Royal Collection, RCIN 403372. Wikimedia Commons / CC BY-SA-3.0. Photo: WGA.

CHAPTER 6

ANTONIA PULCI, ANTONIO MISCOMINI, AND THE TRANSITION TO PRINT

> She also wrote many plays that were beautiful and devout.
>
> Friar Dolciati, 1528[1]

The trauma of the Pazzi conspiracy, which had culminated on Easter Sunday 1478 in the assassination of Giuliano de' Medici during High Mass in the cathedral, resulted in significant self-censorship within the youth confraternities. As we saw in chapter 3, the Medicean confraternity of the Purification hastened to revise its statutes. It made various additions providing for greater oversight of all five companies by a single *preposto* or provost, who would be honoured with a sermon by a *fanciullo* when he visited. Its last two additions related particularly to *feste*. The requirement to attend each other's *feste* was restricted to once every three months, and these *feste* were henceforth to be celebrated only with "beautiful vespers, hymns, prayers, garlands, lights, and greenery, lest by wanting to adorn the walls we sully the inner man." Moreover, there were to be no gatherings of brethren, either in the country or in Florence, without the *guardiano* present. The performance of plays went into abeyance.

The plays themselves, however, did not disappear, because a new medium of 'performance' — through the printing press — had established itself in Florence, and it is at this point that my history of plays becomes also a history of printing in fifteenth-century Florence.[2] In the 1480s, two printers in particular dealt with vernacular texts: Francesco Bonaccorsi and Antonio

---

[1] Antonio Dolciati, dedicatory letter to *De tribus regulis S. Augustini*, BMLF, Gaddi 132, fol. 3ᵛ: "compose *etiam* molte belle e devote rapresentazioni"; cited by Weaver, in Antonia Pulci, *Saints' Lives*, 24, n. 69, with the entire memoir and translation in her Appendix 3, 470–477. On Dolciati, see Zaccaria, "Dolciati."

[2] On this intersection of dramatic manuscripts and printed plays, see Riccò, "Testo per la scena" and "*Su le carte e fra le scene*," 15–91; and Ventrone, "Fra teatro libro e devozione" and *Teatro civile*, 298–330. Ventrone, "Acting and Reading Drama," appeared after this study had been completed.

Miscomini. Bonaccorsi's output was mostly devotional and theological, while the ninety-five titles attributed to Miscomini in the Incunabula Short Title Catalogue (ISTC) include both large- and small-format works, in Latin and in Italian, on classical, devotional, and, importantly, popular subjects. His output includes *novelle, cantari,* and *rappresentazioni,* of which some forty-four are first editions.[3] We know little about the financial basis of Miscomini's printing activities. Over half of his works are signed and dated, but he does not seem to be printing for a commercial publisher since none is named in his colophons. More likely he was printing speculatively (for works that were relatively sure to sell, like Cavalca's *Disciplina degli spirituali* and *Specchio di croce*) or else on commission from the authors. Among the writers who flocked to have their works printed during Miscomini's first period of activity in Florence were Luca and Bernardo Pulci, and their friends Girolamo Benciveni and Bastiano Foresi. The general enthusiasm for the new print technology was ridiculed by the Florentine humanist Bartolomeo Scala, who derided both the vernacular medium and the willingness to publish work that he regarded as second rate.[4]

Close behind those men of the Medici *brigata* came a woman: Antonia Pulci *née* Tanini. I have recently argued that the two-volume anthology, long known as the *Prima* and *Seconda raccolta fiorentina* (First and Second Florentine collections), attributed variously to Bonaccorsi and Miscomini and dated 1490 and "1490|1495," can in fact safely be ascribed to Antonio Miscomini. The first volume bears Antonia's name on the first page, and the year 1483; the implication is that she is responsible for the publication of the anthology, and that 1483 is the year of publication.[5] The two volumes contain thirteen plays, nine in the first (ISTC ir00029680), and four in the second (ISTC ir00029700). Each play is contained within its signatures, so that it could circulate separately as well as in the volume, but it was clearly intended that these should be volumes with substance and durability, and not ephemeral pamphlets. Nevertheless, the plays are exceedingly rare. None survives in

---

[3] Gehl, "Watermark Evidence," 282–283. On Miscomini, see also Avigliano, "Miscomini"; Periti, "L'edizione miscominiana"; Periti, "Contributo," 290–291.

[4] See Scala's letter to Poliziano of 31 December 1493, in Poliziano, *Opera,* fol. f6ʳ; cited in Brown, *Bartolomeo Scala,* 213.

[5] See Newbigin, "Antonia Pulci" (in which I failed to notice the Getty Research Institute's copy of *Arcangelo Raffaello,* PQ4630.P82 F4 1495) and further discussion below. In citations of the two volumes, however, I defer to Scapecchi, *Catalogo degli incunaboli,* 384, BNCF 2399, which accepts "ca. 1484" as the date.

more than four copies, and the total number of extant single plays is forty-four. The only authors whose names appear in the anthology are Antonia Pulci and her husband Bernardo. Three plays are credited to Antonia (*Santa Domitilla*, *Santa Guglielma*, and *San Francesco*) and just one to Bernardo (*Barlaam e Iosafat*). It may be possible to add *Giuseppe, figlio di Giacobbe* from this collection to the list of Antonia's plays, since her biographer, Friar Antonio Dolciati, writing in 1528, says that she "also composed many plays that were beautiful and devout, of Joseph, of David and Saul, of the Prodigal Son, and many others that I don't remember now, for it is more than thirty-six years since I saw them."[6] But it is possible that all the plays are linked to Antonia Pulci and Bernardo Pulci, and possibly even to the most famous member of the family, Luigi Pulci.[7]

Until recently, Antonia's career was all but eclipsed by the men of the Pulci household: Luigi, Luca, and Bernardo. She was regularly noted in

---

[6] Dolciati, dedicatory letter (see n. 1 above): "compose *etiam* molte belle e devote rapresentazioni, di Joseph, di David e Saul, del Figliuolo prodigo e assai altre delle quali ora non mi ricordo, emperoché sono più di trentasei anni non le ho vedute"; see Weaver, in Antonia Pulci, *Saints' Lives*, 473. James Wyatt Cook, in his translation of Antonia Pulci's plays (Antonia Pulci, *Florentine Drama*), included her *Figliuol prodigo*, first published c. 1550 (CNCE 50657), as well as three plays for which corroborating evidence is lacking: *Sant'Antonio della Barba*, first attributed to her in error by Cioni, on the authority of Colomb de Batines where, however, no such attribution is found; *Santa Teodora*, on the grounds of stylistic similarities; and *Reina Rosana*. Flamini, "La vita," 243, attributed *Santa Teodora* to Bernardo (see also D'Ancona, *Origini*, 1:268, n. 3), but this was based on a misconception. The Prologue of Antonio Benivieni the Younger's *Teodora*, (BNCF, II.i.91, mid-sixteenth century, pp. 177–229) reads: "This play is based on the plot of one of our Florentine poets of the Pulci family, the one who truly had the gift of poetry" (La presente favola è ordinata nella trama d'uno de' nostri fiorentini poeti Pulci, quello che hebbe veramente spirito e concetto poetico; p. 177). But Benivieni's *Teodora* is not a *sacra rappresentazione* of the virgin martyr of Antioch. Rather it is the tragedy of Theodora, empress of Constantinople, and the plot is taken from Luca Pulci's *Ciriffo Calvaneo*; see Re, "Un poeta tragico," and Caccioli, "Tragedie." Elissa Weaver adds *Saul e David* to the corpus in Antonia Pulci, *Saints' Lives*. The *San Giuliano* attributed to her is a long-standing lapsus for *Santa Guglielma*.

[7] On Luigi Pulci's anonymity, see Harris, "Sopravvivenze," 183–184. Harris points out that in November 1478, when Ercole d'Este asked his agent in Florence to procure a printed copy of the *Morgante*, the agent knew that they were available from "somebody called Aloysius Pulci who happens to have some" (uno che si chiama Alovise Pulci el quale se ne trova haver), but clearly did not know that this same person was the author. Luigi Pulci at least combined anonymity with intensive marketing. For his likely involvement with the performance of the *San Lorenzo* play, see below, at the end of this chapter.

compendia of Florentine writers, and then, in the second half of the twentieth century, as an exceptional woman writer among so many men, but it was only with the ground-breaking work of Elissa Weaver that Antonia was recognized as a significant author in her own right.[8] Born in about 1452, she was one of six children, mainly daughters, of a Florentine father, Francesco d'Antonio Tanini, and a Roman mother, Iacopa. Judith Bryce has speculated that she may have been educated in a convent school, such as those discussed in Sharon Strocchia's research on two schools for girls, one run by the Hieronymites of San Niccolò dei Frieri in the Oltrarno, and the other by the Observant Augustinians of the convent of Santa Maria del Fiore, also called the "donne di Lapo," on the Via Faentina.[9] Antonia lost her father in 1467 but was sufficiently dowered to be able to marry Bernardo Pulci in 1470.[10] Three of her sisters married, and the others probably became nuns. Bernardo dedicated his verse narrative of the *Passione* to Antonia's sister, "his devout sister in Christ Annalena de' Tanini in the convent of the Murate."[11] His *Barlaam e Iosafat*, discussed in chapter 3, dates to 1474, so plays and their engagement with the confraternity of the Purification must have dated from early in their married life. Bernardo died in 1488, after which Antonia returned to her family home on what is now Piazza San Firenze, where she lived as a *pinzochera* or tertiary until she and her companions took the veil as Augustinian nuns. She then used her dowry and inheritance to found a convent, dedicated to Santa Maria della Misericordia, for women like herself to withdraw to a cloistered but autonomous life. She purchased a house just outside the Porta San Gallo, and at her death on 26 September 1501, she bequeathed the house to her nuns.[12]

---

[8] See Weaver, "Antonia Pulci," "Antonia Tanini," and her introduction to Antonia Pulci, *Saints' Lives*. In addition to these fundamental studies by Elissa Weaver, whom I thank for generous discussions over many years, see Bryce, "Adjusting the Canon," "'Or altra via,'" and "'Les Livres des Florentines',," on female literacy. On the Pulci men, see Carrai, *Le muse dei Pulci*; Decaria, "Pulci, Bernardo," "Pulci, Luca," "Pulci, Luigi," and *Luigi Pulci e Francesco di Matteo Castellani*; Orvieto, *Pulci medievale*, and *Pulci: Luigi*; and Polcri, *Luigi Pulci*.

[9] Bryce, "'Or altra via,'" 23–24; Strocchia, "Learning the Virtues."

[10] Weaver, in Antonia Pulci, *Saints' Lives*, 11–12.

[11] Bernardo Pulci, *Passione* ([Florence: Antonio Miscomini, c. 1485]), ISTC ip01103700, fol. [*]1r: "la divota in Christo suora Annalena de' Tanini nel monasterio delle Murate."

[12] For fuller biographical details, see Weaver, in Antonia Pulci, *Saints' Lives*, 5–30, on which I draw here.

The title page of the first volume of the Miscomini anthology is headed: "Here begins the play of St. Domitilla the Virgin, written and composed in verse by Mona Antonia, wife of Bernardo Pulci, the year 1483" (fig. 6.1).[13] The date does not necessarily indicate the year of publication, but after careful consideration of type, watermarks, and content, I have come to the conclusion that this title page — in lieu of a colophon — marks the beginning of an anthology compiled by Antonia Pulci, containing plays that are closely related to the youth confraternity of the Purification and the Pulci circle, and that 1483 is the year of publication.[14] The anthology, which contains what are probably the first Italian vernacular plays in print, attempts to claim a space for the plays as literature, rather than as popular devotional readings. Even in the absence of a preface, the volume was possibly conceived as a tribute to Lucrezia Tornabuoni (who had died on 25 March 1482) and her son Lorenzo de' Medici, in the same way as Miscomini's editions of Poliziano, Beroaldo, Foresi, and Luca and Luigi Pulci were conceived — as Concetta Bianca has argued — as tributes to Lorenzo.[15]

The two volumes are modestly elegant. Like the works of the Pulci brothers, they are printed in Miscomini's 112R type[16] in a single column and with generous margins. Where the manuscripts distinguished stage directions from dialogue by means of layout and ink-colour, and modern editions use layout and alternating Italic and Roman fonts, Miscomini was limited in practice to a single ink-colour and a single font and used indentation and alignment to distinguish between dialogue and stage direction. He had no precedents in this, and his achievement is remarkable.[17]

But even more remarkable is the revolution that these volumes signalled in the development of the genre of sacre *rappresentazioni*. Here, for the

---

[13] See below, n. 21.

[14] Elissa Weaver has further pointed out to me that the style of Antonia's name, "mona Antonia donna di Bernardo Pulci," indicates that Bernardo was still alive at the time of publication. Bernardo died on 9 February 1487/8.

[15] Bianca, "Le dediche," 67. On Antonia's mother's dealings with Lorenzo and his wife Clarice Orsini, see Weaver, in Antonia Pulci, *Saints' Lives*, 12–15.

[16] Type for our plays is described as Roman or Gothic and its size is expressed as the height in millimetres of twenty lines of type, from the top of the ascenders of the top line to the bottom of the descenders of the bottom line. Twenty lines of Miscomini's Roman type thus measure 112 mm, expressed as 112R.

[17] This presumes that ISTC ir00029680 and ir00029700 are earlier than the Belcari editions ISTC ib00297200, ib00297250, and ib00297300. On stage directions in manuscript and print, see Newbigin, "Rubrics and *Didascalie*."

first time, we find female martyrs and persecuted brides among the subjects treated. If we look back through the manuscript plays, we find scenes from the life of Christ and the Virgin for the liturgical feast days of the Annunciation, Ascension, and Pentecost; stories from the history of Man's salvation, from the Creation to the Last Judgment, performed for the feast of St. John the Baptist; Bible stories and parables, like Belcari's *Abramo* and Muzi's *Vitel sagginato*; tales from the *Vite dei Santi Padri*; miracles of the Virgin; and plays of two male saints, *Sant'Alesso* and *Sant'Eustachio*, both performed by the Purification company. Generally speaking, virtuous women — with the exception of Susanna and St. Cecilia — had not been models for adolescent boys. Now the corpus of plays written and performed in youth confraternities was expanded to include explorations of the female condition written by a woman; virgins, wives, mothers, and widows were held up as models of Christian behaviour.[18] The development was in no way marginal. The plays were not limited to performance by nuns in convents or to domestic settings; in fact, no evidence has been found of such performances in the fifteenth century.[19] Dolciati effectively gives 1492 as the date *ante quem* of Antonia's plays, but does not suggest that they were performed by nuns.[20] Rather, the *rappresentazioni* of the Miscomini anthology come to rest, at least in the first instance, wholly within the tradition of male confraternal performances.

Of the plays in the two volumes, three have been discussed already in chapter 3: Bernardo Pulci's play of *Barlaam e Iosafat*, performed in late 1474; the anonymous play of *Sant'Eustachio*, performed in the garden of Lorenzo de' Medici on 22 February 1476/7; and the play of *Josef, figliuol di Jacob*. I shall now examine the remaining plays of the Miscomini volumes as well as Antonia's *Figliuol prodigo*, not published until the 1550s; the *Distruzione di Saul e il pianto di Davit* attributed to her; the *Bel miracolo di Nostra Donna*, which is found in a codex of Pulci works; and the play of *San Lorenzo quando fu martirizato*, possibly performed in 1460 with the assistance of Francesco Castellani, for whom Luigi Pulci was working as secretary. The plays vary

---

[18] On the programmatic spread of Antonia Pulci's explorations of womanhood, see Carney, "Antonia Pulci's *Rappresentazione*," 12–13; Weaver, in Antonia Pulci, *Saints' Lives*, 61.

[19] Trexler believed that plays were being performed at the convent of Santa Caterina at San Gaggio before Savonarola put a stop to them, but I believe that this view is based on Ginori-Conti's misreading of Pseudo-Burlamacchi; see Trexler, "Florentine Theatre" (rev. 2002), 245 (1496–1498) and below, chapter 9, n. 14.

[20] Weaver, in Antonia Pulci, *Saints' Lives*, 24–25. Simm, "Antonia Pulci," does not provide documentary evidence of performance of Antonia's plays in her convent.

in quality and texture, but they are all close to, if not within, the orbit of the Pulci family.

La rappresentazione di santa Domitilla vergine

The first play of the 'first' volume is *The Play of St. Domitilla the Virgin.*[21] Only two demonstrably earlier plays have a female protagonist: the *Festa di Susanna*, copied after 1464; and the *Rappresentazione di Santa Cicilia vergine*, which Tommaso Leone copied for the Bolognese confraternity of San Girolamo in 1482, and which was performed, according to its later and much abbreviated printed edition, by the youth confraternity of the Vangelista. The appearance of plays about women does not instantly mean that plays are for female actors and audiences; rather we are moving into a society where women become eloquent models of virginal life, chastity, charity, forbearance, and sacrifice, for boys and young men as well as for women. I have already suggested that *Susanna* was a vehicle for the display of the young Daniel's eloquence in the service of virtue wronged, but it is also a reminder that marriage and virtue alone do not protect a woman's chastity and honour. *Santa Cecilia* shows a more perfect union, in which Cecilia's husband accepts her mystical marriage to Christ, converts to Christianity, and joyfully shares her martyrdom. In contrast, Antonia Pulci shows the fate of a would-be husband who does *not* accept his bride's faith and union with Christ.

Various sources have been proposed for Pulci's play, but there can be little doubt that her direct source was the vernacular prose legend that circulated widely from at least the middle of the fourteenth century and was edited by Domenico Maria Manni in the *Vite di alcuni santi* (Some saints' lives).[22] The prose *vita* is prolix; in the *rappresentazione* it is pared down to a

---

[21] *Incomincia La rapresentatione di sancta Domitilla uergine facta & composta in uersi per mona Antonia donna di Bernardo pulci lanno MCCCCLXXXIII* ([Florence: Antonio Miscomini, c. 1484]), ISTC ir00029680, a–b⁸ c⁴; Cioni, *Bibliografia*, 118, xx.1; for modern editions and translation, see Table 2. For commentary, see Weaver, in Antonia Pulci, *Saints' Lives*, 33–37; Carney, "Antonia Pulci's *Rappresentazione*"; Bryce, "Vernacular Poetry," 33–35, and "'Or altra via.'" In this chapter, I quote, where possible, from Weaver's edition of Pulci's text and adapt Cook's translations.

[22] *Vita di s. Domitilla*. For the prose *vita*, see *BAI* online, *Domitilla 2: Vita di s. Domitilla*, beginning, prologue: "Volendo dire alcuna cosa a laude della verginitade, e della castitade" (Wishing to say something in praise of virginity and chastity); text: "Domiziano Imperadore, per cui questa Vergine santa ebbe nome Domitilla, ebbe una sorella, ch'ebbe nome Plautilla" (Emperor Domitian, for whom this holy virgin was called Domitilla, had

minimum: the saint's relationship through her mother Plautilla to St. Paul is not raised; her female companions are unnamed; and much of the didactic element — the instruction of neophyte Christians — is omitted. The play focuses instead on its single and important message of the certainty of virginity and infinite superiority of marriage to Christ (oct. 23–26) over marriage to a carnal husband and all the disappointment and travails that such a union entails (oct. 17–19, 21–22). Even though Aureliano, the husband chosen for her, is at first kind and Domitilla has already accepted his suit, she acts on the advice of her servants (no longer eunuchs, as they had been in the *vita*) and chooses Christ as her *Sposo*, the best and most compassionate spouse, receiving the veil from Pope Clement and distributing alms to the poor. The stanzas of the *rappresentazione* follow the order of events in the *vita*, and only the giving of alms to the poor is not found there. When Domitilla is summoned before her uncle the emperor, she argues the case for preserving her virginity with recourse to history and literature. In response, he exiles her to the island of Ponza (the Purification confraternity later lists a ship among its properties for such contingencies),[23] and Nereo and Achilleo, the faithful servants responsible for her conversion, are martyred. Female companions are sent to Domitilla in her wretched island exile to persuade her to accept her pagan suitor, but they are converted.[24] The companions' suitors, sent to bring them home, are likewise converted. Aureliano recalls Domitilla to Rome, where he has prepared an unseen marriage feast. After he dances himself to death at

---

a sister called Plautilla). Compare, for example, the wording in the play of Domitilla's recollection of her mother's suffering: "Ben mi ricorda che la madre mia | sostenne molte pene tutti gli anni | della suo vita sol per gelosia | del suo marito con sì gravi affanni" (Well do I remember that my mother endured much suffering all the years of her life, just on account of her husband's jealousy which brought deep woe; oct. 20.1–4), with that in the prose *Vita di S. Domitilla*, 273: "Rispuose la Vergine: ben mi ricordo, che mia madre ne fu tribolata molto tempo, imperocché mio padre ne fu molto geloso, e da questa ingiuria ne fu affaticata più tempo" (The virgin replied: well do I remember that my mother was long afflicted, because my father guarded her jealously and she travailed under this affliction for a long time). The Vallombrosan monk Giovanni dalle Celle is said to be the author of a *Vita di Santa Domitilla*, generally (but without secure grounds) identified with the prose *vita*; Giovanni dalle Celle and Marsili, *Lettere*, 1:173–174, n. 1. Bryce, "'Or altra via,'" 37 n. 24. Carney, "Antonia Pulci's *Rappresentazione*," 19, proposes as a source the *Vita Sanctae Domitillae* contained in Mombrizio's *Sanctuarium* [not after 1478].

[23] See inventory below, chapter 9.

[24] In contrast, the *vita* makes much of her joyful life on Ponza, which further provokes Aureliano's wrath; *Vita di S. Domitilla*, 291–292.

the feast, his brother, Lussurio, orders that Domitilla be executed. The Angel bids the audience farewell as the executioner leaves to prepare the bonfire. Since bonfires and battles for the territory on which they stood were a traditional element of Carnival, this ending may indicate that both the play and its bonfire were part of a Carnival entertainment,[25] and the unseen banquet awaited the performers and the audience.

In the *vita*, the physical spaces of Rome and the island of Ponza are described with care, and Domitilla's life is evoked with small details, but in the play, as Weaver notes, the four *luoghi* could be indicated simply by *polizze*, signs indicating the Emperor's palace, Aureliano's palace, Domitilla's house, and Ponza, since these places have no characteristics that are intrinsic to plot development.[26] Music and dancing are part of the initial betrothal (stage direction after oct. 6), but dancing at the wedding feast prepared for Domitilla's return is not explicitly staged; there is nothing between Domitilla asking God for a miracle and a servant reporting Aureliano's death to his brother:

DOMITILLA:

Or si vedrà, Signor, quanto tu m'ami.

UNO SERVO *va a Lussurio e dice come Aureliano ballando è cascato morto:*

Sappi che Domitilla co' sua incanti
ha fatto cader morto il tuo fratello,
così ballando con suoni e con canti.

DOMITILLA:

Now we will see how much you love me,
[Lord!

A SERVANT *goes to Lussurio and tells how Aureliano has fallen dead while dancing:*

I report Domitilla with her spells
has made your brother fall down dead,
[while he
was dancing to the music and the songs.
(oct. 100.8–101.3)

The play could have been performed, like *Santa Cecilia*, in a youth confraternity, but by the sixteenth century it was being performed or read aloud by women, lay and religious, whose names are written in the margins of a copy of the first edition (fig. 6.2).[27] A rare — if fictional — record of a

---

[25] Ginori Conti, ed., *La vita*, 123; Ciappelli, *Carnevale e Quaresima*, 123–131.

[26] Weaver, in Antonia Pulci, *Saints' Lives*, 36. *Polizze* are mentioned in the *Frottola di tre suore*; see Razzolini, "Frottola," 176; and below, chapter 9, n. 207.

[27] The names listed in various late sixteenth-century hands — Maria Vincentia, Ottavia, and Angiola, as well as Jacopa, Maria Gostantia and la Pelagia (?), who have been

performance survives in the Accademia degli Intronati's comedy *L'Ortensio*, performed in Siena in January 1560/1. Ulivetta, a servant, explains that she is going "to the house of Mona Cornelia for the book of the Virgins, because Leonida wants to read me the life of St. Domitilla because tomorrow they are doing the play about her."[28] The details are significant. A mistress reads the legend to her illiterate servant in preparation for attendance at a play written some eighty years earlier. By the mid-sixteenth century, the play has moved into a female sphere, but no details of location or performers are given.

No special devices are required for a performance. The prologue is spoken by an unspecified character in the name of the author: "Good Jesus, by your great almightiness, | grant to my lowly intellect your grace" (O buon Iesù, per la tua gran potenza | concedi grazia al mio basso intelletto; oct. 1.1–2).[29] No realistic horror attends the martyrs' death and no *nugola* descends to collect their souls.

La istoria e leggenda di santa Apollonia vergine e martire di Cristo

The other female martyr of the anthology is St. Apollonia. The title of her play, *The Story and Legend of St. Apollonia, Virgin and Martyr for Christ* (quite exceptionally neither *rappresentazione* nor *festa*),[30] points to the fact that the play is taken from the extended *Legenda di Apollonia di Alessandria vergine e martire*, one of the two vernacular prose legends of Apollonia in circulation in fifteenth-century Florence.[31] The saint does not appear in the canonical *Legenda Aurea*, nor even in the vernacular version with Florentine

---

crossed out, and on other pages Doratea, Suor Maria Angela, Isabella, Maria Angelica, Filippa, Maria Anna, Lodovica, Pace — suggest that the play was performed or read aloud on more than one occasion, with much doubling of roles. Such annotations, from the late sixteenth century onwards and always of women's names, are not uncommon in copies of *rappresentazioni*. Weaver, *Convent Theatre*, 100, n. 9, reads these names as being belonging to nuns.

[28] Accademia degli Intronati, *L'Hortensio*, 117, (III.7): "a casa di Mona Cornelia per il libro delle Vergini, che Leonida mi vuol legger la vita di santa Domitilla, che se ne fa domane la rapresentatione." The book is not St. Ambrose, *De Virginibus*, but more generically an anthology of female saints' lives, such as we find, for example, in BNCF, II.IV.105.

[29] On apology as a female gesture, see discussion of *Jacob ed Esaù*, chapter 3 above.

[30] *Qui comincia lahistoria & leggenda di sancta Apollonia uergine & martyre di Christo* ([Florence: Antonio Miscomini, c. 1484]), ISTC ir00029700, d–f⁸; Cioni, *Bibliografia*, 90, XI.1; for modern editions, see Table 2.

[31] See *BAI* online and, for example, *Apollonia di BMLF*, Ashb. 317, fols. 68ʳ–71ʳ.

additions — despite her importance in Florence as titular saint of the cloistered convent of Camaldolese nuns of Sant'Apollonia, and the timing of her feast day (9 February), which almost always fell during Carnival.[32] The eleven-year-old daughter of the pagan king Tarso is visited by an Angel who tells her to visit a hermit to be instructed in the true faith. The hermit's first response is to fear that she is the Devil, sent to tempt him, but she reassures him and, once he has baptized her (with the help of another Angel), she returns to Alexandria to preach. Meanwhile a maidservant reports to the king that Apollonia is missing, and he, fearing scandal, sends people to search for her. Apollonia preaches in the square and baptizes new converts. Her father's seneschal finds her and obliges her to return to the court. After fierce argument, the king agrees that she should debate with the wisest sages of the realm; she imposes the condition that if she should win, they will accept baptism. They resist simple catechism, but when she cites the wisdom of poets and philosophers — Orpheus, Hesiod, Ovid, Antisthenes, Crispus, Zeno, Anaximenes, Cleanthes, Cicero, Aristotle, and Plato — they realize that she has the better of them and withdraw to discuss their position in Latin (oct. 76–77). They submit, but Tarso chases them out before they can be baptized. Enraged, he orders that Apollonia be beaten mercilessly. She is returned to prison, where yet another Angel appears to her and fortifies her for the final torment that is absolutely central to her identity and her iconography, the breaking of her teeth.

In the *Rappresentazione di San Lorenzo* which will be examined in more detail below, Lorenzo is stripped and beaten about the mouth: "Now the torturers seize him and, having bared his head, they torture him with sticks, scorpion whips, and lead balls, then they strike him in the mouth with stones" (Ora e manigoldi lo pigliano e spogliatolo dal capo gli danno martori con fuste, scarpioni e palle di piombo, poi co' sassi gli percuotono la bocca; stage direction after oct. 92.8), but he is still able to speak eloquently as he is then placed on the grate. Apollonia too has her teeth broken by her torturers,

---

[32] Graesse, followed by Ryan, includes Apollonia with note "this legend is missing in more recent editions" (deest haec legenda in editionibus recentioribus; Jacobus, *Legenda*, ed. Graesse, 293–294, n. 1; Jacobus, *The Golden Legend*, 1:268–269, n. 1), but she is absent from Maggioni's Latin edition (Jacobus, *Legenda Aurea*), and from the *volgarizzamento* (Jacobus, *Leggenda aurea*, based on BRF, Ricc. 1254). In the brief legend (following Eusebius) included by Graesse, Apollonia is old, and her death, after her teeth are beaten out, is in the flames of a pyre. Between 1460 and 1500, the feast day fell during Lent only in 1475, 1478, 1486 and 1497.

but the seneschal informs the king "her teeth are broken and her gums are torn | and no less than before her words come out" (che ha rotti i denti e le gengìe sbarrate | e men che prima non face favela; oct. 98.3–4). Just as conversion to Christianity and angelic instruction made her articulate in the first place, so the torture of her mouth and teeth paradoxically enhances that gift.[33] The effect on the spectators is twofold. They see the extraordinary gifts bestowed by true faith — Apollonia, "all toothless" (tutta sdentata; oct. 101.2) speaks more persuasively than ever — but they are spared anguish at the sight of torture. However realistic the torments may be, they remain fictive and the character transcends them; there is no suggestion that the actor is suffering pain. And at the end, as Apollonia faces her executioner, she is comforted by the voice of Christ who greets her with words that echo the Song of Songs:

La VOCE DI CRISTO *non veduta dice:*	*The* VOICE OF CHRIST, *unseen, says:*
Vienne, diletta mia saggia e fedele.	Come away, my beloved, wise and true.
Vienne, colomba mia tutta formosa.	Come away, my fair dove all beauteous.
Vienne, soave amica più che mele.	Come away, friend, far sweeter yet than honey.
Vienne, sorella mia e cara sposa.	Come away, sister, and my dearest bride.
Esci del mal terribile e crudele	Come forth from sorrow, terrible and cruel,
e la tuo mortal vesta in terra posa.	and let your mortal spoils fall to the ground.
Entra nel gaudio mio che sempre dura,	Enter this everlasting joy of mine,
perfetta pace e gloria sicura.	my perfect peace, and glory ever sure.
Ora alquante donne piangono sopra a	*Now several women weep over St. Apollonia*
santa Apollonia, e una di loro la piglia	*and one of them takes her under her*
sotto il mantello. Un altra ne pone	*mantle. Another places a dummy in her*
quivi una contrafatta che s'assomigli a	*place that looks like St. Apollonia and* THE
santa Apollonia e IL MANIGOLDO *gli*	EXECUTIONER *cuts off her head.*
taglia il capo.	

---

[33] See also *Santa Cristina*: "E tagliatoli le poppe, el Re dice: Fate che la sua lingua gli sia tratta | acciò ch'ella non possa più cantare" (And when her breasts have been cut off, the King says: Tell them to pull her tongue out by the roots | so that she cannot sing another word; oct. 83.1–2). On the 'illegitimacy' of articulate female argumentation and female martyrs, see Wogan-Browne, "Saints' Lives."

Levatevi di qui, mona Dianora,	Get out of here, Madonna Dianora,[34]
che non bisogna far tanto schiamazo.	and there's no need for this almighty din.
Or oltre andate via nella malora	Be on your way to hell, the lot of you:
ch'i' vo' pigliare omai altro sollazo.	I want to have my fun another way.
Volgesi a' compagni:	*He turns to his companions:*
Fate far largo voi sanza dimora	Make everyone stand back without delay,
acciò che noi tornian presto al palazzo.	so that we get home quickly to the palace.
Volgesi al manigoldo.	*He turns to the executioner.*
	(oct. 127–128.6)

It is an unusual ending, with women keening, sleight of hand, and a bloody beheading, but it is without the Angel's farewell, and clearly something has been lost (fig. 6.3).[35] When Miscomini came to reprint *Sant'Apollonia* a decade later, he amended the stage directions, adding the words underlined below, in an attempt to make sense of it, and added a woodcut (fig. 6.4):

Hora alquante donne piangono sopra	*Now several women weep over St.*
Sancta Apollonia e <u>*uno*</u> *di loro la piglia*	*Apollonia and* <u>*one of the men*</u> *takes her*
sotto il mantello, e <u>*un altro*</u> *ne pone quivi*	*under his mantle and* <u>*another*</u> *places a*
una contrafatta che assomigli a santa	*dummy in her place that looks like St.*
Apollonia e il manigoldo <u>*dice a quelle*</u>	*Apollonia and the executioner* <u>*says to*</u>
<u>*donne*</u>:	<u>*those women*</u>:
Levatevi di qui, mona Dianora,	Get out of here, Madonna Dianora,
che non bisogna far tanto schiamazo.	and there's no need for this almighty din.
Hor oltre, andate via nella malhora	Be on your way to hell, the lot of you:
ch'i' vo' pigliar omai altro solazo.	I want to have my fun another way.
Volgesi a' compagni <u>*e dice*</u>:	*He turns to his companions* <u>*and says*</u>:
Fate far largo voi senza dimora	Make everyone stand back without delay,
acciò che noi tornian presto al palazzo.	so that we get home quickly to the palace.

---

[34] Dianora, not previously mentioned, is the name of a talkative servant told to keep quiet in the later *Santa Dorotea*, attributed to Castellano Castellani, oct. 24; see Newbigin, ed., "Dieci sacre rappresentazioni," 336.

[35] The block of type containing the last *ottava* has dropped down the page and the final couplet is missing. The executioner is not the speaker, since the final direction has the speaker turn to address the executioner. The lines may have been intended as supporting type on this page, and have accidentally been left uncovered, but I have not found another play that they belong to.

Ora il manigoldo le <u>tagli</u> il capo. <u>Una</u> <u>nuogola meni l'anima di Sancta Apollonia</u> <u>in cielo.</u>	Now the executioner <u>should cut</u> off her head. <u>A nugola should take the soul of</u> <u>St. Apollonia to heaven.</u>
FINIS	FINIS
	(oct. 128.1–6)

Miscomini's woodcut shows the *nugola* or mandorla, with angels on either side, like the one that the Sant'Agnese company in Santa Maria del Carmine would share with the youth confraternity of Sant'Antonio da Padova in 1483 for their performance of *Reina Rosanna*.[36] The realism of the beheading is now attenuated by having the living soul step into the mandorla and be borne up to heaven unharmed.

Stage directions allow us to glimpse more of how a play was performed. The action takes place in four locations: Tarso's palace, the public square, the cell of the hermit, and the place of execution. Once again, we do not know how these places were expressed — by signs or by some attempt at naturalistic representation — but there is some suggestion in this play, backed up by other martyr plays and the pictorial tradition, that a royal palace or imperial rank can be represented simply by a throne (fig. 6.5), from which the characters rise to speak, and that the throne room stands in opposition to the place of torture and execution.[37] Between these *luoghi* stand the martyr's home and other subsidiary locations.

The woodblock cut expressly for the title page of Miscomini's second edition shows Apollonia tied to a column, with two torturers, one with a rod to break her teeth, and the other with grotesque pincers to pull them out. The emperor is on his throne, and Apollonia's father King Tarso looks on, in an emotionally sparse scene. There is, however, no evidence to link the woodcut to an actual performance rather than to the traditional iconography of the saint in miniatures and in predella panels. The corpus of Italian plays (and Books of Hours), however, offers nothing comparable with Jean Fouquet's elaborate representation of the theatrical torture of Apollonia, in Étienne Chevalier's *Book of Hours* (1452–1460) (fig. 6.6), an illustration that is much debated, in part because no French play of St. Apollonia survives from the

---

[36] For the illustrated edition, *La rapresentatione divota di sancta Apollonia* ([Florence: Antonio Miscomini, 1492–1494]), ISTC ia00922600. For an earlier example, see *San Giovanni Battista decollato* in which, after the Baptist is beheaded, the soul departs for Limbo.

[37] Molinari, *Spettacoli*, 82–83.

mid-century.[38] Moreover, I have found nothing in documents to suggest parallels in Florentine staging to the tiered seating-in-the-round for the audience and for the presence of a narrator or expositor on stage.[39]

In his discussion of Fouquet, Graham Runnalls pointed to a pattern in the French virgin martyr plays that is clearly understood in the Italian plays of Cecilia, Domitilla, Apollonia, and the martyred virgins who will follow them.[40] A previously dutiful child proclaims his or her new-found faith, and refuses to recant in the face of outraged authorities. Those authorities — fathers, governors, emperors, rejected suitors — order a crescendo of torments to subvert the saint's faith, but the saint continues to make converts. The saint transcends suffering, or feels no pain at all, and does not die until finally beheaded. Increasingly, the tortures become the most important part of the plays — *Sant'Agata, Santa Barbara, Santa Cristina,* and *Santa Felicita* and her seven sons will be discussed later — and these could be as simple or as complicated as circumstances allowed. There is also an element of comic irony: the tyrant boasts more and more desperately that he will make the saint see sense, and invariably the saint preaches back to him, becoming increasingly eloquent with every torment, converting those around her. The saint always triumphs. However young the saint, and in defiance of the imagined weaknesses and reticence of her gender, faith brings her the gifts of wisdom, eloquence, and fortitude, and she is rewarded when her soul is transported up to heaven.

In the representation of female saints on stage, an additional question arises: does the appearance of the female martyr, increasingly unclothed and increasingly radiant, arouse sexual as well as spiritual desire?[41] Jocelyn Wogan-Browne has argued that in medieval Britain the collections of lives of female saints and martyrs were read principally by women, and they constituted a "diet of licensed 'body-ripping' [that] seems on the face of it scarcely sustaining literature, even allowing for the possibility of an audience

---

[38] Graham Runnalls demonstrated the existence of a late-fifteenth-century *mistaire* of *saincte Apoline* in the stock of a bookseller in Tours, even though the text does not survive; see Runnalls, "The Catalogue," "Towards a Typology," and "Jean Fouquet's 'Martyrdom,'" 82. His Fouquet article was part of an ongoing debate with Gordon Kipling; see Kipling, "Theatre as Subject" and "Fouquet, St Apollonia."

[39] On this role, see essays in Butterworth, ed., *The Narrator, the Expositor, the Prompter.*

[40] Runnalls, "Jean Fouquet's 'Martyrdom,'" 88.

[41] Winstead, *Virgin Martyrs*; Blanton, "Chaste Marriage"; Carlson, "Using Apollonia," "Spectator Response," and *Performing Bodies in Pain.*

colluding with its own worst interests."[42] But where the actors and audience were the boys and young men of youth confraternities, where the message of the play was the power of faithful virginity and the eloquence that it endows, the entertainment lay not in the violence but in its manner of representation. The audience is not required to participate in the brutality, but rather to be entertained by the skill and ingenuity with which it was represented, and to triumph over it with the saint. I shall return to the subject of virgin martyrs in later chapters.

La rappresentazione della reina Ester

The Play of Queen Esther is the sixth element of the *Domitilla* volume, and like other plays in these two volumes it examines issues of female faith, courage, and integrity.[43] The narrative derives ultimately from a simplified and stream-lined *volgarizzamento* of the Book of Esther, chapters 1–8, from the Ketuvim, the third section of the Hebrew Bible. The Book of Esther was known to Jerome also in an extended Greek version that he accepted as a canonical work of the Vulgate Old Testament. It also circulated independently in several fourteenth-century vernacular prose versions, of which one was used by our author.[44] The subject had already been treated by Lucrezia Tornabuoni, whose *Storia di Ester regina* probably circulated by memorization and

---

[42] Wogan-Browne, "Saints' Lives," 315.

[43] *Incomincia la rappresentatione della reina Hester* ([Florence: Antonio Miscomini, c. 1484]), ISTC ir00029680, q–s⁸ t⁴; Cioni, *Bibliografia*, 127, xxv.1; modern edition and translation, see Table 2. For commentary see Bianchi, "Personaggi." The play is anonymous, but in the Trivulziana copy of the second edition (ISTC ie00111500; Inc. H 431; see below, fig. 8.25) the words "di Abbate Domenico" have been added above the title, fol. a1ʳ, by a later hand, perhaps Anton Maria Salvini; cf. fig. 7.4. The Abbot Domenico, not otherwise identified, is the author of *La rappresentazione di Diecimila Martiri* ([Florence: n. p. 1558]), dedicated to Argentina Malaspina, and thus datable to the period 1502–1512, when her husband Piero Soderini was *gonfaloniere a vita* (see chapter 9 below); the annotation in *Reina Hester* may indicate that he was the owner rather than the author.

[44] The Hebrew text stops at Esther 10:3; the dream recounted by Mordecai at the end of the play and his exhortation (see oct. 137–141) are found in Esther 10:4–13. For an edition of the *volgarizzamento* of the longer version, found in BMVe, It. v.18 (5611), fols. 163ʳ–174ʳ, see *I libri di Tobia di Giuditta e di Ester*, 77–99; see also Cerullo, "Il volgarizzamento," 247. The version published by Zambrini, *Storia della reina Ester*, is shorter and not directly related to the play or to Tornabuoni's poem.

recitation within her own circle.[45] There does not appear to be any direct relationship between the play and the *poemetto* of *Ester*, but it is clear that Esther, like Susanna, Tobit, and John the Baptist, is part of a culture that is shared by the Medici household, its friends, and the play-making confraternities.

The play no longer has its prologue, although the opening stage direction reads "When the Angel's prologue has finished [...]" (Finita l'annuntiatione [...]), and there is no material that would contextualize a performance of the play, but the convoluted and exotic narrative is quickly domesticated into a Florentine setting of palace and garden. Assuero, king of Persia (now commonly identified with Xerxes),[46] summons to his feast the kings of India, Armenia, and Ethiopia, who admire the delights of his palace and garden (oct. 1–19). When Assuero's beautiful queen Vasti refuses to be paraded before them, she is repudiated, stripped of her clothes and crown, and sent away (oct. 20–35). Assuero orders eligible virgins to be brought for his inspection and selects from these the Hebrew orphan Ester, humble, obedient, and beautiful, to be his new queen (oct. 36–47). Two envious courtiers plot against Assuero, but they are overheard by Ester's uncle Mardocheo, who saves Assuero's life by telling Ester to warn the king. The traitors are hanged, and the matter is recorded in Assuero's chronicle (oct. 48–63). Assuero appoints a grand vizier, Aman. When Mardocheo refuses to bow down to him, Aman orders the extermination of all the Jews (oct. 64–80). Mardocheo now seeks Ester's help. She first puts on sackcloth and ashes and prays, then she adorns herself to visit the king. Moved by her swoon, the king promises to grant whatever she asks, and to order a feast to which Aman too will be invited (oct. 81–95). Irony is the mode of the next section. Aman prepares the gallows for Mardocheo and celebrates his triumph with his wife. When night comes, Assuero cannot sleep and asks for a random passage to be read from his chronicle. It is the passage about Mardocheo, and when the king discovers that Mardocheo has received no reward he asks Aman what a man who has served the king well should receive. Aman, believing that he is that man, proposes great pomp, and is then ordered to do such honour to Mardocheo. He obeys, then returns to his wife and reveals his humiliation (oct. 96–106). The next day, Aman arrives late at Ester's banquet. Now Ester reveals her Jewish

---

[45] *Istoria di Ester* with *Vita di Tubia*, in Tornabuoni, *Poemetti biblici*, ed. Ardissino. On Tornabuoni, see above, chapter 3, n. 144.

[46] Only in the first stage direction is the king called Assuero; Ansuero is the form used throughout the play.

identity and her request: that the king should spare her people. The king is astonished to hear that their massacre has been ordered in his name and goes to walk in his garden. Aman pleads with Ester, but she throws herself on her bed and pretends not to hear. In the garden, the king learns of Aman's hatred of Mardocheo, and returns to find Aman apparently attempting to violate Ester. Aman is arrested and he, his wife, and his sons are hanged on the gallows by an enthusiastic executioner (oct. 107–125). Aman's edict is revoked and Mardocheo, appointed in his place, bids farewell to the audience (oct. 126–141).

The scenic space created in the play is highly evocative. It is difficult not to see the palace and garden, which are lavishly praised by the visitors, as a fictionalization of the Medici palace and gardens in the Via Larga.[47] I have no doubt that the three kings of India, Armenia, and Ethiopia who come with their retinues are related to the festive groups who went in procession for the *feste* of the Magi, St. Bartholomew, and St. George, discussed in chapter 5. And Assuero's speech to his guests on *concordia* and communal government (oct. 15–17) belongs more to late-fifteenth-century Florence than to ancient Persia.[48]

The action of the play moves through a series of feasts — or one continuous Carnival feast — as Assuero entertains his barons then celebrates his marriage to Ester, and as Ester organizes the banquet to which Aman is invited. So many of the plays incorporate a feast — the homecoming feast in Muzi's *Vitel sagginato*, Herod's banquet in *San Giovanni decollato*, the governor's banquet with the resurrected fowls in the *Festa del pellegrino*, Holofernes' feast in *Judit ebrea* of 1517/18, as well as wedding banquets in *Santa Cecilia*, *Griselda*, and *Stella*, to name ones that come readily to mind — that it seems reasonable to imagine that the audience, or some part of it, was

---

[47] For a similar palace and garden setting, see the plays of the *Re superbo* and of *Susanna*, both copied before 1464, and of *Barlaam e Iosafat*, performed in 1474, on which see Cicali, "L'occultamento," 63. Discussing the corresponding passage of Tornabuoni's *Hester*, Mario Martelli suggests that her description has various elements in common with Poliziano's description of Venus's palace in the *Stanze*, as well as with the descriptions of pavilions in Pulci's *Morgante*; see M. Martelli, "Lucrezia Tornabuoni," 83, n. 40. On marriage display in the Medici palazzo, see Ventrone, "Medicean Theater," 261–263. See also Marco di Bartolomeo Rustici's description (before 1457) of the imaginary palace of Tolomeo in *Codice Rustici: Dimostrazione*, 2:244–247, cap. 34.

[48] The theme of *concordia* is central to Pico's *Oration on the Dignity of Man* (1486; see Pico della Mirandola, *Oration*), but had long been part of political thinking in a city that professed an abhorrence of factionalism.

regularly part of the banquet and thus part of the spectacle. The stage directions are clearly related to a particular location and recreate that location for the reader. The feast, like the palace and garden, both frames the play and is part of the narrative.

The feast, the palace, and the garden are also represented on wedding chests that appear closely related to the play, both in their narrative and in their visual imagery. A single panel by Marco del Buono Giamberti (1402–1489) now in the Metropolitan Museum of Art in New York,[49] a pair of *cassoni* painted by Filippino Lippi and Sandro Botticelli and their workshop c. 1475–1480 and now dispersed through five different collections,[50] and Jacopo del Sellaio's *spalliera* panels of Esther, c. 1485, now in the Uffizi,[51] all share the play's emotional turmoil framed within opulent display. The play did not go into print before 1483, and is not known to have circulated in manuscript, but the story of Esther was clearly part of a cultural program in which female virtue, in its broadest sense of valour as well as moral virtue, is as essential to the state as male virtue.

The narrative has an ambiguous erotic charge in its feminist and a post-feminist heroines. Vasti proudly refuses to come to Assuero's banquet because she does not wish to be paraded before men, but ultimately, with the patience and humility of Griselda, she accepts being stripped of her crown and robes and her banishment.[52] In contrast, Ester feigns submission in order to assert authority. When the virgins are brought to the palace for Assuero to choose a beautiful and obedient bride, the author is careful to avoid any suggestion that this is a pageant of under-age harlots, or that Ester will be joining a large harem. Instead, the scene is more like that recreated by Judith Bryce in her 2001 essay on dancing, "Performing for Strangers," in which daughters of leading families were required to dance before noble visitors, or that found in the poetic descriptions of chaste dancing before the adolescent Galeazzo Maria Sforza when he visited Florence in 1459.[53] When Ester is selected, her words foreshadow Mary's as she presents herself as *ancilla*:

[49] See Baskins, "Typology, Sexuality"; Bayer, ed., *Art and Love,* 12, 63, 109, 129, 133–34, 298, no. 57, fig. 2 (colour detail), ills. 134–35; C. Campbell, ed., *Love and Marriage,* 24, fig. 8.

[50] Nelson, "Storie di Ester."

[51] Pons, "Storie di Ester."

[52] The play of *Griselda* is probably contemporary; see below.

[53] Bryce, "Performing for Strangers"; *Le onoranze fiorentine,* 98–9, lines 3814–3885. On instances of dancing in the *rappresentazioni,* see A.W. Smith, "References to Dance."

ESTER *s'inginochia e dice:*
Ecco l'ancilla tua; signor, farai
sempre di me ciò che 'l tuo cor disia.

ESTHER *kneels and says:*
Behold your handmaiden; always, my lord,
do whatsoever your heart will desire.

(oct. 43.5–6; cf. 41.8)

But Ester uses her beauty as well as her wits to deceive the king and to protect
herself and her people. When she visits Assuero unannounced and against his
orders, a well-timed swoon and a swift and flattering answer save her from
his wrath:

Le donzelle gli pongono la corona e li
vestimenti reali, e ella appoggiandosi
a uno va a corte, e entrando al re, il
re gli fa mal viso; e lei cade in terra
tramortita, e IL RE *corre, e volendola*
consolare la piglia e istropìcciala, e dice:

Her maids dress her in her crown and her
royal robes, and supported by one of her
servants she goes to the court, and when she
comes into the presence of the king, he looks
at her angrily; and she falls to the ground
in a faint, and THE KING *runs to her, and*
trying to console her he picks her up and
chafes her with his hands and says:

   Gentilissima Ester, diletta sposa,
ch'ha' tu aùto? O Ester, non temere.
Sta un poco IL RE, *e poi dice:*
Deh, non temere, Ester mia graziosa
ché tu puo' venir sempre al tuo piacere.

   Most noble Esther, my beloved bride,
what ails you? Esther, do not be afraid.
THE KING *pauses a moment, and then says:*
Ah, fairest Esther, do not be afraid,
for you can come whenever you should
   [please.

ESTER *si risente e dice:*
I' viddi la tua faccia gloriosa
sì che lo splendor suo mi fe' cadere.

ESTHER *recovers and says:*
I saw the radiant glory of your face,
such that its very splendour made me fall.

(oct. 93)

And later, when Aman throws himself at her feet to beg for mercy, she allows
Assuero to continue under the misapprehension that she was being violated.

   The story of Esther is central to the gynocentric feast of Purim in the
Jewish calendar, celebrating the deliverance of the Jews of Persia from their
enemy Haman. It is a movable feast, falling a month before Passover, around
the fourteenth day of the month of Adar (Esther 9:18, 10:1), that is, in February or March in the Roman calendar. The play, however, gives a specific date:
Aman's massacre will take place on 3 March (oct. 75.3, 76.4), a date so specific

that it suggests a date of performance. The date 3 March fell in the last week of Carnival in 1453/4, 1469/70, and 1480/1, however the complexities of the Julian/Gregorian and Jewish calendar have not allowed me to reconcile these dates with the feast of Purim.

Purim often falls in Carnival and in its celebration of violence — enacted in the play in the boisterous hanging of Aman and his family — it has much in common with the ritual violence of stone fights and bonfires. Purim is now associated with satirical plays but a careful examination of chronology suggests that Purim plays, the *Purim-shpiln* of the Yiddish tradition, are a mid-sixteenth-century grafting of Christian Carnival traditions, particularly the German *Fastnachtspiel*, onto the Jewish holy day of feasting and charity.[54] Even if our author was not aware of the Jewish feast day and its intersections with the Christian calendar, there can be no doubt that he (or she) was fully aware of the Jewish presence in Florence and of the mounting Franciscan campaign to establish Christian loan funds, accompanied by virulent invective against the Jews.[55] Nevertheless, a Jewish heroine is appropriated here as a model of resistance against oppression, and not as a target of invective.

Like its source, the play also examines the role of the ruler and how he can establish and maintain his authority.[56] The two scenes that involve the royal chronicles give an extraordinary glimpse of the ruler, his official historiographer, the twin purposes of Latin and vernacular histories in royal households, and Florentine awareness of how such histories were first created and then used. When King Ansuero has been saved by Mardocheo, he gives orders for the event to be recorded:

Risponde IL RE:	THE KING *replies:*
Scriverrai, cancellier, questo accidente	O chancellor, you'll write of this event
per ordin tutto nella storia nostra.	in all its detail in our history.
El fedel Mardocheo abbi a mente,	Remember faithful Mordecai, and show
e 'l suo gran beneficio a punto mostra.	the act of human kindness he performed.

---

[54] Narrative poems based on the Book of Esther date from at least the fifteenth century. On the genre, Shmeruk, "Purim-Shpil," 16: 744–746. For a sixteenth-century *cantare* of Esther in *ottava rima*, in Italian but transliterated into Hebrew characters, see Busi, *La istoria de Purim*.

[55] Fubini, "Prestito ebraico," 119–120; Delcorno, "The Roles of Jews," 254–260; and see discussion of the *Miracolo del Corpo di Cristo* above, chapter 5.

[56] It is possible to see the Pazzi conspiracy as a subtext within the play (see Delcorno, "The Roles of Jews," 255), but I suspect that *Reina Ester* is earlier than 1478.

Risponde il Cancellieri *con riverenza:*	The Chancellor *replies reverently:*
Scritto sarà, signore, interamente	My lord, it will be written and in full
com'io comprendo esser la voglia vostra;	just as I understand you want it done,
e quel che 'l tempo toglie alla memoria	and what time wipes from memory will be
eterno fia, sendo scritto in istoria.	eternal once it's writ in history.

(oct. 63)

Later, when Assuero cannot sleep he calls for his history to be read to him:

Mentre che le forche si fanno, il Re *dice così:*	*While the gallows are being constructed,* the King *says as follows:*
Poi ch'i' non posso istanotte dormire,	Because I cannot get to sleep tonight
e pur vorrei questo tempo passare,	and yet would want to while this time away,
cancellier, fa' le storie mie venire,	chancellor, have my history brought here
e leggi un po', ch'i' le voglio ascoltare.	and read a while, because I want to listen.
Il Cancellieri *toglie e libri e dice:*	The Chancellor *takes the books and says:*
Ecco la storia tua, potente sire,	Here is your history, most mighty sire,
ch'i' ho composta e ridotta in volgare.	that I've composed and then put in our
El libro, a caso aperto destramente,	[tongue.
dice così nel capitol presente [...]	The book falls open most judiciously,
	and in the present chapter it relates [...]

(oct. 97)

Although the scenes are present both in the Hebrew and the Greek narrative (Esther 2:23, 6:1–2), they are found in only one of the *volgarizzamenti*: the elaboration here is a marker of a new and particularly Florentine commitment to vernacular history and chronicle.[57]

La rappresentazione della Reina Ester *is one of the finest examples of the genre. The author is fully aware of the ambiguities of the story and delights in Esther's guile, allowing it to show through in particularly cohesive dialogue.

---

[57] *I libri di Tobia di Giuditta e di Ester,* 83 and 89; See also Tornabuoni de' Medici, *Sacred Narratives,* 181 and 197. Leonardo Bruni's *Historiarum Florentinarum Libri xii* had been completed in 1442 and translated into Italian by Donato Acciaiuoli in 1473.

La rappresentazione di san Francesco

The fifth element in the first Miscomini volume, *The Play of St. Francis*, is securely attributed to Antonia Pulci.[58] Because it would take too long to recite all the mysteries of his holy life (oct. 3.1–2), the author selects and adapts a series of key moments from the *Legenda major* of St. Bonaventure, known probably through the hugely popular *volgarizzamento* sometimes attributed to Domenico Cavalca.[59] In ninety-six octaves, Pulci links them in a way that has been described as "on the whole pleasing and characterized by a certain variety, [but] formally weak and poorly put together,"[60] although it is no more disconnected than the scenes of the two major St. Francis fresco cycles in Florence, Giotto's scenes in the Bardi Chapel of Santa Croce (c. 1317) and Domenico Ghirlandaio's chapel for the Sassetti family in Santa Trinita (1483–1485). The play covers similar key episodes: St. Francis's charity, his conversion and renunciation of worldly goods, the foundation of his Order and the approval of its rule, his visit to the Sultan and the ordeal by fire, the miracle of the stigmata, his miraculous cure of the widow's son, and his death, surrounded by his followers and assisted by Jacopa da Settesoli. The action thus moves from Assisi to Babylon and La Verna, and back to Assisi.

Weaver has highlighted the play's intimate relationship with Antonia's personal story. Her father's name was Francesco, given to him in an age when Florentines had all but abandoned their congratulatory and augural names like Benvenuto and Dietisalvi and instead named their sons for saints who

---

[58] *Rappresentatione di sancto Francesco composta per mona Antonia donna di Bernardo Pulci* ([Florence: Antonio Miscomini, c. 1484]), ISTC ir00029680, n-o⁸ p⁴; Cioni, *Bibliografia*, 142–143, XXXI.1; for modern editions, see Table 2. For commentary, see Palandri, "Rappresentazioni," 417–430; Ferrigni, "San Francesco"; Cardini, "La figura di Francesco"; A. Mancini, "Francesco nella lauda"; Ulysse, "Un couple," 186–187; Weaver, in Antonia Pulci, *Saints' Lives*, 43–47; Villoresi, *Sacrosante parole*, 119–121.

[59] *Vita di S. Francesco.* The correlated passages are given in Palandri, "Rappresentazioni," 422–430.

[60] Palandri, "Rappresentazioni," 422: "varia ed attraente nell'insieme, slegata e fiacca nella forma"; cited by Weaver, in Antonia Pulci, *Saints' Lives*, 46. Ferrigni further observes "but it is of an academic rather than popular nature, and seems to be made for a reception hall or for a garden (of the Medici perhaps, even of Lucrezia Tornabuoni) rather than for a piazza: for an educated audience rather than for the common people" (ha però carattere piuttosto accademico che popolare, e sembra esser fatta per una sala o per un giardino (di casa Medici forse, di Lucrezia Tornabuoni magari) anziché per una piazza: per un pubblico letterato piuttosto che per una folla popolare); Ferrigni, "San Francesco," 208.

could then be honoured with chapels. Episodes in the life of St. Francis in which Bernardo and Jacopa feature may be intended to pay homage to Antonia's husband and mother respectively, while she omits all mention of St. Clare.[61] The play is remarkable among the lives of St. Francis in the role it attributes to the saint's mother, who overcomes the limitations of her gender and frees him from the prison where his father's wrath has confined him.[62]

No performance is known and the play is undated, but Weaver argues strongly for the play's performability.[63] It does, moreover, reflect many of the values of the youth confraternity plays. Francis is still a youth under his father's jurisdiction when he defies his father's will by renouncing wealth. When faced with his father's wrath, he calls on the God who delivered Jacob from Esau's rage, Daniel from the lion's den, and Esther from the rage of Ahasuerus (oct. 14.2–4, 43.1) — all subjects of youth confraternity plays — and is saved.

La rappresentazione di san Francesco come convertì tre ladroni e fecionsi frati

The second St. Francis play, the last element of the *Domitilla* volume, is more engaging. While Antonia Pulci's play deals with the great themes of the saint's life, the anonymous *Play of How St. Francis Converted Three Thieves and They Became Friars*[64] is taken from the first part of chapter 26 of the *Fioretti di san*

---

[61] On names, see Herlihy, "Tuscan Names"; on Francesco, Jacopa, and Bernardo, see Weaver, in Antonia Pulci, *Saints' Lives*, 46.

[62] On Francis's family dynamics, see Trexler, *Naked before the Father*.

[63] Weaver notes that Pulci must have been familiar with Giotto's frescoes in the Bardi chapel in the Franciscan basilica of Santa Croce (after 1317); in Weaver, in Antonia Pulci, *Saints' Lives*, 44. Santa Croce was home to the flagellant and festive company of San Bartolomeo, which had secondary devotions to St. Francis and to the Archangel Raphael and Tobias; see above, chapter 5 and fig. 5.2. Villoresi relates the play to Ghirlandaio's frescoes of the life of St. Francis in the Sassetti chapel in Santa Trinita, which date to 1483–1485; Villoresi, "San Francesco," 107 and 111, n. 11. Stallini, *Le théâtre*, 192–193, misreading Landucci, suggests that a St. Francis play was performed for Pope Sixtus IV, but in fact Landucci wrote: "And on 15 January [1477/8] Pope Sixtus [...] decreed that the Feast of St. Francis should be observed like feast days of obligation" (E a dì 15 di giennaio [1477/8], fece Papa Sisto [...] che si guardassi la festa di San Francesco come le feste comandate); Landucci, *Diario*, 16.

[64] *Incomincia la rappresentatione di san Francesco come converti tre ladroni et fecionsi frati* ([Florence: Antonio Miscomini, c. 1484]), ISTC ir00029680, aa–bb[8]; Cioni, *Bibliografia*, 143–144, xxxii.1; for modern edition, see Table 2. See commentary in Ferrigni, "San Francesco," 210–212.

Francesco (The little flowers of St. Francis): "How St. Francis converted three murderous thieves, and they became friars; and the most noble vision seen by one of them who became a most holy friar."[65] The scene is a forest, close to the entrance of St. Francis's friary. We are introduced first to a young man (not identified as Frate Agnolo, future *guardiano*) who has resolved to enter the friary, but on his way he meets the Devil, disguised as a lay brother. The Devil claims that there is no point because the friary has just been struck by plague and consumed by flames. The young man insists on going there, if only to bury the dead, leaving the Devil to rue a missed opportunity:

EL DIAVOLO *dice seco medesimo:*

    Non è un'ora colui era dannato,
pe' sua peccati l'alma avea perduta,
e or che s'è pentuto e' s'è salvato
che ha l'alma giù d'inferno riavuta.
Guardisi ognun da uom deliberato
perché gli ha sempre il Signor che l'aiuta.
Volli giuntar colui col morbo e fuoco
e finalmente il ver sempre ha suo loco.

THE DEVIL *says to himself:*

    It's not even an hour since he was
      [damned,
for all his sins his soul was truly lost,
and, now that he's repented, he is saved
and has retrieved his soul from down in hell.
Let all beware when men make up their minds
because the Lord is always there to help.
With plague and fire I tried beguiling him
and in the end the truth has had its way.

(oct. 9)

The young man reaches the friary and is admitted by St. Francis. Next, the three bandits appear, Calcagno, Mazone, and Giunta (Heel, Club, and Cheat). They fall upon a passing merchant who reveals that he is as much a thief as they are. As he lies wounded, he cries: "All my ill-gotten gains, where are they gone, | my false contracts and my usurious loans??" (Dove è la robba mia mal guadagnata, | e falsi mia contratti e molte usure ; oct. 18 1–2), at which the thieves let him go. We see St. Francis leave the friary, and the action returns to the thieves, who now, not having eaten for three days, resolve to raid the friary. Through the door they demand food but they are sent on their way with harsh words by the *guardiano* (oct. 31) and retreat to their cave. When St. Francis returns, he discovers to his dismay that the highwaymen have not been received with charity and sends Frate Agnolo to find them and give them food and invite them to repent. They refuse, but left alone, they examine the food:

---

[65] *Fioretti*, 47–49, XXVI *Come Santo Francesco convertì tre ladroni micidiali, e fecionsi Frati; e della nobilissima visione, che vide uno di loro, il quale fu santissimo Frate.*

E malandrini pigliano el pane in mano	*The thieves pick up the bread to eat it and*
per mangiare e MAZONE *dice così:*	MAZONE *says:*
Forse ch'i' guarderò se gli è muffato	Perhaps I ought to look if there is mould
o se gli è secco i' nol potrò mangiare.	or if it's so dried out that I can't eat.
Io ho il ciel colla terra raccozato	I've brought heaven so close to earth that
che un sol minuzol non ne può cascare.	[not
	a single crumb can fall out of my hand.
Calcagno dice ch'i' sono sdentato	Calcagno says I'm toothless and that's why
ch'i' non so il mio panetto rassettare.	I cannot even chew my loaf of bread.
Guarda s'i' sono al pettine infingardo:	We'll see if I'm a slouch in front of food:
questa la salsa par di san Bernardo.	This sauce looks good enough for St.
	[Bernàrd![66]

(oct. 46)

The rough, colourful language, as Villoresi aptly observes, is reminiscent of Luigi Pulci's Margutte,[67] but the third thief, Calcagno, begins to repent (and to modify his language) and persuades the others to join him in becoming a friar. The Devil falls in with them as they go, this time disguised as a soldier, and tries various tricks with the promise of food, the threat of hunger, even the promise of forgiveness if repentance is postponed. Finally, Calcagno recognizes the Devil and banishes him with the sign of the cross. The three make their way to the friary where they are welcomed by St. Francis and receive their habits "with the customary ceremonies" (con le cerimonie ordinarie; stage direction before oct. 81) and the Angel returns to bid the audience farewell.

The Devil, the evildoings of the thieves, and the lively dialogue are all the invention of the dramatist, who then omits the remaining three-quarters of the story: the vision, and the death of two of the three thieves. The message of the *fioretto* is reworked to highlight the importance of charitable acts in the scheme of God's work; the play communicates that message with a totally captivating contest between good intentions and the Devil. As in the play of *San Bernardo*, about the robber baron and his diabolic scullery hand,[68] and as

---

[66] *la salsa di San Bernardo*: salt and hunger.

[67] Villoresi, *Sacrosante parole*, 120: "Paiono compari di Margutte — come lui, potremmo dire, "cattivi in sin nell'ovo" –, ovvero usciti dalle ottave del *Morgante*" (they seem to be colleagues of Margutte — like him, we might say, "bad from the egg" — as if they had stepped from the octave of the *Morgante*).

[68] See above, chapter 3.

in the play of the *Abataccio*, there is a critique of wealth acquired dishonestly, and a cautionary tale about the wiles of the Devil, who moves in the midst of ordinary people. Here, as in the earlier plays, the Devil is unrecognized by those around him. He is not a medieval pagan devil, with mask and pitchfork and wings; there must have been some more subtle way by which the audience could know, even when other characters in the play did not, that this is the Deceiver who must be vanquished. A much later image, illustrating the Eighth Day of the *Passion de Valenciennes* (fig. 6.7; see also fig. 3.27), shows the Devil, disguised as a hermit, tempting Christ. Christ recognizes him, because his knowledge is perfect; the audience recognizes him because it knows this story well; but at another level, his clawed bird-feet and his horns are invisible. The Devil can lurk unseen and unrecognized in any place. This leaves open the question of the extent to which the Devil was real to the actors and their audience, that is, a monstrous being who might visit them or carry them off, or whether the Devil is entirely a moral construct, a metaphor, made real and present through their performances. The more heinous the sinfulness represented the better, for the way in which the power of Good, expressed through saints or angels, the Virgin, or God himself, is shown to be stronger still.

La rappresentazione di sant'Antonio della Barba romito

A platoon of masked and instantly recognizable devils plays a major role in *The Play of St. Anthony of the Beard, Hermit* (in later editions *Sant'Antonio abbate* [St. Anthony Abbot]), which is the eighth element of the *Domitilla* volume.[69] The starting point is once again Domenico Cavalca's translation of the *Vite dei*

---

[69] *Incomincia la rapresentatione di sancto Antonio della Barba romito* ([Florence: Antonio Miscomini, c. 1484]), ISTC ir00029680, y–z⁸ &⁶; Cioni, *Bibliografia*, 86, x.1; for modern editions, see Table 2. The version "in parlata abruzzese" (in Abruzzese dialect), cited by Cioni, 90, xʙ, does not exist; this is a garbled reference to Toschi's edition of 1927. The edition included in the *Primo libro* of the Giunti collection is titled: *La Rappresentatione di Santo Antonio Abate. Il quale conuerti una sorella, e fecela monaca nel ministero delle Murate di Firenze. E come non uolendo tre ladroni accettare el suo consiglio s'ammazzorno lun laltro e furno portati a casa Satanasso. Et egli fu terribilmente bastonato da i diauoli* (The play of St. Anthony Abbot, who converted his sister and made her a nun in the Murate convent in Florence, and of how three thieves, who did not want to accept his advice, killed each other and were carried off to Satan's, and he was terribly beaten by devils; Florence: [Giunti?], 1555), CNCE 46845. For the problematic attribution to Antonia Pulci, see above, n. 6, and below in this section.

Santi Padri,[70] but the dramatist is dealing with a young Sant'Antonio — and, despite the title, not the aged hermit with very long beard and stick — and he (or she) has added much that is new and charmingly contemporary. One clause in the source, "entrusting his sister to some very holy virgins in a nunnery, so that they might shape her to their example,"[71] is transformed into a whole scene in which Antonio persuades his reluctant sister to abandon everything:

Risponde LA SORELLA *ad Antonio:*	THE SISTER *replies to Antonio:*
Dunque vuo' tu, fratel, ch'io abandoni	So, do you want me, brother, to forsake
le gran magnificenze e la riccheza.	this great magnificence and affluence,
la bella casa e tante possessioni	all my possessions and my lovely house,
e povera diventi, essendo aveza	and to become a pauper, even though
a viver con letizia, e ch'i' mi doni	I love to live in mirth, and give myself
alla religïon con ogni aspreza?	to all the harshness of religious life?
I' ti vo' dire il vero: e' mi par certo	Let me tell you the truth: I really think
che tu sia poco savio e meno esperto.	you're not too smart and even less aware.
	(oct. 25)

She asks whether it is not possible to do good, "living in the non-religious world" (vivendo al mondo non‹ne› religioso; oct. 27.2) but Antonio tells her the risks are too great. She apologizes for her "foolish and wicked words" (parlare stolto e rio; oct. 28.3) and puts herself in his hands. He dispatches her, anachronistically, to the great Florentine convent of the Murate, founded in 1424:

Vo', mona Piera, compagnia le fate,	Take her now, Mona Piera, to the nuns
insino al munister delle Murate.	immured in the Murate nunnery.
	(oct. 28.7–8)

She is not forgotten there. When the Spirit of Apathy tempts Antonio (oct. 54–57), one of his arguments is that Antonio should have found her a husband before he renounced the world:

---

[70] Cavalca, *Vite*, 1:524–583, 1.5–7, 1.20.

[71] Cavalca, *Vite*, 1:526, 1.5.10: "racomandando la sorella ad alquante vergine santissime d'un monasterio, che lla 'nformasseno al loro exemplo."

... dovevi prima maritare	Firstly, you should have found a husband for
la tua sorella, e poi il mondo lasciare.	your sister, then you could have left the
	[world.

Non pensi tu che se le rincrescesse	Just think, if she resented being made
lo star rinchiusa, per la sua sciagura	to live encloistered, to her deep dismay,
e, ritornando al secolo, si desse	and therefore turned to live outside again,
al viver disonesto e con sozura,	and gave herself to wanton, sinful life,
tu saresti cagion ch'ella perdesse	then you would be the reason she would lose
l'anima sua, con fama trista e scura?	her soul and reputation, bleak and black.
Sì che, parlando teco il vero scorto,	And so, this is my message loud and true:
che lasci questi panni i' ti conforto.	I do exhort you, cast this habit off.

(oct. 55.7–56.8)

This topical reference helps to tie the play to the world of Antonia Pulci, even though her name does not appear on it. While other parts of the play locate the action in the landscape of the Desert Fathers around Alexandria and Damiata, the saint's sister is in Florence, and, like Annalena de' Tanini, sister of Antonia Pulci, is a nun in the elite Benedictine convent of the Murate.[72] At about the same time as Miscomini printed the two volumes of plays, he also issued Bernardo Pulci's *Passione*, dedicated to Annalena.[73]

---

[72] Weddle, "Enclosing Le Murate," "'Women in wolves' mouths,'" "Women's Place," and "The Ritual Frame," online.

[73] Bernardo urges her: "Take a good look at the state in which you have been placed, bound in religion to so many most excellent sisters, not only an honour and mirror to our city but also an example and ornament to all Italy, such that it seems not only that you have taken care of yourself but that you have sought the example of the virgins of ancient times, endeavouring to surpass them in obedience, as you swore to do when you took your vows, to desire and not desire whatever your superior wishes. There is no religion, no nun, no convent where there is not obedience, because limbs that are not in accord with the head are the destruction of the body. Strait and arduous is the path that leads us to Glory" (Raguarda bene lo stato in che se' posta: fra quante prestantissime suore riligata. Non solo della nostra città honore e spechio: ma ancora di tutta Italia exemplo e ornamento: acioché paia che non solo di te ti sia curata, ma che degli altri exempli delle antiche virgini tu habbi havuto invidia, cercando l'altre superare in obedientia, e come nel tuo sponsalitio giurasti volere, e non volere, quello che piace al tuo superiore. Non è religione, non monaca o monasterio, dove non è obedienza, peroché le membra discordante dal capo sono destructione del corpo. Arta e difficile è la via che ci conduce alla Gloria), Bernardo Pulci, *Passione* (1486), fol. [*]3ᵛ. On Annalena Tanini, see Weaver, in Antonia Pulci, *Saints' Lives*, 8, n. 18, and 13.

Once Sant'Antonio has dispatched his sister and given away his worldly goods, his real problems begin. Satan summons the Seven Deadly Sins to lead an army of devils to avenge their banishment from heaven. They are to fill men with pride, envy, sins of the flesh, prodigality and avarice, but above all avarice. Sant'Antonio is not defenceless: an Angel reassures him, and he is easily able to recognize and repel the demon of Fornication, who returns to Satan, defeated. Satan sends the demon of Apathy, disguised as a hermit. Antonio confesses his loss of fervour, but when Apathy questions his treatment of his sister, he recognizes him as the Devil. Apathy wishes Gluttony better luck, but when this 'hermit' tells him that grass and water are not good for him, once again Antonio recognizes the Devil. In the next scene, deriving closely from Cavalca's *vita*, Antonio now goes into the desert where he is visited by two pagans from Ethiopia with their interpreter.[74] The visit is inconclusive — the pagans depart without being converted — but the interest lies in the representation of interpreting: the pagans speak lines in Greek — unfortunately not given in the text — that the interpreter translates (oct. 66–72). A fourth devil, the demon of Avarice, visits the desert and places first a silver bowl and then a pile of gold where Sant'Antonio will pass by. He ignores both and leaves for the desert.

The rest of the action (oct. 77–120) brings us three highwaymen, Scaramuccia, Tagliagambe, and Carapello (Scaramouche, Leg-cutter, and Snatch), who had no part in Cavalca's *vita*. They meet Sant'Antonio just after he has been beaten by devils (fig. 6.8) and healed by Christ. He warns them to flee but they ignore his advice. They find the gold, then draw lots to see who should go to buy food. Scaramuccia sets out for Damascus, and on the way decides to buy poison to do away with his two henchmen, but they are lying in wait and kill him on his return, before preparing their supper and drinking the poisoned wine he has brought. In a second major anachronism, Tagliagambe tries to send to Bisticci — the bookshop of Vespasiano da Bisticci near the Florentine Badia — or to the barber at the Canto de' Ricci for the recipe of an antidote (oct. 118.1–3), but it is too late. All three die, and the spirit of Avarice takes their souls to Satan. The Angel returns to remind the audience of the ills that the "accursed wolf" (maladetta lupa) of Avarice (oct. 122.2) brings into the world and to urge them to follow the example of Antonio, who "in his youth forsook possessions and chose poverty" (nella giovinezzza | lasciò

---

[74] Cavalca, *Vite*, 1:582, I.20.1–5.

la robba e la povertà prese; oct. 123.1–2).[75] The episode of the three thieves comes from an unrelated work dating to the last decades of the thirteenth century, known variously as *Le ciento novelle antike* (One hundred ancient tales), or the *Novellino*, in which novella 83 relates "The story of a hermit who was travelling through the wilderness and found a great quantity of treasure."[76]

The question of authorship remains open. Cioni attributes the play to Antonia Pulci, citing Colomb de Batines as his authority, but I have found no such attribution in Colomb de Batines's *Bibliografia* nor in any of the standard incunable reference works. Nevertheless, it appears increasingly likely that this, like most of the works in the two-volume anthology, is by one member or another of the Pulci family. And like so many of the plays that we have examined so far, its eremitic setting and dependence on the *Vite dei Santi Padri*, and its themes of wealth and poverty, avarice and charity, are those near to the heart of the extended Medici household. It increasingly makes sense to see most of the plays of the Miscomini volumes as closely related to the Pulci family.

La rappresentazione della Natività di Cristo

The fame of the intermittent spectacles of the Compagnia dei Magi, staged at Epiphany through the streets of Florence, has all but eclipsed a group of play texts that enact the Nativity of Christ and the surrounding events of shepherds, Magi, the Slaughter of the Innocents, and the vision of Octavian and the Sibyl. The Magi text has already been discussed in connection with the *Festa dei Magi*, and the *Festa di Ottaviano* (before 1462/3) has been set in the context of the *edifici* of St. John the Baptist. I shall now turn to *The Play of the*

---

[75] Villoresi notes in the works of Bernardo Pulci echoes generally of Petrarch, and specifically of Petrarch's *Trionfo del Tempo*, 63–64, and of the *Canzoniere*, 355, 1–2, in oct. 121; Villoresi, *Sacrosante parole*, 121–142.

[76] "Qui conta d'uno romito che andando per un luogo foresto trovò molto grande tesoro." This is the chapter title in *Libro di nouelle*, 86–88, the expurgated edition published by Vincenzio Borghini in 1572. This version is also close in its details to the version contained in *The Pardoner's Tale* in Chaucer's *Canterbury Tales*, and may already have been circulating in the fifteenth century. In the recent critical edition, *Il novellino*, 139–141, the chapter is headed "Come Cristo andando un giorno co' discepoli, videro molto grande Tesoro" (How Christ was walking with his disciples one day and they saw a great pile of treasure), which the editor, Alberto Conte, argues is the original unexpurgated version.

Nativity of Christ, the seventh element of the *Domitilla* volume and among the most frequently reprinted (fig. 6.9).[77]

The *Natività* is more self-consciously constructed than many of our plays, conflating into a single narrative the visit of the shepherds, the visit of the Magi, and the Slaughter of the Innocents. In the church calendar, the visit of the shepherds is celebrated at midnight on Christmas Eve, the Magi at Epiphany on 6 January, and the Holy Innocents on 28 December. In monasteries and cathedrals from the tenth to the sixteenth century, each feast day had its own dramatic office: the *Officium Pastorum* (Office of the Shepherds), in which the midwives greeted the shepherds at the stable with the words "Quem queritis, O Pastores?" (Whom do you seek, Shepherds?); the *Officium Stellae* (Office of the Star), in which the Magi follow the star to Bethlehem; and the *Ordo Herodis* (The Play of Herod) in which Herod's proverbial rage is followed by the Slaughter of the Innocents).[78] In confraternities and in domestic settings, the Nativity would later be enacted with the *presepio* or manger and models of the characters and animals of the narrative who gathered around the Christ Child,[79] but for fifteenth-century Florence, the evidence of popular devotion is largely limited to the proliferation of vernacular *laude* in praise of the Nativity. In the Umbrian *laudari* of the fourteenth and early fifteenth centuries, each Christmas season feast day had its own dramatized *lauda*, but in this *rappresentazione* we find the three feast days brought together in one unified narrative.

The Angel of the prologue turns immediately to the shepherds who are watching over their flocks. Like so many Nativity play shepherds, they are given names that are not formalized like those of the Magi but rather the fruit of a fantastic imagination. Here they are Nencio di Puchio (Nencio, a diminutive form of Lorenzo, is an archetypal rustic name), Bobi del Fatuchio

---

[77] *Incomincia la rappresentatione della Nativita di Christo* ([Florence: Antonio Miscomini, c. 1484]), ISTC ir00029680, u–x[8]; Cioni, *Bibliografia*, 147, XXXIII.1; for modern editions, see Table 2. The edition was reprinted with a Ghirlandaiesque woodcut: *La rappresentatione della Natiuita di Christo* ([Florence: Bartolomeo de' Libri, not after 1495]), ISTC ir00028500; Cioni, *Bibliografia*, 147, XXXIII.2. For commentary, see Eisenbichler, "Nativity"; modern performance, dir. Colin McCormick, Italian Theatre Group, Melbourne, December 1977. For other manuscript Nativity plays, see Table 1; on Italian plays of the Nativity generally, Musumarra, *La sacra rappresentazione*.

[78] Texts are included in Young, *The Drama*, 2:3–196; De Bartholomaeis, *Le origini*, 461–479; Vecchi, *Uffici drammatici*, 6–11, 174–180. See also above, chapter 5, n. 50.

[79] Rauch and Savorelli, *Storia di Natale*, but without details of first appearance.

(Monte Fatucchio, a distinctive cone-shaped mountain in the Valle Santa of the Casentino), Randello ('big stick,' a name that will appear again, as Randellino, in the scene at the beginning of Antonia Pulci's *Figliuol prodigo*, and in Castellani's *Sant'Onofrio*), and the boy Nencetto. The shepherds receive the Angel's instructions but pause to eat a meal on their hillside before they set out for Bethlehem. As they eat, a choir of angels sings a vernacular *lauda*, elsewhere attributed to Antonio Bettini (1396–1487) and based on the *Gloria in excelsis deo* of Luke 2:14.[80] When the angels have finished singing, the action cuts briefly to the stable where Mary and Joseph are adoring the Christ Child. After midnight, the three older shepherds set out from their hillside, leaving Nencetto to tidy up and tend the sheep, even though the child protests that he too wants to come and see the Son of God. The shepherds arrive at the stable and make their offering of gifts; these too the fruit of invention rather than traditional like the gifts of the Magi: six apples, cheeses, and music of the bagpipes. When Mary and Joseph have no hospitality to offer in return, the shepherds (already hungry again) share their wine and cheese, while the six apples (stage direction after oct. 14, and oct. 17.8), no doubt carefully arranged to suggest the balls of the Medici armorial bearings (see fig. 7.9), remain unconsumed at the babe's feet.

As the shepherds depart, the star brings the three kings together. The text distinguishes them only by age and origin (young from the Orient, middle-aged from an unspecified location, and old from the Levant), and not by name, colour, or gift. They have travelled for thirteen days (that is, the time from Christmas to Epiphany), and stop at Herod's court to seek advice. Herod interrogates his three sages before sending the kings to Bethlehem, and as they follow the star, he continues to question his scribes. When the star stops above the stable, the Magi offer their gifts — not gold, frankincense, and myrrh, but simply gifts, in a scene far less complex than that of the adoration of the shepherds. As the kings sleep before making an early start to return to Herod, an Angel appears and advises them, and later the Holy Family, to return home.

---

[80] *Lauda* after oct. 6, "Con giubilante core" (With rejoicing heart). In the earliest printed collection of *laude*, *Laude facte & composte* (1485/6), this *lauda* (fols. cxv^v–cxvi^r) is attributed to "Don Antonio da Siena Ingesuato," to be identified as Antonio Bettini (1396–1487). Wilson, *Singing Poetry* database, gives the *cantasi come* as "Laudate il sommo dio," for which the music is given in Razzi, *Libro primo*, edited in Mancuso, "Serafino Razzi's *Libro primo*," 416–20. Razzi notes a secular text, "Perché son io sì bella," that is sung to the same tune. See Cionacci, "Sopra *Le rime sacre*," col. 25.

The rest of the play — nineteen of the seventy octaves — is dedicated to the Wrath of Herod, his treacherous banquet, and the Slaughter of the Innocents. I have found no precedent for the four rough, bawdy women who assemble for Herod's banquet and behave like fishwives as they chivvy each other about their respective charges. Their names — Tarsia, Calcidonia, Candidora, Monusmelia — suggest chiselled or stony qualities; they are called *balie* (wet nurses), but their words identify them as the mothers rather than the wet nurses of the infants.[81] The women come as a worldly group of four, in clear contrast to the three awestruck shepherds who make the journey to Bethlehem, the three kings who recognize Christ's divinity, and the Holy Family itself. Number symbolism seems to be at work here. As Jacobus de Voragine repeats in the *Legenda Aurea*, "the number four refers to the body and the number three refers to the soul":[82] the tetrad is earthbound, the triad is divine. When all the babies have been slain, Herod returns to boast that his kingdom is safe, and the Angel returns to bid the audience farewell.

The play defies precise dating and attribution. I have already discounted the claim that Pope Eugenius IV witnessed the Archangel Raphael company's performance of a Nativity play in Florence in 1430.[83] The presence of this *Natività* in the Miscomini volumes suggests that it too is the work of somebody in the Pulci group, and thus from the 1460s or 1470s, but there is also another possibility.

The *lauda* sung by the Angel to the shepherds was attributed, as I have indicated, to the Jesuate friar Antonio da Siena.[84] This Antonio Bettini is a

---

[81] In the second (illustrated) edition, ISTC ir00028500, Calcidonia becomes Caladonia.

[82] Jacobus, *Legenda Aurea*, 1:268, cap. xxxv *De ieiuniis quatuor temporum*, 15: "homo constat ex quatuor elementis quantum ad corpus et tribus potentiis, scilicet rationabili, concupiscibili et irascibili, quantum ad animam." Jacobus cites Johannes Beleth as his authority.

[83] See above, chapter 3, n. 40.

[84] See above, n. 80. Two other *laude* in Morsi's anthology are extracted from *sacre rappresentazioni*: Feo Belcari's "Chi serve a Dio con purità di core" (fol. xii[r–v]), from his play of *Abramo*; and Piero di Mariano Muzi's "Deh, sappiatevi guardare" (fols. cxxiii[v]–cxxiv[r]), from Muzi's Prodigal Son play, *Il vitel sagginato*. In those cases, the author of the *lauda* is also the author of the play, but that is not necessarily the case here. As an editor, Jacopo de' Morsi was scrupulous. He made an effort to identify the authors of the *laude* he assembled, and we must wonder how he could attribute this *lauda* to Antonio da Siena when it does not appear to have had a life outside the play. Certainly, the date of the anthology is close enough to the date of publication for authorship to still have been common knowledge.

major figure in the spiritual and economic life of fifteenth-century Italy and in the history of printed books. He entered the Jesuate order, founded by his Sienese compatriot Giovanni Colombini, in 1439, but twenty years later was brought back into the circle of his fellow Sienese, Pope Pius II Piccolomini.[85] Created bishop of Foligno in 1465, he oversaw the creation there of the Monte di Pietà, and his treatise *Monte Santo di Dio* was illustrated with three famous engravings: of the sacred mountain, Christ in Glory, and three-faced Lucifer, the work of Baccio Baldini, probably from designs by Botticelli.[86] He also translated Feo Belcari's biography of the founder of the Jesuates, *La vita del beato Giovanni Colombini*, from Italian into Latin.[87] Bettini travelled extensively and may have visited Florence in the entourage of Pius II in 1459. He was certainly well connected to Florentines, and the Florentine author of this play felt entitled to use his *lauda*. It may be that the author was associated with the former Jesuate friary of Santa Trinita Vecchia and wrote the *rappresentazione* for the youth confraternity of San Giovanni Evangelista. The invocation of the Trinity in the first octave may support this proposition.

La rappresentazione di santa Guglielma

From the familiarity and simplicity of the Nativity I now turn to a new subgenre of *rappresentazioni*: the romantic, even gothic, tales of persecuted women. These women are closer to the damsels of the chivalric romance than to the martyred virgins of the early Church, and they inhabit the forests of northern Europe rather than the deserts of Egypt. They existed in the narrative tradition and are not simply the invention of dramatists. Griselda is the literary archetype of persecuted heroines, the best known and the most versatile. Created by Boccaccio (*Decameron* x.10), translated into Latin by Petrarch and from Latin into the vernacular languages of Europe, Griselda became an allegory of the Christian soul, tested by Christ and finally received by him. The French dramatization, *L'Estoire de Griseldis* (1395), is said to be

---

[85] Prunai, "Bettini." The *incipit* of Bettini's *De divina praeordinatione vitae et mortis humanae* ([Rome: Silber, before 20 August 1480], ISTC ia00885000) names the author as "A. of Siena, by the grace of God bishop of Foligno and member of the Poor Jesuates" (A. de Senis Dei gratia episcopum fulginatensem & de pauperibus Yhesuatis).

[86] Antonio da Siena, *Monte Santo di Dio* (Florence: Niccolò di Lorenzo della Magna, 1477), ISTC ia00886000; see Hind, *Early Italian Engraving* 1 (1938): 97–99. A manuscript of the work, dated 5 April 1444, is in Parma, Biblioteca Palatina, Pal. 303.

[87] For manuscript, dated 1466, see VBAMi, H 26 sup.

the first French secular drama, based on Philippe de Mézières's French prose version.[88] A two-day Florentine play of Griselda from the late fifteenth or early sixteenth century, unfortunately lacking its first folios, is testament to the versatility of the figure of the persecuted bride.[89]

Antonia Pulci's *Play of Santa Guglielma* is the first such play to appear in print,[90] and like the contemporary plays of *Stella* and *Rosana*, it introduces the tale of a persecuted woman who is restored to her rightful state in the world rather than dying and ascending to heaven and to the arms of Christ, her heavenly spouse.

Santa Guglielma is bound as the second play of the *Domitilla* volume of the Miscomini collection and, thanks both to its intrinsic qualities and to the fact that it is securely attributed to Antonia Pulci, it has enjoyed considerable critical attention; in recent times, much research has been done on the complex history of the saint's origins.[91] The play presents the vicissitudes of the English princess, Guglielma (Wilma). It starts in the royal court of Hungary, where the king, newly converted to Christianity, sends his brother to England to sue for the hand of the fair Guglielma, daughter of the English king. Initially reluctant, because she had expected to live her life as a virgin, Guglielma is persuaded to continue to serve God as a chaste bride, and after

---

[88] Roques, ed., *L'Estoire de Griseldis.*

[89] For bibliography, see Morabito, ed., *La circolazione*, "La diffusione," and *Una sacra rappresentazioni*; Albanese, "Fra narrativa." The play of *Griselda*, formerly in the Fiske collection, is now in Cornell University's Kroch Library Rare and Manuscript Collections, 4648 Bd. Ms. 8 +. The manuscript, in *formato bastardello*, 29 × 10 cm approx., lacks the first part of the first day. It is foliated 17–27, and Morabito judges that one half of the folios are missing, but if the days were of equal length, it is possible that only two folios or about fourteen stanzas are missing; *Una sacra rappresentazione*, 9. The codex may have come from the Biblioteca Riccardiana in Florence. Lami's 1756 catalogue of the manuscripts in the Biblioteca Riccardiana includes: "Griselda. *Rappresentazione.* O.IV. *Codex chartac. oblongus* n. XXIII" (Lami, *Catalogus*, 224), but the title does not appear in the Inventario e stima of 1810. Under "Commedie," Lami (142) also lists "Imperfetta. O.III. Codex chartac. oblongus. n. XXIII," which may be a different transcription of the same information. In the library's concordance of old and new shelf-marks, there is no modern shelf-mark to correspond to Ms. O.III.23 or Ms. O.IV.23.

[90] *Comincia la rapresentatione di sancta Guglielma composta per mona Antonia donna di Bernardo Pulci* ([Florence: Antonio Miscomini, c. 1484]), ISTC ir00029680, g–h[8] i[6]; Cioni, *Bibliografia*, 210, LVIII.1; for modern editions and translations, see Table 2.

[91] Pullia, "Due Guglielme," and Pullia and Falvay, "La *sacra rappresentazione*"; Bryce, "'Or altra via'"; Carney, "Antonia Pulci's *Rappresentazione*"; Stallini, "La *sacra rappresentazione*," 301–308; Weaver, in Antonia Pulci, *Saints' Lives*, 37–43.

music and dancing she leaves England and travels with the brother back to the royal court of Hungary. There she is married to the king and, after alms have been distributed by a begrudging seneschal,[92] the newlyweds go to give thanks in church, where Guglielma persuades her husband to visit the Holy Sepulchre in Jerusalem (oct. 20–23). Guglielma cannot accompany him because she must stay and rule as regent, and the king's brother is ordered to obey her as his queen. As soon as the king departs, entrusting himself to the care of the Archangel Raphael, his brother attempts to seduce Guglielma. She escapes his clutches, but is aware of the dangers, and asks God to protect her as he protected Susanna.[93] The brother vows vengeance.

After an absence of just four octaves, a messenger arrives to report that the king is returning. The brother hurries to meet him in an inn and claims that Guglielma has scandalized the court since he left with singing, dancing, and parties too shameful to describe. In dismay, the king sends his brother back to the court to execute her. The judgment is delivered to Guglielma in secret by the captain of the guard; she weeps, takes leave of her maidservants, and entrusts herself to God and the Virgin. The knight who is to execute her, however, recognizes her innocence and burns only her clothes, sending her off into the forest. The Virgin appears to her "dressed as a woman and not revealing who she is" (vestita come donna e non si manifesta chi sia; stage direction after oct. 49) and promises aid. She vanishes just as Guglielma recognizes her as the Virgin.

Two Angels appear to comfort Guglielma. They find a ship and give her a ring with which to pay for her passage; then, like the Virgin, they vanish, unseen by the other characters. In contrast to the captain who kidnapped Sant'Eustachio's wife, this captain and his crew are honest and accompany Guglielma to a remote abbey where the mother abbess takes her in.[94] Guglielma dispenses alms and her fame as a healer grows.

Meanwhile the king's brother has fallen ill with leprosy. The court physicians propose expensive cures, but a servant urges the king to take his brother to the abbey where Guglielma lives. Unrecognized by the two men,

---

[92] The poor are not necessarily undeserving. The character of the seneschal may be the slightest nod to the seneschal episode of the prose legend discussed below, which is omitted in the play.

[93] The play mentions Raphael, Susanna, Isaac, and Daniel, all characters present in earlier confraternal plays.

[94] Stallini suggests that the topos of the *nave spirituale* comes from Antoninus; Stallini, *Le théâtre*, 305–306.

she asks that the brother confess all his sins against the king, and that the king promise to forgive him (fig. 8.6). The brother relates all that he has done, and the king, lamenting the fate of Guglielma but mindful of his promise, forgives him. Through Guglielma's intercession, the brother is healed. At last, Guglielma removes her veil to reveal her identity. The three take their leave of the abbess, return briefly to the court to entrust rule to the barons, then leave for a life of penance in a leafy hermitage.

The legend of the chaste queen, her lecherous brother-in-law, and her miraculous return to her rightful position has many versions,[95] but the immediate source of the play is the anonymous Italian prose version that Antonia has abridged.[96] In the prose legend, which began to circulate in Italy at the end of the thirteenth century, Guglielma is subjected to a second persecution. She is rescued in the forest by men from the court of the king of France, where she once again repels advances, this time of a trusted seneschal, and is accused of killing the king's only son while he is in her care. Again she escapes, and the two men who come to seek a cure for their leprosy are the two kings, of France and Hungary. Both are cured and together they found a hermitage. As Weaver observes, the second ordeal at the hands of the seneschal adds nothing to our understanding of female honour in marriage,[97] and the play is more manageable in Antonia's simpler version. In fact, the play, in only 106 octaves, is stripped to its luminous essentials.

The figure of Guglielma is unknown to historians of tenth- and eleventh-century Hungary and England. But she shares her name with another Guglielma who appeared in Milan in about 1260 and gained a reputation for sanctity, healing, and charismatic teaching.[98] Following her death in 1281, she became the centre of a cult of female priests, and was held to be the incarnation of the Holy Ghost. The rumour that this Guglielma was the daughter of the king of Bohemia is without foundation, and her cult was quickly regarded as heretical. She was condemned posthumously and two of her followers, as

[95] Analogues summarized in D'Ancona, ed., *Sacre rappresentazioni*, 3: 200–208; she appears as Crescenzia, Hildegarde, Florence of Rome, the empress of Rome, and the queen of Poland. See Levi in *Il libro dei cinquanta miracoli*, CXXIV–CXXXVIII; Avalle, "Da santa Uliva."

[96] See Kovács, "Szent Vilma," 126–184, for a list of manuscripts, and *stemma*, p. 219; and synthetically, in Italian, Kovács, "La leggenda," 40–43.

[97] Weaver, *Convent Theatre*, 41.

[98] For the discussion of Guglielma of Bohemia, I rely on Newman, "The Heretic Saint," with bibliography.

well as her bones, were burned. Nevertheless, her memory was cherished by the Visconti family, and her cult remerged in about 1425 in the church of Sant'Andrea Apostolo at Brunate, overlooking Lake Como. It was for the Visconti that Bonifacio Bembo painted the earliest extant deck of tarot cards and included a nun in the brown habit of the Umiliate and wearing a papal tiara. Later called *La papessa*, she is not Pope Joan but, as Gertrude Moakley first argued, the Visconti kinswoman and follower of Guglielma, Maifreda.[99]

In recent years, it has been proposed that the legend of Santa Guglielma was promoted as a cover story to allow the continued veneration of the charismatic heretic,[100] but the legend, revised by Antonio Bonfadini around 1425,[101] is already attested in the 1300s, well before the re-emergence of her cult. It seems more likely that the legend of Santa Guglielma, like those of the other persecuted wives, is initially tied to an over-arching devotion to the Virgin Mary, rather than to a single saint. There is no suggestion that Antonia Pulci had any awareness of or interest in Guglielma's heretical associations; rather Guglielma interests her as a model of piety, of charity, and of forbearance in marriage. There may well have been times when she wished that she too could extract her own brother-in-law, Luigi Pulci, from his wanton pursuits and charges of heresy and withdraw, together with her husband Bernardo, to an eremitic life.

Un miracolo della Nostra Donna, cioè la rappresentazione di Stella

Whereas *Santa Guglielma* was restrained and economical in its narrative, the play of *A Miracle of Our Lady, That Is, the Play of Stella*, includes everything and claims no sainthood for its protagonist. It is the last play in the *Eustachio* volume of the Miscomini collection and, like *Santa Guglielma*, it enjoyed enormous popularity.[102] Wrongly but persistently attributed to

---

[99] Moakley, *The Tarot Cards*, 72–73, cited in Newman, "The Heretic Saint," 28.

[100] Falvay, "Santa Guglielma," "'A Lady,'" 158–169, and "Szent Erzsébet," 66–74; Newman, "The Heretic Saint," 23–27; Pullia, "Due Guglielme"; Pullia and Falvay, "La sacra rappresentazione"; Benedetti, "Di regine," online. The play was performed by students of Albion College, Michigan, at the Ninth International Colloquium of the Société Internationale du Théâtre Médiéval (SITM), Odense, August 1998.

[101] Bonfadini, *Vite*.

[102] *Incomincia uno miracolo della nostra Donna: cioe la rappresentatione di Stella* ([Florence: Antonio Miscomini, c. 1484]), ISTC ir00029700, k–l⁸; Cioni, *Bibliografia*, 279, xcvii.1; for modern editions, see Table 2. The title of the play was evidently too close to the

Muzio Fiordani,[103] the play is probably, like the other works in the Miscomini anthology, the work of close members of the Pulci clan.

The play presents a longer variant — some 164 stanzas — of the persecuted maiden tale. Here, it is the evil queen, jealous of her stepdaughter's beauty, who has her taken into the forest to be killed, but the assassins cut off her hands and leave her to her fate. Stella suffers many vicissitudes before having her hands restored by the Virgin and being elevated to her rightful place as queen. Like the play of *San Bernardo* and the robber baron, and the play of *Teofilo* who sold his soul to the Devil, *Stella* takes its miracle from a popular anthology of miracles of the Virgin that circulated widely in manuscript and went into print in 1475. There we find narrated: "How the glorious Virgin Mary rescued from many snares the daughter of an emperor, whose hands had been cut off."[104]

After a single stanza spoken by the Angel, announcing a miracle of the Virgin, the action opens in the court of Frederick, emperor of France, explained in the prose legend as being "in the time when the Roman empire

---

title of other plays of miracles of the Virgin, and from the second edition the information was reversed, becoming *La rapresentatione divota di Stella cioe un miracolo di Nostra Donna* ([Florence: Antonio Miscomini, 1492–1494]), ISTC ir00029615, not in Cioni. Cioni's "second" edition, xcvii.2, now attributed to Bartolomeo de' Libri or Giovanni Stefano di Carlo, not after 1515, CNCE 19120, is a line-for-line copy of ISTC ir00029615, using the same woodblocks; BNCF, Pal. E.6.5.1v.16bis.

[103] Cioni, and consequently *IGI*, ISTC, and subsequent bibliographers, misattribute this play to Muzio Fiordani (itself a misreading of 'Fiordiani'); Cioni, *Bibliografia*, 279. The name Mutio Fiordiani first appears in the 1606 edition of *La Rapresentazione dell'innocente Stella. Di nuouo partita in due giornate, con i suoi intermedij, e da molte imperfezzioni ricorretta, composta per Mutio Fiordiani* (Siena, Alla Loggia del Papa, 1606); copies BCoR; Chicago, Newberry; BnF). D'Ancona noted the 1609 reprint (offered for sale in Guglielmo Libri's 1859 *Catalogue*, 303, item 2281; now London, British Library, 11426.f.41) and observed judiciously: "this is surely the name of a later poet, making new revisions to the old play" (Questo è certamente il nome di un tardo rapsodo, nuovo editore dell'antica rappresentazione); D'Ancona, ed., *Sacre rappresentazioni*, 3: 318. Fiordiani may have added words to the title, but there is no additional dialogue in the 1606 edition, simply an indication of where *intermezzi* might by introduced if desired.

[104] I cite from *Miracoli della gloriosa Vergine Maria* (1500), fols. b2^r–b4^v, cap. xi *Come la gloriosa vergine Maria campò da molte insidie una figliuola d'uno imperadore alla quale era state tagliate le mani*. On the earlier manuscript printed collections, see Levi's preface to *Il libro dei cinquanta miracoli*, liv–cvii; on the sources of the legend, cviii–cx.

was transferred to the king of France."[105] The emperor, about to depart for England, summons his wife and his daughter and entrusts "this my only daughter, | and your stepdaughter" (questa mia unica figliuola | e tua figliastra; oct. 7.2–3) to the care of the queen. The queen and Stella go into the garden, where the queen overhears two merchants praising Stella's beauty: "If this great lady lives, I am quite sure | her beauty will surpass even the queen's" (Certo se in *vita* dura questa dama, | alla reina ancor torrà la fama; oct. 9.78), the scene that is shown in the woodcut of the second edition (fig. 6.10). Like Snow White's envious stepmother, the queen plots her revenge. She summons two henchmen and orders them to abduct Stella from the garden, kill her in the forest, and bring back her hands. Ugo and Arnaldo lure her away from her maids, and finally tell her that the queen has ordered them to kill her. Stella calls on the Virgin for assistance; Ugo and Arnaldo are moved to pity and resolve simply to cut off her hands (fig. 6.11):[106]

ARNALDO *a Stella:*	ARNALDO *to Stella:*
Pon giù le man sopr'un di questi [ceppi	Lay down your hands upon one of these [stumps
ch'i' te le mozzi: i' ti concedo assai.	that I may sever them: so much I grant.
Di non t'uccider negarti non seppi;	I can't say no to sparing you your life,
questo m'è giuoco forza, e tu nol sai.	but this is what must be, and you don't know.
	(oct. 33.1–4)

Ugo and Arnaldo bring the bloodied hands to the queen and are paid in silver and gold but they quarrel over the division of their payment and Ugo is killed (fig. 6.12).

Stella is found in the forest by the son of the duke of Burgundy (fig. 6.13), who summons his physicians. They confer for so long (oct. 49–52) that a servant tells them to speed it up, but no sooner are Stella's wounds treated than the duke's son falls in love with her and, with his father's blessing, he marries her. Meanwhile, in Paris, the emperor is plunged into melancholy for the loss of his daughter. The queen prescribes a joust to revive his spirits. Letters are sent to the courts of England and Burgundy and the two young

---

[105] *Miracoli della gloriosa vergine Maria* (1500), fol. b2r: "nel tempo nel quale fu translato el romano imperio al Re di Franza."

[106] The hind in the background of the woodcut does not relate directly to the action, but may symbolize Stella's unassailable purity, like Petrarch's white hind in Sonnet 190 that wears a collar on which is written "Let no one touch me" (Nessuno mi tocchi).

nobles arrive with their entourages. After a battle four-on-four — for the stage presumably a stylized *armeggeria* or a *moresca* — the Englishman and the Burgundian do battle hand to hand (oct. 89.4). Both times, the Burgundian triumphs.

Back in Burgundy, Stella has given birth to twins and a messenger is dispatched to Paris with the news. The queen intercepts the messenger and extracts from him the story of the mysterious lady, found in the forest a year before, and realizes that her stepdaughter is still alive. She intercepts the messenger again as he is returning with the Burgundian's joyful reply, drugs him and substitutes a letter of her own, accusing Stella of adultery and asking the duke to order her execution. The duke's servants leave Stella and her babies in the forest where she prays yet again to the Virgin and is rescued by a hermit, who lodges her in a neighbouring cave. She is comforted by the Virgin, who brings her new hands:

Te', ecco qui che per le man terrene,	Here, in the place of your two earthly hands
che ingiustamente ti furon tagliate,	that were cut off unjustly, I give you
ti rendo queste di santità piene,	these two that are quite full of blessedness,
in paradiso per te fabbricate.	created just for you in paradise.

(oct. 127.1–4)

The son of the duke returns to Burgundy to discover what has happened in his absence. He sets off to the forest to look for Stella and his children and finds the hermit who takes him to his family. They return to the Burgundian court, which is filled with rejoicing and praise of the Virgin, then continue to Paris where the emperor is informed of all that has happened. The emperor orders that the queen be burned (fig. 6.14).[107] In an addition to the Marian legend, her crown is given to Stella, and the son of the duke of Burgundy is made governor of all the realm, which is invited to join in the dancing and festivity.

Like so many of the plays discussed so far, the setting requires a garden with a wild forest and two courts, which are possibly represented by no more than a throne where the emperor or queen or duke sits until it is time to speak or act. Stage directions read, for example: "Stella leaves with the maids, and the Queen comes down from her seat and takes the servants by the hand and

---

[107] Before going to her execution, the queen kneels and confesses her sin of envy and asks for prayers for her soul (oct. 160–161). The play ends joyfully, and the woodcut shows a scene that was not necessarily part of the action.

says [...]" (Partesi Stella con le cameriere, e la Regina scende di sedia e piglia e servi per mano e dice [...]; stage direction after oct. 14.8); "Then the Son of the Duke comes down from his seat and, as he loosens his clothes and paces up and down, he says to himself [...]" (Dipoi el Figliuolo del Duca scende di sedia, e sfibbiandosi, andando in qua e in là, dice fra sé medesimo [...]; stage direction after oct. 57.8); "Then [the Seneschal] goes to the Queen's seat and says as he takes the crown from her head [...]" (Di poi [il Siniscalco] va alla sedia della Regina, e dice così cavandoli di testa la corona [....]; stage direction after oct. 159.8). Minor characters come and go, but those with a place that is theirs alone remain in that appointed place in a single extended acting space throughout the action. I cannot say what conventions render them invisible when they are not involved in a scene: a curtain may conceal them, or simply by sitting motionless or looking away they may cease to be 'on stage.' In the early sixteenth century, in nuns' plays with modest scenography, places were identified with *polizze* (signs). Here, the two courts of France and Burgundy may have been indicated by banners or well-known coats of arms. In 2004, when Luciano Alberti directed a production of *Stella* in the Basilica di San Saba in Rome, he addressed the question of how the *rappresentazioni* communicate the passage of time and identify the different places in the plays. Alberti chose to have the stage directions spoken as part of the performance, to ensure that the audience knew who was going where, and why, and the journeys were accompanied by music. For a modern audience that was unfamiliar both with the miracle being enacted and with the staging conventions of the *rappresentazioni*, this proved a surprisingly satisfactory solution.[108]

La rappresentazione della distruzione di Saul e del pianto di Davit

Antonio Dolciati also attributed to Antonia Pulci a play of Saul and David.[109] Elissa Weaver has persuasively identified this with *The Play of the Destruction of Saul and the Lament of David*, printed by Bartolomeo de' Libri no later than 1495 (fig. 6.15).[110] In her introduction she provides an excellent account

---

[108] See discussion of the production by the Compagnia delle Seggiole in Ulysse, "Donne perseguitate."

[109] See n. 6 above.

[110] *La rappresentatione della distructione di Saul & del pianto di Dauit* ([Florence: Bartolomeo de' Libri, not after 1495]), ISTC ir00029500; Cioni, *Bibliografia*, 276, xciiii.1; for modern editions and translations, see Table 2. For commentary, see Weaver, in Antonia

of its complexities and its divergences from the biblical account.[111] The play is not long (just 91 octaves) but is astonishingly complicated in its interweaving of narrative threads and the addition of new ones. Here, as in so many of our plays, brutal, warring armies do battle: Hebrews against Philistines, who are here — in the aftermath of the fall of Constantinople in 1453 — also called Turks. Saul's sons are killed, while Saul meets his death on the sword of his own man-at-arms. A traveller brings the news to David, claiming to have slain Saul himself. David is overcome with grief and has the messenger executed. Pulci however frames the men's battles within a female domestic context, creating an unprecedented narrative of women's plight in war: those who are left behind, like the wife and daughters of the Philistine, and those who are captured and executed, brutally martyred, like the wife of Saul. The Witch of Endor, who conjures up the soul of Samuel and dominates the biblical narrative of 1 Samuel 28, is replaced in the play by these two wives, whose lives are represented as being remarkably similar despite being on opposing sides. Toward the end of the play, angels carry the soul of Saul's queen to Limbo, and the Philistine king Carfase celebrates victory and the marriage of his daughter. But he ends with a dire curse:

EL RE CARFASE *dice*:	KING CARFASE *says*:
Baroni ed altra gente di mie corte,	Barons and other nobles of my court,
vo' questi d'Israel perseguitare,	I want to persecute these Israelites,
e voglio a tutti quanti dar la morte	and put each one to death, to the last man,
ed aspramente fargli tormentare;	and have them tortured bitterly; and if
se n'entra ma' nessun drento a mie porte,	any of them should come within my [gates,
voglio tutti a l'un l'altro dar mangiare;	I will feed them as meat to one another.
se fussin, che non son, dieci cotanti	If there were (and there aren't) ten times [more men,
dispost'ho di distrugger tutti quanti.	I have decided to destroy the lot.

(oct. 91)

Pulci, *Saints' Lives*, 54–61; on dance in *Saul* and in the religious drama in general, see Acone, "La danse," online.

   [111] 1 Samuel 31, recounted also in 1 Chronicles 10, and 2 Samuel 1; retold in Josephus, *Jewish Antiquities*, 4 (1934): 488–517, VI.14.

The Angel returns as usual to bid the audience farewell, thanking them for their attendance "in honour of the Griffin," but the allusion defies explanation.[112] The moral: "King Saul did not obey the orders of | our mighty Lord. See how He's finished him" (Saül non ubbidì el comandamento | del gran Signor. Vedete che l'ha spento; oct. 91.7–8), is in brutal contrast to the joyful promise of a good death at the end of a good life that closed, for example, Belcari's *Abramo*.

La rappresentazione del figliuol prodigo

Antonia Pulci's *Play of the Prodigal Son*, a reworking of the earlier *Festa del vitel sagginato* written by Piero di Mariano Muzi for the Purification company, was not included in the Miscomini anthology and may postdate it. There may have been an edition printed in the 1490s, since the play was almost certainly known to Castellano Castellani in the 1510s, but the earliest surviving edition is the one published around the middle of the sixteenth century.[113] As Weaver demonstrates, Antonia Pulci's *Figliuol prodigo* updates the *Vitel sagginato* with the addition of a short scene of gambling at the beginning, in which the Prodigal Son loses at cards to Randellino, and of a full complement of Deadly Sins, rather than just Pride and his Boon Companions. They are not particularly clever or witty, and there is no attempt to construct comic dialogue — they would scarcely rate as good company. But the representation of emotion and behaviour is not simply allegorical: the Prodigal Son acts out his addiction to gambling, which is not merely sinful but catastrophic for the fact that it places the gambler in the hands of rogues. His lack of respect for his father's bookkeeper, his contempt for his brother, his own downfall, and finally his humility on his return home are all treated with sympathy.

---

[112] "A l'onor del Grifone," oct. 91.5.

[113] Antonia Pulci, *La Rappresentatione del figliuol prodigo nuouamente stampata. Composta per Mona Antonia di Bernardo Pulci.* (Florence: n.p., 1550?), CNCE 50657; Cioni, *Bibliografia*, 138, xxx.1; for modern editions and translation, see Table 2. A "Rappr. del Figliuol Prodigo" in six folios — more probably this one by Pulci than the later one by Castellani in ten fols. — was included in the third volume of the Giunti anthology; see front and back matter of the *Terzo Libro* (1578; CNCE 53305), fol. [4]ʳ, but no copy survives. The copy of CNCE 50657 in BNCF, Pal. E.6.5.1[III.13] has the letters CCC added by hand on fol. a1ʳ, possibly by someone attempting to reconstitute the *Terzo libro*. For commentary, see Weaver, in Antonia Pulci, *Saints' Lives*, 47–54; Eisenbichler, "From *sacra rappresentazione*"; Stallini, *Le théâtre*, 85–105 and 271–282; and Delcorno, *In the Mirror*, in particular 273–283.

The singing, dancing, and banqueting that appeared to involve actors and audience in the *Vitel sagginato* are now disappointingly perfunctory and take place inside the house, where the Older Brother refuses to enter. The Angel dismisses the audience at the end.

Other Plays in the Pulci Orbit: Un bel miracolo di Nostra Donna

To the plays so far discussed I wish to add two more. In BNCF, Magl. vii.293, discussed in chapter 1, are the only known manuscript of Luca Pulci's *Ciriffo Calvaneo*, Bernardo Pulci's *Passione* with its dedication to Annalena de' Tanini, and two plays that I tentatively locate in the Pulci orbit, certainly not far from *Stella*. The two-day play of *San Giorgio* has already been discussed in chapter 5, so it is to the other play, *A Beautiful Miracle of Our Lady*, that I now turn.[114] Like *Uno miracolo di Nostra Donna che per mezzo d'uno peregrino risuscitò el figliuolo d'uno re che cascava di quel malmale* (A miracle of Our Lady who, through a pilgrim, revived the son of a king, who was suffering from falling sickness), later called *Cassiodoro*,[115] it is at heart a romance of star-crossed lovers with a happy ending. I have located no source for either, but they probably come from one of the many collections of miracles that circulated from the Middle Ages onwards. Tiberio, a young prince, is being raised in a palace. He is instructed in the courtly pursuits of singing, dancing, music, and fencing by four expert masters. Despite excellent tutoring in these noble arts, he falls in love with Fiammetta, a young woman who is of lowly birth but pure and chaste, and he asks Ansidonio, her father, for her hand.[116] The tutors take this news to the king, who banishes the girl and her father, sending his Seneschal to abandon them in a forest, where they are rescued by the Virgin Mary. Meanwhile, the Seneschal returns to the palace.

Tiberio and his loyal friend Silestro immediately set out to search for the girl and her father, while the tutors take news of their departure to the king, who realizes that he has now lost everything. Two barons set out to look for Tiberio. Back in the forest, the Virgin comes to the aid of Tiberio

---

[114] *Questa rapresentazione è d'u·bell miracholo di Nostra Donna*, BNCF, Magl. vii.293, fols. 169r–189r; for edition, see Table 1.

[115] *La rapresentatione duno miracolo di nostra donna che per mezo duno peregrino risuscito el figluolo duno Re che chascava di quel malmale* ([Florence: Bartolomeo de' Libri, not after 1494]), ISTC ir00029600; Cioni, *Bibliografia*, 234, lxx.1; for modern editions, see Table 2.

[116] Ansidonio is also the name of a giant in Luca Pulci's *Ciriffo Calvaneo*, iv.68.

too. He is reunited with Fiammetta and Ansidonio, and the lovers rejoice. The barons, however, return to the court and report to the king that Tiberio cannot be found.

The king withdraws to his chamber where he is visited by the Devil in disguise, who reports falsely that he has seen Tiberio being stabbed to death. In despair, the king hangs himself and the Devil carries his soul away. The Second Baron attempts to seize the kingdom, but the loyal Seneschal sets out with the First Baron and the crown to find the rightful heir. They come to the inn where Tiberio, Fiammetta, and Ansidonio are staying, and Tiberio and the Seneschal recognize each other. There in the inn, the Seneschal crowns Tiberio, before they all return to the palace where Tiberio and Fiametta are married. After singing, dancing, and feasting, and first Ansidonio and then the Angel bid the audience farewell. Just as the prologue had promised to show "an old man, with all his might | worshipping the Virgin night and day" (un vecchierel col suo potere | la notte e 'l giorno Maria adorare; oct. 1.5–6), so the Angel invites the audience at the end: "Say your prayers like Ansidonio | and you'll avoid the risk of going to hell" (Come Ansidonio fate orazïone, | ed uscirete d'infernal quistione; oct. 86.7–8).

The genre requires a moral, but the moralizing here is minimal: say your prayers in order to keep safe. Nevertheless, as the action moves from the palace on one side, with its false-speaking courtiers and its artificial pleasures of singing, dancing, music, and fencing, to the inn in the forest on the other, where filial and romantic love bring undying happiness, the play offers unequivocal delight through the celebration of simple values and emotions.

La rappresentazione di San Lorenzo quando fu martirizzato

One last play is associated not with Antonia or Bernardo, but with Luigi Pulci, and it dates to much earlier than the plays discussed so far. Whether this riotous brother, irreligious (but certainly not atheist) and irregular in his emotions, also wrote generally pious plays for boys and young men is a highly contentious proposition, but he is unequivocally associated with the preparation of a play of St. Lawrence in 1460, and there is no reason to exclude the possibility that he, like so many others, was chameleon-like in his ability to put on a mask and perform.[117]

---

[117] Momigliano, *L'indole*, 56–67; see also Polcri, *Luigi Pulci*.

No record has survived of any Florentine performance of a play of St. Lawrence. The festivities for the patron of the Basilica of San Lorenzo, in the heart of Medicean territory, were lavish, and a confraternity of San Lorenzo existed there from the beginning of the fifteenth century. Its connections were such that in 1418 it could borrow ropes and pulley-blocks for its *festa* from the building site of Santa Maria del Fiore,[118] but there is no trace of plays in subsequent records.[119] A play of St. Lawrence was performed, however, in Empoli. A precious indication of how individual actors prepared for the play is found in the *Ricordanze* of Francesco di Matteo Castellani, a Florentine merchant who is even more attentive than most to the individual items of his wardrobe. On the eve of Calendimaggio, or May Day, 1460, Francesco recorded:

> On 30 April, I lent to Taddeo di Nello, the farrier, my little black velvet cloak lined with taffeta, my dark tunic lined with belly fur, and a fine scarlet riding cloak, for a play of *San Lorenzo* they are performing in Empoli. He took them himself, and he said he will bring them back in good condition by 5 May next. [*Later:*] I got the above items back on 4 May. He brought them back himself in good condition, just as he had received them.[120]

In Empoli, St. Lawrence enjoyed a certain prestige, though less than that accorded to the city's patron saint, St. Andrew.[121] On 10 August of the same year, for the feast day of the first Roman martyr, the play was performed there

---

[118] AOSMF, II 1 74, fol. 6ᵛ (7 August 1418): "Item quod provisor dicti Operis possit mutuare taglias et canapos societati Sancti Laurentii de Florentia pro faciendo festum Sancti Laurentii etc." (The chief provedore of the Opera can lend pulley-blocks and ropes to the company of San Lorenzo of Florence to do the *festa* of St. Lawrence).

[119] Ciseri "Scenari festivi," 70, *scheda* 2.5. There was also no youth confraternity attached to the basilica.

[120] F. Castellani, *Ricordanze*, 2 (1995): 90: "Prestai a Taddeo di Nello maniscalcho a dì 30 d'aprile la mia mantellina di velluto nero foderata di taffettà, el mio ucho di chupo foderato di pance e una chovertina di scarlattino fine da cavalcare per una festa di rapresentagione di san Lorenzo fanno a Empoli. Portò e' proprio, e disse rendermi le dette cose salve per tutto 5 di magio proxim'a venire. Riebbi le sopradette chose a dì 4 di magio. Recò e' proprio salve come l'avea ricevute." On Castellani and clothes, see Welch, *Shopping*, 226–235.

[121] *Empoli: Statuti*, 93–94, Capitolo delle ferie (Rubrica xx), 1428. In the collegiate church of Sant'Andrea in Empoli, the chapel of San Lorenzo was situated between the high altar and the chapel of the Immaculate Conception, and was formerly the chapel of the San Lorenzo confraternity, which was "a very large company that rivalled in piety

again. On this occasion Francesco entrusted to his estate manager, Mariotto di ser Antonio of Empoli, sumptuous items of male and female clothing (quite inappropriate to the season), as well as rugs, tapestries, and bench covers with his coat of arms; he also solicited cloaks and dresses from his friends and relatives to lend to Mariotto:

> I record that on 9 August Mariotto di ser Antonio took the following things that I lent him for the play of *San Lorenzo* that they are doing in Empoli. First:
> a black velvet cloak of mine, lined with red taffeta;
> a camlet overdress with a hood and Lombard-style sleeves, with borders of purple velvet and gauze around the bottom and lined with grey cloth;
> an overdress of crimson velvet with tight sleeves, not lined, but faced with fine white cotton, that belongs to Lena;
> a tapestry with figures, 9 *braccia* long;
> a green forest tapestry, 9½ *braccia* long;
> three bench covers with my coat of arms, that is two big lined pieces and one smaller one, unlined.
> And in addition, he took a big piece of cloth, 4 *braccia* long and two wide, with fine blue stripes, to bundle the clothes in.
> He took the following things belonging to Piero Alamanni:
> a cloak of green damask lined with white taffeta;
> an overdress of purple satin velvet with a scalloped border fringed with purple and silver silk.
> And in addition, I received from Jacopo Alamanni these things that I lent to Battista Zeffi by way of Lottieri di Mariotto, on 7 August:
> an overdress of purple damask, lined with white cloth, with hem and edging finished in ermine;
> a jacket of green velvet with the trousers, and the jacket and the cloak were wrapped in big cloth with green stripes.
> And in addition, Mariotto received a big rug, 7 *braccia* long, from my bed.
> [*Later:*] On 14 August Mariotto sent these things back, all except the rug and two of the bench covers, and exchanged a big piece of cloth, 4½ *braccia* long with blue stripes, as noted above.

---

and decorum others that existed in Empoli" (numerosissima e gareggiava nella pietà e nel decoro con altre confraternite esistite in Empoli); Pincetti, *La cappella*, 12 n. (r).

And on 16 August he sent back the rug and the two bench covers; Piero di Fortino brought them.[122]

The costumes for the play of St. Lawrence are luxurious and contemporary, male and female, without any attempt to reproduce classical garb. The *festaiuoli* created a scene adorned with the tapestries and curtains of a world much richer than their own.

Among the texts printed in the last decade of the century is *The Play of St. Lawrence When He Was Martyred*, which might more properly be called "The *festa* of St. Sixtus and of St. Lawrence his deacon," as we find at the end of the play (fol. a10r) (fig. 6.16).[123] The direct source of the play is not to be found in the separate lives of St. Lawrence, of St. Sixtus, and of St. Hippolytus as they are presented in Jacobus de Voragine's *Legenda Aurea*, but rather in the fifth-century *Passio Sancti Laurentii* that survives in some 700 manuscripts and constitutes sections §§11–29 of the much longer *Passio Sancti Polychronii et sociorum*.[124] One striking characteristic of this long prose *passio* is its use of reported speech: it provides the dramatist with all his characters, the order in which they appear, and the basis of what they say. The dramatist's task has been to versify the Latin source.

We know nothing about the play's author, but once again we find ourselves in the ambit of the Pulci clan. Francesco Castellani's secretary in this period was Luigi Pulci, before he moved into the circle of Lucrezia Tornabuoni and Lorenzo de' Medici. He is not named in the preparations, but Castellani's *Ricordanze* show that Luigi Pulci was part of the household when the play was performed.[125] Moreover, St. Lawrence was part of the Pulci family's identity: the decoration of the Pulci family chapel in the northern transept of Santa Croce — Bernardo Daddi's frescoes of the Martyrdom of St.

---

[122] F. Castellani, *Ricordanze*, 2 (1995): 109–110; see appendix, doc. 21. Lena di Francesco di Piero Alamanni was his wife.

[123] *Larapresentatione disancto Lorenzo quando fu martyrizato* ([Florence: Bartolomeo de' Libri, not after 1495]), ISTC il00091500; Cioni, *Bibliografia*, 221, LXIII.1; for editions, see Table 2. The colophon reads: "Finita la festa di sancto Sixto papa & di sancto Lorenzo suo diacano," fol. a10r.

[124] Jacobus, *Legenda Aurea*, 1:830–831, CX *De Sancto Sixto*; 1:840–859, CXIII *De Sancto Laurentio Martyre*; and 2:860–865, CXIV *De Sancto Ypolito*. For the text of the *Passio Sancti Polychronii*, see Delehaye, "Recherches"; for the number of manuscripts, Verrando, "Passio," 181. I have not identified a vernacular version.

[125] Castellani also had dealings with Luca and Bernardo; see Carnesecchi, "Per la biografia," citing from the *Ricordanze*.

Stephen on the left-hand wall and of St. Lawrence on the right — shows their particular devotion to the first Roman martyr (fig. 6.17).[126] Luigi had long left Florence and died a decade before the play was printed, but the text has been prepared meticulously for the press and is illustrated with a fine woodcut prepared expressly for this edition. The text is notable for its clean copy and the near absence of hypo- and hypermetric lines. But no amount of beautiful typography can compensate for the fact that the play is more hagiography than theatre. It is also an almost all-male affair (despite the borrowing of women's clothes), and, as in the *Passio*, the one female character Cirica, a poor, ailing widow who receives alms, plays only a minor role.[127]

The recurring motif of the play is spiritual treasure, attained by renouncing worldly goods. The prologue invites the audience to abandon all attachment to mortal flesh and delight in martyrdom:

Costor vi mosterran quanto sia [accetto	These actors will now show you how [God loves
all'alto Dio chi 'l serve di buon core	all those who serve him with a willing heart,
e quanto più gli piace chi ha 'n dispetto	and how much more He loves the man
la carne propria, che per lo suo amore	[who scorns
ogni martir a lui gli par diletto	his very flesh, since for the love of Him
lasciando 'l mondo cieco e pien [d'errore,	it seems to every martyr a delight to leave this world, so blind and full of sin,
come a san Sisto e Lorenzo vedrete	as you will see with St. Sixtus and Lawrence,
s'attenti con buon cor tutti starete.	if you attend to us with willing hearts.

(oct. 2)

Once it is clear that Pope Sixtus is to die and that Lawrence will follow him, the pope gives orders that his wealth is to be distributed to the poor

---

[126] The woodcut of fig. 6.16 reworks the standard iconography, found also in Daddi's fresco, but relatively rare in Florence. The history of the chapel is not clear. According to one version, it was ceded to the Bardi della Libertà in 1409; see Moïsè, *Santa Croce*, 177; Offner, *A Critical and Historical Corpus*, III.3:122–145. BNCF, Cirri, *Sepoltuario*, 865 (cited in Offner, 122), names Jacopo di Francesco Pulci as founder of the chapel; this is also the name of Luigi Pulci's father, who married Brigida de' Bardi in 1432.

[127] According to tradition, Lawrence was buried by a Christian widow named Ciriaca. Here Lorenzo's body is taken by "a devout Christian man" (uno divoto cristiano; stage direction after oct. 100.8).

(oct. 26). The play thus keeps the focus on the great treasury of merit accumulated by those who dispense charity and mercy, and the horror of their martyrdoms.

The staging requires the usual places — an imperial court, a prison, a collapsing pagan temple — as well as non-speaking parts — devils who escape the ruins of the temple, a choir of Holy Innocents who sing. The stage directions, however, are remarkable for their repeated indications that action is occurring in two places simultaneously:

Ora e sacerdoti, parati a l'usanza degli infedeli, fanno sacrificio al tempio di Giove in presenza dello imperadore e di tutta la baronia ma in mentre che si mettono a ordine al sacrificio SAN SISTO PAPA, *avendo persentito la persecuzione che Decio e Valeriano volevano fare di tutti i cristiani, ragunò tutto il chericato suo dove era Felicissimo e Agabito suoi diacani e, confortandogli con pazienza a sostenere ogni martirio per Gesù Cristo, così dice loro [...]*

Now the priests, robed in the manner of infidels, make their sacrifice in the temple of Jove, in the presence of the Emperor and all the nobles, but while they are arranging the sacrifice, ST. SIXTUS THE POPE, *having heard news of the persecution that Decius and Valerian wanted to wage against all the Christians, gathered together all the clergy, among whom were Felicissimus and Agabitus his deacons, and exhorting them to bear their martyrdom for Jesus Christ with patience, he says to them [...]*

(stage direction after oct. 7)

With the publication of the two unillustrated Miscomini volumes, the drought of *rappresentazioni* was broken. In the Carnival of 1483/4, the youth confraternity of Sant'Antonio da Padova, now known as San Giorgio, swung back into action, using the resources of the adult company of Sant'Agnese in Santa Maria del Carmine, and other confraternities followed. But in the same year 1484, Feo Belcari, the person who almost single-handedly had forged the genre, died, leaving his works still in manuscript. A single copy of the first edition of his *Abramo*, printed in Florence by Franco de' Cenni in about 1485 (fig. 3.5), aligns closely to the manuscript *traditio*, and two other editions, dated October 1485 and 1490, preserve the single column format that had been pioneered in the Miscomini anthology, but a major change in publication practices was imminent, as we will see in chapter 8.

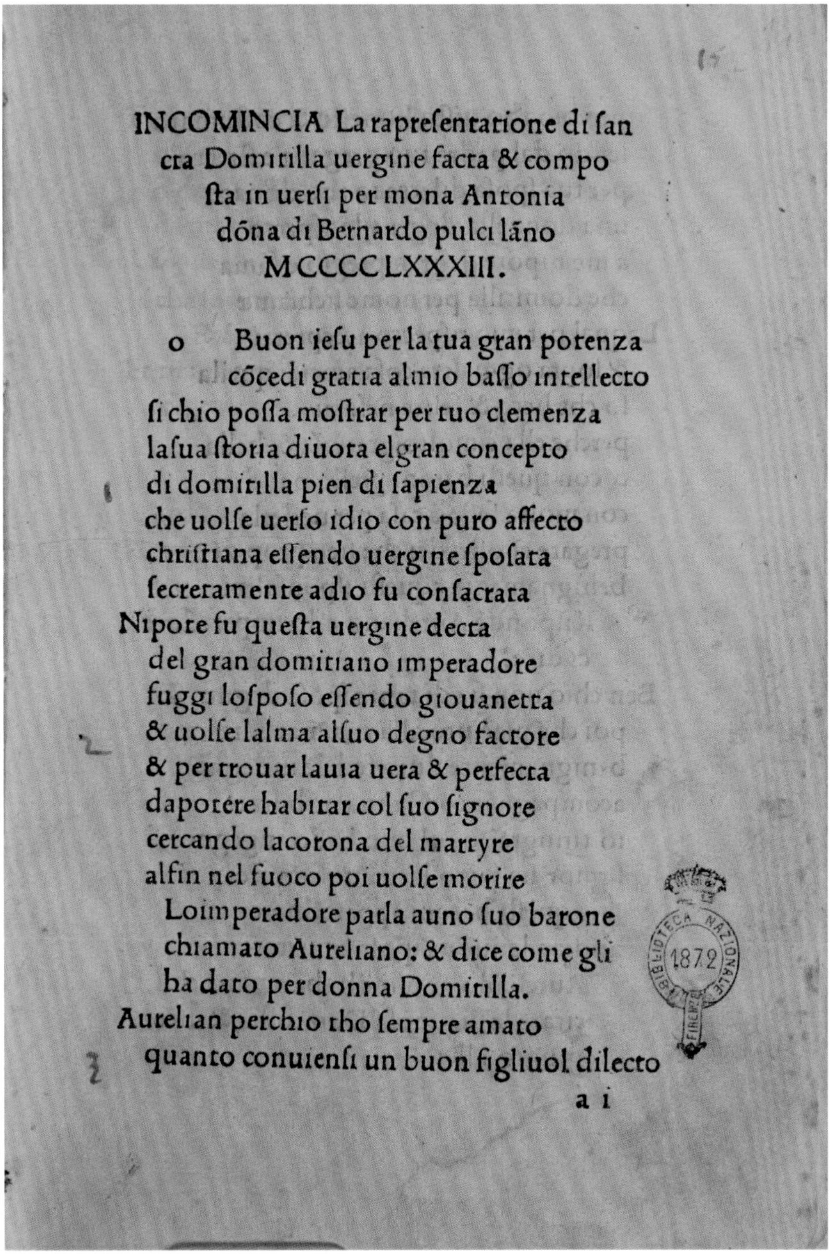

INCOMINCIA La raprefentatione di fan
cta Domitilla uergine facta & compo
fta in uerfi per mona Antonia
dóna di Bernardo pulci láno
M CCCC LXXXIII.

o   Buon iefu per la tua gran potenza
    cócedi gratia almio baffo intellecto
fi chio poffa moftrar per tuo clemenza
lafua ftoria diuota elgran concepto
di domitilla pien di fapienza
che uolfe uerfo idio con puro affecto
chriftiana effendo uergine fpofata
fecreramente adio fu confacrata
Nipote fu quefta uergine decta
    del gran domitiano imperadore
fuggi lofpofo effendo giouanetta
    & uolfe lalma alfuo degno factore
    & per trouar lauia uera & perfecta
dapotere habitar col fuo fignore
cercando lacorona del martyre
alfin nel fuoco poi uolfe morire
    Loimperadore parla auno fuo barone
    chiamato Aureliano: & dice come gli
    ha dato per donna Domitilla.
Aurelian perchio tho fempre amato
    quanto conuienfi un buon figliuol dilecto

a i

Figure 6.1. Antonia Pulci, *Incomincia La rapresentatione di sancta Domitilla uergine* ([Florence: Antonio Miscomini, c. 1484]), fol. a1ʳ. BNCF, P.6.37/1; ISTC ir00029680. © By permission of MiBACT/BNCF. All rights reserved.

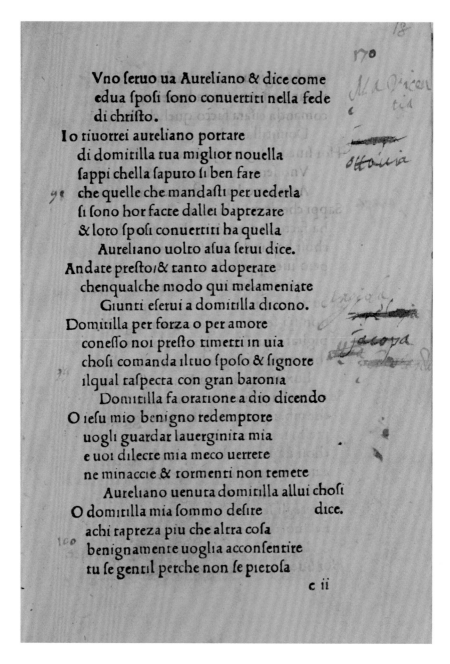

Vno feruo ua Aureliano & dice come
edua fpofi fono conuertiti nella fede
di chrifto.
I o riuorrei aureliano portare
di domitilla tua miglior nouella
fappi chella faputo fi ben fare
che quelle che mandafti per uederla
fi fono hor facte dallei baptezare
& loro fpofi conuertiti ha quella
Aureliano uolto afua ferui dice.
Andate prefto/& tanto adoperare
chenqualche modo qui melameniate
Giunti eferui a domitilla dicono.
Domitilla per forza o per amore
coneffo noi prefto timetti in uia
chofi comanda iltuo fpofo & fignore
ilqual rafpecta con gran baronia
Domitilla fa oratione a dio dicendo
O iefu mio benigno redemptore
uogli guardar lauerginita mia
e uoi dilecte mia meco uerrere
ne minaccie & tormenti non temete
Aureliano uenuta domitilla allui chofi
O domitilla mia fommo defire   dice.
achi rapreza piu che altra cofa
benignamente uoglia acconfentire
tu fe gentil perche non fe pietofa

c ii

Figure 6.2. Antonia Pulci, *Incomincia La rapresentatione di sancta Domitilla uergine* ([Florence: Antonio Miscomini, c. 1484]), fol. c2ʳ. BNCF, P.6.37/1; ISTC ir00029680 © By permission of MiBACT/BNCF. All rights reserved.

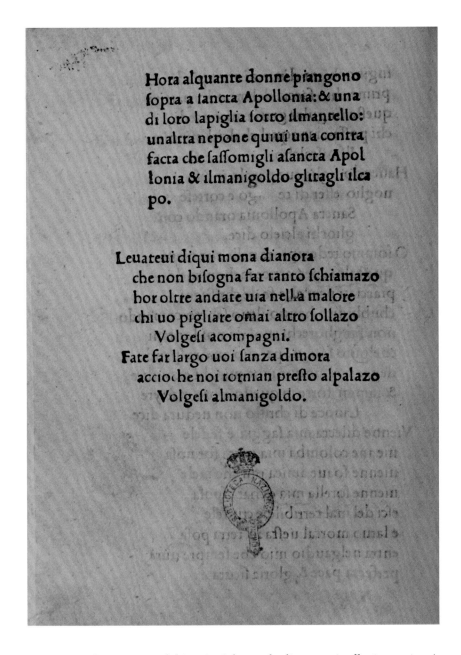

Hora alquante donne piangono
fopra a fancta Apollonia: & una
di loro lapiglia forto ilmantello:
unaltra nepone quiui una contra
facta che faffomigli afancta Apol
lonia & ilmanigoldo gliragli ilca
po.

Leuateui diqui mona dianora
che non bifogna far tanto fchiamazo
hor oltre andate uia nella malore
chi uo pigliare omai altro follazo
        Volgeſi acompagni.
Fate far largo uoi fanza dimora
accioche noi tornian prefto alpalazo
        Volgeſi almanigoldo.

Figure 6.3. *Qui comincia lahistoria & leggenda di sancta Apollonia uergine & martyre di christo* ([Florence: Antonio Miscomini, c. 1484]), fol. f8ᵛ. BNCF, P.6.36/3; ISTC ir00029700. © By permission of MiBACT/BNCF.
All rights reserved.

nõ far lorecchi tuoi da noi lontani
chel puro fãgue p tuo amore fpãdo
degnati dũ̃qz imie prieghi exaudire
& fãmi forte in q̃fto afpro martyre
  Lauoce dixp̃o nõ ueduta dice
Viẽne dilecta mia faggia & fedele
uiẽne colũba mia tutta formofa
uiẽne fuaue amica piu che mele
uiẽne forella mia & cara fpofa
efci delmal terribile & crudele
& latua mortal uefta i terra pofa
entra nel gaudio mio che fepre dura
perfecta paçe & gloria ficura
  Hora alquãte dõne piãgono fo
pra Scã Apollõia & uno diloro

lapiglia fotto ilmãtello: & unal
tro nepone quiui una cõtrafac
ta che affomigli afancta apollo
nia & ilmanigoldo dice aquelle
donne
Leuateui diqui mona dianora
che nõ bifogna far tãto fchiamazo
hor oltre andate uia nella malhora
chi uo pigliar omai altro folazo
  Volgefi acompagni & dice
Fate far largo uoi fenza dimora
accioche noi torniam p̃fto alpalazo
  Hora ilmanigoldo letagli ilca
po una nuogola meni lanima
di Scã Apollonia in cielo
     F   I   N   I   S

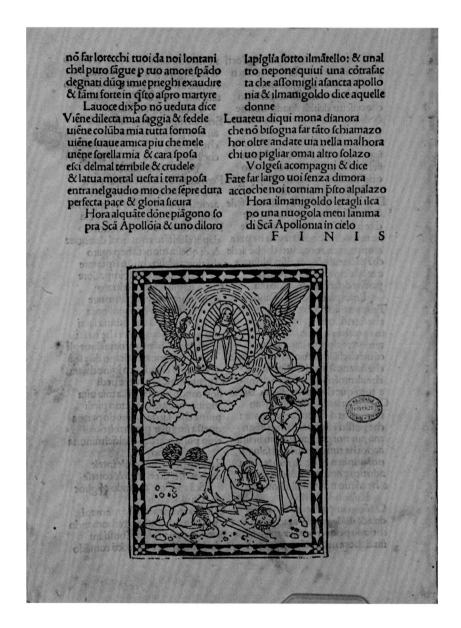

Figure 6.4. *La rapresentatione divota di Sancta Apollonia* ([Florence: Antonio Miscomini, 1492–1494]), fol. b4ᵛ. BNCF, Banco Rari 189.d; ISTC ia00922600. © By permission of MiBACT/BNCF. All rights reserved.

Figure 6.5. *La rapresentatione divota di Sancta Apollonia* ([Florence: Antonio Miscomini, 1492–1494]), fol. a1ʳ. BNCF, Banco Rari 189.d; ISTC ia00922600. © By permission of MiBACT/BNCF. All rights reserved.

Figure 6.6. Jean Fouquet, *The Martyrdom of St. Apollonia*, from *Le Livre d'Heures d'Étienne Chevalier.* 1452–1460. Vellum. Chantilly, Musée Condé, Ms. 71, fragment. Wikimedia Commons / CC BY-SA-3.0.

Figure 6.7. *La Passion et Résurrection de nostre saulveur et rédempteur Jhesucrist, ainsi qu'elle fut juée en Valenchiennes, en le an 1547, par grâce de maistre Nicaise Chamart, seigneur de Alsembergue, alors prevost de la ville,* fol. 89ᵛ. Manuscript on paper, 292 × 205 mm. Paris, BnF, Ms. français 12536, fol. 89ᵛ. By courtesy of Bibliothèque nationale de France.

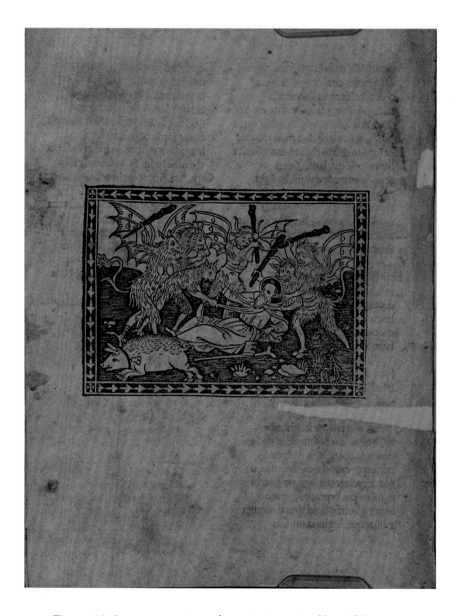

Figure 6.8. *La rapresentatione di sancto Antonio abbate* ([Florence: Bartolomeo de' Libri, not after 1495]), fol. 10ᵛ. BNCF, E.6.7.56ⁱ·⁹; ISTC ia00888500. © By permission of MiBACT/BNCF. All rights reserved.

Figure 6.9. *La rapresentatione della Natiuita di Christo* ([Florence: Bartolomeo de' Libri, not after 1495]), fol. a1ʳ. London, British Library, IA27473; ISTC ir00028500. © The British Library Board.

Figure 6.10. *La rapresentatione divota di Stella: cioe un miracolo di Nostra Donna* ([Florence: Bartolomeo de' Libri or Giovanni Stefano di Carlo, not after 1515]), fol. a1r. BNCF, Pal. E.6.5.1V.16bis; CNCE 19120. © By permission of MiBACT/BNCF. All rights reserved.

Figure 6.11. *La rapresentatione divota di Stella: cioe un miracolo di Nostra Donna* ([Florence: Bartolomeo de' Libri or Giovanni Stefano di Carlo, not after 1515]), fol. a3^v. BNCF, Pal. E.6.5.1$^{V.16bis}$; CNCE 19120. © By permission of MiBACT/BNCF. All rights reserved.

fe lalmo dira firifcalda rnfiamma
iuorro la mia parte a una dramma
    Arnaldo rifponde
Io non ho qui bilancie ne ftadere
cõ che quefto argento & or pefiamo
    Vgho a Arnaldo
Io ho penfiero che mifacci el douere
  & che di tuĉto punto el douidiamo
Arnaldo irato in uerfo Vgho dice
Sentomi montar lira in ful cimiere
io titorro quello che tu hai in mano
& poi darotti certi ftramazoni
come ho in ufo con glialtri poltroni
    Vgo dolendofi dice
Guarda fe per me el cielo ba naccherare
quefto miruba & dice uillania
    Arnaldo glicorre adoffo &
    amazalo & dice
Etua par ghiotti fono ufi a rubare
ebifogna cauarti la pazzia
    Rubalo & dice cofi

Hor chio tho morto come harai a fare
fecondo me fe fuor di fantafia
io lho pur tuĉto:certo a quefte genti
non fiuoraabbe mai fare altrimenti
    Torna la ftoria al figluolo del
    Duca di Borgogna elquale
chiede gratia al Duca fuo padre
dandare a cacciare
Per fuggire otio con cio che tipiaccia
dileĉto padre iuorre far partenza
con certi cortigiani i & gire a caccia
huomini aftuti in ciafcuna fcienza
    El Duca dice al figluolo
La gratia alleta tua par ficonfaccia
figluolo habbi da me piena licenza
    El figluolo con allegrezza dicẽ
    a baroni
Da poi chel Duca mio nõ mha iterdeĉto
alla dimanda, mettianci in affeĉto
    Stella ramaricandofi nel bofco
    dice cofi

Figure 6.12. *La rapresentatione divota di Stella: cioe un miracolo di Nostra Donna* ([Florence: Bartolomeo de' Libri or Giovanni Stefano di Carlo, not after 1515]), fol. a4[r]. BNCF, Pal. E.6.5.1[V.16bis]; CNCE 19120. © By permission of MiBACT/BNCF. All rights reserved.

Io mipensauo gia portar corona
sendo figluola duno imperadore
& hor non par che per me sia persona
a mitigare el mio graue dolore
ciascuno spirto sue forze abandona
& gia per doglia sidiuide el core
triemo tucta & uiémi al pecto lasma
si che ipenso morire per ispasma
  El figluolo del Duca giunto al bo
sco comincia la caccia & dice
Bosco te qui Falcon Martel Sonaglio
Bella Vezzosa Rustica & Villano
tenete tucti ecani fermi al guinzaglio
chi pigli el poggio & chi stia fermo al
uedete uoi di li cola ql taglio (piano
& poi la in ql boscbetto amano amano
io uo apostato al couaccio due lepri
che son da qlle quercie in que ginepri
  Seguita Stella lamentandosi
Doue son hora le pompe mie & uezi
edelicati cibi ebe uestiri
doro & dargento infiniti prezi
non son gia qui ma son degli sospiri
con agi emembri miei sisono auezi

son usa esser seruita da gran siri
hor lassa miritruouo in questo bosco
doue nessun rimedio ciconosco
  El figluol del Duca cacciando dice
State un poco saldi / isento ú mormorio
duna uoce languir che par humana
approximianci col'nome di Dio
afflicta pare:che cosa e/questa stranae
  Vno seruo glirisponde cosi
Ella e/una donzella o signor mio
che/ iginocchiöi & ba meno ogni mana
laqual dimostra desser si sommersa
per labbondante sangue chella uersa
  El figluol del Duca marauiglian
dosi dice
Che uuol dir qsto baron miei carissimi
di questa afflicta & lassa creatura
formosa si di suoi membri bellissimi
nequali mostro suo sforzo la natura
quali cori furon gia mai si crudellissimi
huomini no:ma bestie a chi procura
de che tigioua chel passato predichi
staffu & uienne accio che tu timedichi

Figure 6.13. *La rapresentatione divota di Stella: cioe un miracolo di Nostra Donna* ([Florence: Bartolomeo de' Libri or Giovanni Stefano di Carlo, not after 1515]), fol. a4ᵛ. BNCF, Pal. E.6.5.1[V.16bis]; CNCE 19120. © By permission of MiBACT/BNCF. All rights reserved.

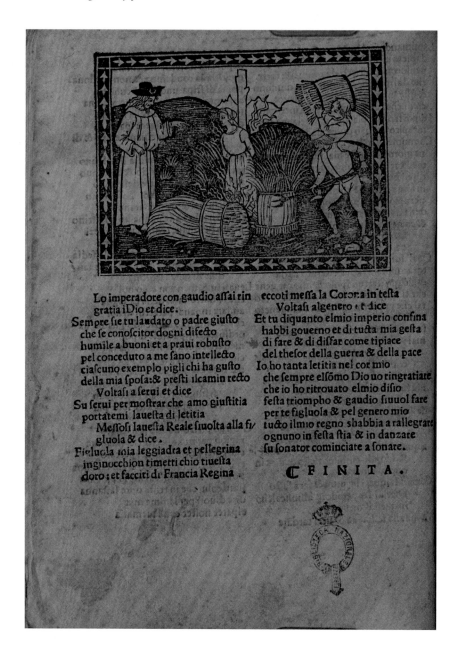

Lo imperadore con gaudio aſſai rin
gratia iDio et dice.
Sempre ſie tu laudato o padre giuſto
che ſe conoſcitor dogni difetto
humile a buoni et a praui robuſto
pel conceduto a me ſano intelletto
ciaſcuno exemplo pigli chi ha guſto
della mia ſpoſa:& preſti ilcamin retto
    Voltaſi a ſerui et dice
Su ſerui per moſtrar che amo giuſtitia
portatemi laueſta di letitia
    Meſſoſi laueſta Reale ſiuolta alla fi/
gluola & dice.
Figluola mia leggiadra et pellegrina
    inginocchion timetti chio tiueſta
doro: et facciti di Francia Regina.

eccoti meſſa la Corona in teſta
    Voltaſi algenero et dice
Et tu diquanto elmio imperio confina
habbi gouerno et di tuta mia geſta
di fare & di diſſar come tipiace
del theſor della guerra & della pace
Io ho tanta letitia nel cor mio
che ſempre elſomo Dio uo ringratiare
che io ho ritrouato elmio diſio
feſta triompho & gaudio ſiuuol fare
per te figluola & pel genero mio
tuto ilmio regno shabbia a rallegrare
ognuno in feſta ſtia & in danzare
ſu ſonator cominciate a ſonare.

C F I N I T A .

Figure 6.14. *La rapresentatione divota di Stella: cioe un miracolo di Nostra Donna* ([Florence: Bartolomeo de' Libri or Giovanni Stefano di Carlo, not after 1515]), fol. c4ᵛ. BNCF, Pal. E.6.5.1ⱽ·¹⁶ᵇⁱˢ; CNCE 19120. © By permission of MiBACT/BNCF. All rights reserved.

Figure 6.15. Antonia Pulci, *La rapresentatione della distructione di Saul &
del pianto di Dauit* ([Florence, Bartolomeo de' Libri, not after 1495]), fol. a1^r.
BRF, Edizioni Rare 686[17]; ISTC ir00029500. © By permission of MiBACT/
BRF. All rights reserved.

Figure 6.16. *Larapresentatione disancto Lorenzo quando fu martyrizato* ([Florence: Bartolomeo de' Libri, not after 1495]), fol. a1ʳ. Milan, Archivio Storico Civico e Biblioteca Trivulziana, Inc. C 322⁶; ISTC il00091500. BEIC / CC BY-SA-4.0.

Figure 6.17. Bernardo Daddi, *Martyrdom of St. Lawrence*. About 1320.
Florence, Basilica di Santa Croce, Pulci-Berardi Chapel. Wikimedia
Commons / CC BY-SA-3.0. Photo: Sailko.